LEARN, TEACH...

SUCCEED...

With **REA's CSET: Mathematics**
test prep, you'll be in a class all your own.

CSET® MATHEMATICS

CALIFORNIA SUBJECT EXAMINATIONS FOR TEACHERS®

TestWare® Edition

Kathryn Porter, Ph.D.
Professor
St. Mary's College
Moraga, California

Research & Education Association

www.rea.com

Research & Education Association
61 Ethel Road West
Piscataway, New Jersey 08854
E-mail: info@rea.com

CSET: Mathematics Test with TestWare® on CD, 4th Edition

Library of Congress Control Number 2012931978

ISBN-13: 978-0-7386-1031-3
ISBN-10: 0-7386-1031-3

The content specifications for the CSET: Mathematics Test were created and implemented by the California Commission on Teacher Credentialing in conjunction with Pearson Education, Inc. For further information visit the CSET® website at *www.cset.nesinc.com*. For all references in this book, CSET® and California Subject Examinations for Teachers® are trademarks of the California Commission on Teacher Credentialing and Pearson Education, Inc., or its affiliate(s), which have not reviewed or endorsed this book.

Cover image: JGI/Blend Images/Getty Images

Windows® is a registered trademark of Microsoft Corporation. All other trademarks cited in this publication are the property of their respective owners.

REA® and TestWare® are registered trademarks of Research & Education Association, Inc.

F12-0101

About Our Author

Dr. Kathryn F. Porter is a Professor of Mathematics at Saint Mary's College of California, where she has held various positions including Coordinator of the Mathematics Preparation Program for future secondary mathematics teachers, Chair of the Department of Mathematics and Computer Science, and Director of the Liberal and Civic Studies Program. She is currently the Director of Mathematics Readiness. Dr. Porter earned her Ph.D. and M.S. in Mathematics at the University of Delaware and her B.S. in Secondary Education and Mathematics at Slippery Rock University. Professor Porter has written many research articles in the mathematical area of topology and has served on numerous committees related to mathematics, teaching, and governance. Professor Porter is one of the founders of the highly regarded *Teachers for Tomorrow* program at Saint Mary's College, and has advised future elementary school teachers as well as future secondary mathematics teachers throughout her twenty years at Saint Mary's.

About Research & Education Association

Founded in 1959, Research & Education Association is dedicated to publishing the finest and most effective educational materials—including software, study guides, and test preps—for students in middle school, high school, college, graduate school, and beyond. Today, REA's wide-ranging catalog is a leading resource for teachers, students, and professionals.

Acknowledgments

In addition to our authors, we would like to thank REA's Larry B. Kling, Vice President, Editorial, for supervising development; Pam Weston, Publisher, for setting the quality standards for production integrity and managing the publication to completion; John Paul Cording, Vice President, Technology, for coordinating the design and development of REA's TestWare®; Kathleen Casey, Senior Editor, for project management and editorial preflight review; Alice Leonard, Senior Editor, and Diane Goldschmidt, Managing Editor, for post-production quality assurance; Heena Patel, software project manager, for her software testing efforts; Weymouth Design and Christine Saul, Senior Graphic Artist, for cover design.

We also gratefully acknowledge Transcend Creative Services for typesetting the manuscript.

CONTENTS

Prologue

Dear Future Mathematics Educator,

Kudos to you for choosing to pursue a career in mathematics education! Our country's schools need well prepared and mathematically knowledgeable teachers. The goal of this prep book is to help you be able to demonstrate your subject matter competence and move you along in your quest to start teaching mathematics.

I began my career in mathematics education as a high school mathematics teacher at Garfield High School in Woodbridge, Virginia. My experiences there enhanced my joy in working with students and increased my love of mathematics. To see the look of understanding on a student's face after many hours of struggle is so satisfying. My time at Garfield High School led me back to the classroom as a graduate student at the University of Delaware, where I taught classes and ran help sessions as I earned my Masters and Ph.D. in mathematics. Afterwards I taught at Ball State University in Indiana, and then Saint Mary's College of California, where I have taught mathematics for many years.

During my time at Saint Mary's College, I have been able to work with many future mathematics teachers through teaching a variety of mathematics classes for future elementary and secondary mathematics teachers. I also was the developer of our department's Mathematics Subject Matter Preparation Program, which was approved by the State of California. Later our department moved to having our students demonstrate their subject matter competencies by taking the CSET exams.

I am passionate about teaching mathematics and the process of preparing others to carry on this noble profession. I often remind myself how lucky I am for being paid to have so much fun! Hopefully you will think the same way about your future career.

I hope you find this book a great help in preparing yourself to be successful in your completion of the CSET exams. Work through all of the practice problems and tests multiple times; read the solutions and explanations. And please pass the word about our book to others who are preparing to follow in your footsteps.

Sincerely,

Kathryn Porter

Passing the CSET: Mathematics Test

ABOUT THIS BOOK AND TESTWARE®

If you're looking to secure certification as a mathematics teacher in California, think of this book as your toolkit to pass your exam.

Deciding to pursue a teaching career already speaks volumes about you. You would not have gotten to this point without being highly motivated and able to synthesize considerable amounts of information.

But, of course, it's a different matter when you have to show what you know on a test. That's where we come in. We're here to help take the mystery and anxiety out of the process. We're here to equip you not only with the nuts and bolts, but, ultimately, with the confidence to succeed alongside your peers across California.

We've put a lot of thought into this, and the result is a book that pulls together all the critical information you need to know to pass the CSET: Mathematics test, which spans the following:

- Mathematics Subtest I (110): Algebra and Number Theory

- Mathematics Subtest II (111): Geometry; Probability and Statistics

- Mathematics Subtest III (112): Calculus; History of Mathematics

In this test prep, REA offers in-depth, up-to-date, objective coverage, with test-specific modules devoted to targeted review and true-to-format practice exams. We strongly recommend that you begin your preparation with the TestWare® practice tests on CD. The software provides the added benefits of timed testing conditions and instantaneous, accurate scoring, which makes it easier to pinpoint your strengths and weaknesses.

ABOUT THE CSET SERIES

CSET is one among a battery of teacher-certification examinations offered by the California Commission on Teacher Credentialing in partnership with Pearson Education, Inc. CSET is shorthand for California Subject Examinations for Teachers. These tests satisfy the subject matter competence requirement by assessing abilities required of entry-level teachers seeking a teaching credential or authorization.

Who Takes the Test?

Candidates are typically nearing completion of, or have completed, their undergraduate work when they take CSET tests. The CSET: Mathematics test is designed to test the knowledge of candidates interested in teaching mathematics from Kindergarten to Grade 12 in California.

When and Where Can I Take the Test?

Pearson and CTC offer these exams six times a year at a number of locations in California and at five out-of-state locations. The usual testing day is Saturday, but examinees may request an administration on an alternate day if a conflict—such as a religious obligation—exists.

How Do I Get More Information on the CSET Exams?

To receive information on upcoming administrations of the CSET: Mathematics test, consult the CSET registration bulletin or website at *www.cset.nesinc.com,* where you will find a CSET test date chart. You can also contact Pearson at:

CSET Program
Evaluation Systems
Pearson
P.O. Box 340880
Sacramento, CA 95834-0880
Phone (9 a.m. - 5 p.m. PST, Mon.-Fri.): (800) 205-3334

Automated Information System: (866) 483-6460 or (916) 928-6110 (available 24 hours daily) E-mail: visit www.cset.nesinc.com

Special accommodations are available for candidates who are visually impaired, hearing impaired, physically disabled, or specific learning disabled. The registration bulletin and website include directions for those requesting such accommodations are available at *www.cset.nesinc. com.*

Is There a Registration Fee?

To take any CSET test there is a fee which is structured per subtest. A complete summary of the registration fees is included in the CSET Registration Bulletin at the website above.

How Do I Register?

You may register online or by U.S. Mail during the regular registration period. For more information visit: *www.cset.nesinc.com.*

Can I Retake the Test?

The CSET can be taken as many times as needed to achieve a passing score. Note: Once you pass a subtest, you do not have to take that subtest again, as long as you use the score toward certification within five years of the test date.

When Should I Start Studying?

It is never too early to start studying for the CSET. The earlier you begin, the more time you will have to sharpen your skills. Do not procrastinate!

A six-week study schedule is provided at the end of this section to assist you in preparing for the CSET: Mathematics Test. This schedule can be adjusted to meet your unique needs. If your test date is only four weeks away, you can halve the time allotted to each section, but keep in mind that this is not the most effective way to study. If you have several months before your test date, you may wish to extend the time allotted to each section. Remember, the more time you spend studying, the better your chances of achieving your goal of a passing score.

FORMAT OF THE TEST

The CSET: Mathematics test is only available as a paper-based test and is given six times a year. Examinations are administered in a morning test session that is five hours in length. The session has a reporting time of 7:30 a.m. and ends at approximately 1:15 p.m.

CSET: Mathematics consists of three subtests, each scored separately and composed of multiple-choice and constructed-response questions. The multiple-choice section of the exam is worth 70% of your total score and the constructed-response section is, therefore, worth 30% of your total score. The following chart details the subtests and their domains and approximate number of questions. The mathematics test represents the combined expertise of California educators, subject area specialists, and district-level educators who worked to develop and validate the test. REA's test prep review and practice tests address each of the broader content areas and the subareas of mathematics as delineated in the table on the next page.

CSET: Mathematics Format

Subtest	Domains	Number of Multiple-Choice Questions	Number of Constructed-Response Questions
I	Algebra	24	3
	Number Theory	6	1
	Subtest Total	30	4
II	Geometry	22	3
	Probability and Statistics	8	1
	Subtest Total	30	4
III	Calculus	26	3
	History of Mathematics	4	1
	Subtest Total	30	4
Total Number of Questions		**90**	**12**

Multiple-Choice Question Formats

The multiple-choice questions assess a beginning teacher's knowledge of certain job-related skills and knowledge. Four choices are available on each multiple-choice question; the options bear the letters A through D.

HOW THE TEST IS SCORED

How are the Multiple-Choice Questions Scored?

The number of raw points awarded on the exams is based on the number of correct answers you tally up. To pass a CSET examination you must earn a passing score on each of the examination's required subtests, which are listed in the CSET registration bulletin. Each CSET subtest is scored separately.

The minimum passing score for each subtest is established by the Commission on Teacher Credentialing based on recommendations from California teachers and teacher educators. Passing status is determined on the basis of total subtest performance. Test results are reported as scaled scores. A scaled score is based on the number of raw score points earned on each section (multiple-choice section and/or constructed-response section) and the weighting of each section. Raw scores are converted to a scale of 100 to 300, with the scaled score of 220 representing the minimum passing score.

A passing subtest score must be achieved at a single CSET administration; performance on sections of subtests cannot be combined across administrations. Once you pass a subtest, you do not have to take that subtest again as long as you use the score toward certification within five years of the test date.

Calculators

Examinees taking CSET: Mathematics Subtest II must bring their own graphing calculator but may not bring a calculator manual. Graphing calculators will not be provided at the test administration. Only the brands and models listed below may be used. Approved calculator brands and models are subject to change; if there is a change, examinees will be notified. Test administration staff will clear the memory of your calculator both before and after testing. Therefore, be sure to back up the memory on your calculator, including applications, to an external device before arriving at the test site. Please note that calculators may **NOT** be used for CSET Math Subtests I and III.

Manufacturer	Approved Calculator Models
Casio	Algebra FX 2.0, CFX-9850G Plus, CFX-9850Ga, CFX-9850Ga Plus, CFX-9850GB Plus, CFX-9850GB Plus-we, CFX-9850GC Plus, FX 1.0 Plus, FX-7400G, FX-7400G Plus, FX-9750G Plus
Hewlett-Packard	HP 49g+
Sharp	EL-9600c, EL-9900
Texas Instruments	TI-73, TI-81, TI-83, TI-83 Plus, TI-83 Plus Silver, TI-84, TI-84 Plus, TI-84 Plus Silver, TI-85, TI-86, TI-89, TI-89 Titanium, TI-Nspire Handheld with TI-84 Plus Keypad*

*Examinees using the TI-Nspire Handheld may not remove the TI-84 Plus Keypad while testing. Violation of this rule, or any other test site rule, may result in the voiding of your scores.

How Will the Constructed-Response Questions be Scored?

Seasoned educators score the constructed responses on examinations based on a four-point rubric. Responses to the constructed-response assignments are scored by at least two qualified California educators using standardized procedures. Scorers focus on the extent to which a response fulfills the following performance characteristics.

• **Purpose:** the extent to which the response addresses the constructed-response assignment's charge in relation to relevant CSET subject matter requirements or relevant CSET content specifications.

• **Subject Matter Knowledge:** the application of accurate subject matter knowledge as described in the relevant CSET subject matter requirements.

• **Support:** the appropriateness and quality of the supporting evidence in relation to relevant CSET subject matter requirements.

• **Depth and Breadth of Understanding:** the degree to which the response demonstrates understanding of the relevant CSET subject matter requirements.

Constructed-Response Scoring Rubric

SCORE POINT	SCORE POINT DESCRIPTION
4	**The "4" response reflects a thorough command of the relevant knowledge and skills as defined in the subject matter requirements for CSET: Mathematics.** • The purpose of the assignment is fully achieved. • There is a substantial and accurate application of relevant subject matter knowledge. • The supporting evidence is sound; there are high-quality, relevant examples. • The response reflects a comprehensive understanding of the assignment.
3	**The "3" response reflects a general command of the relevant knowledge and skills as defined in the subject matter requirements for CSET: Mathematics.** • The purpose of the assignment is largely achieved. • There is a largely accurate application of relevant subject matter knowledge. • The supporting evidence is adequate; there are some acceptable, relevant examples. • The response reflects an adequate understanding of the assignment.
2	**The "2" response reflects a limited command of the relevant knowledge and skills as defined in the subject matter requirements for CSET: Mathematics.** • The purpose of the assignment is partially achieved. • There is limited accurate application of relevant subject matter knowledge. • The supporting evidence is limited; there are few relevant examples. • The response reflects a limited understanding of the assignment.
1	**The "1" response reflects little or no command of the relevant knowledge and skills as defined in the subject matter requirements for CSET: Mathematics.** •The purpose of the assignment is not achieved. • There is little or no accurate application of relevant subject matter knowledge. • The supporting evidence is weak; there are no or few relevant examples. • The response reflects little or no understanding of the assignment.
U	The "U" (Unscorable) is assigned to a response that is unrelated to the assignment, illegible, primarily in a language other than English, or does not contain a sufficient amount of original work to score.
B	The "B" (Blank) is assigned to a response that is blank.

When Will I Receive My Examinee Score Report and in What Form Will It Be?

Since you will be taking a paper-based test, you will be able to access an unofficial score report at 5:00 p.m. PST approximately 1 month after the day of your test. To retrieve your score visit CSET website under *Score Reporting*. Your official score report will be mailed to you in two to four weeks after you take your test.

STUDYING FOR THE TEST

It is critical to your success that you study effectively. The following are a few tips to help get you going:

• Choose a time and place for studying that works best for you. Some people set aside a certain number of hours every morning to study; others may choose to study at night before retiring. Only you know what is most effective for you.

- Use your time wisely and be consistent. Work out a study routine and stick to it; don't let your personal schedule interfere. Remember, six or seven weeks of studying is a modest investment to put you on your chosen path.

- Don't cram the night before the test. You may have heard many amazing tales about effective cramming, but don't kid yourself: most of them are false, and the rest are about exceptional people who, by definition, aren't like most of us.

- When you take the practice tests, try to make your testing conditions as much like the actual test as possible. Turn off your television, radio, and phone. Sit in a quiet area where you are free of distractions, and time yourself.

- As you complete the practice test, score your test and thoroughly review the explanations to the questions you answered incorrectly.

- Keep track of your scores. By doing so, you will be able to gauge your progress and discover your strengths and weaknesses. Carefully study the material relevant to your areas of difficulty. This will build your test-taking skills and your confidence!

- Take notes on material you will want to go over again or research further. Using note cards or flashcards to record facts and information for future review is a good way to study and keep the information at your fingertips in the days to come. You can easily pull out the small note cards and review them at random moments: during a coffee break or meal, on the bus or train as you head home, or just before falling asleep. Using the cards gives you essential information at a glance, keeps you organized, and helps you master the materials.

Study Schedule

The following study schedule allows for thorough preparation to pass CSET: Mathematics. This is a suggested six-week course of study. This schedule can, however, be condensed if you have less time available to study, or expanded if you have more time. Whatever the length of your available study time, be sure to keep a structured schedule by setting aside ample time each day to study. Depending on your schedule, you may find it easier to study throughout the weekend. No matter which schedule works best for you, the more time you devote to studying, the more prepared and confident you will be on the day of the test.

	Study Schedule
Week	**Activity**
Week 1	Read and study Chapter 1, "Passing the CSET: Mathematics Test." This chapter will introduce you to the format of the exam and give you an overview of the subtests on each mathematics exam. Consult the website at *www.cset.nesinc.com* for any further information you may need. Take the first practice test for each of the three subtests. Use the answer key with explanations to identify your areas of strength and those areas where you need more study. Make a list of subject areas where you need additional aid.
Week 2	Study the review section of this book, taking notes, particularly on the sections you need to study most. Writing will aid in your retention of information. Textbooks for college mathematics will help in your preparation. If you have not taken a course on the history of mathematics, start reading one of the suggested texts found at the back of Chapter 7.
Week 3	Review and condense your notes. Develop a structured outline detailing specific acts. It may be helpful to use index cards to aid yourself in memorizing important facts and concepts.
Week 4	Take the second practice test for each of the three subtests in this book. Review the explanations for the questions you answered incorrectly.
Week 5	Re-study any areas you consider to be difficult by using your study materials, references, and notes. Take the REA practice tests again.
Week 6	Work through the sample questions and responses for all three substest which can be located on the CSET website at *www.cset.nesinc.com* under the *Test Guides* navigation bar.

THE DAY OF THE TEST

Before the Test

On the day of the test, make sure to dress comfortably so that you are not distracted by being too hot or too cold while taking the test. Plan to arrive at the test center early. This will allow you to collect your thoughts and relax before the test, and will also spare you the anguish that comes with being late.

You should check your CSET Registration Bulletin and other registration information to find out what time to arrive at the testing center.

Before you leave for the test center, make sure that you have your admission ticket, calculator, and the following identification:

- One piece of current, government-issued identification, in the name in which you registered, bearing your photograph and signature

- One clear and legible photocopy of your original government-issued identification for each test session in which you are testing (i.e., one copy for the morning and/or one copy for the afternoon session)

- One additional piece of identification (with or without a photograph)

Note: If you do not have the required identification, you will be required to complete additional paperwork and have your photograph taken. This additional step will result in a reduction of your available testing time.

Bring at least four sharpened No. 2 pencils and a good eraser, as none will be provided at the test center.

If you would like, you may wear a watch to the test center. However, you may not wear one that has a calculator, or one that makes noise. Dictionaries, textbooks, notebooks, briefcases, laptop computers, packages, and cell phones will not be permitted. Drinking, smoking, and eating are prohibited.

During the Test

You are given five hours to complete the CSET. Restroom breaks are allowed, but they count as testing time. Procedures will be followed to maintain test security. Once you enter the test center, follow all of the rules and instructions given by the test supervisor. If you do not, you risk being dismissed from the test and having your scores cancelled.

When all of the materials have been distributed, the test instructor will give you directions for filling out your answer sheet. Fill out this sheet carefully since this information will be printed on your score report. Once the test begins, mark only one answer per question, completely erase unwanted answers and marks, and fill in answers darkly and neatly.

After the Test

When you finish your test, hand in your materials and you will be dismissed. Then, go home and relax— you deserve it!

Take the test and do your best! Afterward, make notes about the multiple-choice questions you remember. You may not share this information with others, but you may find that the information proves useful on other exams that you take. Go home and relax!

Content Domain I:
Algebra

2.1 Algebraic Structures

> **2.1.1** The California *Mathematics Subject Matter Requirements* stipulate that candidates for any credential program for teaching secondary mathematics must *know the concepts of fields and rings, their properties, and a collection of sets that are or are not fields or rings (e.g., integers, polynomial rings, matrix rings).*

- In the course *Abstract Algebra,* students study algebraic structures such as groups, rings, and fields. An **algebraic structure** is one or more non-empty sets along with one or more binary operations and some properties that the sets and binary operations satisfy. In this section, we look at concepts and examples to help us understand these structures. We begin with the definition of a binary operation, which all of us have used in mathematics since we learned addition in elementary school.

Binary Operations

Let X be a non-empty set. A **binary operation** $\otimes$ **on a set** X is a rule, $\otimes\colon X \times X \to X$, which assigns an element of X to every given ordered pair of elements of X; i.e., for any $(a,b) \in X \times X$, $\otimes\,(a,b) \in X$. It is common to write $a \otimes b$ instead of $\otimes\,(a,b)$ for the result of the operation.

- The word *ordered* in the definition of a binary operation has significance. The element assigned to the ordered pair (a, b) may be different than the element assigned to the ordered pair (b, a).

Examples:

(a) The usual or standard addition, $+$, is a binary operation on the set of all real numbers R because the sum of two real numbers is a real number. It is also a binary operation on other sets, including all (i) integers Z, (ii) rational numbers Q, (iii) positive real numbers R^+, (iv) negative real numbers R^-, and (v) complex numbers C. Standard addition is a binary operation on many sets of numbers but it is not a binary operation on the set of all irrational numbers, I, because there are some pairs of irrationals that when added result in a rational number; e.g., $\sqrt{2} + \left(-\sqrt{2}\right) = 0$, and 0 is rational.

(b) The usual or standard operation of multiplication on the set of all positive integers Z^+ is a binary operation; the product of two positive integers is a positive integer. It is also a binary operation on the set of all (i) integers Z, (ii) real numbers R, (iii) rational numbers Q, (iv) complex numbers C, (v) non-negative real numbers $R^+ \cup \{0\}$. Standard multiplication is a binary operation on many sets but it is not a binary operation on the set of negative real numbers because the product of two negative real numbers is not a negative real number; rather, it is a positive real number.

(c) Standard division on the set of irrational numbers I is not a binary operation because, for example, $\dfrac{\sqrt{2}}{\sqrt{2}} = 1 \notin I$. However, standard division is a binary operation on the non-zero real numbers R^*.

(d) Let X be the collection of all 2×2 matrices with real entries, which is denoted by $M_2(R)$. The usual multiplication of matrices is defined as:

$$\begin{bmatrix} a & b \\ c & d \end{bmatrix} \cdot \begin{bmatrix} e & f \\ g & h \end{bmatrix} = \begin{bmatrix} ae+bg & af+bh \\ ce+dg & cf+dh \end{bmatrix}$$

This multiplication produces a 2×2 matrix, so matrix multiplication is a binary operation on $M_2(R)$.

(e) Consider the operation $*$ on $X = \{0, 1, 2\}$ given in the Cayley table in Figure 2.1. It is a binary operation. Using the table: the result of $0 * 1$ is the entry in intersection of the row 0 with the column 1, which is 1; similarly, $1 * 0$ is the entry in the intersection of row 1 and column 0, which is 2.

*	0	1	2
0	1	1	0
1	2	2	1
2	0	0	1

Figure 2.1

- It is important to notice that the result of a binary operation $\otimes$ on a pair of elements of X must be an element of X. This requirement is called the **Closure Property of** $\otimes$. When $\otimes$ is a given binary operation on a set X, we can say that X **is closed under** $\otimes$ or that X **has the Closure Property of** $\otimes$.

Groups

Let X be a non-empty set with a binary operation $\otimes$ on X that satisfies the following properties:

(a) For all $a, b, c \in X$,   (Associative Property of $\otimes$)
$a \otimes (b \otimes c) = (a \otimes b) \otimes c$.

(b) There exists an element $e \in X$ (Identity Property of $\otimes$)
such that for every $a \in X$,
$a \otimes e = e \otimes a = a$. The element
e is called the **identity element**
of X.

(c) For every element $a \in X$, there   (Inverse Property of $\otimes$)
exists an element $a^* \in X$ such that
$a \otimes a^* = a^* \otimes a = e$. The element a^* is called the **inverse** of a.

Then the pair $(X, \otimes)$ is called a **group**. It is also common to say X is a group when the operation is clear from the context.

Examples:

(a) The following sets are groups with the usual operation of addition: the integers Z, the rational numbers Q, the real numbers R, and the complex numbers C. In all four cases the additive identity is $e = 0$ and the additive inverse is $a^* = -a$ for every a in the set.

(b) Any subset, A, of any of the four sets in example (a) such that $0 \notin A$ fails to be a group under the usual addition because there is no identity element belonging to A. For example, since 0 is not an irrational number, the set of irrational numbers, I, is not a group under addition.

(c) The sets $Q - \{0\}, R - \{0\}$, and $C - \{0\}$ are all groups under the usual operation of multiplication with identity $e = 1$ and inverse $a^* = \dfrac{1}{a}$ for each a in the set. But $Z - \{0\}$ is not a group under the usual multiplication since the inverse of most integers is not an integer.

(d) The set $Z_7 = \{0, 1, 2, 3, 4, 5, 6\}$ is a group with the binary operation of **modular addition**, mod 7, which is defined as follows: $a + b(\mod 7) = r$, where r is the remainder when $a + b$ is divided by 7. For example, $5 + 4(\mod 7) = 2$ since $5 + 4 = 9$ and $9 \div 7 = 1$ with remainder 2. The identity for this group is clearly 0, and each element has an additive inverse ($0+0 = 0$, $1+6 = 7$ $= 0(\bmod\ 7)$, $2+5 = 7 = 0(\bmod 7)$, $3+4 = 7 = 0(\bmod 7)$).

(e) Consider an equilateral triangle ABC as shown on the right. We can rotate the triangle 0°, 120°, or 240°, counterclockwise, about its center and call these functions R_0, R_{120}, and R_{240}, respectively. Note, R_0 leaves the triangle unchanged, so it is the identity function; R_{120} changes the given triangle into triangle CAB as shown in Figure, 2.2; and R_{240} changes the given triangle into triangle BCA.

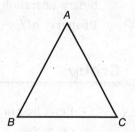

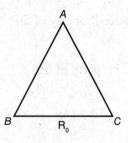 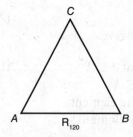 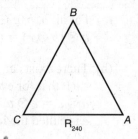

Figure 2.2

We can also reflect triangle ABC over the lines l_1, l_2, and l_3, each of which bisects the triangle; the reflections produce triangle ACB, triangle CBA, and triangle BAC, respectively. Call these functions F_1, F_2, and F_3, respectively. The results of these functions are shown in Figure 2.3.

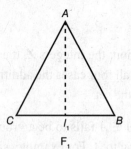 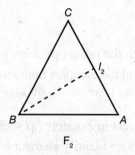 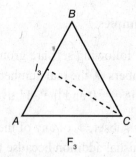

Figure 2.3

The collection of these six functions $X = \{R_0, R_{120}, R_{240}, F_1, F_2, F_3\}$ is called a **symmetry or dihedral group** with the binary operation of composition because the six functions are the symmetries of a regular polygon, an equilateral triangle. The Cayley table in Figure 2.4 shows the results of composing the six functions; so, for example, $F_1 \circ R_{120}$ means to rotate counterclockwise 120° first, then reflect over the line l_1, because in composing two functions $f \circ g$ the function on the right, g, acts first. To find the result of the composition $F_1 \circ R_{120}$, look at the entry in the intersection of the row marked R_{120} and the column marked F_1; the entry is F_2. This means that rotating the original triangle 120° counterclockwise and then reflecting it across the line l_1 produces the same result as simply reflecting the original triangle across the line l_2.

○	R_0	R_{120}	R_{240}	F_1	F_2	F_3
R_0	R_0	R_{120}	R_{240}	F_1	F_2	F_3
R_{120}	R_{120}	R_{240}	R_0	F_2	F_3	F_1
R_{240}	R_{240}	R_0	R_{120}	F_3	F_1	F_2
F_1	F_1	F_3	F_2	R_0	R_{240}	R_{120}
F_2	F_2	F_1	F_3	R_{120}	R_0	R_{240}
F_3	F_3	F_2	F_1	R_{240}	R_{120}	R_0

Figure 2.4

(f) A square $n \times n$ matrix is **invertible** provided there exists an $n \times n$ matrix B such that $AB = BA = I_n$ where I_n is the $n \times n$ matrix with ones on the diagonal and zeroes elsewhere. Let X be the collection of all 2×2 matrices with real entries and which are invertible, along with usual matrix multiplication; here $I_2 = \begin{bmatrix} 1 & 0 \\ 0 & 1 \end{bmatrix}$. This is a group, and I_2 is the multiplicative identity. This group is denoted by $GL_2(\textbf{R})$ and is a **subgroup** of $M_2(\textbf{R})$ the set of all 2×2 matrices with real entries. The notation GL refers to the fact that matrices are general linear transformations. A **subgroup** is a set that is a subset of a group and is a group itself under the same binary operation.

Abelian Groups

Let $(X, \otimes)$ be a group. If it is true that for every $a, b \in X$, $a \otimes b = b \otimes a$, then $(X, \otimes)$ is an **abelian** or **commutative group.**

Examples:

(a) All the examples in parts (a), (c), and (d) of the examples for groups are abelian groups.

(b) The group in part (e) of the examples for groups is non-abelian. To see this, observe, for example, from the Cayley table in Figure 2.4, that $F_2 \circ R_{240} = F_1$ whereas $R_{240} \circ F_2 = F_3$.

(c) Example (f) in the examples for groups is a non-abelian group because matrix multiplication is not always commutative. For example:

$$\begin{bmatrix} 2 & -1 \\ 0 & 3 \end{bmatrix} \begin{bmatrix} -3 & 0 \\ 1 & -2 \end{bmatrix} = \begin{bmatrix} -7 & 2 \\ 3 & -6 \end{bmatrix} \text{ whereas } \begin{bmatrix} -3 & 0 \\ 1 & -2 \end{bmatrix} \begin{bmatrix} 2 & -1 \\ 0 & 3 \end{bmatrix} = \begin{bmatrix} -6 & 3 \\ 2 & -7 \end{bmatrix}$$

However, the collection of all 2×2 diagonal matrices with no zeroes on the diagonal with matrix multiplication is an abelian group. A **diagonal matrix**, A, is a square matrix with zeroes for all non-diagonal entries; i.e., $a_{ij} = 0$ when $i \neq j$.

(d) Let X be $F(\boldsymbol{R}, \boldsymbol{R})$, the collection of all functions with domain and codomain all real numbers with the binary operation composition. Then X is a non-abelian group. To see this, observe that for $f(x) = x^2 + 1$ and $g(x) = 3x$, $f \circ g(x) = (3x)^2 + 1 = 9x^2 + 1$, whereas $g \circ f(x) = 3(x^2 + 1) = 3x^2 + 3$.

Rings

Let X be a non-empty set along with two binary operations, usually called *multiplication*, $\times$, and *addition*, $+$ (even though they may not be the multiplication and addition you are familiar with) satisfying the following:

    i. $(X, +)$ is an abelian group.

    ii. $a \times (b \times c) = (a \times b) \times c$ for all   (Associative Property of $\times$)
       $a, b, c \in X$

    iii. $a \times (b + c) = (a \times b) + (a \times c)$ and   (Left Distributive Property)
       $(b + c) \times a = (b \times a) + (c \times a)$ (Right Distributive Property)
       for all $a, b, c \in X$.

Then, the triple $(X, +, \times)$ is called a **ring.** If multiplication, $\times$, is also commutative, then we say $(X, +, \times)$ is a **commutative ring**. If X has a multiplicative identity, it is called **unity** and $(X, +, \times)$ is called a **ring with unity**.

Examples:

(a) $(\boldsymbol{Z}, +, \cdot)$, where $\boldsymbol{Z}$ is the set of integers, $+$ is the usual addition, and $\cdot$ is standard multiplication, is a commutative ring with unity 1.

(b) $(2\boldsymbol{Z}, +, \cdot)$, where $2\boldsymbol{Z}$ is the set of even integers and $+$ and $\cdot$ are the usual addition and multiplication, respectively, is a commutative ring. The set $2\boldsymbol{Z}$ does not have a unity; although 1 satisfies the conditions of an identity, 1 is not an even integer. Note also that the set of odd integers is not a ring under usual addition and multiplication because the sum of two odd integers is an even integer.

(c) $(X, +, \cdot)$, where X is the set of rational numbers, real numbers, or complex numbers, $+$ is the usual addition, and $\cdot$ is standard multiplication, is a commutative ring with unity equal to 1.

(d) $(\boldsymbol{Z}_n, \oplus, \otimes)$ is a commutative ring with unity, where $\boldsymbol{Z}_n = \{0, 1, 2, \ldots, n - 1\}$, $\oplus$ is modular addition (see example (d) under the examples for groups), and $\otimes$ is **modular multiplication**, which is defined as $a \otimes b \pmod{n} = r$ where r is the remainder when dividing the product ab by n. For example, consider multiplication in $\boldsymbol{Z}_6$. Note that $5 \otimes 4 \pmod{6} = 2$ because 2 is the remainder when 20 is divided by 6.

(e) Let X be the collection, $M_2(\boldsymbol{R})$, of all 2×2 matrices with real entries. It is standard to define addition, $+$, for matrices by adding corresponding entries of the matrices;

i.e., $\begin{bmatrix} a & b \\ c & d \end{bmatrix} + \begin{bmatrix} e & f \\ g & h \end{bmatrix} = \begin{bmatrix} a+e & b+f \\ c+g & d+h \end{bmatrix}$, and, as defined earlier, standard multiplica-

tion of matrices is defined by $\begin{bmatrix} a & b \\ c & d \end{bmatrix} \cdot \begin{bmatrix} e & f \\ g & h \end{bmatrix} = \begin{bmatrix} ae+bg & af+bh \\ ce+dg & cf+dh \end{bmatrix}$.

Then $(X, +, \otimes)$ is a ring that has unity but is not commutative. The unity is the 2×2 identity matrix $I_2 = \begin{bmatrix} 1 & 0 \\ 0 & 1 \end{bmatrix}$.

(f) Let $F = F(\mathbf{R}, \mathbf{R})$ be the collection of all real-valued functions with domain the real numbers, $\mathbf{R}$. Define the binary operations on F as follows: For f and g in F, $(f + g)(x) = f(x) + g(x)$ and $(fg)(x) = f(x) \cdot g(x)$ for each real number x. Then $(F, +, \cdot)$ is a commutative ring with unity function $e(x) = 1$. If instead we change the second operation from multiplication to composition of functions: $f \circ g(x) = f(g(x))$, then we no longer have a ring because the left and right distributive laws fail.

(g) Let $X = Z[x]$, the set of all polynomials in one variable x such that all coefficients are integers; i.e., in $\mathbf{Z}$. These polynomials can be written using summation notation as

$$p(x) = \sum_{i=0}^{n} a_i x^i = a_0 + a_1 x + a_2 x^2 + \cdots + a_{n-1} x^{n-1} + a_n x^n, \text{where } a_0, a_1, ..., a_n \in \mathbf{Z}. \text{ For } p(x) = \sum_{i=0}^{n} a_i x^i$$

and $q(x) = \sum_{i=0}^{m} b_i x^i$ in $Z[x]$, assuming $m \leq n$, we note that $b_i = 0$ for $i = m + 1, m + 2, ..., n$, and define the binary operations of addition and multiplication of polynomials in the usual way, which is as follows:

$$(p+q)(x) = p(x) + q(x) = \sum_{i=0}^{n}(a_i + b_i)x^i$$
$$= (a_0 + b_0) + (a_1 + b_1)x + \cdots + (a_m + b_m)x^m + a_{m+1}x^{m+1} + \cdots + a_n x^n \text{ and}$$

$p(x)q(x) = \sum_{i=0}^{n+m} c_i x^i$, where $c_i = \sum_{j=0}^{i} a_j b_{i-j}$. Then $(Z[x], +, \cdot)$ is a commutative ring with unity $e(x)$

$= 1$ called a **polynomial ring**.

(h) $(R[x], +, \cdot)$ and $(Q[x], +, \cdot)$ are also polynomial rings, where the coefficients of the polynomials are real numbers and rational numbers, respectively.

(i) If we restrict the coefficients in the last example to be elements of Z_n and we define the addition and multiplication of the polynomials as in the example except that the coefficients are determined using modular arithmetic, then $(Z_n[x], +, \cdot)$ is also a polynomial ring.

Fields

Let X be a non-empty set along with two binary operations, called *multiplication*, $\times$ and *addition*, $+$, satisfying the following:

   i. $(X, +)$ is an abelian group with additive identity, which we call 0.

   ii. $(X - \{0\}, \times)$ is an abelian group.

   iii.   For all $a, b, c \in X, a \times (b + c) = (a \times b) + (a \times c).$ (Distributive Law)

   Then the triple $(X, +, \times)$ is called a **field.**

- Another way to think of a field is as a commutative ring in which the non-zero elements under the second operation form a group.

   Examples:

(a) $(\mathbf{Z}, +, \cdot)$, where $\mathbf{Z}$ is the set of integers, $+$ is the usual addition, and $\cdot$ is standard multiplication, is not a field since the property of multiplicative inverses fails; i.e., 2 has no multiplicative inverse that is an integer.

(b) $(2\mathbf{Z}, +, \cdot)$, where $2\mathbf{Z}$ is the set of even integers and $+$ and $\cdot$ are the usual addition and multiplication respectively, is not a field since $2\mathbf{Z}$ is not a group under addition.

(c) $(X, +, \cdot)$, where X is the set of rational numbers or real numbers, $+$ is the usual addition, and $\cdot$ is standard multiplication, is a field.

(d) Consider $(\mathbf{C}, +, \cdot)$, where $\mathbf{C}$ is the set of all complex numbers. The elements of $\mathbf{C}$ are numbers in the form $z = a + bi$, where a and b are real numbers and $i = \sqrt{-1}$; a is called the **real part** of $z = a + bi$ and we write $Re(z) = a$, and b is called the **imaginary part** of z, which we denote by $Im(z) = b$. Standard addition on $\mathbf{C}$ is defined by $z_1 + z_2 = (a + bi) + (c + di) = (a + c) + (b + d)i$, and standard multiplication by $z_1 z_2 = (a + bi)(c + di) = (ac - bd) + (bc + ad)i$. With these operations, $\mathbf{C}$ is a field.

(e) $(\mathbf{Z}_4, +, \cdot)$, where addition and multiplication are modular operations and $\mathbf{Z}_4 = \{0, 1, 2, 3\}$, is not a field because 2 has no multiplicative inverse.

(f) The set $X = \{o, e, a, b\}$ with addition and multiplication given by the Cayley tables in Figure 2.5 is a **finite field**, meaning that there are finitely many elements in X. Note that o is the additive identity, and e is the multiplicative identity.

+	o	e	a	b
o	o	e	a	b
e	e	o	b	a
a	a	b	o	e
b	b	a	e	o

x	o	e	a	b
o	o	o	o	o
e	o	e	a	b
a	o	a	b	e
b	o	b	e	a

Figure 2.5

When computing, for example, $a + b$, the result is the element e in the intersection of the a row and the b column. Similarly, $e \times b$ is equal to the element b in the intersection of the e row and the b column.

(g) The polynomial rings $(\boldsymbol{R}[x], +, \times)$, $(\boldsymbol{Q}[x], +, \times)$, and $(\boldsymbol{Z}[x], +, \times)$ are not fields because of the lack of multiplicative inverses for many polynomials.

- **Theorem**: All fields are rings.

  The proof of this theorem follows directly from the definitions of rings and fields.

- Note that $(\boldsymbol{Z}, +, \cdot)$ is a ring but not a field. So, the **converse** of this theorem (*all rings are fields*) is not true.

Review Problems for Section 2.1.1

1. Let $X = \boldsymbol{I}^{-} \cup \{0\}$, the set of non-positive irrational numbers. Which of the following is a ring property that X with standard addition and multiplication does not satisfy?

    (A) The Commutative Property of Addition

    (B) The Associative Property of Multiplication

    (C) The Multiplicative Identity

    (D) The Closure Property of Multiplication

2. For which of the following addition operations $\oplus$ is the set of integers, $\boldsymbol{Z}$, an abelian group?

    (A) For all $n, m \in Z, n \oplus m = \dfrac{n+m}{2}$, where $+$ is standard integer addition.

    (B) For all $n, m \in Z, n \oplus m = n + m + 1$, where $+$ is standard integer addition.

    (C) For all $n, m \in Z, n \oplus m = n - m$, where $-$ is standard integer subtraction.

    (D) For all $n, m \in Z, n \oplus m = n + 2m$, where $+$ is standard integer addition.

3. Consider $(\boldsymbol{Z}_n, +, \cdot)$, where the operations of addition and multiplication are modular operations. For which value of n is $(\boldsymbol{Z}_n, +, \cdot)$ a field?

    (A) $n = 2$.

    (B) $n = 8$.

    (C) $n = 9$.

    (D) $n = 15$.

4. Let $X = 3Z^+ = \{3, 6, 9, \ldots\}$, the set of all positive integers that are multiples of 3. Let X have the operation: for $n, m \in 3Z^+$, $n \oplus m = n + m - 3$. Which of the following group properties does $(X, \oplus)$ lack?

    (A) Associativity

    (B) Closure

    (C) Inverses

    (D) Identity

5. Let X be the collection of 2×2 matrices in the form $\begin{bmatrix} 1 & a \\ b & 1 \end{bmatrix}$, where a and b are real numbers with the binary operation of "addition" defined by

    $\begin{bmatrix} 1 & a \\ b & 1 \end{bmatrix} \begin{bmatrix} 1 & c \\ d & 1 \end{bmatrix} = \begin{bmatrix} 1 & a+c \\ b+d & 1 \end{bmatrix}$. Which of the following statements is true?

    (A) $(X, \oplus)$ does not have the Closure Property.

    (B) $(X, \oplus)$ has $I = \begin{bmatrix} 1 & 0 \\ 0 & 1 \end{bmatrix}$ as its additive identity.

    (C) $(X, \oplus)$ fails to have the Additive Inverse Property.

    (D) $(X, \oplus)$ does not have the Commutative Property.

Detailed Solutions

1. **D**

    The order of addition of two elements of $X = I^- \cup \{0\}$ does not matter, so the Commutative Property of Addition holds so (A) is not the answer. The grouping for multiplication of elements of X can be changed without altering the result, so X has the Associative Property of Multiplication, so (B) is not the answer. The Multiplicative Identity Property is not a ring property, so even though X does not have a multiplicative identity (1 is neither non-positive nor irrational), the answer (C) cannot be chosen. The product of $-\sqrt{3}$ with itself is 3, which is not an element of X since 3 is neither irrational nor non-positive. Therefore, the correct answer is (D) because X fails to satisfy the Closure Property of Multiplication.

2. **B**

    The integers, Z, with the operation given in (A) is not closed; for example, 2 and 3 are in Z but $2 \quad 3 = \dfrac{2+3}{2} = 2.5$ is not in Z. The addition operation in (B) is a binary operation since $n \oplus m = n + m + 1$ produces another integer. Associativity holds: $n \oplus (m \oplus p) = n \oplus (m + p + 1)$

    $= n + (m + p + 1) + 1 = n + m + p + 2$ and $(n \oplus m) \oplus p = (n + m + 1) \oplus p = (n + m + 1) + p + 1 = n + m + p + 2$. The additive identity here is -1 since $n \oplus -1 = n + -1 + 1 = n$

$= -1 + n + 1 = -1 \oplus n$. The additive inverse of n is $-n + -2$ because $n \oplus (-n + -2)$
$= n + (-n + -2) + 1 = -1$, the identity. Addition is also commutative: $n \oplus m = n + m + 1 = m + n + 1$
$= m \oplus n$. Hence, $\mathbf{Z}$ with the addition operation is (B), which is an abelian group. Note also that the operations in (C) and (D) do not satisfy the Commutative Property; for example, in (C), $3 - 5 \neq 5 - 3$, and in (D), $2 \oplus 3 = 2 + 6 = 8 \neq 7 = 3 + 4 = 3 \oplus 2$.

3.　A

$\mathbf{Z}_n = \{0, 1, 2, \ldots, n\}$ with modular arithmetic (both addition and multiplication are binary operations) satisfies the Associative and Commutative Properties and has 0 as the additive identity. However, as shown in (e) in the examples for fields with $X = \mathbf{Z}_4$, there may be non-zero elements that do not have a multiplicative inverse. So the question is: when does this happen? The answer is that when n is not prime, its divisors (other than 1 and itself) have no additive inverse. For example, in $\mathbf{Z}_9$, 3, which is a divisor of $n = 9$, has no multiplicative inverse. Thus, since 8, 9, and 15 are not prime, $(\mathbf{Z}_8, +, \cdot)$, $(\mathbf{Z}_9, +, \cdot)$, and $(\mathbf{Z}_{15}, +, \cdot)$ are not fields. But $\mathbf{Z}_2$ is a field.

4.　C

The operation $n \oplus m = n + m - 3$ produces a positive multiple of 3, so $3\mathbf{Z}^+$ has the Closure Property with this operation, and (B) is not an answer. Since $n + m - 3 = m + n + -3$, associativity follows from Associativity of Addition, eliminating answer (A). The identity is 3 since $n \oplus 3 = n + 3 - 3 = n = 3 + n - 3 = 3 \oplus n$, so that the Identity Property holds, and (D) is not the answer. The problem therefore must lie in the inverse (answer (C); for example, is there an $n \in 3\mathbf{Z}^+$, such that $12 \oplus n = 3$ (3 is the identity)? The answer is no because $12 \oplus n = 12 + n - 3 = 9 + n$ so that n would need to be -6, which is not an element of $3\mathbf{Z}^+$.

5.　B

Addition is defined by $\begin{bmatrix} 1 & a \\ b & 1 \end{bmatrix} \begin{bmatrix} 1 & c \\ d & 1 \end{bmatrix} = \begin{bmatrix} 1 & a+c \\ b+d & 1 \end{bmatrix}$, and $\begin{bmatrix} 1 & a+c \\ b+d & 1 \end{bmatrix}$ is

an element of X so the closure property holds, and (A) is false.

$\begin{bmatrix} 1 & a \\ b & 1 \end{bmatrix} \begin{bmatrix} 1 & 0 \\ 0 & 1 \end{bmatrix} = \begin{bmatrix} 1 & a \\ b & 1 \end{bmatrix}$ so $I = \begin{bmatrix} 1 & 0 \\ 0 & 1 \end{bmatrix}$ is the additive identity! This is choice (B).

$\begin{bmatrix} 1 & a \\ b & 1 \end{bmatrix} \begin{bmatrix} 1 & -a \\ -b & 1 \end{bmatrix} = \begin{bmatrix} 1 & 0 \\ 0 & 1 \end{bmatrix}$ so X has the Additive Inverse Property, so (C) is false.

$\begin{bmatrix} 1 & a \\ b & 1 \end{bmatrix} \begin{bmatrix} 1 & c \\ d & 1 \end{bmatrix} = \begin{bmatrix} 1 & a+c \\ b+d & 1 \end{bmatrix} = \begin{bmatrix} 1 & c+a \\ d+b & 1 \end{bmatrix} = \begin{bmatrix} 1 & c \\ d & 1 \end{bmatrix} \begin{bmatrix} 1 & a \\ b & 1 \end{bmatrix}$, so the

Commutative Property holds, and (D) is false.

> **2.1.2** The California *Mathematics Subject Matter Requirements* require that candidates for any credential program for teaching secondary mathematics be able to *apply basic properties of real and complex numbers in constructing mathematical arguments* (for example, if $a < b$ and $c < 0$, then $ac > bc$).

Using Properties of the Real Numbers

- **The basic properties of the real numbers** include the properties of a field:

  1. The set of real numbers is closed under both addition and multiplication.

  2. Addition and multiplication of real numbers satisfy the Associative and Commutative Properties.

  3. The set of real numbers has an additive identity, 0, and a multiplicative identity, 1.

  4. Each real number has an additive inverse and each non-zero real number has a multiplicative inverse.

  5. The Distributive Law of Multiplication over Addition holds for the reals.

- **Other properties of the real numbers** include:

  1. Properties of equality for the real numbers:

     (a) If $a, b, c \in R$ and $a = b$, then $a + c = b + c$. (Addition Prop. of Equality)

     (b) If $a, b, c \in R$ and $a = b$, then $ac = bc$. (Multiplication Prop. of Equality)

     (c) If $a \in R$, then $a = a$. (Reflexive Prop. of Equality)

     (d) If $a, b \in R$ and $a = b$, then $b = a$. (Symmetric Prop. of Equality)

     (e) If $a, b, c \in R$ with $a = b$ and $b = c$, then $a = c$. (Transitive Prop. of Equality)

  2. Ordering for real numbers: $a > b$ if and only if $a - b$ is a positive real number.

  3. For any real number a, $a \cdot 0 = 0$.

  4. Properties of inequality for real numbers such as, for $a, b, c \in R$:

     (a) if $a > b$, then $a + c > b + c$. (Addition Prop. of Inequality)

     (b) if $a > b$ and $c > 0$, then $ac > bc$, and (Multiplication Prop. of Inequality)
     if $a > b$ and $c < 0$, then $ac < bc$.

     (c) If $a > b$ and $b > c$, then $a > c$. (Transitive Prop. of Inequality)

     (d) $|a + b| \leq |a| + |b|$ (Triangle Inequality)

Mathematical Arguments Involving the Reals

- The first step in using basic properties of real numbers to establish the validity of statements is to understand the statement. Each given statement has known information (the hypothesis) and a conclusion.

  First, if needed, restate the problem using mathematical terminology and symbols; if possible, phrase the statement in "if−then" form. The *if* part of the statement is called the **hypothesis**, and the *then* part of the statement is the **conclusion**. To begin a direct proof, assume the hypothesis is true. Then work with the basic properties of real numbers and the hypothesis to show the conclusion is true.

Examples:

(a) Prove: Let $a, b, c \in R$ and $a + c = b + c$, then $a = b$. **(Cancellation Law of Addition)**

Proof: Assume $a, b, c \in R$ and $a + c = b + c$. By the existence of additive inverses, $-c \in R$, and $(a + c) + -c = (b + c) + -c$ by the Addition Property of Equality. Using the Associative Property of Addition on both sides of the equation, this statement becomes $a + (c + -c) = b + (c + -c)$, from which it follows from the Additive Inverse Property that $a + 0 = b + 0$. Hence, the Additive Identity Property implies that $a = b$.

Q.E.D.

(b) Prove: Additive inverses in R are unique.

Restatement: Prove: If $a \in R$, then the equation $a + x = 0$ has a unique solution in R.

Proof: Assume $a \in R$. By the Additive Inverse Property, we know there is an element $-a$ in R such that $a + -a = 0$. Suppose there is another element b of R that is a solution of the equation $a + x = 0$; i.e., $a + b = 0$, or $b + a = 0$ by the Symmetric Property of Equality. Then by the Transitive Property of Equality, $a + -a = a + b$. Using the Cancellation Property of Equality from example (a), this equation becomes $-a = b$; i.e., the additive inverse of a is b. Thus, $a + x = 0$ has a unique solution in R.

Q.E.D.

Note that the proofs in examples (a) and (b) are written in a paragraph form with the reasoning given within statements. The next example shows what a proof looks like when the proof is exhibited in column form with the reasoning given in the right column.

(c) Prove that the opposite of any real number is equal to negative one times that number.

Restatement: Prove: If a is any real number, then $-a = -1 \cdot a$.

Proof: Assume a is a real number. Consider $a + (-1 \cdot a)$.

(Comment: This is not part of proof; it is here for instructional purposes. If we can show that this sum is equal to zero, then by the Additive Inverse Property, since for every real number a there is a unique real number b such that a + b = 0, we will have shown −a = −1·a.)

$a + (-1 \cdot a) = 1 \cdot a + (-1 \cdot a)$	Multiplicative Identity Property
$1 \cdot a + (-1 \cdot a) = (1 + -1) \cdot a$	Distributive Property
$(1 + -1) \cdot a = 0 \cdot a$	Additive Inverse Property
$0 \cdot a = 0$	Zero Multiplication
$a + (-1 \cdot a) = 0$	Transitive Property of Equality
$\therefore -a = -1 \cdot a$ for any real number a.	Additive Inverse Property

Q.E.D.

(d) Prove the Transitive Property of >.

Restatement: Prove: For a, b, and $c \in R$, if $a > b$ and $b > c$, then $a > c$.

Proof: Let a, b, and $c \in R$, and suppose $a > b$ and $b > c$. Then it follows by the definition of > that $a - b > 0$ and $b - c > 0$. By the Closure Property of Addition for positive real numbers, the sum of two positive reals is a positive integer, $(a - b) + (b - c) > 0$. But $(a - b) + (b - c) = (a + -b) + (b + -c) = a + (-b + b) + c$ by the definition of subtraction and Associativity. By the Additive Inverse Property, $-b + b = 0$, and using substitution and then the Additive Identity Property, we have $a + (-b + b) + c = a + 0 + c = a + c$. Thus, $a - c = (a - b) + (b - c) > 0$. This means that $a > c$.

Q.E.D.

Properties of the Complex Numbers

The set of **complex numbers, C**, is $C = \{ z = a + bi \mid a, b \in R \text{ and } i = \sqrt{-1} \}$.

The **real part** of z is $Re(z) = a$, and the **imaginary part** of z is $Im(z) = b$.

- **The Basic Operations with Complex Numbers**

1. Addition: $(a + bi) + (c + di) = (a + c) + (b + d)i$

2. Subtraction: $(a + bi) - (c + di) = (a - c) + (b - d)i$

3. Multiplication: $(a + bi)(c + di) = (ac - bd) + (bc + ad)i$

4. Division: $\dfrac{a + bi}{c + di} = \dfrac{a + bi}{c + di} \cdot \dfrac{c - di}{c - di} = \dfrac{(ac + bd) + (bc - ad)i}{c^2 + d^2}$

- For each complex number $z = a + bi$, there is a number $\bar{z} = a - bi$, the **complex conjugate** of z.

- Note $z\bar{z} = (a + bi)(a - bi) = a^2 + b^2 = |z|^2$ (proven in the examples), where $|z|$ is the **modulus** or **absolute value** of z.

- Geometrically, $|z|$ is the distance of the point (a, b) to the origin in the complex plane. The complex plane is formed by a horizontal axis representing the real part of $z = a + bi$, a, and a vertical axis representing the imaginary part b, as shown in Figure 2.6 for $z = 2 + 3i$.

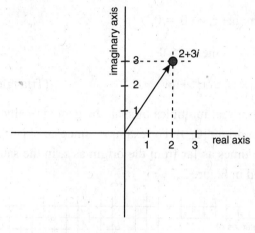

Figure 2.6

- **The basic properties of the complex numbers** include the field properties:

    1. The set of complex numbers is closed under addition and multiplication.

    2. Addition and multiplication of complex numbers satisfy the Associative and Commutative Properties.

    3. The set of complex numbers has an additive identity, $0 + 0i = 0$, and a multiplicative identity, $1 + 0i = 1$.

    4. Each complex number has an additive inverse and each non-zero complex number has a multiplicative inverse.

    5. The Distributive Laws of Multiplication over Addition hold for the complex numbers.

- **Other properties of the complex numbers** include:

    1. Properties of equality for the complex numbers:

a. If $u, w, z \in C$ and $u = w$, then $u + z = w + z$. (Addition Prop. of Equality)

b. If $u, w, z \in C$ and $u = w$, then $uz = wz$. (Multiplication Prop. of Equality)

c. If $z \in C$, then $z = z$. (Reflexive Prop. of Equality)

d. If $w, z \in C$ and $w = z$, then $z = w$. (Symmetric Prop. of Equality)

c. If $u, w, z \in C$ with $u = w$ and $w = z$, then $u = z$. (Transitive Prop. of Equality)

2. For any complex number z, $z \cdot 0 = 0$.

3. For any $z \in C$, if $|z| = 0$, then $z = 0$.

4. If $z, w \in C$, then $|z + w| \leq |z| + |w|$. (Triangle Inequality)

- Let $z \in C$. Then the set of real multiples of z can be geometrically interpreted as the line that passes through z and the origin $(0, 0)$. For example, since $|3z| = 3|z|$, $3z$ is the complex number on the line that is three times as far from the origin as z, in the same direction away from the origin. This is illustrated in Figure 2.7.

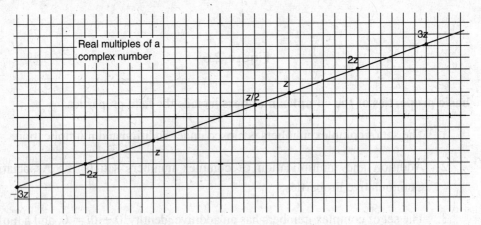

Figure 2.7

- **Properties of the Complex Conjugate of $z = a + bi$**

1. For complex numbers z and w, $\overline{z + w} = \overline{z} + \overline{w}$.

2. For complex numbers z and w, $\overline{z - w} = \overline{z} - \overline{w}$.

3. For complex numbers z and w, $\overline{z \cdot w} = \overline{z} \cdot \overline{w}$.

4. For complex numbers z and w, $\overline{\left(\dfrac{z}{w}\right)} = \dfrac{\overline{z}}{\overline{w}}$.

5. For a complex number z, $\overline{z^n} = (\overline{z})^n$ for all $n \in Z$.

Mathematical Arguments Involving Complex Numbers

Again, first, if needed, restate the problem using mathematical terminology and symbols; if possible phrase the statement in "if–then" form. The *if* part of the statement is called the **hypothesis** and the *then* part of the statement is the **conclusion**. To begin a direct proof, assume the hypothesis is true. Then work with the basic properties of complex numbers and the hypothesis to show the conclusion is true.

Examples:

(a) Prove: For any $z \in C$, $z\bar{z} = |z|^2$.

Proof: Let $z = a + bi \in C$. Then $\bar{z} = a - bi$, so $z\bar{z} = (a + bi)(a - bi) = a^2 + b^2$. By definition, $|z| = \sqrt{a^2 + b^2} \Rightarrow a^2 + b^2 = |z|^2$. Hence, by the Transitive Property of Equality, we see that $z\bar{z} = |z|^2$.

Q.E.D.

(b) Prove the sum of the conjugates of two complex numbers is equal to the conjugates of the sum of the complex numbers.

Restatement: Prove: If $z, w \in C$, then $\overline{z + w} = \bar{z} + \bar{w}$.

Proof: Let $z = a + bi$ and $w = c + di$, then

$\overline{z + w} = \overline{(a + bi) + (c + di)}$	Definition of z and w
$= \overline{(a + c) + (b + d)i}$	Definition of complex addition
$= (a + c) - (b + d)i$	Definition of conjugate
$= a + c - bi - di$	Distributive Property
$= a - bi + c - di$	Commutative Property of Addition
$= \bar{z} + \bar{w}$	Definition of conjugate
$\therefore \overline{z + w} = \bar{z} + \bar{w}$	Transitive Property of Equality

Q.E.D.

Review Problems for Section 2.1.2

1. Prove the **Cancellation Law for Multiplication:** If a, b, and c are real numbers with $a \neq 0$ and $ab = ac$, then $b = c$. Give the reasons for each step.

2. Prove the product of the conjugates of two complex numbers is equal to the conjugates of the product of the complex numbers. Justify your reasoning.

3. Prove the multiplicative identity for real numbers is unique. Give the reasons for each step.

Detailed Solutions

1. Prove: If a, b, and c are real numbers with $a \neq 0$ and $ab = ac$, then $b = c$.

Proof: Assume $a, b, c \in \mathbf{R}$ with $a \neq 0$ and $ac = bc$. Then by the existence of the multiplicative inverse of a, $a^{-1} \in \mathbf{R}$, and $a^{-1}(ab) = a^{-1}(ac)$ by the Multiplication Property of Equality. Using the Associative Property of Multiplication on both sides of the equation, the statement becomes $(a^{-1}a)b = (a^{-1}a)c$. The Inverse Property of Multiplication tells us that $a^{-1}a = 1$, so substituting, we obtain $1 \cdot b = 1 \cdot c$. Therefore, by the Multiplicative Identity Property, $b = c$.

Q.E.D.

2. *Restatement:* Prove: If $z, w \in Z$, then $\overline{zw} = \overline{z}\,\overline{w}$.

Proof: Let $z = a + bi$ and $w = c + di$, then

$$
\begin{aligned}
\overline{zw} &= \overline{(a+bi)(c+di)} && \text{Definition of } z \text{ and } w \\
&= \overline{(ac-bd)+(bc+ad)i} && \text{Definition of complex multiplication} \\
&= (ac-bd)-(bc+ad)i && \text{Definition of conjugate} \\
&= ac-bd-bci-adi && \text{Distributive Property} \\
&= ac-adi-bci-bd && \text{Commutative Property of addition} \\
&= a(c-di)-bi(c-di) && \text{Distributive Property} \\
&= (a-bi)(c-di) && \text{Distributive Property} \\
&= \overline{z}\,\overline{w} && \text{Definition of conjugate} \\
\therefore \overline{zw} &= \overline{z}\,\overline{w} && \text{Transitive Property of Equality}
\end{aligned}
$$

Q.E.D.

3. *Restatement:* Prove: If e is a multiplicative identity of the real numbers, then $e = 1$.

Proof: Suppose e is a multiplicative identity of the real numbers. Then for any real number, a, $a \cdot e = e \cdot a = a$. Also, we know that 1 is a multiplicative identity of the reals, so $a \cdot 1 = 1 \cdot a = a$. By the Transitive Property of Equality, we have $a \cdot e = a \cdot 1$. The Left Cancellation Law for Multiplication implies $e = 1$.

Q.E.D.

2.1.3 The California *Mathematics Subject Matter Requirements* require that candidates for any credential program for teaching secondary mathematics *know that the rational numbers and reals are ordered and the complex numbers are not, and that polynomial equations can be completely solved over the complex field.*

Ordering

Let X be a non-empty set. A **binary relation,** R, is a set of ordered pairs of elements of X, i.e., R is a subset of $X \times X = \{(a, b)|a, b \in X\}$.

Example: Let $R = \{(a, b) \in Z \times Z \,|ab = 20$ and $b > 0 \} = \{(1, 20), (20, 1), (2, 10), (10, 2), (4, 5), (5, 4)\}$. Then R is a binary relation on the integers, Z.

Total Ordering

A set, X, is **ordered** or **totally ordered under a binary relation** R provided the following are true:

    i.   For all $a \in X$, aRa.   (Reflexivity)

    ii. If $a, b \in X$, then either aRb or bRa.   (Totality)

    iii. If $a, b \in X$ such that aRb and bRa, then   (Antisymmetry)
         $a = b$.

    iv. If $a, b, c \in X$ such that aRb and bRc,   (Transitivity)
         then aRc.

Examples:

(a) Let X be the set of even integers, **2Z**, and let R be *"is a divisor of"* e.g., aRb means *a is a divisor of b*, i.e., *there exists a unique integer, c, such that ac = b.* Then, X is not totally ordered by R because, even though R has the transitivity property, R does not satisfy the Totality Property because if $a = b = 0$, there is no unique c such that $ac = b$. Also, R does not have the Antisymmetry Property since $-2R2 = 2R(-2)$ but $2 \neq -2$. In addition, reflexivity fails for $a = 0$.

(b) Let X be the collection of integers and let R be the standard "$\leq$" (less than or equal to). This is a total ordering of the integers.

(c) Let $X = \{ \emptyset, \{1\}, \{1, 2\}, \{1, 2, 3\}, \dots \}$ and let R be "$\subseteq$" (is a subset of). Then R is a total ordering of X.

- **Theorem**: The rationals, Q, and reals, R, are totally ordered by the binary relation "greater than or equal to," which is denoted by $\geq$, where for a, b real numbers, $a \geq b$ if and only if $a - b$ is non-negative.

  Proof: Let $X = R$, the set of all real numbers. (The proof is the same for $X = Q$.)

  i. Assume $a \in X$. It is clear that $a \geq a$ because $a - a = 0$.

  ii. Assume $a, b \in X$. If a is not greater than or equal to b, then $a - b$ is negative. But then the additive inverse of $a - b$, $-(a - b)$, is positive. And since $-(a - b) = b - a$, it is true that $b - a$ is non-negative so that $b \geq a$. Similarly, it can be shown that if b is not greater than a, then $a \geq b$. Hence, if $a, b \in X$ then $a \geq b$ or $b \geq a$.

  iii. Assume $a, b \in X$ such that $a \geq b$ and $b \geq a$. This means that both $a - b$ and $b - a$ are non-negative. But $a - b$ and $b - a$ are additive inverses, so they cannot both be positive real numbers, and so $a - b$ and $b - a$ must both equal zero. Thus, $a = b$.

  iv. Assume $a, b, c \in X$ such that $a \geq b$ and $b \geq c$. Then it follows that $a - b$ and $b - c$ are non-negative, so that their sum is non-negative; i.e., $(a - b) + (b - c) = a - c$ is non-negative. Therefore, $a - c$ is non-negative, which means that $a \geq c$.

  $\therefore$ X is totally ordered by the binary relation $\geq$.

  Q.E.D.

- In actuality, what we know about the set of real numbers is that it is not just totally ordered but that it is an **ordered field**, which means that the real numbers are a field that has a total ordering $\geq$ with the following two properties:

  (a) If $a \geq b$, then $a + c \geq b + c$ for all a, b, c in R.

  (b) If $a \geq 0$ and $b \geq 0$, then $ab \geq 0$.

- We see from property (b) that the complex numbers C cannot be ordered by $\geq$ by asking the question: how do we compare the complex number $i = \sqrt{-1}$ to 0? If we assume that $i \geq 0$, then by property (b), $i \cdot i = i^2 = -1$ is not negative, which we know is not true. If i is not greater than 0 then $-i$ would have to be positive by the second property of a binary relation that is a total order. But then by property (b), $-i \cdot -i = i^2 = -1$ is not negative, which we know is not true. Therefore, C cannot be ordered by $\geq$.

- To truly prove that C is **not an ordered field**, we need a more sophisticated theory than we are able to present here, so we will have to be satisfied with knowing that it is not ordered by the total ordering that makes R an ordered field.

Solvability of Polynomials over the Complex Numbers

The Fundamental Theorem of Algebra: Any polynomial in $C[x]$, the collection of all polynomials with complex coefficients, can be completely factored as a product of linear factors; i.e., if $P(x) = a_n x^n + a_{n-1} x^{n-1} + \cdots + a_1 x + a_0$, where $n > 0$ is a polynomial of degree n so that $a_n \neq 0$, then it can be factored into the form $P(x) = a(x - c_1)(x - c_2) \cdots z(x - c_n)$, where $a, c_1, c_2, c_3, \cdots, c_n$ are complex numbers.

- Note that all real numbers are complex numbers so that when the *Fundamental Theorem of Algebra* says the c_i's are complex numbers, this does not mean that they cannot be real numbers. The *Fundamental Theorem of Algebra* proclaims the existence of n complex roots of an n-degree polynomial, not necessarily all distinct, but does not tell us how to find them. In Section 2.2.3, we look at how to find the roots.

Review Problems for Section 2.1.3

1. Which of the following is a totally ordered set?

   (A) X is the collection of positive integers and R is "is a divisor of."

   (B) X is the collection of 10 people in a room and R is "is taller than."

   (C) X is a collection of four female siblings with R being "is a sister of."

   (D) X is the collection $\{3, 6, 12, \ldots\}$ and R is "is a factor of."

2. The polynomial $P(x) = x^6 - x + 1$ has how many complex roots?

   (A) 1

   (B) 2

   (C) 4

   (D) 6

3. Explain why the complex numbers are not ordered by the usual "$\geq$"; i.e., $a \geq b$ if and only if $a - b \geq 0$.

4. Define the relation zRw, where z, w are complex numbers, zRw if and only if $|z| \geq |w|$. Show that all but one of the properties of a total order are satisfied by R.

Detailed Solutions

1. **D**

   Both "is taller than" and "is a sister of" fail to be reflexive, so neither of choices (B) and (C) is a total order. For choice (A), given the integers 3 and 5, neither is a divisor of the other so "is a divisor of" on the positive integers does not satisfy totality, and hence cannot be a total order. The correct answer is (D) since "is a divisor of" on $X = \{3, 6, 12, \ldots\}$ satisfies all four properties of a total order.

2.   D

It follows from the *Fundamental Theorem of Algebra* that there are six complex roots because the degree of P is 6, so the correct answer is (D).

3.   The binary relation "$\geq$" fails the totality property: Consider trying to compare 0 and i. If we assume that $i \geq 0$, then by the property if $a \geq 0$ and $b \geq 0$ then $ab \geq 0$, $i \cdot i = i^2 = -1$ is not negative, which we know is not true. If i is not greater than 0, then $-i \geq 0$. But then by the property just mentioned, $-i \cdot -i = i^2 = -1$ is not negative, which we know is not true. Thus C cannot be ordered by $\geq$.

4.   It is true that for any complex number $z = a + bi$, zRz since $|z| \geq |z|$, where $|z| = \sqrt{a^2 + b^2}$. Hence the Reflexive Property holds.

Since $|z|$ is a real number for all $z \in C$, it is true that given z and w, complex numbers, either $|z| \geq |w|$ or $|w| \geq |z|$. Thus, the Totality Property holds.

Again, since the modulus is a real number, the Transitive Property holds.

But the Antisymmetry Property does not hold. Consider $z = 4 + 3i$, and $w = 3 - 4i$. $|z| = 5 = |w|$, yet $z \neq w$.

2.2 Polynomial Equations and Inequalities

> **2.2.1** The California *Mathematics Subject Matter Requirements* stipulate that candidates for any credential program for teaching secondary mathematics must *know that the graph of a linear inequality in two variables is a half plane and be able to apply this (e.g., linear programming.)*

Linear Inequalities in Two Variables in Two Dimensions

A **linear inequality in two variables** is an inequality that can be written in the form $ax + by > c$ or $ax + by \geq c$, where a, b, and c are real numbers (constants) and x and y are unknowns (variables).

A **solution** of a linear inequality is an ordered pair (a, b) that, when substituted into the inequality, produces a true statement.

Examples:

(a) Consider the linear inequality $3x + 4y \geq 24$. The solution of this inequality can be broken down into the points that satisfy $3x + 4y = 24$ along with the points that satisfy $3x + 4y > 24$. The first part is a linear equation whose solution can be represented by the line $3x + 4y = 24 \Leftrightarrow y = -\dfrac{3}{4}x + 6$ (the line on the graph in Figure 2.8). Each point on the line has coordinates that satisfy $y = -\dfrac{3}{4}x + 6$.

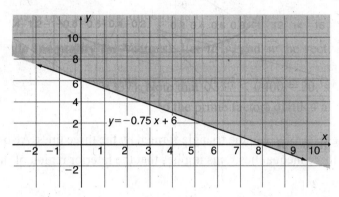

Figure 2.8

The inequality $3x + 4y > 24$ can be represented by all the points above the line $y = -\dfrac{3}{4}x + 6$ since $3x + 4y > 24 \Leftrightarrow y > -\dfrac{3}{4}x + 6$; this indicates that any point (p, q) with q greater than $-\dfrac{3}{4}p + 6$ is in the solution set of $y > -\dfrac{3}{4}x + 6$. To indicate that the region above the line belongs in the solution set of $3x + 4y \geq 24$, we shade the region.

(b) Graph the region represented by the system $\begin{cases} x + 2y < 4 \\ 3x - y \leq 5. \\ x > -1 \end{cases}$

Each of these inequalities represents a region with or without boundaries. The solution set of the system is the intersection of the three regions. To find this solution, we first graph the three lines $x + 2y = 4$, $3x - y = 5$, and $x = -1$; the first and last equations are represented by dashed lines because they are not part of the solution since $x + 2y < 4$ and $x > -1$ are strict inequalities. The three lines are graphed together in Figure 2.9.

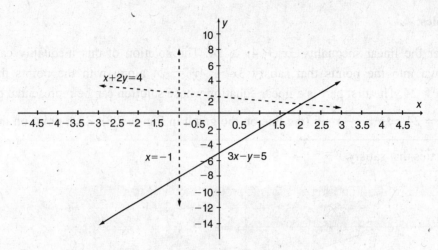

Figure 2.9

Note that the origin $(0, 0)$ lies in the triangle formed by the three lines. Also note that $x = 0$ and $y = 0$ satisfy all three inequalities. This implies that the interior region of the triangle is part of the solution.

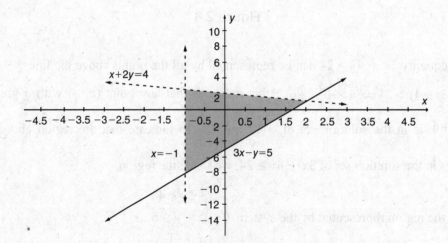

Figure 2.10

This is true because $x + 2y < 4 \Leftrightarrow y < -0.5x + 2$ (shade below the line $x + 2y = 4$), $x > -1$ (shade to the right of the line $x = -1$), and $3x - y < 5 \Leftrightarrow y > 3x - 5$ (shade above the line $3x - y = 5$). Hence, the solution is represented by the graph in Figure 2.10. Note that the vertices or corners (where the three lines intersect) are not part of the solution but that the solid part of the boundary of the triangular region (the part of the line $3x - y = 5$ between $x = -1$ and $x = 2$) is part of the solution.

Linear Programming

A **linear programming** problem is one that is concerned with finding the maximum or minimum (optimal) value of a linear function (called the **objective function**) $z = c_1 x_1 + c_2 x_2 + \ldots + c_n x_n$. The $x_1, x_2, \ldots, x_n$ are called the **decision variables** (or the independent variables), where z is subject to certain problem constraints that are in the form of linear inequalities and/or equations. In addition, there are the nonnegativity constraints $x_1 \geq 0, x_2 \geq 0, \cdots, x_n \geq 0$. The set of points satisfying all the constraints is called the **feasible region**, which is the region of possible solutions for the problem.

We restrict our study of linear programming problems to those involving two decision variables.

Example of a Linear Programming Problem

Minimize the objective function $\quad z = 3x + 4y$
subject to the constraints: $\quad\quad 2x + 3y \geq 6$
$$2x - y \geq 4$$
$$x \geq 0$$
$$y \geq 0$$

Two theorems are necessary for the process of graphically solving linear programming problems: the *Corner Point Theorem* and the *Existence of Solutions Theorem*.

Corner Point Theorem: If a linear programming problem has an optimal solution, then the optimal solution must occur at one (or more) of the corner points.

In the next theorem, we use the term *bounded*. When we say a region S in the plane ($\mathbf{R}^2$) is **bounded**, we mean the region S can be enclosed in a circle.

Existence of Solutions Theorem: Given a linear programming problem with feasible region S and objective function $z = ax + by$:

(a) If S is bounded, then z has both a maximum and a minimum value over S.

(b) If S is unbounded and $a > 0$ and $b > 0$, then z has a minimum value over S but no maximum.

(c) If S is the empty set, then z has neither a maximum nor a minimum value over S.

Note: This theorem does not cover all the possible cases for a and b.

Geometric Solution of a Linear Programming Problem

1. Form a mathematical model for the problem:

    (a) Introduce decision variables and write a linear objective function.

    (b) Write problem constraints using inequalities and/or equations.

    (c) Write the nonnegative constraints.

2. Graph the feasible region and find the corner points.

3. Use the *Existence of Solutions Theorem* to determine if an optimal solution exists.

4. If an optimal solution exists, use the *Corner Point Theorem*. Evaluate the objective function at each corner point to determine the optimal solution.

Examples:

(a) Let's look at the example given on the previous page.

Minimize the objective function $\quad z = 3x + 4y$
subject to the constraints: $\quad 2x + 3y \geq 6$
$$2x - y \geq 4$$
$$x \geq 0$$
$$y \geq 0$$

1. This problem is already modeled with the objective function and constraints.

2. Next, we graph the feasible region. Note that the non-negativity constraints $x \geq 0$ and $y \geq 0$ indicate that the feasible region will lie inside the first quadrant and maybe have boundaries on the positive x- and y- axes and origin. The feasible region is shown in Figure 2.11.

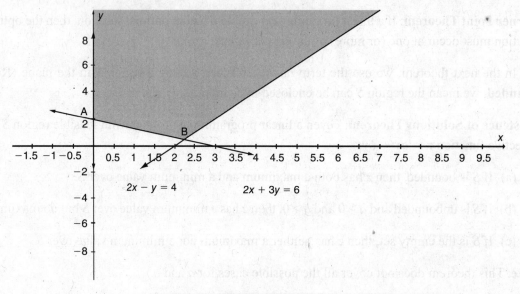

Figure 2.11

The corner point A is clearly $(0, 2)$. But we must find the coordinates of corner point B, which is the intersection of lines $y = -(2/3)x + 2$ and $y = 2x - 4$. Using substitution, we have:

$$-\frac{2}{3}x + 2 = 2x - 4 \qquad 2 + 4 = 2x + \frac{2}{3}x \qquad 6 = \frac{8}{3}x \qquad x = \frac{9}{4} \qquad y = 2\left(\frac{9}{4}\right) - 4 = \frac{1}{2}.$$

So point B has coordinates $(2.25, 0.5)$.

3. Use the *Existence of Solutions Theorem*: Since the feasible region is unbounded, we need to look at the coefficients of the objective function. These are non-negative; hence, the objective function $z = 3x + 4y$ has a minimum.

4. Use the *Corner Point Theorem*: Evaluate the objective function at the two corner points:

corner point	$z = 3x + 4y$
A (0, 2)	8
B (2.25, 0.5)	8.75

Figure 2.12

Thus, the objective function has a minimum value of 8, and this happens when $x = 0$ and $y = 2$. We note that there is no maximum value of the objective function z since x can be made as large as we want while y is zero.

(b) Now let's look at an applied problem.

An office manager needs to purchase new filing cabinets. She knows that *Smart* brand cabinets cost $80 each, require 6 square feet of floor space, and hold 7 cubic feet of files. In contrast, each *Chic* brand cabinet costs $160, requires 8 square feet of floor space, and holds 13 cubic feet of files. Her budget permits her to spend no more than $1120 on files, and the office has floor space for no more than 72 square feet of cabinets. The manager desires the greatest storage capacity within the limitations proposed by funds and space. How many of each type of cabinet should she buy?

1. First, we must model the problem. The office manager wants to maximize the storage capacity. Let x be the number of *Smart* brand file cabinets and y be the number of *Chic* brand file cabinets to buy. Then the storage capacity of x number of *Smart* file cabinets and y number of *Chic* cabinets is $7x + 13y$; thus, the objective function is $z = 7x + 13y$.

   Now let's put the rest of the information in a table, shown in Figure 2.13:

	x	y	constraint
Cost	$80	$160	≤ $1120
Floor space	6 sq. ft.	8 sq. ft.	≤ 72 sq. ft.

Figure 2.13

We form two inequalities from this table, one for each row:

$$80x + 160y \leq 1120 \quad \text{and} \quad 6x + 8y \leq 72$$

And we have also the inequalities $x \geq 0$ and $y \geq 0$.

The model for the linear programming problem is:

Maximize $\quad z = 7x + 13y$

subject to $\quad 80x + 160y \leq 1120$

$\qquad\qquad 6x + 8y \leq 72$

$\qquad\qquad x \geq 0, y \geq 0$

2. Next, we graph the feasible region:

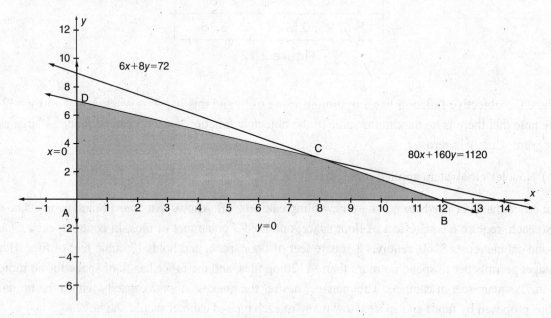

Figure 2.14

The corner points can be seen to be A (0, 0), B (12, 0), C (8, 3), and D (0, 7).

3. Since the feasible region is bounded, there must be a maximum, by the *Existence of Solutions Theorem*.

4. Evaluate the objective function at the corner points:

corner point	$z = 7x + 13y$
A (0, 0)	0
B (12, 0)	84
C (8, 3)	95
D (0, 7)	91

Figure 2.15

Hence, the maximum capacity obtainable is 95 cubic feet and is obtained by buying eight *Smart* brand file cabinets and three *Chic* brand file cabinets.

Review Problems for Section 2.2.1

1. Which of the following regions is the solution set of the system $\begin{cases} 3x - 2y \geq 8 \\ x + y \leq 5 \\ y < -1 \end{cases}$.

(A)

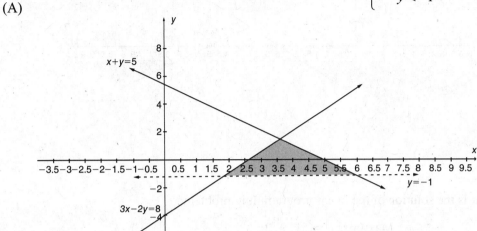

(B)

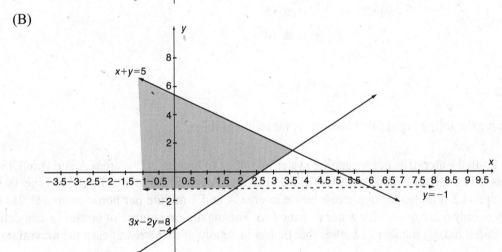

(C)

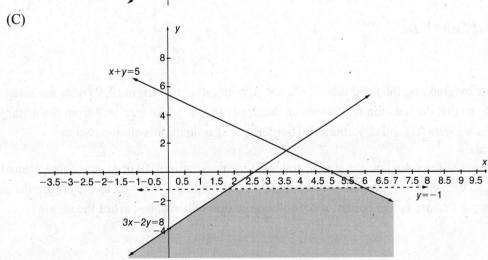

(D)

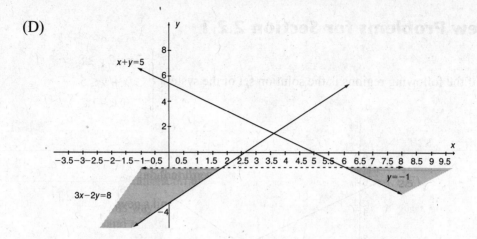

2. What is the solution of the linear programming problem:

$$\text{Maximize } z = 5x_1 + 2x_2$$
$$\text{subject to } x_1 + 3x_2 \leq 15$$
$$2x_1 + x_2 \leq 10$$
$$x_1 \leq 4$$
$$x_1 \geq 0, x_2 \geq 0$$

3. Solve the following applied linear programming problem:

A bottled water distributor supplies water in bottles to houses in two areas A and B in Union-town. The delivery charges per bottle are \$1 in area A and \$1.50 in area B. On average, he has to spend 3 minutes to supply one bottle in area A and 1 minute per bottle in area B. He can spare only 6 hours total for water distribution. The maximum number of bottles he can deliver is 280. Find the number of bottles that he has to supply in each area to earn the maximum.

Detailed Solutions

1. **C**

Start by graphing the solid line $3x - 2y = 8$, noting that the origin $(0, 0)$ does not satisfy the inequality so that the solution region lies on the opposite side of $3x - 2y = 8$ from the origin (this eliminates answers (B) and (D)); the solid border will also lie in the solution region.

Next, graph the solid line $x + y = 5$, and this time the origin $(0, 0)$ does satisfy the inequality $x + y \leq 5$, so the solution region lies on the same side of the line $x + y = 5$ as the origin; the points on $x + y = 5$ that are on the border of the solution region will also be part of the region.

Next, graph the dashed line $y = -1$, and the solution region will lie below this line and not include the line. This eliminates (A). The solution region is (C).

2. First, we graph the feasible region. This includes graphing the lines $x_1 + 3x_2 = 15$, $2x_1 + x_2 = 10$, $x_1 = 4$, $x_1 = 0$, and $x_2 = 0$, then testing the regions in the first quadrant to see what satisfies all the inequalities. The feasible solution is shown in Figure 2.16.

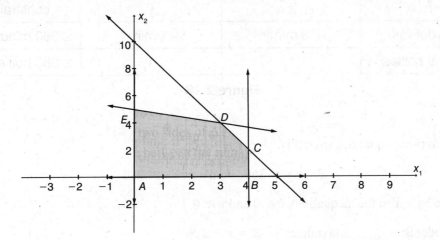

Figure 2.16

We are guaranteed a maximum by the *Existence of Solutions Theorem* since the feasible region is bounded.

Next, we need to find the corner points: A = (0, 0), B = (4, 0), C = (4, 2), and E = (0, 5) are easily read from the graph. Point D is (3, 4), which, if not clear from the graph, can be found by

solving the system of equations $\begin{cases} x_1 + 3x_2 = 15 \\ 2x_1 + x_2 = 10 \end{cases}$.

Next, substitute the corner points into the objective function (Figure. 2.17).

corner point	$z = 5x_1 + 2x_2$
(0, 0)	0
(4, 0)	20
(4, 2)	24
(3, 4)	23
(0, 5)	10

Figure 2.17

Thus, the maximum value of $z = 5x_1 + 2x_2$ is 24, and it occurs when $x_1 = 4$ and $x_2 = 2$.

3. First model the problem. Let x be the number of bottles of water to deliver to Area A and y be the number of bottles of water to deliver to Area B. Then the revenue being brought in from delivering x bottles of water to Area A and y bottles to Area B is $x + 1.5y$; thus, the objective function is $R = x + 1.5y$.

Now put the rest of the information in a table, shown in Figure 2.18.

	x	y	constraint
Time delivering	3 min	1 min	≤ 360 minutes
No. of bottles	1	1	≤ 280 bottles

Figure 2.18

We form two inequalities from this table, one for each row:

$$3x + y \leq 360 \quad \text{and} \quad x + y \leq 280$$

And we have also the inequalities $x \geq 0$ and $y \geq 0$.

The model is: Maximize $R = x + 1.5y$

subject to $3x + y \leq 360$
$x + y \leq 280$
$x \geq 0, y \geq 0$

Next, graph the feasible region:

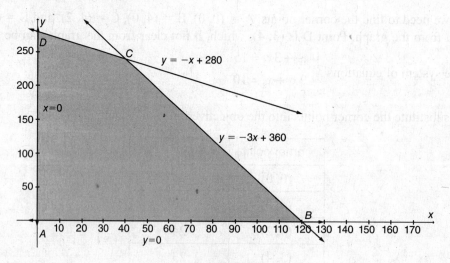

Figure 2.19

The corner points are A (0, 0), B (120, 0), C (40, 240), and D (0, 280).

Since the feasible region is bounded, there must be a maximum, by the *Existence of Solutions Theorem*.

Evaluate the objective function at the corner points, as shown in Figure 2.20.

corner point	$R = x + 1.5y$
A (0, 0)	0
B (120, 0)	120
C (40, 240)	400
D (0, 280)	420

Figure 2.20

Hence, to earn the maximum revenue of $420, the distributor should deliver only in area B and deliver 280 bottles.

> **2.2.2** The California *Mathematics Subject Matter Requirements* stipulate that candidates for any credential program for teaching secondary mathematics must be able to *prove and use each of the following theorems: Rational Root Theorem, Factor Theorem, Conjugate Root Theorem, Quadratic Formula, and Binomial Theorem.*

Important Theorems in Algebra

All of the theorems listed above are important in the development of algebra. We give the proofs and some applications of each.

Rational Root Theorem: If $P(x) = a_n x^n + a_{n-1} x^{n-1} + \cdots + a_1 x + a_0$ is a polynomial with integral coefficients and of degree n, and if $\dfrac{p}{q}$ is a rational root of $P(x)$, where p and q are relatively prime, then p is a divisor of the constant term a_0, and q is a divisor of the leading coefficient a_n.

- Note that the *Rational Root Theorem* first assumes that all the coefficients are integers, so if some coefficients are fractions they must be cleared. Second, the degree is n, which means that the leading coefficient a_n is not equal to zero. If these assumptions are true, then the *Rational Root Theorem* tells us how to look for the rational solutions to the equation $P(x) = 0$; list all rational numbers of the form $\dfrac{p}{q}$, where p and q are **relatively prime** ($\gcd(p, q) = 1$; i.e., they have no common positive divisors other than 1), and compute $P\left(\dfrac{p}{q}\right)$ for each $\dfrac{p}{q}$. If $P\left(\dfrac{p}{q}\right) = 0$ for some rational factor on the list, then it is a solution of $P(x) = 0$.

- **Applying the Rational Root Theorem**

  Example: Find all rational roots of $P(x) = 2x^3 + 3x^2 + 2x + 3$. The p's are the divisors of 3, which are $\pm 1, \pm 3$, and the q's are the divisors of 2, which are $\pm 1, \pm 2$. So, by the *Rational Root Theorem*, if the given polynomial has a rational root, then it must belong to the set of $\frac{p}{q}$'s, which is $\left\{ \pm \frac{1}{2}, \pm 1, \pm \frac{3}{2}, \pm 3 \right\}$. Check:

  $P(\pm .5) \neq 0, P(\pm 1) \neq 0, P(1.5) \neq 0, P(-1.5) = 0, P(\pm 3) \neq 0$.

  So the only rational root is -1.5.

- **Proof of the Rational Root Theorem**

  Proof: Assume $P(x) = a_n x^n + a_{n-1} x^{n-1} + \cdots + a_1 x + a_0$ is a polynomial with integral coefficients and of degree n, and that $\frac{p}{q}$ is a rational root of $P(x)$, where p and q are relatively prime.

  $a_n \left(\frac{p}{q} \right)^n + a_{n-1} \left(\frac{p}{q} \right)^{n-1} + \cdots + a_1 \left(\frac{p}{q} \right) + a_0 = 0$. Multiply each term of this equation by q^{n-1}, resulting in $a_n \left(\frac{1}{q} \right) p^n + a_{n-1} p^{n-1} + a_{n-2} p^{n-2} q + \cdots + a_1 p q^{n-2} + a_0 q^{n-1} = 0$.

  All of the terms after the first one are integers; hence, the first term $a_n \left(\frac{1}{q} \right) p^n$ is also an integer.

  Thus, q divides $a_n p^n$, but since p and q have no common divisors other than 1, q must be a divisor of a_n.

  Now multiply each term $a_n \left(\frac{p}{q} \right)^n + a_{n-1} \left(\frac{p}{q} \right)^{n-1} + \cdots + a_1 \left(\frac{p}{q} \right) + a_0 = 0$ by $\frac{q^n}{p}$ to arrive at $a_n p^{n-1} + a_{n-1} p^{n-2} q + \cdots + a_1 q^{n-1} + a_0 q^n \left(\frac{1}{p} \right) = 0$. The first n terms are integers, hence so is the last term, and this implies that p divides $a_0 q^n$, but since q and p have no common divisors other than 1, p must be a divisor of a_0.

  Q.E.D.

The next important theorem involving divisors is the *Factor Theorem*, which follows from the *Remainder Theorem*. We look at both theorems.

Remainder Theorem: *If $P(x)$ is a polynomial, then the remainder after division by $(x - c)$ is exactly $P(c)$.*

- **Proof**: Let $P(x)$ be a polynomial and consider dividing $P(x)$ by $x - c$. The result is a quotient $Q(x)$ and a constant remainder R. This gives us $P(x) = (x - c)Q(x) + R$. From this, we see that $P(c) = (c - c)Q(c) + R = 0 \cdot Q(c) + R = R$.

  Q.E.D.

Factor Theorem: Let $P(x)$ be a polynomial. Then c is a root of $P(x)$ if and only if $x - c$ is a factor of $P(x)$.

- **Proof**: Let $P(x)$ be a polynomial.

    ($\Rightarrow$)Assume c is a root of $P(x)$. Then $P(c) = 0$. By the *Remainder Theorem*, we know that $P(x) = (x - c)Q(x) + P(c) = (x - c)Q(x)$, and therefore $(x - c)$ is a factor of $P(x)$.

    ($\Leftarrow$) Assume $x - c$ is a factor of $P(x)$. Then $P(x) = (x - c)Q(x)$ for some polynomial Q. Thus, $P(c) = (c - c)Q(c) = 0$, and c is a root of $P(x)$.

    Q.E.D.

- **Applying the Factor Theorem**

    Example: To determine if $x - 2$ or $x + 3$ is a factor of $P(x) = 2x^4 + 6x^3 - x - 3$, we can evaluate $P(2)$ and $P(-3)$: $P(2) = 32 + 48 - 2 - 3 = 75$ and $P(-3) = 162 - 162 + 3 - 3 = 0$. Thus, 2 is not a root of $P(x)$, while -3 is a root. Therefore, we conclude that $x - 2$ is not a factor of $P(x)$ and $x + 3$ is a factor of $p(x)$.

Complex Conjugate Root Theorem: Let $P(x)$ be a polynomial with real coefficients. If the complex number $a + bi$ is a root of $P(x)$, then its conjugate, $a - bi$, is also a root of $P(x)$.

To help understand the theorem, we apply it first, and then prove it.

- **Applying the Complex Conjugate Theorem**

    Example: Show that $2 - 3i$ is a root of $P(x) = 2x^2 - 8x + 26$. We note that the *Complex Conjugate Theorem* tells us that the complex conjugate $2 + 3i$ is also a root. First, show that $2 - 3i$ is a root:

    $$
    \begin{aligned}
    P(2 - 3i) &= 2(2 - 3i)^2 - 8(2 - 3i) + 26 \\
    &= 2(4 - 12i + 9i^2) - 8(2 - 3i) + 26 \\
    &= 2(-5 - 12i) - 16 + 24i + 26 \\
    &= -10 - 24i + 24i + 10 \\
    &= 0
    \end{aligned}
    $$

    Let's check that $2 + 3i$ is also a root:
    $$
    \begin{aligned}
    P(2 + 3i) &= 2(2 + 3i)^2 - 8(2 + 3i) + 26 \\
    &= 2(4 + 12i + 9i^2) - 8(2 + 3i) + 26 \\
    &= 2(-5 + 12i) - 16 - 24i + 26 \\
    &= -10 + 24i - 24i + 10 \\
    &= 0
    \end{aligned}
    $$

So $2 - 3i$ and $2 + 3i$ are both roots of $P(x) = 2x^2 - 8x + 26$.

- **Proving the Complex Conjugate Theorem**

  Proof: Let $P(x) = a_n x^n + a_{n-1}x^{n-1} + \ldots + a_1 x + a_0$, where the coefficients are real numbers, and assume that $z = a + bi$ is a root of $P(x)$. Thus, $P(z) = 0 \Rightarrow \overline{P(z)} = 0$. Using the properties of the complex conjugate, we have:

$$
\begin{aligned}
0 = \overline{P(z)} &= \overline{a_n z^n + a_{n-1}z^{n-1} + \cdots + a_1 z + a_0} \\
&= \overline{a_n z^n} + \overline{a_{n-1}z^{n-1}} + \cdots + \overline{a_1 z} + \overline{a_0} \\
&= \overline{a_n}\,\overline{z^n} + \overline{a_{n-1}}\,\overline{z^{n-1}} + \cdots + \overline{a_1}\,\overline{z} + \overline{a_0} \\
&= a_n \overline{z^n} + a_{n-1}\overline{z^{n-1}} + \cdots + a_a \overline{z} + a_0 \\
&= a_n \left(\overline{z}\right)^n + a_{n-1}\left(\overline{z}\right)^{n-1} + \cdots + a_1 \overline{z} + a_0 \\
&= P\left(\overline{z}\right)
\end{aligned}
$$

Therefore, $\overline{z} = a - bi$ is a root of $P(x)$.

Q.E.D.

Quadratic Formula: Let a, b, and c be real numbers with $a \neq 0$. Then the solutions of the equation $ax^2 + bx + c = 0$ are given by

$$x = \frac{-b \pm \sqrt{b^2 - 4ac}}{2a}$$

- **Proof**: Let a, b, and c be real numbers with $a \neq 0$. Then

$$
\begin{aligned}
ax^2 + bx + c = 0 &\Leftrightarrow x^2 + \frac{b}{a}x = -\frac{c}{a} \\
&\Leftrightarrow x^2 + \frac{b}{a}x + \frac{b^2}{4a^2} = -\frac{c}{a} + \frac{b^2}{4a^2} \\
&\Leftrightarrow \left(x + \frac{b}{2a}\right)^2 = \frac{b^2 - 4ac}{4a^2} \\
&\Leftrightarrow x + \frac{b}{2a} = \frac{\pm\sqrt{b^2 - 4ac}}{2a} \\
&\Leftrightarrow x = \frac{-b \pm \sqrt{b^2 - 4ac}}{2a}
\end{aligned}
$$

Q.E.D.

- **Applying the Quadratic Formula**

  Examples: Use the quadratic formula to solve each of the following quadratic equations.

  (a) $-3x^2 + x = -4$

  (b) $9m^2 - 42m + 49 = 0$

  (c) $z^2 = z - 5$

(a) $-3x^2 + x = -4 \Leftrightarrow -3x^2 + x + 4 = 0$. Set $a = -3$, $b = 1$, and $c = 4$, and substitute these into the quadratic formula:

$$x = \frac{-1 \pm \sqrt{1 - 4(-3)(4)}}{2(-3)} = \frac{-1 \pm \sqrt{49}}{-6} = \frac{-1 \pm 7}{-6} = \frac{1 \pm 7}{6}, \text{ so that the solutions are}$$

$$x = \frac{4}{3} \text{ and } x = -1.$$

(b) $9m^2 - 42m + 49 = 0$. Set $a = 9$, $b = -42$, and $c = 49$; substitute these values into the quadratic formula:

$$m = \frac{42 \pm \sqrt{(-42)^2 - 4(9)(49)}}{2(9)} = \frac{42 \pm 0}{18} = \frac{7}{3}. \text{ So there is a double root, } m = \frac{7}{3}.$$

(c) $z^2 = z - 5 \Leftrightarrow z^2 - z + 5 = 0$. Set $a = 1$, $b = -1$, and $c = 5$ and substitute these values into the quadratic formula:

$$z = \frac{1 \pm \sqrt{(-1)^2 - 4(1)(5)}}{2(1)} = \frac{1 \pm \sqrt{-19}}{2}. \text{ So there are no real solutions but there are two com-}$$

plex solutions, $z = \dfrac{1 + i\sqrt{19}}{2}$ and $z = \dfrac{1 - i\sqrt{19}}{2}$.

Before looking at the **Binomial Theorem**, we introduce some necessary notation.

For any positive integer n, $n!$ (read "***n* factorial**") is computed as follows:

$$n! = n(n - 1)(n - 2) \cdots 3 \cdot 2 \cdot 1.$$

For positive integers n and k with $n \geq k$, we have the combinatorial notation $\dbinom{n}{k} = \dfrac{n!}{k!(n-k)!}$.

Examples:

(a) $5! = 5 \cdot 4 \cdot 3 \cdot 2 \cdot 1 = 120$, $4! = 4 \cdot 3 \cdot 2 \cdot 1 = 24$, $3! = 3 \cdot 2 \cdot 1 = 6$, etc.

(b) $\dbinom{6}{4} = \dfrac{6!}{4!(6-4)!} = \dfrac{6!}{4!2!} = \dfrac{6 \cdot 5}{2!} = 15$. In the third step, we used the following rule:

$$\frac{n!}{k!} = n(n-1)(n-2)\cdots(k+1) \text{ when } n > k.$$

Binomial Theorem: For any positive integer, n,

$$(x + y)^n = \sum_{k=0}^{n} \binom{n}{k} x^{n-k} y^k$$

$$= \binom{n}{0} x^n y^0 + \binom{n}{1} x^{n-1} y^1 + \binom{n}{2} x^{n-2} y^2 + \binom{n}{3} x^{n-3} y^3 + \cdots + \binom{n}{n-1} xy^{n-1} + \binom{n}{n} x^0 y^n$$

$$= x^n + nx^{n-1} y + \frac{n(n-1)}{2!} x^{n-2} y^2 + \frac{n(n-1)(n-2)}{3!} x^{n-3} y^3 + \cdots + nxy^{n-1} + y^n$$

Note again that $\dbinom{n}{k} = \dfrac{n!}{k!(n-k)!}$, where $n! = n(n-1)(n-2)\ldots 3 \cdot 2 \cdot 1$.

- **Proof**: Let P(n) be the statement

$$(x+y)^n = \sum_{k=0}^{n} \binom{n}{k} x^{n-k} y^k$$

$$= \binom{n}{0} x^n y^0 + \binom{n}{1} x^{n-1} y^1 + \binom{n}{2} x^{n-2} y^2 + \binom{n}{3} x^{n-3} y^3 + \cdots + \binom{n}{n-1} x y^{n-1} + \binom{n}{n} x^0 y^n$$

where $n \geq 1$ is an integer.

P(1) is the statement $(x+y)^1 = \sum_{k=0}^{1} \binom{1}{k} x^{1-k} y^k = \binom{1}{0} x^1 y^0 + \binom{1}{1} x^0 y^1 = x+y$, which is true.

Now assume that P(n) is true; that is, assume $(x+y)^n = \sum_{k=0}^{n} \binom{n}{k} x^{n-k} y^k$, where n is any fixed but arbitrary integer such that $n \geq 1$.

Note that P(n + 1) is $(x+y)^{n+1} = \sum_{k=0}^{n+1} \binom{n+1}{k} x^{n+1-k} y^k$

Then, $(x+y)^{n+1} = (x+y)^n (x+y)$ by algebra

$$= \left(\sum_{k=0}^{n} \binom{n}{k} x^{n-k} y^k \right)(x+y) \quad \text{by induction}$$

$$= \sum_{k=0}^{n} \binom{n}{k} x^{n+1-k} y^k + \sum_{k=0}^{n} \binom{n}{k} x^{n-k} y^{k+1} \quad \text{by algebra}$$

$$= \binom{n}{0} x^{n+1} + \binom{n}{1} x^n y + \binom{n}{2} x^{n-1} y^2 + \cdots + \binom{n}{n-1} x^2 y^{n-1} + \binom{n}{n} x y^n \quad \text{by algebra}$$

$$+ \binom{n}{0} x^n y + \binom{n}{1} x^{n-1} y^2 + \cdots + \binom{n}{n-1} x y^n + \binom{n}{n} y^{n+1}$$

$$= x^{n+1} + n x^n y + \frac{n(n-1)}{2} x^{n-1} y^2 + \cdots + n x^2 y^{n-1} + x y^n$$

$$+ x^n y + n x^{n-1} y^2 + \cdots + n x y^n + y^{n+1}$$

$$= x^{n+1} + (n+1) x^n y + \frac{(n+1)n}{2} x^{n-1} y^2 + \cdots + (n+1) x y^n + y^{n+1}$$

$$= \sum_{k=0}^{n+1} \binom{n+1}{k} x^{n+1-k} y^k$$

Hence, for all $n \geq 1$, if P(n) is true, then P(n + 1) is true.

Thus, by the Principle of Mathematical Induction, P(n) is true for all $n = 1, 2, 3,\ldots$

Q.E.D.

- **Applying the Binomial Theorem**

Example: Expand $(2x + 5)^4$.

$$(2x+5)^4 = \binom{4}{0}(2x)^4 + \binom{4}{1}(2x)^3(5) + \binom{4}{2}(2x)^2(5)^2 + \binom{4}{3}(2x)(5)^3 + \binom{4}{4}(5)^4$$

$$= (1)16x^4 + (4)40x^3 + (6)100x^2 + (4)250x + (1)625$$

$$= 16x^4 + 160x^3 + 600x^2 + 1000x + 625$$

Review Problems for Section 2.2.2

1. Use the *Rational Root Theorem* to find all the rational roots of the polynomial $P(x) = 4x^4 - x^2 - 2x - 1$.

2. Use the *Binomial Theorem* to find the third term in the expansion of $(3x - 5i)^6$.

3. Given $q(x) = (x - 1)^2(x + 1)$, find c so that the only real zero of $q(x) + c$ is -3.

4. Find c so that $(2x^4 - x^3 + 5x - 2)/(x + 1) = q(x) + c/(x + 1)$ where $q(x)$ is a polynomial of degree 3.

5. If $a = 2$ and $b = 1 - 3i$ are two of the roots of a cubic polynomial with real coefficients, with the third root being designated by c, find the product abc.

Detailed Solutions

1. The *Rational Root Theorem* says that if a number is a rational root of P, then it must be a rational number in the form $\dfrac{p}{q}$, where p is a divisor of the constant term, -1 here, and q is a divisor of the leading coefficient, 4 here. Thus, we should consider the rational numbers $\pm\dfrac{1}{4}, \pm\dfrac{1}{2}, \pm1$ as the possible roots. So we evaluate $P(x)$ for each of these six numbers, and if any result in $P(x) = 0$, then they are rational roots of P.

$$P\left(-\frac{1}{4}\right) = 4\left(-\frac{1}{4}\right)^4 - \left(-\frac{1}{4}\right)^2 - 2\left(-\frac{1}{4}\right) - 1 = \frac{1}{64} - \frac{1}{16} + \frac{1}{2} - 1 \neq 0$$

$$P\left(\frac{1}{4}\right) = 4\left(\frac{1}{4}\right)^4 - \left(\frac{1}{4}\right)^2 - 2\left(\frac{1}{4}\right) - 1 = \frac{1}{64} - \frac{1}{16} - \frac{1}{2} - 1 \neq 0$$

$$P\left(-\frac{1}{2}\right) = 4\left(-\frac{1}{2}\right)^4 - \left(-\frac{1}{2}\right)^2 - 2\left(-\frac{1}{2}\right) - 1 = \frac{1}{4} - \frac{1}{4} + 1 - 1 = 0$$

$$P\left(\frac{1}{2}\right) = 4\left(\frac{1}{2}\right)^4 - \left(\frac{1}{2}\right)^2 - 2\left(\frac{1}{2}\right) - 1 = \frac{1}{4} - \frac{1}{4} - 1 - 1 \neq 0$$

$$P(-1) = 4(-1)^4 - (-1)^2 - 2(-1) - 1 = 4 - 1 + 2 - 1 \neq 0$$

$$P(1) = 4(1)^4 - (1)^2 - 2(1) - 1 = 4 - 1 - 2 - 1 = 0$$

Hence, the rational roots are $-\dfrac{1}{2}$ and 1.

2. According to the *Binomial Theorem*, the third term in the expansion of $(a + b)^6$ is $\binom{6}{2}a^{6-2}b^2$, so the third term in the expansion of $(3x - 5i)^6 = (3x + (-5i))^6$ is determined to be

$$\binom{6}{2}(3x)^4(-5i)^2 = \frac{6!}{2!(6-2)!}(81x^4)(-25) = (15)(81x^4)(-25) = -30375x^4.$$

3. -3 is a zero of $q(x) + c$ if and only if $q(-3) + c = 0$. Find c: $q(-3) + c = (-3-1)^2(-3+1) + c = -32 + c = 0$, which means that c is 32. Now show that -3 is the only real zero of $q(x) + c$: $q(x) + c = (x-1)^2(x+1) + 32 = x^3 - x^2 - x + 33 = (x+3)(x^2 - 4x + 11)$ so that the other zeroes of $q(x) + c$ are the solutions to $x^2 - 4x + 11 = 0$. Using the *Quadratic Formula Theorem* with $a = 1$, $b = -4$, and $c = 11$, we can find these zeroes: $x = \dfrac{4 \pm \sqrt{16-44}}{2}$, which are complex numbers that are not real numbers. So, -3 is the only real zero of $q(x) + 32$.

4. The expression $(2x^4 - x^3 + 5x - 2)/(x + 1) = q(x) + c/(x + 1)$ can be written in the form $2x^4 - x^3 + 5x - 2 = q(x)(x + 1) + c$. Substituting $x = -1$ into this expression, we see that $2(-1)^4 - (-1)^3 + 5(-1) - 2 = q(-1)\cdot0 + c$, or $c = -4$.

5. Since the cubic polynomial has real coefficients, then by the *Complex Conjugate Root Theorem*, since $1 - 3i$ is a root, its complex conjugate $1 + 3i$ must also be a root, and hence $c = 1 + 3i$. Therefore, $abc = 2(1 - 3i)(1 + 3i) = 2(1 - 9i^2) = 20$.

2.2.3 The California *Mathematics Subject Matter Requirements* stipulate that candidates for any credential program for teaching secondary mathematics must be able to *use the Fundamental Theorem of Algebra to analyze and solve polynomials with real coefficients.*

Fundamental Theorem of Algebra

The short form of the statement of the *Fundamental Theorem of Algebra* is as follows: Any polynomial in $C[x]$ has a root in C.

Another, possibly more familiar, form of the same theorem is: Any polynomial in $C[x]$, the collection of all polynomials with complex coefficients, can be completely factored as a product of linear factors; i.e., if $P(x) = a_nx^n + a_{n-1}x^{n-1} + \cdots + a_1x + a_0$, where $n > 0$ is a polynomial of degree n so that $a^n \neq 0$, then it can be factored into the form $P(x) = a(x - c_1)(x - c_2)\cdots(x - c_n)$, where a, c_1, c_2, c_3, ..., c_n are complex numbers.

This tells us that any polynomial with complex coefficients can be completely factored into a product of linear factors and that it has n (not necessarily distinct) roots.

Examples:

(a) Find all the roots of $P(x) = x^3 + 2x^2 + 3x + 6$. The *Fundamental Theorem of Algebra* tells us that there are three roots, since P is a polynomial of degree 3. From the *Complex Conjugate Theorem*, we know that there must be at least one real root because the complex roots come in pairs. Now we must look for the roots.

Use the *Rational Root Theorem*: if there are rational roots, they must be elements of the set $\{\pm1, \pm 2, \pm3, \pm6\}$. So we evaluate P for these numbers until we find a zero:

$$P(1) = 12, P(-1) = 4, P(2) = 28, P(-2) = 0...\text{stop! We have that} -2 \text{ is a root of } P.$$

This means that $(x + 2)$ is a factor of P. Next we use long division or synthetic division to find the quadratic factor of P:

$$\begin{array}{r} x^2 + 3 \\ x+2 \overline{) x^3 + 2x^2 + 3x + 6} \end{array} \quad \text{so } P(x) = (x + 2)(x^2 + 3) = (x+2)\left(x-\sqrt{3}i\right)\left(x+\sqrt{3}i\right)$$

Hence, the roots of P are $-2, \sqrt{3}i, -\sqrt{3}i$.

(b) Find all roots of $Q(x) = 81x^4 - 1$. This polynomial of degree 4 must have four roots according to the *Fundamental Theorem of Algebra*. This polynomial is a **difference of two squares** binomial, so we can factor it using the formula $a^2 - b^2 = (a - b)(a + b)$. This gives us: $81x^4 - 1 = (9x^2 - 1)(9x^2 + 1)$. But again we have a difference of two squares since $9x^2 - 1 = (3x - 1)(3x + 1)$. Hence we have $81x^4 - 1 = (9x^2 + 1)(3x + 1)(3x - 1)$. Next, we must factor $9x^2 + 1$. If we think of $9x^2 + 1$ as $(3x)^2 - (i)^2$, we again have the difference of two squares and can use this to factor $(3x)^2 - (i) = (3x + i)(3x - i)$. Now we have the factorization: $81x^4 - 1 = (3x + i)(3x - i)(3x + 1)(3x - 1)$, so the four roots are $\frac{1}{3}, -\frac{1}{3}, \frac{i}{3}, -\frac{i}{3}$.

 Review Problems for Section 2.2.3

1. The polynomial $f(x) = x^4 + 2x^3 - 3x^2 + 2x - 4$ has i as a zero. Write f as a product of linear factors.

2. Find all $z \in C$ that satisfy $z^2 + (1 - i)z - i = 0$ and explain why your answer does not contradict the *Complex Conjugate Root Theorem*.

Detailed Solutions

1. $f(x) = x^4 + 2x^3 - 3x^2 + 2x - 4$ has four complex zeroes by the *Fundamental Theorem of Algebra*. The *Complex Conjugate Root Theorem* tells us that since i is a root of $f(x) = 0$, so is $-i$. So we can factor $f(x) = (x - i)(x + i)Q(x)$, where Q is a polynomial of degree 2. Since $(x - i)(x + i) = x^2 + 1$, we can divide f by $x^2 + 1$ to obtain the factorization $x^4 + 2x^3 - 3x^2 + 2x - 4 = (x^2 + 1)(x^2 + 2x - 4)$. To factor $x^2 + 2x - 4$, use the *Quadratic Formula Theorem* with $a = 1$,

$b = 2$, and $c = -4$: $x = \dfrac{-2 \pm \sqrt{4 - (-16)}}{2} = \dfrac{-2 \pm 2\sqrt{5}}{2} = -1 \pm \sqrt{5}$. Hence, we can express f as a product of linear factors: $f(x) = (x - i)(x + i)\left(x + 1 - \sqrt{5}\right)\left(x + 1 + \sqrt{5}\right)$.

2. Once again, the *Fundamental Theorem of Algebra* indicates how many roots we are looking for; in this case, since the polynomial is a quadratic, we are looking for two roots. We can factor $z^2 + (1 - i)z - i = (z + 1)(z - i) = 0$ to see that the roots are $z = i$ and $z = 1$.

   This does not contradict the *Complex Conjugate Root Theorem*, which says the complex conjugates must either both be roots or neither be roots of a polynomial, because the coefficients of the given polynomial are not all real numbers. Hence, the hypothesis of the theorem is not satisfied.

2.3 Functions

> **2.3.1** The California *Mathematics Subject Matter Requirements* stipulate that candidates for any credential program for teaching secondary mathematics must be *able to analyze and prove properties of functions, including domain and range, one-to-one and onto, inverses, composition, and the difference between relations and functions.*

Definitions

   There are several ways to define the concepts of relation and function; here we give two equivalent definitions for each.

   A **relation** from a set X to a set Y is

   (i) a collection of ordered pairs, in which the first element, x, of each pair, (x, y), belongs to the set X, and the second element, y, belongs to Y; or

   (ii) a rule that assigns to some elements, x, of set X, at least one element of the set Y.

   A **function** from a set X to a set Y is

   (i) a collection of ordered pairs, in which the first element, x, of each pair, (x, y), belongs to the set X, while the second element, y, belongs to Y, and each element of X appears in exactly one ordered pair. The two elements of the ordered pair are called **coordinates**; or

   (ii) a given rule that assigns to each element, x, of set X, exactly one element, y, of set Y.

   It should be clear from the definitions of relation and function that every function is a relation. The converse, every relation is a function, is not true, as shown in the next example.

For a function, the set, X, of all first coordinates is called the **domain** of the function and the set of all second coordinates is called the **range**. Note that the range may or may not be equal to Y, which is called the **codomain** of the function.

The difference between a relation and a function is that for a function, each element of X appears in exactly one ordered pair, while in a relation an element of X may appear in no pairs, one pair, or more than one pair. We note that relations and functions are both subsets of the set $X \times Y = \{(x, y) \mid x \in X \text{ and } y \in Y\}$.

Example: Let $X = \{-5, -3, 2, 0\}$ and $Y = \{0, 1, 2, 3\}$, then $\{(2, 1), (2, 0), (0, 1)\}$ is a relation from X to Y but it is not a function because the first coordinate 2 is used more than once and -5 and -3 are not used as first coordinates. The set $\{(2, 3), (-3, 1), (0, 0), (-5, 3)\}$ is an example of a function with domain $\{2, -3, 0, -5\}$ and range $\{3, 1, 0\}$.

Some functions can be described by a formula such as $f(x) = 3x - 5$. The name of the function is f, and we write $f(x)$ (read "f of x") to mean the value or output that the function f assigns to the input x. The variable x, which represents the input, is called the **independent variable** and $y = f(x)$ is the **dependent variable**.

If we say that a function f is defined at x, we mean that x is in the domain of f, which we write as $x \in D_f$. If x is not in the domain of f, then we say that f is undefined at x and we write $x \notin D_f$.

Sometimes when a function is given, the domain is specified, such as in the case $f(x) = x^2$, $x \geq 0$, where the domain is $D_f = [0, +\infty)$. However, if the domain is not specified, we assume the domain is the set of all real numbers that can be substituted into the function formula without causing problems. This is called the **implicit domain**. For example, the function mentioned above, $f(x) = 3x - 5$, has domain $D_f = (-\infty, +\infty)$, all real numbers, whereas the function $g(x) = \dfrac{2x - 3}{x + 7}$ has domain $D_g = (-\infty, -7) \cup (-7, +\infty)$, which is the set of all real numbers not equal to -7 since division by zero is not defined.

The range of a function given by a formula may be more difficult to determine. The function $f(x) = 3x - 5$ has as its range the set of all real numbers. To see this, consider any real number r and set $r = 3x - 5$. Solving for x, we have $x = \dfrac{r + 5}{3}$. This is the input number that produces the output r. In contrast, the function $h(x) = x^2$ never produces a negative number, but the equation $x^2 = r$ can be solved for any non-negative real number r; so we can see that the range is the set $[0, +\infty)$.

Four Ways to Represent a Function

1. **Algebraically:** This is by formula, which we have already seen; for example, $s(t) = \sqrt{t + 1}$. The domain of this function is the set of all real numbers greater than or equal to -1; i.e., $D_s = [-1, +\infty)$. The range of this function is $R_s = [0, +\infty)$ since square roots are non-negative, and $r = \sqrt{t + 1}$ $t = r^2 - 1$ so that an input number t can be found for each non-negative number r.

2. **Numerically:** This we also have seen. Either we are given a set of ordered pairs or the pairs are given in table form, as in Figure 2.21.

u	v
2	9
3	4
5	1
7	4
11	9

Figure 2.21

For the function, $v = v(u)$, given in Figure 2.21, the domain is $D_v = \{2, 3, 5, 7, 11\}$ and the range is $R_v = \{1, 4, 9\}$.

3. **Graphically:** We can plot the ordered pairs in the coordinate plane. Figure 2.22A and Figure 2.22B shows the graphs of the two functions from the algebraic example and the numerical example. It is often easier to determine the range of the function from its graph.

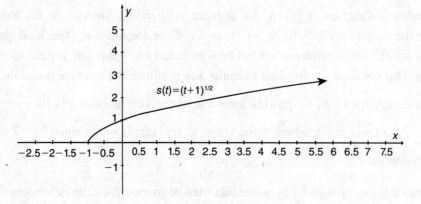

$s(t) = (t+1)^{1/2}$

Figure 2.22A

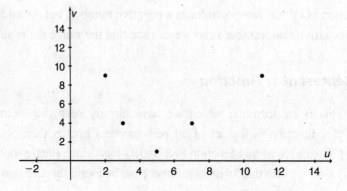

Figure 2.22B

4. **Verbally:** A function can be described in words. For example: The temperature in Indianapolis warmed up throughout the morning, and then suddenly became much cooler around noon when a storm came through. After the storm, it warmed up before cooling off at sunset.

Functions that are defined separately on different subsets of the domain are called **piecewise-defined functions**. Here is an example given first algebraically and then graphically in Figure 2.23.

$$g(x) = \begin{cases} -2x+1, & \text{if } x < 2 \\ x+3, & \text{if } x \geq 2 \end{cases}$$

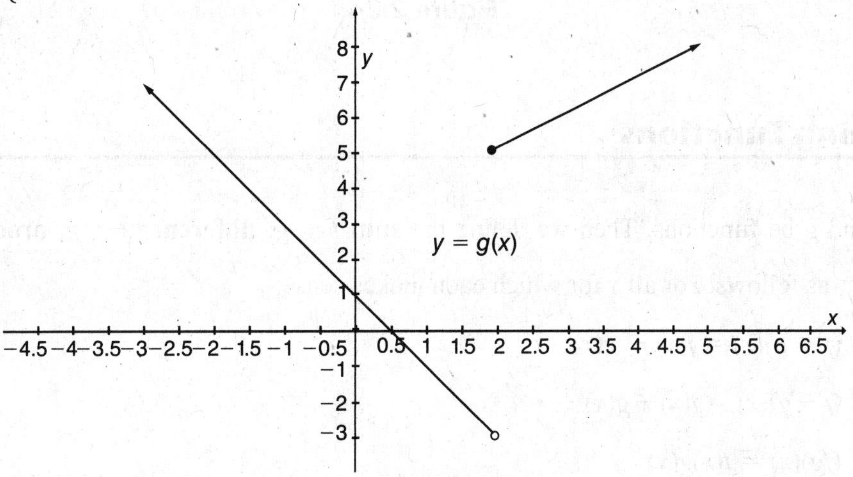

Figure 2.23

The Vertical Line Test: If no vertical line can be drawn that intersects a graph at more than one point, then the graph represents a function.

Figure 2.24 shows a graph that does not represent a function. The vertical dashed line $x = -2$ intersects the graph at three points. We say the graph *fails* the vertical line test, and hence does not represent a function.

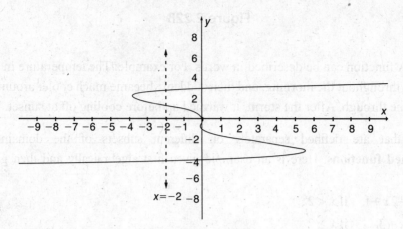

Figure 2.24

Combining Functions

Let f and g be functions. Then we define the **sum** $f + g$, **difference** $f - g$, **product** fg, and **quotient** $\dfrac{f}{g}$ as follows: For all x for which each makes sense,

(a) $(f + g)(x) = f(x) + g(x)$

(b) $(f - g)(x) = f(x) - g(x)$

(c) $(fg)(x) = f(x)g(x)$

(d) $\left(\dfrac{f}{g}\right)(x) = \dfrac{f(x)}{g(x)}, g(x) \neq 0$

Notation: The following rules hold for the domains of the above functions: For functions f and g,

$$D_{f+g} = D_{f-g} = D_{fg} = D_f \cap D_g \text{ and } D_{\frac{f}{g}} = (D_f \cap D_g) - \left\{x \in D_g \mid g(x) = 0\right\}.$$

Composition of Functions

The **composite function**, $f \circ g$, of f and g is defined by $(f \circ g)(x) = f(g(x))$ for each x in the domain of $f \circ g$. The domain of $f \circ g$ is the set of all x in the domain of g such that $g(x)$ is in the domain of f;

i.e., $D_{f \circ g} = \{x \in D_g \mid g(x) \in D_f\}$.

Examples:

Let $f(x) = \dfrac{1}{x-1}$ and $g(x) = \sqrt{x}$. Then $D_f = (-\infty, 1) \cup (1, +\infty)$, and $D_g = [0, +\infty)$.

(a) $(f+g)(x) = \dfrac{1}{x-1} + \sqrt{x}$ $\qquad\qquad D_{f+g} = D_f \cap D_g = [0,1) \cup (1, +\infty)$

(b) $(g-f)(x) = \sqrt{x} - \dfrac{1}{x-1}$ $\qquad\qquad D_{f-g} = D_f \cap D_g = [0,1) \cup (1, +\infty)$

(c) $(fg)(x) = \dfrac{\sqrt{x}}{x-1}$ $\qquad\qquad\qquad D_{fg} = D_f \cap D_g = [0,1) \cup (1, +\infty)$

(d) $\left(\dfrac{f}{g}\right)(x) = \dfrac{1}{\sqrt{x}\,(x-1)}$ $\qquad\qquad D_{\frac{f}{g}} = D_f \cap D_g - \left\{ x \in D_g \mid g(x) = 0 \right\}$

$\qquad\qquad\qquad\qquad\qquad\qquad\qquad\qquad\qquad = [0,1) \cup (1, +\infty) - \{0\}$

$\qquad\qquad\qquad\qquad\qquad\qquad\qquad\qquad\qquad = (0,1) \cup (1, +\infty)$

(e) $(g \circ f)(x) = g(f(x))$ $\qquad\qquad\qquad D_{g \circ f} = \left\{ x \in D_f \mid f(x) \in D_g \right\}$

$\qquad\qquad = \sqrt{f(x)}$ $\qquad\qquad\qquad\qquad\quad = D_f \cap \left\{ x \in R \mid \dfrac{1}{x-1} \in [0, +\infty) \right\}$

$\qquad\qquad = \sqrt{\dfrac{1}{x-1}} = \dfrac{1}{\sqrt{x-1}}$ $\qquad\quad = [(-\infty, 1) \cup (1, +\infty)] \cap (1, +\infty)$

$\qquad\qquad\qquad\qquad\qquad\qquad\qquad\qquad\qquad = (1, +\infty)$

(f) $(f \circ g)(x) = f(g(x))$ $\qquad\qquad\qquad D_{f \circ g} = \left\{ x \in D_g \mid g(x) \in D_f \right\}$

$\qquad\qquad = \dfrac{1}{g(x) - 1}$ $\qquad\qquad\qquad\qquad = D_g \cap \left\{ x \in R \mid \sqrt{x} \in D_f \right\}$

$\qquad\qquad = \dfrac{1}{\sqrt{x} - 1}$ $\qquad\qquad\qquad\qquad = [0, +\infty) \cap [[0,1) \cup (1, +\infty)]$

$\qquad\qquad\qquad\qquad\qquad\qquad\qquad\qquad\qquad = [0,1) \cup (1, +\infty)$

Properties of Functions

A function f with domain D_f and range R_f is a **one-to-one (1−1)** function provided that whenever $a \neq b$ for $a, b \in D_f$, then $f(a) \neq f(b)$. Or equivalently, if $f(a) = f(b)$, then $a = b$.

Examples: The function $f(x) = 3x$ is one-to-one because if $3a = 3b$, i.e., $f(a) = f(b)$, then dividing by 3 on both sides of the equation gives us $a = b$. But $g(x) = x^2$ is not one-to-one because, even though $2 \neq -2$, it is clear that $g(2) = 4 = g(-2)$.

We can use the horizontal line test to check if a graph represents a 1−1 function.

Horizontal line test: If no horizontal line can be drawn that intersects the graph of a function in more than one point, then the function is 1−1.

Look at the graphs of f and g in Figure 2.25. Note that no horizontal line can intersect more than one point of the graph of f but that the line $y = 4$ intersects the graph of g at two points. So f is $1-1$ and g is not.

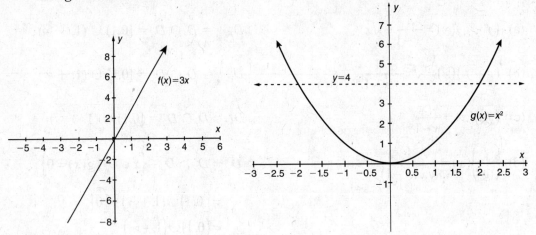

Figure 2.25

A function f with domain D_f, codomain Y, and range R_f is an **onto** function provided $Y = R_f$; i.e., for each $y \in Y$, there is some $x \in D_f$ such that $f(x) = y$.

Example: The function $f(x) = x^2$ would not be considered to be an onto function if it is presented as a real-valued function with domain all reals. In notation, this is $f : \mathbf{R} \to \mathbf{R}$, which means the codomain is $\mathbf{R}$. But the range of f is $R_f = [0, +\infty)$. However if f is given as having codomain $[0, +\infty)$, then we would say that f is onto $[0, +\infty)$. The function $h(x) = 5x$ is onto the reals since its range is all reals and its codomain is also understood to be all reals.

Geometrically, f is onto means that for each b in the codomain, the line $y = b$ intersects the graph of f in at least one point.

Example: In Figure 2.26, we can see that 2 is not in the range of f so that f is not onto $\mathbf{R}$.

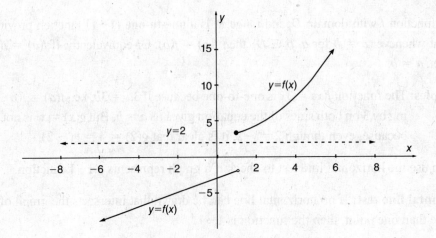

Figure 2.26

Let f be a one-to-one function with domain D_f and range R_f. A function g with domain $D_g = R_f$ and range $R_g = D_f$ is the **inverse function** of f, provided that for all $x \in D_f$ and for all $y \in D_g$, $y = f(x)$ if and only if $x = g(y)$. If g is the inverse of f, we write $g = f^{-1}$.

We also say that f and g are inverses provided that $f \circ g\,(x) = x$ for all $x \in D_g$ and $g \circ f(x) = x$ for all $x \in D_f$.

Example: To prove that $f(x) = x^3 + 1$ is the inverse of $g(x) = (x-1)^{1/3}$ we use this last definition.

Proof: Let f and g be the functions stipulated above. Then.

$$f \circ g(x) = f\left((x-1)^{\frac{1}{3}}\right) = \left((x-1)^{\frac{1}{3}}\right)^3 + 1 = (x-1)+1 = x \text{ for all real numbers } x, \text{ and}$$

$$g \circ f(x) = g(x^3+1) = \left((x^3+1)-1\right)^{\frac{1}{3}} = \left(x^3\right)^{\frac{1}{3}} = x \text{ for all real numbers } x.$$

Therefore, f and g are inverses.

Q.E.D.

When proving f and g are inverses above, we were given the specific functions f and g. We did not have to find the inverse of the function f. So, given a function, how do we find its inverse if it exists?

Finding f⁻¹ Algebraically

1. Verify that f is a one-to-one function on its domain. Note that if f is increasing (or decreasing) on its domain then f is one-to-one.

2. Interchange the x and y variables in the equation $y = f(x)$ to produce the equation $x = f(y)$.

3. Solve the equation $x = f(y)$ for y in terms of x. The result will be $y = f^{-1}(x)$.

   Example: Find the inverse of $f(x) = \dfrac{5x-1}{x+3}$ if it exists. First check if f is $1-1$. Assume

   $$\dfrac{5a-1}{a+3} = \dfrac{5b-1}{b+3} \iff (5a-1)(b+3) = (a+3)(5b-1)$$
   $$\iff 5ab+15a-b-3 = 5ab-a+15b-3$$
   $$\iff b = a$$

So, f is one-to-one. Now let's find f^{-1}:

Switch x and y: $\quad x = \dfrac{5y-1}{y+3}$

Solve for y: $x(y+3) = 5y - 1$

Isolate y: $\Leftrightarrow xy + 3x = 5y - 1$

$\Leftrightarrow xy - 5y = -3x - 1$

$\Leftrightarrow y(x - 5) = -(3x + 1)$

$\Leftrightarrow y = \dfrac{3x + 1}{5 - x}$

So $f^{-1}(x) = \dfrac{3x + 1}{5 - x}$

The **graphical relationship** between f^{-1} and its inverse is that the graph of f^{-1} is the graph of f reflected about the line $y = x$. This is clear from the fact that x and y are interchanged to compute the inverse. Observe the graphs in Figure 2.27 of the two functions from this last example.

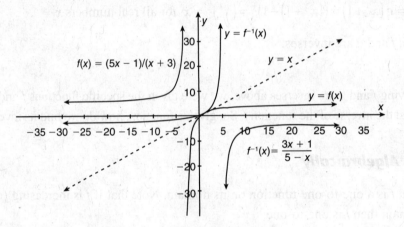

Figure 2.27

A function, f, is **increasing** on an interval (a, b) provided that for all $x_1 \le x_2$ with $x_1, x_2 \in (a, b)$, $f(x_1) \le f(x_2)$. And a function, f, is **decreasing** on an interval (a, b) provided that for all $x_1 \le x_2$ with $x_1, x_2 \in (a, b)$, $f(x_1) \ge f(x_2)$.

We have an intuitive sense of the geometric idea of increasing functions. Increasing means the graph of f is rising from left to right, whereas a decreasing function falls from left to right.

Example: In Figure 2.28, the graphs of g and h are shown. Clearly, h is an increasing function on the real numbers, and g is decreasing on the real numbers.

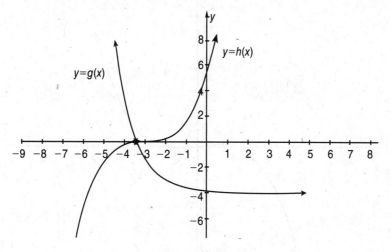

Figure 2.28

A function, *f*, is **even** provided $f(-x) = f(x)$ for all *x* in the domain of *f*. Geometrically this means that the graph of *f* is symmetric with respect to the *y*-axis; i.e., if the graph of *f* is reflected across the *y*-axis, the result is the same as the original graph.

A function, *f*, is called **odd** if $f(-x) = -f(x)$ for all *x* in the domain of *f*. When a function is odd, its graph is symmetric with respect to the origin; i.e., if the graph of *f* is reflected across the *x*-axis and then across the *y*-axis, the result would be the same graph as the original graph.

Example: $f(x) = x^2 + 1$ is an even function because $f(-x) = (-x)^2 + 1 = x^2 + 1 = f(x)$. And $g(x) = 2x^3 - x$ is an odd function because $g(-x) = 2(-x)^3 - (-x) = -2x^3 + x = -g(x)$. Their graphs in Figure 2.29 illustrate the symmetry described in the definitions of odd and even functions.

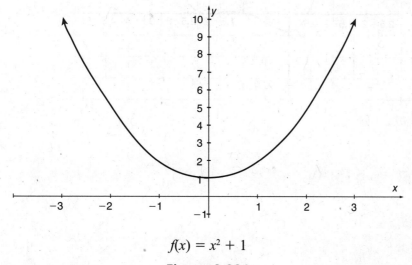

$$f(x) = x^2 + 1$$

Figure 2.29A

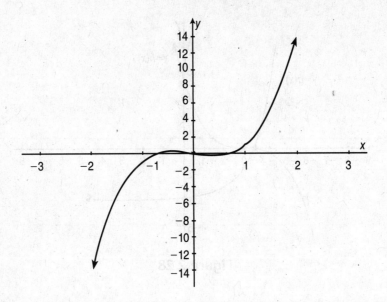

$$g(x) = 2x^3 - x$$

Figure 2.29B

Review Problems for Section 2.3.1

1. Which of the following graphs does not represent a function?

(A)

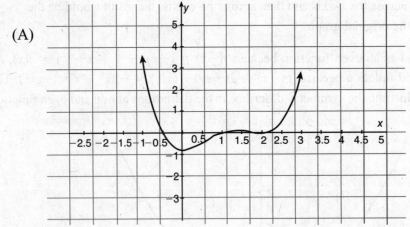

(B)

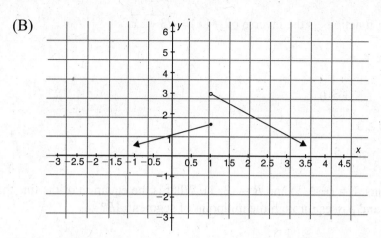

(C)

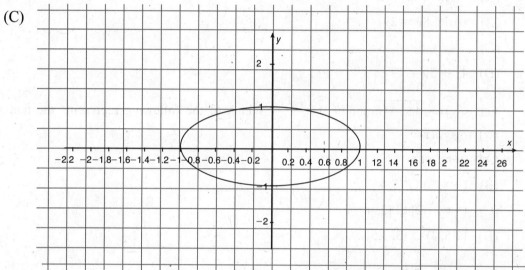

(D)

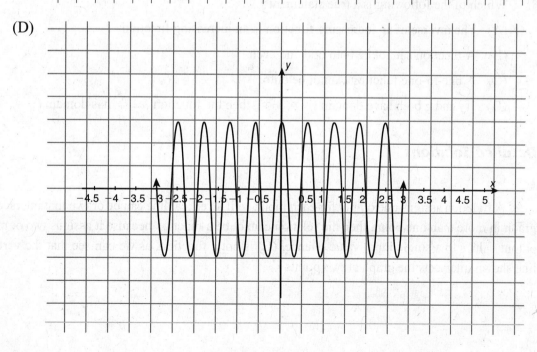

2. Which of the following functions is the inverse of $f(x) = \sqrt{3-2x}$?

(A) $h(x) = \dfrac{1}{\sqrt{3-2x}}, x < 1.5$

(B) $h(x) = -0.5\,x^2 + 1.5, x \geq 0$

(C) $h(x) = \sqrt{2-3x}, x \geq 0$

(D) $h(x) = -\sqrt{3-2x}, x \leq 1.5$

3. Line l contains the points $A = (-2, 5)$ and $B = (3, 1)$. What is the equation of the line that is perpendicular to line l and passes through the midpoint of segment AB?

(A) $-10x + 8y = 19$

(B) $10x + 8y = 29$

(C) $-4x + 5y = 13$

(D) $4x + 5y = 17$

4. Let $g(x) = \sqrt{4x^2 - 16}$ and $h(x) = \dfrac{1}{x-3}$. Which of the following represents the domain of $f(x) = g \circ h(x)$?

(A) $(-\infty, \infty)$

(B) $(-\infty, 3) \cup (3, \infty)$

(C) $(-\infty, -2] \cup [2, \infty)$

(D) $[2.5, 3) \cup (3, 3.5]$

5. Which of the following is a true statement?

(A) The inverse of an increasing function is an increasing function.

(B) A function cannot be both odd and even.

(C) A one-to-one function cannot be onto.

(D) If f and g both have domain $(-\infty, +\infty)$, then the function $h = \dfrac{f}{g}$ has domain $(-\infty, +\infty)$.

Detailed Solutions

1. **C**

A function assigns one output for each input, so if a vertical line can be drawn that intersects a graph in more than one point, then the relation cannot be a function because it assigns two or more output values to a single input value. Hence, (C) is not a function, as we can see that the vertical line shown intersects the graph at two points.

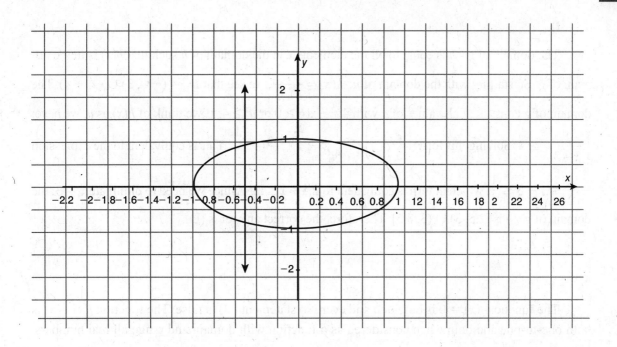

2.   **B**

The inverse of $y = \sqrt{3-2x}$ is $x = \sqrt{3-2y}$. Solving this equation for y:

$$x = \sqrt{3-2y} \iff x^2 = 3-2y$$
$$\iff x^2 - 3 = -2y$$
$$\iff y = -\frac{1}{2}x^2 + \frac{3}{2}$$

So, $f^{-1}(x) = -\frac{1}{2}x^2 + \frac{3}{2}$, and since the domain of f^{-1} equals the range of f, we must also write that $x \geq 0$. Hence the correct answer is (B).

3.   **A**

Line l has slope $m = \dfrac{5-1}{-2-3} = \dfrac{4}{-5}$, so any line that is perpendicular to line l has slope $\dfrac{5}{4}$. The midpoint of the segment AB is $\left(\dfrac{-2+3}{2}, \dfrac{5+1}{2}\right) = \left(\dfrac{1}{2}, 3\right)$. So the line that has slope $\dfrac{5}{4}$ and passes through the point (0.5, 3) is $y - 3 = 1.25(x - 0.5)$ or $y = 1.25x + 2.375$ in slope-intercept form. In standard form, this is $-10x + 8y = 19$.

4.   **D**

The domain of $g \circ h$ is equal to all the elements x in the domain of h such that $h(x)$ is in the domain of g. So starting with the domain of h: $h(x) = \dfrac{1}{x-3}$, we see that $D_h = (-\infty, 3) \cup (3, +\infty)$. The domain of g consists of all values of u with $4u^2 - 16 \geq 0$ or $u^2 \geq 4$. If we think of $h(x)$ as u, we have: $\left(\dfrac{1}{x-3}\right)^2 \geq 4$. Solving this for x: $\left(\dfrac{x-3}{1}\right)^2 \leq \dfrac{1}{4} \Leftrightarrow |x-3| \leq \dfrac{1}{2}$. This is equivalent to the expression $-\dfrac{1}{2} \leq x - 3 \leq \dfrac{1}{2}$, which in turn is equivalent to $2.5 \leq x \leq 3.5$. Since we need to eliminate $x = 3$, the domain of $g \circ h$ is $[2.5, 3) \cup (3, 3.5]$. Therefore, the correct answer is (D).

5.   **A**

The function $f(x) = 0$ is both odd and even, so statement (B) is false. The function $f(x) = x^3$ is both one-to-one and onto when considered as a function with domain and range all real numbers, so statement (C) is false. The functions $f(x) = x$ and $g(x) = x - 1$ both have domain $(-\infty, +\infty)$. But the function $h = \dfrac{f}{g}$ does not have the number 1 in its domain so statement (D) is false.

Basic Functions

Constant Function

The most basic type of function is a **constant function**. For any real number c, the constant function, $f(x) = c$, has domain $D_f = \mathbf{R}$, all real numbers, and its range is the set with one value $R_f = \{c\}$. The graph of f is the horizontal line $y = c$. For example, $f(x) = 3$ is shown in Figure 2.30.

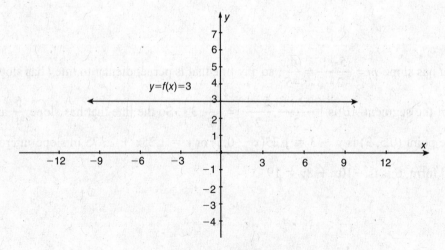

Figure 2.30

Power Function

The second most basic function is a **power function,** which is a function in the form $g(x) = x^r$, where r is a constant. Some special cases of power functions that may be familiar are those with $r = n$, where n is a positive integer; i.e., $g(x) = x^n$. The domain of this function for any positive n is **R**, all real numbers, unless stipulated otherwise.

(a) When $n = 1$, $g(x) = x$ is called a **linear function**. The graph is shown in Figure 2.31. The domain is the set of reals. The range is also seen to be all reals because each horizontal line $y = c$ intersects the graph of $y = x$.

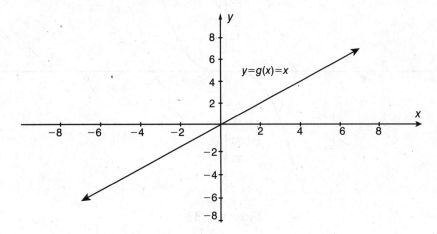

Figure 2.31

(b) When $n = 2$, $g(x) = x^2$, which is called a **quadratic function**. Its graph is called a **parabola**. Note that any horizontal line $y = c$, where $c < 0$, would not intersect the graph, whereas for $c \geq 0$ it would; the range of this function is $R_g = [0, +\infty)$. The graph is shown in Figure 2.32.

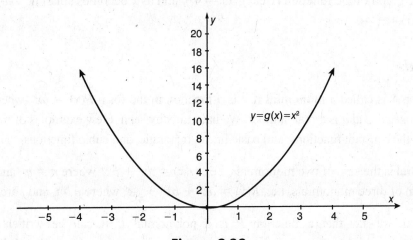

Figure 2.32

Note that the graph of any function $y = x^n$, where n is an even positive integer, will have a graph with the same general shape and behavior as $y = x^2$; i .e., the lowest point on the graph will be $(0, 0)$ and the end behavior (as x becomes large ($x \rightarrow \infty$) or small ($x \rightarrow -\infty$)) of the function is that the graph rises ($g(x) \rightarrow \infty$).

   (c) When $n = 3$, $g(x) = x^n$ is called a **cubic function**; its graph is shown in Figure 2.33.

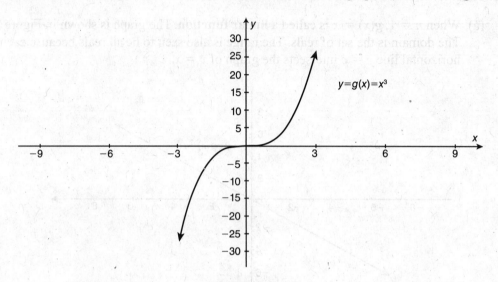

Figure 2.33

Note that any horizontal line $y = c$, where c is any real number, would intersect the graph; the range of this function is all reals.

The graph of any function $y = x^n$, where n is an odd positive integer, will have a graph with the same general shape and behavior as $y = x^3$; i.e., the end behavior as x becomes large ($x \rightarrow \infty$) is that the graph of the function rises ($g(x) \rightarrow \infty$), and as x becomes small ($x \rightarrow -\infty$) the graph falls ($g(x) \rightarrow -\infty$).

Polynomials

A function P is called a **monomial** if it is a function in the form $P(x) = ax^n$, where n is a non-negative integer and a is a real number. We have already seen a few examples of monomials; for example, the constant functions, and basic linear, quadratic, and cubic functions.

A **binomial** is the sum of two monomials, i.e., $Q(x) = ax^n + bx^m$ where $n \neq m$, and a **trinomial** is the sum of three monomials, i.e., $R(x) = ax^n + bx^m + cx^j$ where n, m, and j are distinct.

In general, we say that a function P is a polynomial if it can be written in the form $P(x) = a_n x^n + a_{n-1} x^{n-1} + \cdots + a_2 x^2 + a_1 x + a_0$, where n is a non-negative integer called the **degree of the polynomial**; $a_n, a_{n-1}, \cdots, a_2, a_1, a_0$ are real constants; and $a_n \neq 0$. In general, we always write a polynomial in **standard form,** which means the degrees of the terms are in decreasing order. The term of highest degree is called the **leading term,** and the coefficient of the leading term is called the **leading coefficient**. The term of zero degree, a_0, is called the **constant term**.

The domain of a polynomial function $P(x) = a_n x^n + a_{n-1} x^{n-1} + \cdots + a_2 x^2 + a_1 x + a_0$ is the set of real numbers $(-\infty, +\infty)$. The range of a polynomial of degree n is all real numbers if n is an odd integer; this is because the end behavior of P is the same as that of $Q(x) = a_n x^n$.

The graph of a first-degree polynomial function (**linear function**) $f(x) = mx + b$ is a line. The graph of a second-degree polynomial function (**quadratic function**) $f(x) = ax^2 + bx + c$ is a parabola. A third-degree polynomial function (**cubic function**) is of the form $f(x) = ax^3 + bx^2 + cx + d$.

Figure 2.34 is an example of a graph of a polynomial of degree higher than 3 with local maxima and minima (turning points) at approximately $x = -2, -0.85,$ and 0.6, and zeroes at $x = -2, 0,$ and 1.

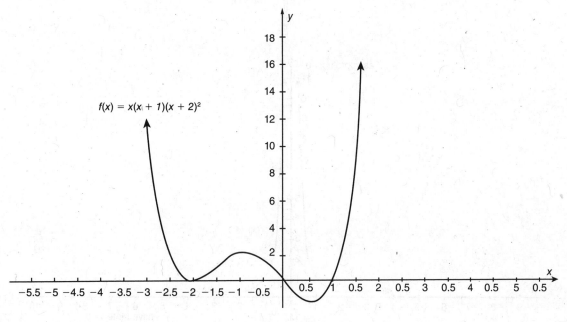

Figure 2.34

Rational Function

A function that can be expressed in the form $f(x) = \dfrac{p(x)}{q(x)}$, where $p(x)$ and $q(x)$ are polynomials and $q(x) \neq 0$, is a **rational function**. The domain of a rational function is the set of all real numbers, x, such that $q(x) \neq 0$. Two basic rational functions are shown in Figure 2.35.

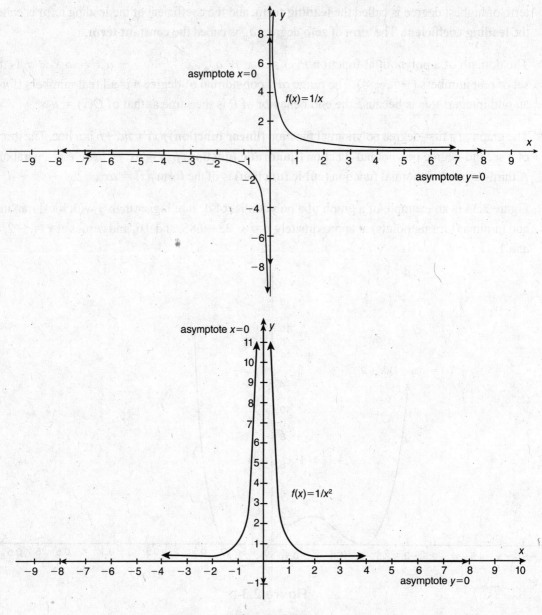

Figure 2.35

A rational function may have **asymptotes**. If the graph of f gets closer and closer to a horizontal line $y = c$ as x **increases or decreases without bound** (i.e., $x \rightarrow +\infty$ or $x \rightarrow -\infty$), then the line $y = c$ is called a **horizontal asymptote**. If the graph of f gets closer and closer to a vertical line $x = a$ as x gets closer and closer to a from one or both sides, then the line $x = a$ is called a **vertical asymptote**.

In Figure 2.35, both rational functions have $y = 0$ as a horizontal asymptote and $x = 0$ as a vertical asymptote.

Note: If $p(x)$ and $q(x)$ have no common factors, then the graph of the rational function $f(x) = \dfrac{p(x)}{q(x)}$ has a vertical asymptote $x = a$ for each value at which $q(a) = 0$. For example, consider the rational function $f(x) = \dfrac{2x}{x^2 - 1}$; since the denominator equals zero when $x = \pm 1$, the graph of f has vertical asymptotes $x = 1$ and $x = -1$, as shown in Figure 2.36.

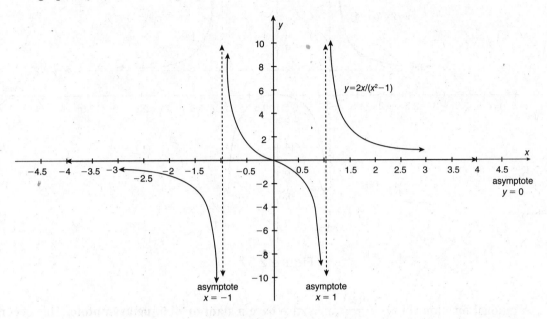

Figure 2.36

The function depicted in Figure 2.36 also has $y = 0$ as a horizontal asymptote. The **Horizontal Asymptote Theorem** indicates how to decide if a rational function has a horizontal asymptote.

Horizontal Asymptote Theorem: The graph of the rational function $f(x) = \dfrac{p(x)}{q(x)}$ $= \dfrac{a_n x^n + a_{n-1} x^{n-1} + \cdots + a_1 x + a_0}{b_m x^m + b_{m-1} x^{m-1} + \cdots + b_1 x + b_0}$, where $a_n \neq 0$, $b_m \neq 0$, has

    (a) a horizontal asymptote $y = 0$ if $n < m$,

    (b) a horizontal asymptote $y = \dfrac{a_n}{b_m}$ if $n = m$,

    (c) no horizontal asymptote if $n > m$.

So for $f(x) = \dfrac{2x}{x^2 - 1}$ shown in Figure 2.36, since the degree of the numerator (1) is less than the degree of the denominator (2), $y = 0$ is a horizontal asymptote. But for the function $g(x) = \dfrac{2x^2}{x^2 - 1}$, $y = 2$ is a horizontal asymptote, as illustrated in Figure 2.37.

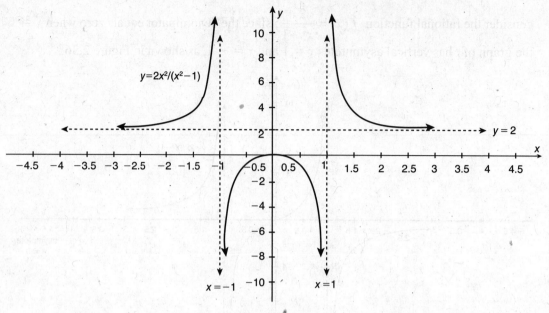

Figure 2.37

A rational function, $r(x) = \dfrac{p(x)}{q(x)}$, may also have **a slant or oblique asymptote.** This occurs when the degree of the polynomial in the numerator, $p(x)$, is one degree greater than the polynomial in the denominator, $q(x)$. This asymptote is a line with non-zero slope.

For example, consider the rational function $r(x) = \dfrac{2x^2 + 3x - 2}{x + 1}$. By dividing the numerator by the denominator using long division, we can rewrite the function r in the form $r(x) = 2x + 1 - \dfrac{3}{x + 1}$.

The graph of r has $y = 2x + 1$ as a slant asymptote and a vertical asymptote $x = -1$, as shown in Figure 2.38.

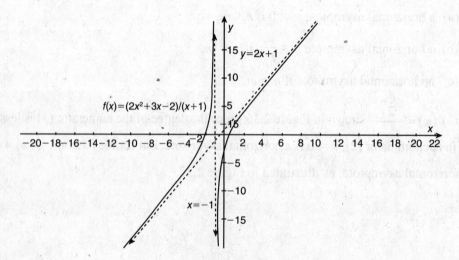

Figure 2.38

If there exists a real number c for which $p(c) = q(c) = 0$, then $r(x) = \dfrac{p(x)}{q(x)}$ is not in completely reduced form. If $r(c)$ is defined once r is completely reduced, then the graph of r has a **hole** $(c, r(c))$.

An example of rational function with a hole in its graph is $r(x) = \dfrac{x^2 - 2x - 3}{x^2 - 3x}$. Note that $r(x) = \dfrac{(x-3)(x+1)}{x(x-3)} = \dfrac{x+1}{x}$, $x \neq 3$. Note that after r is reduced, substituting $x = 3$ into the reduced form produces 4/3; thus the graph of r has a hole $\left(3, \dfrac{4}{3}\right)$. The graph of r also has a horizontal asymptote $y = 1$ and a vertical asymptote $x = 0$, as shown in Figure 2.39.

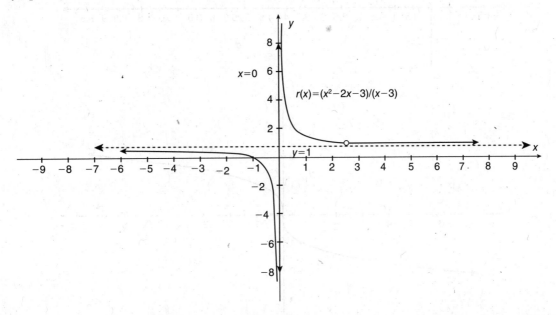

Figure 2.39

Radical Function

A function that can be expressed in the form $f(x) = x^{\frac{1}{n}}$, where n is a positive integer, is called a **root** or **radical function.** In the case that n is an even integer, the function's domain is the set of all non-negative real numbers and its range is the same set. In the case that n is an odd integer, both the domain and range of the root function is the set of all reals. Some example graphs are shown in Figure 2.40.

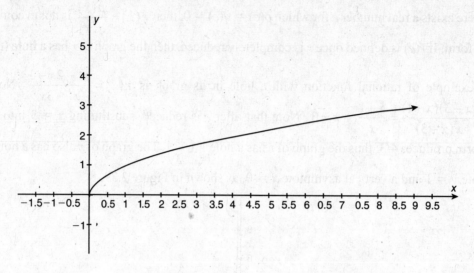

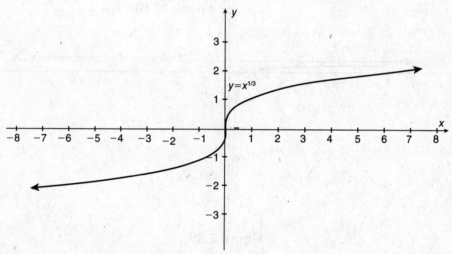

Figure 2.40

Absolute Value Function

Another important function is the **absolute value function** $f(x) = |x|$, which is defined as follows:

$$f(x) = |x| = \begin{cases} x & \text{if } x \geq 0 \\ -x & \text{if } x < 0 \end{cases}$$

The domain of the absolute value function is the set of all reals, and the range is the set of all non-negative real numbers. The graph is shown in Figure 2.41.

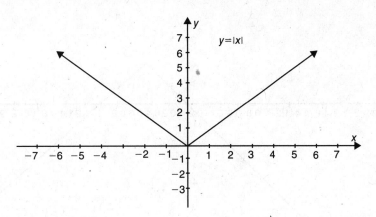

Figure 2.41

Review Problems for Section 2.3.2

1. Which of the following graphs best represents the function $g(x) = -x^2 + x$?

A.

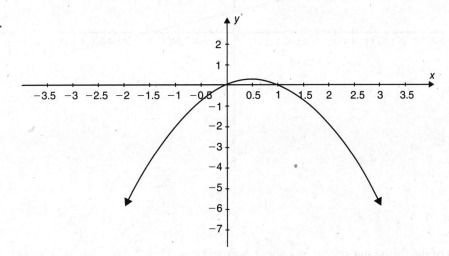

B.

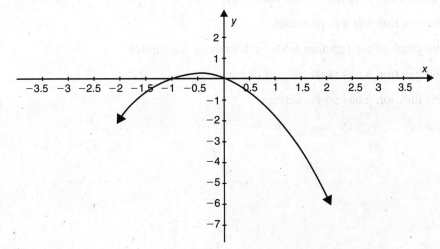

C.

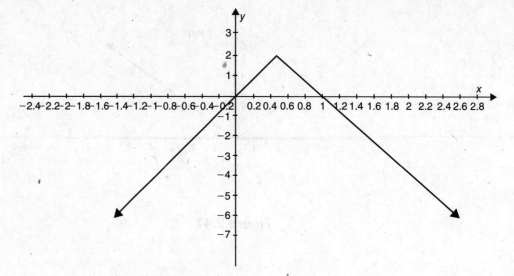

D.

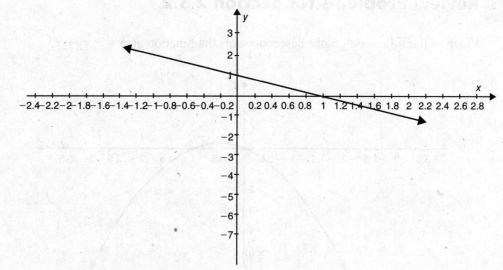

2. Which of the following statements about $h(x) = 3x^5 + x^4 - 2x^3 + x^2 + 3x$ is false?

(A) The function h is a polynomial.

(B) The graph of the function h has no horizontal asymptote.

(C) The function h has range all real numbers.

(D) The function h has no y-intercept.

3. Consider the graph of f shown here. Which of the given statements concerning f could be true?

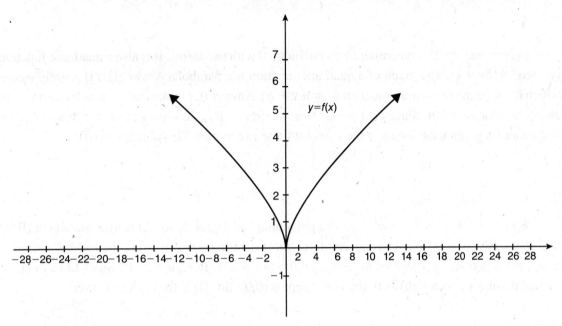

(A) The function is the absolute value function.

(B) The range of f is all real numbers.

(C) The function is a composition of a quadratic and a root function.

(D) The function has asymptotes.

4. Which of the following statements about functions is true?

(A) A polynomial can be an increasing function.

(B) A root function must have all real numbers as its domain.

(C) A rational function must have either a horizontal or vertical asymptote or both.

(D) $x = 3$ is a constant function.

5. A rectangular poster announcing a party is being made on cardboard that has an area of 90 square inches and will have a top and bottom margin of 1 inch. The side margins will be 1.5 inches wide. The printed area needs to be 48 square inches. What should be the dimensions of the printed area?

Detailed Solutions

1. **A**

    $g(x) = -x^2 + x$ is a binomial; i.e., a polynomial with two terms. It is also a quadratic function $(y = ax^2 + bx + c)$. The graph of a quadratic function is a parabola. Answer (D) is a straight line, which is the graph of a linear equation $(y = mx + b)$. Answer (C) looks more like some form of an absolute value function. Since $g(x) = -x^2 + x = -x(x - 1)$, g has two zeroes $(x = 0$ and $x = 1)$, and hence its graph must intersect the x-axis at these two values. This eliminates (B).

2. **D**

    $h(x) = 3x^5 + x^4 - 2x^3 + x^2 + 3x$ is a polynomial of degree 5, so (A) is true. Statement (B) is true since polynomials do not have asymptotes. Statement (C) is true because the end-behavior of h is like the function $y = x^5$, which in turn is similar to $y = x^3$ (see Figure 2.33), which has a range of all real numbers. Since $h(0) = 0$, the y-intercept is $(0,0)$. So (D) is the correct answer.

3. **C**

    The graph of the absolute value function consists of two rays joined at a vertex, which this graph is not, so (A) is false. Statement (B) is false because the range of the graphed function is all non-negative real numbers since the graph does not go below the x-axis. This graph has no asymptotes, so (D) is false. The graph in (C) is similar to the second graph in Figure 2.40 with the $x < 0$ branch of the graph reflected above the x-axis and stretched a bit, such as for $y = x^{\frac{2}{3}} = \left(x^{\frac{1}{3}} \right)^2$.

4. **A**

    The polynomial $y = x^3$ is an increasing function. The function $y = \sqrt{x}$ has the set of all non-negative real numbers as a domain, so (B) is false. Statement (C) is false because the function $y = \dfrac{x^3}{x^2 + 1}$ is a rational function but it does not have either a horizontal or vertical asymptote; its graph is shown on the next page. Statement (D) is false because $x = 3$ is not a function since its graph is a vertical line; hence, the graph fails the vertical line test.

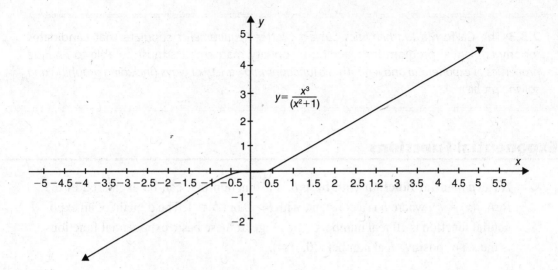

5. Let A be the area of cardboard, which we know equals 90. Let x be the width and y be the length of the printed area. So the width of the cardboard is $x + 3$ and the length is $y + 2$, which makes the area $A = (x + 3)(y + 2)$.

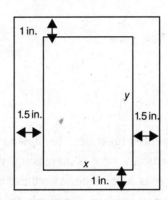

We are also given that the printed region has area 48 inches, so $xy = 48$, or $y = \dfrac{48}{x}$. Substituting

this into our area equation, we obtain $A = (x+3)\left(\dfrac{48}{x}+2\right) = \dfrac{48(x+3)+2x(x+3)}{x} = \dfrac{2(x+3)(x+24)}{x}$.

But $A = 90$, so $90 = \dfrac{2(x+3)(x+24)}{x} \iff 90x = 2x^2 + 54x + 144 \iff 2x^2 - 36x + 144 = 0$.

Solving this quadratic equation is equivalent to finding the x-intercepts of $y = x^2 - 18x + 72$. By factoring, $(x - 6)(x - 12) = 0 \iff x = 6$, or $x = 12$. If $x = 6$, then $y = 8$; if $x = 12$, then $y = 4$. So there are two possible sizes for the printed area, $6'' \times 8''$ and $12'' \times 14''$.

2.3.3 The California *Mathematics Subject Matter Requirements* stipulate that candidates for any credential program for teaching secondary mathematics must be able to *analyze properties of exponential and logarithmic functions in a variety of ways (including graphing and solving problems)*.

Exponential Functions

An **exponential function** with **base** b is a function that can be expressed in the form $f(x) = b^x$, where b is a constant, with $b > 0$ but $b \neq 1$. The domain of an exponential function is all real numbers. The range of these basic exponential functions is the set of positive real numbers $(0, +\infty)$.

Properties of Exponents: If $a > 0$ and $b > 0$, then the following rules hold true for all real numbers x and y:

1. $a^x \cdot a^y = a^{x+y}$

2. $\dfrac{a^x}{a^y} = a^{x-y}$

3. $(a^x)^y = (a^y)^x = a^{xy}$

4. $a^x \cdot b^x = (ab)^x$

5. $\dfrac{a^x}{b^x} = \left(\dfrac{a}{b}\right)^x$

The graphs of some basic exponential functions are shown in Figure 2.42. Note that when the base b is greater than 1, the function $y = b^x$ is increasing; when the base b is less than 1 but greater than 0, the function $y = b^x$ is decreasing. Also these basic exponential functions have a horizontal asymptote, $y = 0$; we can see from the graphs that $b^x \to 0$ (b^x gets closer and closer to 0) when $x \to +\infty$ (x increases without bound) for $0 < b < 1$, and $b^x \to 0$ when $x \to -\infty$ (x decreases without bound) for $b > 1$.

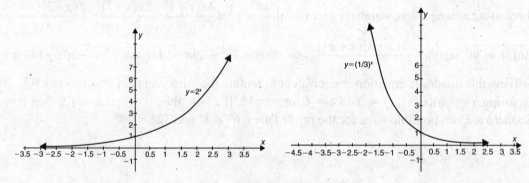

Figure 2.42

Also, if the base b is greater than 1, then we say the graph represents **exponential growth**. If the base is between 0 and 1, the graph represents **exponential decay**.

Note that the exponential functions that have bases less than 1 can be written with a negative exponent in the following way: $y = \left(\dfrac{1}{3}\right)^x = \left(\left(\dfrac{3}{1}\right)^{-1}\right)^x = 3^{-x}$.

For many applications, the best choice for a base is the irrational number $e \approx 2.71828182\ldots$ The number e is called the **natural base**, and the function $f(x) = e^x$ is called the **natural exponential function**. Keep in mind that the letter e is a constant and x is the input variable. Figure 2.43 shows the graphs of $y = e^x$ (solid graph) and $y = e^{-x}$ (dashed graph) on the same set of axes.

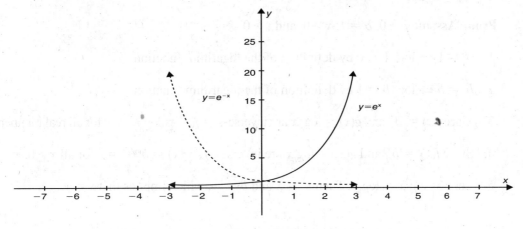

Figure 2.43

The exponential function $f(x) = b^x$ with base b, where $b > 0$ and $b \neq 1$, is a one-to-one function satisfying the horizontal line test, as can be seen from its graph. See, for example, Figure 2.42. Hence, $f(x) = b^x$ has an inverse.

Logarithmic Functions

For $b > 0$, $b \neq 1$, and $x > 0$, we define $y = \log_b x$ to mean $x = b^y$, which is the inverse of $y = b^x$. The function g defined by $g(x) = \log_b x$ is called the **logarithmic function with base b**. The domain of a basic logarithmic function is the set of positive real numbers. The range of the basic logarithmic functions is the set of all real numbers.

Examples: (a) $y = \log_3 x$ is the inverse of $y = 3^x$. (b) $y = \log_{1/3} x$ is the inverse of $y = \left(\dfrac{1}{3}\right)^x$.

Note: The logarithm base 10 is called the **common logarithm**, and we write $\log x$ for $\log_{10} x$. The logarithm base e is called the **natural logarithm**, and we use the notation $\ln x$ to represent $\log_e x$.

Theorem (Basic Properties of Logarithms): For $b > 0$, $b \neq 1$, $x > 0$, and $y > 0$, the following statements are true:

1. $\log_b 1 = 0$.

2. $\log_b b = 1$.

3. $\log_b b^x = x$ for all x in the reals.

4. $b^{\log_b x} = x$ for all $x > 0$.

5. If $\log_b x = \log_b y$ then $x = y$.

   Proof: Assume $b > 0$, $b \neq 1$, $x > 0$, and $y > 0$.

   1. $b^0 = 1 \Leftrightarrow \log_b 1 = 0$ by definition of the logarithm function.

   2. $b^1 = b \Leftrightarrow \log_b b = 1$ by definition of the logarithm function.

   3. Since $f(x) = b^x$ and $g(x) = \log_b x$ are inverses, $g \circ f(x) = \log_b b^x = x$ for all real numbers x.

   4. Since $f(x) = b^x$ and $g(x) = \log_b x$ are inverses, $f \circ g(x) = b^{\log_b x} = x$ for all $x > 0$.

   5. Let $c = \log_b x = \log_b y$. Then $b^c = x$ and $b^c = y$, which implies that $x = y$.

   Q.E.D.

Theorem (More Properties of Logarithms): Let x, y, and b be real numbers such that $b > 0$, $b \neq 1$. Then:

1. $\log_b(xy) = \log_b x + \log_b y$ for all x, y such that $x > 0$ and $y > 0$.

2. $\log_b\left(\dfrac{x}{y}\right) = \log_b x - \log_b y$ for all x, y such that $x > 0$ and $y > 0$.

3. $\log_b(y^x) = x \log_b y$ for all x, y such that $y > 0$ and $x \in \boldsymbol{R}$.

Proof: Let x, y, and b be real numbers such that $b > 0$, $b \neq 1$.

1. Assume $x > 0$ and $y > 0$. Then $b^{\log_b(xy)} = xy$ by the fourth Basic Property of Exponents, and $b^{\log_b x + \log_b y} = b^{\log_b x} b^{\log_b y}$ by the first Basic Property of Exponents. Then, also by the fourth Basic Property of Exponents, $b^{\log_b x} = x$ and $b^{\log_b y} = y$, so that by the Transitive Property of Equality, $b^{\log_b x + \log_b y} = xy$. Hence, it follows that $b^{\log_b(xy)} = b^{\log_b x + \log_b y}$. Since the exponential functions are one-to-one functions, it is true that $\log_b(xy) = \log_b x + \log_b y$ for all x, y such that $x > 0$ and $y > 0$.

2. We leave this proof for the section exercises.

3. Let $y > 0$ and $x \in \boldsymbol{R}$. Then $b^{\log_b(y^x)} = y^x$ and $b^{x\log_b(y)} = \left(b^{\log_b y}\right)^x = y^x$. Thus, $b^{\log_b(y^x)} = b^{x\log_b y}$. Since the exponential function is one-to-one, it follows that $\log_b y^x = x\log_b y$.

Q.E.D.

The graphs of some basic logarithm functions are shown in Figure 2.44. Note that when the base b is greater than 1, the function $y = \log_b x$ is increasing; when the base b is less than 1 but greater than 0, the function $y = \log_b x$ is decreasing. Note also that the logarithm functions have a vertical asymptote $x = 0$. These logarithmic functions have no y-intercept; in fact the domain of these functions is the set of positive real numbers $(0, +\infty)$. The range is all real numbers.

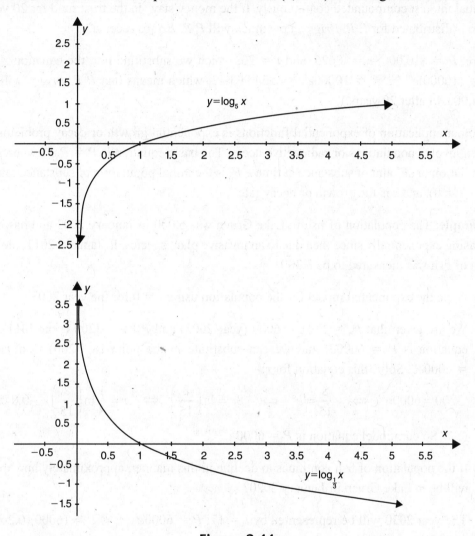

Figure 2.44

We note that the logarithm functions, being the inverse of the exponential functions, are one-to-one functions, as can be seen from the graphs in Figure 2.44.

Applications Using Exponential and Logarithmic Functions

I. One application of exponential functions is in investment earnings or paying interest compounded continuously. The function for such applications is

$$A = Pe^{rt}$$

where P is the **principal** or amount invested, r is the **annual interest rate,** t is the investment **time in years,** and A is the **balance** or **current value** of the investment. The following typical example uses continuous compounding.

Example: An amount of $10,000 is deposited in a trust fund for *P. R. Briggs* that pays 6.25% annual interest compounded continuously. If the money stays in the trust fund for 20 years and then is distributed for *P. R. Briggs*, how much will *P. R. Briggs* receive?

Here, $P = \$10,000$, $r = .0625$, and $t = 20$, which we substitute into the equation $A = Pe^{rt}$: $A = (10000)e^{(0.0625)(20)} = 10000e^{1.25} \approx \$34,903.43$, which means that *P. R. Briggs* will receive $34,903.43 after 20 years.

II. Another application of exponential functions is exponential growth or decay problems, which often involve populations or radioactive decay. The basic equation is $P = P_0 e^{rt}$, where P is the population or amount of substance at time t, P_0 is the initial population or substance (amount at time $t = 0$), and r is the growth or decay rate.

Example: The population of fish in Lake Gruen was 6,000 in January 2003 and has been decreasing exponentially since then due to an invasive plant species. In January 2011, the population of fish was measured to be 3,200.

(a) Write the exponential model for the population using $t = 0$ for the year 2003.

We are given that $P_0 = P(0) = 6000$ (year 2003) and $P(8) = 3200$ (year 2011). So our equation is $P = 6000e^{rt}$ and we can substitute in the point (8, 3200) to obtain $3200 = 6000e^{8r}$. Solve this equation for r:

$$3200 = 6000e^{8r} \iff \frac{8}{15} = e^{8r} \iff 8r = \ln\left(\frac{8}{15}\right) \iff r = \frac{1}{8}\ln\left(\frac{8}{15}\right) \approx -0.07858$$

So our model equation is $P = 6000e^{-0.07858t}$.

(b) If the population of fish continues to decline in this manner, approximately how many fish will be in Lake Gruen in January 2020?

The year 2020 will be represented by $t = 17$: $P = 6000e^{(-0.07858)(17)} \approx (6000)(0.262949) \approx 1577.69$.

Thus, the population of fish in Lake Gruen will be approximately 1,578 in 2020.

III. A third application is a logarithmic model problem.

Example: Automobile sales (in thousands) at *Prasad's Auto Showroom* from 2002 to 2012 can be modeled by the equation: $y = -252 + 315.2 \ln t$ where $t \geq 2$, and $t = 2$ represents the year 2002. Using this model, in what year will sales reach $800,000?

To solve, we set $y = 800$: $800 = -252 + 315.2 \ln t \iff 1052 = 315.2 \ln t \iff \ln t \approx 3.337563 \iff t \approx e^{3.337563} \approx 28.15$. So sales at *Prasad's Showroom* will reach $800,000 in the year 2028.

Review Problems for Section 2.3.3

1. Prove: Let x, y, and b be real numbers such that $b > 0$, $b \neq 1$. Then

   $$\log_b\left(\frac{x}{y}\right) = \log_b x - \log_b y \text{ for all } x, y \text{ such that } x > 0 \text{ and } y > 0.$$

2. Which of the following statements is a true statement?

   (A) Exponential functions are always increasing.

   (B) Logarithmic functions are always increasing.

   (C) Logarithmic functions are $1-1$ functions.

   (D) Exponential functions are onto functions when considering their codomain to be the set of real numbers.

3. The number of bacteria in a culture is growing exponentially. After 3 hours there were 200 bacteria, and after 5 hours there were 300 bacteria. How many bacteria were present after 10 hours?

4. An amount of \$30,000 is currently in a trust fund that has been earning 5% annual interest compounded continuously for 25 years. How much was originally invested?

5. The equation $\beta = 10\log\left(\frac{I}{10^{-12}}\right)$ models the relationship between the number of decibels β and the intensity I of a certain sound measured in watts per square meter. What is the intensity of this sound, which has 100 decibels?

Detailed Solutions

1. **Proof**: Assume $x > 0$ and $y > 0$. Then $b^{\log_b\left(\frac{x}{y}\right)} = \frac{x}{y}$ by the fourth Basic Property of Exponents, and $b^{\log_b x - \log_b y} = b^{\log_b x} / b^{\log_b y}$ by a property of exponents. Then, also by the fourth Basic Property of Exponents, $b^{\log_b x} = x$ and $b^{\log_b y} = y$, so that by the Transitive Property of Equality $b^{\log_b x - \log_b y} = x / y$. Hence, it follows that $b^{\log_b\left(\frac{x}{y}\right)} = b^{\log_b x - \log_b y}$. Since the exponential functions are one-to-one functions, it is true that $\log_b\left(\frac{x}{y}\right) = \log_b x - \log_b y$ for all x, y such that $x > 0$ and $y > 0$.

   Q.E.D.

2. **C**

   Statement (A) is false because the exponential function $y = b^x$ is increasing when $b > 1$ and decreasing when $0 < b < 1$. See Figure 2.42 and 2.43 for examples. The same is true for $y = \log_b x$, which can be seen in Figure 2.44, so (B) is false. The exponential function $y = b^x$ has a range of $(0, \infty)$, so (D) is false. But the logarithmic and exponential functions are one-to-one functions, so the correct answer is (C).

3. Let $P = P_0 e^{rt}$. We are given that at time $t = 3$, $P = 200$, which by substitution gives us the equation $200 = P_0 e^{3r}$ or $P_0 = 200e^{-3r}$. We are also given that at $t = 5$, $P = 300$, which gives the second equation $300 = P_0 e^{5r}$ or $P_0 = 300e^{-5r}$. Solving the two equations simultaneously: $200e^{-3r} = 300e^{-5r} \Leftrightarrow \dfrac{3}{2} = e^{2r} \Leftrightarrow r = \dfrac{1}{2}\ln\left(\dfrac{3}{2}\right) = \ln\sqrt{\dfrac{3}{2}}$. Hence, our equation is

$$P = P_0 e^{t\ln\sqrt{\frac{3}{2}}} = P_0 \left(e^{\ln\left(\sqrt{\frac{3}{2}}\right)}\right)^t = P_0\left(\sqrt{\dfrac{3}{2}}\right)^t = P_0\left(\dfrac{3}{2}\right)^{\frac{t}{2}}.$$ Since $P = 300$ when $t = 3$, we can substitute

into this equation to obtain: $300 = P_0\left(\dfrac{3}{2}\right)^{\frac{3}{2}} \Leftrightarrow P_0 = 300\left(\dfrac{3}{2}\right)^{\frac{-3}{2}} \approx 163$, which we round to a whole number since P is the number of bacteria. To find how many bacteria were present after 10 hours, we substitute: $P = (163)(1.5)^{10/2} \approx 1{,}238$ bacteria after 10 hours.

4. From the problem, we know that $A = 30{,}000$, $t = 25$, and $r = 0.05$; substituting into $A = A_0 e^{rt}$, we have $30000 = A_0 e^{1.25} \Leftrightarrow A_0 = 30000e^{-1.25} \approx 8{,}595.14$. Thus, \$8,595.14 was originally invested.

5. To find I when $\beta = 100$, substitute into $\beta = 10\log\left(\dfrac{I}{10^{-12}}\right)$: $100 = 10\log\left(\dfrac{I}{10^{-12}}\right)$

$10 = \log\left(\dfrac{I}{10^{-12}}\right) \Leftrightarrow 10^{10} = \dfrac{I}{10^{-12}} \Leftrightarrow I = 10^{22}$ watts per square meter is the intensity of this sound.

2.4 Linear Algebra

> **2.4.1** The California *Mathematics Subject Matter Requirements* stipulate that candidates for any credential program for teaching secondary mathematics must be able to *understand and apply the geometric interpretation and basic operations of vectors in two and three dimensions, including their scalar multiples, and scalar (dot) and cross products.*

Introduction to Vectors

- Some physical quantities such as temperature, length, time, and mass can be represented by single real numbers; these are called **scalar quantities**. Concepts such as velocity, acceleration, force, and displacement require two or more numbers for their representation; they are referred to as **vector quantities**.

- Vectors are not completely determined until both direction and magnitude are established. Geometrically, vectors are represented by **directed arrows**. The direction of the arrow specifies the **direction** of the vector, and the length of the arrow specifies the **magnitude** of the vector.

Example: Vector *AB* is denoted by $\overrightarrow{AB}$ or $\vec{v}$, as shown in Figure 2.45.

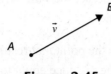

Figure 2.45

The tail, *A*, of the vector is called the **initial point**, and the head, *B*, is called the **terminal point** of the vector.

- Vectors having the same direction and magnitude are called **equivalent vectors**, as seen in Figure 2.46.

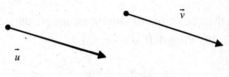

Figure 2.46

When vectors $\vec{u}$ and $\vec{v}$ are equivalent, we write $\vec{u} = \vec{v}$.

- **Vector Addition**: The sum of two vectors, $\vec{u}$ and $\vec{v}$, is a vector $\vec{w}$, which, when the tail of $\vec{v}$ is placed at the head of $\vec{u}$, has the same tail as $\vec{u}$ and the same head as $\vec{v}$, as Figure 2.47 shows.

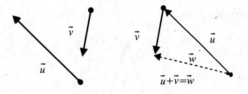

Figure 2.47

- The **Parallelogram Rule for Vector Addition:** If $\vec{v}$ and $\vec{u}$ are vectors in two dimensions ($\mathbf{R}^2$) or three dimensions ($\mathbf{R}^3$) positioned so that their initial points coincide, then the two vectors form adjacent sides of a parallelogram, and the sum $\vec{v} + \vec{u}$ is the vector $\vec{w}$ with tail at the common initial point of $\vec{v}$ and $\vec{u}$ and head at the opposite vertex of the parallelogram. Figure 2.48 shows this parallelogram, and that $\vec{v} + \vec{u} = \vec{u} + \vec{v}$.

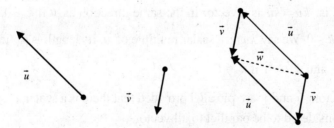

Figure 2.48

- **Vector Addition Viewed Geometrically as Translation**: If the vectors $\vec{v}$, $\vec{w}$, and $\vec{v} + \vec{w}$ are positioned so their initial points coincide, then the terminal point of $\vec{v} + \vec{w}$ can be viewed in two ways:

  1. The terminal point of $\vec{v} + \vec{w}$ is the point that results when the terminal point of $\vec{v}$ is translated in the direction of $\vec{w}$ by the distance equal to the length of $\vec{w}$.

  2. The terminal point of $\vec{v} + \vec{w}$ is the point that results when the terminal point of $\vec{w}$ is translated in the direction of $\vec{v}$ by the distance equal to the length of $\vec{v}$.

  Accordingly we say that $\vec{v} + \vec{w}$ is the translation of $\vec{v}$ by $\vec{w}$, or vice versa.

- The **zero vector**, $\vec{v} = \vec{0}$, is the vector of length zero and can be assigned any direction that is convenient. Note that $\vec{v} + \vec{0} = \vec{v}$ for all vectors $\vec{v}$.

- The **negative** of $\vec{v}$, $-\vec{v}$, is the vector having the same length as $\vec{v}$ but having the opposite direction, as shown in Figure 2.49. Note that $\vec{v} + -\vec{v} = \vec{0}$.

Figure 2.49

- **Subtracting a vector** is the same as adding the opposite vector. By this we mean $\vec{u} - \vec{v} = \vec{u} + -\vec{v}$. Geometrically, $\vec{u} - \vec{v}$ is the vector with initial point at the head of $\vec{v}$ and terminal point at the head of $\vec{u}$, as shown in Figure 2.50.

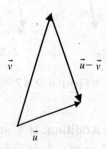

Figure 2.50

- Multiplication of a vector $\vec{u}$ and a scalar (constant), k, is called a **scalar product** or **scalar multiplication**. That is, $k\vec{u} = \overline{ku}$ is a vector in the same direction as $\vec{u}$ if $k > 0$, and in the opposite direction as $\vec{u}$ if $k < 0$. We say $\overline{ku}$ is a scalar multiple of $\vec{u}$. Its length is $|k|$ times the length of $\vec{u}$. Note that $k\vec{0} = \vec{0}$ and $k\vec{u} = \vec{0}$ if $k = 0$.

- Two non-zero vectors $\vec{u}$ and $\vec{v}$ are **parallel** provided that there is a scalar, c, such that $\vec{u} = c\vec{v}$. The zero vector is considered to be parallel to all vectors.

Rectangular Coordinate System in R² and R³

- Let $\vec{v}$ be a vector with initial point $O = (0, 0, 0)$ in $\mathbf{R^3}$ (or $O = (0, 0)$ in $\mathbf{R^2}$). The coordinates of the terminal point (v_1, v_2, v_3) in $\mathbf{R^3}$ (or (v_1, v_2) in $\mathbf{R^2}$) are called the **components of $\vec{v}$**, and we write $\vec{v} = <v_1, v_2, v_3>$ (or $\vec{v} = <v_1, v_2>$ in $\mathbf{R^2}$). In what follows, we work with vectors in $\mathbf{R^3}$.

- Writing vectors in component form makes it easier to perform arithmetic with them. Let $\vec{v} = <v_1, v_2, v_3>$ and $\vec{u} = <u_1, u_2, u_3>$. Then

  (a) $\vec{v} = \vec{u}$ if and only if $v_1 = u_1$, $v_2 = u_2$, and $v_3 = u_3$.

  (b) $\vec{v} \pm \vec{u} = <v_1 \pm u_1, v_2 \pm u_2, v_3 \pm u_3>$.

  (c) $\overline{ku} = <ku_1, ku_2, ku_3>$.

  Example: Let $\vec{v} = <-2, 3, 1>$, $\vec{u} = <1, -4, -1>$, and $k = -4$. Then:

  (a) $\vec{u} + \vec{v} = <1 + -2, -4 + 3, -1 + 1> = <-1, -1, 0>$

  (b) $\vec{u} - \vec{v} = <1 - (-2), -4 - 3, -1 - 1> = <3, -7, -2>$

  (c) $k\vec{v} = -4 <-2, 3, 1> = <8, -12, -4>$

- If $\overline{AB}$ has initial point $A = (x_1, y_1, z_1)$ and terminal point $B = (x_2, y_2, z_2)$, and the origin is $O = (0, 0, 0)$, then $\overline{AB} = \overline{OB} - \overline{OA} = <x_2 - x_1, y_2 - y_1, z_2 - z_1>$. So the **components of a vector** are equal to the coordinates of its terminal point minus the coordinates of its initial point.

  Example: Find the components of $\overline{PQ}$ if $P = (2, -3, 2)$ and $Q = (-6, 1, 1)$.

  $$\overline{PQ} = <-6 - 2, 1 - (-3), 1 - 2> = <-8, 4, -1>$$

- The **norm** or **magnitude** (length) of a vector $\vec{v} = <v_1, v_2, v_3>$ is denoted by $\|\vec{v}\|$ and is defined to be $\|v\| = \sqrt{v_1^2 + v_2^2 + v_3^2}$. Some properties are:

  Theorem: Let $\vec{v}$ be a vector in $\mathbf{R^3}$ and k a scalar. Then

  i. $\|\overline{kv}\| = |k| \|\vec{v}\|$.

  ii. For $\vec{v} \neq \vec{0}$, $\dfrac{\vec{v}}{\|\vec{v}\|}$ is the vector of length 1 with the same direction as $\vec{v}$.

- A vector of length 1 is called a **unit vector**.

- In $\mathbf{R^2}$, the vectors $\vec{i} = <1, 0>$ and $\vec{j} = <0, 1>$ are called the **standard unit vectors**. In $\mathbf{R^3}$, the **standard unit vectors** are $\vec{i} = <1, 0, 0>$, $\vec{j} = <0, 1, 0>$, and $\vec{k} = <0, 0, 1>$.

- We can write all vectors $\vec{u} = <a, b, c>$ in the form $\vec{u} = a\vec{i} + b\vec{j} + c\vec{k}$ as a combination of the standard unit vectors in $\mathbf{R^3}$, and in $\mathbf{R^2}$ vector $\vec{v} = <p, q>$ can be expressed as a combination of the standard unit vectors in the form $\vec{v} = p\vec{i} + q\vec{j}$.

The Dot Product in R² or R³

Let $\vec{u}$ and $\vec{v}$ be vectors in **R²** or **R³**, then we define the **dot product of $\vec{u}$ and $\vec{v}$** by

$$\vec{u} \cdot \vec{v} = \| \vec{u} \| \| \vec{v} \| \cos\theta$$

where θ is the measure of the angle between $\vec{u}$ and $\vec{v}$ and $0 \le \theta \le \pi$ radians.

Example: Let $\vec{u} = \langle 4, 0 \rangle$ and $\vec{v} = \langle 3, 3 \rangle$, so $\theta = 45°$. Then

$$\vec{u} \cdot \vec{v} = (4)(3\sqrt{2})\cos(45°) = (12\sqrt{2})\left(\frac{\sqrt{2}}{2}\right) = 12.$$

- Note that the result of a dot product is a scalar, not a vector.

- If $\vec{u} \cdot \vec{v} = 0$, then $\vec{u}$ and $\vec{v}$ are said to be **orthogonal** or **perpendicular**.

- The zero vector is considered to be orthogonal to all vectors.

An immediate consequence of the definition of the dot product and the fact that $\cos\theta$ has range $[-1, 1]$ is the next important and well-known theorem.

- **Theorem (Cauchy−Schwartz Inequality)**: Let $\vec{u}$ and $\vec{v}$ be vectors in **R²** or **R³**. Then

$$|\vec{u} \cdot \vec{v}| \le \| \vec{u} \| \| \vec{v} \|$$

- **Theorem**: Let $\vec{v} = <v_1, v_2, v_3>$ and $\vec{u} = <u_1, u_2, u_3>$ be vectors in **R³**. Then $\vec{u} \cdot \vec{v} = u_1 v_1 + u_2 v_2 + u_3 v_3$. (In **R²**, this is $\vec{u} \cdot \vec{v} = u_1 v_1 + u_2 v_2$.)

Proof: Let $\vec{v} = <v_1, v_2, v_3>$ and $\vec{u} = <u_1, u_2, u_3>$ be vectors in **R³**. Then, with θ being the measure of the angle between $\vec{u}$ and $\vec{v}$ such that $0 \le \theta \le \pi$ radians, we apply the Law of Cosines:

$$\| \vec{u} - \vec{v} \|^2 = \| \vec{u} \|^2 + \| \vec{v} \|^2 - 2 \| \vec{u} \| \| \vec{v} \| \cos\theta$$

Now, substituting in the components of the vectors and calculating, we have:
$(u_1 - v_1)^2 + (u_2 - v_2)^2 + (u_3 - v_3)^2 = (u_1^2 + u_2^2 + u_3^2) + (v_1^2 + v_2^2 + v_3^2) - 2\vec{u} \cdot \vec{v}$, which is
$u_1^2 - 2u_1 v_1 + v_1^2 + u_2^2 - 2u_2 v_2 + v_2^2 + u_3^2 - 2u_3 v_3 + v_3^2 = (u_1^2 + u_2^2 + u_3^2) + (v_1^2 + v_2^2 + v_3^2) - 2\vec{u} \cdot \vec{v}$.
Eliminating like terms, $-2u_1 v_1 - 2u_2 v_2 - 2u_3 v_3 = -2\vec{u} \cdot \vec{v}$.

Hence, by simplifying, $\vec{u} \cdot \vec{v} = u_1 v_1 + u_2 v_2 + u_3 v_3$.

Q.E.D.

Example: Let $\vec{u} = \langle 2, -1, 2 \rangle$, $\vec{v} = \langle -3, 0, 6 \rangle$, then $\vec{u} \cdot \vec{v} = 2(-3) + -1(0) + 2(6) = 6$.

- **Theorem**: Let $\vec{u}$ and $\vec{v}$ be vectors in **R²** or **R³**, and let θ be the measure of the angle between the two vectors. Then

  (a) $\vec{v} \cdot \vec{v} = \| \vec{v} \|^2$

  (b) If $\vec{u}$ and $\vec{v}$ are non-zero, then

i. θ is acute if $\vec{u}\cdot\vec{v}>0$

ii. θ is obtuse if $\vec{u}\cdot\vec{v}<0$

iii. θ is a right angle if $\vec{u}\cdot\vec{v}=0$

The Cross Product in R³

Let $\vec{v}=<v_1,v_2,v_3>$ and $\vec{u}=<u_1,u_2,u_3>$ be vectors in $\mathbf{R}^3$. Then we define the **cross product of $\vec{u}$ and $\vec{v}$** to be the vector

$$\vec{u}\times\vec{v}=<u_2v_3-u_3v_2,\,u_3v_1-u_1v_3,\,u_1v_2-u_2v_1>$$

The cross product is defined only for vectors in $\mathbf{R}^3$. For the cross product, note that the result is a vector, unlike with the dot product where the result is a scalar.

Example: Let $\vec{u}=<3,-4,-1>$ and $\vec{v}=<4,-2,2>$, then
$\vec{u}\times\vec{v}=<-4(2)-(-1)(-2),(-1)4-3(2),3(-2)-(-4)4>=<-10,\,-10,10>$.

- **Theorem**: Let $\vec{u}$ and $\vec{v}$ be vectors in $\mathbf{R}^3$, and let θ be the measure of the angle between the two vectors; then $\|\vec{u}\times\vec{v}\|=\|\vec{u}\|\|\vec{v}\|\sin\theta$.

- **Righthanded Rule**: For vectors $\vec{a}$ and $\vec{b}$, $\vec{a}\times\vec{b}$ is the vector perpendicular to both $\vec{a}$ and $\vec{b}$, and it points in the direction of your thumb if you were to lay the side of your right hand on $\vec{a}$ with fingers pointing toward the head of $\vec{a}$, and curl your fingers toward $\vec{b}$. This is illustrated in Figure 2.51.

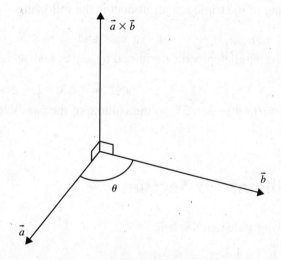

Figure 2.51

- Note that for the standard basis vectors $\vec{i}\times\vec{j}=\vec{k}$, $\vec{j}\times\vec{k}=\vec{i}$, and $\vec{k}\times\vec{i}=\vec{j}$.

- **Theorem**: Let $\vec{u}$ and $\vec{v}$ be vectors in $\mathbf{R}^3$, then $\|\vec{u}\times\vec{v}\|$ is equal to the area of the parallelogram determined by $\vec{u}$ and $\vec{v}$. (See Figure 2.52.)

A geometric application of the cross product is the following.

Example: Use the cross product to find the area of the triangle with vertices $(2, 2, 5)$, $(1, 2, 3)$, and $(-2, 6, 4)$.

Set $A = (2, 2, 5)$, $B = (1, 2, 3)$, and $C = (-2, 6, 4)$. Then the sides of the triangle are the vectors $\overrightarrow{AB} = <-1, 0, -2>$, $\overrightarrow{AC} = <-4, 4, -1>$ and $\overrightarrow{BC} = <-3, 4, 1>$. The area of ΔABC is half of the area of the parallelogram determined by $\overrightarrow{AB}$ and $\overrightarrow{AC}$, as illustrated in Figure 2.52.

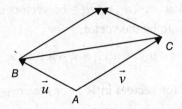

Figure 2.52

The area of the parallelogram is $\| \overrightarrow{AB} \times \overrightarrow{AC} \| = \| <8, 7, -4> \| = \sqrt{64 + 49 + 16} = \sqrt{129}$, so the area of ΔABC is $\dfrac{\sqrt{129}}{2}$ square units.

Let $\vec{u} = <u_1, u_2, u_3>$, $\vec{v} = <v_1, v_2, v_3>$, and $\vec{w} = <w_1, w_2, w_3>$ be vectors in $\mathbf{R}^3$; then we define the **triple scalar product of** $\vec{u}$, $\vec{v}$, and $\vec{w}$ to be

$$\vec{u} \cdot (\vec{v} \times \vec{w})$$

The geometric meaning of the triple scalar product is the following.

- **Theorem**: Let $\vec{u} = <u_1, u_2, u_3>$, $\vec{v} = <v_1, v_2, v_3>$, and $\vec{w} = <w_1, w_2, w_3>$ be vectors in $\mathbf{R}^3$. Then the volume of the parallelepiped determined by $\vec{u}$, $\vec{v}$, and $\vec{w}$ is $|\vec{u} \cdot (\vec{v} \times \vec{w})|$.

Example: Let $\vec{u} = <0, 5, -3>$, $\vec{v} = <1, -1, 2>$, and $\vec{w} = <3, -2, -2>$. Then $\vec{v} \times \vec{w} = <6, 8, 1>$. Then $|\vec{u} \cdot <6, 8, 1>| = |0 + 40 - 3| = 37$, so the volume of the parallelepiped determined by $\vec{u}$, $\vec{v}$, and $\vec{w}$ is 37 cubic units.

Review Problems for Section 2.4.1

1. Which of the following statements is true:

    (A) The length of $\vec{u} = <4, 1, -2>$ is 3.

    (B) The vectors $\vec{u} = <1, -1, 3>$ and $\vec{v} = <-1, 1, -3>$ are orthogonal.

    (C) If $\vec{u}$ is a vector and $\vec{u} \cdot \vec{u} = 0$, then $\vec{u} = \vec{0}$.

    (D) If k is a scalar and $\vec{u}$ is a vector, then the length of $k\vec{u}$ is k times the length of $\vec{u}$.

2. Find the angles of the parallelogram with three adjacent vertices $A\,(2, 4)$, $B\,(4, 1)$, and $C\,(5, 8)$.

3. Find a vector that has direction opposite to $\vec{v} = <2, 5, -1>$ but has length 4.

4. Which of the following statements is false:

(A) If $\vec{u}$ and $\vec{v}$ are non-zero vectors in $\mathbf{R}^3$ such that $\vec{u} \times \vec{v} = \vec{0}$, then $\vec{u} = \vec{v}$.

(B) $\vec{i} \times (\vec{i} \times \vec{j}) = -\vec{j}$.

(C) If $\|\vec{u} \times \vec{v}\| = \|\vec{u}\| \|\vec{v}\|$, then $\vec{u}$ and $\vec{v}$ are orthogonal.

(D) The vector $\vec{u} \times \vec{v}$ is orthogonal to both $\vec{u}$ and $\vec{v}$.

Detailed Solutions

1. **C**

For (A), the length of $\vec{u} = <4, 1, -2>$ is $\sqrt{16+1+4} = \sqrt{21}$. For (B), since $\vec{u} \cdot \vec{v} = -1 + -1 + -9 = -11$, the two vectors are not orthogonal. For (C), if the dot product of a vector, $\vec{u}$, with itself is equal to 0, then it must be true that $\vec{u}$ is the zero vector. If, say, $\vec{u} = <u_1, u_2, u_3>$, then $\vec{u} \cdot \vec{u} = u_1^2 + u_2^2 + u_3^2$. Statement (D) is false since when $k < 0$, k times the length of $\vec{u}$ will be negative, but length cannot be negative.

2. Consider the three points shown on the graph in Figure 2.53 along with the vectors $\overrightarrow{BA} = <-2, 3>$ and $\overrightarrow{BC} = <1, 7>$. Then $\|\overrightarrow{BA}\| = \sqrt{13}$, $\|\overrightarrow{BC}\| = 5\sqrt{2}$, and $\overrightarrow{BA} \cdot \overrightarrow{BC} = 19$, so substituting into the equation $\vec{u} \cdot \vec{v} = \|\vec{u}\| \|\vec{v}\| \cos\theta$ gives us $19 = 5\sqrt{26}\cos\theta$. Solve $\cos\theta = \dfrac{19}{5\sqrt{26}}$ to obtain $\theta = \cos^{-1}\left(\dfrac{19}{5\sqrt{26}}\right)$, which is approximately 0.73 radians, or 41.82 degrees. So the angle at point B (and point D, not shown) in the parallelogram is about 41.82 degrees, and thus the angles at points A and C are about 138.18 degrees.

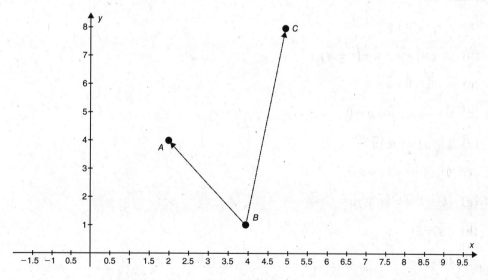

Figure 2.53

3. We need a vector that has the same direction as $-\vec{v} = <-2, -5, 1>$. The length of $\vec{v}$ is $\|\vec{v}\| = \sqrt{4+25+1} = \sqrt{30}$, so if we divide $-\vec{v}$ by $\sqrt{30}$, we obtain a unit vector, and if we then multiply by 4, we will have a vector, $\vec{w}$, with length 4 that is in the opposite direction as $\vec{v}$: $\vec{w} = \dfrac{4}{\sqrt{30}} <-2, -5, 1> = \left\langle \dfrac{-8}{\sqrt{30}}, \dfrac{-20}{\sqrt{30}}, \dfrac{4}{\sqrt{30}} \right\rangle$.

4. A

For (A), if $\vec{u}$ and $\vec{v}$ are non-zero vectors in $\mathbf{R}^3$ such that $\vec{u} \times \vec{v} = \vec{0}$, then using the formula $\|\vec{u} \times \vec{v}\| = \|\vec{u}\| \|\vec{v}\| \sin\theta$, we know that, since neither of the vectors are the zero vector, $\sin\theta = 0$, so for the two vectors are parallel. So it is false that they are orthogonal. Let's look at the other statements. For (B), $\vec{i} \times \vec{j} = \vec{k}$, so $\vec{i} \times (\vec{i} \times \vec{j}) = \vec{i} \times \vec{k} = -\vec{k} \times \vec{i} = -\vec{j}$ is true. If $\|\vec{u} \times \vec{v}\| = \|\vec{u}\| \|\vec{v}\|$, then $\sin\theta = 1$ so that $\theta = \dfrac{\pi}{2}$ radians; hence, the vectors are orthogonal and statement (C) is true. Statement (D) is true; see Figure 2.51. To prove this, show that the dot product of each of $\vec{u}$ and $\vec{v}$ with $\vec{u} \times \vec{v}$ is equal to 0.

2.4.2 The California *Mathematics Subject Matter Requirements* stipulate that candidates for any credential program for teaching secondary mathematics must be able to *prove the basic properties of vectors (e.g., perpendicular vectors have zero dot product).*

Vector Properties

- **Theorem: (Basic Vector Properties):** Let $\vec{u}$, $\vec{v}$, and $\vec{w}$ be vectors in $\mathbf{R}^2$ or $\mathbf{R}^3$, and let k and j be scalars; then

  (a) $\vec{u} + \vec{v} = \vec{v} + \vec{u}$

  (b) $(\vec{u} + \vec{v}) + \vec{w} = \vec{u} + (\vec{v} + \vec{w})$

  (c) $\vec{u} + \vec{0} = \vec{0} + \vec{u} = \vec{u}$

  (d) $\vec{u} + -\vec{u} = -\vec{u} + \vec{u} = \vec{0}$

  (e) $k(j\vec{u}) = (jk)\vec{u}$

  (f) $k(\vec{u} + \vec{v}) = k\vec{u} + k\vec{v}$

  (g) $(k + j)\vec{u} = k\vec{u} + j\vec{u}$

  (h) $1\vec{u} = \vec{u}$

  (i) $0\vec{u} = \vec{0}$

Proof: All of the properties can be proven by using coordinates. Here, we prove parts (a), (c), and (g) for $\mathbf{R}^3$ by using coordinates.

(a) Let $\vec{u} = <u_1, u_2, u_3>$ and $\vec{v} = <v_1, v_2, v_3>$. Then

$$\vec{u} + \vec{v} = <u_1, u_2, u_3> + <v_1, v_2, v_3> \quad \text{(Definition of } \vec{u} \text{ and } \vec{v})$$
$$= <u_1 + v_1, u_2 + v_2, u_3 + v_3> \quad \text{(Definition of vector addition)}$$
$$= <v_1 + u_1, v_2 + u_2, v_3 + u_3> \quad \text{(Commutative Property of + for reals)}$$
$$\quad\quad\quad\quad\quad\quad\quad\quad\quad\quad\quad\quad\quad \text{(Definition of vector addition)}$$
$$= <v_1, v_2, v_3> + <u_1, u_2, u_3> \quad \text{(Definition of } \vec{u} \text{ and } \vec{v})$$
$$= \vec{v} + \vec{u}$$

Q.E.D.

(c) Let $\vec{u} = <u_1, u_2, u_3>$. Then

$$\vec{u} + \vec{0} = <u_1, u_2, u_3> + <0, 0, 0> \quad \text{(Definition of } \vec{u} \text{ and } \vec{0})$$
$$= <u_1 + 0, u_2 + 0, u_3 + 0> \quad \text{(Definition of vector addition)}$$
$$= <u_1, u_2, u_3> \quad \text{(Additive Identity Property of the reals)}$$
$$= <0 + u_1, 0 + u_2, 0 + u_3> \quad \text{(Additive Identity Property of the reals)}$$
$$= <0, 0, 0> + <u_1, u_2, u_3> \quad \text{(Definition of vector addition)}$$
$$= \vec{0} + \vec{u} \quad \text{(Definition of } \vec{u} \text{ and } 0)$$

Q.E.D.

(g) Let $\vec{u} = <u_1, u_2, u_3>$ and let j, k be real numbers. Then

$$(k+j)\vec{u} = (k+j)<u_1, u_2, u_3> \quad \text{(Definition of } \vec{u})$$
$$= <(k+j)u_1, (k+j)u_2, (k+j)u_3> \quad \text{(Definition of scalar multiplication)}$$
$$= <ku_1 + ju_1, ku_2 + ju_2, ku_3 + ju_3> \quad \text{(Distributive Property for reals)}$$
$$= <ku_1, ku_2, ku_3> + <ju_1\ ju_2, ju_3> \quad \text{(Definition of vector addition)}$$
$$= k<u_1, u_2\ u_3> + j<u_1, u_2, u_3> \quad \text{(Definition of scalar multiplication)}$$
$$= k\vec{u} + j\vec{u} \quad \text{(Definition of } \vec{u})$$

Q.E.D.

- **Theorem: (Basic Properties of the Dot Product)**: Let $\vec{u}$, $\vec{v}$, and $\vec{w}$ be vectors in $\mathbf{R}^2$ or $\mathbf{R}^3$, and let k be a scalar. Then

    (a) $\vec{u} \cdot \vec{v} = \vec{v} \cdot \vec{u}$

    (b) $\vec{u} \cdot (\vec{v} + \vec{w}) = \vec{u} \cdot \vec{v} + \vec{u} \cdot \vec{w}$

    (c) $k(\vec{u} \cdot \vec{v}) = (k\vec{u}) \cdot \vec{v} = \vec{u} \cdot (k\vec{v})$

    (d) $\vec{v} \cdot \vec{v} > 0$ if $\vec{v} \neq \vec{0}$ and $\vec{v} \cdot \vec{v} = 0$ if and only if $\vec{v} = \vec{0}$

    (f) $\vec{u} \cdot \vec{v} = 0$ if and only if $\vec{u} \perp \vec{v}$

Proof: We prove parts (b) and (d) in $\mathbf{R}^3$ here.

(b) Let $\vec{u} = <u_1, u_2, u_3>$, $\vec{v} = <v_1, v_2, v_3>$, and $\vec{w} = <w_1, w_2, w_3>$ be vectors in $\mathbf{R}^3$. Then

$$\vec{u} \cdot (\vec{v} + \vec{w}) = \vec{u} \cdot <v_1 + w_1, v_2 + w_2, v_3 + w_3>$$

$$= u_1(v_1 + w_1) + u_2(v_2 + w_2) + u_3(v_3 + w_3)$$

$$= u_1v_1 + u_1w_1 + u_2v_2 + u_2w_2 + u_3v_3 + u_3w_3$$

$$= (u_1v_1 + u_2v_2 + u_3v_3) + (u_1w_1 + u_2w_2 + u_3w_3)$$

$$= \vec{u} \cdot \vec{v} + \vec{u} \cdot \vec{w}$$

(d) Let $\vec{v} = <v_1, v_2, v_3>$ be a vector in $\mathbf{R}^3$. Then $\vec{v} \cdot \vec{v} = v_1^2 + v_2^2 + v_3^2$. If $\vec{v} \neq \vec{0}$, then at least one $v_i \neq 0$, which, along with the fact that $v_i^2 > 0$, implies that $\vec{v} \cdot \vec{v} > 0$. Also, $\vec{v} = \vec{0}$ $\qquad v_1 = v_2 = v_3 = 0$ $\qquad \vec{v} \cdot \vec{v} = 0$.

Q.E.D.

- **Theorem**: Let $\vec{u}$ and $\vec{v}$ be vectors in $\mathbf{R}^3$. Then

  (a) $\vec{u} \cdot (\vec{u} \times \vec{v}) = 0$ $\qquad\qquad\qquad (\vec{u} \perp (\vec{u} \times \vec{v}))$

  (b) $\vec{v} \cdot (\vec{u} \times \vec{v}) = 0$ $\qquad\qquad\qquad (\vec{v} \perp (\vec{u} \times \vec{v}))$

  Proof: Let $\vec{u} = <u_1, u_2, u_3>$ and $\vec{v} = <v_1, v_2, v_3>$, be vectors in $\mathbf{R}^3$,

  (a) $\vec{u} \cdot (\vec{u} \times \vec{v}) = \vec{u} \cdot \langle u_2v_3 - u_3v_2, u_3v_1 - u_1v_3, u_1v_2 - u_2v_1 \rangle$

  $$= u_1(u_2v_3 - u_3v_2) + u_2(u_3v_1 - u_1v_3) + u_3(u_1v_2 - u_2v_1)$$

  $$= u_1u_2v_3 - u_1u_3v_2 + u_2u_3v_1 - u_2u_1v_3 + u_3u_1v_2 - u_3u_2v_1$$

  $$= (u_1u_2v_3 - u_2u_1v_3) + (u_2u_3v_1 - u_3u_2v_1) + (u_3u_1v_2 - u_1u_3v_2)$$

  $$= 0$$

  (b) The proof is similar to the proof for (a).

Q.E.D.

- **Theorem**: (**Some Basic Properties of the Cross Product**): Let $\vec{u}$, $\vec{v}$, and $\vec{w}$ be vectors in $\mathbf{R}^3$, and let k be a scalar. Then

  (a) $\vec{u} \times \vec{v} = -\vec{v} \times \vec{u}$

  (b) $\vec{u} \times (\vec{v} + \vec{w}) = (\vec{u} \times \vec{v}) + (\vec{u} \times \vec{w})$

  (c) $k(\vec{u} \times \vec{v}) = (k\vec{u}) \times \vec{v} = \vec{u} \times (k\vec{v})$

  (d) $\vec{u} \times \vec{0} = \vec{0}$

  (e) $\vec{u} \times \vec{u} = \vec{0}$

  (f) $\vec{u} \times \vec{v} = \vec{0}$ if and only if $\vec{u} \| \vec{v}$

Proof: We prove parts (a) and (d) here.

Let $\vec{u} = <u_1, u_2, u_3>$ and $\vec{v} = <v_1, v_2, v_3>$ be vectors in $\mathbf{R}^3$,

(a) $\vec{u} \times \vec{v} = \left\langle u_2 v_3 - u_3 v_2, u_3 v_1 - u_1 v_3, u_1 v_2 - u_2 v_1 \right\rangle$

$= -\left\langle u_3 v_2 - u_2 v_3, u_1 v_3 - u_3 v_1, u_2 v_1 - u_1 v_2 \right\rangle$

$= -\left\langle v_2 u_3 - v_3 u_2, v_3 u_1 - v_1 u_3, v_1 u_2 - v_2 u_1 \right\rangle$

$= -\vec{v} \times \vec{u}$

(d) $\vec{u} \times \vec{0} = \left\langle 0-0, 0-0, 0-0 \right\rangle$

$= \vec{0}$

Q.E.D.

- **Theorem (Triangle Inequality for Vectors):** Let $\vec{u}$, $\vec{v}$, and $\vec{w}$ be vectors in $\mathbf{R}^2$ or $\mathbf{R}^3$. Then $\| \vec{u} + \vec{v} \| \le \| \vec{u} \| + \| \vec{v} \|$.

Linear Independence of Vectors

- If $S = \left\{ \vec{v_1}, \vec{v_2}, \vec{v_3}, \cdots, \vec{v_n} \right\}$ is a non-empty set of vectors in $\mathbf{R}^n$, then the vector equation $k_1 \vec{v_1} + k_2 \vec{v_2} + \cdots + k_n \vec{v_n} = \vec{0}$ has at least one solution, namely, $k_1 = k_2 = \cdots = k_n = 0$, which is called the **trivial solution**. If this is the only solution, then S is said to be a **linearly independent** set in $\mathbf{R}^n$. If there are solutions in addition to the trivial solution, then S is said to be a **linearly dependent** set in $\mathbf{R}^n$.

Example: Determine whether $\vec{v_1} = \left\langle -1, 2, 1 \right\rangle$, $\vec{v_2} = \left\langle -2, 5, -3 \right\rangle$, and $\vec{v_3} = \left\langle 1, 0, 1 \right\rangle$ are linearly independent or dependent.

Suppose $k_1 \vec{v_1} + k_2 \vec{v_2} + k_3 \vec{v_3} = \vec{0}$. Then $\left\langle -k_1 - 2k_2 + k_3, 2k_1 + 5k_2, k_1 - 3k_2 + k_3 \right\rangle = \left\langle 0, 0, 0 \right\rangle$.

So we need to solve: $\begin{cases} -k_1 - 2k_2 + k_3 = 0 \\ 2k_1 + 5k_2 = 0 \\ k_1 - 3k_2 + k_3 = 0 \end{cases}$. We will solve this system by using the multiplication-addition elimination method. (In the next section, we show how to use matrices to solve such a system.)

Adding two times the first equation to the second equation and then adding the first equation to the third equation to eliminate k_1 from the equations, we arrive at: $\begin{cases} k_2 + 2k_3 = 0 \\ -5k_2 + 2k_3 = 0 \end{cases}$. Next, note that these two equations are not multiples of each other, so since these are homogeneous equations (the constants on the right side of the equations are zero), the only solution is $k_2 = k_3 = 0$. Then, substituting this back into the original equations, we see that $k_1 = 0$ also. Hence, since there is only the trivial solution, the three vectors are linearly independent.

- **Theorem:** A set S with two or more vectors is:

(a) linearly dependent if and only if one of the vectors in S is expressible as a linear combination of the other vectors in S.

(b) linearly independent if and only if no vector in S is expressible as a linear combination of the other vectors in S.

- **Theorem**: The following statements hold for vectors:

  (a) A finite set that contains $\vec{0}$ is linearly dependent.

  (b) A set with exactly one vector is linearly independent if and only if that vector is not the vector $\vec{0}$.

  (c) A set with exactly two vectors is linearly independent if and only if neither vector is a scalar multiple of the other.

- **Theorem**: Let S be a set of r vectors in $\mathbf{R}^n$. If $r > n$, then S is linearly independent.

Review Problems for Section 2.4.2

1. Prove: $\vec{u} \cdot \vec{v} = 0$ if and only if $\vec{u} \perp \vec{v}$.

2. Prove: For $\vec{u}$ in $\mathbf{R}^2$ or $\mathbf{R}^3$, $\vec{u} + -\vec{u} = \vec{0}$.

3. Prove: Let $\vec{u}$, $\vec{v}$, and $\vec{w}$ be vectors in $\mathbf{R}^3$, and let k be a scalar. Then $k(\vec{u} \times \vec{v}) = (k\vec{u}) \times \vec{v}$.

4. Determine whether $\vec{v_1} = \langle 3, -1, 0 \rangle$, $\vec{v_2} = \langle -2, 0, -3 \rangle$, and $\vec{v_3} = \left\langle -4, 1, \frac{-3}{2} \right\rangle$ are linearly independent or dependent.

Detailed Solutions

1. **Proof**: Let $\vec{u}$ and $\vec{v}$ be vectors.

$$\vec{u} \cdot \vec{v} = 0 \iff \|\vec{u}\| \|\vec{v}\| \cos\theta = 0$$

$$\iff \vec{u} = 0 \text{ or } \vec{v} = 0, \text{ or } \theta = \frac{\pi}{2} \text{ radians}$$

$$\iff \vec{u} \perp \vec{v}$$

Q.E.D.

2. **Proof** (for $\mathbf{R}^3$): Let $\vec{u} = <u_1, u_2, u_3>$, then

$$\vec{u} + -\vec{u} = <u_1\, u_2\, u_3> + <-u_1, -u_2, -u_3>$$
$$= <u_1 + (-u_1), u_2 + (-u_2), u_3 + (-u_3)>$$
$$= <0, 0, 0>$$
$$= \vec{0}$$

Q.E.D.

3. **Proof:** Let $\vec{u} = <u_1, u_2, u_3>$, $\vec{v} = <v_1, v_2, v_3>$, and $\vec{w} = <w_1, w_2, w_3>$ be vectors in $\mathbf{R}^3$, and let k be a scalar. Then

$$k(\vec{u} \times \vec{v}) = k(<u_2v_3 - u_3v_2, \ u_3v_1 - u_1v_3, \ u_1v_2 - u_2v_1>)$$

$$= <k(u_2v_3 - u_3v_2), \ k(u_3v_1 - u_1v_3), \ k(u_1v_2 - u_2v_1)>$$

$$= <ku_2v_3 - ku_3v_2, \ ku_3v_1 - ku_1v_3, \ ku_1v_2 - ku_2v_1>$$

$$= <(ku_2)v_3 - (ku_3)v_2, \ (ku_3)v_1 - (ku_1)v_3, \ (ku_1)v_2 - (ku_2)v_1>$$

$$= (k\vec{u}) \times \vec{v}$$

Q.E.D.

4. Suppose $k_1\vec{v_1} + k_2\vec{v_2} + k_3\vec{v_3} = \vec{0}$. Then $\left\langle 3k_1 - 2k_2 - 4k_3, \ -k_1 + k_3, \ -3k_2 - \dfrac{3}{2}k_3 \right\rangle = \langle 0, 0, 0 \rangle$.

So we need to solve: $\begin{cases} 3k_1 - 2k_2 - 4k_3 = 0 \\ -k_1 + k_3 = 0 \\ -3k_2 - \dfrac{3}{2}k_3 = 0 \end{cases}$. Adding three times the second equation to the first

equation and keeping the third equation, we have eliminated k_1 from the first and second equations,

and we obtain: $\begin{cases} -2k_2 - k_3 = 0 \\ -3k_2 - \dfrac{3}{2}k_3 = 0 \end{cases}$. Next, adding $-\dfrac{3}{2}$ times the new first equation to the new second

equation, we obtain $0 = 0$. This means that these two equations are redundant, so we keep the first equation and solve for $k_3 = -2k_2$. The original second equation tells us that $k_1 = k_3$. So the solution set of our original system of equations is the set of all vectors in the form $\left\langle c, \dfrac{-1}{2}c, c \right\rangle$ for any real number c. Hence, since the system has more than the trivial solution, the three vectors are linearly dependent.

2.4.3 The California *Mathematics Subject Matter Requirements* stipulate that candidates for any credential program for teaching secondary mathematics must be able to *understand and apply the basic properties and operations of matrices and determinants (e.g., to determine the solvability of linear systems of equations).*

Systems of Linear Equations

A **linear equation in n variables**, $x_1, x_2, \ldots, x_n$, is an equation that can be written in the form

$$a_1 x_1 + a_2 x_2 + \cdots + a_n x_n = b$$

where $a_1, a_2, a_3, \ldots, a_n$ and b are real **constants**. The x_i's, $i = 1, 2, 3, \ldots, n$ are called the **unknowns** or **variables**.

A **solution of a linear equation** $a_1 x_1 + a_2 x_2 + \cdots + a_n x_n = b$ is a sequence of numbers $s_1, s_2, \ldots, s_n$ such that when the values $x_1 = s_1, x_2 = s_2, \ldots, x_n = s_n$, are substituted into the equation, the result is a true statement.

- The set of all solutions of the equation is called the **solution set** of the equation.

- A finite set of linear equations in the variables $x_1, x_2, x_3, \ldots, x_n$ is called a **system of linear equations** or a **linear system**.

- **A solution of a linear system** is a solution of each of the equations in the system.

Examples:

(i) The values $x = 2, y = 5$, or written as an ordered pair $(2, 5)$, is a solution of $-3x + 2y = 4$.

(ii) The solution set of $-3x + 2y = 4$ consists of all the points on the graph of $-3x + 2y = 4$, which can be written as the set $\{(x, 1.5x + 2)\mid x \in \mathbf{R}\}$.

(iii) $\begin{cases} x + y = 6 \\ 2x + 2y = 5 \end{cases}$ is a system of equations that has no solutions since the graphs of the lines are parallel.

(iv) $\begin{cases} x + y = 6 \\ 2x + 2y = 12 \end{cases}$ is a system of equations that has infinitely many solutions because the two lines coincide.

(v) $\begin{cases} x + y = 6 \\ 2x + y = 7 \end{cases}$ is a system of equations with exactly one solution $(1, 5)$ since the lines intersect at one point.

- A system of equations with no solutions is called **inconsistent**. A system with at least one solution is called **consistent**.

- **Fact**: Every system of linear equations has either no solutions, exactly one solution, or infinitely many solutions.

Augmented Matrix

Given a system of m equations in n unknowns,

$$a_{11}x_1 + a_{12}x_2 + \cdots\cdots + a_{1n}x_n = b_1$$

$$a_{21}x_1 + a_{22}x_2 + \cdots\cdots + a_{2n}x_n = b_2$$

$$a_{31}x_1 + a_{32}x_2 + \cdots\cdots + a_{3n}x_n = b_3$$

$$\cdot \qquad \cdot \qquad \cdot \qquad \cdot \qquad \cdot$$

$$\cdot \qquad \cdot \qquad \cdot \qquad \cdot \qquad \cdot$$

$$\cdot \qquad \cdot \qquad \cdot \qquad \cdot \qquad \cdot$$

$$a_{m1}x_1 + a_{m2}x_2 + \cdots\cdots + a_{mn}x_n = b_m$$

we can write the **augmented matrix** (rectangular array) that corresponds to this system:

$$\left[\begin{array}{cccc|c} a_{11} & a_{12} & \cdots & a_{1n} & b_1 \\ a_{21} & a_{22} & \cdots & a_{2n} & b_2 \\ \cdot & \cdot & \cdots & \cdot & \cdot \\ \cdot & \cdot & \cdots & \cdot & \cdot \\ \cdot & \cdot & \cdots & \cdot & \cdot \\ a_{m1} & a_{m2} & \cdots & a_{mn} & b_n \end{array}\right]$$

and vice versa.

Examples: What is the linear system associated with the augmented matrix:

(a) $\begin{bmatrix} 1 & 0 & \vline & 8 \\ 0 & 1 & \vline & -1 \end{bmatrix}$

Answer: $\begin{cases} x = 8 \\ y = -1 \end{cases}$

(b) $\begin{bmatrix} 1 & 0 & 0 & \bigm| & -2 \\ 0 & 2 & 1 & \bigm| & -3 \\ 0 & 0 & 0 & \bigm| & 0 \end{bmatrix}$

Answer: $\begin{cases} x = -2 \\ 2y + z = -3 \\ 0 = 0 \end{cases}$

- To solve a linear system, we can use the following **elementary operations**:

    1. Multiply an equation by a non-zero constant.

    2. Interchange two equations.

    3. Add a multiple of one equation to another equation.

- The corresponding **elementary row operations** for the augmented matrix are:

    1. Multiply a row by a non-zero constant.

    2. Interchange two rows.

    3. Add a multiple of one row to another row.

- A matrix that is in **reduced row-echelon form** (RREF) has the following properties:

    1. If a row is not all zeroes, then the first non-zero number in the row is a 1. (This is called a **leading 1**.)

    2. If there are any rows that consist entirely of zeroes, then these rows are at the bottom of the matrix.

    3. In any two consecutive rows that are not all zeroes, the leading 1 in the lower row is farther to the right than the leading 1 in the higher row.

    4. Each column that contains a leading 1 has zeroes everywhere else.

A matrix satisfying properties (1), (2), and (3) but not necessarily (4), is said to be in **row-echelon form**.

Examples: Consider the following matrices:

$$A = \begin{bmatrix} 1 & 2 & 1 & \bigm| & -2 \\ 0 & 1 & 0 & \bigm| & -1 \\ 0 & 0 & 1 & \bigm| & -3 \end{bmatrix}, \; B = \begin{bmatrix} 1 & 0 & \bigm| & -1 \\ 1 & 2 & \bigm| & 0 \end{bmatrix}, \; C = \begin{bmatrix} 1 & 0 & 0 & \bigm| & 0 \\ 0 & 1 & 0 & \bigm| & -1 \\ 0 & 0 & 1 & \bigm| & -3 \end{bmatrix}, \; D = \begin{bmatrix} 1 & 0 & 0 & \bigm| & 4 \\ 0 & 1 & 0 & \bigm| & 1 \\ 0 & 0 & 0 & \bigm| & 0 \\ 0 & 0 & 1 & \bigm| & 2 \end{bmatrix}$$

Matrices *A, B,* and *D* are not in RREF, although matrix *A* is in row-echelon form. Matrix *A* is not in RREF because column 2 has a leading 1 in the 2,2 position yet does not have zeroes in all the other positions in that column. Matrix *B* also fails criteria (4) since there is a leading 1 in the 1,1 position but a non-zero number below it. Also, matrix *B* has leading 1s in both rows 1 and 2, but they fail criteria (3) because one is below the other; thus, B is not in row-echelon form. Matrix D fails criteria (2), having a row of zeroes that are not at the bottom of the matrix. Matrix C is in RREF.

- .To **solve a system of linear equations**, change the augmented matrix into either:

    (a) reduced row-echelon form, or

    (b) row-echelon form and use back substitution.

- An augmented matrix that is in reduced row-echelon form, once translated into its corresponding system, **produces the solution** of the original system.

Example: If the matrix is $\begin{bmatrix} 1 & 0 & 0 & | & c_1 \\ 0 & 1 & 0 & | & c_2 \\ 0 & 0 & 1 & | & c_3 \\ 0 & 0 & 0 & | & 0 \end{bmatrix}$, then the corresponding system is: $x_1 = c_1, x_2 = c_2,$

$x_3 = c_3, 0 = 0$. So the solution is $x_1 = c_1, x_2 = c_2, x_3 = c_3$, or the triple (c_1, c_2, c_3).

- **Back-substitution** is a technique used to solve the original system when a matrix is in row-echelon form; beginning with the bottom equation, we successively substitute each equation into the equation above it.

Example: Consider the following matrix, which is in row-echelon form. Use back substitution to solve the original linear system.

$$\begin{bmatrix} 1 & -2 & 3 & | & 1 \\ 0 & 1 & -1 & | & -4 \\ 0 & 0 & 1 & | & 2 \end{bmatrix}$$

The system corresponding to this matrix is $\begin{cases} x - 2y + 3z = 1 \\ y - z = -4 \\ z = 2 \end{cases}$.

We start with $z = 2$ (the third equation) and substitute this value "back" into the other equations, giving $x - 2y + 6 = 1$ and $y - 2 = -4$, or $x - 2y = -5$ and $y = -2$. Next, substitute $y = -2$ into $x - 2y = -5$ to obtain $x + 4 = -5$ or $x = -9$. The solution of the system corresponding to the matrix is $(-9, -2, 2)$.

Gauss-Jordan Elimination

The procedure used to change the augmented matrix into reduced row-echelon form is called **Gauss-Jordan elimination**, which is as follows:

1. Locate the leftmost column that does not consist entirely of zeroes.

2. Interchange the top row with another row, if necessary, to bring a non-zero entry to the top of the column found in step (1).

3. If the entry that is now in the top of the column found in step (1) is a, multiply the first row by $\dfrac{1}{a}$ in order to produce a leading 1.

4. Add suitable multiples of the top row to the rows below the new leading 1 so that all entries below the leading 1 become zeroes.

5. Now cover the top row of the matrix and begin again with step (1) applied to the submatrix that remains. Each time a leading 1 is obtained, add suitable multiples of that row to produce zeroes in all other entries above and below the 1.

6. Continue in this way until the entire matrix is in row-echelon form.

Example: Solve the following system using Gauss-Jordan elimination:

$$\begin{cases} -x + 3y = 5 \\ 2x - y = 3 \end{cases}$$

Step 1: Write the augmented matrix: $A = \begin{bmatrix} -1 & 3 & | & 5 \\ 2 & -1 & | & 3 \end{bmatrix}$

Step 2: Obtain a 1, if possible, in the a_{11} position. Here we can do this by multiplying the first row by -1

$$\begin{bmatrix} -1 & 3 & | & 5 \\ 2 & -1 & | & 3 \end{bmatrix} \quad -1R_1 \quad \begin{bmatrix} 1 & -3 & | & -5 \\ 2 & -1 & | & 3 \end{bmatrix} \quad -2R_1 + R_2 \to R_2 \quad \begin{bmatrix} 1 & -3 & | & -5 \\ 0 & 5 & | & 13 \end{bmatrix}$$

Step 3: Change the a_{21} entry into a zero: Add -2 times row 1 to row 2.

Step 4: Obtain a 1 in the a_{22} entry. Multiply row 2 by $\dfrac{1}{5}$:

$$\begin{bmatrix} 1 & -3 & | & -5 \\ 0 & 5 & | & 13 \end{bmatrix} \quad \frac{1}{5}R_2 \quad \begin{bmatrix} 1 & -3 & | & -5 \\ 0 & 1 & | & 13/5 \end{bmatrix} \quad 3R_2 + R_1 \to R_1 \quad \begin{bmatrix} 1 & 0 & | & 14/5 \\ 0 & 1 & | & 13/5 \end{bmatrix}$$

Step 5: Obtain a zero in the a_{12} position: Add 3 times row 2 to row 1. This matrix is in RREF (reduced row-echelon form), and we can read the solution as $x = 14/5$, $y = 13/5$. We can check our work by using back substitution.

Example: Solve the following system using Gauss-Jordan elimination:

$$\begin{cases} z = 0 \\ x + 3y + 3z = 4 \\ 2x + y + 26z = 4 \end{cases}$$

$$\begin{bmatrix} 0 & 0 & 1 & | & 0 \\ 1 & 3 & 3 & | & 4 \\ 2 & 1 & 26 & | & 4 \end{bmatrix} \quad R_1 \leftrightarrow R_2 \quad \begin{bmatrix} 1 & 3 & 3 & | & 4 \\ 0 & 0 & 1 & | & 0 \\ 2 & 1 & 26 & | & 4 \end{bmatrix} \quad -2R_1 + R_3 \rightarrow R_3 \quad \begin{bmatrix} 1 & 3 & 3 & | & 4 \\ 0 & 0 & 1 & | & 0 \\ 0 & -5 & 20 & | & -4 \end{bmatrix}$$

$$R_2 \leftrightarrow R_3 \quad \begin{bmatrix} 1 & 3 & 3 & | & 4 \\ 0 & -5 & 20 & | & -4 \\ 0 & 0 & 1 & | & 0 \end{bmatrix} \quad -\frac{1}{5} R_2 \leftrightarrow R_2 \quad \begin{bmatrix} 1 & 3 & 3 & | & 4 \\ 0 & 1 & -4 & | & \frac{4}{5} \\ 0 & 0 & 1 & | & 0 \end{bmatrix}$$

$$-3R_2 + R_1 \leftrightarrow R_1 \quad \begin{bmatrix} 1 & 0 & 15 & | & \frac{8}{5} \\ 0 & 1 & -4 & | & \frac{4}{5} \\ 0 & 0 & 1 & | & 0 \end{bmatrix} \quad \begin{matrix} 4R_3 + R_2 \rightarrow R_2 \\ -15R_3 + R_1 \rightarrow R_1 \end{matrix} \quad \begin{bmatrix} 1 & 0 & 0 & | & \frac{8}{5} \\ 0 & 1 & 0 & | & \frac{4}{5} \\ 0 & 0 & 1 & | & 0 \end{bmatrix}$$

The solution is $x = \dfrac{8}{5}$, $y = \dfrac{4}{5}$, $z = 0$, which is a single point in three space.

- A system of linear equations is said to be **homogeneous** provided all the constant terms are zero. Note that every homogeneous system has the **trivial solution** which is $x_i = 0$ for all $i = 1, 2, 3, \ldots, n$. If there are other solutions, they are called **non-trivial solutions**.

  Example: This system is homogeneous:

$$\begin{cases} x + y - z = 0 \\ 2x + 3y - z = 0 \\ -x + 4y - 3z = 0 \end{cases}$$

- **Theorem**: For homogeneous systems, exactly one of the following is true:

  1. The system has only the trivial solution.

  2. The system has infinitely many non-trivial solutions as well as the trivial solution.

  Consider two homogeneous equations in two unknowns! What are the geometric possibilities?

  Homogeneous equations pass through the origin. The first possibility for two homogeneous equations is shown on the left of Figure 2.54, where the lines intersect at one point. The second possibility, shown on the right, is that the lines have the same slope so they coincide and every point on the line is a solution.

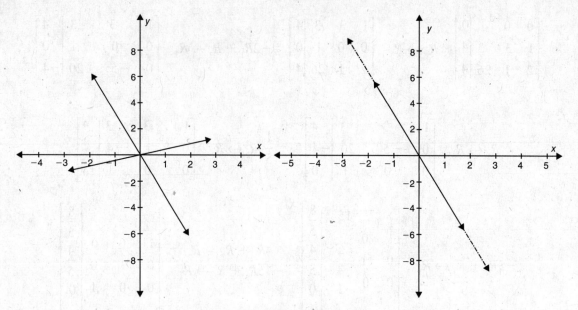

Figure 2.54

- **Theorem:** A homogeneous system of linear equations with more unknowns than equations has infinitely many solutions.

Matrices

A **matrix** is a rectangular array of numbers. The numbers in the array are called **entries**.

- Capital letters are used to represent matrices, and a_{ij} or $(A)_{ij}$ represents the ijth entry in the matrix A, b_{ij} or $(B)_{ij}$ represents the ijth entry in the matrix B, etc.

- The **size** or **dimension** of the matrix is given by $m \times n$ indicating that it has m rows and n columns, and hence has mn entries.

- A **square matrix** of order n, A, is a matrix with n rows and n columns. The entries a_{11}, a_{22}, ..., a_{nn} are said to be on the **main diagonal**.

- A matrix that has size $m \times 1$ is called a **column matrix** or **vector**, and a matrix that has size $1 \times n$ is called a **row matrix** or **vector**.

Example:

$$A = \begin{bmatrix} 2 & 0 & 1 & \sqrt{3} \\ 7 & 2 & 8 & 0 \\ 6 & -1 & 1 & -5 \end{bmatrix}$$ is a 3×4 matrix. $S = \begin{bmatrix} -3 & 2 \\ \frac{1}{2} & -1 \end{bmatrix}$ is a square matrix of size 2×2.

$R = [1\ 1\ 0\ 5]$ is a 1 × 4 row matrix. $C = \begin{bmatrix} 3 \\ 1 \\ -3 \end{bmatrix}$ is a 3 × 1 column matrix.

- When discussing matrices, it is common to refer to numerical quantities as **scalars**. All scalars, unless otherwise indicated, will be real numbers.

- A general $m \times n$ matrix may be written as:

$$A = \begin{bmatrix} a_{11} & a_{12} & \cdots & a_{1n} \\ a_{21} & a_{22} & \cdots & a_{2n} \\ . & . & . & . \\ . & . & . & . \\ a_{m1} & a_{m2} & \cdots & a_{mn} \end{bmatrix}$$

- Two matrices A and B are **equal** ($A = B$) if and only if B and A are the same size and $a_{ij} = b_{ij}$ for all i, j.

Operations on Matrices

- If A and B are the same size, then we **add matrices** as follows: $A + B$ is defined to be the matrix C, where $c_{ij} = a_{ij} + b_{ij}$.

- Similarly, if A and B are the same size, then we **subtract matrices** as follows: $A - B$ is defined to be the matrix C, where $c_{ij} = a_{ij} - b_{ij}$.

- If A is a matrix and c is a scalar then cA is a **scalar multiple** of A and is the matrix D, where $d_{ij} = ca_{ij}$ for all i, j.

Example: For example, compute $3A + B$ and $2A - C$ for:

$$A = \begin{bmatrix} -1 & 4 & 0 \\ 3 & 1 & -2 \end{bmatrix}, \quad B = \begin{bmatrix} 1 & 1 \\ -2 & 3 \end{bmatrix}, \quad C = \begin{bmatrix} 2 & -4 & 6 \\ 1 & 1 & 3 \end{bmatrix}.$$

Matrix $3A$ is 2 × 3 and B is 2 × 2, so they cannot be added, but $2A$ and C both have dimensions 2 × 3.

$$2A - C = \begin{bmatrix} -2 & 8 & 0 \\ 6 & 2 & -4 \end{bmatrix} - \begin{bmatrix} 2 & -4 & 6 \\ 1 & 1 & 3 \end{bmatrix} = \begin{bmatrix} -4 & 12 & -6 \\ 5 & 1 & -7 \end{bmatrix}$$

- Let A be a $m \times n$ matrix and let B be an $n \times p$ matrix; then we define the **dot product** of the ith row of A and jth column of B by

$$A_i \cdot B_j = a_{i1}b_{1j} + a_{i2}b_{2j} + a_{i3}b_{3j} + \cdots + a_{in}b_{nj} = \sum_{k=1}^{n} a_{ik}b_{kj}$$

Example: Let $A = \begin{bmatrix} -1 & 4 & 0 \\ 3 & 1 & -2 \end{bmatrix}$, $B = \begin{bmatrix} 2 & 3 & 5 \\ -2 & 0 & -1 \\ 1 & 2 & -1 \end{bmatrix}$. The dot product of the second

row of A and the third column of B is $\begin{bmatrix} 3 & 1 & -2 \end{bmatrix} \cdot \begin{bmatrix} 5 \\ -1 \\ -1 \end{bmatrix} = 3(5)+1(-1)+-2(-1)=16.$

- Let A be an $m \times r$ matrix and B be an $r \times n$ matrix; then we define the product AB to be the $m \times n$ matrix C, where $c_{ij} = \sum_{k=1}^{r} a_{ik}b_{kj} = A_i \cdot B_j$, the dot product of the ith row of A and the jth column of B.

Example: Let $A = \begin{bmatrix} -1 & 4 & 0 \\ 3 & 1 & -2 \end{bmatrix}$, $B = \begin{bmatrix} 2 & 3 & 5 \\ -2 & 0 & -1 \\ 1 & 2 & -1 \end{bmatrix}$. Then AB is the 2×3 matrix:

$$AB = \begin{bmatrix} -2-8+0 & -3+0+0 & -5-4+0 \\ 6-2-2 & 9+0-4 & 15-1+2 \end{bmatrix} = \begin{bmatrix} -10 & -3 & -9 \\ 2 & 5 & 16 \end{bmatrix}$$

- **Theorem:** Assuming that the sizes of the matrices, A, B, and C, are such that the indicated operations can be performed, and k and l are scalars, the following rules of matrix arithmetic are valid.

(a) $A + B = B + A$ (Commutative Law for Addition)

(b) $A + (B + C) = (A + B) + C$ (Associative Law for Addition)

(c) $A(BC) = (AB)C$ (Associative Law for Multiplication)

(d) $A(B + C) = AB + AC$ (Left Distributive Law)

(e) $(B + C)A = BA + CA$ (Right Distributive Law)

(f) $A(B - C) = AB - AC$ (Left Distributive Law)

(g) $(B - C)A = BA - CA$ (Right Distributive Law)

(h) $k(B + C) = kB + kC$

(i) $k(B - C) = kB - kC$

(j) $(k + l)C = kC + lC$

(k) $(k - l)C = kC - lC$

(l) $k(lC) = (kl)C$

(m) $k(BC) = (kB)C = B(kC)$

- Let A be any $m \times n$ matrix; then the **transpose** of A, denoted by A^T, is defined to be the $n \times m$ matrix that results from interchanging the rows and the columns of A. So, the entries of A^T are $a_{ij}^T = a_{ji}$ for all i and j.

- Let A be a square matrix, then the **trace** of A, tr(A), is the sum of the entries on the main diagonal of A. So if A is $n \times n$, then tr(A) $= a_{11} + a_{22} + \cdots + a_{nn}$.

- The **zero** matrix, O, is an $n \times m$ matrix with all entries equal to zero.

- **Theorem**: Assuming that the sizes of the matrices are such that the indicated operations can be performed, the following rules of matrix multiplication are valid.

  (a) $A + O = O + A = A$

  (b) $A - A = O$

  (c) $O - A = -A$

  (d) $AO = O = OA$

- Recall the **Zero Product Property** for real numbers, which is: If $ab = 0$, then either $a = 0$ or $b = 0$ or both. This property does not hold for matrices.

- Any square matrix with ones on the main diagonal and zeroes as all other entries is called an **identity matrix**, which is denoted by I, or I_n if it is important to designate its size. Hence, if A is a square matrix such that $a_{ij} = 1$ when $i = j$ and 0 otherwise, then A is an identity matrix.

- **Theorem:** If A is an $m \times n$ matrix, then $AI_n = A = I_m A$.

- **Theorem:** If R is the reduced row-echelon form of an $n \times n$ matrix A, then either R has a row of zeroes or R is the identity matrix I_n.

- If A is a square matrix such that a matrix B of the same size exists so that $AB = BA = I$, then A is said to be **invertible** and B is called an **inverse of A**.

- **Theorem:** If B and C are both inverses of the matrix A, then $B = C$.

- Thus, if B is an inverse of the matrix A, it is the unique inverse of A and we write $B = A^{-1}$, and $AA^{-1} = A^{-1}A = I$.

- **Theorem:** The matrix $A = \begin{bmatrix} a & b \\ c & d \end{bmatrix}$ is invertible if and only if $ad - bc \neq 0$, in which case the inverse is given by the formula $A^{-1} = \dfrac{1}{ad-bc} \begin{bmatrix} d & -b \\ -c & a \end{bmatrix}$.

- **Theorem**: If A and B are invertible matrices of the same size, then:

  (a) AB is invertible.

  (b) $(AB)^{-1} = B^{-1}A^{-1}$.

- **Theorem**: If A is an invertible matrix, then

  (a) A^{-1} is invertible and $(A^{-1})^{-1} = A$.

  (b) A^n is invertible and $(A^n)^{-1} = (A^{-1})^n$ for $n = 0, 1, 2, \ldots$

  (c) For any nonzero scalar k, the matrix kA is invertible and $(kA)^{-1} = \dfrac{1}{k}A^{-1}$.

- **Theorem**: Every system of linear equations has either no solutions, exactly one solution, or infinitely many solutions.

- **Theorem**: If A is an invertible $n \times n$ matrix, then for each $n \times 1$ matrix B, the system of equations $AX = B$ has exactly one solution, namely $X = A^{-1}B$.

- **Theorem**: Let A and B be square matrices of the same size. If AB is invertible, then A and B are also both invertible.

- A square matrix in which all of the entries off the main diagonal are zeroes is called a **diagonal matrix**. A general $n \times n$ diagonal matrix D can be written as:

$$D = \begin{bmatrix} d_1 & 0 & \cdots & 0 \\ 0 & d_2 & \cdots & 0 \\ \cdot & \cdot & & \cdot \\ \cdot & \cdot & & \cdot \\ \cdot & \cdot & & \cdot \\ 0 & 0 & \cdots & d_n \end{bmatrix}$$

- **Theorem**: A diagonal matrix is invertible if and only if all of its diagonal entries are non-zero. In the case that the diagonal matrix D is invertible, the inverse is:

$$D^{-1} = \begin{bmatrix} \dfrac{1}{d_1} & 0 & \cdots & 0 \\ 0 & \dfrac{1}{d_2} & \cdots & 0 \\ \cdot & \cdot & & \cdot \\ \cdot & \cdot & & \cdot \\ \cdot & \cdot & & \cdot \\ 0 & 0 & \cdots & \dfrac{1}{d_n} \end{bmatrix}$$

Determinants

- Let A be a 2×2 matrix, $A = \begin{bmatrix} a_{11} & a_{12} \\ a_{21} & a_{22} \end{bmatrix}$. Then the determinant of A is

$$\det(A) = a_{11}a_{22} - a_{12}a_{22}.$$

- Let A be an $n \times n$ matrix. Then the **minor** of entry a_{ij} is denoted by M_{ij} and is defined to be the determinant of the $(n-1) \times (n-1)$ submatrix obtained by deleting the ith row and the jth column of A. The number $C_{ij} = (-1)^{i+j}M_{ij}$ is called the **cofactor** of the entry a_{ij}.

- Let A be an $n \times n$ matrix. Then the number obtained by multiplying the entries of any row (or column) by their cofactors and adding the resulting products is called the **determinant** of A and the sums themselves are called the **cofactor expansions** of A. That is, for each $i = 1, 2, \ldots, n$ and $j = 1, 2, \ldots, n$,

$$\det(A) = \sum_{k=1}^{n} a_{ik}C_{ik} = a_{i1}C_{i1} + a_{i2}C_{i2} + \cdots + a_{in}C_{in} \qquad \text{(Cofactor expansion along the ith row)}$$

or using the columns,

$$\det(A) = \sum_{k=1}^{n} a_{ki}C_{ki} = a_{1i}C_{1i} + a_{2i}C_{2i} + \cdots + a_{ni}C_{ni} \qquad \text{(Cofactor expansion along the ith column)}$$

- **Theorem**: Let A be a square matrix. If A has a row or column of zeroes, then $\det(A) = 0$.

- **Theorem**: Let A be a square matrix. Then $\det(A) = \det(A^T)$.

- **Theorem**: Let A be a square matrix; then:

  (a) If B is the matrix that results when a single row (or column) of A is multiplied by a scalar k, then $\det(B) = k\det(A)$.

  (b) If B is the matrix that results when two rows (or columns) of A are interchanged, then $\det(B) = -\det(A)$.

  (c) If B is the matrix that results when a multiple of one row of A is added to another row (or a multiple of one column is added to another column), then $\det(B) = \det(A)$.

- **Theorem**: If A is a square matrix with two proportional rows or two proportional columns, then $\det(A) = 0$.

- **Theorem**: Let A be a square $n \times n$ matrix and k a scalar. Then $\det(kA) = k^n \det(A)$.

- We note that, in general, $\det(A) + \det(B) \neq \det(A + B)$.

- **Theorem**: A square matrix A is invertible if and only if $\det(A) \neq 0$.

- **Theorem**: If A and B are square matrices of the same size, then $\det(AB) = \det(A)\det(B)$.

- **Theorem**: If A is invertible, then $\det(A^{-1}) = \dfrac{1}{\det(A)}$.

- **Theorem**: If $A \in M_n$, the collection of all $n \times n$ matrices, then the following statements are equivalent:

  (a) A is invertible.

  (b) $AX = 0$ has only the trivial solution.

  (c) The reduced row-echelon form of A is I_n.

  (d) $AX = B$ is consistent for every $n \times 1$ matrix B.

  (e) $AX = B$ has exactly one solution for every $n \times 1$ matrix B.

  (f) $\det(A) \neq 0$.

- **Theorem (Cramer's Rule)**: If $AX = B$ is a system of n linear equations in n unknowns such that $\det(A) \neq 0$, then the system has a unique solution, which is

$$x_1 = \frac{\det(A_1)}{\det(A)}, \quad x_2 = \frac{\det(A_2)}{\det(A)}, \quad \ldots \quad , \quad x_n = \frac{\det(A_n)}{\det(A)}$$

where A_j is the matrix obtained by replacing the entries in the jth column of A by the entries in the column matrix B.

Computing the Inverse of a Matrix

In the previous section, the following formula was given as part of a theorem:

$$A^{-1} = \frac{1}{ad - bc} \begin{bmatrix} d & -b \\ -c & a \end{bmatrix}.$$

So for the matrix $A = \begin{bmatrix} 2 & -3 \\ -4 & 1 \end{bmatrix}$, the inverse is $B = \frac{1}{2-12} \begin{bmatrix} 1 & 3 \\ 4 & 2 \end{bmatrix} = \begin{bmatrix} \frac{-1}{10} & \frac{-3}{10} \\ \frac{-2}{5} & \frac{-1}{5} \end{bmatrix}$. We can check this by multiplying the two matrices A and B to see if the result is I_2, the 2×2 identity matrix.

For larger square matrices, we cannot use this formula. Instead, to find the inverse of an $n \times n$ invertible matrix A, find a sequence of elementary row operations that reduces A to the identity I_n, and then perform that same sequence of operations on I_n to obtain A^{-1}. We do this by writing the augmented $n \times n$ matrix with A augmented by I_n, then performing Gauss-Jordan elimination on the entire matrix.

Example: Find the inverse of $A = \begin{bmatrix} 1 & 0 & -1 \\ -2 & 2 & -1 \\ 3 & 0 & 0 \end{bmatrix}$. First write the augmented matrix and then

perform the elementary row operations to change the left side of the matrix into I while the right side will become A^{-1}:

$$\left[\begin{array}{ccc|ccc} 1 & 0 & -1 & 1 & 0 & 0 \\ -2 & 2 & -1 & 0 & 1 & 0 \\ 3 & 0 & 0 & 0 & 0 & 1 \end{array}\right] \begin{array}{c} 2R_1 + R_2 \rightarrow R_2 \end{array} \left[\begin{array}{ccc|ccc} 1 & 0 & -1 & 1 & 0 & 0 \\ 0 & 2 & -3 & 2 & 1 & 0 \\ 3 & 0 & 0 & 0 & 0 & 1 \end{array}\right] -3R_1 + R_3 \rightarrow R_3$$

$$\left[\begin{array}{ccc|ccc} 1 & 0 & -1 & 1 & 0 & 0 \\ 0 & 2 & -3 & 2 & 1 & 0 \\ 0 & 0 & 3 & -3 & 0 & 1 \end{array}\right] \begin{array}{c} 0.5R_2 \text{ and also } \frac{1}{3}R_3 \end{array} \left[\begin{array}{ccc|ccc} 1 & 0 & -1 & 1 & 0 & 0 \\ 0 & 1 & -\frac{3}{2} & 1 & \frac{1}{2} & 0 \\ 0 & 0 & 1 & -1 & 0 & \frac{1}{3} \end{array}\right] R_3 + R_1 \rightarrow R_1$$

and $\dfrac{3}{2}R_3 + R_2 \rightarrow R_2$ $\left[\begin{array}{ccc|ccc} 1 & 0 & 0 & 0 & 0 & \frac{1}{3} \\ 0 & 1 & 0 & \frac{-1}{2} & \frac{1}{2} & \frac{1}{2} \\ 0 & 0 & 1 & -1 & 0 & \frac{1}{3} \end{array}\right]$. Hence, $A^{-1} = \begin{bmatrix} 0 & 0 & \frac{1}{3} \\ \frac{-1}{2} & \frac{1}{2} & \frac{1}{2} \\ -1 & 0 & \frac{1}{3} \end{bmatrix}$.

Using the Inverse to Solve a Matrix Equation

For a matrix equation $AX = B$, if the coefficient matrix A is invertible, the equation can be solved as $X = A^{-1}B$.

Example: Solve the following system of equations by writing the system in matrix form and then using the inverse of the coefficient matrix.

$$\begin{cases} x - y = 3 \\ x - z = 1 \\ 6x - 2y - 3z = 0 \end{cases}$$

The matrix form is $\begin{bmatrix} 1 & -1 & 0 \\ 1 & 0 & -1 \\ 6 & -2 & -3 \end{bmatrix}\begin{bmatrix} x \\ y \\ z \end{bmatrix} = \begin{bmatrix} 3 \\ 1 \\ 0 \end{bmatrix}$. Next, find the inverse of the coefficient matrix:

$$\left[\begin{array}{ccc|ccc} 1 & -1 & 0 & 1 & 0 & 0 \\ 1 & 0 & -1 & 0 & 1 & 0 \\ 6 & -2 & -3 & 0 & 0 & 1 \end{array}\right] \begin{array}{c} -1R_1 + R_2 \to R_2 \\ -6R_1 + R_3 \to R_3 \end{array} \left[\begin{array}{ccc|ccc} 1 & -1 & 0 & 1 & 0 & 0 \\ 0 & 1 & -1 & -1 & 1 & 0 \\ 0 & 4 & -3 & -6 & 0 & 1 \end{array}\right] \begin{array}{c} R_2 + R_1 \to R_1 \\ -4R_2 + R_3 \to R_3 \end{array}$$

$$\left[\begin{array}{ccc|ccc} 1 & 0 & -1 & 0 & 1 & 0 \\ 0 & 1 & -1 & -1 & 1 & 0 \\ 0 & 0 & 1 & -2 & -4 & 1 \end{array}\right] \begin{array}{c} R_3 + R_1 \to R_1 \\ R_3 + R_2 \to R_2 \end{array} \left[\begin{array}{ccc|ccc} 1 & 0 & 0 & -2 & -3 & 1 \\ 0 & 1 & 0 & -3 & -3 & 1 \\ 0 & 0 & 1 & -2 & -4 & 1 \end{array}\right].$$ So we can

solve the system: $X = \begin{bmatrix} x \\ y \\ z \end{bmatrix} = A^{-1}B = \begin{bmatrix} -2 & -3 & 1 \\ -3 & -3 & 1 \\ -2 & -4 & 1 \end{bmatrix}\begin{bmatrix} 3 \\ 1 \\ 0 \end{bmatrix} = \begin{bmatrix} -9 \\ -12 \\ -10 \end{bmatrix}$. Therefore, the solu-

tion is $x = -9, y = -12, z = -10$.

Review Problems for Section 2.4.3

1. Suppose $A = \begin{bmatrix} a & b & c \\ d & e & f \\ g & h & i \end{bmatrix}$ and $\det(A) = 6$. What is the determinant of

    $B = \begin{bmatrix} 2d & 2e & 2f \\ a & b & c \\ g+4a & h+4b & i+4c \end{bmatrix}$?

2. Use Gauss-Jordan elimination to solve the following system: $\begin{cases} -2x + 3y - z = 2 \\ 3x + y + 5z = 13 \\ 4x + 3y - 4z = -13 \end{cases}$

3. If $A\vec{x} = \vec{b}$ represents a linear system of three equations in three unknowns and $\det(A) = 0$, then which of the following must be true?

    (A) The solution set for the system of equations is a plane.

    (B) The solution set for the system of equations is a line.

    (C) If the solution set is non-empty, then it contains infinitely many points.

    (D) If the solution set is non-empty, then it has exactly one point.

4. Find all values for λ such that $\det(A - \lambda I) = 0$, where $A = \begin{bmatrix} 2 & -3 \\ -1 & 1 \end{bmatrix}$.

5.   Which of the following statements is false?

(A)   The identity matrix is invertible.

(B)   If the main diagonal entries of square matrix A are all zeroes, then A is not invertible.

(C)   All leading 1s in a matrix in row-echelon form must occur in different columns.

(D)   Let A and B be $n \times n$ matrices such that AB is invertible, then B is invertible.

6.   Solve this system by using inverse matrices: $\begin{cases} x+y-4z=4 \\ 3x+y-z=-1 \\ -2x+2x+z=-1 \end{cases}$

Detailed Solutions

1.   To obtain matrix B from matrix A, the following elementary row operations must be done on A:

(a)   Interchange rows 1 and 2.

(b)   Multiply the new row 1 by 2.

(c)   Multiply the new row 2 by 4 and add it to row 3.

Thus, $\det(B) = (-1)(2)\det(A) = -2\det(A) = -2(6) = -12$.

2. $\begin{bmatrix} -2 & 3 & -1 & | & 2 \\ 3 & 1 & 5 & | & 13 \\ 4 & 3 & -4 & | & -13 \end{bmatrix}$ $\begin{matrix} -\frac{1}{2}R_1 \to R_1 \\ -3R_1+R_2 \to R_2 \\ -4R_1+R_3 \to R_3 \end{matrix}$ $\begin{bmatrix} 1 & -3/2 & 1/2 & | & -1 \\ 0 & 11/2 & 7/2 & | & 16 \\ 0 & 9 & -6 & | & -9 \end{bmatrix}$ $\begin{matrix} 2/11R_2 \to R_2 \\ 3/2R_2+R_1 \to R_1 \\ -9R_2+R_3 \to R_3 \end{matrix}$

$\begin{bmatrix} 1 & 0 & 16/11 & | & 37/11 \\ 0 & 1 & 7/11 & | & 32/11 \\ 0 & 0 & -129/11 & | & -387/11 \end{bmatrix}$ $\begin{matrix} -11/129R_3 \to R_3 \\ -16/11R_3+R_1 \to R_1 \\ -7/11R_3+R_2 \to R_2 \end{matrix}$ $\begin{bmatrix} 1 & 0 & 0 & | & -1 \\ 0 & 1 & 0 & | & 1 \\ 0 & 0 & 1 & | & 3 \end{bmatrix}$.

So the solution is the one point in three-space: $(-1, 1, 3)$.

3.   **C**

If $\det(A) = 0$, then A is not invertible, so $AX = B$ either has no solutions or infinitely many solutions. Thus, (C) must be the correct answer.

4. $\det(A - \lambda I) = \det \begin{bmatrix} 2-\lambda & -3 \\ -1 & 1-\lambda \end{bmatrix} = (2-\lambda)(1-\lambda)-(3) = \lambda^2 - 3\lambda - 1 = 0$ when (using the quadratic formula) $\lambda = \dfrac{3 \pm \sqrt{13}}{2}$.

5. **B**

The identity matrix has determinant 1 so it is invertible. In fact, the inverse of I is itself. So statement (A) is true. Statement (B) is false because $A = \begin{bmatrix} 0 & 1 \\ 1 & 0 \end{bmatrix}$ has determinant equal to -1, and so, even though the main diagonal consists of all zero entries, it is invertible. Statement (C) is true; each column or row may have at most one leading 1. Statement (D) is true because if AB is invertible, then $\det(AB)$ is non-zero, and since $\det(AB) = \det(A)\det(B)$, then $\det(B)$ is non-zero.

6. The system in matrix form is $\begin{bmatrix} 1 & 1 & -4 \\ 3 & 1 & -1 \\ -2 & 2 & 1 \end{bmatrix} \begin{bmatrix} x \\ y \\ z \end{bmatrix} = \begin{bmatrix} 4 \\ -1 \\ -1 \end{bmatrix}$. To find the inverse of the coefficient matrix A^{-1}:

$$\left[\begin{array}{ccc|ccc} 1 & 1 & -4 & 1 & 0 & 0 \\ 3 & 1 & -1 & 0 & 1 & 0 \\ -2 & 2 & 1 & 0 & 0 & 1 \end{array}\right] \begin{array}{c} -3R_1 + R_2 \to R_2 \\ \\ 2R_1 + R_3 \to R_3 \end{array} \left[\begin{array}{ccc|ccc} 1 & 1 & -4 & 1 & 0 & 0 \\ 0 & -2 & 11 & -3 & 1 & 0 \\ 0 & 4 & -7 & 2 & 0 & 1 \end{array}\right] \begin{array}{c} \frac{-1}{2}R_2 \to R_2 \\ -R_2 + R_1 \to R_1 \\ -4R_2 + R_3 \to R_3 \end{array}$$

$$\left[\begin{array}{ccc|ccc} 1 & 0 & \frac{3}{2} & \frac{-1}{2} & \frac{1}{2} & 0 \\ 0 & 1 & \frac{-11}{2} & \frac{3}{2} & \frac{-1}{2} & 0 \\ 0 & 0 & 15 & -4 & 2 & 1 \end{array}\right] \begin{array}{c} \frac{1}{15}R_3 \to R_3 \\ \frac{-3}{2}R_3 + R_1 \to R_1 \\ \frac{11}{2}R_3 + R_2 \to R_2 \end{array} \left[\begin{array}{ccc|ccc} 1 & 0 & 0 & \frac{-1}{10} & \frac{3}{10} & \frac{-1}{10} \\ 0 & 1 & 0 & \frac{1}{30} & \frac{7}{30} & \frac{11}{30} \\ 0 & 0 & 1 & \frac{-4}{15} & \frac{2}{15} & \frac{1}{15} \end{array}\right].$$

Then $X = \begin{bmatrix} x \\ y \\ z \end{bmatrix} = A^{-1}B = \begin{bmatrix} \frac{-1}{10} & \frac{3}{10} & \frac{-1}{10} \\ \frac{1}{30} & \frac{7}{30} & \frac{11}{30} \\ \frac{-4}{15} & \frac{2}{15} & \frac{1}{15} \end{bmatrix} \begin{bmatrix} 4 \\ -1 \\ -1 \end{bmatrix} = \begin{bmatrix} \frac{-3}{5} \\ \frac{-7}{15} \\ \frac{-19}{15} \end{bmatrix}.$

So the solution is $x = \frac{-3}{5}, y = \frac{-7}{15}, z = \frac{-19}{15}$.

Content Domain 3: *Number Theory*

3

3.1 Natural Numbers

> **3.1.1** The California *Mathematics Subject Matter Requirements* stipulate that candidates for any credential program for teaching secondary mathematics must be able *to prove and use basic properties of natural numbers (e.g. properties of divisibility).*

Divisibility

In the course *Number Theory,* students study properties of natural numbers. The set of natural numbers, also called the positive integers, is $N = \{1, 2, 3, \ldots\}$. Of particular interest are the concepts of divisors and multiples.

> Let $a, b \in N$. We say that a **divides** b and write $a|b$ if there exists a $c \in N$ such that $ac = b$. We also say that a is a **divisor** of b and that b is a **multiple** of a. If a is not a divisor of b, then we write $a \nmid b$.

If both $c|a$ and $c|b$, we say that c is a **common divisor** of a and b. If d is a common divisor of a and b such that every common divisor of a and b is less than or equal to d, then d is called the **greatest common divisor** of a and b, and we write $d = \gcd(a, b)$.

- If m is a multiple of both a and b, then it is a **common multiple of a and b**. Also, if there is no other common multiple of a and b that is less than m, then m is called the **least common multiple** of m; this is denoted by $m = \text{lcm}(a, b)$.

Examples:

(a) $2|10$ because $2 \cdot 5 = 10$.

(b) $3 \nmid 10$ because there is no integer c such that $3c = 10$.

(c) We can say 9 is a common divisor of 144 and 162 since $9 \cdot 16 = 144$ and $9 \cdot 18 = 162$. But 9 is not the greatest common divisor of these two integers; in fact, $18 = \gcd(144, 162)$.

(d) We can say 90 is a common multiple of 6 and 15, but it is not the least common multiple; note that $\text{lcm}(6, 15) = 30$.

Theorems Involving Divisibility

- **Theorem**: Let a, b, and c be natural numbers. If $a|b$ and $b|c$, then $a|c$.

  Proof: Assume a, b, and c are natural numbers such that $a|b$ and $b|c$. Then by definition of "divides," there exist positive integers d and e such that $ad = b$ and $be = c$. Thus, by substitution, $c = be = (ad)e$, and $(ad)e = a(de)$ by the Associative Property of Addition for positive integers. Hence, by Transitivity, $c = a(de)$. By the Closure Property of Multiplication for positive integers, de is a positive integer, and therefore $a|c$.

  Q.E.D.

- **Theorem**: Let a, b, c, and d be natural numbers. If $a|b$ and $c|d$, then $ac|bd$.

  Proof: Assume a, b, c, and d are natural numbers such that $a|b$ and $c|d$. By the definition of "divides," there exist two positive integers e and f such that $ae = b$ and $cf = d$. Then, multiplying the first equation by d, we have $(ae)d = bd$, and using substitution for d on the left side, $(ae)(cf) = bd$. After applying the properties of Associativity and Commutativity on the left of this equation, the result is $(ac)(ef) = bd$. By the Closure Property of Multiplication for positive integers, ef is a positive integer and hence $ac|bd$.

  Q.E.D.

Review Problems for Section 3.1.1

1. Find the greatest common divisor of 24 and 180.

2. Find the least common multiple of 15 and 18.

3. Let a, b, and c be natural numbers. Prove that if $a|b$ and $a|c$, then $a|(b + c)$.

4. Let a, b, and c be natural numbers. Prove that if $a|b$ and c is any natural number, then $a|bc$.

Detailed Solutions

1. The positive integer divisors of 24 are: 1, 2, 3, 4, 6, 8, 12, 24. The divisors of 180 are 1, 2, 3, 4, 5, 6, 9, 10, 12, 15, 18, 20, 30, 36, 45, 60, 90, 180. So the greatest common divisor of 24 and 180 is 12.

2. The multiples of 15 are: 15, 30, 45, 60, 75, 90, 105, 120, … The first multiple of 15 for which 18 is a divisor is 90. Thus, the least common multiple of 15 and 18 is 90.

3. **Proof**: Assume a, b, and c are natural numbers. Suppose $a|b$ and $a|c$. Then there exists positive integers n and m such that $an = b$ and $am = c$. Then, using the Addition Property of Equality, we obtain $an + am = b + c$. By factoring the left side of this equation, we arrive at $a(n + m) = b + c$. Thus, since $n + m$ is a positive integer by the Closure Property of Addition for positive integers, it follows that $a|(b + c)$.

    Q.E.D.

4. **Proof**: Assume a, b, and c are natural numbers. Suppose $a|b$; then there exists a positive integer n such that $an = b$. Then $(an)c = bc$ by the Multiplication Property of Equality. But by the Associative Property of Multiplication, $(an)c = a(nc)$, so $a(nc) = bc$, since nc is a positive integer by the Closure Property of Multiplication for positive integers, we can say, $a|bc$.

    Q.E.D.

3.1.2 The California *Mathematics Subject Matter Requirements* require that candidates for any credential program for teaching secondary mathematics be able to *use the Principle of Mathematical Induction to prove results in number theory.*

Mathematical Induction

Mathematical induction is similar to the process of knocking over dominoes. Suppose we stand up dominoes in a row and want to knock them all down. If we do not knock over the first one, none of the others will fall. Also, if the gap between the two adjacent dominoes is too large, then when one falls it may not knock over the next one. Two conditions must be met in order to knock over all of the dominoes. We can state this requirement as follows:

1. If we knock over the first domino in the row, and

2. as each domino is knocked over, it causes the next domino to fall, then all the dominoes will fall. In mathematical terms, we state the **Principle of Mathematical Induction (PMI)** as follows:

Principle of Mathematical Induction: Let m be a positive integer and let $P(k)$ be a mathematical statement, where $k \geq m$ is a positive integer. Suppose that

1. $P(m)$ is a true statement, and

2. if $P(k)$ is true, then $P(k+1)$ is true for each $k \geq m$.

Then $P(k)$ is true for all $k = m, m+1, m+2, \ldots$.

Several observations need to be made. First, often in step (1), $m = 1$, but not always. Also, the assumption in step (2) is called the **induction hypothesis**.

Examples:

Note: In the following proofs that use PMI, statements in italics are comments and not part of the proof; these comments are there to help explain the process.

(a) Use the Principle of Mathematical Induction to prove:

$k^2 > k + 1$ for all $k = 2, 3,\ldots$

Illustration: Remember the dominoes. We can imagine that on the face of each domino is a mathematical statement that we are going to prove is true. In this case, the initial step corresponds to $m = 2$, and for $k = 2, 3,\ldots, 8$, the dominoes appear as in Figure 3.1.

$2^2 > 2+1$ $k=2$	$3^2 > 3+1$ $k=3$	$4^2 > 4+1$ $k=4$	$5^2 > 5+1$ $k=5$	$6^2 > 6+1$ $k=6$	$7^2 > 7+1$ $k=7$	$8^2 > 8+1$ $k=8$

Figure 3.1

Clearly, each statement in the figure is true. We are going to use induction to show that $k^2 > k + 1$ for all $k = 2, 3,\ldots$ Now on to the proof!

Proof: Let $P(k)$ be the statement $k^2 > k + 1$, where $k \geq 2$ is an integer.

Initial step: We must show that the statement p(m) is true for m = 2:

$P(2)$ is the statement $2^2 > 2 + 1$, or $4 > 3$, which is true.

Next comes the Induction step: Assume that $P(k)$ is true; that is, assume $k^2 > k + 1$, where k is any fixed but arbitrary integer such that $k \geq m$.

Now we must show that it follows from our assumption that $P(k+1)$ is true. Note that $P(k+1)$ is the statement $(k+1)^2 > (k+1) + 1$. Let's do it! Beginning with the left side of $P(k+1)$,

we have $(k+1)^2 = k^2 + 2k + 1$ by algebra

$$> (k+1) + 2k + 1 \qquad \text{by the induction hypothesis}$$

$$\text{so } (k+1)^2 > 3k + 2 \qquad \text{by algebra}$$

$$> k + 2 \qquad \text{since } 3k > k \text{ for } k \geq 2$$

$$\text{and } (k+1)^2 > (k+1) + 1 \qquad \text{by algebra}$$

Hence, for all $k \geq 2$, if $P(k)$ is true, then $P(k+1)$ is true.

Now write the conclusion:

Hence, by the Principle of Mathematical Induction, $P(k)$ is true for all $k = 2, 3, \ldots$

Q.E.D.

(b) Use the Principle of Mathematical Induction to prove: If $x > -1$, then $(1+x)^k \geq 1 + kx$ for all $k = 0, 1, 2, \ldots$

Proof: Assume $x > -1$. Let $P(k)$ be the statement $(1+x)^k \geq 1 + kx$, where $k \geq 0$ is an integer.

Initial step: We must show that the statement is true for $k = 0$: $P(0)$ is the statement $(1+x)^0 \geq 1 + (0)x$, or $1 \geq 1$, which is true.

Induction step:

Assume that $P(k)$ is true; that is, assume $(1+x)^k \geq 1 + kx$, where k is any fixed but arbitrary integer such that $k \geq 1$.

Now we must show that it follows from our assumption that $P(k+1)$ is true. Note that $P(k+1)$ is $(1+x)^{k+1} \geq 1 + (1+k)x$. Let's do it! Again, beginning with the left side of $P(k+1)$, we have,

$$(1+x)^{k+1} = (1+x)^k(1+x) \qquad \text{by algebra}$$

$$\geq (1+kx)(1+x) \qquad \text{by the induction hypothesis}$$

$$\text{so } (1+x)^{k+1} > 1 + (k+1)x + kx^2 \qquad \text{by algebra}$$

$$\text{and } (1+x)^{k+1} \geq 1 + (k+1)x \qquad \text{since } kx^2 \geq 0$$

Hence, for all $k \geq 0$, if $P(k)$ is true, then $P(k+1)$ is true.

Thus, by the Principle of Mathematical Induction, $P(k)$ is true for all $k = 0, 1, \ldots$

Q.E.D.

(c) Prove: $1 + 2 + 3 + \cdots + k = \dfrac{k(k+1)}{2}$ for all positive integers k.

Proof: Let $P(k)$ be the statement $1 + 2 + 3 + \cdots + k = \dfrac{k(k+1)}{2}$, where $k \geq 1$ is a positive integer.

$P(1)$ is the statement $1 = \dfrac{(1)(2)}{2}$, or $1 = 1$, which is true.

Assume that $P(k)$ is true, that is, assume $1+2+3+\cdots+k = \dfrac{k(k+1)}{2}$, where k is any fixed but arbitrary integer such that $k \geq 1$.

Note: $P(k+1)$ is $1+2+3+\cdots+k+(k+1) = \dfrac{(k+1)((k+1)+1)}{2}$.

Again, beginning with the left side of $P(k+1)$:

Then, $\qquad 1+2+3+\cdots+k+(k+1) = \dfrac{k(k+1)}{2}+(k+1) \qquad$ by the induction hyp.

$$= \frac{k(k+1)}{2}+\frac{2(k+1)}{2} \qquad \text{by algebra}$$

$$= \frac{(k+1)(k+2)}{2} \qquad \text{by algebra}$$

$$= \frac{(k+1)((k+1)+1)}{2} \qquad \text{by algebra}$$

Hence, for all $k \geq 1$, if $P(k)$ is true, then $P(k+1)$ is true.

Thus, by the Principle of Mathematical Induction, $P(k)$ is true for all $k = 1, 2,\ldots$

$\qquad\qquad$ Q.E.D.

Review Problems for Section 3.1.2

Use the Principle of Mathematical Induction to prove each of the following:

1. $k < 2^k$ for all positive integers k.

2. $1 + 3 + 5 + \cdots + (2k-1) = k^2$ for all $k = 1, 2, 3, \ldots$.

Detailed Solutions

1. **Proof**: Let $P(k)$ be the statement $k < 2^k$, where $k \geq 1$ is a positive integer.

$P(1)$ is the statement $1 < 2^1$, or $1 < 2$, which is true.

Assume that $P(k)$ is true, that is, assume $k < 2^k$, where k is any fixed but arbitrary integer such that $k \geq 1$.

Note: $\qquad P(k+1)$ is $(k+1) < 2^{k+1}$.

Then, $\qquad k+1 < 2^k+1 \qquad\qquad$ by the induction hypothesis.

$\qquad\qquad < 2^k+2^k \qquad\qquad$ since $1 < 2^x$ for any positive real number x

$\qquad\qquad = 2 \cdot 2^k \qquad\qquad$ by algebra

$$= 2^{k+1} \qquad \text{by algebra}$$

Hence, for all $k \geq 1$, if $P(k)$ is true, then $P(k + 1)$ is true.

Thus, by the Principle of Mathematical Induction, $P(k)$ is true for all $k = 1, 2,...$

Q.E.D.

2. **Proof**: Let $P(k)$ be the statement $1 + 3 + 5 + \cdots + (2k - 1) = k^2$, where $k \geq 1$ is a positive integer.

$P(1)$ is the statement $1 = 1^2$, or $1 = 1$, which is true.

Assume that $P(k)$ is true, that is, assume $1 + 3 + 5 + \cdots + (2k - 1) = k^2$, where k is any fixed but arbitrary integer such that $k \geq 1$.

Note: $P(k + 1)$ is $1 + 3 + 5 + \cdots + (2k - 1) + (2(k + 1) - 1) = (k + 1)^2$.

Then, $1 + 3 + 5 + \cdots + (2k - 1) + (2(k + 1) - 1) = k^2 + (2(k + 1) - 1)$ by the induction hypothesis.

$$= k^2 + 2k + 2 - 1 \qquad \text{by algebra}$$

$$= k^2 + 2k + 1 \qquad \text{by algebra}$$

$$= (k + 1)^2 \qquad \text{by algebra}$$

Hence, for all $k \geq 1$, if $P(k)$ is true, then $P(k + 1)$ is true.

Thus, by the Principle of Mathematical Induction, $P(k)$ is true for all $k = 1, 2,...$

Q.E.D.

3.1.3 The California *Mathematics Subject Matter Requirements* stipulate that candidates for any credential program for teaching secondary mathematics must *know and be able to apply the Euclidean Algorithm.*

The Division and Euclidean Algorithms

An algorithm in mathematics is a finite set of steps that solves a problem. The Division Algorithm is not actually an algorithm; it is a theorem that describes the procedure of long division as we learn it in elementary school. From this theorem, we set up the Euclidean Algorithm, which is an algorithm for finding the greatest common divisor of two integers.

The Division Algorithm Theorem: Let a and b be integers with $a > 0$. Then there exist unique integers q and r such that $b = aq + r$ with $0 \leq r, < a$.

To complete the proof of the Division Algorithm Theorem we use the **Well-Ordering Principle for Natural Numbers**, which is: *Every non-empty subset of the natural numbers (positive integers) has a least element.*

Proof (of the Division Algorithm): Let a and b be integers with $a > 0$. Let S be the set of all non-negative integers w such that $w = b - aq$ for some integer q. To see that S is a non-empty set, look at b: if $b > 0$, choose $q = 0$, and then $w = b$ would be in S; if $b < 0$, let $q = b$, so that $w = b - aq = b - ba = -b(a - 1)$. Note that $-b > 0$, and since $a > 0$, it follows that $a - 1 \geq 0$. Hence, $w \geq 0$, and S again is non-empty. Therefore, by the Well-Ordering Principle, S has a least element, call it r, and let q' be an integer such that $r = b - aq'$. By definition of S, $r \geq 0$. Suppose that $r \geq a$, then $r - a \in S$ because $r - a = b - aq' - a = b - a(q' + 1)$. But $r - a \leq r$, so this would contradict the fact that r is the least element of S; thus, our supposition that $r \geq a$ is incorrect; so $0 \leq r < a$. (This means we have shown the existence of q and r as stipulated in the theorem, but we must still prove their uniqueness).

Note that if q is unique, then so is r since $r = b - aq$. So, suppose there exist q and q^* such that $b = aq + r$, $b = aq^* + r^*$, where $0 \leq r < a$ and $0 \leq r^* < a$ and, without loss of generality, $q \geq q^*$. Then, subtracting the two equations for b gives us the equation $0 = a(q - q^*) + r - r^*$, or $a(q - q^*) = r^* - r$. This means that a divides $r^* - r$. Since $a > 0$ and $q \geq q^*$, $r^* - r \geq 0$, and $r^* < a \leq a + r$; therefore, $0 \leq r^* - r \leq a$. But a divides $r^* - r$ so either $a \leq r - r^*$ or $r - r^* = 0$. In either case, $q = q^*$. This shows that q, and hence r, is unique.

Q.E.D.

Example:

Let $a = 11$ and $b = 316$, then $q = 28$ and $r = 8$; i.e., $316 = (11)(28) + 8$.

In order to prove the Euclidean Algorithm we need the following lemma (helping theorem).

Lemma: Let a, b, c, and k be integers such that $0 < a < b$ and $b = ak + c$ with $0 \leq c < a$, Then $\gcd(a, b) = \gcd(b, c)$.

Proof: Let a, b, c, and k be integers such that $0 < a < b$, $b = ak + c$, and $0 \leq c < a$.

Let $g = \gcd(a, b)$. Since $c = b - ak$ and g divides both a and b, g must also divide c. Because $c < a$, it follows that $g = \gcd(b, c)$.

Q.E.D.

The Euclidean Algorithm: This algorithm is used for calculating the greatest common divisor of two numbers. Suppose that a and b are integers with $a > 0$. Repeatedly apply the Division Algorithm as follows:

1. $b = aq_1 + r_1 \qquad 0 \leq r_1 < a,$

2. $a = r_1 q_2 + r_2 \qquad 0 \leq r_2 < r_1$

3. $r_1 = r_2 q_3 + r_2 \qquad 0 \leq r_3 < r_2$

Continue this algorithm until one obtains a zero remainder; i.e. $r_{n+1} = 0$ and $r_n \neq 0$. Then gcd $(a, b) = r_n$.

Proof: Suppose that a and b are integers with $a > 0$. Repeatedly apply the Division Algorithm as follows:

1. $b = aq_1 + r_1$ $0 \leq r_1 < a$

2. $a = r_1 q_2 + r_2$ $0 \leq r_2 < r_1$

3. $r_1 = r_2 q_3 + r_2$ $0 \leq r_3 < r_2$

Continue this algorithm until we obtain a zero remainder; i.e., $r_{n+1} = 0$ and $r_n \neq 0$. These remainders form a strictly decreasing sequence of non-negative integers, and therefore from the lemma we have: $\gcd(a, b) = \gcd(a, r_1) = \gcd(r_1, r_2) = \ldots = \gcd(r_n, 0) = r_n$.

Q.E.D.

Examples:

(a). Compute the gcd(408, 126):

$408 = \mathbf{126}(3) + \mathbf{30}$

$126 = \mathbf{30}(4) + \mathbf{6}$

$30 = \mathbf{6}(5) + \mathbf{0}$

So, gcd(408, 126) = 6

(b). Find the gcd(344, 2206):

$2206 = \mathbf{344}(6) + \mathbf{142}$

$344 = \mathbf{142}(2) + \mathbf{60}$

$142 = \mathbf{60}(2) + \mathbf{22}$

$60 = \mathbf{22}(2) + \mathbf{16}$

$22 = \mathbf{16}(1) + \mathbf{6}$

$16 = \mathbf{6}(2) + \mathbf{4}$

$6 = \mathbf{4}(1) + \mathbf{2}$

$4 = \mathbf{2}(2) + 0$

So, the gcd(344, 2206) = 2

Review Problems for Section 3.1.3

1. Find the greatest common divisor of

    (a) 165 and 465.

    (b) 192 and 120

2. Find x and y such that $27x + 15y = \gcd(27, 15)$.

Detailed Solutions for Review Problems Section 3.1.3

1. (a) $465 = \mathbf{165}(2) + \mathbf{135}$
        $165 = \mathbf{135}(1) + \mathbf{30}$
        $135 = \mathbf{30}(4) + \mathbf{15}$
        $\ \ 30 = \mathbf{15}(2) + 0$
    So the $\gcd(465, 165) = 15$

    (b) $192 = \mathbf{120}(1) + \mathbf{72}$
        $120 = \mathbf{72}(1) + \mathbf{48}$
        $\ \ 72 = \mathbf{48}(1) + \mathbf{24}$
        $\ \ 48 = \mathbf{24}(2) + 0$
    So the $\gcd(192, 120) = 24$

2. First we work through the Euclidean Algorithm to get the $\gcd(27, 15)$ (which we know is 3). Then we work backwards:

    $27 = \mathbf{15}(1) + 12$
    $15 = \mathbf{12}(1) + 3$
    $12 = \mathbf{3}(4) + 0$
    So $3 = 15 - 12(1) = 15 - (27 - 15(1)) = 27(-1) + 15(2)$.
    Thus, $x = -1$ and $y = 2$.

3.1.4 The California *Mathematics Subject Matter Requirements* stipulate that candidates for any credential program for teaching secondary mathematics must be able to *apply the Fundamental Theorem of Arithmetic.*

Fundamental Theorem of Arithmetic

A positive integer is a **prime number** provided it has exactly two distinct positive integer divisors (1 and itself). A positive integer greater than 1 that is not prime is called a **composite number**. The number 1 is neither prime nor composite.

> **Theorem (Fundamental Theorem of Arithmetic)**: Any integer greater than 1 has a factorization into primes. This factorization is unique up to the order of the primes.

Examples:

(a) The first 15 prime numbers are: 2, 3, 5, 7, 11, 13, 17, 19, 23, 29, 31, 37, 41, 43, 47.

(b) The first 15 composite numbers are 4, 6, 8, 9, 10, 12, 14, 15, 16, 18, 20, 21, 22, 24, 25.

(c) Write the prime factorization of 424.

$$424 = 2 \cdot 212 = 2 \cdot 2 \cdot 106 = 2^2 \cdot 2 \cdot 53 = 2^3 \cdot 53$$

(d) Write the prime factorization of 18975.

$$18975 = 3 \cdot 6325 = 3 \cdot 5 \cdot 1265 = 3 \cdot 5^2 \cdot 253 = 3 \cdot 5^2 \cdot 11 \cdot 23$$

Some Divisibility Rules to Know When Factoring Large Numbers

1. A positive integer is divisible by 2 if and only if its last digit (units place) is even.

2. A positive integer is divisible by 3 if and only if the sum of its digits is divisible by 3.

3. A positive integer is divisible by 4 if and only if the number named by its last two digits (tens and units places) is divisible by 4.

4. A positive integer is divisible by 5 if and only if its units digit is 0 or 5.

5. A positive integer is divisible by 6 if and only if it is divisible by both 2 and 3.

6. To check whether a positive integer is divisible by 7: Take the last digit and double it then subtract this from the rest of the digits of the original number. Is this number divisible by 7? If yes, then the original number is divisible by 7. Repeat this for large numbers. (For example, let's

take 5732: double 2 to get 4 and subtract this from 573 to get 569. Repeat: double 9 to get 18 and subtract this from 56 to get 38, which is not divisible by 7. So 5732 is not divisible by 7.)

7. A positive integer is divisible by 8 if and only if the number named by its last three digits (hundreds, tens, and units places) are divisible by 8. (For example, 19224 is divisible by 8 because 224 is divisible by 8)

8. A positive integer is divisible by 9 if and only if the sum of its digits is divisible by 9.

9. A positive integer is divisible by 10 if and only if it is divisible by both 2 and 5, or its units digit is 0.

A Guide for Factoring

When looking for divisors/factors of a positive integer, how high should I look for divisors/factors? The following theorem helps.

Theorem: If an integer, $n > 1$, has no prime divisors $\leq \sqrt{n}$, then n is prime.

This tells us that we need to check prime divisors only up to $\sqrt{n}$.

Example: Is 857 a prime number? $\sqrt{857} \leq \sqrt{900} = 30$, so check only whether the prime numbers less than 30 divide 857:

857 is not divisible by 2 since its units place number is 7, which is not even.

857 is not divisible by 3 since the sum of the digits of 857 is $8 + 5 + 7 = 20$, which is not divisible by 3.

857 is not divisible by 5 since its units place digit is not 0 or 5.

To check divisibility by 7, take the units digit, 7, and double it, 14, then subtract it from the remaining digits to get $85 - 14 = 71$. Since 71 is not divisible by 7, 857 is not divisible by 7.

857 divided by 11 is 77 with remainder 10, so 857 is not divisible by 11.

857 divided by 13 is 65 with remainder 12, so 857 is not divisible by 13.

857 divided by 17 is 50 with remainder 7, so 857 is not divisible by 17.

857 divided by 19 is 45 with remainder 2, so 857 is not divisible by 19.

857 divided by 23 is 37 with remainder 6, so 857 is not divisible by 23.

857 divided by 29 is 29 with remainder 16, so 857 is not divisible by 29.

This, since 857 is not divisible by any prime number less than or equal to $\sqrt{857}$, it is prime.

Review Problems for Section 3.1.4

1.   Write the prime factorization of 4044.

2.   Write the prime factorization of 11385.

3.   Find the greatest power of 3 that divides 11799.

4.   Show whether or not 4207 is prime.

Detailed Solutions

1. $4044 = 2(2022) = 2^2(1011) = 2^2 \cdot 3(337)$. Note that $\sqrt{337} < \sqrt{400} = 20$, so the largest prime to check as a divisor is 19. None are factors, so the prime factors of 4044 are $2^2 \cdot 3 \cdot 337$.

2. $11385 = 3(3795) = 3 \cdot 5(759) = 3 \cdot 5 \cdot 3(253) = 3^2 \cdot 5 \cdot 11(23)$.

3.   Since the sum of the digits of 11799 equals 27, which is divisible by 9, we know that $9 = 3^2$ divides 11799, and $11799 = 3^2(1311)$. The sum of the digits of 1311 is 6, which is not divisible by 9 but is divisible by 3, so 3^3 divides 11799 but 3^4 does not. So the greatest power of 3 that divides 11799 is 3^3.

4.   The number 4207 is not divisible by 2 since its units digit is an odd number. It is also not divisible by 3 since the sum of the digits is 13, which is not divisible by 3. It cannot be divisible by 5 because the units digit is not 0 or 5. The last digit, 7, doubled is 14, and subtracting this from 42 gives 28, which is divisible by 7, so 4207 is not a prime number.

Content Domain 2: *Geometry*

4.1 Parallelism

> **4.1.1** The California *Mathematics Subject Matter Requirements* stipulate that candidates for any credential program for teaching secondary mathematics must *know the Parallel Postulate and its implications, and justify its equivalents (e.g., the Alternate Interior Angle Theorem, the angle sum of every triangle is 180 degrees).*

Euclidean Plane Geometry

With the writing of Book I of his treatise, *The Elements,* around 300 B.C.E., Euclid developed Euclidean plane geometry, beginning with 23 definitions, some assumptions called *common notions,* and 5 postulates, which also are assumptions.

Euclid's Definitions: We show Euclid's definition in italics followed by a modern definition or explanation.

1. *A **point** is that which has no part.* Euclid's definition means that a **point** cannot be subdivided into parts. Hence, although we represent a point by a dot, it has no width, length, or depth, but it does have location. Points are denoted by capital letters.

2. *A **line** is breadthless width.* Euclid is defining a **line segment** here. A line segment has just one dimension, length, but no thickness.

2. *A **line** is breadthless width.* Euclid is defining a **line segment** here. A line segment has just one dimension, length, but no thickness.

3. *The **ends of a line** are points.* Euclid is referring to the **endpoints** of a line segment.

4. *A **straight line** is a line which lies evenly with the points on itself.* Most people interpret this to mean that Euclid is differentiating between a curved line and a straight line.

5. *A **surface** is that which has length and breadth only.* Euclid defines a surface as something with two dimensions. This could mean a plane or something else such as a sphere, cone, disk, or a rectangle with its interior.

6. *The **edges** of a surface are lines.* In this definition, Euclid indicates that if the surface has edges, such as in the case of a disk or a cone, the edges or **boundaries** are lines or line segments, either of which could be straight or curved. The boundary of a disk is a circle, which is a line segment that has coinciding endpoints, and the edge of a cone is a circle.

7. *A **plane surface** is a surface which lies evenly with the straight lines on itself.* Euclid is defining a **plane** here. If two points lie in a plane, then the entire line segment must lie in the plane.

8. *A **plane angle** is the inclination to one another of two lines in a plane which meet one another and do not lie in a straight line.* Euclid's angles in this definition can have curved sides and share a point, which we would call a **vertex**.

9. *And when the lines containing the angle are straight, the angle is called **rectilinear**.* A rectilinear angle is the union of two straight rays sharing their endpoints. This is what we call an **angle** in modern geometry.

10. *When a straight line standing on a straight line makes the adjacent angles equal to one another, each of the equal angles is right, and the straight line standing on the other is called a perpendicular to that on which it stands.* Euclid is saying that if two lines intersect so that adjacent angles have the same measure, then the angles are called **right angles** and the two lines are **perpendicular**. Note that since the two adjacent angles have equal measure and form a straight line, they must have measure equal to 90°. Also, the modern term **congruent** is used when referring to things that have the same measure.

11. *An **obtuse angle** is an angle greater than a right angle.* So an obtuse angle has measure greater than 90°. We also assume that an obtuse angle has measure less than 180°.

12. *An **acute angle** is an angle less than a right angle.* Thus, an acute angle is an angle with measure less than 90°, but greater than 0°.

13. *A **boundary** is that which is an extremity of anything.* Euclid seems to say that if one moves past a boundary point, then one is no longer a part of the object.

14. *A **figure** is that which is contained by any boundary or boundaries.* In modern terminology, a figure is a bounded object; i.e., can be contained in a circle with finite radius.

15. *A **circle** is a plane figure contained by one line such that all the straight lines falling upon it from one point among those lying within the figure equal one another.* A circle is a set of points in a plane that are equidistant from a specified point.

16. *And the point is called the **center of the circle**.*

17. *A **diameter** of the circle is any straight line drawn through the center and terminated in both directions by the circumference of the circle, and such a straight line also bisects the circle.* A diameter of a circle is a line segment with endpoints lying on the circle and containing the center of the circle.

18. *A **semicircle** is the figure contained by the diameter and the circumference cut off by it. And the center of the semicircle is the same as that of the circle.* A semicircle is a diameter of a circle along with a half of the circle on one side of the line containing the diameter. If we also include the points inside these curves then we would call this a **half-disk**.

19. ***Rectilinear figures** are those which are contained by straight lines, trilateral figures being those contained by three, quadrilateral those contained by four, and multilateral those contained by more than four straight lines.* Rectlinear figures are **polygons**. Polygons with three sides are called **triangles** and four-sided polygons are **quadrilaterals**.

20. *Of trilateral figures, an **equilateral triangle** is that which has its three sides equal, an **isosceles triangle** that which has two of its sides alone equal, and a **scalene triangle** that which has its three sides unequal.* A triangle with three congruent sides is an equilateral triangle, one with exactly two congruent sides is called an isosceles triangle, and a triangle with sides of three different lengths is called scalene.

21. *Further, of trilateral figures, a right-angled triangle is that which has a right angle, an obtuse-angled triangle that which has an obtuse angle, and an acute-angled triangle that which has its three angles acute.* A triangle with a right angle is called a **right triangle,** one with an obtuse angle is named an **obtuse triangle,** and a triangle with three acute angles is called an **acute triangle.**

22. *Of quadrilateral figures, a square is that which is both equilateral and right-angled; an oblong that which is right-angled but not equilateral; a rhombus that which is equilateral but not right-angled; and a rhomboid that which has its opposite sides and angles equal to one another but is neither equilateral nor right-angled. And let quadrilaterals other than these be called trapezia.* A **square** is a quadrilateral that has four congruent sides and four right angles. A **rectangle** (oblong) is a quadrilateral that has four right angles. A **rhombus** is a quadrilateral with four congruent sides. A quadrilateral with congruent opposite angles and sides is a **parallelogram** (rhomboid). Euclid then says all other quadrilaterals will be called **trapezia**, but we do not use this terminology; in fact, a **trapezoid** is the term for a quadrilateral with exactly one pair of opposite sides being parallel.

23. *Parallel straight lines are straight lines which, being in the same plane and being produced indefinitely in both directions, do not meet one another in either direction.* **Parallel lines** are lines that lie in the same plane and do not meet.

Euclid's Common Notions (ideas that are self-evident): Euclid's statements are presented in italics followed by an equivalent modern statement.

1. *Things which are equal to the same thing are also equal to one another.* **Transitivity Property of Equality**: If $a = b$ and $b = c$, then $a = c$.

2. *If equals be added to equals, the wholes are equal.* **Addition Property of Equality**: If $a = b$, then $a + c = b + c$ for any real number c.

3. *If equals be subtracted from equals, the remainders are equal.* **Addition Property of Equality** with subtraction viewed as adding the opposite: If $a = b$ then $a + (-c) = b + (-c)$, which is equivalent to $a - c = b - c$.

4. *Things which coincide with one another are equal to one another.* If one object can be placed on another object so that one can see the objects are exactly the same, then the two objects are equal; in the case of plane figures, we say they are **congruent**.

5. *The whole is greater than the part.* Anything is greater than a proper subset of itself.

The Five Postulates of Euclid: These are five assumptions on which Euclid bases his geometry. As before, Euclid's original statements are presented in italics followed by the equivalent modern statement.

1. *A straight line may be drawn between any two points.* Through any two points, there is exactly one line.

2. *A piece of straight line may be extended indefinitely.* A line segment can be extended in both directions to create a line.

3. *A circle may be drawn with any given radius and an arbitrary center.* Given a point and a set length, there exists a circle with the point as the center and the length as the radius of the circle.

4. *That all right angles equal one another.* All right angles are congruent.

5. *If a straight line crossing two straight lines makes the interior angles on the same side less than two right angles, then the two straight lines, if extended indefinitely, meet on that side on which the angles are less than the two right angles.* If a line (transversal) intersects two other lines with the sum of the measures of the interior angles on the same side less than 180°, then the lines intersect on that side.

Neutral or Absolute Geometry

The geometry based on Euclid's 23 definitions, axioms, and the first four postulates above is called **neutral** or **absolute geometry**. The first 28 propositions of Euclid's Book I of *The Elements* can be proven from assuming only these 23 definitions, axioms, and the first four postulates. The 28 propositions, rewritten in today's mathematical language, follow. The figures are the originals from Euclid's *The Elements*, Book I.

- **Proposition 1:** Given a line segment, an equilateral triangle can be constructed with the given segment as one of the sides (Figure 4.1).

- **Proposition 2:** Given line segment PQ and a point A, point B can be found such that $AB \cong PQ$ (where the symbol $\cong$ is read as "is congruent to").

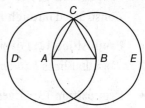

Figure 4.1

- **Proposition 3:** Given $\overline{AB}$ and $\overline{CD}$ with $AB > CD$, a point E can be found on $\overline{AB}$ such that $AE \cong CD$ (Figure 4.2).

- **Proposition 4 (Side-Angle-Side (SAS)):** If two sides and the included angle of one triangle are congruent to two sides and the included angle of a second triangle, respectively, then the third pair of sides of the triangles are congruent, and the two triangles are congruent, meaning that all the corresponding parts of the triangles are congruent.

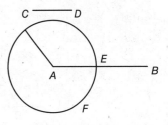

Figure 4.2

- **Proposition 5:** The base angles of an isosceles triangle are congruent, and, if the congruent sides of the isosceles triangle are extended, the angles under the base are also congruent to each other (Figure 4.3).

- **Proposition 6:** If in a triangle two angles are congruent, then the sides opposite the congruent angles are also congruent.

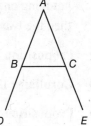

- **Proposition 7:** Given $\overline{AB}$ and point C not on the line through points A and B, it is not possible to find a point D different from C but on the same side of line $\overleftrightarrow{AB}$ as point C such that $\triangle ABC \cong \triangle ABD$ (Figure 4.4).

Figure 4.3

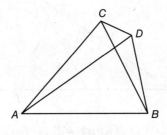

Figure 4.4

- **Proposition 8:** If two isosceles triangles have three pairs of congruent corresponding sides, then the triangles are congruent and, hence, the vertex angles of the two triangles are congruent.

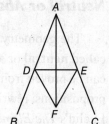

Figure 4.5

- **Proposition 9:** Every plane angle can be bisected (Figure 4.5).

- **Proposition 10:** Every line segment can be bisected (Figure 4.5).

- **Proposition 11:** Given a line l and a point P on l, a unique line m can be constructed through P so that lines l and m are perpendicular.

- **Proposition 12:** Given a line l and a point P not on l, a unique line m can be constructed through P so that lines l and m are perpendicular (Figure 4.6).

- **Proposition 13:** Given a line l and a point P on l, any ray $\overline{PQ}$ forms two angles with l such that sum of the two angles is 180°, and it might be true that both angles are right angles (Figure 4.7).

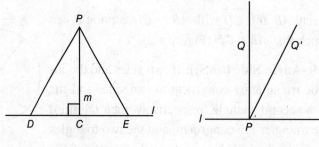

Figure 4.6   **Figure 4.7**

- **Proposition 14:** Given any line l, and a point P on the line, if two rays emanating from P and not lying on the same side of l make the sum of the measures of the adjacent angles equal 180°, then the two rays are collinear.

- **Proposition 15:** When two lines intersect, the vertical angles are congruent.

- **Corollary:** If two lines are perpendicular, then they form four right angles.

- **Proposition 16:** In any triangle, if one of the sides is extended, then the measure of the exterior angle is greater than the measure either of the two interior non-adjacent angles (Figure 4.8).

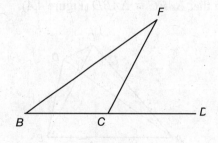

Figure 4.8

- **Proposition 17:** In any triangle, the sum of the measures of any two angles is less than 180° (Figure 4.9).

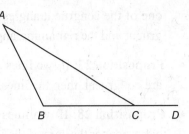

- **Proposition 18:** In any triangle, the angle opposite the longest side has the greatest measure.

- **Proposition 19:** In any triangle, the side opposite the angle of greatest measure is the longest.

Figure 4.9

- **Proposition 20:** In any triangle, the sum of the lengths of any two sides is greater than the length of the remaining side (Triangle Inequality).

- **Proposition 21:** If, from the endpoints of one of the sides of a $\triangle ABC$, two lines are constructed that meet in the interior of $\triangle ABC$, then the sum of the lengths of the constructed lines is less than the sum of the remaining two sides of $\triangle ABC$, but the constructed lines form an angle with greater measure than the angle between the remaining two sides of $\triangle ABC$.

- **Proposition 22:** Given three line segments, a triangle can be constructed with sides congruent to the given line segments, provided that the sum of the lengths of any two of the line segments is greater than that of the remaining side (Figure 4.10).

- **Proposition 23:** Given an angle, a congruent angle can be constructed on a given line segment at a specified point (Figure 4.11).

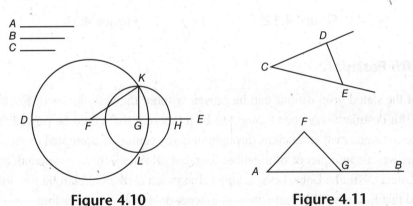

Figure 4.10   **Figure 4.11**

- **Proposition 24:** If two sides of one triangle are congruent to two of another triangle, but the angle contained by the two sides in one triangle has a measure greater than the angle included in the other triangle, then the third side in the triangle with the larger angle is longer than the third side of the other triangle.

- **Proposition 25:** If two sides of one triangle are congruent to two sides of another triangle, but the third sides are non-congruent, then the angles between the congruent sides are not congruent, and the one with the longer opposite side has greater measure.

- **Proposition 26 (Angle-Side-Angle (ASA)** and **Angle-Angle-Side (AAS)):** If two angles in one triangle are congruent to two angles in another triangle, and a side in one triangle is congruent to a side in the other triangle (either the side adjoining the congruent angles, or that opposite one of the congruent angles) then the respective remaining sides in the two triangles are congruent and the remaining angles, respectively, are congruent.

- **Proposition 27:** If two lines are intersected by a transversal so that the alternate interior angles are congruent, then the lines are parallel (Figure 4.12).

- **Proposition 28:** If two lines are intersected by a transversal so that corresponding angles are congruent or the sum of the interior angles on the same side of the transversal equals 180°, then the lines are parallel (Figure 4.13).

- **Note:** Corresponding angles are a pair of angles that when 2 lines are cut by a transversal the angles are one exterior and one interior angle on the same side of the transversed but are not adjacent.

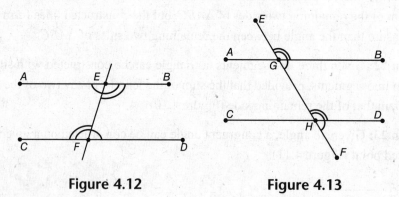

Figure 4.12   Figure 4.13

Euclid's Fifth Postulate

All 28 of the stated propositions can be proven without the assumption of Euclid's Fifth Postulate. The Fifth Postulate was once thought to be a theorem that could be proven from the other four postulates. Various mathematicians throughout many centuries attempted to show that Euclid's Fifth Postulate was a consequence of the other four, but all failed. In the nineteenth century, a Russian mathematician, Nikolai Lobachevsky, and a Hungarian mathematician, János Bolyai, independently proved that Euclid's Fifth Postulate was independent from the other four.

Recall Euclid's Fifth Postulate in modern language: If a line (transversal) intersects two other lines with the sum of the measures of the interior angles on the same side less than 180°, then the lines intersect on that side.

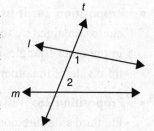

Figure 4.14

- Euclid defines lines in a plane as **parallel** if they do not intersect even when extended indefinitely.

- Euclid's Fifth Postulate is illustrated in Figure 4.14. The lines l and m are intersected by line t such that angles 1 and 2, which are the interior angles on the same side of t, have measures with sum less than 180°; i.e., less than the sum of two right angles.

Some Statements Equivalent to the Parallel Postulate

Playfair's Postulate: Given any point in a plane and a line in the plane not containing the given point, there exists exactly one line in the plane that contains the given point and is parallel to the given line. This postulate is also called the **Euclidean Parallel Postulate.**

- **Theorem**: The Euclidean Parallel Postulate and the Euclid's Fifth Postulate are equivalent.

Proof: Assume that Euclid's Fifth Postulate is true. Let l be a line in the plane and let P be a point in the plane not lying on l. By Proposition 12, line m may be constructed through point P perpendicular to line l (Figure 4.15). Let Q be the point where lines m and l intersect. By Proposition 11, line n can be constructed through point P perpendicular to line m. Thus, line m is a transversal of line l and n, and the alternate interior angles are right angles and, hence, congruent; thus, by Proposition 27, lines l and n are parallel. So there exists at least one line through P parallel to line l.

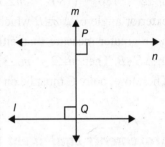

Figure 4.15

Now assume line j contains point P and is parallel to line l, and point R lies on j but not on line n. Then $\angle RPQ$ is not a right angle. If $m\angle RPQ < 90°$, then the interior angles on that side of the transversal have sum less than 180° (less than two right angles) and hence, by Euclid's Fifth Postulate, lines j and l must meet. This contradicts our assumption that j and l are parallel. If $m\angle RPQ > 90°$, then we can similarly show that j and l meet on the side of the transversal opposite point R. Hence, the parallel line n is unique.

Conversely, assume the Euclidean Parallel Postulate is true. Let l and m be two distinct lines cut by another line t (transversal) such that the sum of the interior angles on one side of t is less than 180°. Let A and B be the points of intersection of lines l and t, and m and t, respectively. Let C and D be points on lines l and m, respectively, such that both lie on the same side of t as where the sum of the measures of the interior angles is less than 180° (Figure 4.16A). So, $m\angle CAB + m\angle ABD < 180°$.

Let E be on line l such that point E is on the opposite side of the transversal t from C and D. Then $m\angle EAB + m\angle CAB = 180°$ and thus, $m\angle ABD < m\angle EAB$. So there is a ray $\overline{BF}$ such that $m\angle ABF = m\angle EAB$ (Figure 4.16B). Let n be the line containing points B and F. Since $\angle ABF$ and $\angle EAB$ are congruent alternate interior angles, then by Proposition 27 lines l and n are parallel. So by the Euclidean Parallel Postulate, m cannot be parallel to l and thus, must intersect l, say, in some point G.

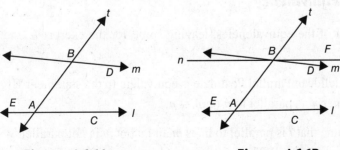

Figure 4.16A   **Figure 4.16B**

To show that point G is on the same side of t as D, assume that G is on the opposite side of t as D. Consider Figure 4.16C as labeled with the knowledge that $m\angle 2 + m\angle 4 < 180°$ by our original assumption. So $m\angle 2 < 180° - m\angle 4$. We also know that $m\angle 3 + m\angle 4 = 180°$ so $m\angle 4 = 180° - m\angle 3$. Then substituting we have $m\angle 2 < 180° - (180° - m\angle 3) = m\angle 3$. But $\angle 2$ is an exterior angle of $\triangle GAB$ which by Proposition 16 must have greater measure than either remote interior angle in $\triangle GAB$. Then $m\angle 2 < m\angle 3$ which is a contradiction.

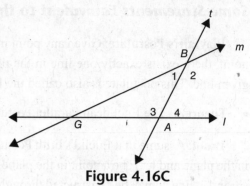

Figure 4.16C

Therefore, point G must lie on the side of line t where the interior angles sum to less than 180 degrees.

Q.E.D.

Statements Equivalent to the Euclidean Parallel Postulate and Euclid's Fifth Postulate

1. If l is parallel to lines m and n, then either m is parallel to n or $m = n$.

2. If l and m are parallel lines and line n intersects line l, then n also intersects m.

3. If two parallel lines are cut by a transversal, then the alternate interior angles are congruent (the converse of Proposition 27).

4. If line $l \perp$ line m and $m \parallel n$, then $l \perp n$.

5. The sum of the measures of the interior angles of a triangle is $180°$.

6. Fundamental Theorem of Similar Triangles: Two triangles are similar if and only if their corresponding sides are in proportion.

7. Wallis's Postulate: Given any $\triangle ABC$ and any line segment $\overline{DE}$, there exists a triangle $\triangle DEF$ such that $\triangle ABC \sim \triangle DEF$, where $\sim$ means the triangles are similar.

8. The Pythagorean Theorem.

9. If three angles of a quadrilateral are right angles, then the fourth angle is a right angle.

A Few Proofs of Equivalency

We prove several of the equivalencies, leaving some for the exercises, and the remaining for the reader.

- **Theorem**: The Euclidean Parallel Postulate is equivalent to the statement "If l is parallel to lines m and n, then either m is parallel to n or $m = n$."

  Proof: $(\Rightarrow)$ Assume that l is parallel to lines m and n but m is not parallel to n and $m \neq n$. Then m and n intersect at a point P. Thus, there are at least two distinct lines passing through point P and parallel to line l, contradicting the Euclidean Parallel Postulate.

($\Leftarrow$) Assume the second statement. Let lines m and n both be parallel to line l through a point P not on l. Then either $m = n$ or $m \parallel n$. If $m \parallel n$, this is a contradiction of the Euclidean Parallel Postulate; hence, it must be true that $m = n$, and the postulate holds.

Q.E.D.

- **Theorem**: The Euclidean Parallel Postulate is equivalent to the statement "The sum of the measures of the interior angles of a triangle is 180°."

Proof: ($\Rightarrow$) Consider $\triangle ABC$.

Let line l be the unique line through point B that is parallel to the line through side $\overline{AC}$, as stipulated in the Euclidean Parallel Postulate. Let D be a point on line l on the same side as point C, and let point E be another point on l on the same side as point A (Figure 4.17).

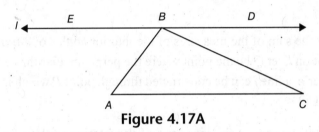

Figure 4.17A

Then $m\angle EBA + m\angle ABC + m\angle DBC = 180°$. But, by the converse of Proposition 27, the angles $\angle DBC$ and $\angle BCA$ are alternate interior angles, as are the angles $\angle EBA$ and $\angle BAC$, and so each pair is congruent.

Thus, by substitution, $m\angle BAC + m\angle ABC + m\angle BCA = 180°$.

($\Leftarrow$) Assume that the sum of the measures of the interior angles of any triangle is 180°. Let point P and line l be such that point P does not lie on line l. Let line m be the line perpendicular to line l containing point P. Let n be the line perpendicular to line m through point P (see Figure 4.17B) Then we have congruent alternate interior angles, so by Proposition 27 $n \parallel m$. Thus, there is at least one line through a point not on the given line parallel to the given line.

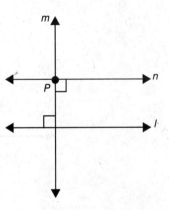

Figure 4.17B

Now we must show that line n is the unique line passing through point P and parallel to line l. To this end, suppose line k, not equal to line n, passes through point P and is parallel to line l. Label the illustration as in Figure 4.16C so that $m\angle VPQ < 90°$. (This must happen on one side of line m since n and k are not the same line.) Let $\varepsilon = 90° - m\angle VPQ$. Then by the Lemma following this proof, we can construct line j through P which intersects line l at some point U and such that $\angle PUQ < \varepsilon$. In $\triangle PQU$, $m\angle QPU = 90° - m\angle PUQ > 90° - \varepsilon = m\angle VPQ$. Therefore, $\overrightarrow{PV}$ is between rays $\overrightarrow{PQ}$ and $\overrightarrow{PU}$, and thus, must intersect $\overline{UQ}$ (Crossbar Theorem). Therefore n is unique.

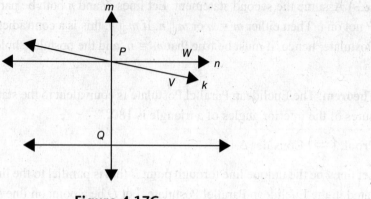

Figure 4.17C

Q.E.D.

Lemma: Assume that the sum of the measures of the interior angles of a triangle is 180°. Given a line l and a point P not on l, let Q be the point where the perpendicular through P intersects l. Then for any positive number ε, a line j can be constructed through point P which intersects line l at point U and such that $m\angle PUQ < \varepsilon$.

Proof: Assume that the sum of the measures of the interior angles of a triangle is 180°. Let line l be given along with point P not on l. Construct the perpendicular $\overrightarrow{PQ}$ from the point P to the line; choose point R on line l so that $PQ = QR$, and, hence, $m\angle QRP = m\angle QPR = 45°$. Now choose S on line l (with R between Q and S as in Figure 4.17D) so that $PR = RS$. Then $m\angle PRS = 135°$, $m\angle RPS = m\angle RSP = 22.5°$, since the sum of the measures of the interior angles of any triangle is 180°. Thus, $m\angle RSP = \frac{1}{2} m\angle PRQ$. Let $\varepsilon > 0$ be given. If $m\angle RSP = 22.5° > \varepsilon$, repeat the construction as many times as necessary to obtain an angle with measure less than ε.

Q.E.D.

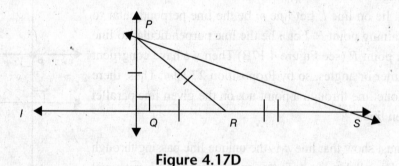

Figure 4.17D

Q.E.D.

- **Theorem:** The Euclidean Parallel Postulate is equivalent to the Pythagorean Theorem.

There are many proofs of the Pythagorean Theorem. Some rely on the existence of similar triangles and others use the existence of squares. Assuming the Euclidean Parallel Postulate, one can prove either the existence of similar triangles or the existence of squares from which it follows that the Pythagorean Theorem is true conversely, assuming the Pythagorean Theorem is true, we have the existence of rectangles, from which we can show that the Euclidean Parallel Postulate holds.

The Remaining Propositions

- **Proposition 29:** If two parallel lines are crossed by a transversal, the alternate interior angles are congruent; corresponding angles are also congruent, and the sum of the measures of the interior angles on the same side of the transversal is 180°.

- **Proposition 30:** Lines that are parallel to the same line are parallel to each other.

- **Proposition 31:** Through a given point not on a given line, there is a line parallel to the given line.

- **Proposition 32:** If one side of a triangle is extended, then the measure of the exterior angle is equal to the sum of the measures of the two remote interior angles. Also, the sum of the three interior angles of a triangle is 180°.

- **Proposition 33:** If two sides of a quadrilateral are congruent and parallel, then the quadrilateral is a parallelogram.

- **Proposition 34:** In a parallelogram, the opposite sides and angles are congruent and a diagonal bisects the area.

- **Proposition 35:** Parallelograms on the same base and with the same parallels have equal areas. (In Figure 4.18, area of parallelogram $ABCD$ = area of parallelogram $FEBC$.)

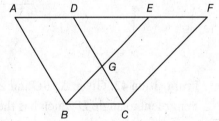

- **Proposition 36:** Parallelograms with congruent bases that lie on the same parallel lines have equal areas.

Figure 4.18

- **Proposition 37:** Triangles with the same base and with the third vertex on the same line that is parallel to the line through the base have equal areas. (In Figure 4.19, area of $\triangle ABC$ = area of $\triangle DCB$.)

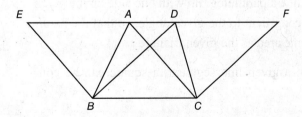

Figure 4.19

- **Proposition 38:** Triangles with congruent bases on the same line with the third vertex on the same line that is parallel to the line through the bases have equal areas.

- **Proposition 39:** Triangles with equal areas that have the same base and lie on the same side of it are situated such that the third vertex lies on the same line, which is parallel to the base.

- **Proposition 40:** For triangles which have equal areas and congruent bases which lie on the same line, if the triangles lie on the same side of the line containing the base then their third vertices lie on the same line which is parallel to the give line. (Figure 4.20A)

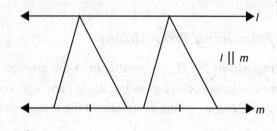

Figure 4.20A

- **Proposition 41:** If a parallelogram and a triangle have the same base and the third vertex of the triangle is on the line containing the opposite side of the parallelogram, the area of the parallelogram is double the area of the triangle. (In Figure 4.20, the area of parallelogram *ABCD* is double the area of Δ*EBC*.)

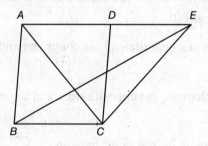

Figure 4.20

- **Proposition 42:** Given Δ*ABC* and ∠*D*, it is possible to construct a parallelogram with one angle congruent to angle *D* which has the same area as Δ*ABC*.

- **Proposition 43:** Given parallelogram *ABCD* with point *K* on its diagonal and in its interior as shown in Figure 4.20B, then the area of parallelogram *HDFK* is equal to the area of parallelogram *BEKG*.

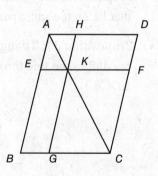

- **Proposition 44:** Given a line, a triangle and an angle, it is possible to construct on the line a parallelogram with one side on the given line and one angle congruent to the given angle, so that the parallelogram has the same area as the given triangle.

- **Proposition 46:** On a given line segment, a square can be constructed.

Figure 4.20B

- **Proposition 47 (Pythagorean Theorem):** In a right triangle, the square of the length of the hypotenuse is equal to the sum of the squares of the lengths of the legs (the sides that form the right angle).

- **Proposition 48 (Converse of Pythagorean Theorem):** If the square of length of a side of triangle equals the sum of the squares of the other two sides, then the angle contained by those two sides is a right angle.

Review Problems for Section 4.1.1

1. Determine which of the following statements can be proven without assuming Euclid's Fifth Postulate and then prove it.

   (A) A rectangle exists.

   (B   If a line is perpendicular to one of two parallel lines, it is perpendicular to the other.

   (C) If two lines intersect, the vertical angles are congruent.

   (D) The sum of the measures of the interior angles of a triangle is 180°.

2. Which of the following statements is not equivalent to Euclid's Fifth Postulate?

   (A) If two lines are cut by a transversal so that the alternate interior angles are congruent, then the lines are parallel.

   (B) Given any point in a plane and a line in the plane not containing the given point, there exists exactly one line in the plane that contains the given point and is parallel to the given line.

   (C) The Pythagorean Theorem holds.

   (D) If two distinct lines are each parallel to a distinct third line, then the two lines are parallel.

3. Prove that the following statement follows from neutral geometry and the assumption of Euclid's Fifth Postulate.

   Wallis's Postulate: If $\triangle ABC$ and $\overline{DE}$ are given, then there exists a point F such that $\triangle ABC \sim \triangle DEF$.

4. Assuming the Euclidean Parallel Postulate, if lines m and n are parallel, what must be the value of x?

   (A) 30

   (B) 60

   (C) 70

   (D) 110

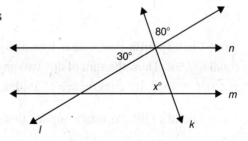

Figure 4.21

Detailed Solutions

1. (C)

Statement (C) does not need Euclid's Fifth Postulate in its proof. Here is the proof.

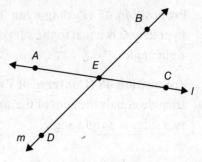

Proof: Let lines l and m intersect at point E and let points A, B, C, and D be on lines l and m as shown in Figure 4.22.

Figure 4.22

Since l is a line, $m\angle AEB + m\angle BEC = 180°$. Similarly, m is a line, so we also have $m\angle BEC + m\angle CED = 180°$. Hence, by Transitivity, $m\angle AEB + m\angle BEC = m\angle BEC + m\angle CED$. Using the Addition Property of Equality, we obtain $m\angle AEB = m\angle CED$, or $\angle AEB \cong \angle CED$.

Using the same argument, we can show $\angle AED \cong \angle BEC$.

$\therefore$ The vertical angles are congruent.

Q.E.D.

2. (A)

Statement (B) is the Euclidean Parallel Postulate, (C) is the Pythagorean Theorem; these are well-known to be equivalent to Euclid's Fifth Postulate. If we did not assume the Fifth Postulate, then the two lines in statement (D) could be intersecting since there would be no rule that there is only one line through a given point parallel to a given line; therefore, (D) is equivalent to Euclid's Fifth Postulate. Statement (A) is Proposition 27, which is part of neutral geometry.

3. Proof: Assume Euclid's Fifth Postulate is true.

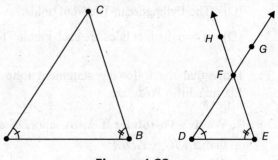

Assume that $\triangle ABC$ and $\overline{DE}$ are given. By Proposition 23, an angle can be constructed at point D that is congruent to $\angle BAC$. Let G be a point on the ray such that $\angle BAC \cong \angle EDG$. Also, an angle can be constructed at E such that $\angle CBA \cong \angle DEH$, and point H is on the same side of $\overline{DE}$ as point G.

Figure 4.23

Since Euclid's Fifth Postulate is true, it follows that the sum of the three angles of any triangle is equal to 180°. Thus, the sum of any two angles of a triangle is less than 180°. Therefore, $m\angle CAB + m\angle ABC < 180°$. By congruence of angles, we also know $m\angle GDE + m\angle HED < 180°$.

Thus, Euclid's Fifth Postulate implies that $\overline{DG}$ and $\overline{EH}$ meet at a point, say F.

By angle addition and subtraction, $\angle BCA \cong \angle EFD$.

Thus, by the definition of similar triangles, $\triangle ABC \sim \triangle DEF$.

Q.E.D.

4. (C)

Since vertical angles are congruent, the measure of angle 1 is 80°, so the measure of angle 2 then must be $180 - (30 + 80) = 70°$. Lines n and m will be parallel if the alternate interior angles are congruent, which will happen if $x = 70$.

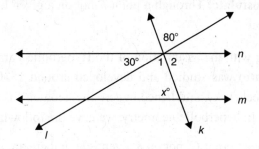

Figure 4.24

4.1.2 The California *Mathematics Subject Matter Requirements* require that candidates for any credential program for teaching secondary mathematics *know that variants of the Parallel Postulate produce non-Euclidean geometries (e.g, spherical, hyperbolic).*

Non-Euclidean Geometries

Euclidean Geometry is an **axiomatic system**. Axiomatic systems must be consistent, complete, and independent. A system is **consistent** provided the axioms (basic assumptions) of the system do not contradict each other. Also, if a system is consistent, one should not be able to prove two contradictory statements are true in the system. A **complete** collection of assumptions means that for any two contradictory statements involving concepts in the system, at least one of the statements can be proven. The last property, **independence**, can be described in the following way: Let X be an axiom of a system S of axioms. If X cannot be proven from the other axioms in the system, then X is called independent of the other axioms in system S. If all the axioms in S are independent, then the entire system S is called independent. In other words, none of the axioms of the system are redundant; no axiom duplicates information given by the others.

As we stated previously, the geometry based on all of Euclid's axioms, definitions, and the first four of Euclid's postulates is called **Absolute** or **Neutral Geometry**. We have seen that the first 28 propositions of Euclid's are part of this geometry. Euclidean geometry is based on all the information for neutral geometry along with Euclid's Fifth Postulate. Non-Euclidean geometries are geometries based on neutral geometry along with a fifth postulate, which is contradictory to Euclid's Fifth Postulate.

Variants of the Parallel Postulate

Hyperbolic Geometry

Hyperbolic Parallel Postulate: Through a point P not on a given line l, there are at least two lines that do not intersect line l.

The geometry resulting with the assumption of the Hyperbolic Parallel Postulate (also called the **Characteristic Postulate**) was studied and developed around 1830 independently by mathematicians Bolyai and Lobechevsky, and hence hyperbolic geometry is sometimes called **Bolyai-Lobechevskian geometry**. In hyperbolic geometry, we have the following theorems:

- **Theorem**: Through a given point C, not on a given line, l, there are an infinite number of lines not intersecting the given line l.

- **Theorem:** The sum of the interior angles of a triangle is less than $180°$.

A consequence of this theorem is that there are no rectangles in hyperbolic geometry due to the following corollary.

- **Corollary:** The sum of the interior angles of a quadrilateral is less than $360°$.

The **Saccheri quadrilateral** is a convex quadrilateral with two adjacent angles being right angles. The side between these angles is called the **base** and the opposite side is the **summit**. The other two sides are congruent and are simply called the **sides**. The two angles that share the summit as a side are called **summit angles** (Figure 4.25).

In Euclidean geometry, this quadrilateral would be a rectangle, but not so in hyperbolic geometry.

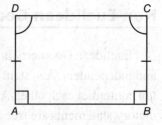

Figure 4.25

- **Theorem:** In a Saccheri quadrilateral, the summit angles are congruent and acute.

The second interesting quadrilateral in geometry is the **Lambert quadrilateral**. It is a convex quadrilateral with three right angles. In Euclidean geometry, this quadrilateral would again be a rectangle. But in hyperbolic geometry, we have the following:

- **Theorem:** In a Lambert quadrilateral, the fourth angle is an acute angle.

In hyperbolic geometry, there is no difference between similar and congruent triangles.

- **Theorem:** All similar triangles are congruent.

In hyperbolic geometry, the first lines in either direction through a point that do not intersect a given line are called **parallel lines**. These lines are sometimes called **sensed parallel lines.** Lines through a point not intersecting the given line, and not parallel to it, are called **nonintersecting lines,** or sometimes **ultraparallel lines.** Thus, there are exactly two parallel lines through a given point not on a given line. They are called the **left-hand** and **right-hand parallels** (according to what side of the point they are on). The interior angles that are formed at the given point with the parallels and the line through the point perpendicular to the given line are called the **angles of parallelism**; they are indicated by θ in Figure 4.26.

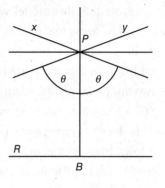

- **Theorem**: The two angles of parallelism for the same segment are congruent and acute.

In hyperbolic geometry, two parallel lines are said to meet in an **ideal point**. We call the two ideal points (one for each parallel) Ω and Ω'. These are not actual points. In hyperbolic geometry, an **omega** or **asymptotic triangle** is a three-sided figure with one ideal vertex.

Figure 4.26

- **Theorem**: The **Axiom of Pasch** (If a line, not passing through any vertex of a triangle, meets one side of the triangle, then it meets another side) holds for an omega triangle, whether the line enters at a vertex or at a point that is not a vertex.

- **Theorem**: For any omega triangle $AB\Omega$, the measures of the exterior angles formed by extending $\overline{AB}$ are greater than the measures of their opposite interior angles.

- **Theorem**: Omega triangles $AB\Omega$ and $A'B'\Omega'$ are congruent if the sides of finite length are congruent and if a pair of corresponding angles at A and A' or B and B' are congruent.

Elliptic Geometry

In the mid 1800s, Bernhard Riemann, a German mathematician, developed an area of mathematics called Riemannian geometry, which includes the area of **elliptic geometry.** Elliptic geometry is designated as a non-Euclidean geometry because it does not have any parallel lines.

Elliptic Parallel Postulate: Given a line l and a point P not on l, there are no lines containing P and parallel to l.

Consequences of this postulate are the following theorems.

- **Theorem:** In elliptical geometry, all lines intersect.

- **Theorem:** The sum of the interior angles of a triangle is greater than 180°.

- **Corollary:** The sum of the interior angles of a quadrilateral is greater than 360°.

Note that this last corollary implies that there are no rectangles in the elliptic geometry system, since a rectangle would have four 90° angles.

In the spherical model for elliptical geometry the lines are the great circles of the sphere. A great circle is the intersection of the sphere and a plane containing the center of the sphere. Elliptical geometry is also called **spherical** geometry for this reason.

Note that this model violates Euclid's first postulate since if one considers two great circles it is easy to see they must have two points of intersection (P and Q in Figure 4.27), so there can be no parallel lines. In fact there are infinitely many lines that pass through any two antipodal points. Riemann replaced Euclid's first postulate to read *"Given any two points, there is at least one line containing the points."* This does not change any of the other results of neutral geometry and allows mathematicians to use the sphere as an elliptical geometry model. Due to Riemann's adjustment, this geometry is also called **Riemannian geometry.**

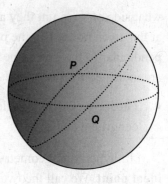

Figure 4.27

Review Problems for Section 4.1.2

1. Which of the following statements is true in hyperbolic geometry?

    (A) The sum of the measures of the interior angles in a triangle is greater than 180°.

    (B) Through a point not on a given line there are no parallel lines.

    (C) There are no rectangles.

    (D) The Pythagorean Theorem holds.

2. The statement "is parallel to" is an equivalence relation in which of the following?

    (A) Elliptic geometry

    (B) Euclidean geometry

    (C) Hyperbolic geometry

    (D) None of the above geometries

3. Which of the following statements is true in elliptic geometry?

    (A) The sum of the measures of the interior angles in a triangle is equal to 180°.

    (B) Through a point not on a given line there are no parallel lines.

    (C) Vertical angles are not congruent.

    (D) The Pythagorean Theorem holds.

Detailed Solutions

1. **(C)**

    In hyperbolic geometry, the sum of the measures of the interior angles of a triangle is less than 180°, so (A) is false. Statement (B) is false because the Hyperbolic Postulate states there is at least one line through a point off a given line that is parallel to the given line. Statement (D) is false because Euclid's Fifth Postulate is replaced by the Hyperbolic Postulate. Statement (C) is true because the sum of the measures of the interior angles of a quadrilateral is less than 360°.

2. (D)

None of the geometries have "is parallel to" as a reflexive property since a line cannot be parallel to itself. So, "is parallel to" cannot be an equivalence relation in any of these geometries.

3. (B)

Statement (A) is false; the sum of the measures of the interior angles of a triangle in elliptic geometry is greater than 180°. Statement (C) is false because vertical angles are congruent in all three geometries, as it is one of the neutral geometry propositions. The Elliptic Postulate replaces the Euclidean Fifth Postulate, so (D) is false.

4.2 Congruence and Similarity

4.2.1 The California *Mathematics Subject Matter Requirements* stipulate that candidates for any credential program for teaching secondary mathematics must be able to *prove theorems and solve problems involving similarity and congruence.*

Congruence

Two objects are **congruent** if they have the same shape and size.

An elementary way of showing that two objects are congruent is to make a tracing of the first object and lay the tracing on top of the second object so that it matches.

The mathematical symbol $\cong$ is read as "is congruent to."

Some Definitions

- $\overline{AB} \cong \overline{CD}$ if and only if $AB = CD$, read as *line segment AB is congruent to line segment CD if and only if the length of $\overline{AB}$ is equal to the length of $\overline{CD}$.*

- $\angle ABC \cong \angle DEF$ if and only if $m \angle ABC = m\angle DEF$, read as *angle ABC is congruent to angle DEF if and only if the measure of angle ABC is equal to the measure of angle DEF.*

- **Two circles are congruent** if and only if their radii are congruent.

- **Arc ABC is congruent to arc DEF** if and only if the circles of which they are a part are congruent and the arcs themselves are the same length.

- $\triangle ABC$ **is congruent to** $\triangle DEF$ ($\triangle ABC \cong \triangle DEF$) **if and only if** $\angle A \cong \angle D$ $\angle B \cong \angle E$, $\angle C \cong \angle F$, $\overline{AB} \cong \overline{DE}$, $\overline{BC} \cong \overline{EF}$, and $\overline{AC} \cong \overline{DF}$.

The angles that are paired in the definition of congruent triangles are called pairs of **corresponding angles** of the triangle, and the sides that are paired are called pairs of **corresponding sides** of the triangle.

The important idea here is that **corresponding parts of congruent triangles are congruent.** This fact is often used in proofs, and is abbreviated to CPCTC.

Note: It is crucial that the letters of corresponding angles lie in the same position of the name of the respective triangles. For example, in the triangles in Figure 4.28, it is true that $\triangle ABC \cong \triangle DEF$ but it is false that $\triangle ABC \cong \triangle DFE$.

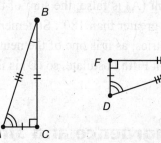

Figure 4.28

- **Two polygons are congruent** if and only if by creating a one-to-one correspondence between their vertices, then all pairs of corresponding angles and all pairs of corresponding sides are congruent.

Examples:

(a) Given that M is the midpoint of $\overline{AB}$, prove $AM = \frac{1}{2} AB$.

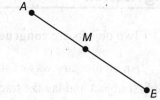

Proof:

Statements	Reasons
1. M is the midpoint of $\overline{AB}$	1. Given
2. $\overline{AM} \cong \overline{MB}$	2. Definition of midpoint
3. $AM = MB$	3. Definition of congruent segments
4. $AM + MB = AB$	4. A whole is the sum of its parts
5. $AM + AM = AB$	5. Substitution
6. $2AM = AB$	6. Addition
7. $AM = \frac{1}{2} AB$	7. Multiplication Property of Equality

Q.E.D.

(b) Prove that all right angles are congruent.

First we restate the problem: Given that $\angle A$ and $\angle B$ are right angles, prove $\angle A \cong \angle B$.

Proofs can be written in column form, as shown in example (a), or as a paragraph. We will do this proof in paragraph form.

Proof: Assume $\angle A$ and $\angle B$ are right angles, then by the definition of right angles, $m\angle A = 90°$ and $m\angle B = 90°$. So by the Transitive Property of Equality, $m\angle A = m\angle B$. Therefore, $\angle A \cong \angle B$ by the definition of congruent angles.

Q.E.D.

Triangle Congruences

There are six parts of a triangle, three sides and three angles, and the definition of congruent triangles states that two triangles are congruent provided the six corresponding parts are congruent. However, we will not have to show that all six parts are congruent in order to be satisfied that the triangles are congruent.

- **Theorem (Side-Side-Side (SSS))**: If the three sides of one triangle are congruent, respectively, to the three sides of a second triangle, then the triangles are congruent.

In Figure 4.29, the corresponding congruent sides are marked by the same number of slashes. This is the conventional way we indicate segment congruences. For Figure 4.29, the congruence is $\Delta ABC \cong \Delta DEF$.

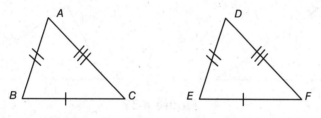

Figure 4.29

- **Theorem (Side-Angle-Side (SAS))**: If two sides and the included angle of one triangle are congruent to two sides and the included angle of another triangle, respectively, then the two triangles are congruent.

Note how the congruent angles are marked the same in Figure 4.30; this figure illustrates $\Delta ABC \cong \Delta DEF$.

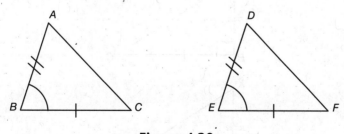

Figure 4.30

- **Theorem (Angle-Side-Angle (ASA)):** If two angles and the included side of one triangle are congruent to two angles and the included side of another triangle, respectively, then the two triangles are congruent. Figure 4.31 illustrates the ASA markings and that $\triangle ABC \cong \triangle DEF$.

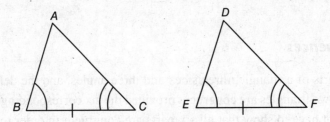

Figure 4.31

- **Theorem (Angle-Angle-Side (AAS)):** If two angles and a non-included side of one triangle are congruent to two angles and the corresponding side of another triangle, respectively, then the two triangles are congruent. Figure 4.32 shows the AAS markings and that $\triangle ABC \cong \triangle DEF$.

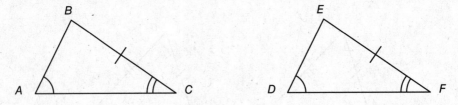

Figure 4.32

- **Theorem (Leg-Leg (LL)):** If the two legs of one right triangle are congruent to the two legs of another right triangle, the two triangles are congruent. Figure 4.33 illustrates the LL relationship and that $\triangle ABC \cong \triangle XYZ$.

Note that LL is equivalent to SAS in right triangles.

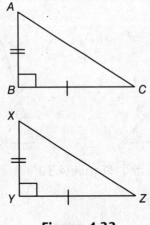

Figure 4.33

- **Theorem (Hypotenuse-Leg (HL)):** If the hypotenuse and one leg of one right triangle are congruent to the hypotenuse and one leg of another right triangle, respectively, then the two triangles are congruent. Figure 4.34 illustrates the HL congruence.

This theorem follows from using the Pythagorean Theorem to arrive at SSS.

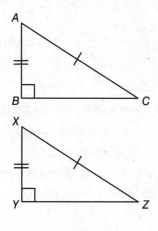

Figure 4.34

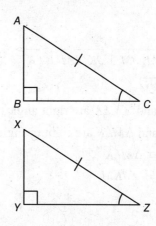

Figure 4.35

- **Theorem (Hypotenuse-Angle (HA)):** If the hypotenuse and an acute angle of one right triangle are congruent to the hypotenuse and an acute angle of another right triangle, respectively, then the two triangles are congruent. Figure 4.35 illustrates the HA congruence.

Note that HA is AAS in right triangles.

Examples:

(a) Prove: If $\overline{AD} \parallel \overline{CB}$ and $\overline{AD} \cong \overline{BC}$, then $\triangle ADP \cong \triangle BCP$.

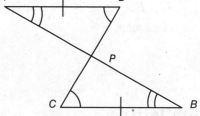

Figure 4.36

Proof:

Statements	Reasons
1. $\overline{AD} \parallel \overline{CB}$, $\overline{AD} \cong \overline{BC}$	1. Given
2. $\angle DAP \cong \angle CBP$ and $\angle ADP \cong \angle BCP$	2. If two parallel lines are cut by a transversal, the alternate interior angles are congruent.
3. $\triangle ADP \cong \triangle BCP$	3. ASA

Q.E.D.

(b) Given: $\overline{JM} \cong \overline{LM}$, $\overline{JM} \perp \overline{JK}$, $\overline{LM} \perp \overline{LK}$.

Prove: $\angle LKM \cong \angle JKM$.

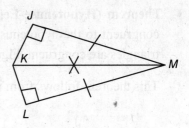

Figure 4.37

Proof:

Statements	Reasons
1. $\overline{JM} \cong \overline{LM}$, $\overline{JM} \perp \overline{JK}$, $\overline{LM} \perp \overline{LK}$	1. Given
2. $\overline{KM} \cong \overline{KM}$	2. Reflexive Property of $\cong$.
3. $\angle MJK$ and $\angle MLK$ are right angles	3. Perpendicular lines form right angles
4. $\triangle MJK$ and $\triangle MLK$ are right triangles	4. Definition of right triangle
5. $\triangle MJK \cong \triangle MLK$	5. HL (hypotenuse-leg)
6. $\angle LKM \cong \angle JKM$	6. CPCTC (corresponding parts of congruent triangles are congruent)

Q.E.D.

(c) Given: $\overline{BC} \cong \overline{DC}$, $\angle 1 \cong \angle 2$. Prove: $\triangle ACE$ is isosceles.

Proof: Assume $\overline{BC} \cong \overline{DC}$, $\angle 1 \cong \angle 2$. Since any angle is congruent to itself by the Reflexive Property of $\cong$, $\angle BCE \cong \angle DCA$. Therefore, $\triangle CBE \cong \triangle CDA$ by AAS. So by CPCTC, $\overline{AC} \cong \overline{EC}$. Then, by the definition of isosceles triangle, $\triangle ACE$ is isosceles.

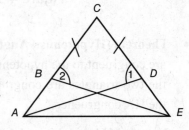

Figure 4.38

Q.E.D.

Similarity

Two objects are **similar** if they have the same shape.

The mathematical symbol $\sim$ is read as "is similar to."

Triangles are similar provided there is a correspondence between their vertices such that the corresponding angles are congruent. So $\triangle ABC \sim \triangle PQR$ if and only if $\angle A \cong \angle P$, $\angle B \cong \angle Q$, $\angle C \cong \angle R$.

- **Theorem (Angle-Angle (AA))**: Two triangles are similar provided two of the pairs of the corresponding angles are congruent.

Proof: If two pairs of the corresponding angles are congruent, then the third pair must also be congruent since the sum of the measures of the interior angles of a triangle is 180°.

Q.E.D.

Some other theorems involving similarity are stated next without proof.

- **Theorem**: Suppose line k intersects side $\overline{AB}$ at a point between A and B and is parallel to side $\overline{AC}$ of $\triangle ABC$ (Figure 4.39). Then k also intersects $\overline{BC}$ in such a way that it divides the lengths of the two sides proportionally; i.e., $\dfrac{BD}{DA} = \dfrac{BE}{EC}$.

- **Theorem (Fundamental Theorem of Similarity)**: The measures of the corresponding sides of similar triangles are in proportion. Specifically, if $\triangle ABC \sim \triangle PQR$, then $\dfrac{AB}{PQ} = \dfrac{BC}{QR} = \dfrac{AC}{PR}$.

  Example: Referring to Figure 4.40, if the lines containing $\overline{AC}$ and $\overline{DE}$ are parallel, what is x?

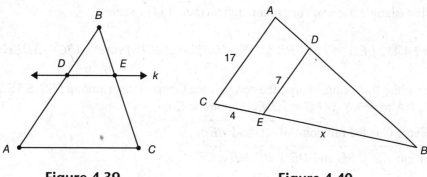

Figure 4.39　　　　　　　　　　Figure 4.40

Since the lines are parallel, corresponding angles are congruent, so $\angle BDE \cong \angle BAC$, and $\angle BED \cong \angle BCA$. Thus, by AA, $\triangle BDE \sim \triangle BAC$. Then, by the Fundamental Theorem of Similarity,

$$\frac{x}{4+x} = \frac{7}{17}.$$

This is equivalent to $17x = 28 + 7x$, which in turn can be solved to obtain $x = 2.8$.

- **Theorem**: If two triangles are congruent, then they are similar.

  The converse of this theorem is false; simply consider the two isosceles right triangles, one with hypotenuse of length 1 unit and the other with hypotenuse of length 2 units; clearly, these triangles are both 45°-45°-90° triangles.

- **Theorem (SAS for Similarity)**: If an angle of one triangle is congruent to the corresponding angle of another triangle and the lengths of the sides including these angles are in proportion, the triangles are similar.

- **Theorem**: If the ratio of the lengths of corresponding sides of similar triangles is $a{:}b$, then the ratio of the areas of the triangles is $a^2{:}b^2$.

Review Problems for Section 4.2.1

1. Which of the following statements is true?

    (A) Triangles with the same areas are congruent.

    (B) Squares with the same areas are congruent.

    (C) Angles with the same vertex are congruent.

    (D) Rectangles with the same areas are congruent.

2. Prove: If a triangle has two congruent angles, then it is isosceles.

3. In Figure 4.41, $\overline{BE} \perp \overline{AB}$ and $\overline{BE} \perp \overline{DE}$, $\angle DFB \cong \angle ACE$. Prove $\triangle ABC \sim \triangle DEF$.

4. For each of the following, choose the congruence theorem from among SSS, SAS, AAS, ASA, HL, LL, HA to prove $\triangle ABC \cong \triangle DEC$ (Figure 4.42).

    (a) Given: C is the midpoint of $\overline{AD}$ and $\overline{BE}$.

    (b) Given: $\overline{AB} \perp \overline{BE}$ and $\overline{DE} \perp \overline{BE}$, $\overline{AB} \cong \overline{DE}$.

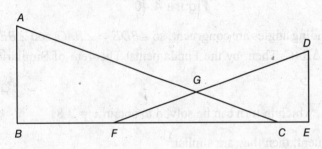

Figure 4.41

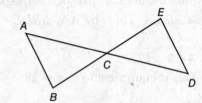

Figure 4.42

Detailed Solutions

1. (B)

Consider two right triangles, one with legs that have lengths 1 inch and 10 inches and the other with legs of lengths 2 inches and 5 inches. Both right triangles have area 5 square inches but they are not congruent, so (A) is false. Given an area of a square, say x, there is only one square with that area (one with sides length $\sqrt{x}$), so (B) is true. Statement (C) is false because there can be infinitely many different sized angles with a given point as a vertex. Statement (D) is false since a 2′ by 6′ rectangle and a 3′ by 4′ rectangle have the same area.

2. *Restatement*: Given $\triangle ABC$ (Figure 4.43) with $\angle B \cong \angle C$, prove $\triangle ABC$ is an isosceles triangle.

Proof: Consider $\triangle ABC$ with $\angle B \cong \angle C$. Let ray $\overrightarrow{AP}$ be the angle bisector of $\angle A$, where P is the point where the ray intersects side $\overline{BC}$. Then $\angle BAP \cong \angle CAP$ by the definition of angle bisector. Since $\overline{AP} \cong \overline{AP}$ by the Reflexive Property of Congruence, $\triangle APB \cong \triangle APC$ by AAS. Therefore, $\overline{AB} \cong \overline{AC}$ by CPCTC. Hence, $\triangle ABC$ is an isosceles triangle.

Q.E.D.

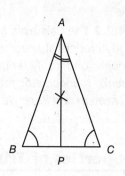

Figure 4.43

3. **Proof**:

Statements	Reasons
1. $\overline{BE} \perp \overline{AB}$ and $\overline{BE} \perp \overline{DE}$, $\angle DFB \cong \angle ACE$.	1. Given
2. $\angle ABC$ and $\angle DEF$ are right angles.	2. Definition of right angles
3. $\angle ABC \cong \angle DEF$	3. All right angles are congruent
4. $m\angle DFB + m\angle DFE = 180°$ $m\angle ACE + m\angle ACB = 180°$	4. Straight lines form supplementary angles
5. $m\angle DFB + m\angle DFE = m\angle ACE + \angle ACB$	5. Transitive Property of Equality
6. $m\angle DFB = m\angle ACE$	6. Definition of congruent angles
7. $m\angle DFE = m\angle ACB$	7. Addition Property of = (subtraction)
8. $\angle DFE \cong \angle ACB$	8. Definition of congruent angles
9. $\triangle ABC \sim \triangle DEF$	9. AA theorem

Q.E.D.

4. (a) Since C is the midpoint of $\overline{AD}$ and $\overline{BE}$, $\overline{AC} \cong \overline{CD}$ and $\overline{BC} \cong \overline{CE}$. In addition, $\angle ACB \cong \angle DCE$ because they are vertical angles. This gives congruence of triangles by SAS.

(b) Again we have congruent vertical angles $\angle ACB \cong \angle DCE$. We also have right angles at B and E, so these angles are congruent. We are given $\overline{AB} \cong \overline{ED}$; hence, the triangles are congruent by LA or AAS.

4.2.2 The California *Mathematics Subject Matter Requirements* stipulate that candidates for any credential program for teaching secondary mathematics must be able to *understand, apply, and justify properties of triangles (e.g., the Exterior Angle Theorem, concurrence theorems, trigonometric ratios, Triangle Inequality, Law of Sines, Law of Cosines, the Pythagorean Theorem and its converse).*

Properties of Triangles

Classifications of Triangles

Classification by sides (Figure 4.44):

- **Scalene** triangles have no congruent sides.

- **Isosceles** triangles have exactly two congruent sides.

- **Equilateral** triangles have three congruent sides.

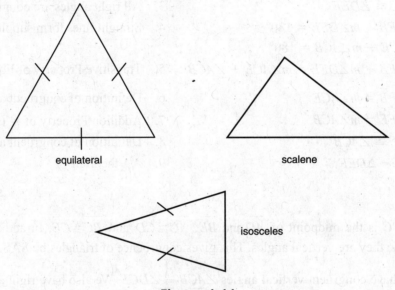

equilateral   scalene

isosceles

Figure 4.44

Classification by angles (Figure 4.45):

- **Acute** triangles have three acute angles.

- **Obtuse** triangles have one obtuse angle.

- **Right** triangles have one right angle.

- **Equiangular** triangles have three congruent angles.

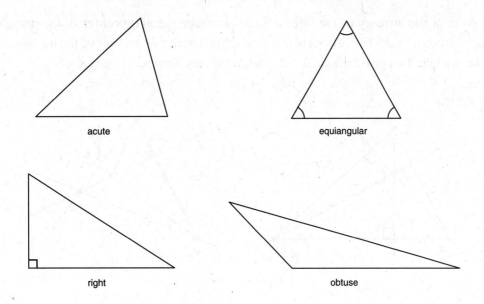

Figure 4.45

Concurrence in Triangles

Three lines are **concurrent** if there is a point P such that P lies on all three of the lines. The point P is called the **point of concurrency**.

Three **line segments are concurrent** if they all have an interior point in common.

- The segment joining a vertex of a triangle to the midpoint of the opposite side is called a **median** of the triangle.

- **Median Concurrence Theorem:** The three medians of any triangle are concurrent; that is, if $\triangle ABC$ is a triangle and D, E, and F are the midpoints of the sides opposite A, B, and C, respectively, then $\overline{AD}$, $\overline{BE}$, and $\overline{CF}$ all intersect in a common point G (Figure 4.46).

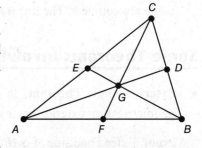

Moreover, $AG = 2GD$, $BG = 2GE$, and $CG = 2GF$.

The point of concurrency of the three medians is called the **centroid** of the triangle.

Figure 4.46

- An **altitude** of a triangle is a line segment from a vertex to the line containing the opposite side of the triangle that is perpendicular to that side. The point at which an altitude intersects the line through the opposite side of a triangle is called the **foot** of the altitude.

- **Altitude Concurrence Theorem:** The three altitudes of any triangle are concurrent.

- The point of concurrency of the three altitudes is called the **orthocenter** of the triangle. It is usually denoted by H. The orthocenter can be in the interior or exterior of the triangle, or even on the triangle. Two possibilities, ΔABC and ΔDEF, are shown in Figure 4.47.

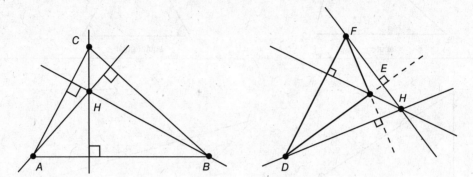

Figure 4.47

- A **perpendicular bisector of a side** of a triangle is a line containing the midpoint of a side of the triangle such that it is perpendicular to that side.

- **The Perpendicular Bisector Theorem:** The three perpendicular bisectors of a triangle are concurrent.

- The point of concurrency of the three perpendicular bisectors of the sides of a triangle is called the **circumcenter** of the triangle. The circum-

Figure 4.48

center is usually denoted by O (Figure 4.48). A circle with center O and radii $OA = OB = OC$ can be circumscribed about ΔABC.

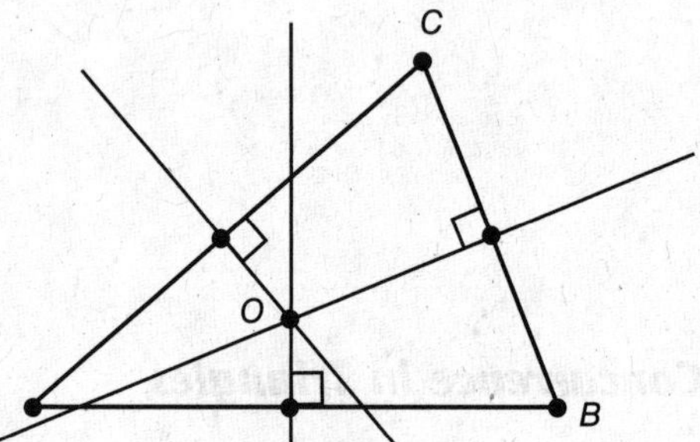

- **Euler Line Theorem:** The orthocenter H, the circumcenter O, and the centroid G of any triangle are collinear. The line that contains the three points is called the **Euler line.**

Some Theorems Involving Triangles

- **Exterior Angle Theorem:** In neutral geometry (and hence in Euclidean and non-Euclidean geometries), an exterior angle of ΔABC is greater than either of its remote interior angles.

    Proof: Extend one side of ΔABC, say $\overline{BC}$, and choose any point D on $\overrightarrow{BC}$ so that C lies between B and D. Then $\angle ACD$ (which does not contain point B in its interior) is an exterior angle of ΔABC. Then bisect $\overline{AC}$ and call the midpoint E. Draw $\overrightarrow{BE}$, and find point F on the ray so that $BE = EF$. Draw segment FC and $\overline{AC}$; choose a point G on the ray such that C lies between A and G (see Figure 4.49).

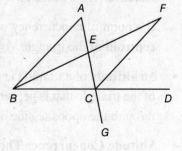

Figure 4.49

We know $\overline{AE} \cong \overline{EC}$ and $\overline{BE} = \overline{EF}$. Also, $\angle BEA \cong \angle FEC$ because they are vertical angles. Hence, $\triangle BEA \cong \triangle FEC$ by SAS. Thus, from CPCTC, $\angle BAE \cong \angle ECF$.

Note that $m\angle ACD > m\angle ECF$, so $m\angle ACD > m\angle BAE$.

We could repeat the same argument to show that $m\angle ACD > m\angle CAB$ by bisecting $\overline{CB}$ and following similar steps.

Q.E.D.

- **The Pythagorean Theorem**: For a right triangle, the sum of the squares of the lengths of the legs is equal to the square of the length of the hypotenuse.

  Proof (outline): Let $\triangle ABC$ be a right triangle with right angle at C, and let $\overline{CD}$ be the perpendicular from C to the hypotenuse $\overline{AB}$, as shown in Figure 4.50.

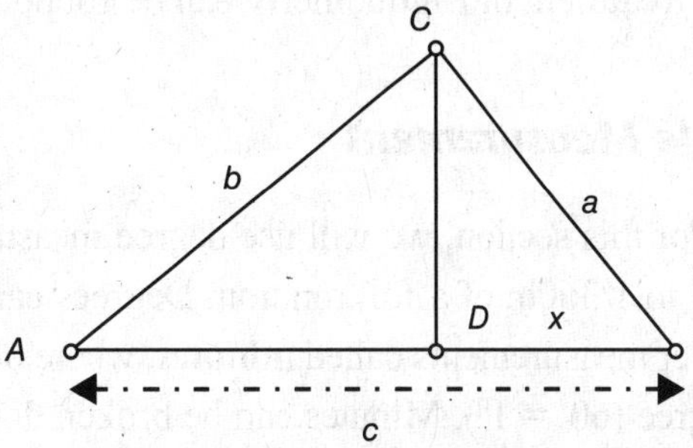

  Show $\triangle CAB$ is similar to $\triangle DAC$ and then show $\triangle CAB$ is similar to $\triangle DCB$.

Figure 4.50

Next, let $\overline{BD}$ have length x, so that AD has length $c - x$. Then, by similar triangles, $\dfrac{x}{a} = \dfrac{a}{c}$ and $\dfrac{c-x}{b} = \dfrac{b}{c}$. We can then eliminate x from these two equations to arrive at $a^2 + b^2 = c^2$.

Q.E.D.

- **Converse of the Pythagorean Theorem**: In a triangle, if the sum of the squares of the lengths of two sides is equal to the square of the length of the third side, then the triangle is a right triangle.

- **The Triangle Inequality Theorem**: In any triangle, the length of any side of a triangle is less than the sum of the lengths of the other two sides of the triangle. This is Euclid's Proposition 20, true in neutral geometry.

  Restatement: Given any triangle ABC, $BC < AB + AC$.

  Proof: Given $\triangle ABC$, extend side BA and choose point D on $\overrightarrow{BA}$ such $AD \cong AC$, as in Figure 4.51. Note that $m\angle BCD > m\angle DCA$. $\triangle ADC$ is isosceles and $\angle ABC \cong \angle DCA$, so $m\angle BCD > m\angle ADC$. The side opposite the greater angle is longer than the side opposite the smaller angle; hence, $BD > BC$. Note that $BD = AB + AD$. Using that $AD = AC$ by congruence, $AB + AC > BC$.

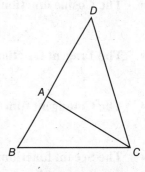

Figure 4.51

Q.E.D

Example: Is there a triangle with sides of length 2, 4, and 7 inches?

Note that $2 + 4 = 6$ is not greater than 7, so if there were such a triangle it would invalidate the Triangle Inequality. So there is no such triangle.

Some Trigonometry

We discuss right triangle ratios and the Law of Sines and Cosines in this section. A more thorough treatment of trigonometry can be found in Chapter 6.

Angle Measurement

For this section, we will use degree measurement of angles. A **degree** is an angle measurement equal to 1/360th of a full rotation. Degrees can be broken into smaller measurements called **minutes**, where 60 minutes equals 1 degree ($60' = 1°$). Minutes can be broken down into **seconds** ($60'' = 1'$).

Trigonometric Ratios

There are six trigonometric functions defined from a set of angle measurements to a ratio of the lengths of the sides of a right triangle. Consider $\triangle ABC$ in Figure 4.52.

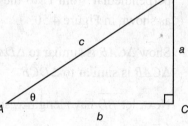

Figure 4.52

For these functions, $0 < \theta < 90°$.

- **The Sine function:** $\quad \sin(\theta) = \dfrac{BC}{AB} = \dfrac{\text{length of the side opposite } \angle A}{\text{length of the hypotenuse}} = \dfrac{opp}{hyp}$

- **The Cosine function:** $\quad \cos(\theta) = \dfrac{AC}{AB} = \dfrac{\text{length of the side adjacent to } \angle A}{\text{length of the hypotenuse}} = \dfrac{adj}{hyp}$

- **The Tangent function:** $\quad \tan(\theta) = \dfrac{BC}{AC} = \dfrac{\text{length of the side opposite } \angle A}{\text{length of the side adjacent to } \angle A} = \dfrac{opp}{adj}$

- **The Cotangent function:** $\cot(\theta) = \dfrac{AC}{BC} = \dfrac{\text{length of the side adjacent to} \angle A}{\text{length of the side opposite } \angle A} = \dfrac{adj}{opp}$

- **The Secant function:** $\quad \sec(\theta) = \dfrac{AB}{AC} = \dfrac{\text{length of the hypotenuse}}{\text{length of the side adjacent to } \angle A} = \dfrac{hyp}{adj}$

- **The Cosecant function:** $\quad \csc(\theta) = \dfrac{AB}{BC} = \dfrac{\text{length of the hypotenuse}}{\text{length of the side opposite } \angle A} = \dfrac{hyp}{opp}$

Some Identities

From the previous definitions, it is true that for all $0 < \theta < 90°$,

1. $\sin(\theta) = \dfrac{1}{\csc(\theta)}$

2. $\cos(\theta) = \dfrac{1}{\sec(\theta)}$

3. $\tan(\theta) = \dfrac{1}{\cot(\theta)} = \dfrac{\sin(\theta)}{\cos(\theta)}$

4. $\sin^2(\theta) + \cos^2(\theta) = 1$ (using the Pythagorean Theorem)

5. $\tan^2(\theta) + 1 = \sec^2(\theta)$ (divide identity (4) by $\cos^2(\theta)$)

6. $1 + \cot^2(\theta) = \csc^2(\theta)$ (divide identity (4) by $\sin^2(\theta)$)

Example: Suppose θ is an acute angle in a triangle such that $\cos(\theta) = \dfrac{1}{3}$. Use the identities to find the values of the other five trigonometric functions for θ.

$\sec(\theta) = 3$ because $\sec(\theta) = \dfrac{1}{\cos(\theta)}$. Since $\sin^2(\theta) + \cos^2(\theta) = 1$,

$\sin(\theta) = \sqrt{1 - \left(\dfrac{1}{3}\right)^2} = \dfrac{2\sqrt{2}}{3}$, which then since $\csc(\theta)$ is the reciprocal, $\csc(\theta) = \dfrac{3\sqrt{2}}{4}$.

$\tan(\theta) = \dfrac{\sin(\theta)}{\cos(\theta)} = 2\sqrt{2}$, and $\cot(\theta)$ is the reciprocal, which is $\dfrac{\sqrt{2}}{4}$.

Note: An alternative method of finding the values of the other trigonometric functions is to label a right triangle, use the Pythagorean Theorem to find the length of the third side of the triangle, and then use the triangle to find the values of the other five functions.

Special Right Triangles

30°–60°–90° Triangle

A 30°–60°–90° triangle is half an equilateral triangle, so the length of the base is half the length of the hypotenuse. Thus, if, as in Figure 4.53, we let the length of each side of the equilateral triangle equal 2, then the base of the right triangle has length 1. Then, using the Pythagorean Theorem, the altitude of the equilateral triangle, and the third side, h, of the 30°–60°–90° triangle is equal to $\sqrt{3}$. We can use this triangle to compute the values of the six trigonometric functions for $\theta = 30°$ and 60°. See Figure 4.55.

45°–45°–90° Triangle

A 45°–45°–90° triangle is an isosceles right triangle. Let the legs of the triangle have length 1, and then by the Pythagorean Theorem, the hypotenuse H has length $\sqrt{2}$ (Figure 4.54). We can use this triangle to compute the values of the six trigonometric functions for $\theta = 45°$. See Figure 4.55.

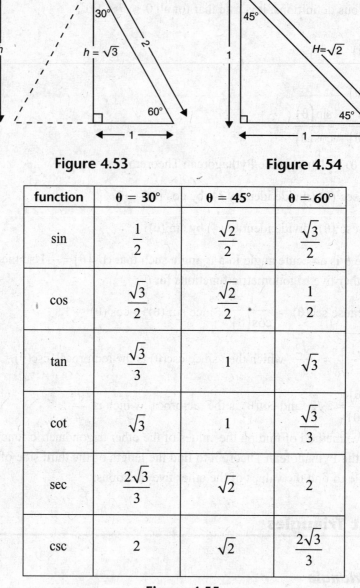

Figure 4.53   **Figure 4.54**

function	θ = 30°	θ = 45°	θ = 60°
sin	$\dfrac{1}{2}$	$\dfrac{\sqrt{2}}{2}$	$\dfrac{\sqrt{3}}{2}$
cos	$\dfrac{\sqrt{3}}{2}$	$\dfrac{\sqrt{2}}{2}$	$\dfrac{1}{2}$
tan	$\dfrac{\sqrt{3}}{3}$	1	$\sqrt{3}$
cot	$\sqrt{3}$	1	$\dfrac{\sqrt{3}}{3}$
sec	$\dfrac{2\sqrt{3}}{3}$	$\sqrt{2}$	2
csc	2	$\sqrt{2}$	$\dfrac{2\sqrt{3}}{3}$

Figure 4.55

Laws of Sines and Cosines

The Laws of Sines and Cosines are used for triangles that are not right triangles; the terminology for such triangles is **oblique.**

- An **acute** triangle is one in which all of the angles have measure less than 90°. An **obtuse** triangle is one in which there is an angle with measure greater than 90°.

- To solve oblique triangles, we will need to know the measure of at least one side and any two other parts of the triangle. Here are the four possible cases:

1. two angles and any side (AAS or ASA)

2. two sides and an angle opposite one of them (SSA, the **ambiguous case**)

3. three sides (SSS)

4. two sides and their included angle (SAS)

The first two cases can be solved by using the **Law of Sines**, and the second two cases can be solved by using the **Law of Cosines**.

- **Law of Sines**: Given $\triangle ABC$ with sides a, b, and c (Figure 4.56), it is true that

$$\frac{a}{\sin(A)} = \frac{b}{\sin(B)} = \frac{c}{\sin(C)}$$

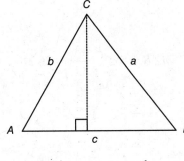

A is an acute angle

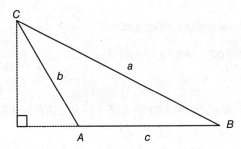

A is an obtuse angle

Figure 4.56

The Law of Sines can be used to find a side or angle of a triangle only if we are given one of the following sets of measures:

i. two sides and the non-included angle

ii. two angles and the side between them

iii. two angles and a side not included between them

Example: If $m\angle A = 35°$, $m\angle B = 15°$, and $c = 5$ inches, solve the triangle.

Solving the triangle means to find the missing measures. First $m\angle C = 180° - (35 + 15)°$ $= 130°$. Then we set up the extended proportion of the Law of Sines to find the sides:

$\dfrac{5}{\sin(130°)} = \dfrac{a}{\sin(35°)} = \dfrac{b}{\sin(15°)}$. Solving this proportion, we obtain $a = \dfrac{5\sin(35°)}{\sin(130°)} \approx 3.74$

inches and $b = \dfrac{5\sin(15°)}{\sin(130°)} \approx 1.69$ inches

- **Law of Cosines:** Given $\triangle ABC$ with sides a, b, and c, it is true that

$$\begin{cases} a^2 = b^2 + c^2 - 2bc\cos(A) \\ b^2 = a^2 + c^2 - 2ac\cos(B) \\ c^2 = a^2 + b^2 - 2ab\cos(C) \end{cases}$$

You will need to use the Law of Cosines if you are given the following measures:

   i.   two sides and the included angle

   ii.   three sides

Example: Given $a = 8$ cm, $b = 6$ cm, and $c = 12$ cm, solve the triangle.

Using the first equation of the Law of Cosines (we could start with any of them):

$$64 = 36 + 144 - 144\cos(A) \Rightarrow \cos(A) = \frac{116}{144} = \frac{29}{36} \Rightarrow m\angle A = \cos^{-1}\left(\frac{29}{36}\right) \approx 36.3°$$

Using the second equation:

$$36 = 64 + 144 - 192\cos(B) \Rightarrow \cos(B) = \frac{172}{192} = \frac{43}{48} \Rightarrow m\angle B = \cos^{-1}\left(\frac{43}{48}\right) \approx 26.38^c$$

Then $m\angle C = 180° - (36.3 + 26.38)° = 117.32°$

Review Problems for Section 4.2.2

1. In Figure 4.57, the medians of $\triangle ACE$, $\overline{AD}$, $\overline{EB}$, and $\overline{CF}$, meet at point G. If the length of $\overline{FG} = 12$ cm, what is the length, in centimeters, of $\overline{GC}$?

    (A) 24

    (B) 12

    (C) 6

    (D) 4

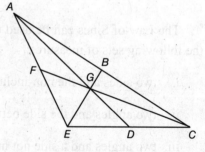

Figure 4.57

2. Prove a triangle is equilateral if and only if its centroid and circumcenter are the same point.

3. In $\triangle ABC$, $AB = 12$ ft, $BC = 16$ ft, and $m\angle BAC = 60°$. Find AC to the nearest tenth of a foot.

    (A) 10.5 ft

    (B) 13.7 ft

    (C) 15.9 ft

    (D) 18.2 ft

4. If $\sin(\alpha) = \dfrac{2}{5}$, where α is an acute angle in a right tri-angle, use the identities to find the values of the other five trigonometric functions for α.

5. If $\overline{CD} \perp \overline{AB}$ in Figure 4.58, what is the value of x to the nearest hundredth?

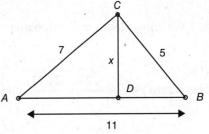

Figure 4.58

Detailed Solutions

1. (A)

The relationship between the lengths of the segments on the median, where G is the median, is $GC = 2FC = 24$.

2. Proof: ($\Rightarrow$) Assume $\triangle ABC$ is an equilateral triangle. To show that the centroid and the circumcenter are the same point, we can show that the medians are the perpendicular bisectors of the sides. So, referencing Figure 4.59, we know $AB \cong AC \cong BC$ because $\triangle ABC$ is equilateral, $BD \cong DC$ because AD is a median, and AD is congruent to itself, so $\triangle ABD \cong \triangle ACD$ by SSS. Thus, by CPCTC, $\angle ADB \cong \angle ADC$. But these angles are supplementary since they are a linear pair. Hence, $\angle ADB$ and $\angle ADC$ are right angles. So $AD \perp BC$. Therefore, the median is perpendicular to the opposite side. $\therefore$ The centroid must be the circumcenter.

($\Leftarrow$) Now suppose the centroid of $\triangle ABC$ is the same as the circumcenter. This implies that the median is perpendicular to the other side. So, referring to Figure 4.59, this means we know that $BD \cong DC$ since D must be the midpoint of side BC, $AD \perp BC$ so that $\angle ADB \cong \angle ADC$ and they are right angles, and $\overline{AD} \cong \overline{AD}$. Hence, $\triangle ABD \cong \triangle ACD$ by the Leg-Leg theorem. By CPCTC, $\overline{AB} \cong \overline{AC}$. We could repeat this argument using the median from point B to side AC to show that $AB \cong BC$. Then by transitivity, $\triangle ABC$ is an equilateral triangle.

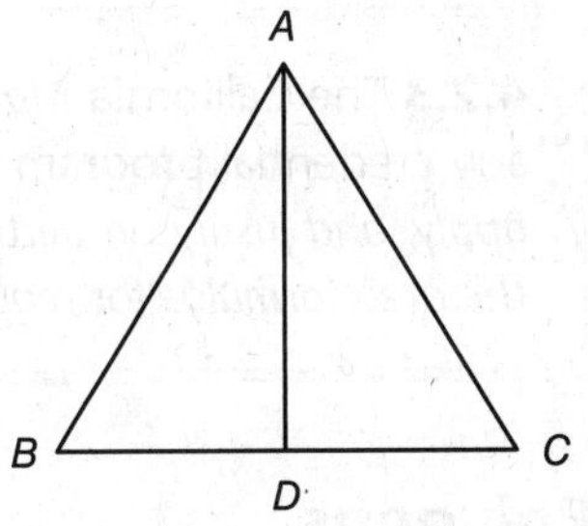

Figure 4.59

Q.E.D.

3. (D)

Since we are given SSA and we want the third side of the triangle, we must use the Law of Cosines: $BC^2 = AB^2 + AC^2 - 2(AB)(AC)\cos(A)$. Using x for AC:

$$256 = 144 + x^2 - 24x\left(\cos(60°)\right) \Rightarrow 0 = x^2 - 12x - 112 \quad \Rightarrow \quad x = \frac{12 \pm \sqrt{144 - (-448)}}{2}$$

$x = 6 \pm \dfrac{\sqrt{592}}{2} = 6 \pm 2\sqrt{37}$. Since x cannot be negative, we have $x = 6 + 2\sqrt{37} \approx 18.17$. The correct answer is (D).

4. We know $\sin(\alpha) = \dfrac{2}{5}$, so $\cos(\alpha) = \sqrt{1-\left(\dfrac{2}{5}\right)^2} = \dfrac{\sqrt{21}}{5}$.

Then $\tan(\alpha) = \dfrac{2}{5} \div \dfrac{\sqrt{21}}{5} = \dfrac{2\sqrt{21}}{21}$, $\cot(\alpha) = \dfrac{1}{\tan(\alpha)} = \dfrac{\sqrt{21}}{2}$, $\sec(\alpha) = \dfrac{1}{\cos(\alpha)} = \dfrac{5\sqrt{21}}{21}$, and

$\csc(\alpha) = \dfrac{1}{\sin(\alpha)} = \dfrac{5}{2}$.

5. Let $AD = y$, then $DB = 11 - y$. Using the Pythagorean Theorem on right triangles $\triangle ADC$ and $\triangle BDC$: $x^2 + y^2 = 49$ and $x^2 + (11 - y)^2 = 25$. Solving these simultaneously:

$(49 - y^2) + (121 - 22y + y^2) = 25 \implies 145 = 22y \implies y = \dfrac{145}{22}$. To find x, we substitute in the value

of y: so $x^2 + \left(\dfrac{145}{22}\right)^2 = 49 \implies x^2 \approx 5.5599$, so $x \approx 2.36$.

4.2.3 The California *Mathematics Subject Matter Requirements* stipulate that candidates for any credential program for teaching secondary mathematics must be able to *understand, apply, and justify properties of polygons and circles from an advanced standpoint (e.g., derive the area formulas for regular polygons and circles from the area of a triangle).*

Polygons

A **polygon** is the union of line segments all in the same plane such that each segment intersects exactly two others, one at each of its endpoints. The line segments are the **sides** of the polygon and the points where they intersect are called **vertices** (**vertex** is singular). A polygon has three or more sides.

A polygon has the same number of angles as sides. Some examples of polygons are shown in Figure 4.60.

Examples of Polygons

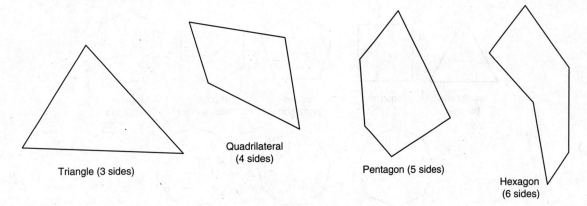

Triangle (3 sides)

Quadrilateral
(4 sides)

Pentagon (5 sides)

Hexagon
(6 sides)

Figure 4.60

- A polygon is **convex** if no line segment joining two points on the polygon contains a point in the exterior of the polygon. The only polygon in Figure 4.60 that is not convex is the hexagon. In a convex polygon, each interior angle is less than 180°.

- A polygon is **equilateral** if all of its sides have the same length.

- A polygon is **equiangular** if all of its angles are of equal measure.

- A **regular polygon** is a polygon that is both equilateral and equiangular.

Quadrilaterals

- A **rhombus** is an equilateral quadrilateral; i.e., it has four congruent sides.

- An equiangular quadrilateral has four right angles and is called a **rectangle**.

- A **square** is a quadrilateral that is both a rectangle and a rhombus.

- A quadrilateral with two pairs of adjacent congruent sides is called a **kite**.

- A quadrilateral with two pairs of opposite sides that are parallel is a **parallelogram.**

- A quadrilateral with exactly one pair of parallel sides is called a **trapezoid.**

Regular Polygons

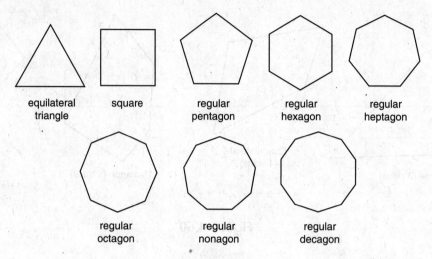

Figure 4.61

- A **diagonal** of a polygon is a line segment that joins two non-adjacent vertices.

- The number of diagonals that can be drawn from a single vertex of a polygon with n sides is $n - 3$; this polygon is generally called an ***n*-gon.** Figure 4.62 shows a hexagon ($n = 6$) with three diagonals drawn from one vertex. Note that these diagonals subdivide the area inside the hexagon into four triangular regions.

- **Theorem**: There are a total of $\dfrac{n(n-3)}{2}$ diagonals in an n-gon.

- **Theorem**: The sum of the measures of the interior angles of an n-gon is $(n-2)180°$.

- **Theorem**: The measure of one angle of a regular n-gon is $\dfrac{(n-2)180°}{n}$.

   Example: Consider the nonagon in Figure 4.63. Each interior angle has measure $\dfrac{7(180°)}{9} = 140°$.

- **Theorem**: The sum of the measures of the exterior angles of an n-gon is $360°$.

   This is easy to see for a regular n-gon. Each exterior angle of an n-gon is supplementary to an interior angle and so has measure $180° - \dfrac{(n-2)180°}{n} = \dfrac{360°}{n}$ (Figure 4.64).

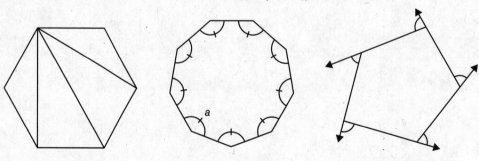

Figure 4.62   **Figure 4.63**   **Figure 4.64**

- The **perimeter** of a polygon is the sum of the lengths of the sides.

- The **perimeter of a regular *n*-gon** is $P = ns$, where s is the length of one side.

Areas of Regular Polygons

- The **apothem** of a regular polygon is the distance from the center of the polygon to a side. The word *apothem* often refers to the line segment itself. This segment is perpendicular to a side of the polygon (Figure 4.65).

- The **area of a regular polygon** is given by

$$A = \frac{1}{2}aP$$

where P is the perimeter of the polygon and a is the apothem. This can be seen by considering a regular polygon with *n*-sides. If the *n* radii of the *n*-gon are drawn from the center, the *n*-gon is partitioned into *n* isosceles triangles, each with area $\frac{1}{2}a \cdot s$, where s is the length of a side of the polygon (Figure 4.66). Taking the sum of these *n* triangles gives the area of the regular *n*-gon as $A = \frac{1}{2}a \cdot ns = \frac{1}{2}a \cdot P$.

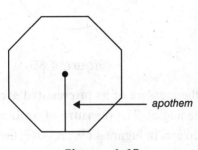

Figure 4.65

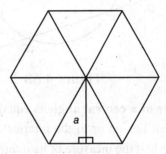

Figure 4.66

Circles

- A circle is the set of points in a plane that are equidistant from a given point called the **center** of the circle. The distance from the center to the points on the circle is the **radius**, *r*, of the circle. The word *radius* is also often used to represent the segment interior to the circle with one endpoint at the center of the circle and the other on the circle (Figure 4. 67).

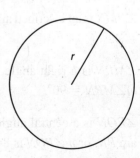

Figure 4.67

- A **chord** of a circle is a line segment that joins two points on the circle. The longest chord is the **diameter**, which joins two **antipodal points**. In Figure 4.68, $\overline{AB}$ and $\overline{EF}$ are chords of circle O that are not diameters, and $\overline{JD}$ is a diameter.

- A **secant** is a line that intersects a circle in two points. In Figure 4.68, $\overrightarrow{GE}$ is a secant line of circle O.

- A **tangent** is a line that intersects the circle at one point. Line $\overleftrightarrow{HC}$ is a tangent line to circle O in Figure 4.68. Point C is called the **point of tangency**.

- **Theorem**: If a chord is perpendicular to a radius of the circle, then the radius bisects the chord.

- **Theorem**: If two chords are equidistant from the center of a circle, they are congruent.

- **Theorem**: Any pair of opposite angles in a quadrilateral inscribed in a circle are supplementary.

- An angle with vertex at the center of a circle is called a **central angle**, and an **inscribed angle** is formed by two chords in a circle with a common endpoint. In Figure 4.69, $\angle APB$ is a central angle of circle P and $\angle DEC$ is an inscribed angle.

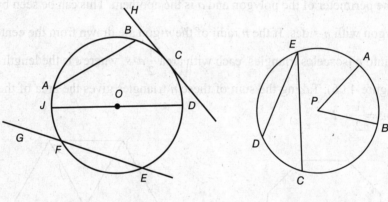

Figure 4.68　　　　**Figure 4.69**

- The **measure of a central angle** is equal to the measure of its **intercepted arc** (the portion of the circle that lies on or in the interior of the angle). The **measure of an inscribed angle** is equal to one-half the measure of its intercepted arc. In Figure 4.69, arc AB is the intercepted arc of central $\angle APB$, and arc CD is the intercepted arc of incribed $\angle DEC$.

Example: In Figure 4.70, arc MP has measure 96°, and arc PN has measure 84°. Find the measure of $\angle PMN$, $\angle MPN$, and $\angle PQN$.

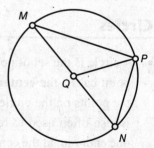

Figure 4.70

$\angle PMN$ is an inscribed angle, so its measure is half of arc PN, or $m\angle PMN = 42°$.

$\angle MPN$ is a right angle because its intercepted arc is a semi-circle, so $m\angle MPN = 90°$.

$\angle PQN$ is a central angle, so its measure is the same as its intercepted arc PN, or $m\angle PQN$ is 84°.

- The measure of an angle formed by the intersection of a chord and a tangent at the point of tangency is one half the measure of the intercepted arc.

- The measure of an angle formed by two chords intersecting in the interior of a circle is one-half the sum of the intercepted arcs.

- The measure of an angle formed by two tangents, or two chords, or a chord and a tangent, that intersect in the exterior of a circle is one-half the difference of the intercepted arcs.

- For any two non-antipodal points X and Y, on a circle, two arcs are formed. An arc XY with lesser measure is called the **minor arc XY**, and the arc with greater measure is called **major arc XY**.

  Example: In Figure 4.71, the measures of arcs PS and QS are $165°$ and $53°$, respectively. The measure of $\angle U$ is $42°$. Find the measures of minor arc VT and $\angle R$.

  The measure of $\angle U$ is one half the difference between the measures of major arc VT and minor arc VT. Let x be the measure of the minor arc; then the measure of the major arc is $360° - x$, so $42° = (360° - x) - x$, and $x = 159°$.

  The measure of $\angle R = \frac{1}{2}(165° - 53°) = 56°$.

- A triangle is **inscribed** in a circle if all of its angles are inscribed angles (Figure 4.72).

- **Theorem**: A triangle inscribed in the circle with one side a diameter is a right triangle (Figure 4.72).

- **Theorem**: In a circle with chords $\overline{DB}$ and $\overline{AC}$ intersecting at interior point P, $DP \cdot PB = AP \cdot PC$ (Figure 4.73).

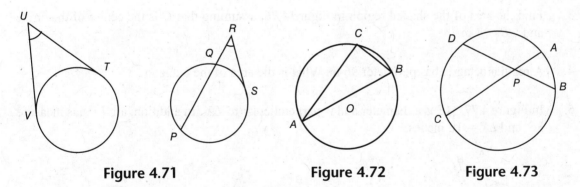

| Figure 4.71 | Figure 4.72 | Figure 4.73 |

- The **circumference** (perimeter) **of a circle** is $C = 2\pi r$. This formula can be derived by using limits and trigonometry or arc length and integrals in calculus.

- The **area of a circle** is given by the formula $A = \pi r^2$.

  To see where this formula comes from, consider that the area of a regular n-gon inscribed in a circle has area $A = \frac{1}{2}aP$, where a is the apothem and P is the perimeter of the n-gon (Figure 4.74). As n increases and becomes very large, the apothem becomes closer and closer to the radius of the circle while the perimeter of the n-gon becomes closer and closer to the circumference of the circle. Hence,

$$\text{the area of a circle} = \lim_{n \to \infty}(\text{the area of an } n\text{-gon}) = \lim_{n \to \infty}\frac{1}{2}a\,P = \frac{1}{2}r \cdot C = \frac{1}{2}r \cdot 2\pi r = \pi r^2.$$

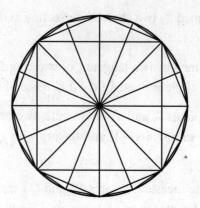

Figure 4.74

Theorem: In a plane, two distinct circles intersect in at most two points.

◼ Review Problems for Section 4.2.3

1. Regular pentagon *LMNOP* is formed by joining the midpoints of the sides of regular pentagon *ABCDE* (Figure 4.75). What is $m\angle AML$?

2. A regular polygon has an exterior angle with measure 15°. How many sides does the polygon have?

3. Find the area of the shaded region in Figure 4.76, assuming that *O* is the center of the circle and $OB = 3$ m.

4. A regular octagon has perimeter 96 in. What is the area of the octagon?

5. In Figure 4.77, $\overline{AE}$ is a diameter and is perpendicular to $\overline{LX}$. In addition, arc *LE* has measure 36° and $LX = 10$ inches.

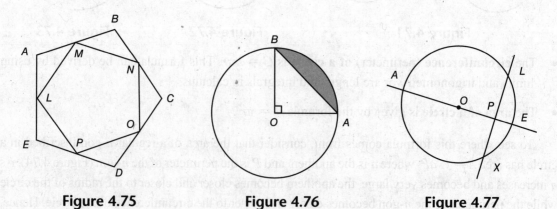

Figure 4.75   **Figure 4.76**   **Figure 4.77**

What is the length of $\overline{PX}$ and what is the measure of arc *AL*?

6. If the area of a circle is 20π square yards, what is the circumference of the circle?

7. Prove: If a chord is perpendicular to a radius of a circle, then the radius bisects the chord.

Detailed Solutions

1. $\triangle AML$ is an isosceles triangle, so $\angle AML \cong \angle ALM$. Since the pentagon is regular, $m\angle MAL = \dfrac{3(180^\circ)}{5} = 108^\circ$. Thus, $m\angle AML = (180^\circ - 108^\circ)/2 = 36^\circ$.

2. The sum of the measures of the exterior angles of a polygon is 360°, and since a regular polygon has congruent exterior angles, each angle has measure $\dfrac{360^\circ}{n}$, where n is the number of sides. So, if an exterior angle has measure 15°, the regular polygon has $360/15 = 24$ sides.

3. The area of the circle is $A = \pi(3)^2 = 9\pi$ square meters. So a quarter of the circle has area 2.25π square meters. The triangle ABO has area $\dfrac{1}{2}(3)(3) = 2.25$ square meters. The area of the shaded region is equal to the area of the quarter of the circle minus the area of the triangle ABO, which is $(2.25\pi - 2.25)$ square meters.

4. If a regular octagon has perimeter equal to 96 inches, then each side has length $96/8 = 12$ inches. Each of the triangles with vertex at the center O of the octagon and other two vertices as consecutive vertices of the octagon is an isosceles triangle with base equal to 12 (Figure 4.78). The altitude of the triangle is a; this is the apothem's length. Consider right triangle OAB. Since $m\sphericalangle AOP = \dfrac{360^\circ}{8} = 45^\circ$, $m\sphericalangle POB = 22.5^\circ$. Thus, $\tan 22.5^\circ = \dfrac{6}{a}$ or $a = \dfrac{6}{\tan 22.5} \approx 14.49$. Hence, the area of the regular octagon is $\dfrac{1}{2}aP \approx \dfrac{1}{2}(14.44)(96) \approx 695.52$ square inches.

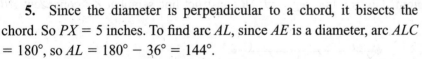

Figure 4.78

5. Since the diameter is perpendicular to a chord, it bisects the chord. So $PX = 5$ inches. To find arc AL, since AE is a diameter, arc $ALC = 180^\circ$, so $AL = 180^\circ - 36^\circ = 144^\circ$.

6. We know that $\pi r^2 = 20\pi$, so $r = 2\sqrt{5}$ yards. Thus, the circumference of the circle is $C = 2\pi r = 4\sqrt{5}\pi$ yards.

7. We can restate this problem in terms of Figure 4.77: If $\overline{XL} \perp \overline{OE}$, where O is the center of the circle, then $\overline{LP} \cong \overline{PX}$.

Proof: Assume $\overline{XL} \perp \overline{OE}$ and O is the center of the circle. Then $\angle LPO$ and $\angle XPO$ are right angles. Since (not shown) $\overline{OX}$ and $\overline{OL}$ are both radii of circle O, they are congruent. By reflexivity, $\overline{OP}$ is congruent to itself. By the HL theorem, $\Delta LOP \cong \Delta XOP$. Hence, using CPCTC, $\overline{LP} \cong \overline{XP}$.

Q.E.D.

4.2.4 The California *Mathematics Subject Matter Requirements* stipulate that candidates for any credential program for teaching secondary mathematics must be able to *justify and perform the classical constructions (e.g., angle bisector, perpendicular bisector, replicating shapes, regular n-gons for n equal to 3, 4, 5, 6, and 8).*

Geometric Constructions

A **geometric construction** is a task in which, given some geometric elements such as points, segments, angles, or circles, other objects are drawn by using a straightedge and compass. In ancient times, people used geometric constructions to measure and copy figures for architectural and artistic purposes. Euclid set up the rules of construction with a straightedge and compass with his first three axioms:

1. *A straight line may be drawn between any two points.*

2. *A piece of straight line may be extended indefinitely.*

3. *A circle may be drawn with any given radius and an arbitrary center.*

The first two rules involve using only the straightedge, whereas the third rule uses the compass. A straightedge is not a ruler; it has no markings of measurement on it.

- **Copying a line segment:** Given a line segment AB construct line segment KY congruent $\overline{AB}$ (Figure 4.79).

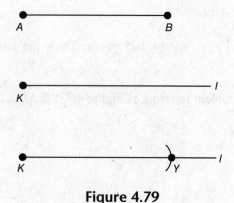

Figure 4.79

1. Using a straightedge, draw a line segment, *l*, on which you wish to construct the segment *KY*. Label an endpoint *K*.

2. Place the point of the compass at *A*. Open the compass so that the pencil end is on point *B*. Now place the point of the opened compass at point *K*. Make an arc through the line *l*. Mark the point of intersection *Y*.

    $\therefore \overline{AB} = \overline{KY}$

- **Copying a circle:** Given a line segment $\overline{AB}$ with $AB = r$ and a point *O*, construct a circle with center at *O* and radius *r* (Figure 4.80).

    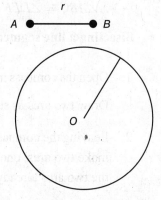

1. Open the compass the width of *AB* by placing the compass point at point *A* and the pencil end at point *B*.

2. Place the compass point at point *O*, leaving the compass opening as found in step 1, and draw the circle with this radius.

- **Copying an angle:** Given ∠*ABC*, and a line *l*, construct ∠*DEF* on line *l* congruent to ∠*ABC* (Figures 4.81A and B).

    Figure 4.80

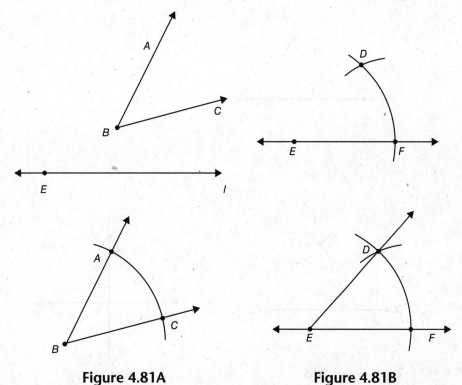

Figure 4.81A   **Figure 4.81B**

1. Choose a point *E* on line *l*.

2. Place the compass point on point *B* and draw an arc so that it intersects both sides of ∠*ABC* and passes through the interior of ∠*ABC*. Set the compass opening to the length of $\overline{BC}$.

3. Now place the compass point at point E, leaving the compass opening as found in step 2, and draw a large arc through l. Label the point F where the arc passes through l. Now place the point of the compass at point F and draw an arc that intersects the large arc; label the point of intersection D.

4. Use the straightedge to draw in ray $\overline{ED}$.

$$\therefore \angle ABC \cong \angle DEF$$

- **Bisecting a line segment:** Given $\overline{AB}$, find its midpoint (Figures 4.82A and B).

1. Open the compass more than $\dfrac{1}{2} AB$ but less than AB. Place the point of the compass at point A. Draw two arcs as shown, one above the line segment and one below.

2. Leaving the compass open as it was in step 1, place the point of the compass on point B and make two arcs, one above the line segment and one below, each of which intersects one of the two arcs already there. Label the two points of intersection P and Q.

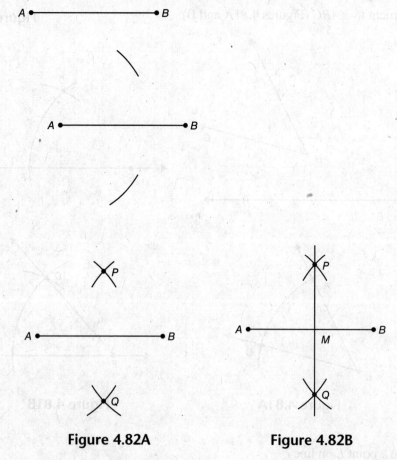

| **Figure 4.82A** | **Figure 4.82B** |

3. Draw a line through points P and Q. Label the point of intersection of $\overline{AB}$ and $\overline{PQ}$, M.

$$\therefore M \text{ is the midpoint of } \overline{AB}.$$

- **Bisecting an Angle:** Given $\angle PQR$, bisect $\angle PQR$ (Figures 4.83A and B).

  1. Open the compass the length of $\overline{QP}$. Place the point of the compass on point Q and then draw an arc through both sides of $\angle PQR$. Label the point S where the arc intersects $\overrightarrow{QR}$.

  2. Leaving the compass open the same width as in step 1, place the compass point on P and make a small arc in the interior of $\angle PQR$, as shown in Figure 4.83A. Then, placing the point of the compass on point S, make another small arc in the interior of the angle that intersects the first arc.

  3. Draw the ray from point Q through point T, as shown in Figure 4.83B.

  $\therefore \angle PQT \cong \angle TQS$

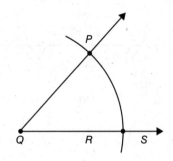

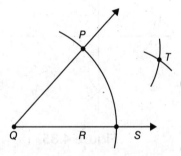
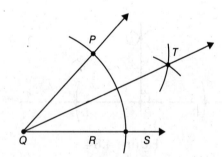

Figure 4.83A   **Figure 4.83B**

- **Constructing a perpendicular through a given point on a given line:** Given line k with point P on k, construct a line through P perpendicular to k (Figure 4.84).

  1. Open the compass a comfortable amount, place the compass point on point P, and then draw a small arc on each side of P that intersects line k. Label these points C and D.

  2. Open the compass width more than the amount it was open in step 1. Place the compass point on C and draw a small arc above the line. Place the compass point on point D and draw a small arc above the line that intersects the first arc; label this point Q.

  3. Draw a line through points P and Q.

  $\therefore \overline{PQ} \perp \overleftrightarrow{k}$

- **Constructing a perpendicular through a given point not on a given line:** Given line k with point P not on k, construct a line through P perpendicular to k (Figure 4.85).

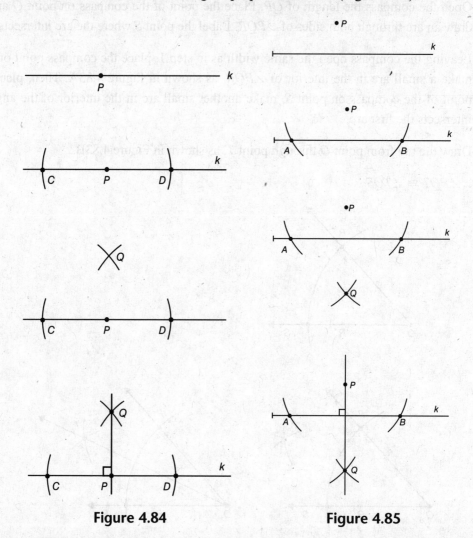

Figure 4.84   **Figure 4.85**

1. Open the compass enough so that when the compass point is on point P, the pencil will reach a bit below line k. Swing the compass so that it makes two small arcs through line k as shown in the figure. Label the two points of intersection A and B.

2. Place the compass point on point A and make a small arc on the other side of line k. Repeat this with the compass point on point B such that the second arc intersects the first arc. Mark the point of intersection Q.

3. Draw a line through points P and Q.

   $$\therefore \overline{PQ} \perp \overline{AB}$$

- **Constructing a line parallel to a given line through a given point:** Given line l with point P not on it, construct a line through P parallel to l (Figure 4.86).

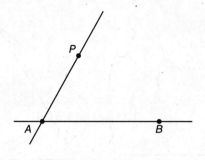

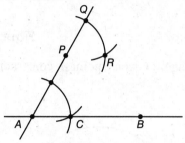

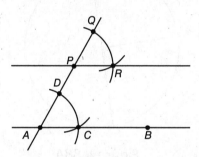

Figure 4.86

1. With a straightedge, draw a line through point P that intersects line l. Label the point of intersection A. Also label another point on l as B so that $\angle PAB$ is an acute angle.

2. Copy $\angle PAB$ at point P so that $\angle QPR$ is congruent to $\angle PAB$, thereby having the corresponding angles congruent.

    $\therefore \overrightarrow{PR} \parallel \overrightarrow{AB}$

- **Constructing an equilateral triangle**: Given a line segment $\overline{AB}$, construct an equilateral triangle with all sides congruent to $\overline{AB}$ (Figures 4.87A and B).

1. Open the compass the length of $\overline{AB}$. Then, placing the point of the compass on A, make an arc above the middle of $\overline{AB}$. Placing the point of the compass on point B, make another arc above $\overline{AB}$ that intersects the first arc; label this point C.

2. Using point C as the third vertex, draw $\overline{AC}$ and $\overline{BC}$.

    $\therefore \Delta ABC$ is an equilateral triangle.

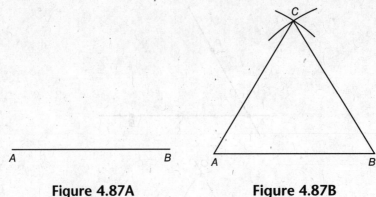

Figure 4.87A   **Figure 4.87B**

- **Constructing a regular pentagon**: Given a point A, construct a regular pentagon with A as the center (Figures 4.88A and B).

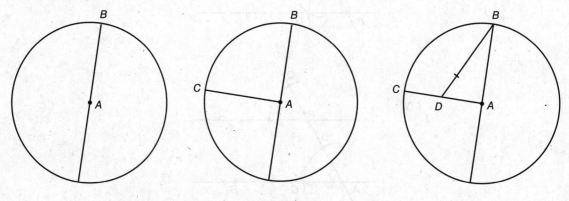

Figure 4.88A

1. Viewing A as the center, use your compass to draw a circle of any comfortable radius. This circle will circumscribe the pentagon. Draw a diameter through point A, labeling one of the endpoints as B. (Figure 4.88A left)

2. Construct radius $\overline{AC} \perp \overline{AB}$. (Figure 4.88A middle)

3. Find the midpoint of $\overline{AC}$ by constructing the perpendicular bisector of $\overline{AC}$. Label it D. Draw $\overline{BD}$. (Figure 4.88A right)

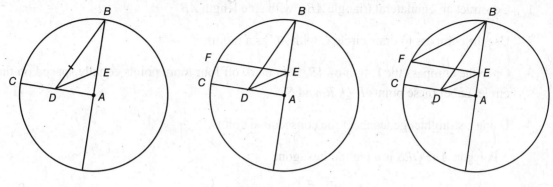

Figure 4.88B

4. Bisect ∠*BDA*. Mark the point *E* where the angle bisector intersects $\overline{AB}$. (Figure 4.88B left)

5. Construct a line parallel to $\overline{AC}$ through point *E*. Label the point *F* where this line intersects the circle on the same side of line $\overline{AB}$. (Figure 4.88B middle)

6. Draw segment $\overline{FB}$. This is one side of the pentagon. (Figure 4.88B right)

7. Open the compass the length of $\overline{FB}$ and then, placing the point of the compass on point *F*, make an arc that intersects the circle below *F*; label the point *G*. Repeat this with the point of the compass at *G*, and continue, labeling the last vertex *I*. (Figure 4.88C)

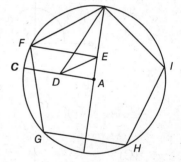

8 Using a straightedge, connect the consecutive points.

∴Polygon *BFGHI* is a regular pentagon.

- **Constructing a regular hexagon given a side:** Given a line segment *AB* construct a regular hexagon with *AB* as a side (Figures 4.89A and B).

Figure 4.88C

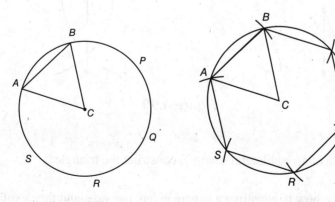

Figure 4.89A   **Figure 4.89B**

1. Construct an equilateral triangle *ABC* with side length *AB*.

2. Use the compass to draw circle *C* with *AC* as a radius.

3. Open the compass the length of *AB*, then mark off four more points equally spaced on the circle. Label these points *P, Q, R,* and *S*.

4. Using a straightedge, connect the consecutive points.

∴ Polygon *ABPQRS* is a regular hexagon.

Review Problems for Section 4.2.4

1. Which diagram in Figure 4.90 shows the construction of the perpendicular bisector of $\overline{AB}$?

(A)   (B)

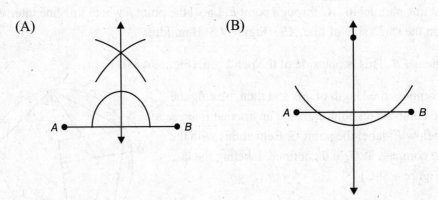

(C)   (D)

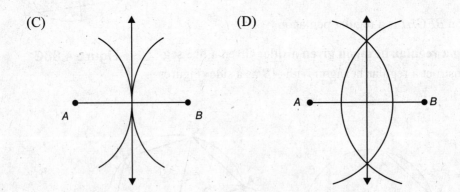

Figure 4.90

2. Given the altitude of an equilateral triangle, construct the triangle.

3. In words, describe how to construct a square given one side, and then explain how you know it is a square.

4. Given a line segment, construct a regular octagon with the line segment as a diagonal.

Detailed Solutions

1. (D)

Given a line segment, we need to find two points off the line segment through which the perpendicular bisector will pass. Then once the bisector is drawn, we can see the midpoint of the given segment. In (A) and (C), it appears that we already know where the midpoint is. In (B), a point off the line was given to start.

2. Follow these steps:

• Start with a line segment that will be the altitude of the equilateral triangle. This could be a given segment or one you draw yourself. Arrange the paper so that the segment is vertical (Figures 4.91 A and B).

• Next, construct a perpendicular line through point A.

• Open the compass a distance less than the length of $\overline{AB}$ and construct the vertices of an equilateral triangle BEF similar to the construction shown in Figures 4.87A and B. This creates a 60° angle at B, and $\triangle BEF$ is equilateral. Extend the sides to form $\overline{BC}$ and $\overline{BD}$.

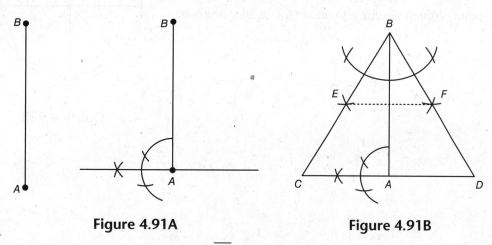

Figure 4.91A   **Figure 4.91B**

∴ $\triangle BCD$ is an equilateral triangle with $\overline{AB}$ as the altitude.

3. Construct a square in this way: Starting with a segment $\overline{AB}$, construct a line perpendicular to AB through A. Open the compass to the length AB and, placing your compass point on point A, mark this length off along the new segment above A. Call this point C. Now, leaving the compass open the length AB, place the compass point on B and make an arc above point B. Then place the compass point on point C and make an arc that intersects the first arc; the point of intersection is the fourth vertex of the square, point D.

We have constructed a quadrilateral with four congruent sides and one right angle. If we call this quadrilateral $ABCD$ with angle B being the known right angle, we can prove $\triangle ABC \cong \triangle CDA$, by using the SSS theorem. Then $\angle D$ would also be a right angle by the CPCTC theorem. Next we could use CPCTC to state that $\angle DAC \cong \angle BCA$; these angles are alternate interior angles; hence,

the opposite sides $\overline{AD}$ and $\overline{BC}$ are parallel. But then it follows that
angles $\angle A$ and $\angle C$ are also right angles since interior angles on the
same side of the transversal (the diagonal) are supplementary. Therefore, quadrilateral $ABCD$ is a square.

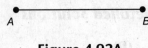

Figure 4.92A

4. Given line segment $\overline{AB}$, construct a regular octagon with
AB as a diagonal.

1. First construct the perpendicular bisector of $\overline{AB}$ to find
the midpoint M (Figures 4.92A and B).

2. Then draw the circle with center M and radius MB. Label the ends of the perpendicular bisector as C and D.

3. Construct the angle bisectors of $\angle CMA$ and $\angle CMB$.
Mark the two points of intersection with each bisector
and the circle.

4. Then use a straightedge to connect the eight consecutive
points around the circle to obtain the regular octagon.

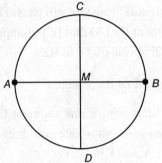

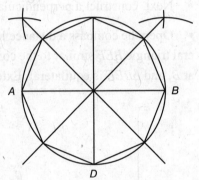

Figure 4.92B

> **4.2.5** The California *Mathematics Subject Matter Requirements* stipulate that candidates
> for any credential program for teaching secondary mathematics must be able to *use tech-*
> *niques in coordinate geometry to prove geometric theorems.*

Coordinate Geometry

Coordinate geometry involves studying geometric concepts using algebraic methods. These
methods utilize the coordinates in the two- or three-dimensional coordinate system.

The two-dimensional coordinate system is also called the **Cartesian plane** (Figure 4.93). The Cartesian plane has two perpendicular lines, which serve as the **axes**. **The horizontal axis** is called the *x*-axis, and **the vertical axis** is the *y*-axis. The point of intersection of these two lines is called the **origin**.

Quadrants

- Points that lie above the *x*-axis and to the right of the *y*-axis are said to be in the first quadrant, or **Quadrant I**.

- Points that lie above the *x*-axis and to the left of the *y*-axis are said to be in the second quadrant, or **Quadrant II**.

- Points that lie below the *x*-axis and to the left of the *y*-axis are said to be in the third quadrant, or **Quadrant III**.

- Points that lie below the *x*-axis and to the right of *y*-axis are said to be in the fourth quadrant, or **Quadrant IV**.

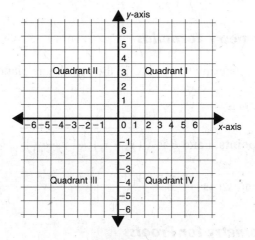

Figure 4.93

Each point in the plane has a unique pair of real numbers (a, b) assigned to it; the first coordinate, or the **x-coordinate**, indicates the point's horizontal distance from the *y*-axis, and the second coordinate, or the **y-coordinate**, gives the point's vertical distance from the *x*-axis. A negative first coordinate means the point is to the left of the *y*-axis, whereas a positive *x*-coordinate shows that the point is to the right of the *y*-axis; a first coordinate of 0 indicates that the point is on the *y*-axis. Similarly, a negative second coordinate means the point is below the *x*-axis, whereas a positive *y*-coordinate shows that the point is above the *x*-axis; a second coordinate of 0 indicates that the point is on the *x*-axis.

Figure 4.94 shows how the coordinates represent the different points. The Cartesian plane is also called the **rectangular coordinate system**; this is due to being able to travel from the origin to a point in a rectangular fashion. For example, in Figure 4.95, to reach a point(2,3) from the origin, we could move first two units right then three units upwards, or starting at the origin, we could move three units upward and then two units right. These paths form a rectangle.

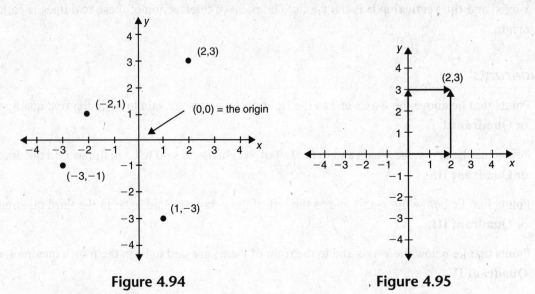

Figure 4.94   **Figure 4.95**

Some Coordinate Geometry Formulas

Let $A(x_1, y_1)$ and $B(x_2, y_2)$ be any two points in the coordinate plane.

- The **slope of line** $\overrightarrow{AB}$ is $m = \dfrac{y_2 - y_1}{x_2 - x_1}$.

- The **distance between points** A and B is $\sqrt{\left(x_2 - x_1\right)^2 + \left(y_2 - y_1\right)^2}$.

- The **midpoint** of segment $\overline{AB}$ is $\left(\dfrac{x_1 + x_2}{2}, \dfrac{y_1 + y_2}{2}\right)$.

Using Coordinate Geometry for Proofs

Coordinate systems can make geometric ideas easier to prove and clearer to understand. The first step is to set up an illustration using the coordinate plane. If possible, have the geometric figure include the origin. Assign coordinates to the given points. Next, rewrite the statement you wish to prove in terms of the coordinate illustration. Then use coordinate formulas such as those for the slope, distance, and midpoint, along with other known concepts, to establish the conclusion.

Examples

(a) Prove that quadrilateral *ABCD* with vertices *A*(1,2), *B*(2,5), *C*(5,7), and *D*(4,4) is a parallelogram.

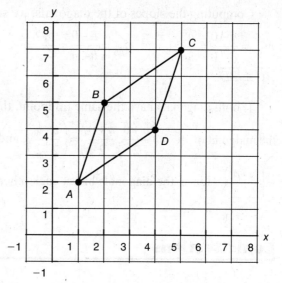

Proof: Consider the four points *A*(1,2), *B*(2,5), *C*(5,7), and *D*(4,4) and the quadrilateral *ABCD* in Figure 4.96.

We compute the following slopes:

$$m_{\overline{AB}} = \frac{5-2}{2-1} = 3$$

$$m_{\overline{DC}} = \frac{7-4}{5-4} = 3$$

$$m_{\overline{AD}} = \frac{4-2}{4-1} = \frac{2}{3}$$

$$m_{\overline{BC}} = \frac{7-5}{5-2} = \frac{2}{3}$$

Figure 4.96

Since lines with equal slopes are parallel, we have two pairs of opposite sides parallel.

Hence, quadrilateral *ABCD* is a parallelogram.

Q.E.D.

(b) Prove: The diagonals of a square are congruent and are perpendicular bisectors of each other.

First we draw a coordinate illustration (Figure 4.97).

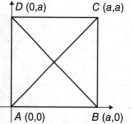

Figure 4.97

Then we restate the problem with respect to the picture.

Given square *ABCD* in Figure 4.97 with diagonals $\overline{AC}$ and $\overline{BD}$, prove $\overline{AC} \cong \overline{BD}$, $\overline{AC} \perp \overline{BD}$, and $\overline{AC}$ and $\overline{BD}$ bisect each other.

Proof: Consider square *ABCD* with diagonals $\overline{AC}$ and $\overline{BD}$, where the points have coordinates *A*(0,0), *B*(a,0), *C*(a,a), and *D*(0,a).

Using the distance formula, we obtain:

$$AC = \sqrt{(a-0)^2 + (a-0)^2} = \sqrt{2a^2} = \sqrt{2}a$$

$$BD = \sqrt{(a-0)^2 + (0-a)^2} = \sqrt{2a^2} = \sqrt{2}a$$

$$\therefore \overline{AC} \cong \overline{BD}$$

Computing the slopes of the diagonals, we see:

$m_{\overline{AC}} = \dfrac{a-0}{a-0} = \dfrac{a}{a} = 1$ and $m_{\overline{BD}} = \dfrac{a-0}{0-a} = \dfrac{a}{-a} = -1$, and since the slopes are negative reciprocals, $\overline{AC} \perp \overline{BD}$.

If both diagonals have the same midpoint, then they bisect each other. To this end, the midpoint of $\overline{AC} = \left(\dfrac{a+0}{2}, \dfrac{a+0}{2} \right) = \left(\dfrac{a}{2}, \dfrac{a}{2} \right)$, and the midpoint of $\overline{BD} = \left(\dfrac{a+0}{2}, \dfrac{0+a}{2} \right)$

$= \left(\dfrac{a}{2}, \dfrac{a}{2} \right)$. Hence, the diagonals bisect each other.

Q.E.D.

Conic Sections

Conic sections are the plane curves formed by the intersection of a plane and a right circular double cone. There are four non-degenerate conic sections: the parabola, ellipse, circle, and hyperbola; these are illustrated in Figure 4.98. There also some degenerate conic sections, which are (i) the empty set, (ii) one point, (iii) one line, and (iv) two lines. We are most interested in the non-degenerate conic sections, which we discuss next.

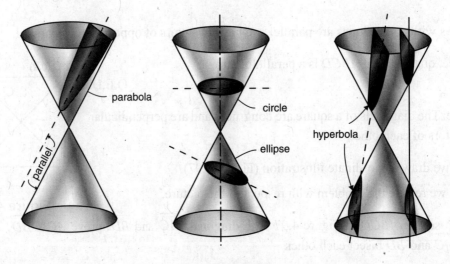

Figure 4.98

The Parabola

A **parabola** is a **locus** (collection) of points in the plane, each of which is equidistant from a fixed line (the **directrix**) and a fixed point (the **focus**). The line that passes through the focus and is perpendicular to the directrix is the **line of symmetry**. The point where the axis of symmetry intersects the parabola is called the **vertex** of the parabola.

• The standard forms of the equation of a parabola with vertex (h, k) are

i. $y = a(x - h)^2 + k$ if the graph opens upward ($a > 0$) or downward ($a < 0$).

ii. $x = b(y - k)^2 + h$ if the graph opens to the right ($b > 0$) or to the left ($b < 0$).

- The vertex is the point which is half the distance from the focus to the directrix.

- Define $p = \dfrac{1}{4a}$.

- In case (i) the focus is $(h, k + p)$, the directrix is $y = k - p$, and the axis of symmetry is $x = h$.

- In case (ii) the focus is $(h + p, k)$, the directrix is $x = h - p$, and the axis of symmetry is $y = k$.

Example: Describe and graph the locus $y = -3\left(x + 5\right)^2 + 2$.

This is a downward-opening parabola with vertex $(-5, 2)$, focus $\approx (-5, 1.9166)$, directrix $y \approx 2.0833\ldots$, and axis of symmetry $x = -5$.

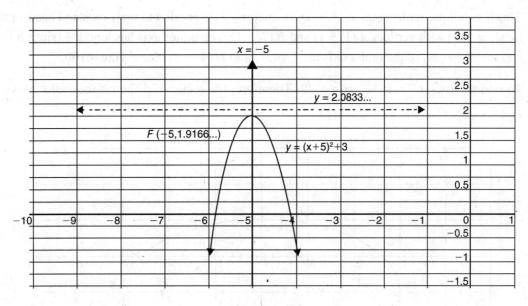

Figure 4.99

The Ellipse

An **ellipse** is a locus in the plane, the sum of whose distances from two fixed points (the **foci**, plural of focus) is a constant. The midpoint of the line segment between the foci is called the **center** of the ellipse.

- The standard form of the equation of an ellipse with center (h, k) is

$$\frac{\left(x - h\right)^2}{a^2} + \frac{\left(y - k\right)^2}{b^2} = 1.$$

i.   If $a > b$, then the vertices of the ellipse are $(a + h, k)$ and $(-a + h, k)$, which are the endpoints of the **major axis** of the ellipse (length $2a$). The **minor axis** has length $2b$ and has endpoints $(h, k + b)$ and $(h, k - b)$.

In this case, $c^2 = a^2 - b^2$, where c is the distance between a focus and the center, and the foci are $(h + c, k)$ and $(h - c, k)$.

The sum of the distances from the foci to any point on the ellipse is $2a$.

ii.   If $a < b$, then the vertices are $(h, k + b)$ and $(h, k - b)$, which are the endpoints of the **major axis** of the ellipse (length $2b$). The **minor axis** has length $2a$ and has endpoints $(h + a, k)$ and $(h - a, k)$.

In this case $c^2 = b^2 - a^2$, where c is the distance between a focus and the center, and the foci are $(h, k + c)$ and $(h, k - c)$.

The sum of the distances from the foci to any point on the ellipse is $2b$.

Example: Describe and graph the locus of $\dfrac{(x-4)^2}{9} + \dfrac{(y+1)^2}{4} = 1$.

This is an ellipse with center at $(4, -1)$. Its major axis is parallel to the x-axis and has length 6 (since $a = 3$) with vertices $A\,(1, -1)$ and $B\,(7, -1)$. The minor axis has length 4 (since $b = 2$) and the endpoints of the minor axis are $C\,(4, 1)$ and $D\,(4, -3)$. See Figure 4.100.

To find the foci: $c^2 = 9 - 4$, so $c = \sqrt{5}$. Therefore, the foci, which lie on the major axis, are $F_1\left(4 - \sqrt{5}, -1\right)$ and $F_2\left(4 + \sqrt{5}, -1\right)$.

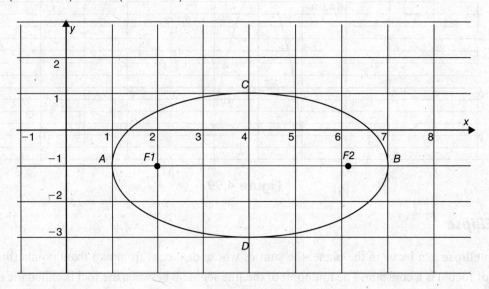

Figure 4.100

The Circle

A **circle** is a locus in the plane whose distance from a given point (the **center**) is constant. This constant is called the **radius** of the circle; we also call any line segment from the center to a point of the circle a radius.

- The standard form of the equation of a circle with **center** (h, k) and **radius** r is

$$(x - h)^2 + (y - k)^2 = r^2$$

Example: Describe and graph the locus that satisfies $x^2 + y - 4x + 6y - 3 = 0$.

Rearrange the terms and complete the square for both the x's and y's:

$(x - 2)^2 + (y + 3)^2 = 16$. This is a circle with center $(2, -3)$ and radius 4 (Figure 4.101).

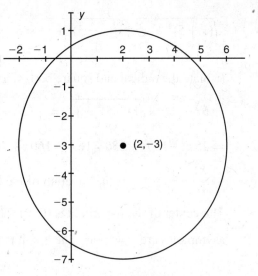

Figure 4.101

The Hyperbola

A hyperbola is a locus in the plane, the difference of whose distances from two fixed points (the **foci**) is a constant. The midpoint of the line segment between the foci is called the **center** of the hyperbola.

- The standard forms of the equation of a hyperbola with center (h, k) is

$$\text{i.} \quad \frac{(x-h)^2}{a^2} - \frac{(y-k)^2}{b^2} = 1, \text{ or}$$

$$\text{ii.} \quad \frac{(y-k)^2}{b^2} - \frac{(x-h)^2}{a^2} = 1$$

We assume $c^2 = a^2 + b^2$ for hyperbolas in both cases. The **transverse axis** of a hyperbola is the line that contains the vertices and the foci; the hyperbola opens along this line. The hyperbola has two linear asymptotes: $y = \pm\frac{b}{a}(x - h) + k$, which are usually represented in the graph of a hyperbola by dotted lines.

Case (i). The vertices in this case are $(a + h, k)$ and $(-a + h, k)$, and the foci are $(c + h, k)$ and $(-c + h, k)$. The difference of the distances from the foci to any point on the hyperbola is $2a$.

Case (ii). The vertices in this case are $(h, k + b)$ and $(h, k - b)$, and the foci are $(h, k + c)$ and $(h, k - c)$. The difference of the distances from the foci to any point on the hyperbola is $2b$.

Example: Find the locus in the plane for which the difference of the distances from the points to the foci $F_1 = (5, 0)$ and $F_2 = (-5, 0)$ is always 8. Find the equation and then graph the figure.

This is clearly a hyperbola. If the point $P = (x, y)$ is on the hyperbola, then the difference of the distances $\overline{PF_1} = \sqrt{(x-5)^2 + y^2}$ and $\overline{PF_2} = \sqrt{(x+5)^2 + y^2}$ is 8. We set up the equation, isolate one of the radicals, and square both sides of the equation:

$$\Rightarrow x^2 + 10x + 25 + y^2 = 64 + 16\sqrt{(x-5)^2 + y^2} + x^2 - 10x + 25 + y^2$$

$$\sqrt{(x+5)^2 + y^2} - \sqrt{(x-5)^2 + y^2} = 8 \implies \left(\sqrt{(x+5)^2 + y^2}\right)^2 = \left(8 + \sqrt{(x-5)^2 + y^2}\right)^2$$

(isolate the radical and square both sides again)

$$\implies 5x - 16 = 4\sqrt{(x-5)^2 + y^2} \implies (5x-16)^2 = \left(4\sqrt{(x-5)^2 + y^2}\right)^2$$

$$\implies 25x^2 - 160x + 256 = 16x^2 - 160x + 400 + 16y^2 \implies 9x^2 - 16y^2 = 144$$

$$\implies \frac{x^2}{16} - \frac{y^2}{9} = 1 \quad \text{is the equation of the hyperbola.}$$

The center of the hyperbola is (0, 0). The vertices of the hyperbola are (4, 0) and (−4, 0). The asymptotes are $y = \pm\frac{3}{4}x$. The graph is shown in Figure 4.102.

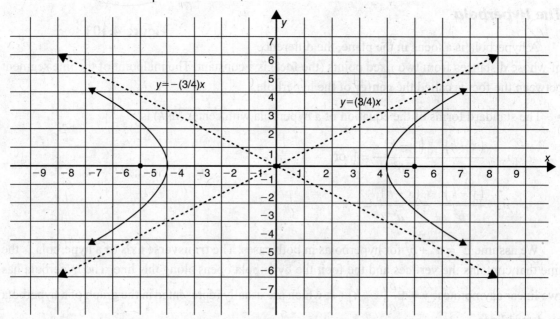

Figure 4.102

Review Problems for Section 4.2.5

1. The vertices of a triangle are $A(0,0)$, $B(8,0)$, and $C(2,6)$. What are the coordinates of the centroid of $\triangle ABC$?

2. Prove that quadrilateral $ABCD$ is an isosceles trapezoid, where A is $(0,-2)$, B is $(9,1)$, C is $(4, 6)$, and D is $(1,5)$.

3. Given that A $(0, 5)$ and B $(0, -3)$ are two points in the Cartesian plane and point P has the coordinates (x, y). If the length of $\overline{PA}$ is three times the length of $\overline{PB}$, which of the following correctly describes the locus of points satisfying these conditions?

    (A) A circle with center $(0, 1)$ and radius 4

    (B) A parabola with vertex $(0, 1)$

    (C) A circle with center $(0, 4)$ and radius 3

    (D) A parabola with vertex $(0, 4)$

4. Find the equation of the curve traced by a point that moves so that the distances to the point $(1, 3)$ and the line $x = -3$ are equal. Graph the curve.

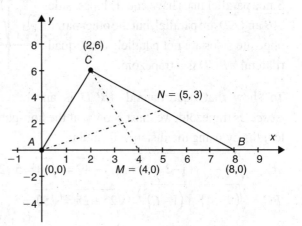

Figure 4.103

Detailed Solutions

1. First find the midpoints of two of the sides:

The midpoint of $\overline{AB} = \left(\dfrac{0+8}{2}, \dfrac{0+0}{2}\right) = (4, 0)$

(label it M), and the midpoint of $\overline{BC} = \left(\dfrac{2+8}{2}, \dfrac{6+0}{2}\right) = (5, 3)$ (label this point N). See Figure 4.103.

The centroid is the point where the segments $\overline{CM}$ and $\overline{AN}$ intersect.

The slope of line $\overleftrightarrow{CM}$ is $m = \dfrac{6-0}{2-4} = -3$, so since the point $(4, 0)$ lies on $\overleftrightarrow{CM}$, the equation of $\overleftrightarrow{CM}$ is $y = -3x + 12$.

The slope of line $\overleftrightarrow{AN}$ is $m = \dfrac{3-0}{5-0} = \dfrac{3}{5}$, so the equation of line $\overleftrightarrow{AN}$ is $y = \dfrac{3}{5}x$ because it passes through the origin.

To find the intersection, solve the two equations simultaneously:

$\dfrac{3}{5}x = -3x + 12 \implies \dfrac{18}{5}x = 12 \implies x = \dfrac{10}{3}$

$\Rightarrow y = \dfrac{3}{5}\left(\dfrac{10}{3}\right) = 2$. So the centroid has coordinates $\left(\dfrac{10}{3}, 2\right)$.

2. Proof: To show that quadrilateral $ABCD$ is a trapezoid, we need to show there is exactly one pair of opposite sides parallel. So we compute the slopes of the lines containing the sides.

$$m_{\overline{AB}} = \frac{1-(-2)}{9-0} = \frac{1}{3}$$

$$m_{\overline{BC}} = \frac{6-1}{4-9} = -1$$

$$m_{\overline{CD}} = \frac{5-6}{1-4} = \frac{1}{3}$$

$$m_{\overline{AD}} = \frac{5-(-2)}{1-0} = 7$$

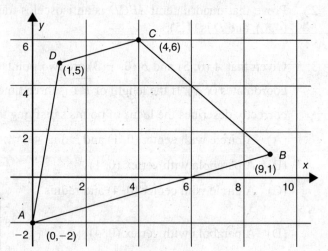

Since parallel lines have equal slopes, sides $\overline{AB}$ and $\overline{CD}$ are parallel, but the other pair of opposite sides are not parallel. Thus, quadrilateral $ABCD$ is a trapezoid.

Figure 4.104

To show that quadrilateral $ABCD$ is an *isosceles* trapezoid, we must show that the non-parallel sides are congruent. Thus, we compute their lengths by using the distance formula:

$$AD = \sqrt{(0-1)^2 + (-2-5)^2} = \sqrt{1+49} = \sqrt{50} = 5\sqrt{2}$$

$$BC = \sqrt{(9-4)^2 + (1-6)^2} = \sqrt{25+25} = \sqrt{50} = 5\sqrt{2}.$$

$\therefore$ Quadrilateral $ABCD$ is an isosceles trapezoid. See Figure 4.104.

Q.E.D.

3. (C)

If the length of $\overline{PA}$ is three times the length of $\overline{PB}$, then $\sqrt{(x-0)^2 + (y-5)^2} = 3\sqrt{(x-0)^2 + (y+3)^2}$. Squaring both sides of the equation and expanding the expressions, we obtain $x^2 + y^2 - 10y + 25 = 9x^2 + 9y^2 + 54y + 81$, which simplifies to $8x^2 + 8y^2 + 64y + 56 = 0$, or $x^2 + y^2 + 8y + 7 = 0$. Completing the square for the y terms, we have: $(x-0)^2 + (y-4)^2 = 9$. This is a circle with center $(0, 4)$ and radius 3.

4. Let $P = (x, y)$ be a point on the curve being traced. The distance between P and the given point is $d = \sqrt{(x-1)^2 + (y-3)^2}$. The distance between P and the line $x = -3$ is $|x + 3|$. Setting these equal and squaring, we obtain: $x^2 - 2x + 1 + y^2 - 6y + 9 = x^2 + 6x + 9$. Rewriting and simplifying, we arrive at $(y-3)^2 = 8(x+1) \Rightarrow x + 1 = \dfrac{1}{8}(y-3)^2$. This is a parabola that opens to the right and has a vertex at $(-1, 3)$. Since $a = \dfrac{1}{8}$, $p = \dfrac{1}{4a} = 2$. So the focus is $(-1 + 2, 3) = (1, 3)$ and the directrix is $x = -3$. Figure 4.105 shows the graph of the parabola with its focus and directrix.

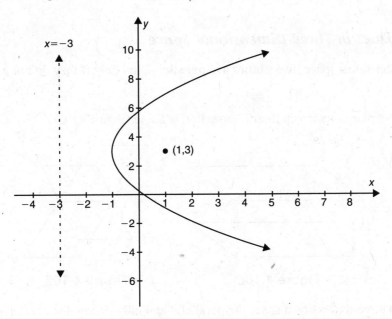

Figure 4.105

4.3 Three-Dimensional Geometry

4.3.1 The California *Mathematics Subject Matter Requirements* stipulate that candidates for any credential program for teaching secondary mathematics must be able to *demonstrate an understanding of parallelism and perpendicularity of lines and planes in three dimensions.*

Planes and Lines

Preliminaries

Three-dimensional space is denoted by $\mathbf{R}^3$ (or sometimes $\mathbf{E}^3$).

- For any three non-collinear points, there is exactly one plane that contains all three.

- If a plane contains two points, the plane contains the entire line determined by these points.

- There is exactly one plane containing any line and a point not on that line.

- There is exactly one plane containing two intersecting non-collinear lines.

Planes and Lines in Three-Dimensional Space

- In three-dimensional space, two **planes are parallel** if and only if they do not intersect (Figure 4.106).

- If two distinct planes intersect, their intersection is a line (Figure 4.107).

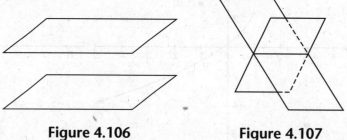

Figure 4.106   **Figure 4.107**

- Two lines in three-dimensional space are parallel if and only if they do not intersect and there is a plane that contains both of the lines (i.e., they are coplanar) (Figure 4.108).

- Lines that do not intersect and are not coplanar are called **skew lines** (Figure 4.109).

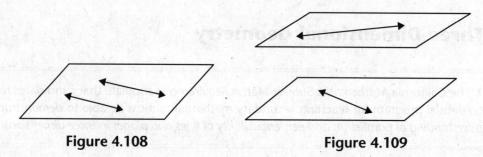

Figure 4.108   **Figure 4.109**

- When the intersection of two planes is a line, the angle between the planes is the same as the angle formed by two rays perpendicular to the line of intersection at the same point but in different planes. An angle between two planes is called a **dihedral angle** (Figure 4.110).

- **Perpendicular planes** are planes that intersect and form four right dihedral angles (Figure 4.111).

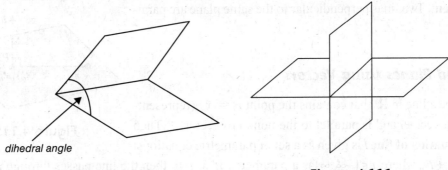

Figure 4.110   **Figure 4.111**

- **Theorem**: If a line not lying in a plane intersects a plane, then the intersection of the line and plane is one point (Figure 4.112).

- A line is **perpendicular to a plane** if it is perpendicular to every line in the plane that passes through the point of intersection of the line and the plane (Figure 4.113).

Figure 4.112

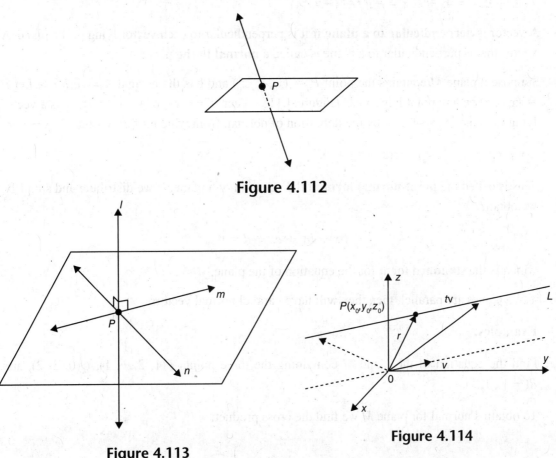

Figure 4.113   **Figure 4.114**

- **Theorem**: If a line is perpendicular to two intersecting lines through their point of intersection, then the line is perpendicular to the plane determined by the intersecting lines (Figure 4.113).

- **Theorem**: Two planes are perpendicular if and only if one plane contains a line perpendicular to the other plane.

- **Theorem**: Two lines perpendicular to the same plane are parallel.

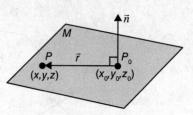

Lines and Planes Using Vectors

- Let L be a line in $\mathbf{R}^3$ that contains the point $P = \bar{x}_0$ (represented as a vector) and is parallel to the non-zero vector $\vec{v}$. Then the **equation of line** l is given as a set of parametric equations: $\vec{x} = \vec{x}_0 + t\vec{v}$, where $t \in (-\infty, \infty)$ is a parameter. If $\bar{x}_0 = \bar{0}$, then the line passes through the origin and the equation is $\vec{x} = t\vec{v}$ (Figure 4.114).

    Figure 4.115

    Example: Write the equation of the line containing the points $(2, 1, 0)$ and $(0, -3, 1)$.

    A vector parallel to the line is $\vec{v} = <2, 4, -1>$. So a set of parametric equations for line L is $x = 2t + 2, y = 4t + 1, z = -t, t \in (-\infty, \infty)$.

- A vector is **perpendicular to a plane** if it is perpendicular to each vector lying in the plane. A vector that is perpendicular to a plane is called a **normal to the plane.**

- Suppose a plane M contains the point $P_0 = (x_0, y_0, z_0)$ and has the normal $\bar{n} = <a, b, c>$. Let $P = (x, y, z)$ be any point lying in M (Figure 4.115). Then $\vec{r} = <x - x_0, y - y_0, z - z_0>$ is a vector lying in plane M. So $\vec{r} \perp \bar{n}$, by the definition of normal, from which it follows that $\vec{r} \cdot \bar{n} = 0$ or

    $$a(x - x_0) + b(y - y_0) + c(z - z_0) = 0.$$

    This is called the **point-normal form** of the equation of a plane. If we distribute and simplify, we obtain

    $$ax + by + cz + d = 0$$

    which is the **standard form** for the equation of the plane.

- If two planes are parallel, then they will have parallel normal vectors.

    Examples:

(a) Find the equation of the plane M containing the three points $P(1, 2, -1)$, $Q(0, 3, 2)$, and $R(-1, 1, 5)$.

    To obtain a normal for plane M we find the cross product:

$\vec{n} = \overrightarrow{PQ} \times \overrightarrow{PR} = <-1, 1, 3> \times <-2, -1, 6> = <9, 0, 3>$. Then, using point P, the equation in point-normal form is $9(x-1) + 0(y-2) + 3(z-1) = 0$, or in standard form, $9x + 3z - 6 = 0$.

(b) Given the equation of the plane $2x - y + 3z + 1 = 0$, identify a normal to the plane.

The coefficients of x, y, and z are the components of a normal vector, so we can say $\vec{n} = <2, -1, 3>$.

- **Theorem**: The distance D between point $P_0(x_0, y_0, z_0)$ and the plane $ax + by + cz + d = 0$ is

$$D = \frac{|ax_0 + by_0 + cz_0 + d|}{\sqrt{a^2 + b^2 + c^2}}$$

Example: Find the distance from the point $(2, -5, 1)$ to the plane $3x - 4y + z + 1 = 0$.

$$D = \frac{|3(2) - 4(-5) + 1(1) + 1|}{\sqrt{9 + 16 + 1}} = \frac{28}{\sqrt{26}}$$

■ Review Problems for Section 4.3.1

1. Planes M and N are distinct planes. Both are perpendicular to line k. Which of the following statements is true?

   (A) Plane M is perpendicular to plane N.

   (B) Plane M is parallel to plane N.

   (C) Planes M and N form an acute dihedral angle.

   (D) Plane M bisects plane N.

2. Consider the following two statements.

   I. A line perpendicular to a given plane is perpendicular to every line in the plane.

   II. Two distinct planes that are both perpendicular to another plane are perpendicular to each other.

   Which of the following is correct?

   (A) Only statement I is true.

   (B) Only statement II is true.

   (C) Both statements I and II are true.

   (D) Neither statement I nor II is true.

3. Let plane M be given by the equation $-2x + 5y - z = 8$ and let plane P be given by the equa-

tion $-2x + 5y - z = 4$.

(a) Find the distance between planes M and P.

(b) Write parametric equations for line, l, which is orthogonal (perpendicular) to plane M and passes through the point $(-1, 3, 7)$.

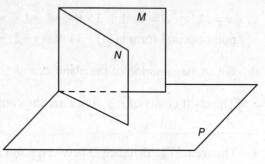

Figure 4.116

Detailed Solutions

1. (B)

If two planes are perpendicular to the same line, then they have parallel normal vectors. So they must either be parallel to each other (distinct planes) or be the same plane. But planes M and N are distinct planes. So they must be parallel and (B) is correct. Note that planes cannot be bisected, as they are not finite, so statement (D) is false.

2. (D)

A line perpendicular to a plane is perpendicular to only the lines in the plane that intersect it. So statement I is false, and (A) and (C) are incorrect.

Two planes perpendicular to the same plane could be perpendicular to each other. But they could also be parallel to each other or neither. For example, planes M and N in Figure 4.116 form an acute dihedral angle but both are perpendicular to plane P. So (B) is incorrect.

So neither statement is true.

3. (a) Let X be point $(-4, 0, 0)$ in the first given plane. Using the formula for distance from a point to a plane, where X is the point and the second plane's equation is $-2x + 5y - z - 4 = 0$, we obtain:

$$D = \frac{|-2(-4) + 5(0) + -1(0) - 4|}{\sqrt{(-2)^2 + (5)^2 + (-1)^2}} = \frac{4}{\sqrt{30}}$$ as the distance between the two planes.

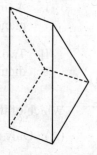

(b) Use the normal of the plane $\vec{n} = <-2, 5, -1>$ as the vector parallel to the line.

$$\begin{cases} x = -2t - 1 \\ y = 5t + 3 \\ z = -t + 7 \end{cases}$$ with $t \in (-\infty, \infty)$ is the set of parametric equations for the line.

Figure 4.117

4.3.2 The California *Mathematics Subject Matter Requirements* stipulate that candidates for any credential program for teaching secondary mathematics must be able to *understand, apply, and justify properties of three-dimensional objects from an advanced standpoint (e.g., derive the volume and surface area formulas for prisms, pyramids, cones, cylinders, and spheres).*

Three-Dimensional Objects

Prisms

- A **polyhedron** is a three-dimensional closed figure formed by the union of polygonal regions. The polygonal figures intersect on their boundaries, which are called the **edges** of the polyhedron. The intersections of the edges of the polyhedron are called **vertices**. The polygonal figures themselves are called the **faces** of the polyhedron (Figure 4.117).

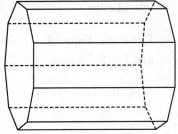

Figure 4.120

- The word **polyhedra** is the plural of the word *polyhedron*.

- A **prism** is a polyhedron with a pair of sides that are congruent and lie in parallel planes and whose other sides are all parallelograms. The sides that are in parallel planes are called the **bases**, and the other sides are called the **lateral faces**. The intersections of the lateral faces are called the **lateral edges**.

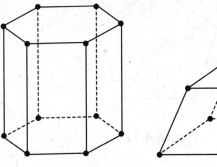

Figure 4.118

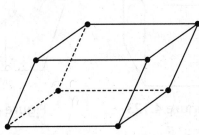

Figure 4.119

- A **right prism** (Figure 4.118) is a prism in which all the lateral faces are perpendicular to the bases. The lateral faces of a right prism are rectangles. Prisms that are not right prisms are called **oblique prisms** (Figure 4.119).

- A **regular prism** is a prism that has regular polygons as its bases (Figures 4.118 and 4.120).

- A **parallelepiped** is a prism in which all faces are parallelograms (Figure 4.119).

- A **rectangular parallelepiped** is a parallelepiped in which all faces are rectangles (Figure 4.121).

- A **cube** is a rectangular parallelepiped in which all faces are squares (Figure 4.122).

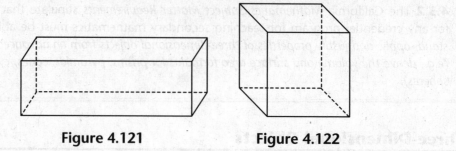

Figure 4.121   Figure 4.122

Surface Area

- The **surface area of a prism** is the sum of the areas of its faces.

- The **surface area of a regular right prism** is $SA = 2B + nsl$, where B is the area of a base, n is the number of sides in the base, s is the length of one side of the base, and l is the length of a lateral edge.

  Example: Figure 4.123 shows a regular right pentagonal prism, so $n = 5$. Suppose $s = 4$ inches and $l = 5.5$ inches.

  Then the area of each base is $\frac{1}{2}aP$, where a is the apothem and P is the perimeter. $P = 20$ inches, so $B = 10a$.

  To find the apothem, we need to use the Law of Sines:

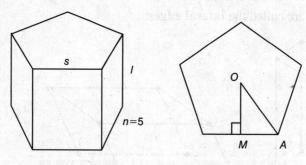

Figure 4.123   Figure 4.124

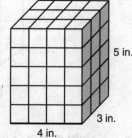

5 in.

4 in.   3 in.

Figure 4.125

In Figure 4.124, $\overline{OM} \perp \overline{MA}$ and $m\angle AOM = \dfrac{360°}{10} = 36°$, so $m\angle OAM = 54°$.

We know $MA = 2$, and we want to find $a = OM$. Using the Law of Sines:

$$\frac{a}{\sin(54°)} = \frac{2}{\sin(36°)} \quad \Rightarrow \quad a = \frac{2\sin(54°)}{\sin(36°)} \approx 2.753$$

The area of $\triangle AOM = \frac{1}{2}(2)a = a$. So the area of the pentagon is $B = 10a \approx 27.53$ square inches, and thus the area of the two bases is approximately 55.06 square inches.

The lateral area is $L = 5ls = 110$ square inches.

Thus, the approximate surface area of the pentagonal prism is 165.06 square inches.

- The **surface area of a cube** is $SA = 6s^2$, where s is the length of the edge of the cube.

  Example: If the surface area of a cube is 480 square meters, what is the length of an edge of the cube?

  We write the following equation and solve for s: $6s^2 = 480 \Rightarrow s^2 = 80$, so $s = 4\sqrt{5}$ meters.

- The **volume of a prism** is the area of the base times the height of an altitude; so $V = Bh$. In the case of a rectangular parallelepiped, the formula is $V = lwh$, and for a cube it is $V = s^3$.

  Example: The volume of the rectangular parallelepiped (box) in Figure 4.125 is, by definition, $V = (4)(3)(5) = 60$ cubic inches.

Observe that there are 60 cubes of side length 1 inch in the box; that is the meaning of the terminology *cubic inches*.

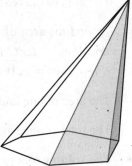

Figure 4.126

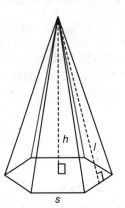

Figure 4.127

Pyramids

- A **pyramid** is a three-dimensional figure with one side, called a **base**, which is a polygon with n sides, and n **lateral faces**, all of which are triangles. The lateral faces each meet the base on one edge and meet two other lateral adjacent faces. The lateral faces all meet at a point called the **vertex** (Figure 4.126).

  The altitude of the pyramid is the line segment with one endpoint at the vertex and which forms a right angle in the plane that contains the base. The **height** of the pyramid is the length of the altitude.

- A **regular** pyramid is a pyramid with a regular polygon for a base and the foot of the altitude at the center of the base. The **slant height** of a regular pyramid is the height of each lateral face, which is an isosceles triangle (Figure 4.127).

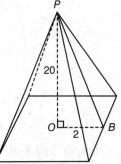

Figure 4.128

- The **surface area of a pyramid** is the area of the base (n-gon) plus the sum of the areas of the n lateral faces. For a **regular pyramid**, this is $SA = B + n(1/2 \, sl)$, where B is the area of the base, n is the number of sides of the base, s is the length of one side of the base, and l is the slant height of the pyramid.

Example: Find the surface area of a square pyramid with base side length 4 mm and height 20 mm.

The area of the base is $B = 4^2 = 16$ square mm.

To find the area of the lateral faces, we need to know the slant height. Consider Figure 4.128 and look at $\triangle POB$. We can use the Pythagorean Theorem to find PB: $2^2 + 20^2 = PB^2$, so $PB = \sqrt{404} = 2\sqrt{101}$.

The area of one lateral face is $\frac{1}{2}(4)(2\sqrt{101}) = 4\sqrt{101}$ square mm.

The total surface area of the square pyramid is thus $16 + 16\sqrt{101}$ square mm.

- The **volume of a pyramid** is $V = \frac{1}{3}Bh$, where B is the area of the base and h is the height of the pyramid. To prove that this is the formula for the volume of a pyramid, we would need to use methods of calculus, so we defer this proof until Chapter 6.

Example: Find the volume of the pyramid shown in Figure 4.129.

To find the volume we need the area of the base and also the height. We are given the length of one side of the base to be 6 feet and a side of a lateral face to be 18 feet.

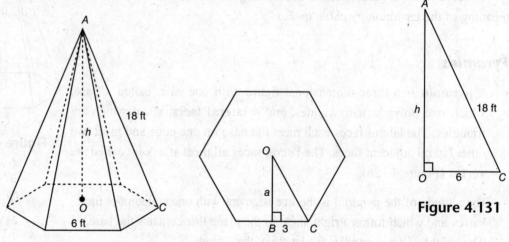

| Figure 4.129 | Figure 4.130 | Figure 4.131 |

The base is shown in Figure 4.130. Since angle COB has measure of 30°, the apothem has length $3\sqrt{3}$ feet. The area of the base is $\frac{1}{2}aP = \frac{1}{2}(3\sqrt{3})(36) = 54\sqrt{3}$ square feet.

To find the volume of the pyramid, consider Figure 4.131 to find h. We use the Pythagorean Theorem: $BC = 3$ so OC is 6 in Figure 4.130.

$h^2 = 18^2 - 6^2 = 288$

$h \approx 12\sqrt{2}$ feet

So the volume of the pyramid is $V = \frac{1}{3}(54\sqrt{3})(12\sqrt{2}) \approx 529$ cubic feet.

Cylinders

- A **cylinder** is a closed figure in three-dimensional space that has two **bases** that lie in parallel planes, and every cross section parallel to the bases is the same as the bases. The surface that is not part of the bases is called the **lateral surface**.

- A cylinder in which the altitude is the line segment joining the centers of the bases is called a **right cylinder.** In the case that the bases are circles, the figure is called a **circular cylinder**.

- For example, in Figure 4.132, the cylinder on the left is a circular cylinder but is not a right cylinder. The cylinder in the middle is a right circular cylinder, and the cylinder on the right is a **right elliptical cylinder** since the bases are ellipses.

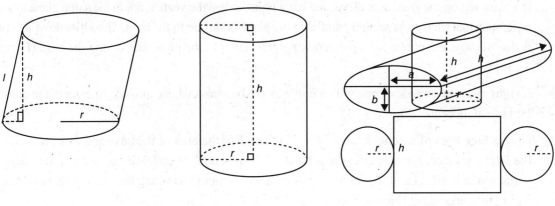

Figure 4.132 **Figure 4.133**

- The **surface area of a cylinder** is the area of the two bases plus the area of the lateral surface. For a circular cylinder, the area of a base is πr^2, and the area of the lateral surface is $2\pi rh$. This last part can be visualized by thinking of cutting off the circular bases and then slicing along the slant height l; laying this surface flat you will have a parallelogram with one side $2\pi r$ (the circumference of the base) and the altitude equal to h. This is called a **net** of the surface and is illustrated for a right circular cylinder in Figure 4.133.

- The surface area of a right circular cylinder is $SA = 2\pi r^2 + 2\pi rh$.

  Example: If the height of a right circular cylindrical is 2 feet and the radius is 8 inches, what is the surface area of the cylinder?

  First, note that the units must be in the same measurement, so let $h = 24$ inches and $r = 8$ inches.

  Then, $SA = 2\pi(8)^2 + 2\pi(8)(24) = 128\pi + 384\pi = 512\pi$ square inches.

- The **volume of a cylinder** is equal to $V = Bh$, where B is the area of the base and h is the height. In the case of a **circular cylinder**, the volume is $V = \pi r^2 h$. We can prove this by using calculus, so we defer it to the section on *Volumes of Revolution* in chapter six.

- Note that a prism is a type of cylinder.

Example: A closed cylindrical can has a radius of 5 cm and has a surface area of 170π square cm. What is the volume of the can in cubic centimeters?

$SA = 2\pi(5)^2 + 2\pi(5)h = 50\pi + 10\pi h = 10\pi(5 + h) = 170\pi$. So $h + 5 = 17$, or $h = 12$ cm.

Therefore, $V = Bh = (25\pi)(12) = 300\pi$ cubic cm.

Figure 4.134

Cones

- A **cone** is a closed figure in three dimensions that has exactly one base that is a plane region enclosed by a curve, and has a point, called the **vertex**, not in the same plane as the base, such that each cross section parallel to the plane is similar to the base. The **altitude of a cone** is the line segment drawn from the vertex perpendicular to the plane containing the base (Figure 4.134).

- A **right circular cone** is a cone with a circle as the base and whose altitude intersects the circular base at its center (Figure 4.135).

- The **surface area of a cone** is $SA = B + L$, where B is the area of the base and L is the area of the lateral surface. For a right circular cone, $B = \pi r^2$ and $L = \pi r l$. We can see that the lateral surface area is the area of the sector that is created by slicing up along the slant height and then laying the surface flat (Figure 4.136).

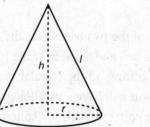
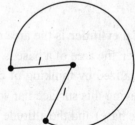

Figure 4.135   **Figure 4.136**

The area of the sector is equal to α times the area of the circle with radius l, where α is the fraction of the circle that the sector defines. The fraction α is equal to the ratio of the arc of the sector ($2\pi r$) to the circumference of the circle with radius l ($2\pi l$), so $\alpha = \dfrac{r}{l}$. Thus, the area of the sector is $\alpha\left(\pi l^2\right) = \dfrac{r}{l}\left(\pi l^2\right) = \pi r l$.

Thus, for a right circular cone with radius r and slant height l, the surface area is

$SA = \pi r^2 + \pi r l = \pi r (r + l)$.

- The volume of a cone is $V = \dfrac{1}{3} Bh$, where B is the area of the base and h is the height of the cone. This formula can be developed by using calculus. In Chapter 6, we show this development in the section on *Volumes of Solids of Revolution*.

Example: If the height of a right circular cone is 20 cm and the slant height is 25 cm, what are the volume and surface area of the cone?

The radius, height, and slant height form a right triangle, so by using the Pythagorean Theorem: $r^2 + 400 = 625$, so $r = 15$ cm. Therefore, the volume is $V = \frac{1}{3}\pi(15)^2(20) = 1500\pi$ cubic cm, and the surface area is given by

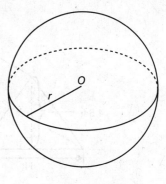

Figure 4.137

$$SA = \pi(15)^2 + \pi(15)(25) = 600\pi \text{ square cm.}$$

Spheres

- A **sphere** is the set of all points in three-dimensional space that are equidistant from a given point. The given point O is called the **center of the sphere**, and the distance is **radius** of the sphere (Figure 4.137).

- **The equation of a sphere** with center (a, b, c) and radius r is $(x - a)^2 + (y - b)^2 + (z - c)^2 = r^2$. This formula comes from the formula for the distance between two points in three-dimensional space.

- The **surface area** of a sphere is $SA = 4\pi r^2$, and the **volume** is $V = \frac{4}{3}\pi r^3$. Both of these formulas need calculus for their proofs.

Review Problems for Section 4.3.2

1. The volume of a circular cylinder is 528 cm³. The height of the cylinder is 12 cm. Find the radius of the cylinder to the nearest tenth of a centimeter.

2. Find the surface area of the solid shown in Figure 4.138.

3. A right circular cone has a base with a radius of 9 meters, and a volume of 189 cubic meters. Find the lateral surface area of the cone.

4. Find the volume of a sphere inscribed in a cube if each edge of the cube is 16 mm (Figure 4.139).

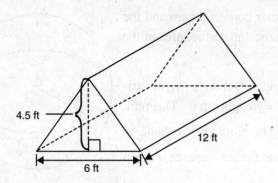

Figure 4.138

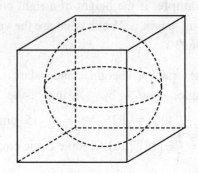

Figure 4.139

Detailed Solutions

1.   The volume of a circular cylinder is Bh, so $12B = 528$. Thus, $B = 44$ square cm. Since $B = \pi r^2$, $r = \sqrt{\dfrac{44}{\pi}} \approx 3.74 \, \text{cm}$.

2.   The surface area of the triangular prism is $SA = 2B + 3ls = 2\left(\dfrac{1}{2}(4.5)(6)\right) + 3(12)(6) = 243$ square feet.

3.   Since $V = \dfrac{1}{3}Bh$, we have $189 = \dfrac{1}{3}\left(9^2\pi\right)h \ \Rightarrow \ h = \dfrac{189}{27\pi} = \dfrac{7}{\pi}$. The lateral surface area of the cone is $L = \pi r l = 9\pi l$. To find the slant height, we can use the Pythagorean Theorem: $l^2 = r^2 + h^2 = 81 + \dfrac{49}{\pi^2} \ \Rightarrow \ l \approx 9.27$. The lateral area of the cone is approximately $9\pi(9.27) = 262.15$ square meters.

4.   The edge of the cube is 16 mm, so the diameter of the sphere is also 16 mm. Thus, the radius is 8 mm. The volume is then $V = \pi(8)^3 = 512\pi$ cubic millimeters.

4.4 Transformational Geometry

4.4.1 The California *Mathematics Subject Matter Requirements* stipulate that candidates for any credential program for teaching secondary mathematics must be able to *demonstrate an understanding of the basic properties of isometries in two- and three-dimensional space (e.g., rotation, translation, reflection).*

Transformations

A **transformation**, T, from a set A into a set B is a one-to-one mapping T of A onto B.

The essential characteristic of the transformations of Euclidean geometry is that distance is preserved; i.e., distance is an invariant property. A transformation T is called an **isometry** of A onto B if it preserves distances. This means for any two points, P_1 and P_2, the distance between P_1 and P_2 is equal to the distance between $T(P_1)$ and $T(P_2)$. In mathematical distance notation, this is $d(P_1, P_2) = d(T(P_1), T(P_2))$. The word isometry is derived from the Greek words *iso* (same) and *metry* (distance or measure).

In Euclidean geometry, the distance in $\mathbf{R^2}$ (two-space) between two points P (x_1, y_1) and Q (x_2, y_2) is defined by $d(P, Q) = \sqrt{(x_2 - x_1)^2 + (y_2 - y_1)^2}$, and in $\mathbf{R^3}$ (three-space), the distance between two points P (x_1, y_1, z_1) and Q (x_2, y_2, z_2) is given by the extended formula $d(P, Q) = \sqrt{(x_2 - x_1)^2 + (y_2 - y_1)^2 + (z_2 - z_1)^2}$. These formulas follow from the Pythagorean Theorem.

If an isometry exists between two segments, we say the **segments are congruent**.

Euclidean geometry involves the study of motions of the plane $\mathbf{R^2}$ or space $\mathbf{R^3}$, where when we say motion we mean an isometry of a set of points onto a set of points. In the 1800s, Felix Klein, a German mathematician, defined geometry as the study of invariant properties of a set of points under a group of transformations.

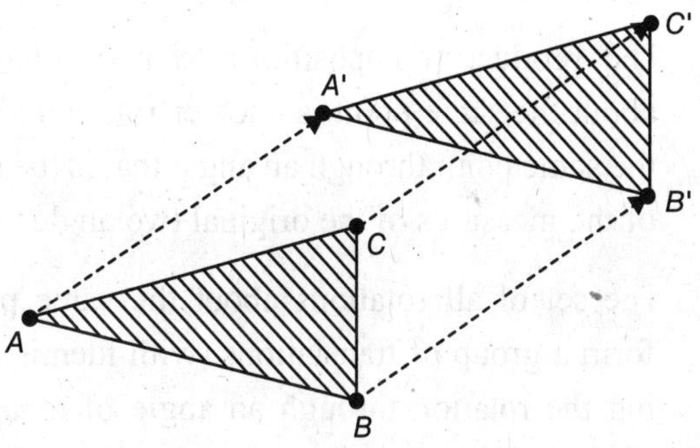

Figure 4.140

Transformations in R²

The plane motions are: translation, rotation, reflection, and glide-reflection.

- A **translation** is a correspondence between points and their image points so that each image point is the same distance in the same direction from the original point. In function notation, a translation that moves points a units horizontally and b units vertically is

    $T(x. y) = (x + a, y + b)$.

Some facts about a translation:

- A segment is translated into a parallel segment.

- All vectors connecting corresponding points are equal.

- The inverse of a translation is another translation the same distance in the opposite direction.

- The product (composition) of translations is a translation.

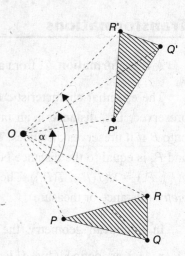

- The set of all translations forms a group with identity the zero vector.

  Example: Figure 4.140 illustrates the translation of $\triangle ABC$ along the translation vector $\overline{AA'} \cong \overline{BB'} \cong \overline{CC'}$, resulting in the image $\triangle A'B'C'$.

- The symbol R(O, α) represents a **rotation through an angle of $\alpha°$ about the point O.** A counterclockwise rotation is associated with a positive angle.

  A rotation about the origin O through an angle α can be given by the function

  $T(x,y) = (x\cos(\alpha) - y\sin(\alpha), x\sin(\alpha) + y\cos(\alpha)).$

Figure 4.141

Some facts about a rotation:

- A segment is usually not parallel to its image.

- The inverse of a rotation R(O, α) is the rotation R(O, $-\alpha$).

- The product (composition) of two rotations about the same point is another rotation about the same point through an angle that is the sum of the measures of the original two angles.

- The set of all rotations about the same point form a group of translations (with identity being the rotation through an angle of measure $0°$).

- Rotations with center O with angles α and $\alpha \pm 360°n$ are the same rotation for $n = 0, 1, 2, \ldots$

  Example: Figure 4.141 illustrates the rotation of $\triangle PQR$ about the point O through an angle of α, resulting in the image $\triangle P'Q'R'$.

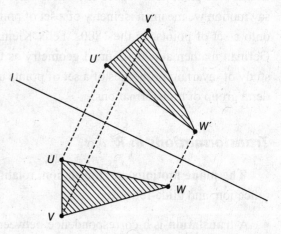

Figure 4.142

- The set of all translations and rotations is called the set of **rigid motions** or **displacements.**

- A **reflection** is also a motion of the plane. We denote a reflection about a line m by R$_m$. R$_m$ takes a point P onto a point P_0 such that m is the perpendicular bisector of $\overline{PP_0}$.

Some facts about a reflection:

- A segment is usually not parallel to its image.

- The inverse of a reflection is the same reflection.

- The product (composition) of two reflections about the different lines is not a reflection.

- A reflection cannot be considered a translation in the plane.

    Example: Figure 4.142 illustrates the reflection of ΔUVW about the line l, resulting in the image $\Delta U'V'W'$.

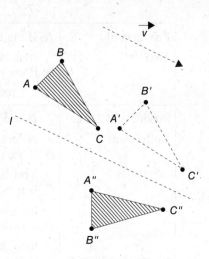

Figure 4.143

Some reflections can be represented in function notation, In particular,

i. A reflection about the x-axis is $T(x, y) = (x, -y)$.

ii. A reflection about the y-axis is $T(x, y) = (-x, y)$.

iii. A reflection about the line $y = x$ is $T(x, y) = (y, x)$.

- The product (composition) of a reflection and a translation parallel to the fixed line of reflection, in either order, is called a **glide-reflection**.

    Example: In Figure 4.143 we begin with ΔABC along with a translation vector, $\vec{v}$ and a line l over which we will reflect. If we first translate all the points of ΔABC, we obtain the image $\Delta A'B'C'$. Next we reflect over the line l to arrive at the image $\Delta A''B''C''$.

- **Theorem**: The four types of Euclidean motions of the plane constitute a group of transformations with composition (which is often called *product*) as its binary operation.

    Recall what this means:

    i. **Closure Property of Compositions**: The composition of any two plane motions is a plane motion.

    ii. **Associative Property of Compositions**: If f, g, h are plane motions, then $f \circ (g \circ h)(x, y) = (f \circ g) \circ h(x, y)$ for all points (x, y) in $\mathbf{R}^2$.

    iii. **Identity Property of Composition**: The identity transformation can be considered a translation of distance 0 or a rotation of 0°; it is denoted by $e(x, y) = (x, y)$ for all $(x, y) \in \mathbf{R}^2$, and $(f \circ e)(x, y) = f(x, y) = (e \circ f)(x, y)$.

    iv. **Inverse Property of Composition**: The inverse of a translation is a translation, the inverse of a rotation is a rotation, and the inverse of a reflection is a reflection.

- **Theorem**: A transformation is a plane motion if and only if it is the product of three or fewer reflections.

- **The possible results of products (compositions) of reflections**

Products of Two Reflections	A. If the two lines of reflection are parallel, then the motion is a translation. B. If the two lines of reflection are non-parallel, then the motion is a rotation.
Products of Three Reflections	A. If two of the lines of reflection coincide, then the motion is a reflection. B. If the three lines of reflection are parallel, then the motion is a reflection. C. If two lines of reflection intersect at a point on a third, then the motion is a reflection. D. If two lines of reflection intersect at a point not on a third, then the motion is a reflection.

An **invariant point** is a point that is its own image under a transformation.

- A translation has no invariant points; a rotation has one invariant point; a reflection has infinitely many invariant points (all the points on the line of reflection); a glide-reflection has no invariant points.

- The properties studied in elementary geometry, such as congruence of segments, triangles, and angles, area of regions, and intersection of lines, are all properties of sets of points that are invariant under the group of motions.

Transformations in R^3

The **space motions** are translation, rotation, reflection, and glide-reflection.

- In function notation, a translation that moves points a units parallel to the x-axis, b units parallel to the y-axis, and c units parallel to the z-axis is $T(x, y, z) = (x + a, y + b, z + c)$.

The facts about translations listed in the previous section on *Transformations in R^2* are also true for translations in R^3.

- The symbol R(L, α) represents a **rotation through an angle of $\alpha°$ about the line L**. A counter-clockwise rotation is associated with a positive angle.

A rotation R(L, α) can be given by the function

i. $T(x, y, z) = (x, y\cos(\alpha) - z\sin(\alpha), y\sin(\alpha) + z\cos(\alpha))$ when L is the x-axis.

ii. $T(x, y, z) = (x\cos(\alpha) - z\sin(\alpha), y, x\sin(\alpha) + z\cos(\alpha))$ when L is the y-axis.

iii. $T(x, y, z) = (x\cos(\alpha) - y\sin(\alpha), x\sin(\alpha) + y\cos(\alpha), z)$ when L is the z-axis.

The facts about rotations listed in the previous section on *Transformations in R^2* are also true for rotations in R^3, except the rotations are about a line rather than a point.

- A **reflection** is also a motion of space. We denote a reflection about a plane M by R_M. R_M takes a point P onto a point P_0 such that M is the perpendicular bisector of $\overline{PP_0}$.

  The facts about reflections listed in the previous section on *Transformations in R^2* are also true for reflections in R^3, except the reflections are about a plane rather than a line.

  Again, some reflections can be represented in function notation. In particular,

  i.   A reflection about the xy-plane is $T(x, y, z) = (x, y, -z)$.

  ii. A reflection about the yz-plane is $T(x, y, z) = (-x, y, z)$.

  iii. A reflection about the xz-plane is $T(x, y, z) = (x, -y, z)$.

- The product (composition) of a reflection across a plane and a translation parallel to the fixed plane of reflection, in either order, is called a **glide-reflection**.

- **Theorem**: The four types of Euclidean motions of space constitute a group of transformations with composition (which is often called *product*) as its binary operation.

Using Matrices to Represent Transformations

- A **linear transformation** is a function $T: \mathbf{R}^n \to \mathbf{R}^n$ such that for all $\vec{u}, \vec{v} \in \mathbf{R}^n$ and real numbers a, $T\left(\vec{u} + \vec{v}\right) = T\left(\vec{u}\right) + T\left(\vec{v}\right)$ and $T\left(c\vec{v}\right) = cT\left(\vec{v}\right)$.

  Example: The transformation $T(x, y) = (x + 2, y - 3)$ is a translation. To see if it is a linear transformation: $T((x, y) + (u, v)) = T(x + u, y + v) = (x + u + 2, y + v - 3)$, whereas $T(x, y) + T(u, v) = (x + 2, y - 3) + (u + 2, v - 3) = (x + u + 4, y + v - 6)$; so the first condition for linear transformation fails. In general, translations are not linear transformations. But the transformation $T(x, y) = (2y, x)$ is a linear transformation because $T((x, y) + (u, v)) = T(x + u, y + v) = (2(y + v), x + u) = (2y, x) + (2v, u) = T(x, y) + T(u, v)$ and $T(c(x, y)) = T(cx, cy) = (2cy, cx) = c(2y, x) = cT(x, y)$ for all (x, y), and $(u, v) \in \mathbf{R}^2$ and $c \in \mathbf{R}$.

- **Theorem**: If A is an $n \times m$ matrix, then there is an **induced linear transformation** $T_A: \mathbf{R}^m \to \mathbf{R}^n$ such that $T_A\left(\vec{x}\right) = A\vec{x}$ for all $\vec{x} \in \mathbf{R}^n$. This is matrix multiplication.

- **Theorem**: If $T: \mathbf{R}^m \to \mathbf{R}^n$ is a linear transformation, then there exists an $n \times m$ matrix A such that $T = T_A$. The matrix A is often called the **standard** or **associated matrix**. In fact, the columns of A are $T\left(\vec{e_j}\right)$ for each j, where $\vec{e_j}$ is the vector in $\mathbf{R}^m$ that has all components equal to 0 except the jth one, which equals 1.

Example: Let $T(x, y) = (x, -y)$, the reflection about the x-axis. We could show that T is a linear transformation and $T(1, 0) = (1, 0)$, $T(0, 1) = (0, -1)$, so that T can be represented by

$$T(x, y) = \begin{bmatrix} 1 & 0 \\ 0 & -1 \end{bmatrix} \begin{bmatrix} x \\ y \end{bmatrix}.$$

If we look back at the transformations representing our plane and space motions, we would see:

1. Translations are not linear transformations and so do not have the associated (standard) matrix A.

2. Rotations that do have associated matrices are:

   (a) Counterclockwise rotation about the origin through an angle α:

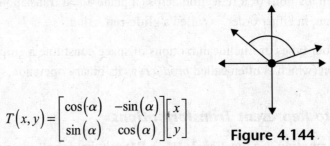

   $$T(x, y) = \begin{bmatrix} \cos(\alpha) & -\sin(\alpha) \\ \sin(\alpha) & \cos(\alpha) \end{bmatrix} \begin{bmatrix} x \\ y \end{bmatrix}$$

   Figure 4.144

   (b) Counterclockwise rotation (in three dimensions) about the x-axis through an angle α:

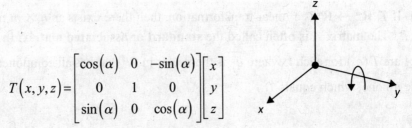

   $$T(x, y, z) = \begin{bmatrix} 1 & 0 & 0 \\ 0 & \cos(\alpha) & -\sin(\alpha) \\ 0 & \sin(\alpha) & \cos(\alpha) \end{bmatrix} \begin{bmatrix} x \\ y \\ z \end{bmatrix}$$

   Figure 4.145

   (c) Counterclockwise rotation (in three dimensions) about the y-axis through an angle α:

   $$T(x, y, z) = \begin{bmatrix} \cos(\alpha) & 0 & -\sin(\alpha) \\ 0 & 1 & 0 \\ \sin(\alpha) & 0 & \cos(\alpha) \end{bmatrix} \begin{bmatrix} x \\ y \\ z \end{bmatrix}$$

   Figure 4.146

(d) Counterclockwise rotation (in three dimensions) about the z-axis through an angle α:

$$T(x, y, z) = \begin{bmatrix} \cos(\alpha) & -\sin(\alpha) & 0 \\ \sin(\alpha) & \cos(\alpha) & 0 \\ 0 & 0 & 1 \end{bmatrix} \begin{bmatrix} x \\ y \\ z \end{bmatrix}$$

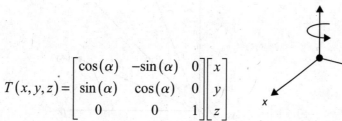

Figure 4.147

3. Reflections that have associated matrices:

   (a) Reflection about the x-axis:

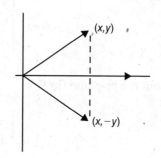

$$T(x, y) = \begin{bmatrix} 1 & 0 \\ 0 & -1 \end{bmatrix} \begin{bmatrix} x \\ y \end{bmatrix}$$

Figure 4.148

   (b) Reflection about the y-axis:

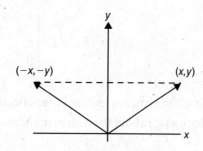

$$T(x, y) = \begin{bmatrix} -1 & 0 \\ 0 & 1 \end{bmatrix} \begin{bmatrix} x \\ y \end{bmatrix}$$

Figure 4.149

   (c) Reflection across the y = x line:

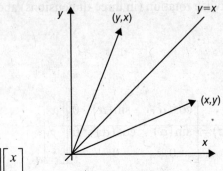

$$T(x,y) = \begin{bmatrix} 0 & 1 \\ 1 & 0 \end{bmatrix} \begin{bmatrix} x \\ y \end{bmatrix}$$

Figure 4.150

(d) Reflection about the xy-plane (in $\mathbf{R}^3$)

$$T(x,y,z) = \begin{bmatrix} 1 & 0 & 0 \\ 0 & 1 & 0 \\ 0 & 0 & -1 \end{bmatrix} \begin{bmatrix} x \\ y \\ z \end{bmatrix}$$

(e) Reflection about the yz-plane (in $\mathbf{R}^3$)

$$T(x,y,z) = \begin{bmatrix} -1 & 0 & 0 \\ 0 & 1 & 0 \\ 0 & 0 & 1 \end{bmatrix} \begin{bmatrix} x \\ y \\ z \end{bmatrix}$$

(f) Reflection about the xz-plane (in $\mathbf{R}^3$)

$$T(x,y,z) = \begin{bmatrix} 1 & 0 & 0 \\ 0 & -1 & 0 \\ 0 & 0 & 1 \end{bmatrix} \begin{bmatrix} x \\ y \\ z \end{bmatrix}$$

Example: What is the standard matrix for a reflection about the xz-plane followed by a 30° rotation (counterclockwise) about the x-axis in three-dimensional space?

Let A_1 be the standard matrix for the reflection and let A_2 be the standard matrix for the rotation. Then the associated/standard matrix for the reflection followed by the rotation is

$$A = A_2 A_1 \text{ since } T(x, y, z) = = A_2 \left(A_1 \begin{bmatrix} x \\ y \\ z \end{bmatrix} \right)$$

Since $A_1 = \begin{bmatrix} 1 & 0 & 0 \\ 0 & -1 & 0 \\ 0 & 0 & 1 \end{bmatrix}$ and $A_2 = \begin{bmatrix} 1 & 0 & 0 \\ 0 & \cos(30°) & -\sin(30°) \\ 0 & \sin(30°) & \cos(30°) \end{bmatrix} = \begin{bmatrix} 1 & 0 & 0 \\ 0 & \dfrac{\sqrt{3}}{2} & \dfrac{-1}{2} \\ 0 & \dfrac{1}{2} & \dfrac{\sqrt{3}}{2} \end{bmatrix},$

$$A = A_2 A_1 = \begin{bmatrix} 1 & 0 & 0 \\ 0 & \dfrac{\sqrt{3}}{2} & \dfrac{-1}{2} \\ 0 & \dfrac{1}{2} & \dfrac{\sqrt{3}}{2} \end{bmatrix} \begin{bmatrix} 1 & 0 & 0 \\ 0 & -1 & 0 \\ 0 & 0 & 1 \end{bmatrix} = \begin{bmatrix} 1 & 0 & 0 \\ 0 & \dfrac{-\sqrt{3}}{2} & \dfrac{-1}{2} \\ 0 & \dfrac{-1}{2} & \dfrac{\sqrt{3}}{2} \end{bmatrix}$$ is the associated matrix for the reflec-

tion followed by the rotation.

Review Problems for Section 4.4.1

1. Let $T(x, y, z) = (y, -3x, z)$. Find a matrix A that represents T.

2. After a reflection in the y-axis, $(4, -7)$ is the image of point P. What is P?

3. What is the image under the translation $T(x, y) = (x + 3, y - 2)$ of $\triangle ABC$ with coordinates $A(2, 6)$, $B(0, 10)$, and $C(8, -5)$?

4. What is the image of point $(8, -4, 2)$ under the 90° rotation (counterclockwise) about the z-axis?

   (A) $(8, 4, 2)$

   (B) $(4, 8, 2)$

   (C) $(-4, 8, 2)$

   (D) $(-4, -8, -2)$

5. Which translation is equivalent to the composition $R_1 \circ R_2$, where R_1 is the reflection about the y-axis and R_2 is the reflection about the line $y = x$?

   (A) A rotation

   (B) A reflection

   (C) A translation

   (D) A glide-reflection

6. Describe completely the transformation shown in Figure 4.151 on the next page.

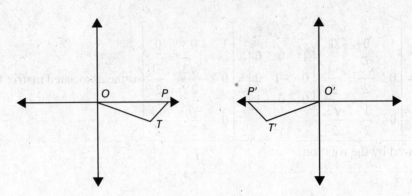

Figure 4.151

Detailed Solutions

1. The columns of the associated matrix will be $T(1, 0, 0)$, $T(0, 1, 0)$, $T(0, 0, 1)$ if T is a *linear* transformation. Check:

$$T((x, y, z) + (u, v, w)) = T(x + u, y + v, z + w) = (y + v, -3(x + u), z + w) = (y, -3x, z)$$
$$+ (v, -3u, w) = T(x, y, z) + T(u, v, w)$$

$$T(c(x, y, z)) = T(cx, cy, cz) = (cy, -3cx, cz) = c(y, -3x, z) = cT(x, y, z)$$

T is a linear transformation.

$T(1,0,0) = (0, -3, 0), T(0,1,0) = (1,0,0), T(0,0,1) = (0,0,1)$. So the associated or standard matrix

$$A = \begin{bmatrix} 0 & 1 & 0 \\ -3 & 0 & 0 \\ 0 & 0 & 1 \end{bmatrix}.$$

2. The inverse of a reflection is itself. Reflecting $(4, -7)$ over the y-axis gives $P = (-4, -7)$.

3. The transformation T is a translation; translations map a figure to a congruent figure. So $\triangle ABC$ is mapped to $\triangle DEF$, where $D = T(2,6) = (5, 4)$, $E = T(0, 10) = (3, 8)$, and $F = T(8, -5) = (11, -7)$, and $\triangle ABC \cong \triangle DEF$.

4. **(B)**

A $90°$ rotation about the z-axis is given by $T(x, y, z) = \begin{bmatrix} \cos(90°) & -\sin(90°) & 0 \\ \sin(90°) & \cos(90°) & 0 \\ 0 & 0 & 1 \end{bmatrix} \begin{bmatrix} x \\ y \\ z \end{bmatrix}$, or

$T(x, y, z) = \begin{bmatrix} 0 & -1 & 0 \\ 1 & 0 & 0 \\ 0 & 0 & 1 \end{bmatrix} \begin{bmatrix} x \\ y \\ z \end{bmatrix}$. Therefore, $T(8, -4, 2) = \begin{bmatrix} 0 & -1 & 0 \\ 1 & 0 & 0 \\ 0 & 0 & 1 \end{bmatrix} \begin{bmatrix} 8 \\ -4 \\ 2 \end{bmatrix} = \begin{bmatrix} 4 \\ 8 \\ 2 \end{bmatrix}$.

5. (A)

The rule says that if the lines of reflection are parallel, the product is a translation; otherwise, it is a rotation. The y-axis and the line $y = x$ are not parallel, so the result must be a rotation.

If we do not know the rules of what a composition of reflections produces, we could look at it graphically; choose a triangle and draw the image under the reflections. If the image does not look like a translation, then it must be a rotation.

6. The transformation is a reflection about the y-axis in $\mathbf{R}^2$ taking $\triangle OPT$ to $\triangle O'P'T'$.

4.4.2 The California *Mathematics Subject Matter Requirements* stipulate that candidates for any credential program for teaching secondary mathematics must be able to *understand and prove the basic properties of dilations (e.g., similarity transformations or change of scale).*

Dilation

A **dilation** with **center** C and a **scale factor** k is a transformation that maps every point P to a point P' so that the following properties are true:

i.   If P is not the center point C, then the image point P' lies on ray $\overrightarrow{CP}$. The scale factor k is a positive number such $k = \dfrac{CP'}{CP}$ and $k \neq 1$.

ii. If P is the center point C, then $P = P'$ and $k = 1$.

Example: Consider the dilation shown in Figure 4.152. $\triangle ABC \sim \triangle DEF$. Since corresponding sides are in proportion, we can see that $\dfrac{DE}{AB} = 2$ must be the scale factor.

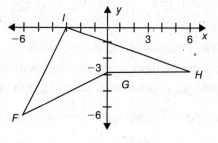

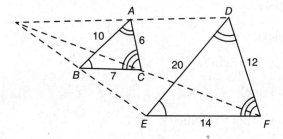

Figure 4.152

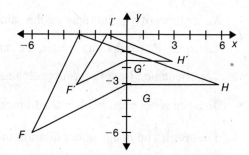

Figure 4.153

A dilation changes the size of a figure but not its shape, which means the image and preimage are similar. The dilation is a **contraction** (reduction or shrink) if $0 < k < 1$, and it is an **expansion** (enlargement or stretch) if $k > 1$. Sometimes the word *dilation* refers to this linear transformation only when $k > 1$.

For a dilation with scale factor k and center the origin, the image of a point x is the point $\overline{kx}$. This means that the associated transformation and matrix:

i. in $\mathbf{R}^2$ is $T(x, y) = (kx, ky) = \begin{bmatrix} k & 0 \\ 0 & k \end{bmatrix}\begin{bmatrix} x \\ y \end{bmatrix}$

ii. in $\mathbf{R}^3$ is $T(x, y, z) = (kx, ky, kz) = \begin{bmatrix} k & 0 & 0 \\ 0 & k & 0 \\ 0 & 0 & k \end{bmatrix}\begin{bmatrix} x \\ y \\ z \end{bmatrix}$

Example: Use matrices to find the image of quadrilateral *FGHI* shown in Figure 4.153 when the center of dilation is the origin and the scale factor is ½.

$T(x, y) = \begin{bmatrix} \frac{1}{2} & 0 \\ 0 & \frac{1}{2} \end{bmatrix}\begin{bmatrix} x \\ y \end{bmatrix}$. We can find all four images of the vertices in one multiplication by the

matrix operator:

$\begin{bmatrix} \frac{1}{2} & 0 \\ 0 & \frac{1}{2} \end{bmatrix}\begin{bmatrix} -6 & 0 & 6 & -3 \\ -6 & -3 & -3 & 0 \end{bmatrix} = \begin{bmatrix} -3 & 0 & 3 & \frac{-3}{2} \\ -3 & \frac{-3}{2} & \frac{-3}{2} & 0 \end{bmatrix}$

The columns of the second matrix on the left side are the vertices of *FGHI*, and the resulting matrix on the right side gives the coordinates of the vertices of the image quadrilateral *F'G'H'I'*. The image is shown in the second graph in Figure 4.153.

- Properties preserved (invariant) under a dilation:

  1. angle measures (remain the same)

  2. parallelism (parallel lines remain parallel)

  3. collinearity (points stay on the same lines)

  4. midpoint (midpoints remain the same in each figure)

  5. orientation (lettering order remains the same)

- Distance is not preserved under dilation, so it is not an isometry.

Theorem: The image under dilation of a line segment is a parallel line segment.

Proof: Choose $\overline{PQ}$ non-collinear with the origin; make a coordinate system with point *O* at the origin and label points *P* and *Q* as (*a, b*) and (*c, d*), respectively (Figure 4.154). By definition of dilation, $k = \dfrac{OP'}{OP} = \dfrac{OQ'}{OQ}$, and since Q' lies on ray OQ and P' lies on ray OP, we have $\angle O \cong \angle O$. So by SAS for similarity, $\triangle POQ \sim \triangle P'OQ'$. So $\angle OQP \cong \angle OQ'P'$. For the lines $\overleftrightarrow{QP}$ and $\overleftrightarrow{Q'P'}$ the corresponding angles are congruent, so $\overleftrightarrow{QP} \parallel \overleftrightarrow{Q'P'}$.

Q.E.D.

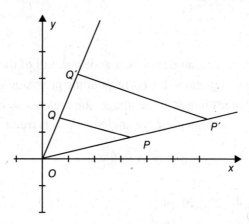

Figure 4.153

Review Problems for Section 4.4.2

1. In the *Star Wars* movies, Darth Vader is 77 inches tall in his black suit. The Scifi Toy Company is making a Darth Vader doll that will be 14 inches tall. What is the scale factor they will use to make the doll?

2. When $\triangle ABC$ undergoes a dilation with a scale factor of 3, its image is $\triangle PQR$. Which of the following statements is true?

   (A) $\overline{AB} \cong \overline{DE}$

   (B) The perimeter of $\triangle ABC$ = the perimeter of $\triangle DEF$

   (C) The area of $\triangle DEF$ = 3(the area of $\triangle ABC$)

   (D) $\angle ACB \cong \angle DFE$

3. Use matrices to find the image under dilation of rectangle $ABCD$ with $A(1, 2)$, $B(5, 2)$, $C(5, 4)$, and $D(1, 4)$. Use the origin as the center and use a scale factor of 4. How does the perimeter of the preimage compare to the perimeter of the image?

4. Prove that the image under a dilation of a midpoint of a segment is the midpoint of the segment.

Detailed Solutions

1. The scale factor will be $k = \dfrac{14}{77} = \dfrac{2}{11}$.

2. **(D)**

   If the scale factor is 3, then the triangle is larger and so are all of the sides. So the image's sides will be 3 times larger and not congruent to the corresponding preimage sides. So (A) and (B) cannot be true. Since each side is 3 times larger in the image, the area of the image is 9 times the area of the preimage, so (C) is false. Dilations preserve angles, so (D) is true.

3. $T(x,y) = \begin{bmatrix} 4 & 0 \\ 0 & 4 \end{bmatrix}\begin{bmatrix} x \\ y \end{bmatrix}$ so we can compute as follows:

$$\begin{bmatrix} 4 & 0 \\ 0 & 4 \end{bmatrix}\begin{bmatrix} 1 & 5 & 5 & 1 \\ 2 & 2 & 4 & 4 \end{bmatrix} = \begin{bmatrix} 4 & 20 & 20 & 4 \\ 8 & 8 & 16 & 16 \end{bmatrix}.$$

   So the image is rectangle $PQRS$ with vertices $P(4, 8)$, $Q(20, 8)$, $R(20, 16)$, and $S(4, 16)$. The perimeter of rectangle $PQRS = 2PQ + 2QR = 2(16) + 2(8) = 48$. The perimeter of the preimage is 12. So the perimeter also increases by a factor of 4.

4. **Proof**: Let $T(x, y) = (kx, ky)$ be a dilation, and let points A and B have coordinates (a, c) and (b, d), respectively. Then the midpoint of $\overline{AB}$ is point $M = \left(\dfrac{a+b}{2}, \dfrac{c+d}{2}\right)$.

   Let A' and B' be the images of points A and B, respectively. Then the coordinates of these points are (ka, kc) and (kb, kd), respectively. Thus, the midpoint of $\overline{A'B'}$ is the point $M' = \left(\dfrac{ka+kb}{2}, \dfrac{kc+kd}{2}\right) = k\left(\dfrac{a+b}{2}, \dfrac{c+d}{2}\right)$. So the midpoint of $\overline{AB}$ maps to the midpoint of $\overline{A'B'}$.

   Q.E.D.

Content Domain 4: *Probability and Statistics*

5.1 Probability

> **5.1.1** The California *Mathematics Subject Matter Requirements* stipulate that candidates for any credential program for teaching secondary mathematics must be able to *prove and apply basic principles of permutations and combinations.*

Sets

- A **set** is a collection of objects.

  Example: The set of positive integers between 3 and 11 is {4, 5, 6, 7, 8, 9, 10}.

- The objects in the set are called the **elements** or **members** of the set.

  Notation: Consider the set $A = \{2, 4, 6, 8\}$. The number 6 is an element of set A. In symbols, we write $6 \in A$. Also, 5 is not an element of A is denoted by $5 \notin A$.

- A set with no elements is called the **empty** or **null** set and is denoted by $\varnothing$ or { }, but not {$\varnothing$}, which happens to be a set with one element, $\varnothing$, in it!

- Two sets are **equal** if they contain exactly the same elements.

- A set can also be given in **set-builder notation**.

  Example: The set of all even positive integers can be written as: $\{n \in Z+ \,|\, n \text{ is even}\}$.

- The **universal set**, U, for a particular discussion is a set that includes all the objects under discussion.

  Example: If we are discussing the solutions of an equation, our universal set might be all real numbers.

- A set A is a **subset** of a set B ($A \subseteq B$) if every element of A is also in B.

  Notation: To indicate that B is not a subset of C, we write $B \not\subseteq C$.

  Example: Let $U = \{1, 2, 3, \ldots, 20\}$, $A = \{1, 2, 3, 5, 7, 10, 12\}$, $B = \{2, 3, 5, 7\}$, and $C = \{1, 4, 10, 12\}$.

  True or False: (a) $A \subseteq B$, (b) $B \subseteq A$, (c) $B \subseteq C$, (d) $C \subseteq A$, (e) $C \subseteq C$, (f) $\varnothing \subseteq B$, (g) $C \subseteq \varnothing$

  Answers: (a) False, (b) True, (c) False, (d) False, (e) True, (f) True, (g) False.

  Note: For any set A, $\varnothing \subseteq A$ and $A \subseteq A$.

Venn Diagrams

Let A and B be sets with universal set U. The basic operations and their Venn diagrams are shown in Figure 5.1.

Operation (Figures 5.1A and 5.1B)	**Venn Diagram**

The **complement** of set A is the set, A', of all objects in the universal set U that are *not* in A.

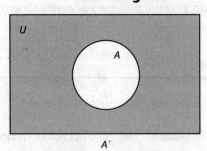

The **intersection** of sets A and B is the set $A \cap B$, which contains all elements of U that belong to both A and B.

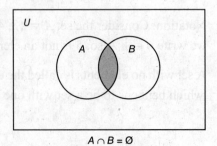

$A \cap B = \varnothing$

Figure 5.1A

Operation (Figures 5.1A and 5.1B)

Two sets, A and B, are **disjoint** ($A \cap B = \varnothing$) if they have no elements in common.

Venn Diagram

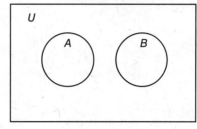

$A \cap B = \varnothing$

The **union** of two sets A and B is the set, $A \cup B$, of all elements belonging to either A or B (or both).

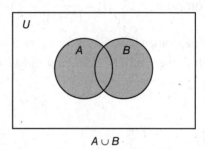

$A \cup B$

Figure 5.1B

Permutations and Combinations

To work with permutations and combinations, we must understand factorials.

Factorials

- For all non-negative integers n, $n!$ is read as **n-factorial** and is defined by

$$n! = n\,(n-1)\,(n-2)\ldots 3 \cdot 2 \cdot 1$$

We define 0! to be equal to 1.

Examples: $3! = (3)(2)(1) = 6$, $4! = (4)(3)(2)(1) = 3!(4) = 24$, $5! = 4!(5) = 120$

Note that $\dfrac{7!}{3!} = \dfrac{7 \cdot 6 \cdot 5 \cdot 4 \cdot 3 \cdot 2 \cdot 1}{3 \cdot 2 \cdot 1} = 7 \cdot 6 \cdot 5 \cdot 4$

- This illustrates the rule: $\dfrac{n!}{r!} = n \cdot (n-1) \cdot (n-2)\ldots(n-r)$ for $n \geq r$.

Permutations

- An arrangement or selection of objects (without replacement) for which the selection order is important is called a **permutation**.

  Example: How many different arrangements of the letters R, A, and T can be made?

  RAT, RTA, ART, ATR, TAR, TRA. So we see the answer is $6 = 3(2)$ or $6!$.

- **The number of permutations of n objects taken r at a time** ($r \leq n$) is denoted by $_nP_r$ and is defined as

$$_nP_r = \frac{n!}{(n-r)!} = n \cdot (n-1) \cdot (n-2) \ldots (n-r+1)$$

Examples:

(a) Compute $_8P_5$: $\quad _8P_5 = \frac{8!}{(8-5)!} = \frac{8!}{3!} = 8 \cdot 7 \cdot 6 \cdot 5 \cdot 4 = 6{,}720$

(b) Nine women have formed a softball team. How many ways can three of them be chosen to play left fielder, center fielder, and right fielder?

$$_9P_3 = \frac{9!}{(9-3)!} = \frac{9!}{6!} = 9 \cdot 8 \cdot 7 = 504$$

So there are 504 different ways for the team to choose the three outfield positions.

(c) A club has 15 members. In how many ways can a president, vice-president, secretary, and treasurer be chosen?

$$_{15}P_4 = \frac{15!}{(15-4)!} = \frac{15!}{11!} = 15 \cdot 14 \cdot 13 \cdot 12 = 32{,}760$$

So there are 32,760 ways the club can select a president, vice-president, treasurer, and secretary.

(d) Which one of the following problems is a permutation problem and why?

  (i) There are six students in a club. Three will be chosen to go to a convention to represent the club. How many different ways can the three representatives be chosen?

  (ii) There are six students in a group. Three will be chosen to go to a convention to represent the group, and will be labeled Delegate 1, Delegate 2, Delegate 3. How many different ways can the three delegates be chosen?

The order is important in the second problem because if we choose Jo, Jose, and Jim to be Delegate 1, 2, and 3, respectively, we could also choose Jim, Jo, and Jose to be Delegate 1, 2, and 3, respectively, and this would be a different choice.

There are $_6P_3 = \frac{6!}{3!} = 6 \cdot 5 \cdot 4 = 120$ ways to choose three people to go to the convention labeled as Delegate 1, 2, and 3.

How is problem (i) different than problem (ii)?

If Moe, Chloe, and Joe are chosen, in problem (i) to represent the group at the convention, we cannot choose Chloe, Moe, and Joe as a different choice, as we could have in problem (ii). Changing the order of the names does not give us a different choice. This problem is an example of a **combination.**

Combinations

- An arrangement or selection of objects (without replacement) in which the order is not important is called a **combination**.

   Example: Look back at the previous problem i: *There are six students in a group. Three will be chosen to go to a convention to represent the group. How many ways can the three be chosen?*

   When the order mattered (i.e., changing the order gave us a different valid selection), there were 120 different selections. But in the case of combinations, some of the permutation selections are not viewed as different, such as "Moe, Chloe, Joe"; "Chloe, Moe, Joe"; "Moe, Joe, Chloe"; "Chloe, Joe, Moe"; "Joe, Moe, Chloe"; and "Joe, Chloe, Moe." So we can choose three objects three at a time six ways, or 3! Hence, we can choose three people from six in $\frac{120}{6} = 20$ ways.

   This is an example of a combination of 6 objects taken 3 at a time. Sometimes we say this is "6 choose 3" and we may write it as $\binom{6}{3}$ or as in the following definition.

- The number of **combinations of *n* objects taken *r* at a time** ($r \le n$) is defined to be:

$$_nC_r = \frac{_nP_r}{r!} = \frac{n!}{r!(n-r)!} = \binom{n}{r}$$

Examples:

(a) Compute $_{11}C_6 = \binom{11}{6} = \frac{11!}{6!(11-6)!} = \frac{11!}{6! \cdot 5!} = \frac{11 \cdot 10 \cdot 9 \cdot 8 \cdot 7}{5 \cdot 4 \cdot 3 \cdot 2 \cdot 1} = 11 \cdot 3 \cdot 2 \cdot 7 = 462$

(b) How many different ways can we choose 5 cards from an ordinary deck of 52 cards? That is, how many different 5-card hands are there?

   This is a combination problem because if you are holding five cards and then you change the order in which you are holding the five cards, you do not have a different collection of five cards.

$$\binom{52}{5} = \frac{52!}{5!47!} = \frac{52 \cdot 51 \cdot 50 \cdot 49 \cdot 48}{5 \cdot 4 \cdot 3 \cdot 2 \cdot 1} = 2,598,960$$

There are 2,598,960 different five-card hands.

Review Problems for Section 5.1.1

1.   Compute the following:

   (a) $\dfrac{13!}{10!}$

   (b) $_{18}C_3$

   (c) $_{22}P_4$

   (d)   If $U = \{1, 2, 3, ..., 25\}$, $E = \{2, 4, 6, ..., 24\}$, $O = \{1, 3, 5, ..., 25\}$, $A = \{5, 10, 15, 20, 25\}$, find

          i. $A \cap E$

          ii. $(A \cup O)'$

2.   A chapel has nine bells in its bell tower. Before each church service, six bells are rung in sequence. No bell is rung more than once. How many possible sequences are there?

   (a)   504

   (b)   5,040

   (c)   16,440

   (d)   60,480

3.   An exam with 15 questions is given in a math class. Students are required to answer any 10 questions. How many choices of 10 questions are there?

   (a)   150

   (b)   1505

   (c)   3003

   (d)   5432

4.   Draw the Venn Diagram representing:

   (a) $A' \cap B$

   (b) $A \cup (B \cap C)$

Detailed Solutions

1. (a) $\dfrac{13!}{10!} = 13 \cdot 12 \cdot 11 = 1,716$

    (b) $_{18}C_3 = \dfrac{18!}{3!15!} = \dfrac{18 \cdot 17 \cdot 16}{3 \cdot 2 \cdot 1} = 3 \cdot 17 \cdot 16 = 816$

    (c) $_{22}P_4 = \dfrac{22!}{18!} = 22 \cdot 21 \cdot 20 \cdot 19 = 175,560$

    (d) (i) $A \cap E = \{10, 20\}$

        (ii) $A \cup O = \{1, 3, 5, 7, 9, 10, 11, 13, 15, 17, 19, 20, 21, 23, 25\}$ so that
        $(A \cup O)' = U - (A \cup O) = \{2, 4, 6, 8, 12, 14, 16, 18, 22, 24\}$

2. **D**

    Since the order is important (i.e., if you change the order you get another possible answer), this is a permutation problem of 9 objects 6 at a time: $_9P_6 = \dfrac{9!}{3!} = 9 \cdot 8 \cdot 7 \cdot 6 \cdot 5 \cdot 4 = 60,480$. Thus there are 60,480 different sequences to ring the bells.

3. **C**

    Since choosing problem 1 and 2 is the same as choosing problem 2 and 1, the order does not matter (i.e., changing the order does not produce another possibility). Therefore, this is a combination: $_{15}C_{10} = \dfrac{15!}{10!5!} = \dfrac{15 \cdot 14 \cdot 13 \cdot 12 \cdot 11}{5 \cdot 4 \cdot 3 \cdot 2 \cdot 1} = 3,003$. There are 3,003 ways to choose 10 problems.

4. (a) $A' \cap B$ is everything in B that is not in A.
    (b) $A \cup (B \cap C)$ is everything in A along with the objects in the intersection of B and C.

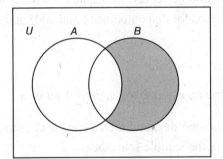
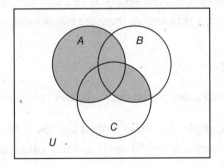

Figure 5.2

5.1.2 The California *Mathematics Subject Matter Requirements* require that candidates for any credential program for teaching secondary mathematics must be able *to illustrate finite probability using a variety of examples and models (e.g., the fundamental counting principles).*

Probability Experiments

In probability, an **experiment** is an activity or occurrence with an observable result. Each repetition of an experiment is called a **trial**. Experiments in which there is no predictability, such as flipping a coin, are called **random experiments**. **Probability** is the area of mathematics that studies random experiments. From this point on, when we say "experiment" we mean "random experiment."

A **probability** is a ratio, which may be expressed as a fraction, decimal, or percent. The ratio is determined from considering possible results of an experiment. The results of an experiment are called **outcomes**. The set of all possible outcomes of an experiment is called the **sample space**.

The outcomes of an experiment must be chosen so that when the experiment is performed one and only one of the outcomes occurs.

Examples:

(a) Two coins, a penny and a nickel, are flipped, and the face that is upward is recorded. The sample space for this experiment is (where the penny is recorded first). $S = \{(heads, heads), (heads, tails), (tails, heads), (tails, tails)\}$. There are four elements in the sample space; we indicate this by $n(S) = 4$.

(b) Which of the following is not a sample space for the experiment "rolling a die?" $\{1, 2, 3, 4, 5, 6\}$, $\{odd, 1, 2, 4, 6\}$, $\{even, odd\}$?

The first and last set could be a sample space, but the middle set cannot because if a die is rolled and a 1 is facing up there are two possible representations for that outcome (1 and odd) in the set.

Events

- Given a sample space, S, for an experiment, we define an **event** E to be any subset of S.

Example: A coin is flipped and the side facing up is recorded, and then a card is chosen from an ordinary deck of 52 cards and the suit is recorded. Let the sample space be

$S = \{(heads, D), (heads, H), (heads, S), (heads, C), (tails, D), (tails, H), (tails, S), (tails, C)\}$, where D is diamonds, H is hearts, S is spades, and C is clubs.

Find the following events.

(a) A head is observed on the coin.

$E = \{(heads, D), (heads, H), (heads, S), (heads, C)\}$

(b) A tail is observed and the suit is black.

$E = \{(tails, S), (tails, C)\}$

(c) A head is observed and the suit is hearts.

$E = \{(heads, H)\}$

- For a sample space S with **equally likely outcomes** (i.e., one outcome is just as likely to occur as the other), the **probability of an event E** is

$$P(E) = \frac{n(E)}{n(S)}$$

- When we assume that the outcomes are **equally likely**, we are determining the probability **theoretically**. Unless it is indicated otherwise, we are computing probabilities theoretically.

Example: A ball is randomly chosen from a jar that contains 30 balls numbered 1 through 30. The sample space is $S = \{1, 2, 3, \ldots, 29, 30\}$. Find the probability of choosing a ball with:

(a) The number five on it. $E = \{5\}$, so $P(E) = \dfrac{n(E)}{n(S)} = \dfrac{1}{30}$

(b) A number divisible by 3 on it. $E = \{3, 6, 9, 12, 15, 18, 21, 24, 27, 30\}$, so we obtain $P(E) = \dfrac{10}{30} = \dfrac{1}{3}$.

(c) A positive number on it. $E = S$, so $P(E) = 1$.

(d) A zero on it. $E = \varnothing$, so $P(E) = 0$.

- Since $\varnothing \subseteq E \subseteq S$ for any event E, and $0 = n(\varnothing) \leq n(E) \leq n(S)$, we have $0 = P(\varnothing) \leq P(E) \leq P(S) = 1$, or **probabilities have values only from 0 to 1.**
- Events can be classified according to their probabilities.

(1) If $E = S$, then E is called a **certain event**.

$$P(S) = 1$$

(2) If the event $E = \varnothing$ (the empty set), then E is called an **impossible event**.

$$P(\varnothing) = 0$$

(3) If an event E contains only one outcome, then it is called a **simple event**. If $S = \{E_1, E_2, E_3, \ldots, E_n\}$, where the E_i are simple events, then $P(S) = 1 = \sum_{i=1}^{n} P(E_i).$

$$P(S) = \sum_{i=1}^{n} P(E_i) = 1$$

Examples:

(a) Suppose we flip three coins, a penny, nickel, and dime, in this order. (**Note**: S = {HHH, HHT, HTH, THH, HTT, THT, TTH, TTT}, $n(S)$ = 8.) What is the probability of each of the following?

   (i) Exactly 3 heads. E = {HHH}, thus $P(E) = 1/8 = 0.125$.

   (ii) Two tails and a head, in that order. E = {TTH}, so $P(E) = 1/8 = 0.125$.

   (iii) Two tails and a head, in any order. E = {TTH, THT, HTT}, so $P(E) = 3/8 = 0.375$.

(b) Two fair (or uniform) dice are thrown, one red and the other green (S = ((1,1), (1,2), (1,3),..., (5,6), (6,6)}; $n(S)$ = 36). What is the probability of each of the following:

   (i) The numbers on both dice are greater than 6. $E = \varnothing$, so $P(E) = 0$.

   (ii) The numbers on the dice are the same. E = {(1,1), (2,2), (3,3), (4,4), (5,5), (6,6)}, therefore $P(E) = 6/36 = 1/6$.

Rules for Computing Probabilities

- **The Union Rule**: For any events E and F,

$$P(E \cup F) = P(E) + P(F) - P(E \cap F)$$

- If $E \cap F = \varnothing$, then E and F are called **mutually exclusive events**. Hence $P(E \cap F) = 0$; therefore,

$$P(E \cup F) = P(E) + P(F)$$

- For any event E, the **complement of E** is the set $E' = S - E$, and since E and E' are mutually exclusive,

$$P(E') = 1 - P(E)$$

Example: Two dice are rolled, one red and the other white. What is the probability that the sum of the dots on the upward faces of the dice is:

(a) at least 4?

The sample space consists of pairs of numbers. The sample space (with the red die's number first) is

S = {(1, 1), (1, 2), (1, 3), (1, 4), (1, 5), (1, 6), (2, 1), (2, 2), (2, 3), (2, 4), (2, 5), (2, 6), (3, 1), (3, 2), (3, 3), (3, 4), (3, 5), (3, 6), (4, 1), (4, 2), (4, 3), (4,4), (4, 5), (4, 6), (5, 1), (5, 2), (5, 3), (5, 4), (5, 5), (5, 6), (6, 1), (6, 2), (6, 3), (6, 4), (6, 5), (6, 6)}.

So $n(S)$ = 36.

The event E is having a sum of at least 4. Note that it is easier to list the complement event, E', *less than or equal to 3*. So we use the complement rule. E' = {(1, 1), (1, 2), (2, 1)} and $P(E) = 1 - P(E') = 1 - 1\dfrac{3}{36} = \dfrac{33}{36} = \dfrac{11}{12}$.

(b) greater than 9 or both dice show an odd number?

The sample space is the same as in part (a). Let E be the event *the sum is greater than* 9 and let F be the event *both dice show an odd number*. Then

E = {(4, 6), (5, 5), (5, 6), (6, 4), (6, 5), (6, 6)}

F = {(1, 1), (1, 3), (1, 5), (3, 1), (3, 3), (3, 5), (5, 1) (5, 3) 5, 5)}

$E \cap F$ = {(5, 5)}.

So, $n(E)$ = 6, $n(F)$ = 9, $n(E \cap F)$ = 1 and

$$P(E \text{ or } F) = P(E \cup F) = P(E) + P(F) - P(E \cap F) = \frac{6}{36} + \frac{9}{36} - \frac{1}{36} = \frac{14}{36} = \frac{7}{18}.$$

(c) greater than or equal to 8 and both dice show a prime number?

The sample space is the same as in part (a). Let E be the event *the sum is greater than or equal to 8* and let F be the event *both dice show a prime number*. Then

E = {(2, 6), (3, 5), (3, 6), (4, 4), (4, 5), (4, 6), (5, 3), (5, 4), (5, 5), (5, 6), (6, 2), (6, 3), (6, 4), (6, 5), (6, 6)}

F = {(2, 2), (2, 3), (2, 5), (3, 2), (3, 3), (3, 5), (5, 2), (5, 3), (5, 5)}.

So, $E \cap F$ = {(3, 5), (5, 3), (5, 5)}, hence, $P(E \cap F) = \dfrac{3}{36} = \dfrac{1}{12}$.

(d) less than 4 or equal to 7?

The sample space is the same as in part (a). Let E be the event *the sum is less than 4* and let F be the event *the sum is equal to 7*.

E = {(1, 1), (1, 2), (1, 3)}

F = {(1, 6), (2, 5), (3, 4), (4, 3), (5, 3), (6, 1)}

These events are mutually exclusive, so $P(E \cap F) = 0$.

Then $P(E \cup F) = P(E) + P(F) = \dfrac{3}{36} + \dfrac{6}{36} = \dfrac{9}{36} = \dfrac{1}{4}$.

- **The Fundamental Counting Principle** is used to determine the total possible choices when combining groups of items. If you can choose one item from a group of M possibilities, and another from a group of N possibilities, then the total number of two-item choices is MN.

  This principle can be extended to n choices: If you can choose one item each from n groups with $M_1 \cdot M_2, \cdots, M_n$ possibilities, respectively, then the total number of n-item choices is $M_1 \cdot M_2 \cdots M_n$.

  Example: A pizza can be ordered with three size choices (small, medium, or large), three crust choices (thin, thick, or regular), and six topping choices (beef, sausage, pepperoni, bacon, extra cheese, or mushroom). How many different one-topping pizzas can be ordered?

  There are $3 \cdot 3 \cdot 6 = 54$ different one-topping pizzas that can be ordered.

Empirical Probability

- A **probability distribution** is a sample space, $S = \{s_1, s_2, s_3, ..., s_n\}$, for an experiment, along with a set of numbers $p_1, p_2, ..., p_n$ that satisfy the following two conditions:

  1. For each $i = 1, 2, \ldots, n$, $0 \le p_i \le 1$

  2. $p_1 + p_2 + \cdots + p_n = 1$

  The number p_i is the **empirical probability** of the outcome s_i.

  Example: Suppose we toss a die 200 times and find that a one comes up 43 times, a two 25 times, a three 53 times, a four 31 times, a five 35 times, and a six 13 times. We can summarize this in a **frequency table** (Figure 5.3).

Outcome	Frequency
1	43
2	25
3	53
4	31
5	35
6	13

Figure 5.3

- In general, if we conduct an experiment n times and an outcome s_i occurs with frequency $f(s_i)$, then the ratio $\dfrac{f(s_i)}{n}$ is called the **empirical probability**.

Example: The **probability distribution** for the previous example is:

Outcome	Frequency	Probability
1	43	$\dfrac{43}{200} = 21.5\%$
2	25	$\dfrac{25}{200} = 12.5\%$
3	53	$\dfrac{53}{200} = 26.5\%$
4	31	$\dfrac{31}{200} = 15.5\%$
5	35	$\dfrac{35}{200} = 17.5\%$
6	13	$\dfrac{13}{200} = 6.5\%$

Figure 5.4

- Once we have a probability distribution, we define the **probability of an arbitrary event** E, denoted by $P(E)$, as follows:

1. If E is the empty set, then $P(E) = 0$.

2. If $E = \{t_1, t_2, ..., t_q\}$ and the probability of t_i is p_i for each $i = 1, 2, ..., q$,

   then $P(E) = p_1 + p_2 + \cdots + p_q$.

3. If $E = S$, then $P(E) = P(S) = 1$.

Example: Using the probability distribution from the last example (see Figure 5.4), what is the probability of rolling:

(a) an even number?

   $E = \{2, 4, 6\}$, $P(E) = P(2) + P(4) + P(6) = (12.5 + 15.5 + 6.5)\% = 34.5\%$

(b) a number greater than 2?

   $E = \{3, 4, 5, 6\}$, $E' = \{1, 2\}$, $P(E) = 1 - P(E') = 1 - (.215 + .125) = .66 = 66\%$

(c) a number divisible by 7?

   $E = \varnothing$, $P(E) = 0$

(d) a nonnegative number?

$E = S, P(E) = 1.$

Review Problems for Section 5.1.2

1. One marble is randomly chosen from a box with 7 red, 3 blue, and 9 green marbles. What is the probability that a blue one is chosen?

2. Given: $P(A) = .43, P(B) = .62, P(A \cap B) = .22$

    (a) Find $P(A')$.

    (b) Find $P(A \cup B)$.

    (c) Are A and B mutually exclusive? Why or why not?

3. A card is randomly chosen from a standard deck of 52 cards. What is the probability that the card is:

    (a) not a heart?

    (b) a spade and a club?

    (c) red or black?

    (d) a red king or queen?

4. Four coins are flipped 1,000 times, giving the following frequency table:

Outcomes	Frequency
4 heads	72
3 heads	104
2 heads	322
1 heads	363
0 heads	139

    Figure 5.5

    What is the probability that if you flip four coins you get at least two heads? Make a relative frequency table.

5. A bag contains three red marbles, two green marbles, one pearl blue marble, two yellow marbles, and three orange marbles. If you grab five marbles from the bag at random, what is the probability that you have all the red ones and that you have the pearl blue marble?

6. A door has a four-digit security access code. Each digit can be any number from 0 to 9 inclusive.

(a) How many access codes are possible if each digit can be used only once and the first digit cannot be a 0 or 1?

(b) If we randomly choose a four digit access code as described in part (a), what is the probability that the code is correct?

Detailed Solutions

1. There are 19 total marbles and 3 blue, so the probability of choosing a blue marble is $\frac{3}{19}$.

2. (a) $P(A') = 1 - P(A) = 1 - 0.43 = 0.57$

   (b) $P(A \cup B) = P(A) + P(B) - P(A \cap B) = 0.43 + 0.62 - 0.22 = 0.83$

   (c) A and B are mutually exclusive events if and only if they do not intersect. They don't intersect if and only if $P(A \cap B) = 0$, which is not the case in this problem. So A and B are not mutually exclusive.

3. The sample space is the set of 52 cards so $n(S) = 52$.

   (a) If H is the event *a card is a heart* then $P(H) = \frac{13}{52} = 0.25$, since $n(H) = 13$. Then $P(H') = 1 - 0.25 = 0.75$.

   (b) The events *a card is a spade* and a *card is a club* are mutually exclusive, so $P(spade \cap club) = 0$.

   (c) All 52 cards in the sample space are either *red* or *black*, so this is a certain event and $P(red \cup black) = 1$.

   (d) Let R be the event that *a card is red* and let C be the event *a card is either a king or queen*. Then, $P(R \cap C) = \frac{4}{52} = \frac{1}{13}$. Hence, there is a 1/13 probability that a card is a red king or queen.

4. The relative frequency table is:

Outcomes	Frequency	Relative Frequency or Probability
4 heads	72	7.2%
3 heads	104	10.4%
2 heads	322	32.2%
1 head	363	36.3%
0 heads	139	13.9%
total	1000	100%

Figure 5.6

The probability of at least two heads is 1 – (the probability that there are 1 or 0 heads) $= 1 - (0.363 + 0.139) = 1 - 0.502 = 49.8\%$.

5. The number of different ways to choose five marbles is $_{11}C_5 = \dfrac{11!}{6!5!} = 462$.

The number of ways to choose one pearl blue, then three red, and then another marble is

$_1C_1 \cdot {}_3C_3 \cdot {}_7C_1 = 1 \cdot 1 \cdot 7 = 7$.

Therefore, the probability that you choose five marbles, where one is pearl blue and three are red is $\dfrac{7}{462} = \dfrac{1}{66} = 0.015151515... \approx 0.015 = 1.5\%$

6. (a) We use the *Fundamental Theorem of Counting* here: There are 8 choices for the first number of the access code (no 0 or 1), then 9 choices for the second number (cannot use the number you chose for the first number), then 8 choices for the third number, and 7 choices for the fourth number. So there are 4,032 ways to choose an access code.

(b) The probability of getting the correct access code is $\dfrac{1}{4032} = 0.000248$

5.1.3 The California *Mathematics Subject Matter Requirements* stipulate that candidates for any credential program for teaching secondary mathematics must be able to *use and explain the concept of conditional probability*.

Conditional Probability

The probability of an event A given an event B is called the **conditional probability of A given B** and is denoted by $P(A|B)$.

$$P(A\,|\,B) = \frac{P(A \cap B)}{P(B)} = \frac{n(A \cap B)}{n(B)}, \text{ where } P(B) \neq 0$$

Example: Suppose a Finite Mathematics class contains 50 students. Of these, 35 are freshmen, 30 are business majors, and 25 are both.

(a) What is the probability that a student randomly selected from the class is a business major?

S is the set of all the students in the class, F is the set of all freshman in the class, and B is the set of all business majors in the class.

$n(S) = 50$, $n(F) = 35$, $n(B) = 30$, $n(F \cap B) = 25$, $P(B) = \dfrac{n(B)}{n(S)} = \dfrac{30}{50} = 60\%$.

Thus, the probability that a randomly chosen student is a business major is 60%.

(b) A student is randomly selected from the class. If we know that the student is a freshman, what is the probability that the student is a business major?

This is conditional probability. $P(B/F) = \dfrac{n(F \cap B)}{n(F)} = \dfrac{25}{35} \approx 71.3\%$.

Therefore, the probability that a random student chosen from the class is a business major, when we know the student is a freshman, is 71.3%

(c) A certain company of 1000 employees has 400 employees who participate in the profit-sharing plan, 800 employees who have major medical insurance, and 340 who do both. What is the probability that an employee chosen randomly has major medical insurance if we know the employee is in the profit-sharing plan?

Let A be the set of employees who have major medical insurance, and let B be the set of employees who participate in the profit-sharing plan. Then

$$P(A \mid B) = \frac{n(A \cap B)}{n(B)} = \frac{340}{400} = 85\%.$$

Thus, the probability that an employee chosen randomly has major medical given they participate in the profit-sharing plan is 85%.

Product Rule of Probability

Note that the formula $P(A \mid B) = \dfrac{P(A \cap B)}{P(B)}$ can be written in the following form:

$$\boxed{P(A \cap B) = P(A|B) \cdot P(B)}$$

This is called the **Product Rule of Probability**.

Example: A firm has six accountants, three women and three men. If two of the accountants are randomly selected to attend a seminar, what is the probability that the two who are chosen are both men?

Let M = the set of all male accountants.

$P(M \cap M)$ = the probability of choosing 2 men. $P(M|M)$ is the probability of choosing a man on the second pick if the first one chosen is a male.

Figure 5.7 shows a **tree diagram**. On the first choice of an accountant there is a 50-50 chance of picking either a male or female since there are 3 males and 3 females. This is illustrated on the first set of branches. The second set of branches represents conditional probability since the first selection has already been made. The product of these numbers gives the probabilities of arriving at the selection of the two accountants.

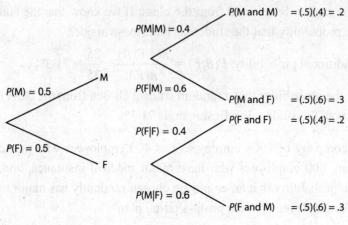

$$P(M|M) = 0.4 \qquad P(M \text{ and } M) = (.5)(.4) = .2$$

M

$$P(M) = 0.5 \qquad P(F|M) = 0.6$$
$$P(M \text{ and } F) = (.5)(.6) = .3$$
$$P(F \text{ and } F) = (.5)(.4) = .2$$
$$P(F|F) = 0.4$$

$$P(F) = 0.5$$

F

$$P(M|F) = 0.6$$
$$P(F \text{ and } M) = (.5)(.6) = .3$$

Figure 5.7

The probability of choosing 2 males is 20%.

 Review Problems for Section 5.1.3

1. Given: $P(A) = .43$, $P(B) = .62$, $P(A \cap B) = .22$, find $P(A|B)$ and $P(B|A)$.

2. A collection of 22 laptops includes 16 defective laptops. If a sample of 3 laptops is randomly chosen from the collection, what is the probability that at least one laptop in the sample will be defective?

3. Use a tree diagram to solve the following: (label the diagram completely). If two people are chosen randomly from among eight men and six women, what is the probability that the two people are of the same gender?

Detailed Solutions

1. $P(A \mid B) = \dfrac{P(A \cap B)}{P(B)} = \dfrac{.22}{.62} = \dfrac{11}{31} \approx 35.5\%. \quad P(B \mid A) = \dfrac{P(B \cap A)}{P(A)} = \dfrac{.22}{.43} = \dfrac{22}{43} \approx 51.2\%.$

2. The complement of choosing *at least one defective laptop* is choosing *no defective laptops*. So we will compute the latter and then subtract from 1.

    We use the *Fundamental Counting Principle* as we choose each of the three laptops.

    P(three non-defective laptops) = P(first laptop not defective)·P(second laptop not defective| first laptop not defective)·P(third laptop not defective| first two laptops not defective)

    $= \dfrac{16}{22} \cdot \dfrac{15}{21} \cdot \dfrac{14}{20} = \dfrac{4}{11} \approx 0.3636.$ So the probability of at least one defective laptop) $\approx 1 - 0.3636$

    $= 0.6364 \approx 63.6\%.$

3. Make the tree diagram (Figure 5.8).

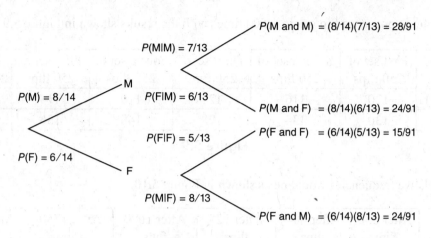

Figure 5.8

So the probability that the two chosen people are of the same gender is

$$P(\text{M and M}) + P(\text{F and F}) = \frac{28}{91} + \frac{15}{91} = \frac{43}{91} \approx 47.3\%$$

5.1.4 The California *Mathematics Subject Matter Requirements* stipulate that candidates for any credential program for teaching secondary mathematics must be able to *interpret the probability of an outcome.*

Interpreting Probabilities

In the previous sections, we have mainly looked at the classical notion of probability (**classical probability**) in a theoretical way such that simple events are equally likely to occur.

Another interpretation that is most frequently used and most easily understood is based on experiments (**empirical probability**) and the concept of **relative frequencies**.

Consider an experiment that can be repeatedly performed in an identical and independent fashion (such as flipping a coin), and let A be an event consisting of a fixed set of outcomes of the experiment. Simple examples of such repeatable experiments include coin-flipping and die-tossing experiments. If the experiment is performed n times (n **trials**), on some of the trials, event A will occur (the outcome will be in the set A), and on others, A will not occur. Let $n(A)$ denote the number of trials on which A does occur. Then the ratio $\frac{n(A)}{n}$ is called the **relative frequency of occurrence of the event A in the sequence of n trials.**

Example: Suppose we flip a coin 1,500 times with the results shown in Figure 5.9.

Outcome	First set of 250 flips	Second set of 250 flips	Third set of 250 flips	Fourth set of 250 flips	Fifth set of 250 flips	Sixth set of 250 flips
Heads (H)	120	116	122	110	114	100
Tails (T)	130	134	128	140	136	150

Figure 5.9

Then the relative frequencies would be as shown in Figure 5.10.

	After 250 flips	After 500 flips	After 725 flips	After 1000 flips	After 1250 flips	After 1500 flips
Relative frequency of H	$\frac{120}{250} = 0.48$	$\frac{236}{500} = 0.472$	$\frac{358}{750} \approx 0.478$	$\frac{468}{1000} \approx 0.468$	$\frac{582}{1250} \approx 0.466$	$\frac{682}{1500} \approx 0.455$
Relative frequency of T	$\frac{130}{250} = 0.52$	$\frac{264}{500} = 0.528$	$\frac{392}{750} \approx 0.522$	$\frac{532}{1000} \approx 0.532$	$\frac{668}{1250} \approx 0.534$	$\frac{818}{1500} \approx 0.545$

Figure 5.10

The results of many such repeatable experiments have indicated that any relative frequency of this sort will stabilize as the number of replications n increases. That is, as n gets arbitrarily large, $\frac{n(A)}{n}$ approaches a limiting value referred to as the **limiting (or long-run) relative frequency of the event** A.

The objective interpretation of probability identifies this limiting relative frequency with $P(A)$.

For example, suppose that probabilities are assigned to events in accordance with their limiting relative frequencies. Then a statement such as "The probability of a package being delivered within one day of mailing is .62" means that of a large number of mailed packages, approximately 62% will arrive within one day. It does *not* say anything about a specific package.

Similarly, if B is the event that a certain brand refrigerator will need service while under warranty, then $P(B) = 0.2$ is interpreted to mean that in the long run 20% of such refrigerators will need warranty service. This does not mean that exactly 2 out of 10 will need service, or that exactly 20 out of 100 will need service, because 10 and 100 are not the long run.

This relative frequency interpretation of probability is said to be **objective** because it rests on a property of the experiment rather than on any particular item involved with the experiment.

For a fair coin, $P(H) = P(T) = 0.5$, and for a fair die $P(1) = \ldots = P(6) = 1/6$. These probabilities have been shown by the limiting relative frequencies of these events.

Because the objective interpretation of probability is based on the concept of the limiting relative frequency, its applicability is limited to experimental situations that can be repeated. Yet the language of probability is often used in connection with situations that are inherently unrepeatable. Examples include: "The chances are good for rain today," "It is likely that 70% of the class will get at least a B+ on the exam," and "Because their best receiver is injured, I expect them to score no more than 10 points against us."

In such situations, we would like to assign numerical probabilities to various outcomes and events. Interpretations in such situations are hence termed **subjective**.

In the subjective approach, we define probability as **the degree of belief that we hold in the occurrence of an event.** That is, **subjective probability** is based on opinion, not facts.

 ## Review Problems for Section 5.1.4

1. Classify each of the following statements as an example of classical probability, subjective probability, or empirical probability.

    (a) On the basis of a study of 2000 American cars, a randomly chosen American car will have a white exterior 42% of the time.

    (b) I think there is a 50% chance of rain tomorrow.

    (c) The probability of flipping a coin and obtaining *tails* is 50%.

2. You are told that the probability that the new bicycle you are buying has a 90% probability of lasting 10 years. What does this mean?

3. What does it mean when a friend of yours tells you that if he flips the coin he has in his hand, the probability that a head will land up is 50%?

Detailed Solutions

1. (a) This is empirical probability because the probability is based on an experiment (sampling).

    (b) This is subjective probability because it is based on an opinion.

    (c) We are assuming the coin is a fair coin and that each side has an equally likely chance of facing upward. This is classical or theoretical probability.

2. This means that out of many, many bicycles of this type and brand, approximately 90% will last at least 10 years. It does not mean your particular bicycle has a 90% probability of lasting 10 years.

3. Your friend is assuming that the coin is a fair coin and that each of the two sides of the coin is equally likely to land upwards.

5.1.5 The California *Mathematics Subject Matter Requirements* stipulate that candidates for any credential program for teaching secondary mathematics must be able to *use normal, binomial, and exponential distributions to solve and interpret probability problems.*

The Binomial Distribution

- A **binomial experiment** is a probability experiment that satisfies all of the following conditions:

  (1) The experiment is repeated for a fixed number, n, of trials, where each trial is independent of the others.

  (2) There are only two possible outcomes of each trial. The outcomes can be labeled S for success and F for failure.

  (3) The probability of success $P(S)$ is the same for every trial.

  (4) The random variable x counts the number of successful trials.

  Example: An octahedral die is rolled, and it is noted whether or not the number rolled is less than 4. This is done ten times, and three times the number 1, 2, or 3 faces upward.

  So, $n = 10$; S = rolling a 1, 2, or 3; F is rolling a 4, 5, 6, 7, or 8; $P(S) = \dfrac{3}{8}$, $P(F) = \dfrac{5}{8}$, and $x = 3$.

- In a binomial experiment, **the probability of exactly x successes in n trials** is

$$P(x) = {}_nC_x p^x q^{n-x} = \frac{n!}{(n-x)!x!} p^x q^{n-x}, \text{ where } p = P(S), \text{ and } q = P(F) = 1 - p.$$

  Example: Jackie is taking a multiple-choice quiz that has five questions. Each question has four possible answers, only one of which is correct. If Jackie randomly guesses the answers to the questions, what is the probability that she gets at least four answers correct?

  First, we compute the probability of getting exactly four correct, then exactly five correct. Lastly add the two results together using the union rule.

  Exactly four correct: $P(4) = {}_5C_4 p^4 q = 5\left(\dfrac{1}{4}\right)^4\left(\dfrac{3}{4}\right) \approx 0.0146$

  Exactly five correct: $P(5) = {}_5C_5 p^5 q^0 = \left(\dfrac{1}{4}\right)^5 \approx 0.00098$

  So the probability that Jackie guesses and gets at least four correct is $0.01558 \approx 1.6\%$.

- A **binomial distribution** is a list of the possible values for x along with the values of $P(x)$ for each. It is a type of **discrete probability distribution,** which means it has a finite number of values for x.

Graphing a Binomial Distribution

Suppose we know that 78% of all households in the United States own at least one cell phone. We randomly choose 10 households and ask whether they own at least one cell phone. To construct a probability distribution for the random variable x, we compute $P(x)$ for each x, where $P(x) = {}_{10}C_x(.78)^x(.22)^{10-x}$.

x	P(x)
0	0.0000003
1	0.0000094
2	0.00015024
3	0.00142044
4	0.00881320
5	0.03749617
6	0.11078415
7	0.22444581
8	0.29841091
9	0.23511162
10	0.08335776
sum	1

Figure 5.11

Graph the information using a histogram.

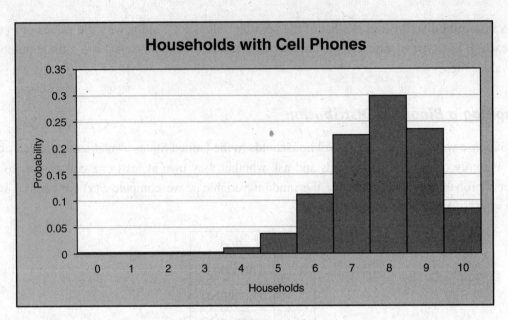

Figure 5.12

We can see from the histogram that it is usual for the ten households to have at least one cell phone.

Normal Distributions

- A **continuous random variable** has an infinite number of possible values, which can be represented by an interval on a number line. Its probability distribution is called a **continuous probability distribution**.

- The **normal distribution** is the most widely known and widely used of all distributions. Because the normal distribution approximates many natural phenomena (blood pressure, height, etc.) so well, it has developed into a standard of reference for many probability problems.

- A normal distribution is a continuous probability distribution for a random variable x. The graph of a normal distribution is called a **normal curve**.

- A normal distribution can have any mean, μ, and positive standard deviation, σ. These two parameters determine the shape of the curve.

- The mean is the center of the data and the line of symmetry occurs at μ.

- The standard deviation determines how spread out the data are and hence the width of the curve.

- A normal distribution (Figure 5.13) must have the following properties:

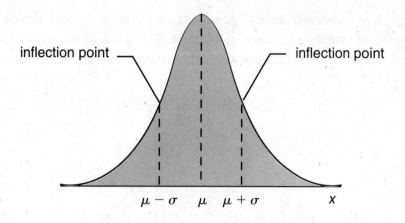

Figure 5.13

(1) The mean, mode, and median are equal.

(2) The normal curve is bell-shaped and is symmetric about the mean.

(3) The total area under the curve and above the horizontal axis is 1.

(4) The normal curve approaches but never intersects the x-axis as it extends farther and farther away from the mean.

(5) Between $\mu - \sigma$ and $\mu + \sigma$ the graph is concave down and is concave up when $x > \mu + \sigma$ or $x < \mu - \sigma$. The curve has inflection points when $x = \mu \pm \sigma$.

μ is the **mean** and σ is the **standard deviation.**

We use a histogram to graph a discrete probability distribution, but a continuous probability curve can be given by a **probability density function, or pdf**. The normal curve is given by the **normal probability density function** $y = \dfrac{1}{\sigma\sqrt{2\pi}} e^{\frac{-(x-\mu)}{2\sigma^2}}$.

Figure 5.14 shows some examples of normal distributions.

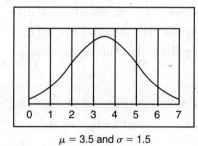

$\mu = 3.5$ and $\sigma = 1.5$

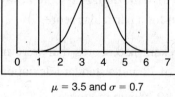

$\mu = 3.5$ and $\sigma = 0.7$

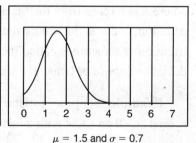

$\mu = 1.5$ and $\sigma = 0.7$

Figure 5.14

From the graph of the normal curve (Figure 5.15), we can see that approximately 68.2% of the data lies within one standard deviation of the mean, 95.7% lies within two standard deviations of the mean, and 99.7% of all data lies within three standard deviations of the mean.

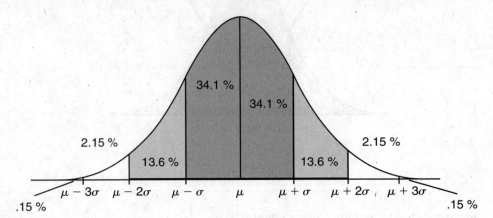

Figure 5.15

Example: The lifetime of a battery *is normally distributed* with a mean life of 44 hours and a standard deviation of 1.5 hours. Find the probability that a randomly selected battery lasts longer than 47 hours.

Since 47 hours is two standard deviations above the mean, the percentage of data that lies above this is about 2.15 + .15 = 2.3%. So the probability that a battery would last beyond 47 hours is 2.3%.

The Standard Normal Distribution

The **standard normal distribution** is a normal distribution with a mean of 0 and a standard deviation of 1. Normal distributions can be transformed to standard normal distributions by the formula

$$z = \frac{x - \mu}{\sigma}$$

where x is a score from the original normal distribution, μ is the mean of the original normal distribution, and σ is the standard deviation of original normal distribution. The standard normal distribution is sometimes called the *z* **distribution**. A *z*-score always reflects the number of standard deviations above or below the mean for a particular score.

Example: Suppose a history exam had scores that were normally distributed and a person scored an 80 on a test with a mean of 72 and a standard deviation of 5. Converting the test score to a *z*-score would give $z = \frac{80 - 72}{5} = 1.9$, shown in Figure 5.16.

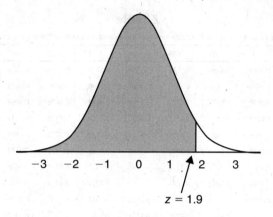

$z = 1.9$

Figure 5.16

The area under the standard normal curve is the probability that z lies in a particular interval. So, $P(a < z < b)$ represents the probability that a standard normal random variable is between a and b and is the area under the curve over the interval $[a, b]$; $P(z > a)$ represents the probability that a standard normal random variable is greater than a; and $P(z < a)$ represents the probability that a standard normal random variable is less than a. We do not distinguish between strict ($<$, $>$) and non-strict ($\leq$, $\geq$) inequalities.

Figure 5.17 presents a standard z-score table. We can use it to find probability.

Examples:

(a) Suppose the average miles per gallon for a Toyota is 33 with a standard deviation of 4. How many miles to the gallon do the top 10% of Toyota cars average?

We are looking for the z-score where 10% of the area lies to the right or 90% lies to the left. So we look at the z-score table (Figure 5.17) and locate the closest z-score that goes with .9000. The z-score of 1.28 has .8997, so we use this to compute x.

$z = \dfrac{x - \mu}{\sigma} \Rightarrow 1.28 = \dfrac{x - 33}{4} \Rightarrow x = 38.12$. So the top 10% of Toyotas would average 38.12 miles per gallon.

Z Table

Entries in the body of the table represent area under the curve between μ and z

z	0.00	0.01	0.02	0.03	0.04	0.05	0.06	0.07	0.08	0.09
0.0	0.5000	0.5040	0.5080	0.5120	0.5160	0.5199	0 5239	0.5279	0.5319	0.5359
0.1	0.5398	0.5438	0,5478	0.5517	0.5557	0.5596	0.5436	0.5675	0.5714	0.5753
0.2	0.5793	0.5832	0.5871	0.5910	0.5948	0.5987	0.6026	0.6064	0.6103	0.6141
0.3	0.6179	0 6217	0.6255	0.6293	0 6331	0.6368	0.6406	0.6443	0 6480	0.6517
0.4	0.6554	0 6591	0.6628	0 6664	0.6700	0 6736	0 6772	0 6808	0 6844	0 6879
0.5	0.6915	0.6950	0 6985	0.7019	0.7054	0.7088	0.7123	0.7157	0 7190	0.7224
0.6	0.7257	0.7291	0.7324	0.7357	0.7389	0.7422	0.7454	0.7486	0.7517	0.7549
0.7	0.7580	0.7011	0 7642	0.7673	0 7704	0.7734	0 7764	0 7794	0 7823	0.7152
0.8	0.7881	0 7910	0 7939	0 7967	0 7995	0 8023	0 8051	0.8078	0 8106	0.8133
0.9	0.8159	0.8186	0 8212	0.8238	0 8264	0.8289	0 8315	0.8340	0 8365	0.8389
1.0	0.8413	0.8438	0 8461	0.8485	0 8508	0.8531	0.8554	0.8577	0.8599	0.8621
1.1	0.8643	0.8665	0.8686	0.8708	0.8729	0 8749	0 8770	0.8790	0.8810	0.8830
1.2	0.8849	0.8869	0.8888	0.8907	0 8925	0.8944	0.8962	0.8980	0.8997	0.9015
1.3	0.9032	0.9049	0.9066	0.9082	0.9099	0.9115	0.9131	0.9147	0.9162	0.9177
1.4	0.9192	0.9207	0.9222	0.9236	0 9251	0.9265	0.9279	0 9292	0 9306	0.9319
1.5	0.9332	0 9545	0 9557	0 9570	0 9582	0 9394	0.9406	0.9418	0 9429	0 9441
1.6	0.9452	0 9463	0.9474	0 9484	0.9495	0.9505	0 9515	0.9525	0.9535	0.9545
1.7	0.9554	0.9564	0.9573	0.9582	0.9591	0.9599	0 9408	0.9616	0.9625	0.9633
1.8	0.9641	0.9649	0.9656	0.9664	0.9671	0.9678	0.9686	0.9693	0.9699	0.9706
1.9	0.9713	0 9719	0.9726	0.9732	0 9738	0.9744	0.9750	0.9756	0.9761	0 9767
2.0	0.9772	0.9778	0.9783	0.9788	0 9793	0.9798	0.9803	0 9808	0.9812	0.9817
2.1	0.9821	0.9826	0.9830	0.9834	0 9838	0.9842	0.9846	0.9850	0.9854	0.9857
2.2	0.9861	0.9864	0.9868	0.9871	0.9875	0.9878	0.9881	0.9884	0.9887	0.9890
2.3	0.9893	0 9896	0 9898	0 9901	0 9904	0 9906	0.9909	0.9911	0.9913	0.9916
2.4	0.9918	0.9920	0.9922	0.9925	0 9927	0.9929	0 9931	0.9932	0.9934	0.9936
2.5	0.9938	0.9940	0.9941	0 9943	0 9945	0.9946	0.9948	0.9949	0 9951	0.9952
2.6	0.9953	0 9955	0 9956	0 9957	0 9959	0 9960	0 9961	0 9962	0 9963	0.9964
2.7	0.9965	0.9966	0 9967	0 9968	0 9969	0.9970	0 9971	0.9972	0 9973	0 9974
2.8	0.9974	0.9975	0.9974	0.9977	0.9977	0.9978	0.9979	0.9979	0.9980	0.9981
2.9	0.9981	0.9982	0.9982	0.9983	0 9984	0.9984	0.9985	0.9985	0.9986	0.9986
3.0	0.9987	0.9987	0 9987	0 9988	0 9989	0 9989	0 9989	0 9989	0.9990	0.9990

Figure 5.17

(b) Suppose that SAT math scores have a normal distribution with mean 500 and standard deviation 120. What percentage of people taking the math SAT test should have scores between 600 and 700?

$$P(600 < x < 700) = P(x < 700) - P(x < 600)$$

We need to have the z-scores for $x < 600$ and $x < 700$:

$$z = \frac{600-500}{120} \approx 0.8333 \quad \text{and} \quad z = \frac{700-500}{120} \approx 1.6667.$$ So, using the table:

Look in the row for 0.8 and column. 0.03, which is 0.7967, meaning that $P(x < 600) \approx 79.67\%$.

Now look in the row for 1.6 and the column for 0.07 to obtain 0.9525, which means that $P(x < 700) \approx 95.25\%$.

So, $P(600 < x < 700) = P(x < 700) - P(x < 600) \approx 95.25 - 79.67 = 15.58\%$.

Approximately 15.58% of all test takers would earn a score on the math portion of the SAT between 600 and 700 (inclusive, actually).

Exponential Distribution

An **exponential distribution** can be used to describe various physical phenomena, such as the time t for a radioactive nucleus to decay or the time x for a component to fail. The exponential distribution is characterized by the single parameter, λ. The distribution (Figure 5.18) can be given by the equation

$$f(x) = \lambda e^{-\lambda x} \text{ for } x \geq 0, \lambda > 0$$

The mean and variance for the exponential distribution are $\mu = \dfrac{1}{\lambda}$ and $\sigma^2 = \left(\dfrac{1}{\lambda}\right)^2$, respectively.

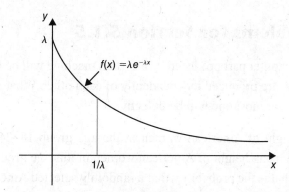

Figure 5.18

The exponential distribution is used to model the time between successive events, or the waiting time. The exponential distribution has the property of having no memory, i.e., knowing the time that the last event occurred does not assist in the prediction of when the next event may occur. For example, if you've already been waiting for a few minutes, the total amount of time you expect to wait is *the same*.

Note that $\int\limits_{0}^{\infty} \lambda e^{-\lambda x} dx = 1$. The **probability that x is greater than s** is the area under the curve

from s onward. $P(x > s) = \int\limits_{s}^{\infty} \lambda e^{-\lambda x} dx = 1 - \int\limits_{0}^{s} \lambda e^{-\lambda x} dx = e^{-\lambda s}$, where $e \approx 2.71828182$ is known as the

natural base.

$$\boxed{P(x > s) = e^{-\lambda s}}$$

The **conditional probability** $P(x > s + t \mid x > t) = P(x > t)$ means that the probability that x is greater than $s + t$, given that t minutes has already passed, is equal to the probability that x is greater than $(s + t) - t = s$.

$$P(x > s + t \mid x > t) = P(x > t)$$

Example: Suppose that the amount of time a person spends in a bank is exponentially distributed with mean 10 minutes. What is the probability that a customer will spend more than 20 minutes in a bank? What is the probability that a customer will spend more than 20 minutes in the bank, given that she is still in the bank after 10 minutes?

The mean is 10 so $\lambda = 1/10$. Then $P(x > 20) = e^{-\left(\frac{1}{10}\right)(20)} = e^{-2} \approx 0.1353$. So the probability that a person will be in a bank for more than 20 minutes is approximately 13.5%.

Also, $P(x > 20 \mid x > 10) = P(x > 10) = e^{-\left(\frac{1}{10}\right)(10)} = e^{-1} \approx 0.3678$. Therefore, the probability that a customer will be in a bank more than 20 minutes if she has already been in the bank 20 minutes is approximately 36.8%.

Review Problems for Section 5.1.5

1. It is known that a computer part produced by a certain machine will be defective with probability 0.1, and that parts are produced independently of each other. What is the probability that in a sample of 10 items, at most one will be defective?

2. Suppose that the height of American women in the age group 18–24 years is normally distributed and that the mean height of American women in this age group is 67″ with a standard deviation of 1.5″. What is the probability that a randomly selected American woman in this age group is less than 70″ tall?

3. If a normally distributed data set has a mean of 35.0 and a standard deviation of 2, in which of the following graphs does the shaded area represent the probability that a given member of the set is greater than or equal to 32 and less than or equal to 33?

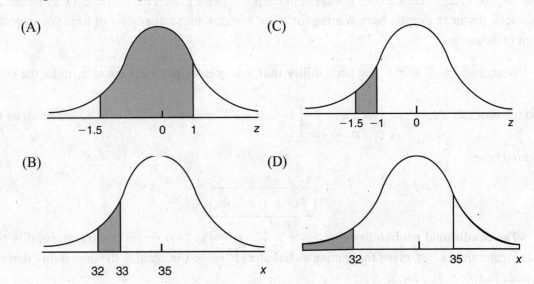

4. Suppose the time X it takes a puppy to run and get a ball follows an increasing exponential distribution with a mean of 30 seconds. What is the probability that it takes the puppy more than 50 seconds to get the ball?

5. A soda machine is filled with cans of soda that should hold 12 oz of soda. It is found that the volumes of the cans are normally distributed with a mean of 11.9 oz and a standard deviation of 0.045 oz. What is the probability that a randomly chosen can of soda from this machine will contain at least 12 oz of soda?

Detailed Solutions

1. This is a binomial distribution problem since we have "success" if the part is "a defective part." The probability of having *at most one defective part* is: (Let $x =$ the number of defective parts)

$$P(x = 0) + P(x = 1) = {}_{10}C_0(.1)^0(.9)^{10} + {}_{10}C_1(.1)^1(.9)^9$$

$$= (1)(1)(.348678) + (10)(.1)(.38742) \approx 0.7361$$

The probability that in a sample of 10 items at most one will be defective is 73.6%.

2. We want $P(x \leq 70) = P(x \leq 67) + P(67 \leq x \leq 70) = .50 + .477 = .977$ since the interval $[67, 70]$ is 2 standard deviations above the mean. Thus, the probability that a randomly selected American woman in the 18–24 year age group is less than 70″ tall is 97.7%.

3. **C**

   $P(32 < x < 33)$ is the area under the curve over the z interval (standard normal) corresponding to the z-scores that correspond with the x scores of 32 and 33:

   $$z = \frac{32 - 35}{2} = -1.5 \quad \text{and} \quad z = \frac{33 - 35}{2} = -1.$$

4. $\lambda = \frac{1}{\mu} = \frac{1}{30}$. So $P(X \geq 50) = e^{-\left(\frac{1}{30}\right)(50)} = e^{\frac{-5}{3}} \approx 0.1889$. The probability that the puppy will take more than 50 seconds is approximately 18.9%.

5. $z = \frac{12 - 11.9}{.045} \approx 2.22$. Using the z table, we look in the row for 2.2 and the column for .02 to obtain .9868. This number is the probability that the volume is less than or equal to 12 oz. So the probability that a randomly chosen soda can has at least 12 oz is approximately $1 - 0.9868 = 1.32\%$.

5.2 Statistics

> **5.2.1** The California *Mathematics Subject Matter Requirements* stipulate that candidates for any credential program for teaching secondary mathematics must be able to *compute and interpret the mean, median, and mode of both discrete and continuous distributions.*

Measures of Central Tendency

- A **population** is the collection of all outcomes, responses, measurements, or counts that are of interest, whereas a **sample** is a subset, or part, of the population.

  Example: In a survey, 2,000 adults in Mexico were asked if they thought there was good evidence that global warming exists. Of these, 1,146 responded yes. What are the population and the sample? Describe the sample data set.

  The population is the set of all responses of all the adults in Mexico. The sample is the set of responses of the 2,000 adults in Mexico who were surveyed. The data set consists of two sets: one is the 1,146 surveyed adults who responded *yes,* and the other is the 854 surveyed adults who said *no.*

- A **parameter** (or population statistic) is a numerical description of a characteristic of a *population,* whereas a **statistic** is a numerical description of a characteristic of a *sample.*

  Examples:

  (a) The average starting salary of teachers in 2010 was $30,500. The $30,500 is a parameter because it is based on a population.

  (b) In a recent survey of 1,000 teachers in California, it was found that their average starting salary in 2010 was $34,200. The $34,200 is a statistic because it is a numerical description of a sample.

Discrete Data Sets

Discrete data are data whose values are distinct and separate, whereas **continuous data** are data that are an interval.

- The **mean** of a data set is the sum of all the data values divided by the total number of data values.

- The **mode** of a data set is the number that occurs most often in the data. There can be more than one mode.

- The **median** of a data set is the middle score of the data when the data are put in order (lowest to highest or highest to lowest). If there is an even number of data numbers, then the median is the mean of the middle two numbers.

Examples: What are the mean, median, and mode for each data set below?

(a) $A = \{10, 7, 6, 8, 7, 9, 10, 10, 3, 4, 10\}$

The sum of the 11 numbers is 84, so the mean is $\frac{84}{11} = 7\frac{7}{11}$. List the scores from high to low: 10, 10, 10, 10, 9, 8, 7, 7, 6, 4, 3. The middle score is the 6th score, since there are 11 numbers, so the median is 8. Clearly, 10 is the mode since it occurs more times than all the other numbers.

(b) $B = \{6, 11, 7, 4, 2, 2, 3, 6\}$

The mean is the sum of the numbers, 41, divided by 8 which is 41/8 = 5.125. Again, we list the scores from high to low: 11, 7, 6, 6, 4, 3, 2, 2. Since there is an even number of numbers the median is the average of the two middle scores 6 and 4; the median is 5. There are two modes: 6 and 2. We say in this instance that the data are **bimodal**.

Continuous Distributions

A **probability density function,** pdf, of a continuous random variable x is a non-negative function, f, such that

(1) f is continuous on all intervals (a, b) on which f is positive, and

(2) the area under the curve but above the x-axis is normalized to equal 1, which means

$$\int_{-\infty}^{\infty} f(x)dx = 1.$$

(3) $P(a \le x \le b) = \int_{a}^{b} f(x)dx$ = the area under the curve $y = f(x)$ over the interval $[a, b]$.

A **continuous distribution** is a distribution that can be represented by a probability density function.

By definition, we have that P($X = x$) = 0 for continuous random variables. Continuous probability tells us only the probability that a random variable lies in an interval, not the specific value. The measures of central tendency for an example continuous distribution are shown in Figure 5.19.

- The **mean of a continuous distribution**, μ_x, is also called the **expected value**, $E(x)$. It is computed by $\mu_x = E(x) = \int_{-\infty}^{\infty} xf(x)dx$.

• The **median of a continuous distribution** is the value c, for which the area under the distribution curve lying to the left of $x = c$ is 0.5. So $\int_{-\infty}^{c} f(x)\,dx = \int_{c}^{\infty} f(x)\,dx = 0.5$.

• The **mode of a continuous distribution** is the value b where f has its maximum.

Example:

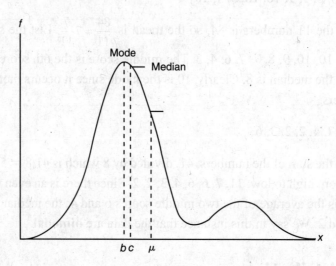

Figure 5.19

Find the mean, mode, and median for the continuous distribution with pdf

$$f(x) = \begin{cases} .2x^3 - 1.2x^2 + 2.4x - 1.4 & \text{if } 1 \le x \le 3.774 \\ 0 & \text{otherwise} \end{cases}$$

We graph the pdf in Figure 5.20 to help visualize the concepts.

(a) To find the mean, compute: $\displaystyle\int_{1}^{3.774} xf(x)\,dx = \int_{1}^{3.774} \left(.2x^4 - 1.2x^3 + 2.4x^2 - 1.4x\right) dx$

$$\int_{1}^{3.774} \left(.2x^4 - 1.2x^3 + 2.4x^2 - 1.4x\right) dx = \left(.04x^5 - 0.3x^4 + 0.8x^3 - 0.7x^2\right)\Big|_{1}^{3.774} \approx 2.958$$

(b) To compute the median, solve for $\displaystyle\int_{1}^{c} \left(.2x^3 - 1.2x^2 + 2.4x - 1.4\right) dx = 0.5$

$$\int_{1}^{c} \left(.2x^3 - 1.2x^2 + 2.4x - 1.4\right) dx = .05c^4 - 0.4c^3 + 1.2c^2 - 1.4c - 0.55 = 0.5$$

$.05c^4 - 0.4c^3 + 1.2c - 1.4c - 1.05 = 0$, so $c \approx 3.2115$

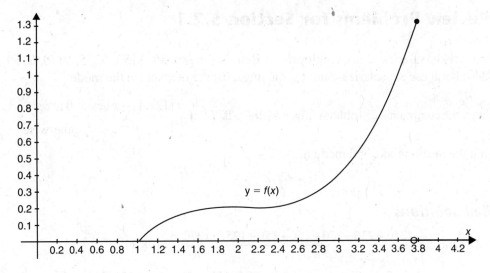

Figure 5.20

(c) The mode is the greatest value, which is $f(3.774) \approx 1.3166$

Skewed Distributions

A distribution is **skewed** if one of its tails is longer than the other.

The distribution on the left in Figure 5.21 has a **positive (or right) skew**. This means that it has a long tail in the positive (right) direction. The distribution in the center of Figure 5.21 has a **negative (or left) skew** since it has a long tail in the negative (left) direction. The third distribution is symmetric and has no skew.

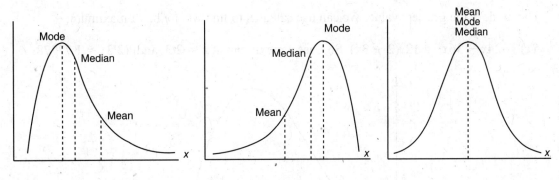

Figure 5.21

Review Problems for Section 5.2.1

1. The weekly salaries of six employees at Betty's Burgers are $150, $235, $170, $150, $125, $240. For these six salaries, find: (a) the mean (b) the median (c) the mode.

2. Given the continuous distribution given by the pdf $f(x) = \begin{cases} 12x^2(1-x) & \text{if } 0 \le x \le 1 \\ 0 & \text{otherwise} \end{cases}$

    Find the mean, mode, and median.

Detailed Solutions

1. (a) The mean is $\dfrac{240+235+170+150+150+125}{6} = \dfrac{1070}{6} \approx \$178.33$.

    (b) List the values from high to low: 240, 235, 170, 150, 150, 125. The median is the middle score. Since there is an even number of salaries, we average the two middle numbers to obtain $160 as the median.

    (c) The mode is $150 since it occurs twice in the data and the other numbers occur only once.

2. To help visualize these concepts, look at the graph of f shown in Figure 5.22.

    The mean is $E(x) = \int_0^1 xf(x)\,dx = \int_0^1 12x^3(1-x)\,dx = \int_0^1 \left(12x^3 - 12x^4\right) dx = \left(3(1)^4 - \dfrac{12}{5}(1)^5\right) = 0.6$

    To find the median, solve: $\int_0^c \left(12x^2 - 12x^3\right) dx = 0.5$

    $\int_0^c (12x^2 - 12x^3)\,dx = 4c^3 - 3c^4 = 0.5$. Using a graph to solve this, we get $c \approx 0.614275$.

    The mode is the greatest value. We can use calculus to find when f has a maximum:

    $f(x) = 24x - 36x^2 = 12x(2 - 3x)$. So f has a maximum at $x = 2/3$, and $f(2/3) \approx 1.77778$.

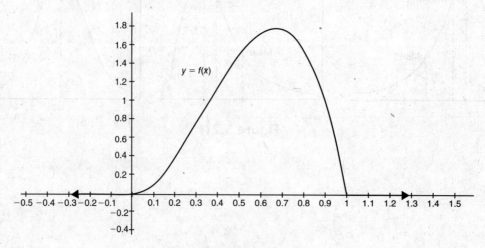

Figure 5.22

> **5.2.2** The California *Mathematics Subject Matter Requirements* stipulate that candidates for any credential program for teaching secondary mathematics must be able to *compute and interpret quartiles, range, variance, and standard deviation of both discrete and continuous distributions.*

Discrete Distributions

- Given a set of data, the **range** of the set is the difference between the greatest element of the data set and the least.

- The middle element of the data set, when it is listed from least to greatest, is called the median or the **second quartile** Q_2. The median breaks the data into a lower half of data and an upper half. The median of the lower half of the data is called the **first quartile** or **lower quartile** Q_1. The median of the upper half of the data is the **third quartile** or **upper quartile** Q_3.

- Twenty-five percent of all data lies below Q_1, which can be called the 25th percentile. Fifty percent of all data lies below Q_2, which is the 50th percentile. Seventy-five percent of all data lies below Q_3, which is also called the 75th percentile.

- Note that quartiles are not intervals, they are numbers.

- The **interquartile range (IQR)** is the difference between the third quartile and first quartile: $IQR = Q_3 - Q_1$

- **Percentiles** are like quartiles except they separate the data into 100 equal parts. Percentiles are used to compare the relative standing in a population. For example, having the 12th highest grade out of 80 students places a student in the 85th percentile $[(80-12)/80 = 68/80 = 85\%]$, whereas having the 12th highest grade out of 130 students places a student in the 90th percentile $[(130 - 12)/130 = 118/130 \approx 90.8\%]$.

Box Plots

A **box plot** or **box-and-whiskers plot** is a pictorial summary that illustrates the center, spread, extent, and nature of any symmetry/asymmetry in the distribution and identifies any outliers.

To Construct a box plot, follow these steps:

1. Draw a horizontal axis (number line) to use for measurement purposes.

2. Construct a rectangle whose left edge lies directly above Q_1 and whose right side lies above Q_3.

3. Draw a vertical line segment through the inside of the rectangle directly above Q_2.

4. Extend line segments from each end of the rectangle (box) out to the farthest observations.

Each of the data points outside the box that fall between 1.5 and 3 standard deviations from the nearest side of the box are called **mild outliers** and those that fall more than 3 standard deviations from the nearest side of the box are called **extreme outliers**.

Example: The following numbers are the heights in feet of the ten tallest buildings in Springcity, PA: 24, 55, 58, 64, 66, 68, 75, 88, 92, 220.

The calculations are shown in Figure 5.23.

x	$x - \bar{x}$	$(x - \bar{x})^2$
24	−57	3249
55	−26	676
58	−23	529
64	−17	289
66	−15	225
68	−13	169
75	−6	36
88	7	49
92	11	121
220	139	19321
$\bar{x} = 81$	$s^2 =$	2740.444

$Q_2 = (66 + 68)/2 = 67$

$Q_1 = 58, Q_3 = 88$

$s \approx 52.35$

$1.5s \approx 78.53$

$3s \approx 157$

So 220 is the only outlier and it is a mild outlier.

Figure 5.23

The box plot for this example is shown in Figure 5.24.

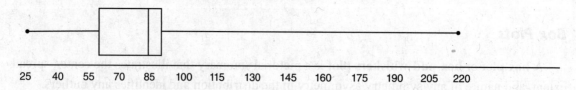

25   40   55   70   85   100   115   130   145   160   175   190   205   220

Figure 5.24

Variance

- **Variability** is a term that describes the spread of a distribution of data. **Variance** and **standard deviation** are ways of measuring, or quantifying, variability, with standard deviation simply being the square root of variance.

- The **variance of a sample** s^2 is computed using the formula $s^2 = \dfrac{\sum\limits_{i=1}^{n}\left(x_i - \bar{x}\right)^2}{n-1}$, where n is the number of items in the data and $\bar{x}$ is the sample mean.

- The **standard deviation** of a sample s is $s = \sqrt{\dfrac{\sum\limits_{i=1}^{n}\left(x_i - \bar{x}\right)^2}{n-1}}$.

- **For a population,** the variance is $\sigma^2 = \dfrac{\sum\limits_{i=1}^{n}\left(x_i - \bar{x}\right)^2}{n}$ and the standard deviation is $\sigma = \sqrt{\dfrac{\sum\limits_{i=1}^{n}\left(x_i - \bar{x}\right)^2}{n}}$.

In both cases, the smaller the variance the closer the data are together.

Example: Two charts of data are shown in Figure 5.25. Chart 1 shows a data set with mean 3 and variance 1.5. Chart 2 shows a data set with the same mean but with a larger variance, since the data are not clustered.

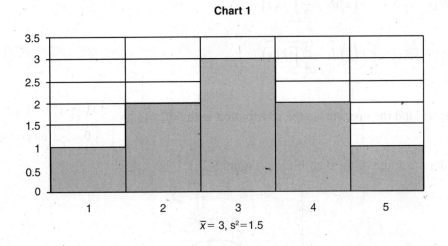

Figure 5.25

Continuous Distributions

The definitions of range, first, second, and third quartiles are the same for continuous distributions as for discrete distributions, but how to find the quartiles is different.

- Given a set of data, the **range** of the set is the difference between the greatest element of the data set and the least. The range could be infinite.

- The middle value of the data set is called the median or the **second quartile Q_2**. The median breaks the data into a lower half of data and an upper half. The median of the lower half of the data is called the **first quartile** or **lower quartile Q_1**. The median of the upper half of the data is the **third quartile** or **upper quartile Q_3**. To find these variables we must solve the following equations:

To find Q_1, solve: $\int_{-\infty}^{Q_1} f(x)\,dx = \frac{1}{4}\int_{-\infty}^{\infty} f(x)\,dx$

To find Q_2, solve: $\int_{-\infty}^{Q_2} f(x)\,dx = \frac{1}{2}\int_{-\infty}^{\infty} f(x)\,dx$

To find Q_3, solve: $\int_{-\infty}^{Q_3} f(x)\,dx = \frac{3}{4}\int_{-\infty}^{\infty} f(x)\,dx$

Example: Find the quartiles in the distribution with pdf $f(x) = \begin{cases} \frac{1}{2}x(3-x) & \text{for } 0 \le x \le 3 \\ 0 & \text{otherwise} \end{cases}$.

Consider the graph of the distribution (Figure 5.26).

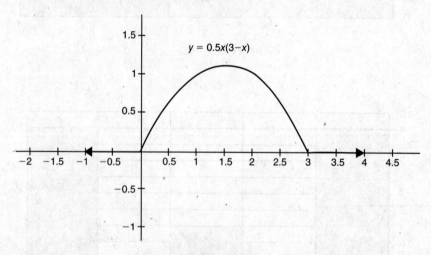

Figure 5.26

The graph is symmetric, so $Q_2 = 1.5$.

$\int_{0}^{3} \frac{1}{2}x(3-x)\,dx = \left(\frac{3}{4}x^2 - \frac{1}{6}x^3\right)\Big|_{0}^{3} = \frac{27}{4} - \frac{9}{2} = \frac{9}{4}$ is the area under the graph.

To find the first quartile, solve for a: $\int_0^a \frac{1}{2}x(3-x)\,dx = \frac{1}{4}\left(\frac{9}{4}\right) = \frac{9}{16}$: $\frac{3}{4}a^2 - \frac{1}{6}a^3 = \frac{9}{16}$, or $8a^3 - 36a^2 + 27 = 0$. To solve this, graph the function $y = 8x^3 - 36x^2 + 27$ and zoom in on the value between 0 and 3 where the graph crosses the x-axis (Figurie 5.27).

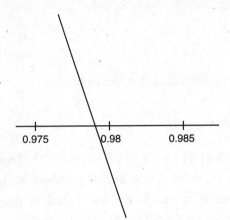

The value where the function crosses the axis is approximately 0.979, so this is the approximate value of a or Q_1.

Figure 5.27

To find the third quartile, we can use symmetry. Since the first quartile is approximately 0.979, the third quartile must be the same distance from the right endpoint of the interval, so that $Q_3 \approx 3 - 0.979 = 2.021$.

The IQR $\approx 2.021 - 0.979 = 1.042$

- Recall that the mean for a continuous distribution with pdf $y = f(x)$ is

$\mu = E(x) = \int_{-\infty}^{\infty} xf(x)\,dx$. The formula **variance** for continuous distributions comes from the discrete formula but using integrals (which are limits of sums) instead of sums. The formula is:

$V(x) = E(x^2) - u^2$, where $E(x^2) = \int_{-\infty}^{\infty} x^2 f(x)\,dx$.

Example: Find the variance in the distribution with pdf $f(x) = \begin{cases} \frac{3}{4}x(2-x) & \text{for } 0 \le x \le 2 \\ 0 & \text{otherwise} \end{cases}$.

$E(x) = \mu = \int_0^2 \frac{3}{4}x^2(2-x)\,dx = \left(\frac{1}{2}x^3 - \frac{3}{16}x^4\right)\Big|_0^2 = 1$

$E(x^2) = \int_0^2 \frac{3}{4}x^3(2-x)\,dx = \left(\frac{3}{8}x^4 - \frac{3}{20}x^5\right)\Big|_0^2 = 6 - \frac{24}{5} = 1.2$

So the variance is $V(x) = 1.2 - 1^2 = 0.2$

- The **standard deviation** of a continuous distribution is the square root of the variance.

In the previous example the variance is 0.2, so the standard deviation is $\sqrt{0.2} \approx 0.447$

Review Problems for Section 5.2.2

1. Find the interquartile range for the following data set:

    15 10 50 68 61 71 29 52 48 41 63 70 41

2. Let $f(x) = \begin{cases} 2e^{-2x} & \text{if } x \geq 0 \\ 0 & \text{otherwise} \end{cases}$.

    Find the mean, mode, median, and variance for the distribution with f as the pdf.

Detailed Solutions

1. Write the entries from lowest to highest: 10 15 29 41 41 48 50 52 61 63 68 70 71. There are 13 numbers. The median is the middle number: $Q_2 = 50$. There are six numbers below 50. The first quartile is the average of the two middle scores in the lower half of the data: $Q_1 = \dfrac{29+41}{2} = 35$. The third quartile is the average of the two middle scores out of the upper six scores: $Q_3 = \dfrac{63+68}{2} = 65.5$.

    Hence, the IQR = $65.5 - 35 = 30.5$.

2. The mean is $E(x) = \displaystyle\int_0^\infty 2xe^{-2x}dx = \lim_{c\to\infty}\int_0^c 2xe^{-2x}dx$.

    Using integration by parts, we can compute the indefinite integral: Let $u = 2x$ and $dv = e^{-2x}dx$, so that $du = 2dx$ and $v = \dfrac{-1}{2}e^{-2x}$. Then $\displaystyle\int 2xe^{-2x}dx = (2x)\left(\dfrac{-1}{2}e^{-2x}\right) - \int\dfrac{-1}{2}e^{-2x}(2dx) = -xe^{-2x} - \dfrac{1}{2}e^{-2x} + C$.

    Substitute this back into the above definite integral:

    $E(x) = \displaystyle\int_0^\infty 2xe^{-2x}dx = \lim_{c\to\infty}\int_0^c 2xe^{-2x}dx = \lim_{c\to\infty}\left[-ce^{-2c} - \dfrac{1}{2}e^{-2c} + \dfrac{1}{2}\right] = \dfrac{1}{2}$ (after using L'Hopital's rule).

    The mode is 0 since f has its maximum there.

    The area under the curve is $\displaystyle\int_0^\infty 2e^{-2x}dx = \lim_{c\to\infty}\int_0^c 2e^{-2x}dx = \lim_{c\to\infty}\left[-e^{-2c} + 1\right] = 1$ so the median is the value m, where $\displaystyle\int_0^m 2e^{-2x}dx = \dfrac{1}{2}$ or when $-e^{-2m} + 1 = \dfrac{1}{2} \Leftrightarrow e^{-2m} = \dfrac{1}{2} \Leftrightarrow m = \dfrac{1}{2}\ln(2)$. The median is $\dfrac{1}{2}\ln(2)$.

    To obtain the variance, we need: $E(x^2) = \displaystyle\int_0^\infty 2x^2e^{-2x}dx = \lim_{c\to\infty}\int_0^c 2x^2e^{-2x}dx$. We again must rely on integration by parts but we need to apply it twice: Let $u = 2x^2$ and let $dv = e^{-2x}dx$, so that $du = 4xdx$ and $v = \dfrac{-1}{2}e^{-2x}dx$:

$$\int 2x^2 e^{-2x} dx = \left(2x^2\right)\left(\frac{-1}{2}e^{-2x}\right) - \int \frac{-1}{2}e^{-2x}\left(4x\,dx\right) = -x^2 e^{-2x} + \int 2x e^{-2x} dx.$$ But we already know that

$$\int 2x e^{-2x} dx = -x e^{-2x} - \frac{1}{2}e^{-2x} + C;$$ hence,

$$\int 2x^2 e^{-2x} dx = -x^2 e^{-2x} + \int 2x e^{-2x} dx = -x^2 e^{-2x} - x e^{-2x} - \frac{1}{2}e^{-2x} + C.$$ Substituting back into the

definite integral: $\displaystyle\int_0^\infty 2x^2 e^{-2x} dx = \lim_{c\to\infty} \int_0^c 2x^2 e^{-2x} dx = \lim_{c\to\infty}\left[-c^2 e^{-2c} - c e^{-2c} - \frac{1}{2}e^{-2c} + \frac{1}{2}\right] = \frac{1}{2}$

$$V(x) = E(x^2) - \mu^2 = \frac{1}{2} - \frac{1}{4} = \frac{1}{4}.$$ The variance is $\frac{1}{4}$.

5.2.3 The California *Mathematics Subject Matter Requirements* stipulate that candidates for any credential program for teaching secondary mathematics must be able to *select and evaluate sampling methods appropriate to a task (e.g., random, systematic, cluster, convenience sampling) and display the results.*

Probability Sampling Methods

A **sample** is a collection of units selected from a larger group (the population), sometimes called the **sampling frame**. By studying the sample, one hopes to draw valid conclusions about the larger group.

The main types of probability sampling methods are simple random sampling, stratified sampling, cluster sampling, multistage sampling, and systematic random sampling. The main benefit of probability sampling methods is that they guarantee that the sample chosen is representative of the population. This ensures that the statistical conclusions will be valid.

- A **simple random sampling** is any sampling method such that

   i.   the population consists of N objects,

   ii. the sample consists of n objects,

   iii. all possible samples of n objects are equally likely to occur.

There are various ways to obtain a simple random sample. One way would be the lottery method in which each of the N population members is given a different number. The numbers are placed in a bag and mixed. Then, a blind-folded person selects n numbers. Population members having the selected numbers are included in the sample. Another way would be to number all the people and use a random number generator to choose them.

- With **stratified sampling**, the population is divided into homogeneous subgroups, called **strata**, based on some characteristic. Then, within each subgroup, a simple random sampling is used, and the results are combined.

  We might use this method when a population can be split into different sized groups that may have some reason to answer differently on a survey. If we were to randomly choose people from the entire population, we may have too many from one group, which could create a bias.

  Example: Suppose the student population at Smart University is 60% women and 40% men and we are doing a survey on funding for the baseball program. It is likely that men and women might have differing opinions on this matter. So we break the population into the strata *female* and *male*. Then we would choose 60 women and 40 men using a simple random method; this way, we eliminate the possibility of choosing 100 people randomly and ending up with 70 males and 30 females, which would not represent the student population fairly.

- To conduct **cluster sampling**, each member of the population is assigned to a unique subgroup called a cluster. Next a sample of clusters is randomly chosen. Then all the individuals within the sampled clusters are surveyed.

  The difference between cluster sampling and stratified sampling is that with stratified sampling, the sample includes elements from each stratum, but with cluster sampling, the sample includes only elements from sampled clusters.

- With **multistage sampling**, we select a sample by using combinations of different sampling methods.

  For example, in Stage 1, we might use cluster sampling to choose clusters from a population. Then, in Stage 2, we might use systematic sampling to select a subset of elements from each chosen cluster for the final sample.

- With **systematic random sampling**, we create a list of every member of the population. From the list, we randomly choose one member. Then we select every mth name on the population list, starting from the selected member.

  This method is different from simple random sampling since every possible sample of n elements is not equally likely.

All of the types of sampling listed above are types of **probability sampling** because in each method every element has a known nonzero probability of being sampled and each method involves random selection at some point.

There are also non-probability sampling methods, which do not have one or both of the properties above. **Convenience sampling** is a type of nonprobability sampling that involves the sample being drawn from that part of the population that is close at hand. That is, a population is selected because it is readily available and convenient. The researcher using such a sample cannot scientifically make generalizations about the total population from this sample because it would not be representative enough.

Problems with Sampling

In statistics, problems can arise when sampling is done in such a way that some members of the population are less likely to be chosen for the sample. This is called **sample bias**.

- Telephone sampling is common in marketing surveys. A simple random sample may be chosen from the sampling frame consisting of a list of telephone numbers of people in the area being surveyed. This is a type of convenience sampling. Telephone sampling, however, excludes people who do not have a phone or who have only a cell phone that has an area code not in the region being surveyed. It will also not include people who do not wish to be surveyed. Thus the method systematically excludes certain types of consumers in the area. This is an example of having an **incomplete sampling frame**.

- In a **voluntary response sample**, a large group of individuals are invited to participate and all who respond are counted. This method is used in call-in voting for television shows, Internet polls, and letters written to government agencies. The responses from such sampling are often biased since those with strongly held opinions are often the people who do respond.

- **Undercoverage** can also cause bias. This occurs when certain portions of the population are not sampled at all or a percentage of the sample is much smaller than the percentage of this group within the population. For example, at a conservative political rally with 10,000 attendees, wewould not find many liberals, so conducting a survey about politics in general at the rally would create a bias.

- **Non-response bias** can be caused by a certain group not responding to a survey.

- **Response bias** is caused by anything that influences people's responses. This includes wording questions in such a way that favors certain responses. Some questions may be considered too personal to some people, and these people may decline to respond. In addition, people often tend to tailor their responses to fool or to please an interviewer.

- **Convenience sampling** can also create bias. To save time and money, people sometimes choose individuals who are easy for them to reach. For instance, suppose we are interested in how much the people in our town enjoy reading books. Going to a local library to sample opinions might give a biased response since the people at the library probably enjoy reading more than somebody we might just meet on the street.

Review Problems for Section 5.2.3

1. A survey was done at a high school basketball game attended by 1500 people. Name the sampling method used in each of the following:

   (a) Since 2/3 of the people were fans of the home team, 100 people were chosen from that group and 50 from the away-team fans.

   (b) 150 people were chosen by picking ticket numbers out of a hat.

(c) The tickets were numbered 1 to 1500. A person randomly chose a first number to start with and then every 10th number was chosen, beginning with the first number.

(d) The survey was done by the 150 people sitting in the first section of the gym nearest the door.

(e) The people were divided into eight sections by where they were sitting. Then three sections were chosen for sampling. In each of these three sections 50 people were randomly chosen to be surveyed.

2. Cathy's Chili is a small company that produces 15 cases of chili each day, with each case holding 16 cans of chili. Each evening, Cathy chooses three jars to weigh and then samples to ensure product quality. If today's cases are labeled Oct15–01 through Oct15–12:

(a) What type of sampling method would be appropriate?

(b) Explain how you would complete the sampling.

3. Discuss the bias or lack of bias in each of the following sampling situations:

(a) Every 10th person entering an ice cream shop is asked whether they like ice cream (i) a lot, (ii) some, or (iii) not at all.

(b) A survey asks a random group of Americans the question, "Why do you believe the media has a negative effect on elections?"

(c) Two groups, 1,000 urban and 1,000 rural senior citizens, are asked about their experience with prescription drugs.

(d) A voter poll in the morning on Election Day is conducted by telephone.

(e) From a complete list of students at a local elementary school, 400 students are randomly chosen and asked their opinions on the school cafeteria food.

Detailed Solutions

1. (a) This is an example of stratified sampling.

(b) This is simple random sampling.

(c) This is an example of systematic sampling.

(d) This is convenience sampling.

(e) This is cluster sampling.

2. (a) Randomly choosing three cases from the 12 by using the case numbers (puting them on slips of paper in a hat) and then randomly choosing one can from each case would be appropriate.

(b) To choose the can in each case, number the cans and then randomly choose a number from 1 to 12 for each case. This is cluster sampling.

3. (a) This is biased because people entering the store have made an effort to come to an ice cream shop, so they at least like it a little. So the sample is skewed toward a positive response. It's also a convenience sampling.

(b) The question has response bias. The wording of the question assumes that it's a fact that the media have a negative effect on elections, so the question is leading toward the negative response.

(c) This is stratified sampling. Some bias (it's difficult to have none) may be that more senior citizens may live in the urban versus rural areas. Also, this survey leaves out the suburban senior citizens.

(d) This poll uses an incomplete sampling frame since it uses morning telephone polling—some people do not have telephones and some people are not at home in the morning.

(e) This is simple random sampling. Some bias might occur, however, because some students do not buy lunch at school.

5.2.4 The California *Mathematics Subject Matter Requirements* stipulate that candidates for any credential program for teaching secondary mathematics must be able to *know the method of least squares and apply it to linear regression and correlation.*

Linear Regression

Linear regression is a method of finding the linear equation that comes closest to fitting a collection of data points in a certain way.

Example: Figure 5.28 shows the number of households in Certaintown, USA, with cable television.

Year (x) ($x = 0$ is 2000)	0	1	2	3	4
Households with cable (y) (in thousands)	44	49	56	62	66

Figure 5.28

If we plot these data, we get the following graph:

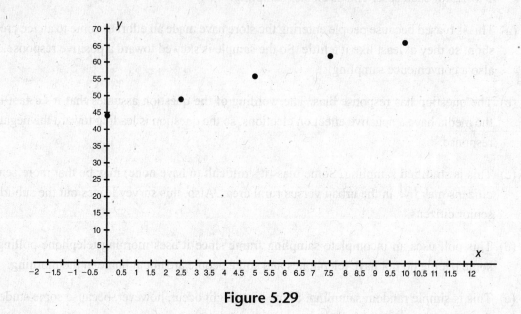

Figure 5.29

Although no single line passes exactly through these four points, many lines pass *close* to them. One of them is shown in Figure 5.30.

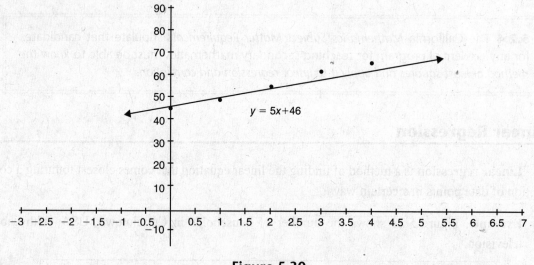

$$y = 5x + 46$$

Figure 5.30

Suppose that we used the line rather than the data points to estimate the number of households with cable. Then we would get slightly different values from the original observed values shown in Figure 5.29.

These values are called **predicted values**, as shown in Figure 5.31.

Year (x)	0	1	2	3	4
Observed value y	44	49	56	62	66
Predicted value ŷ	46	50	54	58	62

Figure 5.31

- The better our choice of line, the closer the predicted values will be to the observed values. The difference between the predicted value and the observed value is called the **residual.**

  Residual = Observed Value − Predicted Value = $y - \hat{y}$

- The residuals measure the vertical distances on the graph between the (observed) data points and the line (Figure 5.32), and they tell us how far off the linear model is in predicting the number of households with cable.

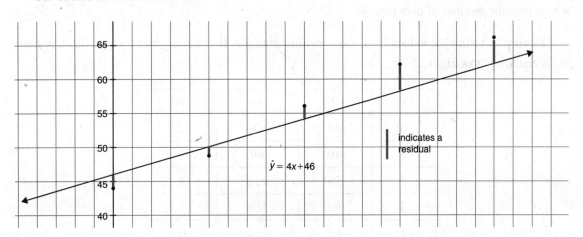

Figure 5.32

Sum-of-Squares Error

For our graph, the residuals are shown in the table in Figure 5.33.

Year (x)	0	1	2	3	4
Observed value y	44	49	56	62	66
Predicted value ŷ	46	50	54	58	62
residuals	−2	−1	2	4	4

Figure 5.33

- Notice that some residuals are positive and others are negative. If we add up the squares of the residuals, we get a measure of how well the line fits, called the **sum-of-squares error, SSE.**

$$SSE = \sum_{i=1}^{n}\left(y_i - \hat{y}_i\right)^2$$

In our example, the sum-of-squares error is $(-2)^2 + (-1)^2 + 2^2 + 4^2 + 4^2 = 41$

- Note that the smaller the SSE, the better the approximating function fits the data. This is the idea of **least squares**. The idea is to find the line that gives the least value for the SSE.

The **regression line (least squares line, best-fit line)** associated with the points (x_1, y_1), (x_2, y_2), ... , (x_n, y_n) is the line that gives the minimum SSE. The regression line is

$$\hat{y} = mx + b$$

where m and b are computed as follows:

$$m = \frac{n(\sum xy) - (\sum x)(\sum y)}{n(\sum x^2) - (\sum x)^2} \qquad b = \frac{\sum y - m(\sum x)}{n}$$

where n = the number of data points.

Example: Using the values from the previous example, find the regression line. Start by making a chart, such as Figure 5.34.

x	y	xy	x^2
0	44	0	0
1	49	49	1
2	56	112	4
3	62	186	9
4	66	264	16
$\sum x = 10$	$\sum y = 277$	$\sum xy = 611$	$\sum x^2 = 30$

Figure 5.34

$$m = \frac{5(611) - (10)(277)}{5(30) - (10)^2} = 5.7 \text{ and } b = \frac{277 - (5.7)(10)}{5} = 44.$$

The equation of the regression line is thus $y = 5.7x + 44$. Graph the regression line with the data (Figure 5.35).

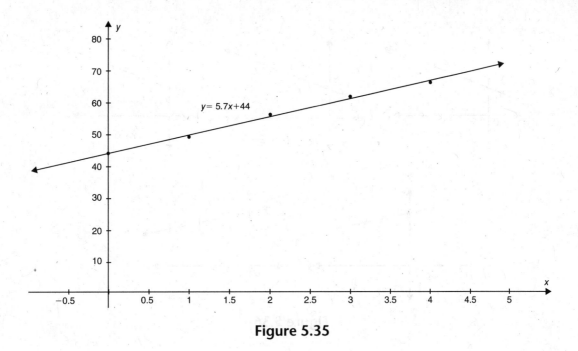

$$y = 5.7x + 44$$

Figure 5.35

Correlation

Correlation quantifies the extent to which two quantitative variables, x and y, have a good relationship. When high values of x are associated with high values of y, we say a **positive correlation** exists. When high values of x are associated with low values of y, we say a **negative correlation** exists. We are particularly interested in linear relationships between the quantitative variables.

Suppose we are starting with a set of data points. If all the data points do not lie on one straight line, we would like to be able to measure how closely they can be approximated by a straight line.

Recall that SSE measures the sum of the squares of the deviations from the regression line; therefore, it is a measurement of goodness of fit. For instance, if SSE = 0, then all the data points lie on a straight line. However, SSE depends on the units we use to measure y, and also on the number of data points (the more data points we use, the larger SSE tends to be). Thus, while we can use SSE to compare the goodness of fit of two lines to the same data, we cannot use it to compare the goodness of fit of one line to one set of data with that of another to a different set of data.

To remove this dependency, mathematicians have found a related number that can be used to compare the goodness of fit of lines to different sets of data. This quantity, called the **coefficient of correlation**, or **correlation coefficient**, denoted by r, is between -1 and 1, inclusive. The closer r is to -1 or 1, the better the fit; i.e., the more linear is the relationship between the two variables.

- For an *exact* fit, we would have $r = -1$ (for a line with negative slope) or $r = 1$ (for a line with positive slope). For a bad fit, we would have r close to 0.

- Several collections of data points with least squares lines and the corresponding values of r are shown in Figure 5.36.

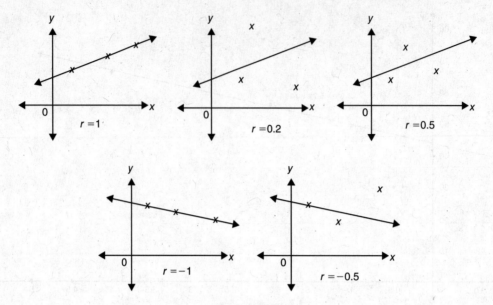

Figure 5.36

- The coefficient of correlation of the n data points (x_1, y_1), (x_2, y_2), ..., (x_n, y_n) is

$$r = \frac{n(\Sigma xy) - (\Sigma x)(\Sigma y)}{\sqrt{n(\Sigma x^2) - (\Sigma x)^2}\sqrt{n(\Sigma y^2) - (\Sigma y)^2}}$$

- The value of r measures how closely the data points (x_1, y_1), (x_2, y_2), ..., (x_n, y_n) fit the regression line.

   Example: Let's look at the points from the previous example for which we found the equation of the regression line (Figure 5.37).

x	y	xy	x^2	y^2
0	44	0	0	1936
1	49	49	1	2401
2	56	112	4	3136
3	62	186	9	3844
4	66	264	16	4356
$\Sigma x = 10$	$\Sigma y = 277$	$\Sigma xy = 611$	$\Sigma x^2 = 30$	$\Sigma y^2 = 15673$

Figure 5.37

$r = \dfrac{(5)(611) - (10)(277)}{\sqrt{5(30) - (10)^2}\sqrt{5(15673) - (277)^2}} = \dfrac{285}{\sqrt{50}\sqrt{1636}} \approx \dfrac{285}{286.007} \approx 0.996$. This number is close to 1,

so the regression line in this example is a good fit.

- How close to 1 or -1 does r have to be to be considered a good fit?

  The sign of the correlation coefficient determines whether the correlation is positive or negative. The magnitude of the correlation coefficient determines the strength of the correlation. Although there are no fixed rules for describing correlational strength, a general guideline is this:

  $0 < |r| < .3$ weak correlation

  $0.3 < |r| < .7$ moderate correlation

  $|r| > 0.7$ strong correlation

Review Problems for Section 5.2.4

1. Consider the following data:

x	1	3	4	6
y	2	5	3	6

   Compute the sum-of-squares error for both of the lines below and explain which line is a better fit to the data.

   line 1: $y = x - 1$ line 2: $y = 0.8x + 1.2$

2. Find the correlation coefficient for these data. Is the regression line a good fit? What is its equation?

x	y
0	9
2	9
4	10
6	11
8	11
10	12
12	13
14	13

   Figure 5.38

3. Which of the following is the best approximation for the coefficient of correlation for the data in Figure 5.39?

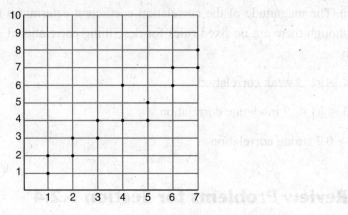

(A) 1

(B) 0.8

(C) 0

(D) – 0,7

Detailed Solutions

1. Make a chart (Figure 5.40):

x	Observed y	Predicted $\hat{y}$ for line 1	Residuals^2 for line 1	Predicted $\hat{y}$ for line 2	Residuals^2 for line 2
1	2	0	4	2	0
3	5	2	9	3.6	1.96
4	3	3	0	4.4	1.96
6	6	5	1	6	0
			SSE = 14		SSE = 3.92

Figure 5.40

Because the SSE for line 2 is smaller than that of line 1, line 2 is a better representative of the data.

2. Make the chart:

x	y	xy	x^2	y^2
0	9	0	0	81
2	9	18	4	81
4	10	40	16	100
6	11	66	36	121
8	11	88	64	121
10	12	120	100	144
12	13	156	144	169
14	13	182	196	169
Σ(Sum)	56	88	670	560	986

Figure 5.41

Substituting the values from the chart in Figure 5.41 into the formula, we get

$$r = \frac{n(\Sigma xy) - (\Sigma x)(\Sigma y)}{\sqrt{n(\Sigma x^2) - (\Sigma x)^2} \cdot \sqrt{n(\Sigma y^2) - (\Sigma y)^2}}$$

$$= \frac{8(670) - (56)(88)}{\sqrt{8(560) - 56^2} \cdot \sqrt{8(986) - 88^2}} \approx 0.982.$$

Thus, the fit of the regression line is a good one, that is, the x and y values of the given points have a good linear relationship.

To find the equation of the regression line:

$$m = \frac{8(670) - (56)(88)}{8(560) - (56)^2} \approx 0.321 \text{ and } b = \frac{88 - (0.32)(56)}{8} = 8.75.$$ Thus, the equation of the regres-

sion line is $y = 0.321x + 8.75$. Graph the data and the regression line to check (Figure 5.42).

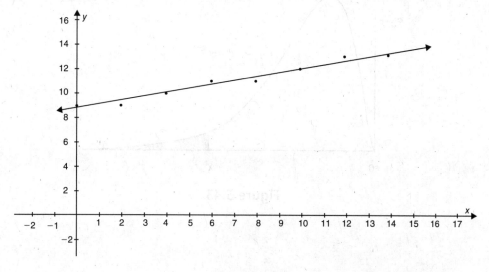

Figure 5.42

3. **B**

The data definitely have a positive correlation since it rises as x increases. The data are not perfectly linear, so the coefficient of correlation should be positive but not equal to 1.

5.2.5 The California *Mathematics Subject Matter Requirements* stipulate that candidates for any credential program for teaching secondary mathematics must be able to *know and apply the chi-square test.*

Chi-Square Test

A **chi-square goodness-of-fit test** is used to test whether a frequency distribution fits an expected distribution when the data are categorical rather than numerical.

A **chi-square**, χ^2, is a positively-skewed distribution that has a minimum value of 0 and no maximum value. The curve obtains a maximum to the right of 0 and then gradually decreases and approaches—but never quite touches—the horizontal axis. For each value of the degree of freedom, there is a different χ^2. The mean of a χ^2 is equal to the degree of freedom (df), and the standard deviation is 2df. As the degree of freedom increases, the distribution is more spread out, with its maximum point farther to the right. As a result, for any given level of significance, the critical region begins at a greater value for a greater degree of freedom.

Figure 5.43 shows the χ^2 distribution for df = 5. The horizontal axis represents the values of χ^2 and the vertical axis is the probability of each χ^2 value. The α denotes the level of significance.

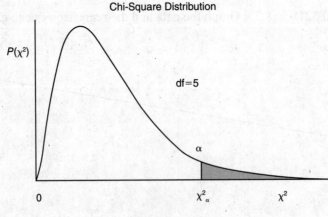

Chi-Square Distribution

Figure 5.43

Some terminology:

- The **null hypothesis** is a statement that can be shown to be false by using the chi-square goodness-of-fit test. Usually it corresponds with a general or default position. For example, the null hypothesis might be that there is or is not a relationship between two measurements. This is the statement that the chi-square test will determine whether the null hypothesis is to be accepted or not.

- The **alternative hypothesis** is the negation of the null hypothesis. If the null hypothesis is rejected, then this statement is accepted and vice versa.

- The **expected values** arise from the null hypothesis, which gives the hypothesized proportion of each category.

- The **residuals** are the differences between the observed values and the expected values.

- The **component** for each category is the square of the residual divided by the expected value.

- The **chi-square statistic** is the sum of the components.

- The **degree of freedom** is the number of values in the final calculation of a statistic that are free to vary. For the chi-square test, this is $n - 1$.

- In statistics, the word *significance* is related to the word *truth* rather than the word *importance*. The **level of significance** is the probability (level of acceptance) at which the hypothesis is to be accepted; it is sometimes called the **critical P-value**. It can also be viewed as the maximum allowable probability of making an error by rejecting the null hypothesis when in fact it is true.

We will work through an example as we explain the steps of the χ^2 test.

Example: A healthcare researcher wants to determine the proportions of people who use different healthcare facilities for non-emergency situations. A previous survey claims that the distribution is as follows: 35%, primary care physician; 25%, teaching hospitals; 20%, healthcare clinics; 15%, mobile healthcare units; 5%, none. The researcher randomly surveys 600 people. The results are shown in Figure 5.44. The researcher would like to know if he should reject the results of his survey at the 5% significance level.

Category	frequency
Primary care physicians	202
Teaching hospitals	142
Healthcare clinics	126
Mobile healthcare units	106
No treatment	24

Figure 5.44

Step 1: State the **null hypothesis H_0** and the **alternative hypothesis H_a**.

For our example, we have:

H_0: The distribution of healthcare facilities for non-emergency situations is 35% primary care physician, 25% teaching hospitals, 20% healthcare clinics, 15% mobile health care units, 5% none.

H_a: The distribution of healthcare facilities for non-emergency situations is not as stated in the null hypothesis.

Step 2: Find the **expected values**.

There are 600 responses in the survey so:

35% of 600 = 210, 25% of 600 = 150, 20% of 600 = 120, 15% of 600 is 90, 5% of 600 = 30. We put these numbers in a table. See the *expected value* column in Figure 5.45.

Step 3: Compute the **residuals**.

We subtract the expected values from the observed values. See the *residuals* column in Figure 5.45.

Step 4: Compute the **components**.

Each component is $= \dfrac{\left(\text{residual}\right)^2}{\text{expected value}} = \dfrac{\left(\text{observed value} - \text{expected value}\right)^2}{\text{expected value}}$. See the *components* column in Figure 5.45.

Step 5: Find the **chi-square statistic**, which is the sum of the components.

For our example, this is 5.075873.

Step 6: Determine the **degrees of freedom**, which is equal to the number of categories minus 1.

Our example has five categories, so this example has $5 - 1 = 4$ degrees of freedom.

Step 7: **Test the hypothesis.** Look up the critical value in a table of chi-square values, using the degrees of freedom and the given **level of significance.**

The level of significance that the researcher in this experiment has decided upon is 5%.

Our critical number, 10.409206 is greater than the P-number for 4 degrees of freedom at the 5% level of significance (from Figure 5.46, there is a 5% probability of a χ^2 statistic being greater than 9.49), so the researcher rejects the null hypothesis.

Category	Observed Value	Expected value	Residuals	Residuals²	Components
Primary care physicians	202	210	− 8	64	0.304762
Teaching hospitals	142	150	− 8	64	0.426667
Healthcare clinics	126	120	6	36	0.300000
Mobile healthcare units	106	90	16	256	2.844444
No treatment	24	30	−6	36	1.200000
					χ^2 **statistic = 5.075873**

Figure 5.45

Chi-square Distribution Table

Degrees of Freedom	Probability of a larger value of χ^2								
	0.99	0.95	0.90	0.75	0.50	0.25	0.10	0.05	0.01
1	0.000	0.004	0.016	0.102	0.455	1.32	2.71	3.84	6.63
2	0.020	0.103	0.211	0.575	1.386	2.77	4.61	5.99	9.21
3	0.115	0.352	0.584	1.212	2.366	4.11	6.25	7.81	11.34
4	0.297	0.711	1.064	1.923	3.357	5.39	7.78	9.49	13.28
5	0.554	1.145	1.610	2.675	4.351	6.63	9.24	11.07	15.09
6	0.872	1.635	2.204	3.455	5.348	7.84	10.64	12.59	16.81
7	1.239	2.167	2.833	4.255	6.346	9.04	12.02	14.07	18.48
8	1.647	2.733	3.490	5.071	7.344	10.22	13.36	15.51	20.09
9	2.088	3.325	4.168	5.899	8.343	11.39	14.68	16.92	21.67
10	2.558	3.940	4.865	6.737	9.342	12.55	15.99	18.31	23.21
11	3.053	4.575	5.578	7.584	10.341	13.70	17.28	19.68	24.72
12	3.571	5.226	6.304	8.438	11.340	14.85	18.55	21.03	26.22
13	4.107	5.892	7.042	9.299	12.340	15.98	19.81	22.36	27.69
14	4.660	6.571	7.790	10.165	13.339	17.12	21.06	23.68	29.14
15	5.229	7.261	8.547	11.037	14.339	18.25	22.31	25.00	30.58
16	5.812	7.962	9.312	11.912	15.338	19.37	23.54	26.30	32.00
17	6.408	8.672	10.085	12.792	16.338	20.49	24.77	27.59	33.41
18	7.015	9.390	10.865	13.675	17.338	21.60	25.99	28.87	34.80
19	7.633	10.117	11.651	14.562	18.338	22.72	27.20	30.14	36.19
20	8.260	10.851	12.443	15.452	19.337	23.83	28.41	31.41	37.57

Figure 5.46

Example: Pat claims that his 1964 Kennedy half dollar is a fair coin. To test this, Pat has a friend flip the coin 400 times and they record the results; *heads* came up 182 times. What does the chi-square test at the 5% level of significance tell them about the coin?

First we write the hypotheses:

H_0: Pat's 1964 Kennedy half dollar is a fair coin.

H_a: Pat's 1964 Kennedy half dollar is not a fair coin.

Category	Observed Value	Expected value	Residuals	Residuals^2	Component
heads	182	200	− 18	324	1.62
tails	218	200	18	324	1.62
					χ^2 statistic $=3.24$

Figure 5.47

The P-value from the table (Figure 5.46) for $n = 1$ df and level of significance 5% is 3.84; so since the χ^2 statistic is less than the P-value, Pat should accept his null hypothesis and consider the coin to be fair.

Review Problems for Section 5.2.5

1. What is the P-value when:

   (a) $n = 6$ at the 10% level of significance?

   (b) $n = 3$ at the 5% level of significance?

2. What can you say about the null hypothesis if

   (a) the critical value (χ^2 statistic) is 6.25 and the P-value is 9.342?

   (b) the critical value is 13.5 and the P-value is 4.107?

3. Chris wants to test the fairness of a six-sided die. So Chris has a fellow student roll the die 300 times, obtaining the results in Figure 5.48. Use the chi-square test with level of significance at 1% to determine the outcome of fairness of the die.

outcome	frequency
1	38
2	64
3	55
4	49
5	62
6	32

Figure 5.48

Detailed Solutions

1. (a) If $n = 6$ then df $= 5$. So looking in the df $= 5$ row and the 0.10 column, the P-value is 9.24.

   (b) For $n = 3$, df $= 2$, so look in the df $= 2$ row with the .05 column to obtain the P-value of 5.99.

2. (a) Since the critical value is below the P-value, accept the null hypothesis.

   (b) Since the critical value is above the P-value, reject the null hypothesis.

3.

Category	Observed Value	Expected value	Residuals	Residuals²	Component
1	38	50	−12	144	2.88
2	64	50	14	196	3.92
3	55	50	5	25	0.5
4	49	50	−1	1	0.02
5	62	50	12	144	2.88
6	32	50	−18	324	6.48
					χ^2 **statistic = 16.68**

Now, the P-value for df $= 5$ and level of significance 1% is 15.09. Since the P-value is less than the χ^2 statistic, Chris should reject the null hypothesis and not accept the die as fair.

Content Domain 5: *Calculus*

6.1 Trigonometry

> **6.1.1** The California *Mathematics Subject Matter Requirements* stipulate that candidates for any credential program for teaching secondary mathematics must be able to *prove that the Pythagorean Theorem is equivalent to the trigonometric identity $\sin^2 x + \cos^2 x = 1$ and that this identity leads to $1 + \tan^2 x = \sec^2 x$ and $1 + \cot^2 x = \csc^2 x$.*

Pythagorean Theorem

Consider the right triangle in Figure 6.1. The **Pythagorean Theorem** in terms of this triangle is

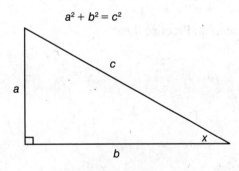

$$a^2 + b^2 = c^2$$

Figure 6.1

The definitions of the trigonometric functions say that for this right triangle,

$$\sin x = \frac{a}{c} \text{ and } \cos x = \frac{b}{c}.$$

So, $a = c\sin x$ and $b = c\cos x$. Substituting into the equation $a^2 + b^2 = c^2$, we obtain

$$a^2 + b^2 = (c\sin x)^2 + (c\cos x)^2 = c^2\sin^2 x + c^2\cos^2 x = c^2\left(\sin^2 x + \cos^2 x\right) = c^2.$$

Therefore, the original equation $a^2 + b^2 = c^2$ is equivalent to $\sin^2 x + \cos^2 x = 1$ for the right triangle in Figure 6.1.

If we divide $\sin^2 x + \cos^2 x = 1$ by $\cos^2 x$, we have $\frac{\sin^2 x}{\cos^2 x} + 1 = \frac{1}{\cos^2 x}$ or $\tan^2 x + 1 = \sec^2 x$.

If we divide $\sin^2 x + \cos^2 x = 1$ by $\sin^2 x$, we obtain $1 + \frac{\cos^2 x}{\sin^2 x} = \frac{1}{\sin^2 x}$ or $1 + \cot^2 x = \csc^2 x$.

Therefore, the following statements are all equivalent to the conclusion of the Pythagorean Theorem and to each other:

$$\sin^2 x + \cos^2 x = 1$$

$$\tan^2 x + 1 = \sec^2 x$$

$$1 + \cot^2 x = \csc^2 x$$

Review Problems for Section 6.1.1

1. Start with the statement of the Pythagorean Theorem and develop the trigonometric identity $\sin^2 x + \cos^2 x = 1$.

2. Show how to obtain the trigonometric identities $\tan^2 x + 1 = \sec^2 x$ and $1 + \cot^2 x = \csc^2 x$ from the identity $\sin^2 x + \cos^2 x = 1$.

Detailed Solutions

These are shown in the section. Practice these!

6.1.2 The California *Mathematics Subject Matter Requirements* require that candidates for any credential program for teaching secondary mathematics must be able to *prove the sine, cosine, and tangent sum formulas for all real values, and derive special applications of the sum formulas (e.g., double-angle, half angle).*

Sum and Difference Formulas

To derive the sum and difference formulas, consider Figure 6.2.

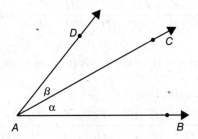

Figure 6.2

Insert the following constructions (see Figure 6.3):

- Construct the perpendicular from point D to $\overline{AB}$; name the foot E.

- Construct the perpendicular from point D to $\overline{AC}$; name the foot F.

- Construct the perpendicular from point F to $\overline{AB}$; name the foot G.

- Construct the perpendicular from point F to $\overline{DE}$; name the foot H.

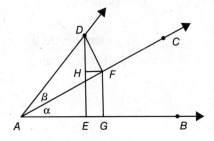

Figure 6.3

Then, for right triangle DEA, $\sin(\alpha + \beta) = \dfrac{DE}{AD}$.

Claim: $m\angle HDF = \alpha$

Line $\overleftrightarrow{HF} \parallel \overleftrightarrow{AB}$ and $\overleftrightarrow{AC}$ is a transversal, so $\angle CAB \cong \angle AFH$, since alternate interior angles are congruent. Also, $\angle DFH$ is complementary to $\angle HFA$ because they are adjacent angles that form a right angle. In addition, $\angle HDF$ is complementary to $\angle DFH$ because they are the two acute angles in right triangle HDF. Hence, $m\angle HDF = \alpha$

We have: $\sin \alpha = \dfrac{FG}{AF} = \dfrac{HF}{DF}$, $\sin \beta = \dfrac{FD}{AD}$, $\cos \alpha = \dfrac{DH}{FD} = \dfrac{AG}{AF}$, and $\cos \beta = \dfrac{AF}{AD}$

Note that $ED = DH + HE = DH + FG = FG + DH$,

so $\sin(\alpha + \beta) = \dfrac{ED}{AD} = \dfrac{FG}{AD} + \dfrac{DH}{AD} = \dfrac{FG}{AF} \cdot \dfrac{AF}{AD} + \dfrac{DH}{FD} \cdot \dfrac{FD}{AD} = \sin \alpha \cos \beta + \cos \alpha \sin \beta$.

$$\sin(\alpha + \beta) = \sin \alpha \cos \beta + \cos \alpha \sin \beta$$

Referring again to Figure 6.3, similarly,

$\cos(\alpha + \beta) = \dfrac{AE}{AD} = \dfrac{AG}{AD} - \dfrac{EG}{AD} = \dfrac{AG}{AF} \cdot \dfrac{AF}{AD} - \dfrac{EG}{DF} \cdot \dfrac{DF}{AD} = \dfrac{AG}{AF} \cdot \dfrac{AF}{AD} - \dfrac{HF}{DF} \cdot \dfrac{DF}{AD}$

$= \cos \alpha \cos \beta - \sin \alpha \sin \beta$.

$$\cos(\alpha + \beta) = \cos \alpha \cos \beta - \sin \alpha \sin \beta$$

Using these two formulas we obtain:

$\tan(\alpha + \beta) = \dfrac{\sin(\alpha + \beta)}{\cos(\alpha + \beta)} = \dfrac{\sin \alpha \cos \beta + \cos \alpha \sin \beta}{\cos \alpha \cos \beta - \sin \alpha \sin \beta}$. Divide each term in this last expression by $\cos \alpha \cos \beta$ to obtain: $\tan(\alpha + \beta) \dfrac{\tan \alpha + \tan \beta}{1 - \tan \alpha \tan \beta}$.

$$\tan(\alpha + \beta) = \dfrac{\tan \alpha + \tan \beta}{1 - \tan \alpha \tan \beta}$$

Double-Angle Formulas

Using the formulas for the sum of angles, we can now derive the double-angle formulas:

(i) $\sin(2\alpha) = \sin(\alpha + \alpha) = \sin \alpha \cos \alpha + \cos \alpha \sin \alpha = 2 \sin \alpha \cos \alpha$

(ii) $\cos(2\alpha) = \cos(\alpha + \alpha) = \cos \alpha \cos \alpha - \sin \alpha \sin \alpha = \cos^2 \alpha - \sin^2 \alpha$

(iii) $\tan(2\alpha) = \dfrac{\tan \alpha + \tan \alpha}{1 - \tan \alpha \tan \alpha} = \dfrac{2\tan \alpha}{1 - \tan^2 \alpha}$

Formula (ii) has two other useful forms:
$\cos(2\alpha) = \cos^2 \alpha - \sin^2 \alpha = (1 - \sin^2 \alpha) - \sin^2 \alpha = 1 - 2 \sin^2 \alpha$
$\cos(2\alpha) = \cos^2 \alpha - \sin^2 \alpha = \cos^2 \alpha - (1 - \cos^2 \alpha) = 2 \cos^2 \alpha - 1$

$$\sin(2\alpha) = 2\sin a \cos a$$

$$\cos(2\alpha) = \cos^2\alpha - \sin^2\alpha$$

$$= 1 - 2\sin^2\alpha$$

$$= 2\cos^2\alpha - 1$$

$$\tan(2\alpha) = \frac{2\tan\alpha}{1-\tan^2\alpha}$$

Half-Angle Formulas

Using the double-angle formulas, we can obtain the half-angle formulas:

- $\cos(\alpha) = \cos\left(2\left(\frac{1}{2}\alpha\right)\right) = 1 - 2\sin^2\left(\frac{1}{2}\alpha\right)$, so $\sin\left(\frac{1}{2}\alpha\right) = \pm\sqrt{\frac{1-\cos\alpha}{2}}$, with the sign depending on the angle $\left(\frac{1}{2}\alpha\right)$.

- Also, $\cos(\alpha) = \cos\left(2\left(\frac{1}{2}\alpha\right)\right) = 2\cos^2\left(\frac{1}{2}\alpha\right) - 1$, so $\cos\left(\frac{1}{2}\alpha\right) = \pm\sqrt{\frac{1+\cos\alpha}{2}}$, with the sign depending on the angle $\left(\frac{1}{2}\alpha\right)$.

- The half-angle formula for tangent comes from the ratio of the half-angle formulas for sine and cosine:

$$\tan\left(\frac{1}{2}\alpha\right) = \frac{\sin\left(\frac{1}{2}\alpha\right)}{\cos\left(\frac{1}{2}\alpha\right)} = \pm\sqrt{\frac{1-\cos\alpha}{1+\cos\alpha}},$$ with the sign depending on the angle $\left(\frac{1}{2}\alpha\right)$.

$$\sin\left(\frac{1}{2}\alpha\right) = \pm\sqrt{\frac{1-\cos\alpha}{2}}$$

$$\cos\left(\frac{1}{2}\alpha\right) = \pm\sqrt{\frac{1+\cos\alpha}{2}}$$

$$\tan\left(\frac{1}{2}\alpha\right) = \pm\sqrt{\frac{1-\cos\alpha}{1+\cos\alpha}}$$

where the sign for each depends on the angle $\left(\frac{1}{2}\alpha\right)$

Review Problems for Section 6.1.2

1. Show how the sum of the angles formulas are developed for the sine and cosine function, starting with a basic illustration of two adjacent angles with measures α and β.

2. Obtain the sum of angles formula for the tangent function using the sum of angles formulas for sine and cosine.

3. Develop the double-angle formulas, $\sin(2\alpha) = 2\sin\alpha\cos\alpha$ and $\cos(2\alpha) = \cos^2\alpha - \sin^2\alpha$, from the sum of angles formulas for sine and cosine, respectively.

4. Show that $\cos(2\alpha) = 1 - 2\sin^2\alpha = 2\cos^2\alpha - 1$.

5. Obtain the double-angle formula for tangent from the double-angle formulas for sine and cosine.

6. Demonstrate how to obtain the three half-angle formulas beginning with the double-angle formula for the cosine.

Detailed Solutions

All six of the problems are shown in the section material. Practice!

6.1.3 The California *Mathematics Subject Matter Requirements* stipulate that candidates for any credential program for teaching secondary mathematics must be able to *analyze properties of trigonometric functions in a variety of ways (e.g., graphing and solving problems).*

Analyzing Trigonometric Functions

The previous two sections discussed the trigonometric functions defined only for acute angles. Here extend the definitions of the trigonometric functions to any measure of angle. These definitions coincide with the right triangle definitions for acute angles.

Definitions

Let θ be the measure of an angle O in **standard position**; i.e., the initial side of $\angle O$ lies on the positive x-axis and the vertex is at the origin. Let (x, y) be any point on the terminal side of $\angle O$ except O and $r = \sqrt{x^2 + y^2}$. (Figure 6.4). Note that r cannot be 0 or negative.

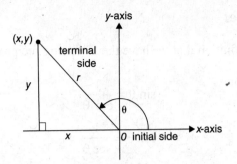

Figure 6.4

Define:

$$\sin \theta = \frac{y}{r} \qquad \cos \theta = \frac{x}{r}$$

$$\tan \theta = \frac{y}{x} \qquad \cot \theta = \frac{x}{y}$$

$$\sec \theta = \frac{r}{x} \qquad \csc \theta = \frac{r}{y}$$

Each angle with measure θ corresponds to a right triangle so these definitions correlate with the right triangle definitions of the previous sections.

From this point forward, we use radian measure unless measurement by degrees is specifically given. Recall that radian measure and degree measure are related by: $180° = \pi$ radians.

It is sometimes simpler to think of the trigonometric functions in terms of the unit circle; i.e, the circle with radius 1 and center at the origin. Then the trigonometric functions are defined as follows.

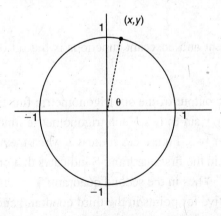

Figure 6.5

$$\sin \theta = y \qquad \cos \theta = x$$

$$\tan \theta = \frac{y}{x} \qquad \cot \theta = \frac{x}{y}$$

$$\sec \theta = \frac{1}{x} \qquad \csc \theta = \frac{1}{y}$$

Trigonometric Identities

It is clear from either definition that we have the following reciprocal identities:

$$\sin\theta = \frac{1}{\csc\theta}$$

$$\cos\theta = \frac{1}{\sec\theta}$$

$$\tan\theta = \frac{1}{\cot\theta}$$

By symmetry of the circle (and also from the right triangle definitions given in Section 4.2.2), the following complementary identities hold:

$$\sin(90° - \theta) = \cos\theta \qquad \cos(90° - \theta) = \sin\theta$$

$$\tan(90° - \theta) = \cot\theta \qquad \cot(90° - \theta) = \tan\theta$$

$$\sec(90° - \theta) = \csc\theta \qquad \csc(90° - \theta) = \sec\theta$$

Also, from the definitions, we can see the following:

- The domain of both sine and cosine is the set of all real numbers, $\mathbf{R} = (-\infty, \infty)$.

- The domain of the tangent and secant functions is the set of all real numbers except for $\theta = \frac{\pi}{2} \pm n\pi, n = 0, 1, 2,\ldots$

- The domain of the cotangent and cosecant functions is the set of all real numbers except for $\theta = \pm n\pi, n = 0, 1, 2,\ldots$

In addition, the sign of the output of the six trigonometric functions depends on the quadrant in which the point ($x = \cos\theta, y = \sin\theta$) lies. Each trigonometric function is positive for two quadrants and negative for the other two. Figure 6.6 indicates when they are positive. **A** indicates that all are positive when (x, y) lies in the first quadrant; **S** indicates that only the sine and its reciprocal, cosecant, are positive when (x, y) lies in the second quadrant; **T** means that only the tangent and its reciprocal, cotangent, are positive for points in the third quadrant; and **C** indicates that only cosine and its reciprocal, secant, are positive for points in the fourth quadrant.

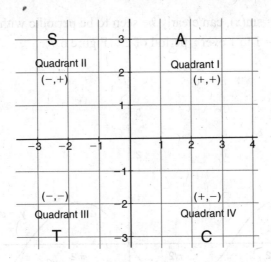

Figure 6.6

From this we can see that only cosine and secant are even functions, so the following are identities:

$$\sin(-\theta) = -\sin(\theta) \qquad \cos(-\theta) = \cos(\theta)$$

$$\tan(-\theta) = -\tan(\theta) \qquad \cot(-\theta) = -\cot(\theta)$$

$$\sec(-\theta) = \sec(\theta) \qquad \csc(-\theta) = -\csc(\theta)$$

The Graphs of the Six Trigonometric Functions

A **periodic function** is a function for which there exists a number k such that for every x in the domain of f, $f(x + k) = f(x)$. If k is the least positive number such that the condition is true, then we say that f is a periodic function with **period k**.

The trigonometric functions all have the property that $f(x + 2\pi) = f(x)$ because as the point on the unit circle travels around the circle, each revolution passes through the same points. Four of the six trigonometric functions have period 2π: sine, cosine, secant, and cosecant. Tangent and cotangent also satisfy $f(x + \pi) = f(x)$ for x in the domain; their period is π.

The graphs of the trigonometric functions are shown in Figures 6.7–6.12. The graphs show that when the point (x, y) lies on one of the axes, some of the functions are undefined because one of the coordinates of the point equals 0.

The **amplitude** of the sine and cosine functions, $y = \sin x$ and $y = \cos x$, is equal to half the distance between the maximum and minimum value of the function; i.e., $\frac{1}{2}(1 - (-1)) = 1$. The other four trigonometric functions do not have amplitude since they don't have a minimum or maximum value.

The sine function, $y = \sin(x)$, can clearly be seen to be periodic with amplitude 1 as its graph waves up and down from -1 to 1 over a period of 2π (Figure 6.7).

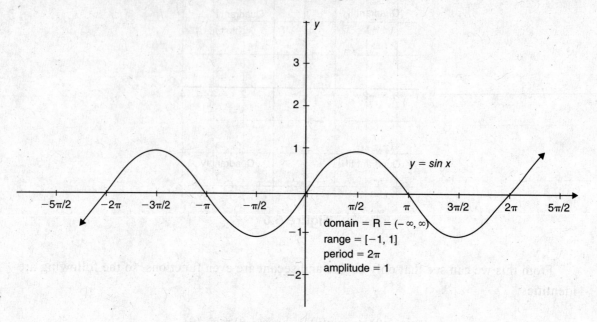

Figure 6.7

The graph of the cosine function, $y = \cos(x)$, is the graph of the sine function translated $\dfrac{\pi}{2}$ units to the left (Figure 6.8).

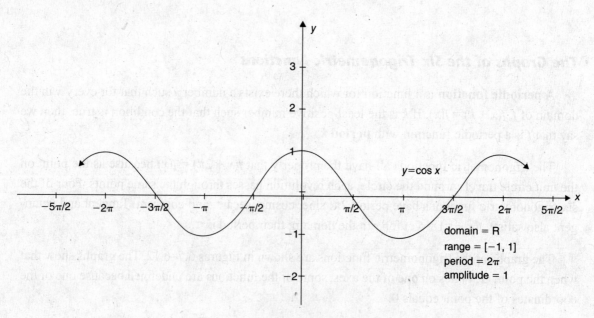

Figure 6.8

The tangent function, $y = \tan(x)$, can be seen to have period π (Figure 6.9).

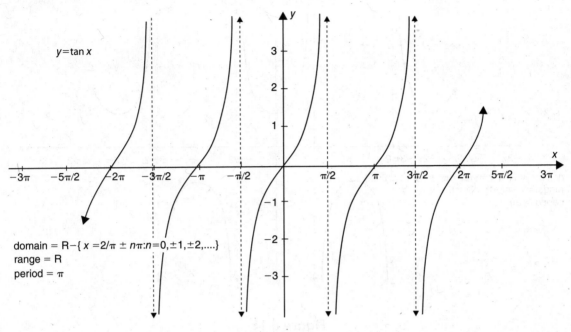

domain = R−{ $x = 2/\pi \pm n\pi : n = 0, \pm 1, \pm 2, ...$}
range = R
period = π

Figure 6.9

The graph of the cotangent function $y = \cot(x)$ is the graph of the tangent function reflected over the y-axis and then translated $\dfrac{\pi}{2}$ to the left (Figure 6.10).

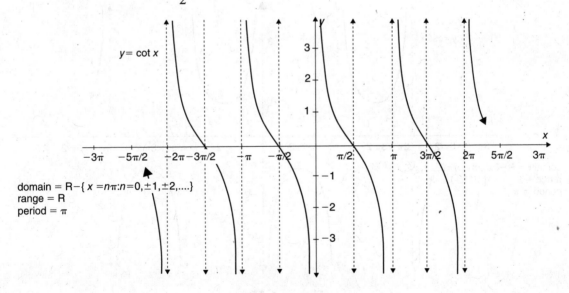

domain = R−{ $x = n\pi : n = 0, \pm 1, \pm 2, ...$}
range = R
period = π

Figure 6.10

The graph of the secant function $y = \sec(x)$ illustrates that the period is 2π (Figure 6.11).

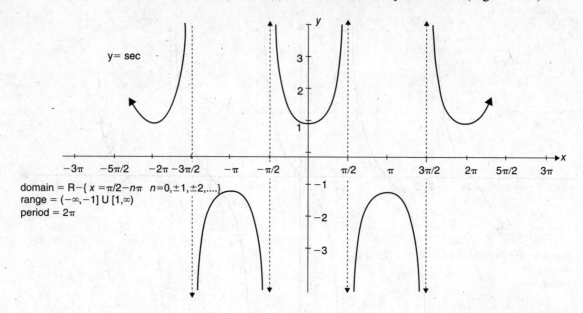

domain = $R - \{\, x = \pi/2 - n\pi \quad n = 0, \pm1, \pm2, \ldots \}$
range = $(-\infty, -1] \cup [1, \infty)$
period = 2π

Figure 6.11

The graph of the cosecant function is the graph of the secant function translated $\dfrac{\pi}{2}$ units to the right (Figure 6.12).

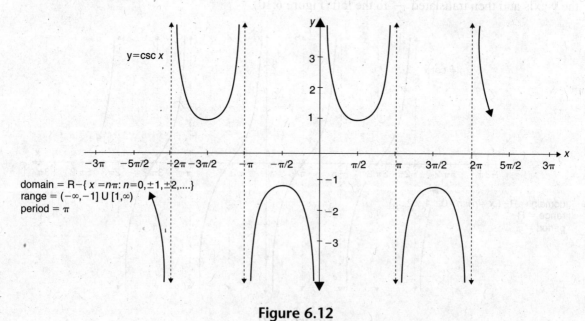

domain = $R - \{\, x = n\pi : n = 0, \pm1, \pm2, \ldots \}$
range = $(-\infty, -1] \cup [1, \infty)$
period = π

Figure 6.12

Translations and Scaling

Sine and Cosine

Consider the functions $y = A\sin(Bx + C) + D$ and $y = A\cos(Bx + C) + D$. Each of the numbers A, B, C, and D indicates something specific about the graphs of these two functions.

- The value $|A|$ is the amplitude of the function.

- The value $\dfrac{2\pi}{B}$ is the period of the function.

- The number AC indicates that there has been a horizontal translation (shift) of the graph $\dfrac{C}{B}$ to the right if $\dfrac{C}{B} < 0$ and to the left if $\dfrac{C}{B} > 0$. The number $\dfrac{C}{B}$ is called the **phase shift**.

- If $D > 0$, then there has been a vertical translation of the graph D units upward, and if $D < 0$, the translation is D units downward.

Examples:

(a) Graph $y = 2\sin\left(3x - \dfrac{\pi}{2}\right)$.

The graph of $y = \sin(x)$ is shown in Figure 6.13 as a dotted line. The graph of $y = 2\sin\left(3x - \dfrac{\pi}{2}\right)$, shown as a solid black curve, is the graph of $y = \sin(x)$ shrunk horizontally so that the period is $\dfrac{2\pi}{3}$, then translated $\dfrac{\pi}{6}$ to the right, and then stretched vertically by a factor of 2 so that the amplitude is 2.

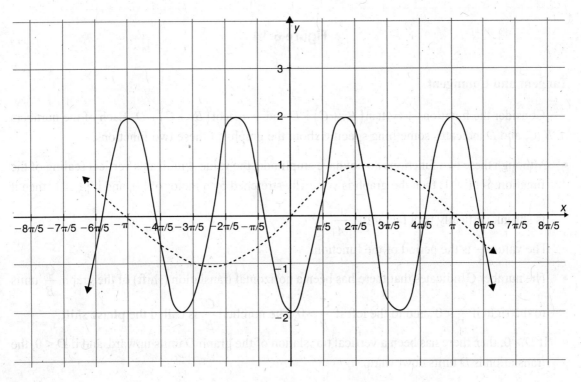

Figure 6.13

(b) Graph $y = \frac{1}{3}\cos\left(\frac{1}{2}x\right) + 1$.

The graph of $y = \cos(x)$ is shown in Figure 6.14 as a dotted line. The graph

$y = \frac{1}{3}\cos\left(\frac{1}{2}x\right) + 1$, shown as a solid black curve, is the graph of $y = \cos(x)$

stretched horizontally so that the period is 4π, then shrunk vertically so that

the amplitude is $\frac{1}{3}$. Lastly, the graph is translated 1 unit upward.

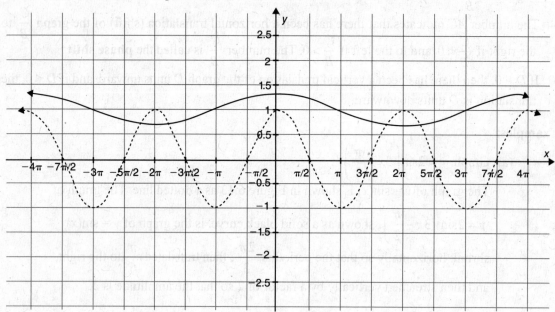

Figure 6.14

Tangent and Cotangent

Consider the functions $y = A\tan(Bx + C) + D$ and $y = A\cot(Bx + C) + D$. Each of the numbers A, B, C, and D indicates something specific about the graphs of these two functions.

- Although these two functions do not have amplitude, the value A indicates vertical scaling of the function; if $|A| > 1$, then the graph is vertically stretched by a factor of $|A|$, and if $|A| < 1$, then it is shrunk vertically by a factor of $\frac{1}{|A|}$.

- The value $\frac{\pi}{B}$ is the period of the function.

- The number C indicates that there has been a horizontal translation (shift) of the graph $\frac{C}{B}$ units to the right if $\frac{C}{B} < 0$, and to the left if $\frac{C}{B} > 0$. The number $\frac{C}{B}$ is called the **phase shift**.

- If $D > 0$, then there has been a vertical translation of the graph D units upward, and if $D < 0$, the translation is D units downward.

Examples:

(a) Graph $y = 4\tan\left(3x - \dfrac{\pi}{2}\right)$.

The graph of $y = \tan(x)$ is shown in Figure 6.15 as a dotted line. The graph

$y = 4\tan\left(3x - \dfrac{\pi}{2}\right)$, shown as a solid black curve, is the graph of $y = \tan(x)$

shrunk horizontally so that the period is $\dfrac{\pi}{3}$, then translated $\dfrac{\pi}{6}$ to the right, and

finally stretched vertically by a factor of 4. Since $D = 0$, there is no vertical

translation.

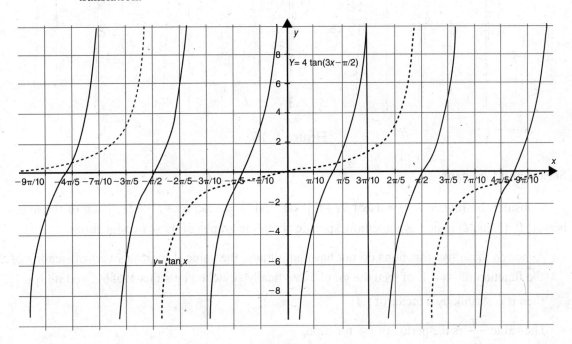

Figure 6.15

(b) Graph $y = \dfrac{1}{6}\cot\left(\dfrac{1}{3}x\right) + 2$.

The graph of $y = \cot(x)$ is shown in Figure 6.16 as a dotted line. The graph

$y = \dfrac{1}{6}\cot\left(\dfrac{1}{3}x\right) + 2$, shown as a solid black curve, is the graph of $y = \cot(x)$

stretched horizontally so that the period is 3π, then shrunk vertically by a

factor of $\dfrac{1}{6}$, and lastly translated 2 units upward.

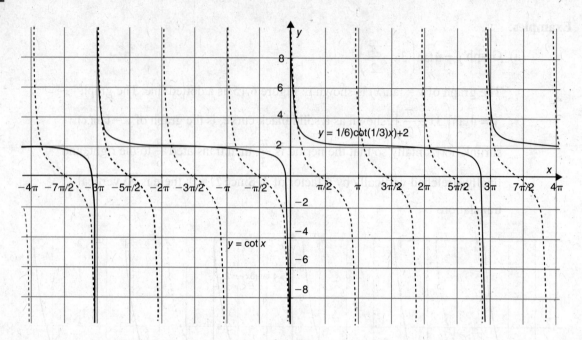

Figure 6.16

Secant and Cosecant

Consider the functions $y = A\sec(Bx + C) + D$ and $y = A\csc(Bx + C) + D$. Each of the numbers A, B, C, and D indicates something specific about the graphs of these two functions.

- Although these two functions do not have amplitude, the value A indicates vertical scaling of the function; if $|A| > 1$, of then the graph is vertically stretched by a factor of $|A|$, and if $|A| < 1$, then it is shrunk by a factor of $|A|$.

- The value $\dfrac{2\pi}{B}$ is the period of the function.

- The value C indicates that there has been a horizontal translation (shift) of the graph $\dfrac{C}{B}$ to the right if $\dfrac{C}{B} < 0$ and to the left if $\dfrac{C}{B} > 0$. The number $\dfrac{C}{B}$ is called the **phase shift**.

- If $D > 0$, then there has been a vertical translation of the graph D units upward, and if $D < 0$, the translation is D units downward.

Examples:

(a) $y = \dfrac{2}{5}\sec\left(3x + \dfrac{\pi}{4}\right)$.

The graph of $y = \sec(x)$ is shown in Figure 6.17 as a dotted line. The graph $y = \dfrac{2}{5}\sec\left(3x + \dfrac{\pi}{4}\right)$. shown as a solid black curve, is the graph of $y = \sec(x)$ shrunk horizontally so that the period is $\dfrac{2\pi}{3}$, then translated $\dfrac{\pi}{12}$ to the left, and then shrunk vertically by a factor of $\dfrac{2}{5}$.

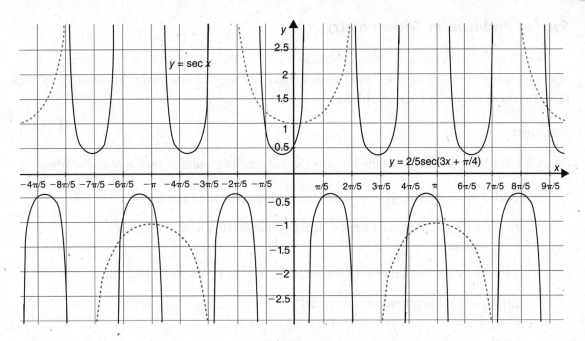

Figure 6.17

(b) Graph $y = 4\csc\left(\dfrac{1}{4}x\right) - 3$.

(ii) The graph of $y = \csc(x)$ is shown in Figure 6.18 as a dotted line. The graph a
$y = 4\csc\left(\dfrac{1}{4}x\right) - 3$, shown as a solid black curve, is the graph of $y = \csc(x)$

stretched horizontally so that the period 8π, then stretched vertically by a factor of 4 and finally translated 3 units downward.

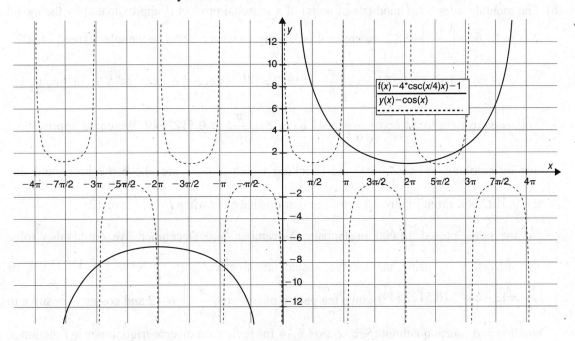

Figure 6.18

Solving Problems in Trigonometry

In Chapter 4, we practiced solving problems involving the definition of the trigonometric functions and using the Laws of Sines and Cosines. Here, we use our knowledge about the graphs of these functions to answer some questions.

Examples:

(a) A Ferris wheel is built so that the height in feet above the ground of each seat on the wheel can be modeled by $h(t) = 60\sin\left(\dfrac{1}{10}t\right) + 64$, where t is measured in seconds.

   (i) How long will it take a person riding on the Ferris wheel to make one revolution?

   (ii) What is the maximum height a person riding the Ferris wheel will obtain?

   (iii) What is the amplitude of the model?

   (i) The question is asking how long it takes the Ferris wheel to pass through one period. The period of $h(t) = 60\sin\left(\dfrac{1}{10}t\right) + 64$ is $\dfrac{2\pi}{1/10} = 20\pi \approx 62.83$. So it takes approximately 62.83 seconds for the Ferris wheel to make one revolution.

   (ii) h has a maximum when the sine equals 1. At this point h has the value $60 + 64 = 124$. So the maximum height reached by a person on the Ferris wheel is 124 feet.

   (iii) The amplitude is 60 feet.

(b) The monthly sales S (in hundreds of units) of a seasonal product is approximated by the model $S(t) = 81.6\cos\left(\dfrac{\pi}{6}t\right) + 98.2$, where $t = 1$ is January. In what months do the sales exceed 14,000?

We want to solve $S(t) = 81.6\cos\left(\dfrac{\pi}{6}t\right) + 98.2 > 140$ (since the units of S is in hundreds).

This is equivalent to $81.6\cos\left(\dfrac{\pi}{6}t\right) > 41.8$, or $\cos\left(\dfrac{\pi}{6}t\right) > 0.5122549$. We could approximate this by graphing $y = \cos\left(\dfrac{\pi}{6}t\right)$ and checking which months are above the horizontal line $y = 0.5122549$. From Figure 6.19, we see that this happens when $t = 1, 11,$ or 12.

So the sales exceed 14,000 in January, November, and December. We could also solve the inequality by using the inverse cosine and a calculator: $\dfrac{\pi t}{6} = \cos^{-1}(0.5122549)$, or $\dfrac{\pi t}{6} = 12 - \cos^{-1}(0.5122549)$ since the period of $y = \cos\left(\dfrac{\pi}{6}t\right)$ is 12 and cosine is positive in the first and fourth quadrant (See section 6.14 for review on inverse trigonometric functions). Solving this equation gives us $t \approx 1.972$ or $t \approx 10.02$. In the first quadrant, cosine is decreasing, so the function is greater than 140 when $t = 1$, and in the fourth quadrant the function is increasing, so we get $t = 11$ or 12. So again we obtain that the sales exceed 14,000 in January, November, and December.

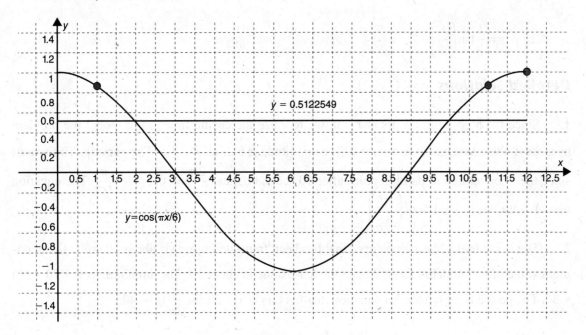

Figure 6.19

Review Problems for Section 6.1.3

1. A buoy oscillates in **simple harmonic motion** (behaves like a sine or cosine curve) as waves go past. The buoy moves a total of 3 feet from its low point to its high point, and it returns to its high point every 10 seconds. Write an equation that describes the motion of the buoy if its high point occurs when $t = 0$.

2. Figure 6.20 is a plot of average weekly temperatures in a given city in England. Find an equation that models this curve.

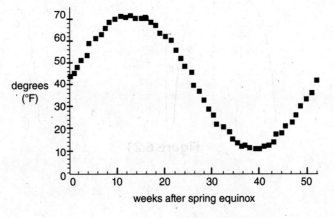

Figure 6.20

3.   Graph the following functions:

(a) $y = 3\sec\left(x - \dfrac{\pi}{2}\right) + 2$

(b) $y = \dfrac{1}{3}\tan\left(\dfrac{x}{4}\right) - 2$

Detailed Solutions

1.   Since the high point occurs at $t = 0$, we will use the cosine function to model the problem because it obtains its maximum at $t = 0$. The amplitude is half of 3 or 1.5. The period is 10 seconds since the buoy returns to its high point after 10 seconds; thus, $\dfrac{2\pi}{B} = 10$ or $B = \dfrac{\pi}{5}$. The equation that satisfies this is $y = 1.5\cos\left(\dfrac{\pi}{5}t\right)$.

2.   The curve looks like a sine curve that has been translated upwards about 40 units; the maximum value of the model is about 70 and the least value is about 10. The amplitude is $0.5(70 - 10)$ $= 30$. The period is 52 weeks. An equation that fits this is $y = 30\sin(\dfrac{\pi}{26}t) + 40$.

3.   (a) The graph of $y = 3\sec\left(x - \dfrac{\pi}{2}\right) + 2$ is the graph of $y = \sec x$ translated $\dfrac{\pi}{2}$ units to the right, then stretched vertically by a factor of 3, and lastly translated 2 units upward (Figure 6.21).

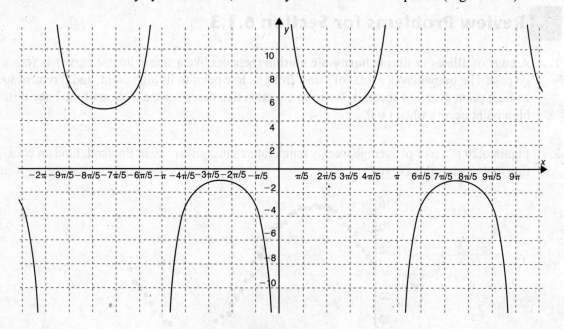

Figure 6.21

(b)   The graph of $y = \dfrac{1}{3}\tan\left(\dfrac{x}{4}\right) - 2$ is the graph of $y = \tan x$ stretched horizontally so that the period is 4π, then shrunk vertically by a factor of $\dfrac{1}{3}$, and lastly translated 2 units downward (Figure 6.22).

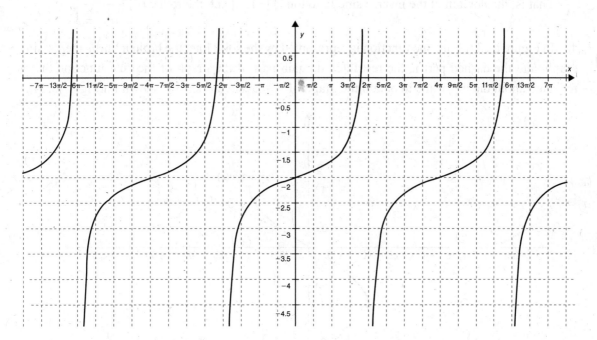

Figure 6.22

6.1.4 The California *Mathematics Subject Matter Requirements* stipulate that candidates for any credential program for teaching secondary mathematics must be able to *know and apply the definitions and properties of inverse trigonometric functions (i.e., arcsin, arccos, and arctan).*

Inverse Trigonometric Functions

None of the six trigonometric functions are one-to-one. So to create inverse trigonometric functions, we restrict the domain of each trigonometric function so that each is one-to-one and then look at the inverse functions of these functions.

Inverse Sine Function

The **inverse sine function**, denoted by $\sin^{-1}$ or arcsin, is defined by

$$y = \sin^{-1}x \text{ if and only if } x = \sin y \text{ for } x \in [-1, 1] \text{ and } y \in \left[-\frac{\pi}{2}, \frac{\pi}{2}\right].$$

That is, the domain of the inverse sine function is $[-1, 1]$ and the range is $\left[-\frac{\pi}{2}, \frac{\pi}{2}\right]$.

In Figure 6.23 the arcsine function is represented by the solid line; the broken line is the $y = \sin x$ graph, and the dashed part is the restricted domain part of the graph of the sine function that is reflected about the $y = x$ line to obtain the graph of $y = \arcsin x = \sin^{-1} x$, shown in (Figure 6.24).

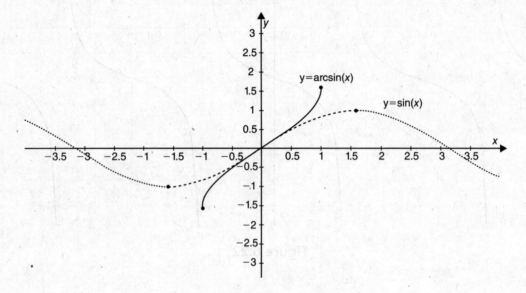

Figure 6.23

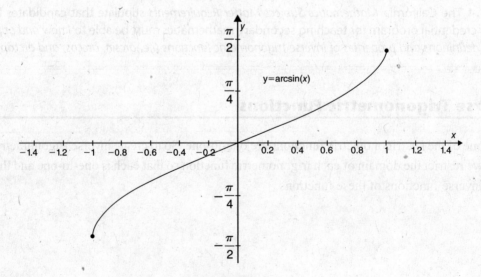

Figure 6.24

Examples: Find the exact value of:

(a) $\arcsin\left(\dfrac{-\sqrt{3}}{2}\right)$ (b) $\sin^{-1} 0$ (c) $\sin^{-1} 3$

(a) Let $a = \arcsin\left(\dfrac{-\sqrt{3}}{2}\right)$. This is the same as $\sin a = \left(\dfrac{-\sqrt{3}}{2}\right)$, where $a \in \left[-\dfrac{\pi}{2}, \dfrac{\pi}{2}\right]$. Thus, $a = \dfrac{-\pi}{3}$.

(b) Let $b = \sin^{-1} 0 \Leftrightarrow \sin b = 0$, $b \in \left[-\dfrac{\pi}{2}, \dfrac{\pi}{2}\right]$. Hence, $b = 0$.

(c) Let $c = \sin^{-1} 3 \Leftrightarrow \sin c = 3$. But $|\sin c| \le 1$. So there is no value $c = \sin^{-1} 3$.

Inverse Cosine Function

The **inverse cosine function**, denoted by $\cos^{-1}$ or arccos, is defined by

$$y = \cos^{-1} x \text{ if and only if } x = \cos y \text{ for } x \in [-1, 1] \text{ and } y \in [0, \pi].$$

That is, the domain of the inverse cosine function is $[-1, 1]$ and the range is $[0, \pi]$.

In Figure 6.25, the arccosine function is represented by the solid line; the broken line is $y = \cos x$ graph, and the dashed part is the restricted domain part of the graph of the cosine function that is reflected about the $y = x$ line to obtain the graph of $y = \arccos x = \cos^{-1} x$, shown in Figure 6.26.

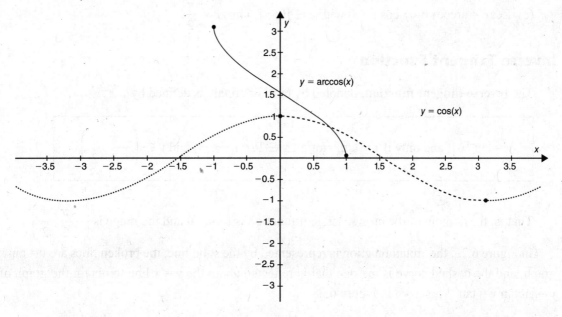

Figure 6.25

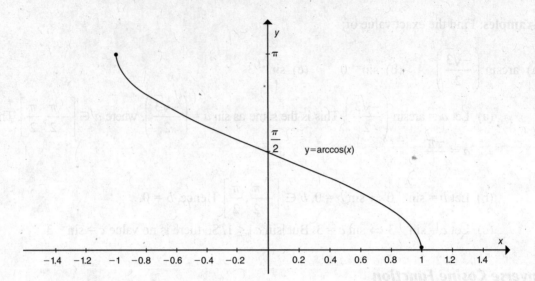

Figure 6.26

Examples: Find the exact value of:

(a) $\arccos\left(\dfrac{1}{2}\right)$ (b) $\cos^{-1}(-1)$ (c) $\arccos 0$

(a) Let $a = \arccos\left(\dfrac{1}{2}\right)$. This is the same as $\cos a = \left(\dfrac{1}{2}\right)$, where $a \in [0, \pi]$. So, $a = \dfrac{\pi}{3}$.

(b) Let $b = \cos^{-1}(-1) \Leftrightarrow \cos b = -1$, $b \in [0, \pi]$. Hence, $b = \pi$.

(c) Let $c = \arccos 0 \Leftrightarrow \cos c = 0$ with $c \in [0, \pi]$. Thus $c = \dfrac{\pi}{2}$

Inverse Tangent Function

The **inverse tangent function**, denoted by $\tan^{-1}$ or arctan, is defined by

$$y = \tan^{-1}x \text{ if and only if } x = \tan y \text{ for all } x \in \mathbf{R} = (-\infty, \infty) \text{ and } y \in \left(-\frac{\pi}{2}, \frac{\pi}{2}\right).$$

That is, the domain of the inverse tangent function is $(-\infty, \infty)$ and the range is $\left(-\dfrac{\pi}{2}, \dfrac{\pi}{2}\right)$.

In Figure 6.25, the arctan function is represented by the solid line; the broken lines are $y = \tan x$ graph, and the dashed curve is the one that is reflected about the $y = x$ line to obtain the graph of $y = \arctan x = \tan^{-1}x$, shown in Figure 6.28.

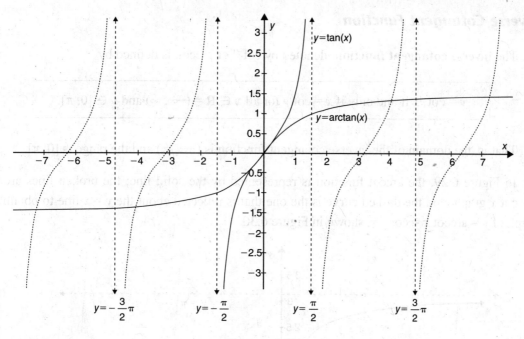

Figure 6.27

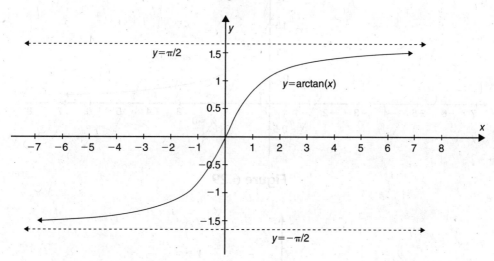

Figure 6.28

Examples: Find the exact value of:

(a) $\tan^{-1}(-1)$ (b) $\arctan 0$ (c) $\tan^{-1} \dfrac{1}{\sqrt{3}}$

(a) Let $a = \tan^{-1}(-1)$, or $\tan a = -1$, where $a \in \left(-\dfrac{\pi}{2}, \dfrac{\pi}{2}\right)$. Thus, $a = \dfrac{-\pi}{4}$.

(b) Let $b = \arctan 0 \Leftrightarrow \tan b = 0$, $b \in \left(-\dfrac{\pi}{2}, \dfrac{\pi}{2}\right)$. Hence, $b = 0$.

(c) Let $c = \tan^{-1}\left(\dfrac{1}{\sqrt{3}}\right) \Leftrightarrow \tan c = \dfrac{1}{\sqrt{3}}$ with $c \in \left(-\dfrac{\pi}{2}, \dfrac{\pi}{2}\right)$. So, $c = \dfrac{\pi}{6}$.

Inverse Cotangent Function

The **inverse cotangent function**, denoted by $\cot^{-1}$ or arccot, is defined by

$$y = \cot^{-1}x \text{ if and only if } x = \cot y \text{ for all } x \in \mathbf{R} = (-\infty, \infty) \text{ and } y \in [0, \pi].$$

That is, the domain of the inverse cotangent function is $(-\infty, \infty)$ and the range is $[0, \pi]$.

In Figure 6.29, the arccot function is represented by the solid line; the broken lines are the $y = \cot x$ graph, and the dashed curve is the one that is reflected about the $y = x$ line to obtain the graph of $y = \text{arccot } x = \cot^{-1} x$, shown in Figure 6.30.

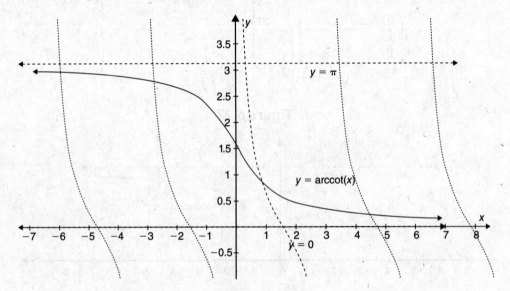

Figure 6.29

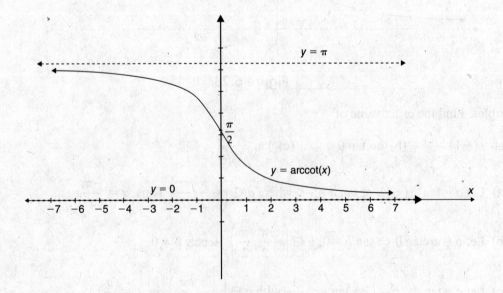

Figure 6.30

Inverse Secant Function

The **inverse secant function**, denoted by $\sec^{-1}$ or arcsec, is defined by

$$y = \sec^{-1}x \text{ if and only if } x = \sec y \text{ for all } x \in (-\infty, -1] \cup [1, \infty) \text{ and } y \in \left[0, \frac{\pi}{2}\right) \cup \left(\frac{\pi}{2}, \pi\right].$$

That is, the domain of the inverse secant function is $(-\infty, -1] \cup [1, \infty)$ and the range is $\left[0, \frac{\pi}{2}\right) \cup \left(\frac{\pi}{2}, \pi\right]$.

In Figure 6.31, the arcsec function is represented by the solid line; the broken lines are $y = \sec x$ graph, and the dashed lines are those that are reflected about the $y = x$ line to obtain the graph of $x = \sec^{-1}x$, shown in Figure 6.32.

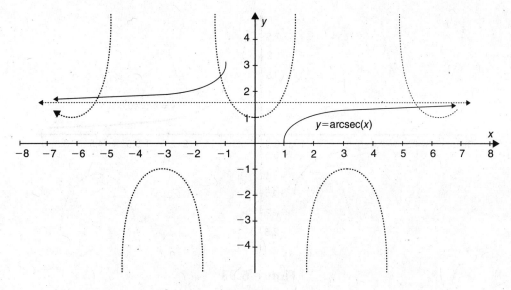

Figure 6.31

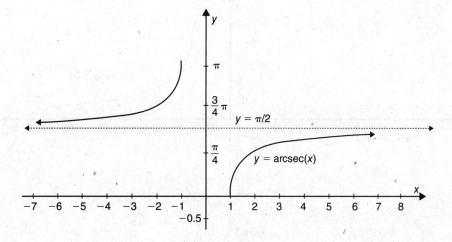

Figure 6.32

Inverse Cosecant Function

The **inverse cosecant function**, denoted by $\csc^{-1}$ or arccsc, is defined by

$$y = \csc^{-1} x \text{ if and only if } x = \csc y \text{ for all } x \in (-\infty, -1] \cup [1, \infty) \text{ and } y \in \left[-\frac{\pi}{2}, 0 \right) \cup \left(0, \frac{\pi}{2} \right].$$

Thai is, the domain of the inverse cosecant function is $(-\infty, -1] \cup [1, \infty)$ and the range is $\left[-\frac{\pi}{2}, 0 \right) \cup \left(0, \frac{\pi}{2} \right]$.

In Figure 6.33, the arccsc function is represented by the solid line; the broken lines are $y = \csc x$ graph, and the dashed lines are those that are reflected about the $y = x$ line to obtain the graph of $x = \csc^{-1} x$, shown in Figure 6.34.

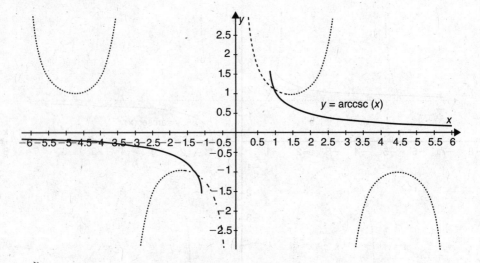

Figure 6.33

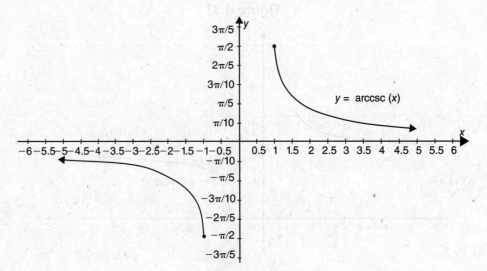

Figure 6.34

Properties That Follow from the Definitions

If $-1 \le x \le 1$ and $\dfrac{-\pi}{2} \le y \le \dfrac{\pi}{2}$, then $\sin(\arcsin x) = x$ and $\arcsin(\sin y) = y$.

If $-1 \le x \le 1$ and $0 \le y \le \pi$, then $\cos(\arccos x) = x$ and $\arccos(\cos y) = y$.

If x is a real number and $\dfrac{-\pi}{2} < y < \dfrac{\pi}{2}$, then $\tan(\arctan x) = x$ and $\arctan(\tan y) = y$.

If x is a real number and $0 < y < \pi$, then $\cot(\text{arccot } x) = x$ and $\text{arccot}(\cot y) = y$.

If $|x| \ge 1$ and $y \in \left[0, \dfrac{\pi}{2}\right) \cup \left(\dfrac{\pi}{2}, \pi\right]$, then $\sec(\text{arcsec } x) = x$ and $\text{arcsec}(\sec y) = y$.

If $|x| \ge 1$ and $y \in \left[-\dfrac{\pi}{2}, 0\right) \cup \left(0, \dfrac{\pi}{2}\right]$, then $\csc(\text{arccsc } x) = x$ and $\text{arccsc}(\csc y) = y$.

Examples If possible, find the exact value:

(a) $\arctan\left(\tan\left(\dfrac{7\pi}{3}\right)\right)$ (b) $\sec(\cot^{-1}(-1))$ (c) $\sin\left(\arccos\left(\dfrac{2}{3}\right)\right)$

(a) $\arctan\left(\tan\left(\dfrac{7\pi}{3}\right)\right) = \arctan\left(\tan\left(\dfrac{\pi}{3}\right)\right) = \dfrac{\pi}{3}$

(b) $\sec(\cot^{-1}(-1)) = \sec\left(\dfrac{3\pi}{4}\right) = -\sqrt{2}$

(c) Let $\theta = \arccos\left(\dfrac{2}{3}\right)$, so that $\cos\theta = \dfrac{2}{3}$. Label a right triangle as shown. Use the Pythagorean Theorem to find the length of the other leg. Then from the triangle, $\sin\theta = \dfrac{\sqrt{5}}{3}$.

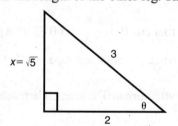

Review Problems for Section 6.1.4

1. Find the exact value of each of the following without using a calculator.

(a) $\text{arccsc}(0)$ (b) $\arctan\left(-\sqrt{3}\right)$ (c) $\arcsin\left(\dfrac{\sqrt{2}}{2}\right)$

(d) $\cos^{-1}(1)$ (e) $\text{arcsec}\left(\dfrac{2}{\sqrt{3}}\right)$ (f) $\cot^{-1}(1)$

2. Evaluate:

(a) $\arccos(\cos(0))$

(b) $\tan(\tan^{-1}\frac{8}{3})$

(c) $\sin\left(\operatorname{arccsc}(4)\right)$

(d) $\operatorname{arccot}\left(\sin\left(\frac{-9\pi}{2}\right)\right)$

(e) $\csc\left(\cos^{-1}\left(\frac{-4}{7}\right)\right)$

Detailed Solutions

1. (a) Let $x = \operatorname{arccsc}(0) \Leftrightarrow \csc x = 0$. The cosecant never equals zero; its range is $\{\, y \mid |y| \geq 1 \,\}$; thus arcse(0) does not exist.

(b) Let $x = \arctan\left(-\sqrt{3}\right) \Leftrightarrow \tan x = -\sqrt{3}$, with $|x| < \frac{\pi}{2}$. Hence, $x - \frac{\pi}{3}$.

(c) Let $y = \arcsin\left(\frac{\sqrt{2}}{2}\right) \Leftrightarrow \sin y = \frac{\sqrt{2}}{2}$, with $|x| \leq \frac{\pi}{2}$. Thus, $y = \frac{\pi}{4}$.

(d) Let $y = \cos^{-1}(1) \Leftrightarrow \cos y = 1$, with $0 \leq y \leq \pi$; $y = 0$.

(e) Let $\theta = \operatorname{arcsec}\left(\frac{2}{\sqrt{3}}\right)$. Then $\sec\theta = \frac{2}{\sqrt{3}}$, and θ must be in the first quadrant. So $\theta = \frac{\pi}{6}$.

(f) Let $y = \cot^{-1}(1)$, then $\cot y = 1$ and $y = (0, \pi)$, hence $y = \frac{\pi}{4}$.

2. (a) $\operatorname{Arccos}(\cos(0)) = \arccos(1) = 0$.

(b) $\operatorname{Tan}(\tan^{-1}\frac{8}{3}) = \frac{8}{3}$ since $\tan(\tan^{-1}p) = p$ for all real numbers.

(c) Let $\theta = \left(\operatorname{arccsc}(4)\right)$. Then $\csc\theta = 4$. Therefore, $\sin(\theta) = \frac{1}{4}$, and $\theta \approx .08\pi$

(d) $\operatorname{arccot}\left(\sin\left(\frac{-9\pi}{2}\right)\right) = \operatorname{arccot}(-1) = \frac{3\pi}{4}$.

(e) Let $\theta = \left(\cos^{-1}\left(\frac{-4}{7}\right)\right)$ so that $\cos\theta = \frac{-4}{7}$ and $\theta \in [0, \pi]$. Label a right triangle (think of it in the second quadrant since the adjacent side is -4) to represent this. The other leg is $\sqrt{49-16} = \sqrt{33}$ by the Pythagorean Theorem. Then $\csc\left(\cos^{-1}\left(\frac{-4}{7}\right)\right) = \csc\theta = \frac{7}{\sqrt{33}}$.

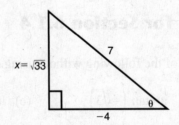

$x = \sqrt{33}$ 7 -4 θ

6.1.5 The California *Mathematics Subject Matter Requirements* stipulate that candidates for any credential program for teaching secondary mathematics must be able to understand and *apply polar representations of complex numbers (e.g., DeMoivre's Theorem).*

Polar representation of complex Numbers

A complex number, z, is a number that can be written in the form $z = a + bi$, where a and b are real numbers and $i = \sqrt{-1}$. The value a is called the real part of z, or $\text{Re}(z) = a$, and b is called the imaginary part of z, or $\text{Im}(z) = b$. The pair (a, b) can be represented in the **complex plane,** where the horizontal axis (**real axis**) represents the real part of z and the vertical axis (**imaginary axis**) represents the imaginary part of z. In Figure 6.35, (a, b) represents the complex number z'.

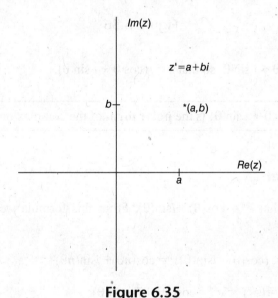

Figure 6.35

The **modulus** or **length** of $z = a + bi$, denoted by $|z|$, is defined as the distance between the point (a, b) and the origin, or the length of the vector that which represents z: $|z| = \sqrt{a^2 + b^2}$.

Let z be a non-zero complex number of modulus $r > 0$. Define $\hat{z} = \dfrac{1}{r} z$. Then $\hat{z}$ has modulus 1. Hence, the point representing $\hat{z}$ lies on the unit circle, which means it has coordinates $(\cos \theta, \sin \theta)$, where θ is the angle between the positive real axis and the vector representing z (Figure 6.36). Note that $\tan(\theta) = \dfrac{y}{x}$ where $(x, y) = (\cos \theta, \sin \theta)$ represents $\hat{z}$ in the complex plane.

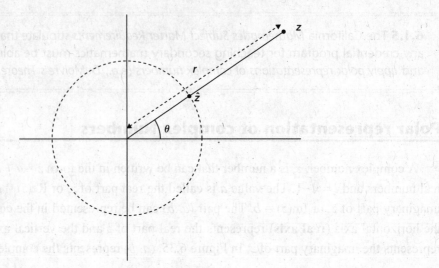

Figure 6.36

Thus, $\hat{z} = \dfrac{1}{r} z = \cos\theta + i\sin\theta$, so that $z = r(\cos\theta + i\sin\theta)$.

$z = r(\cos\theta + i\sin\theta)$ is the **polar form** of the complex number z.

De Moivre's Theorem

Euler's Identity states that $e^{i\theta} = \cos(\theta) + i\sin(\theta)$. From this formula we can prove **De Moivres Theorem**:

For any positive integer n, $(\cos(\theta) + i\sin(\theta))^n = \cos(n\theta) + i\sin(n\theta)$

Proof: $(\cos(\theta) + i\sin(\theta))^n = (e^{i\theta})^n = e^{in\theta} = \cos(n\theta) + i\sin(n\theta)$.

Q.E.D.

- If $z \neq 0$, then $(\cos(\theta) + i\sin(\theta))^n = \cos(n\theta) + i\sin(n\theta)$ is also true when n is a negative integer.

Examples:

(a) If $z = -1 + i$, find z^{13}.

$|z| = \sqrt{(-1)^2 + 1^2} = \sqrt{2}$ and $\tan(\theta) = -1$ so that $\theta = \dfrac{3\pi}{4}$ since the point $(-1, 1)$ lies in the second

quadrant. So $z = \sqrt{2}\left(\cos\left(\dfrac{3\pi}{4}\right) + i\sin\left(\dfrac{3\pi}{4}\right)\right)$, thus $z^{13} = \left(\sqrt{2}\right)^{13}\left(\cos\left(\dfrac{39\pi}{4}\right) + i\sin\left(\dfrac{39\pi}{4}\right)\right)$

$= 64\sqrt{2}\left(\cos\left(\dfrac{7\pi}{4}\right) + i\sin\left(\dfrac{7\pi}{4}\right)\right) = 64\sqrt{2}\left(\dfrac{\sqrt{2}}{2} - i\dfrac{\sqrt{2}}{2}\right) = 64 - 64i$.

(b) Find all complex cube roots of 125*i*.

We want to find all z such that $z^3 = 125i$. So we write z^3 in polar form: $|z^3| = 125$ and $\theta = \dfrac{\pi}{2}$ since the point representing z^3 in the complex plane is $(0, 125)$. Hence, we have that

$z^3 = 125\left(\cos\left(\dfrac{\pi}{2}\right) + i\sin\left(\dfrac{\pi}{2}\right)\right)$, so $z = 5(\cos(\beta) + i\sin(\beta))$, where $3\beta = \left(\dfrac{\pi}{2}\right) + 2\pi k$, k is an integer. Therefore, $\beta = \dfrac{\pi}{6} + \dfrac{2\pi}{3}k$. The possibilities for the complex cube roots of 125*i* are:

$\beta = \dfrac{\pi}{6}$, so that $z_1 = 5\left(\cos\left(\dfrac{\pi}{6}\right) + i\sin\left(\dfrac{\pi}{6}\right)\right) = \dfrac{5}{2}\sqrt{3} + \dfrac{5}{2}i$

$\beta = \dfrac{5\pi}{6}$, so that $z_2 = 5\left(\cos\left(\dfrac{5\pi}{6}\right) + i\sin\left(\dfrac{5\pi}{6}\right)\right) = -\dfrac{5}{2}\sqrt{3} + \dfrac{5}{2}i$

$\beta = \dfrac{3\pi}{2}$, so that $z_3 = 5\left(\cos\left(\dfrac{3\pi}{2}\right) + i\sin\left(\dfrac{3\pi}{2}\right)\right) = -5i$

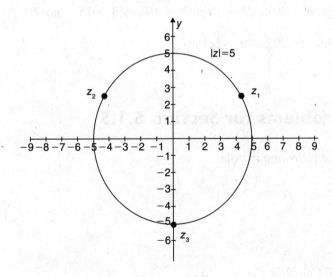

Figure 6.37

Note that the three complex cube roots are equally spaced about the circle with radius 5, as shown in Figure 6.37.

(c) Prove that $\cos(5\theta) = 16\cos^5\theta - 20\cos^3\theta + 5\cos\theta$.

Proof:

By the Binomial Theorem:

$(\cos\theta + i\sin\theta)^5 =$

$(\cos\theta)^5 + \binom{5}{1}(\cos\theta)^4(i\sin\theta)^1 + \binom{5}{2}(\cos\theta)^3(i\sin\theta)^2 + \binom{5}{3}(\cos\theta)^2(i\sin\theta)^3$

$+ \binom{5}{4}(\cos\theta)^1(i\sin\theta)^4 + \binom{5}{5}(\cos\theta)^0(i\sin\theta)^5$

$= \cos^5\theta + 5\cos^4\theta(i\sin\theta) + 10(\cos^3\theta)(i^2\sin^2\theta) + 10(\cos^2\theta)(i^3\sin^3\theta) + 5(\cos\theta)(i^4\sin^4\theta) + (i^5\sin^5\theta)$

$= \cos^5\theta + i5\cos^4\theta\sin\theta - 10\cos^3\theta\sin^2\theta - i10\cos^2\theta\sin^3\theta + 5\cos\theta\sin^4\theta + i\sin^5\theta$

$= (\cos^5\theta - 10\cos^3\theta\sin^2\theta + 5\cos\theta\sin^4\theta) + i(5\cos^4\theta\sin\theta - 10\cos^2\theta\sin^3\theta + \sin^5\theta)$

By De Moivre's Theorem, $(\cos\theta + i\sin\theta)^5 = \cos5\theta + i\sin5\theta$.

So, $\cos5\theta + i\sin5\theta = (\cos^5\theta - 10\cos^3\theta\sin^2\theta + 5\cos\theta\sin^4\theta)$
$$+ i(5\cos^4\theta\sin\theta - 10\cos^2\theta\sin^3\theta + \sin^5\theta)$$

The real parts must be equal, so $\cos(5\theta) = \cos^5\theta - 10\cos^3\theta\sin^2\theta + 5\cos\theta\sin^4\theta$. Then, since $\sin^2\theta = 1 - \cos^2\theta$,

$$\cos(5\theta) = \cos^5\theta - 10\cos^3\theta(1 - \cos^2\theta) + 5\cos\theta(1 - \cos^2\theta)^2$$

$$= \cos^5\theta - 10\cos^3\theta = 10 - \cos^5\theta + 5\cos\theta(1 - \cos^2\theta + \cos^4\theta)$$

$$= 11\cos^5\theta - 20\cos^3\theta + (5\cos\theta - 10\cos^3\theta - 15 - \cos^5\theta)$$

$$= 16\cos^5\theta - 20\cos^5\theta + 5\cos\theta$$

Q.E.D.

Review Problems for Section 6.1.5

1. Write each of the following in polar form:

    (a) $5i$

    (b) $3 - 3i$

    (c) $\sqrt{3}$

2. Let $z = 1 + \sqrt{3}\,i$. Calculate z^9.

3. Find all complex fourth roots of $z = 1 - i$.

4. Prove that $\sin(4\theta) = 4\cos\theta\sin\theta - 8\cos\theta\sin^3\theta$

Detailed Solutions

1. (a) $z = 0 + 5i$, $|z| = 5$ and $\theta = \dfrac{\pi}{2}$, so in polar form $z = 5(\cos\dfrac{\pi}{2} + i\sin\dfrac{\pi}{2})$.

    (b) $z = 3 - 3i$, $|z| = \sqrt{9+9} = 3\sqrt{2}$, $\theta = \dfrac{7\pi}{4}$, so in polar form $z = 3\sqrt{2}\,(\cos\dfrac{7\pi}{4} + i\sin\dfrac{7\pi}{4})$.

(c) $z = \sqrt{3} + 0i$, $|z| = \sqrt{3}$ and $\theta = 0$, so in polar form $z = \sqrt{3}(\cos 0 + i\sin 0)$.

2. $z = 1 + \sqrt{3}i$, $|z| = \sqrt{1+3} = 2$ and $\theta = \tan^{-1}(\sqrt{3}) = \dfrac{\pi}{3}$. So, $z = 2(\cos \dfrac{\pi}{3} + i\sin \dfrac{\pi}{3})$.
Then $z^9 = 2^9(\cos 3\pi + i\sin 3\pi) = -512$.

3. We want to find all z such that $z^4 = 1 - i$. So write z^4 in polar form: $|z^4| = \sqrt{2}$ and
$\theta = \dfrac{7\pi}{4}$ since the point representing z^4 in the complex plane is $(1, -1)$. Hence, we have that

$$z^4 = \sqrt{2}\left(\cos\left(\frac{7\pi}{4}\right) + i\sin\left(\frac{7\pi}{4}\right)\right), \text{ so } z = \sqrt[8]{2}\ (\cos(\beta) + i\sin(\beta)) \text{ where } 4\beta = \frac{7\pi}{4} + 2\pi k, k \text{ is an integer.}$$

Therefore, $\beta = \dfrac{7\pi}{16} + \dfrac{\pi}{2}k$. The possibilities for the complex cube roots of $1 - i$ are:

$z_1 = \sqrt[8]{2}\ (\cos \dfrac{7\pi}{16} + i\ \sin \dfrac{7\pi}{16})$, $z_2 = \sqrt[8]{2}\ (\cos \dfrac{15\pi}{16} + i\ \sin \dfrac{15\pi}{16})$, $z_3 = \sqrt[8]{2}\ (\cos \dfrac{23\pi}{16}$)

$+ i\ \sin \dfrac{23\pi}{16})$, and $z_4 = \sqrt[8]{2}\ (\cos \dfrac{31\pi}{16} + i\ \sin \dfrac{31\pi}{16})$. The four complex fourth roots are shown in

Figure 6.38.

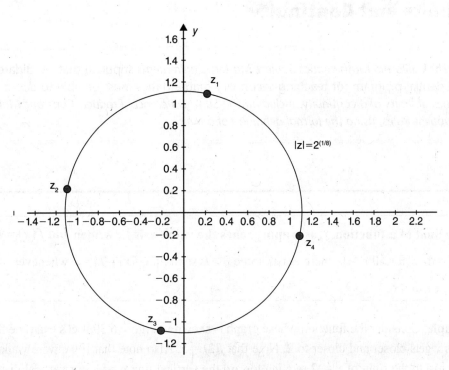

Figure 6.38

4.   **Proof:**

$(\cos \theta + i \sin \theta)^4$

$= (\cos \theta)^4 + \binom{4}{1}(\cos \theta)^3(i\sin \theta) + \binom{4}{2}(\cos \theta)^2(i\sin \theta)^2 + \binom{4}{3}(\cos \theta)(i\sin \theta)^3 + \binom{4}{4}(i\sin \theta)^4$

$= \cos^4 \theta + 4\cos^3 \theta(i\sin \theta) + 6\cos^2 \theta\,(i^2\sin^2 \theta) + 4\cos \theta\,(i^3\sin^3 \theta) + (i^4\sin^4 \theta)$

$= (\cos^4 \theta - 6\cos^2 \theta \sin^2 \theta) + \sin^4 \theta) + i(4\cos^3 \theta \sin \theta - 4\cos \theta \sin^3 \theta)$

But $(\cos\theta + i\sin\theta)^4 = \cos(4\theta) + i\sin(4\theta)$, hence equating the imaginary parts we have
$\sin(4\theta) = 4\cos^3 \theta \sin\theta - 4\cos\theta \sin^3 \theta$.

Then since $\cos^2 \theta = 1 - \sin^2$,
$$\sin(4\theta) = 4\cos\theta \sin\theta\,(1 - \sin^2\theta) - 4\cos\theta \sin^3\theta$$
$$= 4\cos\theta \sin\theta - 8\cos\theta \sin^3\theta$$

Q.E.D.

6.2 Limits and Continuity

6.2.1 *The California Mathematics Subject Matter Requirements* stipulate that candidates for any credential program for teaching secondary mathematics must be able to *derive basic properties of limits and continuity, including the Sum, Difference, Product, Constant Multiple, and Quotient Rules, using the formal definition of a limit.*

Limits

> **The limit of a function, f, as x approaches the value a, is L,** written $\lim\limits_{x \to a} f(x) = L$ if and only if for all $\varepsilon > 0$, there exists some $\delta > 0$ such that $|f(x) - L| < \varepsilon$ whenever $0 < |x - a| < \delta$.

Example: Consider the function whose graph is shown in Figure 6.39. Let's examine the limit of $f(x)$ as x gets closer and closer to 2. Note that $f(2) = 5$. Also note that if we were walking on the curve just to the right of $x = 2$ moving toward the vertical line $x = 3$, our vertical distance from the x-axis becomes closer and closer to 3. The same is true if we were walking on the curve to the left of $x = 2$ moving toward the vertical line $x = 2$. Informally, this means the limit is $L = 3$.

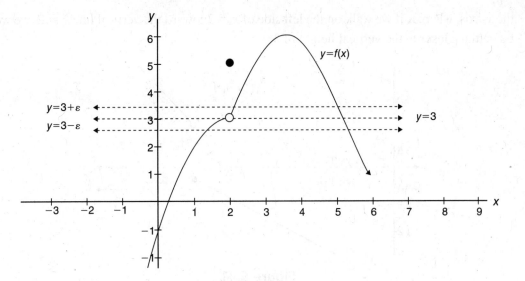

Figure 6.39

This is the same as saying that for any positive number ε there is a horizontal strip between the lines $y = 3 + \varepsilon$ and $y = 3 - \varepsilon$, and for x values really close to 2 (how close to 2?...within some positive number δ), the function values must stay in that horizontal strip.

Hence, for every $\varepsilon > 0$, there must be another positive number δ such that if we choose $x \neq 2$ but such that $2 - \delta < x < 2 + \delta$, then $3 - \varepsilon < f(x) < 3\,\varepsilon$ (Figure 6.40).

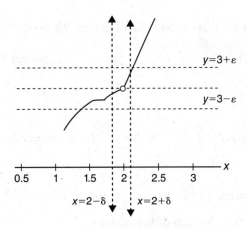

Figure 6.40

Example: Consider the following function $f(x) = \begin{cases} x + 1, & \text{if } x \leq 2 \\ 2x, & \text{if } x > 2 \end{cases}$. The graph is shown in Figure 6.41.

This function does not have a limit as x gets closer to 2. If we were walking on the function's graph to the right of 2 toward the vertical line $x = 2$, we would be getting closer to 4 units above the x-axis, whereas if we walk on the left side of $x = 2$ toward the vertical line $x = 2$, we would be getting closer to the vertical height of 3.

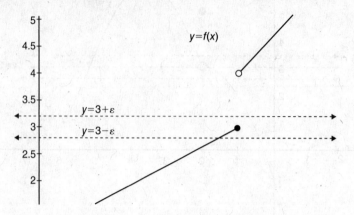

Figure 6.41

Example: Prove $\lim\limits_{x \to 4}(1 - 3x) = -11$.

Proof: Let $\varepsilon > 0$ be given. Choose $\delta = \dfrac{\varepsilon}{3}$; then when $0 < |x - 4| < \delta = \dfrac{\varepsilon}{3}$, it follows that

$$|(1 - 3x) - (-11)| = |12 - 3x| = 3|x - 4| < 3\left(\dfrac{\varepsilon}{3}\right) = \varepsilon.$$

Therefore, $\lim\limits_{x \to 4}(1 - 3x) = -11$.   Q.E.D.

Note: The numbers $\delta = \dfrac{\varepsilon}{3}$ is not just plucked out of the air. We need $|f(x) - L| < \varepsilon$, so looking at that

statement for this problem: $|(1 - 3x) - (-11)| = 3|x - 4| < \varepsilon$, we see that we must choose $\delta \le \dfrac{\varepsilon}{3}$.

Limit Theorems

Let c be a constant and let $\lim\limits_{x \to a} f(x) = L$ and $\lim\limits_{x \to a} g(x) = M$, where $L, M \in \mathbf{R}$, Then the following statements (theorems) are true:

1. $\lim\limits_{x \to a}\big[f(x) + g(x)\big] = \lim\limits_{x \to a} f(x) + \lim\limits_{x \to a} g(x) = L + M$.

    (The limit of the sum is the sum of the limits.)

2. $\lim\limits_{x \to a}\big[f(x) - g(x)\big] = \lim\limits_{x \to a} f(x) - \lim\limits_{x \to a} g(x) = L - M$.

    (The limit of the difference is the difference of the limits.)

3. $\lim\limits_{x \to a}\big[cf(x)\big] = c\lim\limits_{x \to a} f(x) = cL$.

    (The limit of a constant times a function is the constant times the limit of the function.)

4. $\lim\limits_{x \to a}\big[f(x) \cdot g(x)\big] = \lim\limits_{x \to a} f(x) \cdot \lim\limits_{x \to a} g(x) = L \cdot M$.

    (The limit of the product is the product of the limits.)

5. $\lim\limits_{x \to a} \left[\dfrac{f(x)}{g(x)} \right] = \dfrac{\lim\limits_{x \to a} f(x)}{\lim\limits_{x \to a} g(x)} = \dfrac{L}{M}$, provided $M \neq 0$.

    (The limit of the quotient is the quotient of the limits, provided the limit of the denominator is not zero.)

6. $\lim\limits_{x \to a} \left[f(x) \right]^n = \left[\lim\limits_{x \to a} f(x) \right]^n = L^n$.

    (The limit of the nth power of a function is the nth power of the limit of the function.)

7. $\lim\limits_{x \to a} c = c$.

    (The limit of a constant is the constant.)

8. $\lim\limits_{x \to a} x = a$.

    (The limit of the linear function $h(x) = x$ as x approaches a is a.)

9. $\lim\limits_{x \to a} \sqrt[n]{x} = \sqrt[n]{a}$, where n is a positive integer. If n is even, we need $a \geq 0$.

10. $\lim\limits_{x \to a} \sqrt[n]{f(x)} = \sqrt[n]{\lim\limits_{x \to a} f(x)} = \sqrt[n]{L}$ where n is a positive integer, and if n is even, we need $L > 0$.

Examples:

(a) $\lim\limits_{x \to a} \left[f(x) + g(x) \right] = \lim\limits_{x \to a} f(x) + \lim\limits_{x \to a} g(x)$.

Proof: Assume $\lim\limits_{x \to a} f(x) = L$ and $\lim\limits_{x \to a} g(x) = M$. Let $\varepsilon > 0$ be given. Then there exists $\delta' > 0$

and $\delta'' > 0$ such that if $0 < |x - a| < \delta'$, $|f(x) - L| < \dfrac{\varepsilon}{2}$, and if $0 < |x - a| < \delta''$, $|g(x) - M| < \dfrac{\varepsilon}{2}$.

Choose $\delta = \min\{\delta', \delta''\}$. Then if $0 < |x - a| < \delta'$, using the triangle inequality for real numbers, $|(f(x) + g(x)) - (L + M)| \leq |f(x) - L| + |g(x) - M| < \dfrac{\varepsilon}{2} + \dfrac{\varepsilon}{2} = \varepsilon$.

Hence, $\lim\limits_{x \to a} \left[f(x) + g(x) \right] = \lim\limits_{x \to a} f(x) + \lim\limits_{x \to a} g(x)$.

Q.E.D.

(b) Prove: $\lim\limits_{x \to a} \left[cf(x) \right] = c \lim\limits_{x \to a} f(x)$.

Proof: Assume that $\lim\limits_{x \to a} f(x) = L$. If $c = 0$, then the statement is clearly true as $0 = 0$. So assume $c \neq 0$.

Let $\varepsilon > 0$ be given. Then there exists some $\delta > 0$ such that if $0 < |x - a| < \delta$, then $|f(x) - L| < \dfrac{\varepsilon}{|c|}$.

Now assume $0 < |x - a| < \delta$. Then $|cf(x) - cL| = |c/|f(x) - L| < |c| \cdot \dfrac{\varepsilon}{|c|} = \varepsilon$.

Therefore, $\lim\limits_{x \to a} \left[cf(x) \right] = c \lim\limits_{x \to a} f(x)$.

Q.E.D.

(c) Prove: $\lim\limits_{x \to a}\left[\dfrac{f(x)}{g(x)}\right] = \dfrac{\lim\limits_{x \to a} f(x)}{\lim\limits_{x \to a} g(x)} = \dfrac{L}{M}$, provided $M \neq 0$.

Proof: First we will prove: $\lim\limits_{x \to a}\left[\dfrac{1}{g(x)}\right] = \dfrac{1}{M}$, where $M \neq 0$.

Assume $\lim\limits_{x \to a} g(x) = M$ and $M \neq 0$. Let $\varepsilon > 0$ be given. (We don't need to use this right now, but we will state it here.)

Since $\lim\limits_{x \to a} g(x) = M$ and $|M| > 0$, for $\varepsilon^* = \dfrac{|M|}{2}$ there exists $\delta^* > 0$ such that $|g(x) - M| < \varepsilon^*$ $= \dfrac{|M|}{2}$ whenever $0 < |x - a| < \delta^*$.

Then for x such that $0 < |x - a| < \delta^*$, $|M| = |M - g(x) + g(x)| \leq |M - g(x)| + |g(x)|$ by the triangle inequality. But $|M - g(x)| = |g(x) - M|$, so $|M - g(x)| + |g(x)| \leq \dfrac{|M|}{2} + |g(x)|$. It follows that $|M| \leq \dfrac{|M|}{2} + |g(x)|$, which simplifies to $\dfrac{|M|}{2} \leq |g(x)|$. This is equivalent to $\dfrac{1}{|g(x)|} \leq \dfrac{2}{|M|}$.

Now, because $\lim\limits_{x \to a} g(x) = M$ and $\dfrac{|M|^2}{2}\varepsilon > 0$ there exists a $\delta' > 0$ such that $|g(x) - M| < \dfrac{|M|^2}{2}\varepsilon$ whenever $0 < |x - a| < \delta'$.

Choose $\delta = \min\{\delta^*, \delta'\}$. Then, whenever $0 < |x - a| < \delta$,

$$\left|\frac{1}{g(x)} - \frac{1}{M}\right| = \left|\frac{M - g(x)}{Mg(x)}\right|$$

$$= \frac{1}{|M|}\frac{1}{|g(x)|}|M - g(x)|$$

$$< \frac{1}{|M|}\frac{2}{|M|}|M - g(x)|$$

$$= \frac{2}{|M|^2}|M - g(x)|$$

$$< \frac{2}{|M|^2}\frac{|M|^2}{2}\varepsilon$$

$$= \varepsilon$$

Hence, $\lim\limits_{x \to a}\left[\dfrac{1}{g(x)}\right] = \dfrac{1}{M}$, where $M \neq 0$.

Now, assume that $\lim\limits_{x \to a} f(x) = L$ and $\lim\limits_{x \to a} g(x) = M \neq 0$. Then

$$\lim_{x \to a}\left[\frac{f(x)}{g(x)}\right] = \lim_{x \to a}\left[f(x)\frac{1}{g(x)}\right] = \lim_{x \to a}\left[f(x)\right]\lim_{x \to a}\left[\frac{1}{g(x)}\right] = L \cdot \frac{1}{M} = \frac{L}{M}.$$

Q.E.D.

(d) Evaluate each of the following using the Theorems.

(i) $\lim_{x \to 2}\left(3x^3 - x + 5\right)$ (ii) $\lim_{x \to -1}\left(\frac{x+5}{2-x}\right)$ (iii) $\lim_{x \to 0}\left(\sqrt{4-x^2}\right)\left(2^x + 1\right)$

(i) $\lim_{x \to 2}\left(3x^3 - x + 5\right) = \lim_{x \to 2}\left(3x^3\right) - \lim_{x \to 2}\left(x\right) + \lim_{x \to 2}\left(5\right)$ (limit of sum/difference)

$\qquad = 3\lim_{x \to 2}\left(x^3\right) - \lim_{x \to 2}\left(x\right) + \lim_{x \to 2}\left(5\right)$ (limit of a constant times a function)

$\qquad = 3\lim_{x \to 2}\left(x^3\right) - \lim_{x \to 2}\left(x\right) + 5$ (limit of a constant)

$\qquad = 3\left(\lim_{x \to 2} x\right)^3 - \lim_{x \to 2}\left(x\right) + 5$ (limit of a power of a function)

$\qquad = 3(2)^3 - 2 + 5 = 27$ (limit of x)

(ii) $\lim_{x \to -1}\left(\frac{x+5}{2-x}\right) = \dfrac{\lim_{x \to -1}\left(x+5\right)}{\lim_{x \to -1}\left(2-x\right)}$ (limit of a quotient)

$\qquad = \dfrac{\lim_{x \to -1} x + \lim_{x \to -1} 5}{\lim_{x \to -1} 2 - \lim_{x \to -1} x}$ (limit of sum/difference)

$\qquad = \dfrac{\lim_{x \to -1} x + 5}{2 - \lim_{x \to -1} x}$ (limit of a constant)

$\qquad = \dfrac{-1+5}{2-(-1)} = \dfrac{4}{3}$ (limit of x)

(iii) $\lim_{x \to 0}\left(\sqrt{4-x^2}\right)\left(2^x + 1\right) = \lim_{x \to 0}\left(\sqrt{4-x^2}\right)\lim_{x \to 0}\left(2^x + 1\right)$ (limit of product)

$\qquad = \left(\sqrt{\lim_{x \to 0}\left(4-x^2\right)}\right)\lim_{x \to 0}\left(2^x + 1\right)$ (limit of a root)

$\qquad = \left(\sqrt{\lim_{x \to 0} 4 - \lim_{x \to 0}\left(x^2\right)}\right)\left(\lim_{x \to 0} 2^x + \lim_{x \to 0} 1\right)$ (limit of sum/difference)

$\qquad = \left(\sqrt{4 - \lim_{x \to 0}\left(x^2\right)}\right)\left(\lim_{x \to 0} 2^x + 1\right)$ (limit of a constant)

$\qquad = \left(\sqrt{4 - \left(\lim_{x \to 0} x\right)^2}\right)\left(\lim_{x \to 0} 2^x + 1\right)$ (limit of a power)

$\qquad = \left(\sqrt{4 - (0)^2}\right)\left(2^0 + 1\right) = 4$ (limit of x)

One-Sided Limits

- $\lim\limits_{x \to a^+} f(x) = L$ is the **right-hand limit**. It means that $f(x) \to L$ as $x \to a$ from the right (i.e., for values of $x > a$).

- $\lim\limits_{x \to a^-} f(x) = L$ is the **left-hand limit**. It means that $f(x) \to L$ as $x \to a$ from the left (i.e., for values of $x < a$.)

- The two-sided limit, $\lim\limits_{x \to a} f(x) = L$, exists if and only if both of the one-sided limits exist and are equal to L.

Example:

(a) Let $g(x) = \begin{cases} x - 1 & \text{if } x \le 3 \\ x^2 & \text{if } x > 3 \end{cases}$. Then $\lim\limits_{x \to 3+} g(x) = \lim\limits_{x \to 3+} x^2 = 9$ and

$$\lim\limits_{x \to 3-} g(x) = \lim\limits_{x \to 3-} x - 1 = 2$$

So the two-sided limit does not exist.

(b) The graph of a function g is shown in Figure 6.42. This function does not have a limit (2-sided) as $x \to 0$ since the left-hand limit equals -7 and the right-hand limit equals 4. The limit as $x \to 2$ exists since both one-sided limits equal -4, even though there is no function value at $x = 2$. The limit exists at all other values of the function g's domain.

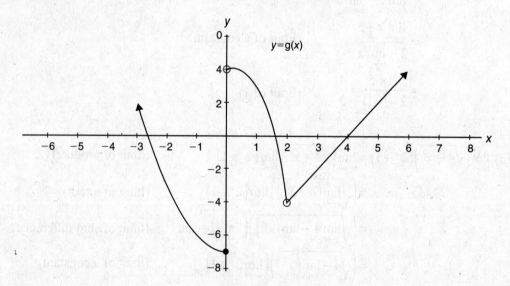

Figure 6.42

- $\lim\limits_{x \to \infty} f(x) = L$, read as *the limit of f(x) as x approaches ∞ equals L*, means that $f(x)$ is getting closer to L as x increases without bound.

- $\lim\limits_{x \to -\infty} f(x) = L$, read as *the limit of f(x) as x approaches $-\infty$ equals L*, means that $f(x)$ is getting closer to L as x decreases without bound.

- The line $y = L$ is a **horizontal asymptote** of the graph of a function f provided $\lim\limits_{x \to \infty} f(x) = L$ or $\lim\limits_{x \to -\infty} f(x) = L$.

Example: In the graph in Figure 6.43, we see a function, h, whose behavior indicates that $\lim\limits_{x \to \infty} h(x) = \pi$ and $\lim\limits_{x \to -\infty} h(x) = 0$. Both lines $y = 0$ and $y = \pi$ are horizontal asymptotes of h.

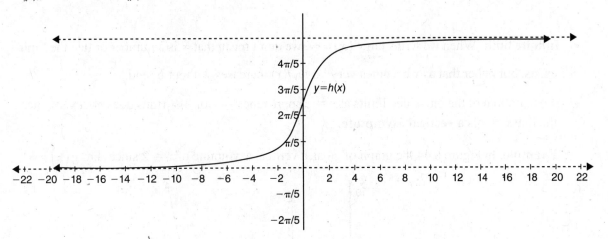

Figure 6.43

- Rational functions often have horizontal asymptotes. In order to find them we take the limits as $x \to \pm\infty$, but for these functions we also can use a certain algebraic technique. We divide each term of the numerator and denominator by x^n, where n is the degree of the polynomial in the denominator. Then we take advantage of knowing that $y = \dfrac{1}{x^n} \to 0$ as $x \to \pm\infty$, for all $n > 0$.

Examples:

(a) $\lim\limits_{x \to \infty} \dfrac{3x^5 - x^4 + 2x^2 + 5}{2x^6 + x - 1} = \lim\limits_{x \to \infty} \dfrac{3x^5 - x^4 + 2x^2 + 5}{2x^6 + x - 1} \quad \dfrac{\div x^6}{\div x^6}$

$\qquad = \lim\limits_{x \to \infty} \dfrac{\dfrac{3}{x} - \dfrac{1}{x^2} + \dfrac{2}{x^4} + \dfrac{5}{x^6}}{2 + \dfrac{1}{x^5} - \dfrac{1}{x^6}} = \dfrac{0}{2} = 0$

(b) $\lim\limits_{x \to -\infty} \dfrac{x^5 - 2x^2 + 3}{2x^4 + 2x - 1} = \lim\limits_{x \to -\infty} \dfrac{x^5 - 2x^2 + 3}{2x^4 + 2x - 1} \quad \dfrac{\div x^4}{\div x^4}$

$\qquad = \lim\limits_{x \to -\infty} \dfrac{x - \dfrac{2}{x^2} + \dfrac{3}{x^4}}{2 + \dfrac{2}{x^3} - \dfrac{1}{x^4}} = \dfrac{-\infty}{2} = -\infty$

(c) $\displaystyle \lim_{x \to \infty} \frac{3x^3 + 5}{2x^3 + x - 1} = \lim_{x \to \infty} \frac{3x^3 + 5}{2x^3 + x - 1} \cdot \frac{\div x^3}{\div x^3}$

$\displaystyle = \lim_{x \to \infty} \frac{3 + \dfrac{5}{x^3}}{2 + \dfrac{1}{x^2} - \dfrac{1}{x^3}} = \frac{3}{2}$

- **Infinite limit**: When we write $\displaystyle \lim_{x \to a} f(x) = \infty$, we don't mean that ∞ is a number or that the limit exists, but rather that as x becomes very large, $f(x)$ increases without bound.

- If one or both of the one-sided limits at $x = c$ approaches $-\infty$ or $+\infty$ (thus does not exist), then the line $x = c$ is a **vertical asymptote**.

  Example: In Figure 6.44 the graph of g has a vertical asymptote of $x = 2$ since $\displaystyle \lim_{x \to 2-} g(x) = \infty$.

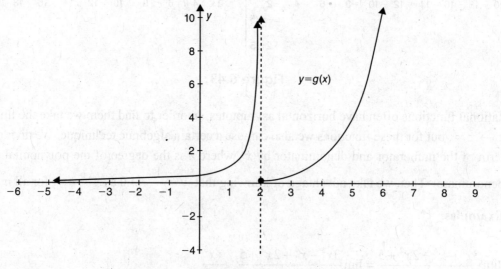

Figure 6.44

- **"Rules" involving infinity**

  1. The expression $\dfrac{1}{\pm\infty}$ should be expressed as 0.

  2. For any positive number k, $k \cdot \pm\infty = \pm\infty$.

  3. $\infty + \infty = \infty$

  4. $\infty - \infty$ is indeterminate, meaning we cannot determine what this is equal to in this form.

  5. The expression $\dfrac{k}{0}$ is undefined for $k \neq 0$.

  6. The expression $\dfrac{\infty}{\infty}$ is indeterminate.

Other Facts about Limits

Theorem (Limits of equal functions): Suppose that f and g are functions such that $f(x) = g(x)$ for all x, except possibly at $x = a$; then $\lim\limits_{x \to a} f(x) = \lim\limits_{x \to a} g(x)$.

Example: $\lim\limits_{x \to 3} \dfrac{x^2 - 3x}{x^2 - 9} = \lim\limits_{x \to 3} \dfrac{x(x-3)}{(x-3)(x+3)} = \lim\limits_{x \to 3} \dfrac{x}{(x+3)} = \dfrac{3}{6} = \dfrac{1}{2}$. We used the fact that

$\dfrac{x(x-3)}{(x-3)(x+3)} = \dfrac{x}{(x+3)}$ except at $x = 3$ to evaluate the limit.

Theorem: If f is a polynomial or rational function and a is in the domain of f, then $\lim\limits_{x \to a} f(x) = f(a)$.

Theorem (Limits of inequalities): Suppose $\lim\limits_{x \to a} f(x) = L$ and $\lim\limits_{x \to a} g(x) = M$. If $f(x) \leq g(x)$ for all x close to a, except possibly at a itself, then $L \leq M$.

The Squeeze (or Sandwich) Theorem: If $f(x) \leq g(x) \leq h(x)$ for all x close to a, except possibly at a, and $\lim\limits_{x \to a} f(x) = L = \lim\limits_{x \to a} h(x)$, then $\lim\limits_{x \to a} g(x) = L$.

Example: $h(x) = -x^2 \leq x^2 \sin\left(\dfrac{1}{x}\right) \leq x^2 = f(x)$ For all x near 0, and $\lim\limits_{x \to 0} f(x) = 0 = \lim\limits_{x \to 0} h(x)$,

hence $\lim\limits_{x \to 0} x^2 \sin\left(\dfrac{1}{x}\right) = 0$ (Figure 6.45).

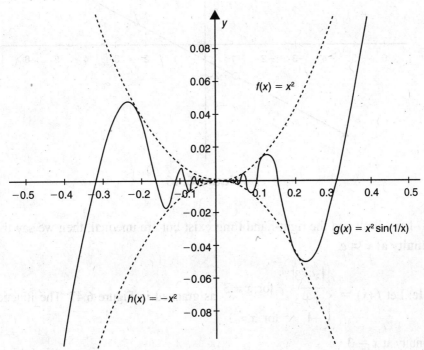

Figure 6.45

Continuity

A function f is said to be **continuous at $x = c$**, where $c \in \mathbf{R}$, provided all three of the following conditions are true:

1. $f(c)$ exists.

2. $\lim\limits_{x \to c} f(x)$, exists.

3. $\lim\limits_{x \to c} f(x) = f(c)$.

- If f is not continuous at $x = c$, then we say that f is **discontinuous at $x = c$** or that f has a **discontinuity** at $x = c$.

- If f is discontinuous at $x = c$ but $\lim\limits_{x \to c} f(x)$ exists, then we say that f has a **removable discontinuity** at $x = c$.

Example: Consider $f(x) = \dfrac{x^2 - 1}{x + 1}$ (Figure 6.46). The function f is not defined at $x = -1$, but $\lim\limits_{x \to -1} \dfrac{x^2 - 1}{x + 1} = \lim\limits_{x \to -1} (x - 1) = -2$. Thus, f has a removable discontinuity because we can *remove it* by defining f at the one point. Here, we would define $f(-) = -2$.

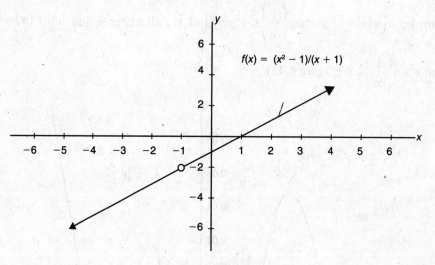

Figure 6.46

- If the left-hand limit and the right-hand limit exist but are unequal, then we say that f has a **jump discontinuity at $x = c$**.

Example: Let $f(x) = \begin{cases} \dfrac{|x+3|}{x+3} & \text{for } x \neq 3 \\ -1 & \text{for } x = 3 \end{cases}$ as graphed in Figure 6.47. The function f has a jump discontinuity at $x = 3$.

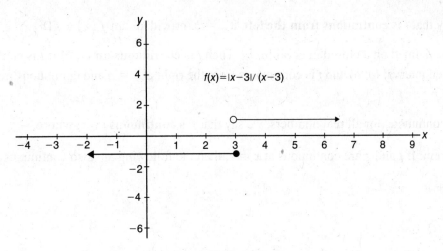

Figure 6.47

- If one (or both) of the one-sided limits approaches $-\infty$ or $+\infty$ (thus does not exist), then the line $x = c$ is a **vertical asymptote** and we say that there is an **infinite or asymptotic discontinuity** at $x = c$.

   Example: In Figure 6.48, the function f has asymptotic discontinuities at $x = 3$ and $x = -1$.

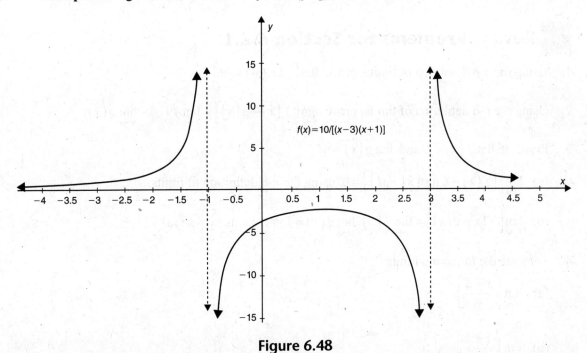

Figure 6.48

- If f is continuous at every real number c in an open interval (a, b), then we say that f is **continuous on (a, b)**.

- We say that f is **continuous from the right** at $x = a$, provided $\lim\limits_{x \to a^+} f(x) = f(a)$

- We say that f is **continuous from the left** at $x = b$, provided $\lim\limits_{x \to b^-} f(x) = f(b)$.

- Let f be defined on a closed interval $[a, b]$. Then f is **continuous on $[a, b]$** if f is continuous on the open interval (a, b) and f is continuous from the right at $x = a$ and continuous from the left at $x = b$.

- If f is continuous for all real numbers, we say that f is **continuous everywhere**.

   Theorem: If f and g are continuous at $x = c$, then the following are also continuous at $x = c$:

   1. $f + g$

   2. $f - g$

   3. fg

   4. $\dfrac{f}{g}$, provided $g(c) \neq 0$.

   Theorem: If $\lim\limits_{x \to c} g(x) = b$ and if f is continuous at b, then

   $$\lim_{x \to c}(f \circ g)(x) = \lim_{x \to c} f(g(x)) = f\left(\lim_{x \to c} g(x)\right) = f(b)$$

Review Problems for Section 6.2.1

1. Using the ε-δ definition of limits, prove $\lim\limits_{x \to 5}(-2x + 4) = -6$.

2. Using the ε-δ definition of limits, prove $\lim\limits_{x \to a}[f(x) - g(x)] = \lim\limits_{x \to a} f(x) - \lim\limits_{x \to a} g(x)$.

3. Prove: if $\lim\limits_{x \to a} f(x) = L$ and $\lim\limits_{x \to a} g(x) = M$,

   (a) $\lim\limits_{x \to a}\big[(f(x) - L)(g(x) - M)\big] = 0$, using the ε-δ definition of limits,

   (b) $\lim\limits_{x \to a}[f(x) \cdot g(x)] = \lim\limits_{x \to a} f(x) \cdot \lim\limits_{x \to a} g(x) = L \cdot M$ by using part (a).

4. Evaluate the following limits:

   (a) $\lim\limits_{x \to -1}\left(\dfrac{x+2}{x}\right)$

   (b) $\lim\limits_{x \to 0+}\left(\dfrac{x+2}{x}\right)$

   (c) $\lim\limits_{x \to -1}\left(\dfrac{x^2 + x - 2}{x^2 - x}\right)$

   (d) $\lim\limits_{x \to -\infty}\left(\dfrac{x^2 + x - 2}{3x^2 - x}\right)$

(e) $\lim\limits_{x\to\infty}\left(\dfrac{x^3+x-2}{x^2+5x}\right)$

(f) $\lim\limits_{x\to\infty}\left(\dfrac{3x-5}{x^3+5x}\right)$

5. (a) Using the definition of continuity, explain where the function in Figure 6.49 is discontinuous and why.

(b) For each of the discontinuities in Figure 6.49, classify the discontinuity as a removable, jump, or infinite discontinuity.

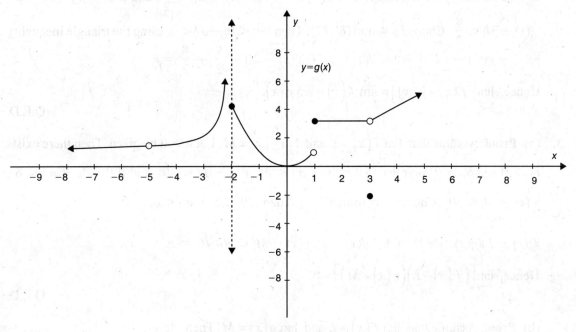

Figure 6.49

6. Practice the following proofs that are done in the section:

(a) $\lim\limits_{x\to a}\left[f(x)+g(x)\right]=\lim\limits_{x\to a}f(x)+\lim\limits_{x\to a}g(x)$

(b) $\lim\limits_{x\to a}\left[cf(x)\right]=c\lim\limits_{x\to a}f(x)$

(c) $\lim\limits_{x\to a}\left[\dfrac{f(x)}{g(x)}\right]=\dfrac{\lim\limits_{x\to a}f(x)}{\lim\limits_{x\to a}g(x)}$

Detailed Solutions

1. **Proof:** Let $\varepsilon > 0$ be given. Choose $\delta = \dfrac{\varepsilon}{2}$. Then when $0 < |x - 5| < \delta = \dfrac{\varepsilon}{2}$, it follows that

$$|(-2x+4) - (-6)| = |10 - 2x| = 2|x - 5| < 2\left(\frac{\varepsilon}{2}\right) = \varepsilon.$$

Therefore, $\lim\limits_{x \to 5}(-2x+4) = -6$.

Q.E.D

2. **Proof:** Assume that $\lim\limits_{x \to a} f(x) = L$ and $\lim\limits_{x \to a} g(x) = M$. Let $\varepsilon > 0$ be given. Then there exists $\delta' > 0$ and $\delta'' > 0$ such that if $0 < |x - a| < \delta'$, $|f(x) - L| < \dfrac{\varepsilon}{2}$, and if $0 < |x - a| < \delta''$, $|g(x) - M| < \dfrac{\varepsilon}{2}$. Choose $\delta = \min\{\delta', \delta''\}$. Then if $0 < |x - a| < \delta$, using the triangle inequality

$$|(f(x) - g(x)) - (L - M)| < |f(x) - L| + |g(x) - M| < \frac{\varepsilon}{2} + \frac{\varepsilon}{2} = \varepsilon.$$

Hence, $\lim\limits_{x \to a}\left[f(x) - g(x)\right] = \lim\limits_{x \to a} f(x) - \lim\limits_{x \to a} g(x)$.

Q.E.D.

3. (a) **Proof:** Assume that $\lim\limits_{x \to a} f(x) = L$ and $\lim\limits_{x \to a} g(x) = M$. Let $\varepsilon > 0$ be given. Then there exists $\delta' > 0$ and $\delta'' > 0$ such that if $0 < |x - a| < \delta'$, $|f(x) - L| < \sqrt{\varepsilon}$ and if $0 < |x - a| < \delta''$, $|g(x) - M| < \sqrt{\varepsilon}$. Choose $\delta = \min\{\delta', \delta''\}$. Then if $0 < |x - a| < \delta$,

$$|(f(x) - L)(g(x) - M) - 0| < |f(x) - L|\,|g(x) - M| < \sqrt{\varepsilon}\sqrt{\varepsilon} = \varepsilon.$$

Hence, $\lim\limits_{x \to a}\left[(f(x) - L)(g(x) - M)\right] = 0$.

Q.E.D.

(b) **Proof:** Assume that $\lim\limits_{x \to a} f(x) = L$ and $\lim\limits_{x \to a} g(x) = M$. Then

$$\lim_{x \to a} f(x)g(x) = \lim_{x \to a}\left\{\left[(f(x) - L)(g(x) - M)\right] + Mf(x) + Lg(x) - LM\right\}$$

$$= \lim_{x \to a}\left[(f(x) - L)(g(x) - M)\right] + \lim_{x \to a} Mf(x) + \lim_{x \to a} Lg(x) - \lim_{x \to a} LM$$

$$= 0 + M\lim_{x \to a} f(x) + L\lim_{x \to a} g(x) - LM$$

$$= ML + LM - LM = LM$$

Therefore, $\lim\limits_{x \to a}\left[f(x) \cdot g(x)\right] = \lim\limits_{x \to a} f(x) \cdot \lim\limits_{x \to a} g(x) = L \cdot M$.

Q.E.D

4. (a) $\lim\limits_{x \to -1}\left(\dfrac{x+2}{x}\right) = \dfrac{-1+2}{-1} = -1$

(b) $\lim\limits_{x\to 0+}\left(\dfrac{x+2}{x}\right)=+\infty,=\lim\limits_{x\to 0^+}\left(1+\dfrac{2}{x}\right)$ limit does not exist.

(c) $\lim\limits_{x\to -1}\left(\dfrac{x^2+x-2}{x^2-x}\right)=\lim\limits_{x\to -1}\left(\dfrac{(x-1)(x+2)}{x(x-1)}\right)=\lim\limits_{x\to -1}\left(\dfrac{x+2}{x}\right)=-1$

(d) $\lim\limits_{x\to -\infty}\left(\dfrac{x^2+x-2}{3x^2-x}\right)=\lim\limits_{x\to -\infty}\left(\dfrac{x^2+x-2}{3x^2-x}\right)\cdot\dfrac{\div x^2}{\div x^2}=\lim\limits_{x\to -\infty}\left(\dfrac{1+\dfrac{1}{x}-\dfrac{2}{x^2}}{3-\dfrac{1}{x}}\right)=\dfrac{1+0-0}{3-0}=\dfrac{1}{3}$

(e) $\lim\limits_{x\to \infty}\left(\dfrac{x^3+x-2}{x^2+5x}\right)=\lim\limits_{x\to \infty}\left(\dfrac{x^3+x-2}{x^2+5x}\right)\cdot\dfrac{\div x^2}{\div x^2}=\lim\limits_{x\to \infty}\left(\dfrac{x+\dfrac{1}{x}-\dfrac{2}{x^2}}{1+\dfrac{5}{x}}\right)=\dfrac{\infty+0+0}{1}=\infty$, the limit

does not exist.

(f) $\lim\limits_{x\to \infty}\left(\dfrac{3x-5}{x^3+5x}\right)=\lim\limits_{x\to \infty}\left(\dfrac{3x-5}{x^3+5x}\right)\cdot\dfrac{\div x^3}{\div x^3}=\lim\limits_{x\to \infty}\left(\dfrac{\dfrac{3}{x^2}-\dfrac{5}{x^3}}{1+\dfrac{5}{x^2}}\right)=\dfrac{0-0}{1+0}=0$

5. (a) g is discontinuous at $x=-5$ because $g(-5)$ does not exist.

   g is discontinuous at $x=-2$ because $\lim\limits_{x\to -2}g(x)$ does not exist.

   g is discontinuous at $x=1$ because $\lim\limits_{x\to 1}g(x)$ does not exist.

   g is discontinuous at $x=3$ because $\lim\limits_{x\to 3}g(x)=3\neq g(3)=-2$.

   (b) g has removable discontinuities at $x=-5$ and 3, an infinite discontinuity at $x=-2$, and a jump discontinuity at $x=1$.

6. Practice!

6.2.2 The California *Mathematics Subject Matter Requirements* stipulate that candidates for any credential program for teaching secondary mathematics must be able to *show that a polynomial function is continuous at a point.*

Continuity of a Polynomial

Theorem: Every polynomial is continuous everywhere.

Proof: Every polynomial can be written in the form $p(x) = c_n x^n + c_{n-1} x^{n-1} + \cdots + c_1 x + c_0$, where n is the degree of the polynomial and $c_n, c_{n-1}, \ldots, c_1, c_0$ are constants with $c_n \neq 0$. Then for any real number a,

$$\lim_{x \to a} p(x) = \lim_{x \to a} \left(c_n x^n + c_{n-1} x^{n-1} + \cdots + c_1 x + c_0 \right)$$

$$= \lim_{x \to a} \left(c_n x^n \right) + \lim_{x \to a} \left(c_{n-1} x^{n-1} \right) + \cdots + \lim_{x \to a} \left(c_1 x \right) + \lim_{x \to a} \left(c_0 \right) \qquad \text{the limit of a sum}$$

$$= c_n \lim_{x \to a} \left(x^n \right) + c_{n-1} \lim_{x \to a} \left(x^{n-1} \right) + \cdots + c_1 \lim_{x \to a} \left(x \right) + \lim_{x \to a} \left(c_0 \right) \qquad \text{the limit of a constant times a function}$$

$$= c_n \lim_{x \to a} \left(x^n \right) + c_{n-1} \lim_{x \to a} \left(x^{n-1} \right) + \cdots + c_1 \lim_{x \to a} \left(x \right) + \left(c_0 \right) \qquad \text{the limit of a constant}$$

$$= c_n \left(\lim_{x \to a} x \right)^n + c_{n-1} \left(\lim_{x \to a} x \right)^{n-1} + \cdots + c_1 \lim_{x \to a} \left(x \right) + \left(c_0 \right) \qquad \text{the limit of a power}$$

$$= c_n a^n + c_{n-1} a^{n-1} + \cdots + c_1 a + c_0 \qquad \text{the limit of } x$$

$$= p(a).$$

Therefore, p is continuous at each $a \in \mathbf{R}$.

Q.E.D.

Theorem: All rational functions $f(x) = \dfrac{g(x)}{h(x)}$ are continuous for all values $a \in \mathbf{R}$ such that $h(a) \neq 0$.

Proof: Let $f(x) = \dfrac{g(x)}{h(x)}$, where g and h are polynomials and hence continuous eveywhere.

Let $a \in \mathbf{R}$ such that $h(a) \neq 0$. Then $\lim\limits_{x \to a} f(x) = \lim\limits_{x \to a} \dfrac{g(x)}{h(x)} = \dfrac{\lim\limits_{x \to a} g(x)}{\lim\limits_{x \to a} h(x)}$, since the limit of a quotient is the quotient of the limits. Since we know that polynomial functions are continuous everywhere, we have $\dfrac{\lim\limits_{x \to a} g(x)}{\lim\limits_{x \to a} h(x)} = \dfrac{g(a)}{h(a)} = f(a)$. Thus f is continuous at a.

Q.E.D.

Review Problems for Section 6.2.2

1. Prove that all polynomials are continuous everywhere.

2. Prove that rational functions are continuous on their domain.

Detailed Solutions

These are shown in the section. Practice!

6.2.3 The California *Mathematics Subject Matter Requirements* stipulate that candidates for any credential program for teaching secondary mathematics must be able to *know and apply the Intermediate Value Theorem, using the geometric implications of continuity.*

The Intermediate Value Theorem

The *Intermediate Value Theorem* (IVT) If f is continuous on a closed interval $[a, b]$ and w is any number between $f(a)$ and $f(b)$, then there is at least one number $c \in (a, b)$ such that $f(c) = w$ (Figure 6.50).

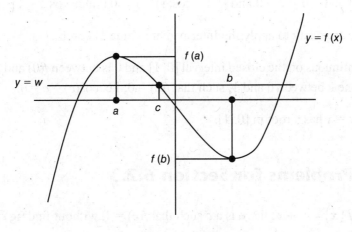

Figure 6.50

Geometrically, this says that if a function f is continuous on an interval $[a, b]$ the graph of f must intersect every horizontal line $y = w$ somewhere on the interval (a, b), where w is between $f(a)$ and $f(b)$.

Examples:

(a) Use the Intermediate Value Theorem (IVT) to show that there is a positive number c such that $c^2 = 2$.

Let $f(x) = x^2$. Then f is continuous since it is a polynomial, and $f(0) = 0 < 2 < 4 = f(2)$. By the IVT, there is a number $c \in (0, 2)$ such that $c^2 = f(c) = 2$.

(b) If $g(x) = x^5 - 2x^3 + x^2 + 2$, show that there is a $c \in \mathbf{R}$ such that $g(c) = -1$.

First, g is continuous everywhere, because it is a polynomial, and $g(0) = 2$ and $g(-2) = -10$. Therefore, $g(-2) < -1 < g(0)$. By the IVT, there is a $c \in (-2, 0)$ such that $g(c) = -1$.

(c) Show that $\cos x = x$ has a root between 0 and 1.

We can use the Intermediate Value Theorem to show that the equation $\cos x = x$ has a root between 0 and 1.

Step 1. Create a new function by subtracting the right-hand side of the equation from the left-hand side, i.e. $f(x) = \cos x - x$. By doing this, we come up with a new problem, which is equivalent to the original one: is there a value c for x between 0 and 1 such that $f(c) = 0$?

In order to apply the IVT, we need to verify that the two conditions in the theorem are satisfied; i.e., the function f is continuous in [0, 1], and the value 0 is between $f(0)$ and $f(1)$.

Step 2. The cosine function and the power functions are both continuous everywhere, so f, as the difference of two continuous functions, is also continuous everywhere. In particular, f is continuous on the interval [0, 1].

Step 3. Calculate the values $f(0)$ and $f(1)$, and compare them with 0.

$f(0) = \cos(0) - 0 = 1 - 0 = 1 > 0$ and $f(1) = \cos(1) - 1 < 0$ (since $\cos x \leq 1$).

Step 4. Now we are ready to apply the Intermediate Value Theorem.

Since $f(x)$ is continuous on the closed interval [0, 1] and 0 is between $f(0)$ and $f(1)$, by IVT, there exists at least one c between 0 and 1, such that $f(c) = 0$; i.e. $\cos(c) - c = 0$.

Therefore $\cos x = x$ has a root in [0, 1].

Review Problems for Section 6.2.3

1. Show that if $f\left(x\right) = x^4 + x$, there is a c such that $f(c) = 4$, without finding c.

2. Show that $\ln(x) = e - x$ has a root between 1 and 3.

Detailed Solutions

1. $f(1) = 2$ and $f(2) = 18$. Since f is a polynomial, it is continuous everywhere so f is certainly continuous on [0, 2]. By the Intermediate Value Theorem, there is a $c \in (1, 2)$ such that $f(c) = 4$, since $f(1) < 4 < f(2)$.

2. Let $f(x) = \ln(x) + x - e$ (Figure 6.51). Then f is continuous on the interval [1, 3] since it is the sum of functions that are continuous on [1, 3], $f(1) = 1 - e < 0$ and $f(3) = \ln(3) + 3 - e > 0$. Hence, since $f(0) < 0 < f(3)$, there is a value $c \in (1, 3)$ such that $f(c) = 0$, which implies that $\ln(c) = e - c$.

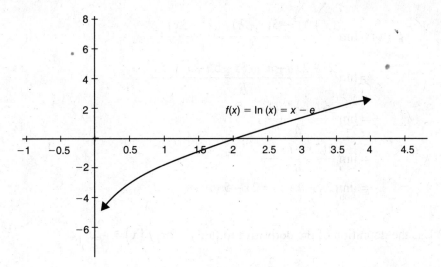

Figure 6.51

6.3 Derivatives and Applications

> **6.3.1** The California *Mathematics Subject Matter Requirements* stipulate that candidates for any credential program for teaching secondary mathematics must be able *derive the rules of differentiation for polynomial, trigonometric, and logarithmic functions using the formal definition of derivative.*

Derivatives

Let f be a function. The **derivative of f at x** is the function denoted by $f9(x)$, which is defined by $f'(x) = \lim\limits_{h \to 0} \dfrac{f(x+h) - f(x)}{h}$ provided the limit exists.

- The function expression $\dfrac{f(x+h) - f(x)}{h}$ is called the **difference quotient** for f.
- Other notations for the derivative include: $y' = f'(x) = \dfrac{dy}{dx} = D_x f$

Examples:
  (a) Use the definition of the derivative to find f' for $f(x) = x^2 - 5x$.

$$f'(x) = \lim_{h \to 0} \frac{(x+h)^2 - 5(x+h) - (x^2 - 5x)}{h}$$

$$= \lim_{h \to 0} \frac{x^2 + 2xh + h^2 - 5x - 5h - x^2 + 5x}{h}$$

$$= \lim_{h \to 0} \frac{2xh + h^2 - 5h}{h}$$

$$= \lim_{h \to 0} \frac{h(2x + h - 5)}{h}$$

$$= \lim_{h \to 0} (2x + h - 5) = 2x - 5$$

(b) Use the definition of the derivative to find f' for $f(x) = \dfrac{2}{\sqrt{x}}$.

$$f'(x) = \lim_{h \to 0} \frac{\dfrac{2}{\sqrt{x+h}} - \dfrac{2}{\sqrt{x}}}{h}$$

$$= \lim_{h \to 0} \left(\frac{\dfrac{2}{\sqrt{x+h}} - \dfrac{2}{\sqrt{x}}}{h} \right) \cdot \frac{\sqrt{x}\sqrt{x+h}}{\sqrt{x}\sqrt{x+h}}$$

$$= \lim_{h \to 0} \frac{2\sqrt{x} - 2\sqrt{x+h}}{h\sqrt{x}\sqrt{x+h}}$$

$$= \lim_{h \to 0} 2\left(\frac{\sqrt{x} - \sqrt{x+h}}{h\sqrt{x}\sqrt{x+h}} \right)\left(\frac{\sqrt{x} + \sqrt{x+h}}{\sqrt{x} + \sqrt{x+h}} \right)$$

$$= \lim_{h \to 0} 2\left(\frac{x - (x+h)}{h\sqrt{x}\sqrt{x+h}\left(\sqrt{x} + \sqrt{x+h}\right)} \right)$$

$$= \lim_{h \to 0} 2\left(\frac{-h}{h\sqrt{x}\sqrt{x+h}\left(\sqrt{x} + \sqrt{x+h}\right)} \right)$$

$$= \lim_{h \to 0} 2\left(\frac{-1}{\sqrt{x}\sqrt{x+h}\left(\sqrt{x} + \sqrt{x+h}\right)} \right)$$

$$= \frac{-2}{x\left(\sqrt{x} + \sqrt{x}\right)} = \frac{-1}{x\sqrt{x}}$$

Rules of Differentiation

Derivative of a Constant

For any real number c, $\dfrac{d}{dx}(c) = 0$.

Proof: Let $f(x) = c$ for all x. Then

$$f'(x) = \lim_{h \to 0} \frac{f(x+h) - f(x)}{h} = \lim_{h \to 0} \frac{c-c}{h} = \lim_{h \to 0} \frac{0}{h} = \lim_{h \to 0} 0 = 0.$$

Q.E.D.

Derivative of x

$$\boxed{\frac{d}{dx}(x) = 1.}$$

Proof: Let $f(x) = x$ for all x. Then

$$f'(x) = \lim_{h \to 0} \frac{f(x+h) - f(x)}{h} = \lim_{h \to 0} \frac{(x+h) - x}{h} = \lim_{h \to 0} \frac{h}{h} = \lim_{h \to 0} 1 = 1.$$

Q.E.D.

Derivative of a Sum

If f and g are differentiable functions, then $(f + g)'(x) = f'(x) + g'(x)$.

Proof: Assume f and g are differentiable. Then

$$(f + g)'(x) = \lim_{h \to 0} \frac{(f+g)(x+h) - (f+g)(x)}{h}$$

$$= \lim_{h \to 0} \frac{f(x+h) + g(x+h) - f(x) - g(x)}{h}$$

$$= \lim_{h \to 0} \left[\frac{f(x+h) - f(x)}{h} + \frac{g(x+h) - g(x)}{h} \right]$$

$$= \lim_{h \to 0} \left[\frac{f(x+h) - f(x)}{h} \right] + \lim_{h \to 0} \left[\frac{g(x+h) - g(x)}{h} \right]$$

$$= f'(x) + g'(x)$$

Q.E.D.

Derivative of a Difference

If f and g are differentiable functions, then $(f - g)'(x) = f'(x) - g'(x)$.

Proof: Similar to the last proof. Exercise.

Derivative of a Product

If f and g are differentiable functions, then $(f \cdot g)'(x) = f(x)\, g'(x) + g(x)\, f'(x)$.

Proof: Assume f and g are differentiable. Then

$$(f \cdot g)'(x) = \lim_{h \to 0} \frac{(f \cdot g)(x+h) - (f \cdot g)(x)}{h}$$

$$= \lim_{h \to 0} \frac{f(x+h)g(x+h) - f(x)g(x)}{h}$$

$$= \lim_{h \to 0} \frac{f(x+h)g(x+h) - f(x+h)g(x) + f(x+h)g(x) - f(x)g(x)}{h}$$

$$= \lim_{h \to 0} \frac{f(x+h)\left[g(x+h) - g(x)\right] + g(x)\left[f(x+h) - f(x)\right]}{h}$$

$$= \lim_{h \to 0} \frac{f(x+h)\left[g(x+h) - g(x)\right]}{h} + \lim_{h \to 0} \frac{g(x)\left[f(x+h) - f(x)\right]}{h}$$

$$= \lim_{h \to 0} f(x+h) \lim_{h \to 0} \frac{\left[g(x+h) - g(x)\right]}{h} + \lim_{h \to 0} g(x) \lim_{h \to 0} \frac{\left[f(x+h) - f(x)\right]}{h}$$

$$= f(x)g'(x) + g(x)f'(x)$$

Q.E.D.

Derivative of a Quotient

If f and g are differentiable functions, then $\left(\dfrac{f}{g}\right)'(x) = \dfrac{g(x)f'(x) - f(x)g'(x)}{[g(x)]^2}$

Proof: Assume f and g are differentiable functions. First, we find prove $\left(\dfrac{1}{g}\right)'(x) = \dfrac{-g'(x)}{[g(x)]^2}$

$$\left(\frac{1}{g}\right)'(x) = \lim_{h \to 0} \frac{\left(\frac{1}{g}\right)(x+h) - \left(\frac{1}{g}\right)(x)}{h} = \lim_{h \to 0} \frac{\left(\frac{1}{g(x+h)}\right) - \left(\frac{1}{g(x)}\right)}{h}$$

$$= \lim_{h \to 0} \frac{\frac{g(x) - g(x+h)}{g(x+h)g(x)}}{h}$$

$$= \lim_{h \to 0} \left[\frac{1}{g(x+h)g(x)} \frac{g(x) - g(x+h)}{h}\right]$$

$$= \lim_{h \to 0} \left[\frac{1}{g(x+h)g(x)}\right] \lim_{h \to 0} \left[\frac{g(x) - g(x+h)}{h}\right]$$

$$= \frac{1}{[g(x)]^2} \cdot (-g'(x))$$

$$= \frac{-g'(x)}{[g(x)]^2}$$

Now, using the rule for the derivative of a product,

$$\left(\frac{f}{g}\right)'(x) = \left(f \cdot \frac{1}{g}\right)'(x)$$

$$= f(x)\left(\frac{1}{g}\right)'(x) + \left(\frac{1}{g}\right)(x)f'(x)$$

$$= f(x) \cdot \frac{-g'(x)}{\left[g(x)\right]^2} + \frac{f'(x)}{g(x)}$$

$$= \frac{g(x)f'(x) - f(x)g'(x)}{\left[g(x)\right]^2}$$

Q.E.D.

The Power Rule

$$\frac{d}{dx}\left(x^n\right) = nx^{n-1} \text{ for all positive integers } n.$$

Proof: Let S be the statement that $\frac{d}{dx}\left(x^n\right) = nx^{n-1}$, where n is a positive integer.

Since $\frac{d}{dx}\left(x\right) = 1 = x^0$, S is true for $n = 1$.

Now assume that S is true for some $n > 1$, where n is a fixed but arbitrary integer. This means $\frac{d}{dx}\left(x^n\right) = nx^{n-1}$. Then, by the product rule for derivatives, $\frac{d}{dx}\left(x^{n+1}\right) = \frac{d}{dx}\left(x \cdot x^n\right) = x\frac{d}{dx}\left(x^n\right) + x^n\frac{d}{dx}\left(x\right)$.

So $\frac{d}{dx}\left(x^{n+1}\right) = x\left(nx^{n-1}\right) + x^n\left(1\right)$ by the assumption that S is true for n. This simplifies to $\frac{d}{dx}\left(x^{n+1}\right) = nx^n + x^n = \left(n+1\right)x^n$. Hence, S is true for $n + 1$ whenever the statement S is true for n.

Therefore, S is true for all positive integers n by the Principle of Mathematical Induction.

Q.E.D.

- This result can be shown to be generalized so that $\frac{d}{dx}\left(x^n\right) = nx^{n-1}$ for all non-zero numbers n.

Implicit Differentiation

There are two ways to define functions, *implicitly* and *explicitly*. Most equations we use are explicit equations, such as $y = \frac{1}{x}$, which we can denote by $y = f(x) = \frac{1}{x}$. But the equation $xy = 1$ describes the same function as an implicit definition of y as a function of x.

We can take the derivative of an implicit function just as we take the derivative of an explicit function. In the case of an implicit equation, we take the derivative of each side of the equation, remembering to treat the independent variable as a function of the dependent variable, apply the rules of differentiation, and solve for the derivative.

Example: $xy = 1 \Rightarrow \frac{d}{dx}(xy) = \frac{d}{dx}(1)$. When differentiating the left side, we must remember that $y = y(x)$:

$$x \cdot \frac{dy}{dx} + y \cdot 1 = 0 \quad \Rightarrow \quad \frac{dy}{dx} = \frac{-y}{x}.$$

Since we can rewrite $xy = 1$ as $y = \frac{1}{x}$, we can substitute this into the derivative to obtain

$$\frac{dy}{dx} = \frac{-y}{x} = \frac{-\frac{1}{x}}{x} = \frac{-1}{x^2}.$$

We could have obtained the same result using an explicit equation:

$$y = x^{-1} \text{ so using the power } y' = -1 \cdot x^{-2} = \frac{-1}{x^2}.$$

But we cannot always solve an equation explicitly, so the method of implicit differentiation is useful.

Example: Find $\frac{dy}{dx}$ for $x^2 y + xy^2 = 6 - y^3$

$$\frac{d}{dx}(x^2 y + xy^2) = \frac{d}{dx}(6 - y^3)$$

$$x^2 \frac{dy}{dx} + 2xy + x\left(2y\frac{dy}{dx}\right) + y^2 = 0 - 3y^2 \frac{dy}{dx}$$

$$\left(x^2 + 2xy + 3y^2\right)\frac{dy}{dx} = -2xy - y^2$$

$$\frac{dy}{dx} = \frac{-2xy - y^2}{x^2 + 2xy + 3y^2}$$

Derivatives of Special Functions

Derivatives of Exponentials

Let $f(x) = a^x$. Then $f'(x) = \lim_{h \to 0} \frac{a^{x+h} - a^x}{h} = \lim_{h \to 0} \frac{a^x(a^h - 1)}{h} = a^x \lim_{h \to 0} \frac{a(a^h - 1)}{h}$.

Let's look at this last limit graphically for $a = 2$ and $a = 3$ (Figures 6.52 and 6.53). In each, we see that as x gets very close to 0 the value of $\frac{a^h - 1}{h}$ gets extremely close to $\ln(a)$.

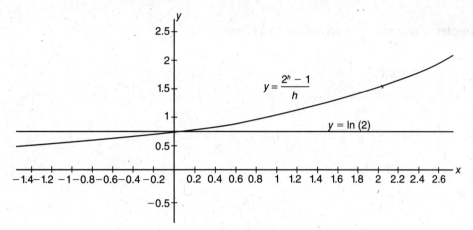

Figure 6.52

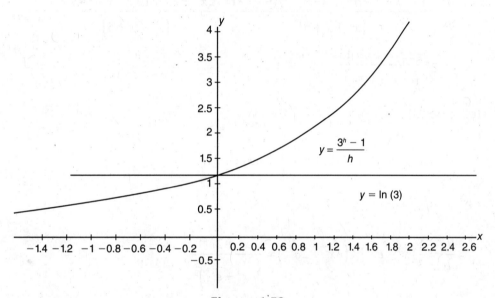

Figure 6.53

We will accept that $\lim\limits_{h\to 0}\dfrac{\left(a^h-1\right)}{h}=\ln a$; hence, $\dfrac{d}{dx}\left(a^x\right)=a^x\ln a$ for all $a>0$.

Theorem:

Chain Rule (Differentiation of Composite Functions): If f and g are differentiable functions, then

$$\frac{d}{dx}\big(f(g(x))\big)=f'(g(x))\cdot g'(x).$$

Examples: Compute $\dfrac{dy}{dx}$ each of the following:

(a) $y = x^3 - 5\sqrt{x} - \dfrac{1}{x^2} + \pi^4$

$$\frac{dy}{dx} = 3x^2 - 5\left(x^{\frac{1}{2}}\right)' - \left(x^{-2}\right)' + 0 = 3x^2 - \frac{5}{2}x^{\frac{-1}{2}} + 2x^{-3} = 3x^2 - \frac{5}{2\sqrt{x}} + \frac{2}{x^3}$$

(b) $y = \dfrac{2x-3}{x^2+x+5}$

$$\frac{dy}{dx} = \frac{\left(x^2+x+5\right)(2) - (2x-3)(2x+1)}{\left(x^2+x+5\right)^2} = \frac{2x^2+2x+10-4x^2+4x+3}{\left(x^2+x+5\right)^2}$$

$$= \frac{-2x^2+6x+13}{\left(x^2+x+5\right)^2}$$

(c) $y = x^2 3^x$

$$\frac{dy}{dx} = x^2\left(3^x \ln 3\right) + 3^x(2x) = x3^x\left((\ln 3)x + 2\right)$$

(d) $y = \sqrt[3]{x^3 + e^{2x}}$

$$\frac{dy}{dx} = \frac{1}{3}\left(x^3 + e^{2x}\right)^{\frac{-2}{3}}\left(3x^2 + 2e^{2x}\right) = \frac{3x^2 + 2e^{2x}}{3\left(x^3 + e^{2x}\right)^{\frac{2}{3}}}$$

Derivatives of Logarithms

We now can use the method of implicit differentiation to derive the derivative of the logarithm:

$$y = \log_b x \iff x = b^y$$

$$\frac{d}{dx}(x) = \frac{d}{dx}(b^y) \iff 1 = b^y \ln b \frac{dy}{dx} \iff \frac{dy}{dx} = \frac{1}{\ln b}\frac{1}{b^y} = \frac{1}{\ln b}\frac{1}{x}$$

$$\boxed{\frac{d}{dx}(\log_b x) = \frac{1}{\ln b}\frac{1}{x}}$$

Examples: Calculate $\dfrac{dy}{dx}$:

(a) $\dfrac{d}{dx}\left(\log_5 x\right)$

$$\dfrac{d}{dx}\left(\log_5 x\right) = \dfrac{1}{\ln}$$

(b) $\ln\left(xy\right) = x^2 - y^2$

$$\dfrac{1}{xy}\left(x\dfrac{dy}{dx} + y\right) = 2x - 2y$$

$$\left(\dfrac{1}{y} + 2y\right)\dfrac{dy}{dx} = 2x - \dfrac{1}{x}$$

$$\left(\dfrac{\left(1 + 2y^2\right)}{y}\right)\dfrac{dy}{dx} = \dfrac{\left(2x^2 -\right.}{x}$$

$$\dfrac{dy}{dx} = \dfrac{y\left(2x^2 - 1\right)}{x\left(1 + 2y^2\right)}$$

Derivatives of the Trigonometric Functions

There are several important limits that we need in deriving the derivatives of the trigonometric functions. These are:

Theorem: (a) $\displaystyle\lim_{\theta \to 0}\dfrac{\sin\theta}{\theta} = 1$

(b) $\displaystyle\lim_{\theta \to 0}\dfrac{\cos\theta - 1}{\theta} = 0$

Proof: (a) Assume $0 < \theta < \dfrac{\pi}{2}$ since we look at small values of θ when we take the limit. So at first we are only looking at the right-hand limit. Consider Figure 6.54 with the unit circle and point $P = (x, y)$ on the circle. We can see that the area of $\Delta OAP <$ area of sector OBP $<$ area of ΔOBQ. These areas are demonstrated in Figure 6.55.

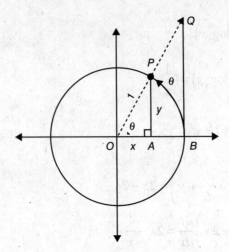

Figure 6.54

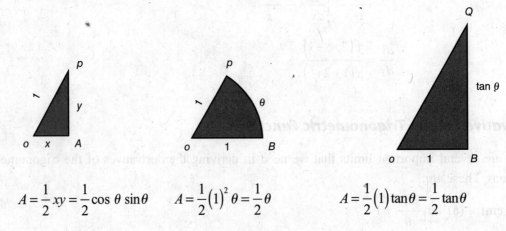

$$A = \frac{1}{2}xy = \frac{1}{2}\cos\theta\sin\theta \qquad A = \frac{1}{2}(1)^2\theta = \frac{1}{2}\theta \qquad A = \frac{1}{2}(1)\tan\theta = \frac{1}{2}\tan\theta.$$

Figure 6.55

So, $\dfrac{1}{2}\cos\theta\sin\theta < \dfrac{1}{2}\theta < \dfrac{1}{2}\tan\theta \iff \cos\theta\sin\theta < \theta < \tan\theta \iff \cos\theta < \dfrac{\theta}{\sin\theta} < \dfrac{1}{\cos\theta}$

$\iff \dfrac{1}{\cos\theta} > \dfrac{\sin\theta}{\theta} > \cos\theta.$

Thus $\displaystyle\lim_{\theta\to0+}\dfrac{1}{\cos\theta} > \lim_{\theta\to0+}\dfrac{\sin\theta}{\theta} > \lim_{\theta\to0+}\cos\theta$ and since $\displaystyle\lim_{\theta\to0+}\dfrac{1}{\cos\theta} = 1$ and $\displaystyle\lim_{\theta\to0+}\cos\theta = 1$, by the Squeeze

Theorem $\displaystyle\lim_{\theta\to0+}\dfrac{\sin\theta}{\theta} = 1.$

For negative values of θ, the proof is similar.

Q.E.D.

(b)

$$\lim_{\theta \to 0} \frac{\cos\theta - 1}{\theta} = \lim_{\theta \to 0} \frac{\cos\theta - 1}{\theta} \cdot \frac{\cos\theta + 1}{\cos\theta + 1} = \lim_{\theta \to 0} \frac{\cos^2\theta - 1}{\theta(\cos\theta + 1)} = \lim_{\theta \to 0} \frac{-\sin^2\theta}{\theta(\cos\theta + 1)}$$

$$= \lim_{\theta \to 0} \frac{\sin\theta}{\theta} \cdot \lim_{\theta \to 0} \frac{-\sin\theta}{(\cos\theta + 1)} = 1 \cdot \lim_{\theta \to 0} \frac{-\sin\theta}{(\cos\theta + 1)} = 1 \cdot \frac{0}{1+1} = 1 \cdot 0 = 1$$

Q.E.D.

Theorem: $\dfrac{d}{dx}\left(\sin x\right) = \cos x.$

Proof: $\dfrac{d}{dx}(\sin x) = \lim_{h \to 0} \dfrac{\sin(x+h) - \sin x}{h}$

$$= \lim_{h \to 0} \frac{\sin x \cos h + \cos x \sin h - \sin x}{h}$$

$$= \lim_{h \to 0} \sin x \lim_{h \to 0} \frac{\cos h - 1}{h} + \lim_{h \to 0} \cos x \lim_{h \to 0} \frac{\sin h}{h}$$

$$= \sin x \cdot 0 + \cos x \cdot 1$$

$$= \cos x$$

Q.E.D.

Theorem: $\dfrac{d}{dx}\left(\cos x\right) = -\sin x.$

Proof: $\dfrac{d}{dx}(\cos x) = \dfrac{d}{dx}\left(\sin\left(\dfrac{\pi}{2} - x\right)\right) = \cos\left(\dfrac{\pi}{2} - x\right)\dfrac{d}{dx}\left(\dfrac{\pi}{2} - x\right) = -\cos\left(\dfrac{\pi}{2} - x\right) = -\sin x$

Q.E.D.

Theorem: $\dfrac{d}{dx}\left(\tan x\right) = \sec^2 x$

Proof:

$$\frac{d}{dx}(\tan x) = \frac{d}{dx}\left(\frac{\sin x}{\cos x}\right) = \frac{\cos x \dfrac{d}{dx}(\sin x) - \sin x \dfrac{d}{dx}(\cos x)}{\cos^2 x}$$

$$= \frac{\cos x (\cos x) - \sin x (-\sin x)}{\cos^2 x}$$

$$= \frac{\cos^2 x + \sin^2 x}{\cos^2 x}$$

$$= \frac{1}{\cos^2 x} = \sec^2 x$$

Q.E.D.

Theorem: $\dfrac{d}{dx}\left(\cot x\right) = -\csc^2 x.$

Proof: Similar to that for $\dfrac{d}{dx}\left(\tan x\right) = \sec^2 x.$

Theorem: $\dfrac{d}{dx}\left(\sec x\right) = \sec x \tan x.$

Proof: $\dfrac{d}{dx}(\sec x) = \dfrac{d}{dx}\left(\dfrac{1}{\cos x}\right) = \dfrac{-(\cos x)'}{\cos^2 x} = \dfrac{\sin x}{\cos^2 x} = \sec x \tan x$

Theorem: $\dfrac{d}{dx}(\csc x) = -\csc x \cot x.$

Proof: Similar to the one for secant.

Examples: Find $\dfrac{dy}{dx}$ for each of the following:

(a) $y = x\tan\left(x^3\right)$

$$\frac{dy}{dx} = x\left(\sec^2\left(x^3\right)\cdot 3x^2\right) + \tan\left(x^3\right)\cdot 1 = 3x^3\sec^2\left(x^3\right) + \tan\left(x^3\right)$$

(b) $y = 2^{\csc(3x)}$

$$\frac{dy}{dx} = 2^{\csc(3x)}\ln 2 \cdot \frac{d}{dx}\left(\csc(3x)\right) = 2^{\csc(3x)}\ln 2 \cdot \left(-\csc(3x)\cot(3x)3\right)$$

$$= -3\ln 2 \cdot 2^{\csc(3x)}\left(\csc(3x)\cot(3x)\right)$$

(c) $x^2\cos y + \sin(2y) = xy$

$$x^2\left(-\sin y\frac{dy}{dx}\right) + \cos y(2x) + \cos(2y)\left(2\frac{dy}{dx}\right) = x\frac{dy}{dx} + y\cdot 1$$

$$\left(2\cos(2y) - x^2\sin y - x\right)\frac{dy}{dx} = y - 2x\cos y$$

$$\frac{dy}{dx} = \frac{y - 2x\cos y}{2\cos(2y) - x^2\sin y - x}$$

Review Problems for Section 6.3.1

1. Derive the following rules of differentiation using the formal definition of derivative:

(a) For any real number, $\dfrac{d}{dx}(c) = 0.$

(b) $\dfrac{d}{dx}(x) = 1.$

(c) If f and g are differentiable functions $(f + g)'(x) = f'(x) + g'(x).$

(d) If f and g are differentiable functions $(f - g)'(x) = f'(x) - g'(x).$

(e) If f and g are differentiable functions $(f\cdot g)'(x) = f(x)g'(x) + g(x)f'(x).$

(f) If f and g are differentiable functions $\left(\dfrac{f}{g}\right)'(x) = \dfrac{g(x)f'(x) - f(x)g'(x)}{[g(x)]^2}$.

(g) $\dfrac{d}{dx}(x^n) = nx^{n-1}$ for all positive integers

(h) $\dfrac{d}{dx}(\log_b x) = \dfrac{1}{\ln b}\dfrac{1}{x}$ for any $b > 0$ and $x > 0$

(i) $\dfrac{d}{dx}(\sin x) = \cos x$

2. Derive the formula for the derivatives of the other five trigonometric functions using $\dfrac{d}{dx}(\sin x) = \cos x$.

3. Find $\dfrac{dy}{dx}$ each of the following:

    (a) $y = e^2 + \dfrac{1}{x} - \cot\left(x^3 - 5\sqrt{2x}\right)$

    (b) $y = \dfrac{\sin x + 1}{\cos x - 1}$

    (c) $\log_6\left(y + 2^{xy}\right) = y^2 - 5x^e$

Detailed Solutions

1. All of these derivations are shown in the section. Practice!

2. The only ones that are not shown in the section are the cotangent and the cosecant, which are shown here:

$$\dfrac{d}{dx}(\cot x) = \dfrac{d}{dx}\left(\dfrac{\cos x}{\sin x}\right) = \dfrac{\sin x(-\sin x) - \cos x(\cos x)}{(\sin x)^2} = \dfrac{-\sin^2 x - \cos^2 x}{(\sin x)^2}$$

$$= \dfrac{-(\sin^2 x + \cos^2 x)}{(\sin x)^2} = \dfrac{-1}{(\sin x)^2} = -\csc^2 x$$

$$\dfrac{d}{dx}(\csc x) = \dfrac{d}{dx}\left(\dfrac{1}{\sin x}\right) = \dfrac{-\cos x}{(\sin x)^2} = -\cot x \csc x$$

3. (a) $y = e^2 + \dfrac{1}{x} - \cot\left(x^3 - 5\sqrt{2x}\right)$

$$\frac{dy}{dx} = 0 + \left(x^{-1}\right)' - \left(-\csc^2\left(x^3 - 5\sqrt{2x}\right) \cdot \left(x^3 - 5\sqrt{2x}\right)'\right)$$

$$= -1x^{-2} + \csc^2\left(x^3 - 5\sqrt{2x}\right) \cdot \left(3x^2 - 5\left(\sqrt{2}\right)\left(\sqrt{x}\right)'\right)$$

$$= \frac{-1}{x^2} + \csc^2\left(x^3 - 5\sqrt{2x}\right) \cdot \left(3x^2 - 5\left(\sqrt{2}\right)\left(\frac{1}{2}x^{\frac{-1}{2}}\right)\right)$$

$$= \frac{-1}{x^2} + \left(3x^2 - \frac{5\sqrt{2}}{2\sqrt{x}}\right)\csc^2\left(x^3 - 5\sqrt{2x}\right)$$

(b) $y = \dfrac{\sin x + 1}{\cos x - 1}$

$$\frac{dy}{dx} = \frac{(\cos x - 1)(\cos x) - (\sin x + 1)(-\sin x)}{(\cos x - 1)^2} = \frac{\cos^2 x - \cos x + \sin^2 x + \sin x}{(\cos x - 1)^2} = \frac{1 - \cos x + \sin x}{(\cos x - 1)^2}$$

(c) $\log_6\left(y + 2^{xy}\right) = y^2 - 5x^e$

$$\left(\frac{1}{\ln 6}\frac{1}{y + 2^{xy}}\left(y + 2^{xy}\right)'\right) = 2y\frac{dy}{dx} - 5ex^{e-1}$$

$$\left(\frac{1}{\ln 6}\frac{1}{y + 2^{xy}}\left(\frac{dy}{dx} + 2^{xy}\ln 2\,(xy)'\right)\right) = 2y\frac{dy}{dx} - 5ex^{e-1}$$

$$\left(\frac{1}{\ln 6}\frac{1}{y + 2^{xy}}\left(\frac{dy}{dx} + 2^{xy}\ln 2\left(x\frac{dy}{dx} + y \cdot 1\right)\right)\right) = 2y\frac{dy}{dx} - 5ex^{e-1}$$

$$\left(\frac{1}{\ln 6}\frac{1}{y + 2^{xy}}\frac{dy}{dx} + \frac{1}{\ln 6}\frac{1}{y + 2^{xy}}2^{xy}\ln 2x\frac{dy}{dx} + \frac{1}{\ln 6}\frac{1}{y + 2^{xy}}2^{xy}\ln 2y\right) = 2y\frac{dy}{dx} - 5ex^{e-1}$$

$$\left(\frac{1}{\ln 6}\frac{1}{y + 2^{xy}} + \frac{\ln 2}{\ln 6}\frac{x^2 2^{xy}}{y + 2^{xy}} - 2y\right)\frac{dy}{dx} = -5ex^{e-1} - \frac{\ln 2}{\ln 6}\frac{2^{xy}xy}{y + 2^{xy}}$$

$$\frac{dy}{dx} = \left(-5ex^{e-1} - \frac{\ln 2}{\ln 6}\frac{2^{y}xy}{y + 2^{xy}}\right) \div \left(\frac{1}{\ln 6}\frac{1}{y + 2^{xy}} + \frac{\ln 2}{\ln 6}\frac{x\,2^{xy}}{y + 2^{xy}} - 2y\right)$$

$$= \left(\frac{-\left(5e\ln 6x^{e-1}\left(y + 2^{xy}\right) + \ln 2 \cdot 2^{xy}xy\right)}{\ln 6\left(y + 2^{xy}\right)}\right) \div \left(\frac{1 + \ln 2\left(x\,2^{xy}\right) - 2y\left(\ln 6\left(y + 2^{xy}\right)\right)}{\ln 6\left(y + 2^{xy}\right)}\right)$$

$$= \frac{-\left(5e\ln 6x^{e-1}\left(y + 2^{xy}\right) + \ln 2 \cdot 2^{xy}xy\right)}{1 + \ln 2\left(x\,2^{xy}\right) - 2y\left(\ln 6\left(y + 2^{xy}\right)\right)}$$

> **6.3.2** The California *Mathematics Subject Matter Requirements* stipulate that candidates for any credential program for teaching secondary mathematics must be able to *interpret the concept of derivative geometrically, numerically, and analytically (i.e., slope of the tangent, limit of difference quotients, extrema, Newton's method, and instantaneous rate of change).*

Interpreting the Derivative

The previous section introduced the concept of derivative algebraically as the limit of a difference quotient:

> Let f be a function. The **derivative of f at x** is the function denoted by $f'(x)$, which is defined by
> $$f'(x) = \lim_{h \to 0} \frac{f(x+h) - f(x)}{h}$$
> provided the limit exists.

And defined the derivative for a value a as follows:

> Let f be a function. The derivative of f at $x = a$ is the number denoted by $f'(a)$, which is defined by
> $$f'(a) = \lim_{h \to 0} \frac{f(a+h) - f(a)}{h}$$
> provided the limit exists.

A **secant line** of a graph of a function is a line that passes through two specified points on the graph. In Figure 6.56, secant line l_1 passes through the points $(0, 2)$ and $(1, 1)$ on the graph of $y = f(x)$ is shown. The slope of this secant line is $m = \dfrac{\Delta y}{\Delta x} = \dfrac{y_2 - y_1}{x_2 - x_1} = \dfrac{2-1}{0-1} = -1.$

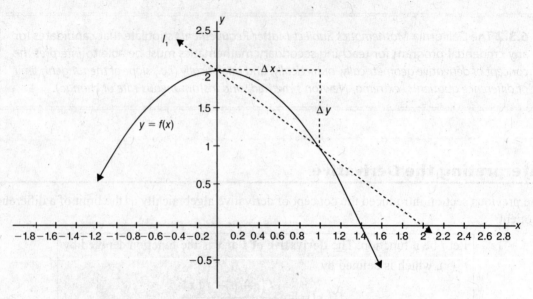

Figure 6.56

Now consider the graph of the same function (on Figure 6.57) with other secant lines, l_2 and l_3, along with another line t. All lines pass through the point (1, 1) but l_2 passes through (0.6, 1.64) and l_3, passes through (0.8, 1.36). The slope of line l_2 is –1.6, the slope of line l_3 is – 1.8, and the slope of t is – 2. Note that as the x value of the points (0, 2), (0.6, 1.64), and (0.8, 1.36) approaches 1, the slope of the secant line gets closer to the slope of the line t. Line t is called the **tangent line** of f at $x = 1$. The tangent line is the limiting line of the secant lines through points P(a fixed point) and Q as point Q is moved closer to P (i.e., $Q_i \rightarrow P$); as this happens $-x \rightarrow 0$, and we have

$$\lim_{\Delta x \to 0} m_{\text{secant}} = m_{\text{tangent}} \quad \lim_{\Delta x \to 0} \frac{\Delta y}{\Delta x} = m_{\text{tangent}}$$

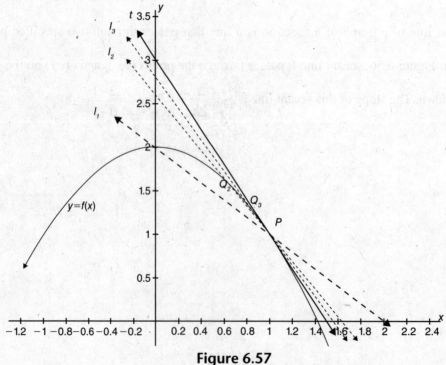

Figure 6.57

Now, to clarify this idea and connect it to the derivative, let us use the same notation that we did when defining the derivative at $x = a$. Let $(a, f(a))$ be a point on the graph of f and choose a value $b = a + h$, where h is not zero but is close to zero (Figure 6.58). Then the slope of the secant line through $(a, a + h)$ and $(b, f(b)) = (a + h, f(a + h))$ is $\dfrac{f(a+h) - f(a)}{(a+h) - a} = \dfrac{f(a+h) - f(a)}{h}$, which you might recognize as the difference quotient.

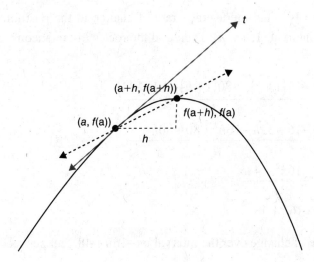

Figure 6.58

> The **slope of the tangent line at $x = a$** is given by
> $$f'(a) = \lim_{h \to 0} \frac{f(a+h) - f(a)}{h}$$

Example: Find the equation of the tangent to the graph of $f(x) = x2^x$ at $x = 1$.

$f'(x) = x2^x \ln 2 + 2^x$ using the product rule. So, $m_{\tan} = f'(1) = 2(\ln 2 + 1)$. The point of tangency $(1, f(1)) = (1, 2)$. Thus: $y = 2(\ln 2 + 1)(x - 1) + 2$ or $y = 2(\ln 2 + 1)x - 2\ln 2$ is the equation of the tangent line.

We can also look at the difference quotient as the **average rate of change of a function f over an interval**:

> The **average rate of change of a function f over the interval $[a, a + h]$ or $[a - h, a]$** is given by
> $$\frac{f(a+h) - f(a)}{h}$$

Then, by taking the limit, we are shortening the interval $[a, a + h]$ or $[a + h, h]$ until the interval represents the value a, and we obtain:

The **instantaneous rate of change** in f at $x = a$ is given by

$$f'(a) = \lim_{h \to 0} \frac{f(a+h) - f(a)}{h}$$

Example: A rock has been thrown, and its position in feet at time t is given by $s(t) = -16t^2 + 80t + 10$. Find the average rate of change in the position of the rock (average velocity) over the interval $[1, 1 + h]$. Then find the rock's instantaneous rate of change in position (velocity) at $t = 1$.

$$\frac{f(1+h) - f(1)}{h} = \frac{-16(1+h)^2 + 80(1+h) + 10 - (74)}{h}$$

$$= \frac{-16 - 32h - 16h^2 + 80 + 80h - 64}{h}$$

$$= \frac{-16h^2 + 48h}{h}$$

$$= -16h + 48$$

So the average rate of change over the interval is $-16h + 48$ feet per second.

The instantaneous velocity or rate of change at $t = 1$ is $s'(1) = \lim_{h \to 0}(-16h + 48) = 48$ feet per second.

A Note on Notation: There are various notations for all of these notions. All of the following are the same:

$$f'(a) = \lim_{h \to 0} \frac{f(a+h) - f(a)}{h} \Leftrightarrow f'(a) = \lim_{\Delta x \to 0} \frac{f(a + \Delta x) - f(a)}{\Delta x} \Leftrightarrow f'(a) = \lim_{b \to a} \frac{f(b) - f(a)}{b - a}$$

Extrema

- Let f be a function with domain D. Then $f(c)$ is the:

  (a) **absolute (or global) maximum value** on D if and only if $f(c) \geq f(x)$ for all $x \in$ D.

  (b) **absolute (or global) minimum value** on D if and only if $f(c) \leq f(x)$ for all $x \in$ D.

- Absolute (or global) maximum and minimum values are also called **absolute extrema** (plural of extremum). Sometimes we just omit the term absolute or global and just say maximum or minimum.

Extreme Value Theorem: Let f be continuous on a closed interval $I = [a, b]$. Then f has both absolute maximum and minimum value's on the interval i.e., there exists $c, d \in [a, b]$ such that $f(c)$ is the maximum value of f on $[a, b]$ and $f(d)$ is the minimum value of f on $[a, b]$.

- This important theorem guarantees that a continuous function on a closed and bounded interval has a maximum and minimum point. It does not say where it occurs or whether it occurs when the derivative is a certain value.

- Let c be an interior point of the domain of the function f. Then $f(c)$ is a

  (a) **local maximum value** at $x = c$ if and only if $f(c) \geq f(x)$ for all values of x in some open interval containing c.

  (b) **local minimum value** at $x = c$ if and only if $f(c) \leq f(x)$ for all values of x in some open interval containing c.

- Local extrema are also called **relative extrema**.

- A function f has a local maximum or minimum **at an endpoint** c if the appropriate inequality holds for all x in some half-open interval with c as the included endpoint.

- These extrema are illustrated in the example graph in Figure 6.59.

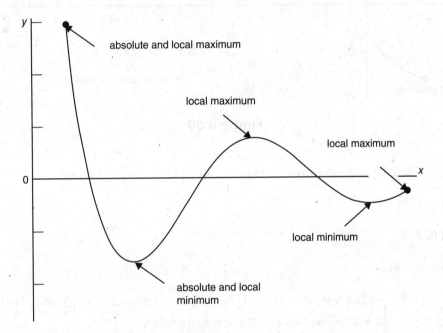

Figure 6.59

Theorem: If f has a local maximum or minimum at an interior point c of its domain and if $f(c)$ exists, then $f'(c) = 0$.

- What this theorem does not say is that if $f'(c) = 0$, then there is a local maximum or minimum at c, but what is true is that the candidates for where local extrema occur are points in the domain of f where $f'(x) = 0$, $f'(x)$ does not exist, or an endpoint of an interval (Figure 6.60).

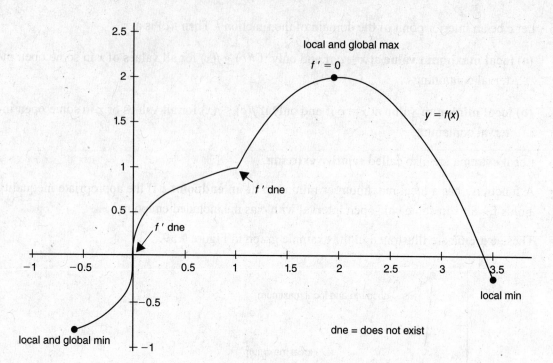

Figure 6.60

Example: Find the local and absolute extrema of $f(x) = x^3 - 6x^2 + 9x$ on

(a) $[-1, 5]$

(b) $[0.5, 5)$

(c) $(-\infty, +\infty)$

$f'(x) = 3x^2 - 12x + 9 = 3(x-3)(x-1)$. So $f'(x) = 0$ when $x = 1$ or 3, and f' exists everywhere. Test the sign of the first derivative (Figure 6.61).

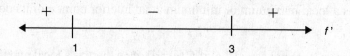

Figure 6.61

This indicates that f is increasing on $(-\infty, 1) \cup (3, +\infty)$ and decreasing on $(1, 3)$

(a) So, on $[-1, 5]$, by the Extreme Value Theorem, there must be an absolute max and min. The local maximums and minimums occur at $x = -1, 1, 3$, and 5: $f(-1) = -16, f(1) = 4, f(3) = 0$, and $f(5) = 20$. So f has an absolute maximum of 20 at $x = 5$ and an absolute minimum of -16 at $x = -1$. f has local maxima at $x = 1$ and 5 and local minima at $x = -1$ and 3.

(b) On [0.5, 5), there is no guarantee of global extrema since the interval is not closed. The function f, starting at $x = 0.5$, $f(0.5) = 3.125$, and then increases to $4a+x = 1$. Then the function decreases to 0 at $x = 3$, then increases, getting close to 20 near $x = 5$. So f on [0.5, 5) has a global minimum of 0 but no global maximum. The local extrema are: local maximum of 3.125 at $x = 0.5$ and local minimum of 0 at $x = 3$.

(c) On $(-\infty, +\infty)$, f has no global extrema since $\lim_{x \to +\infty} \left(x^3 - 6x^2 + 9x \right) = \lim_{x \to +\infty} x^3 = +\infty$ and $\lim_{x \to -\infty} \left(x^3 - 6x^2 + 9x \right) = \lim_{x \to -\infty} x^3 = -\infty$. But f has a local maximum of 4 at $x = 1$ and a local minimum of 0 at $x = 3$.

Theorem (The Second Derivative Test): Suppose f'' is continuous near c.

(a) If $f'(c) = 0$ and $f''(c) > 0$ for all x in an interval I, then f has a local minimum at c.

(b) If $f'(c) = 0$ and $f''(c) < 0$ for all x in an interval I, then f has a local maximum at c.

Newton's Method

Newton's method is a technique for finding zeroes of differentiable functions:

1. Find $a, b \in \mathbf{R}$ such that $f(a) > 0$ and $f(b) < 0$ or vice versa. Then, by the Intermediate Value Theorem, there is a zero of f in (a, b).

2. Choose $x_1 \in (a, b)$ such that $f'(x_1) \neq 0$; x_1 is our first guess for the zero (maybe choose the midpoint of the interval).

Look at the tangent to $y = f(x)$ at $x = x_1$. Its equation is

$$y = f'(x_1)(x - x_1) + f(x_1)$$

3. Find the x-intercept of the tangent at x_1, this is its zero. Call it x_2. So the point $(x_2, 0)$ is on the tangent (Figure 6.62). Substitute this into the equation of the tangent at x_1 and solve for x_2:

$$0 = f'(x_1)(x_2 - x_1) + f(x_1) \iff x_2 = x_1 - \frac{f(x_1)}{f'(x_1)}$$

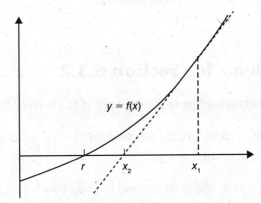

Figure 6.62

4. Repeat this process until the degree of accuracy needed is achieved.

Theorem (Newton's Method): Let f be a differentiable function and suppose r is a real zero of f. If x_n is an approximation to r, then the next approximation is:

$$x_{n+1} = x_n - \frac{f(x_n)}{f'(x_n)}$$

provided $f'(x_n)$ exists.

- Convention: If an approximation to k decimal places is desired, we shall approximate each of the $x_1, x_2, x_3, \ldots$ to $k+1$ decimal places, continuing until two consecutive approximations are the same to the kth decimal place.

Example: Estimate the fifth root of 23 by using Newton's Method with five-decimal place accuracy.

Let $x = \sqrt[5]{23} \Leftrightarrow x^5 - 23 = 0$. Set $f(x) = x^5 - 23$ and note that $f(1) = -22 < 0$, whereas $f(2) = 9 > 0$. $f'(x) = 5x^4$, so our formula is $x_{n+1} = x_n - \frac{x_n^5 - 23}{5x_n^4} = x_n - 0.2x_n - 4.6x_n^{-4}$. We compute using six decimal places to the right of the decimal point. We used Excel. to get Figure 6.63. Thus, we have $\sqrt[5]{23} \approx 1.87217$.

n	x_n
1	1.5
2	2.108642
3	1.919587
4	1.874457
5	1.872177
6	1.872171

Figure 6.63

Review Problems for Section 6.3.2

1. Find the equation of the tangent line to the curve of $f(x) = x\cos(2x) - 3$ at $x = 0$.

2. What is the average rate of change in the function $g(x) = \frac{2}{3x+4}$ over the interval [1, 3]? What is the instantaneous rate of change at $x = 1$?

3. The height of a rocket, in feet, above the ground is given by $s(t) = -16t^2 + 160t + 16$, where t is in seconds. What is the velocity of the rocket after 2 seconds? When does the rocket reach its maximum height?

4. Find the local and global extrema of $h(x) = x^4 - 5x^2$.

5. Use Newton's method to find a root of the equation $\cos x = x$ with accuracy to six decimal places.

6. State and explain the Extreme Value Theorem.

Detailed Solutions

1. $f(x) = x\cos(2x) - 3$, so the derivative $f'(x) = x(-2\sin(2x)) + \cos(2x)$. Then $f'(0) = -2$ and $f(0) = -3$, so the equation of the tangent line is $y = -2x - 3$.

2. The average rate of change in $g(x) = \dfrac{2}{3x+4}$ over $[1, 3]$ is $\dfrac{g(3) - g(1)}{3-1} = \dfrac{\frac{2}{13} - \frac{2}{7}}{2} = -\dfrac{6}{91}$, whereas the instantaneous rate of change at $x = 1$ is $g'(1)$. $g'(x) = -2(3x+4)^{-2}(3x+4)' = \dfrac{-6}{(3x+4)^2}$, so $g'(1) = \dfrac{-6}{49}$.

3. $s(t) = -16t^2 + 160t + 16$, so the velocity is $v(t) = s'(t) = -32t + 160$, and $v(2) = -32(2) + 160 = 96$ ft/sec. The rocket reaches its maximum height when $v(t) = 0$, which is at $t = 5$ seconds.

4. $h(x) = x^4 - 5x^2$, so $h'(x) = 4x^3 - 10x = 2x(2x^2 - 5)$. Extrema occur at $h'(x) = 0$, or when $x = 0$ or $\pm\sqrt{2.5}$. Using the First Derivative Test (Figure 6.64), we see that h has a local minimum of $h(\sqrt{2.5}) = -6.25$ and a local maximum $h(0) = 0$.

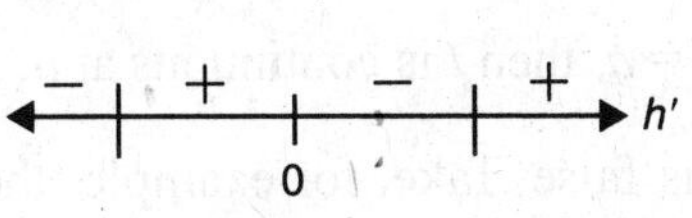

Figure 6.64

Since the function's end behavior is the same as its leading term x^4, its ends go up, so there is no absolute maximum but the global minimum is -6.25, and it occurs at $x = \pm\sqrt{2.5}$.

5. $\cos x = x \iff x - \cos x = 0$, so let $f(x) = x - \cos x$. Note that $f(0) = -1 < 0$ and $f\left(\dfrac{\pi}{2}\right) = \dfrac{\pi}{2} > 0$, so we choose a number x_1 between 0 and $\dfrac{\pi}{2}$, say, $x_1 = 1$. $f'(x) = 1 + \sin x$, So our iteration formula will be $x_{n+1} = x_n - \dfrac{x_n - \cos x_n}{1 + \sin x_n}$. Using Excel to compute we obtain Figure 6.65. Thus, $\cos x = x$ at about $x = 0.739085$

n	x_n
1	1.0000000
2	0.7503639
3	0.7391129
4	0.7390851
5	0.7390851

Figure 6.65

6. This is shown in the section. Practice!

6.3.3 The California *Mathematics Subject Matter Requirements* stipulate that candidates for any credential program for teaching secondary mathematics must be able to *interpret both continuous and differentiable functions geometrically and analytically and apply Rolle's Theorem, the Mean Value Theorem, and L'Hôpital's rule.*

Continuous and Differentiable Functions

Why Continuity and Differentiability Matter!

Theorem: If f is continuous at $x = a$, then $\lim_{x \to a} f(x) = f(a)$.

*   Without this theorem, we are limited in our calculations of limits.

Theorem: If f is differentiable at $x = a$, then f is continuous at a.

*   The converse of this theorem is false. Take, for example, the function $f(x) = |x|$. The graph is shown in Figure 6.66. The derivative does not exist at $x = 0$, but f is clearly continuous at 0.

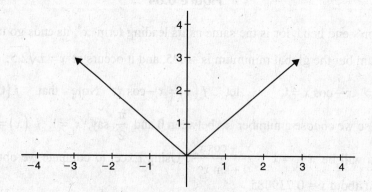

Figure 6.66

The right-hand derivative at $x = 0$ is $\displaystyle\lim_{h\to0^+}\frac{f(0+h)-f(0)}{h}=\lim_{h\to0^+}\frac{f(h)}{h}=\lim_{h\to0^+}\frac{h}{h}=\lim_{h\to0^+}1=1$, and the

left-hand derivative at $x = 0$ is $\displaystyle\lim_{h\to0^-}\frac{f(0+h)-f(0)}{h}=\lim_{h\to0^-}\frac{f(h)}{h}=\lim_{h\to0^-}\frac{-h}{h}=\lim_{h\to0^-}(-1)=-1.$ Since
the right- and left-handed derivatives are unequal, the derivative at $x = 0$ does not exist.

Rolle's Theorem: Let f be continuous on a closed interval $[a, b]$ and differentiable on the open interval (a, b). If $f(a) = f(b)$, then there is at least one point c in (a, b) where $f'(c) = 0$.

- Rolle's Theorem indicates that if f is continuous on a closed and bounded interval $[a, b]$ where the function values are equal at the endpoints, and differentiable on (a, b) then somewhere in the interval (a, b) there is a tangent to the graph of f that is horizontal (Figure 6.67).

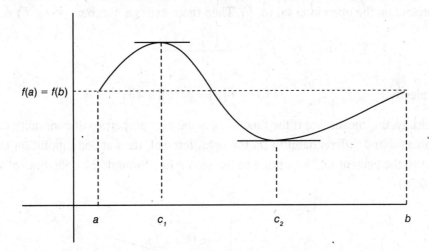

Figure 6.67

- Note that both continuity and differentiability are necessary for the conclusion of Rolle's Theorem. In Figure 6.68, there is a function that is continuous but not differentiable at $x = 0$ and there is no value for x where $f'(x) = 0$. In Figure 6.69, we see an example of a function that is not continuous at $x = 0$ and also has no value for where $f'(x) = 0$.

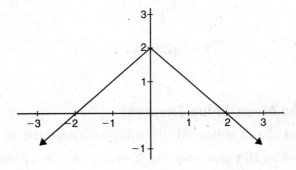

Figure 6.68

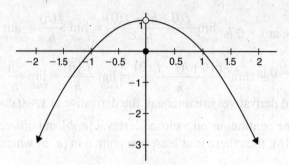

Figure 6.69

The Mean Value Theorem (for Derivatives): Let f be continuous on a closed interval $[a, b]$ and differentiable on the open interval (a, b). Then there exists a number $c \in (a, b)$ such that

$$f'(c) = \frac{f(b) - f(a)}{b - a}$$

or equivalently,

$$f(b) - f(a) = f'(c)(b - a).$$

- Geometrically, this means that if the function has the nice properties of continuity on the entire closed interval and differentiability on the open interval, then at some point on the graph in the interval, the tangent line is parallel to the secant line through the endpoints of the interval (Figure 6.70).

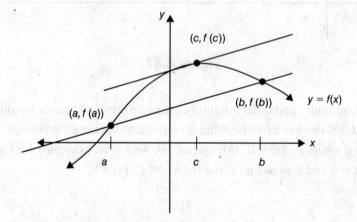

Figure 6.70

Consequences of the Mean Value Theorem

Theorem: If $f'(x) = 0$ for all x in an interval I, then $f(x) = c$, a constant, for all x in I.

Theorem: If $f'(x) = g'(x)$ for all x in an interval I, then $f(x) - g(x) = c$, a constant, for all x in I.

L'Hôpital's Rule

Theorem (L'Hôpital): Suppose f and g are differentiable functions and that $g'(x) \neq 0$ near a, except possibly at a, and suppose that $\lim\limits_{x \to a} f(x) = 0 = \lim\limits_{x \to a} g(x)$ or $\lim\limits_{x \to a} f'(x) = \pm\infty = \lim\limits_{x \to a} g'(x)$, then

$$\lim_{x \to a} \frac{f(x)}{g(x)} = \lim_{x \to a} \frac{f'(x)}{g'(x)},$$

provided the limit on the right exists.

When $\lim\limits_{x \to a} f(x) = 0 = \lim\limits_{x \to a} g(x)$, we say that $\lim\limits_{x \to a} \dfrac{f(x)}{g(x)}$ is in the **indeterminate form** $\dfrac{0}{0}$, and when

$\lim\limits_{x \to a} f(x) = \pm\infty = \lim\limits_{x \to a} g(x)$, we say that $\lim\limits_{x \to a} \dfrac{f(x)}{g(x)}$ is in the **indeterminate form** $\dfrac{\infty}{\infty}$.

- L'Hôpital's Rule is also valid for one-sided limits and limits at either of the infinities.

  Examples:

  (a) $\lim\limits_{x \to 1} \dfrac{\ln x}{x - 1}$ has the indeterminate $\dfrac{0}{0}$ form since $\lim\limits_{x \to 1} \ln x = 0 = \lim\limits_{x \to 1}(x - 1)$. So, using

  L'Hôpital's rule: $\lim\limits_{x \to 1} \dfrac{\ln x}{x - 1} = \lim\limits_{x \to 1} \dfrac{\frac{1}{x}}{1} = 1$

  (b) $\lim\limits_{x \to \infty} \dfrac{5x + e^{-x}}{6x^2}$ has the indeterminate form $\dfrac{\infty}{\infty}$ since $\lim\limits_{x \to \infty}(5x + e^{-x}) = \infty = \lim\limits_{x \to \infty} 6x^2$. Thus,

  $\lim\limits_{x \to \infty} \dfrac{5x + e^{-x}}{6x^2} = \lim\limits_{x \to \infty} \dfrac{5 - e^{-x}}{12x} = \dfrac{5}{\infty} = 0$

  (c) $\lim\limits_{x \to 1} \dfrac{\sin 2x}{x}$. L'Hôpital's Rule cannot be used for this limit since it is not indeterminate, but

  often people will try to use it. In fact, $\lim\limits_{x \to 1} \dfrac{\sin 2x}{x} = \sin 2$, but if someone erroneously used

  L'Hôpital their "result" would be $\lim\limits_{x \to 1} \dfrac{\sin 2x}{x} = \lim\limits_{x \to 1} \dfrac{2\cos 2x}{1} = 2\cos 2$.

Other Indeterminate Forms

- A limit of a product $f(x)g(x)$ is called an **indeterminate form of type $0 \cdot \infty$** if $\lim\limits_{x \to a} f(x) = 0$ and

  $\lim\limits_{x \to a} g(x) = \pm\infty$. To evaluate a limit of this form, convert the problem to indeterminate form $\dfrac{0}{0}$ or $\dfrac{\infty}{\infty}$.

  Example: $\lim\limits_{x \to -\infty} xe^x = \lim\limits_{x \to -\infty} \dfrac{x}{e^{-x}} = \lim\limits_{x \to -\infty} \dfrac{1}{-e^{-x}} = \lim\limits_{x \to -\infty}(-e^x) = 0$

- **Indeterminate forms** $0^0, \infty^0,$ or 1^∞: To evaluate a limit of any of these forms:

  1. Let $y = f(x)^{g(x)}$.

  2. Take the natural logarithm: $\ln y = \ln f(x)^{g(x)} = g(x) \cdot \ln f(x)$.

  3. Evaluate $\lim (\ln y) = \lim[g(x) \cdot \ln f(x)]$.

  4. If $\lim \ln y = L$, then $\lim y = e^L$.
     If $\lim \ln y = +\infty$, then $\lim y = \infty$.
     If $\lim \ln y = -\infty$, then $\lim y = 0$.

Example: $\lim\limits_{x \to \infty} \left(1 + \dfrac{2}{x}\right)^x$. This is an indeterminate form 1^∞.

Let $y = \left(1 + \dfrac{2}{x}\right)^x$; then $\ln y = \ln \left(1 + \dfrac{2}{x}\right)^x = x \ln \left(1 + \dfrac{2}{x}\right)$.

Next, taking the limit, we obtain a $0 \cdot \infty$ indeterminate form: $\lim\limits_{x \to \infty} \ln y = \lim\limits_{x \to \infty} x \ln \left(1 + \dfrac{2}{x}\right)$.

Rewriting this and using L'Hôpital's Rule: $\lim\limits_{x \to \infty} x \ln \left(1 + \dfrac{2}{x}\right) = \lim\limits_{x \to \infty} \dfrac{\ln \left(\dfrac{x+2}{x}\right)}{\dfrac{1}{x}} = \lim\limits_{x \to \infty} \dfrac{\left(\dfrac{x}{x+2}\right)\left(-2x^{-2}\right)}{-x^{-2}}$.

Then, simplifying, we obtain:

$$\lim_{x \to \infty} \ln y = \lim_{x \to \infty} \dfrac{\left(\dfrac{x}{x+2}\right)\left(-2x^{-2}\right)}{-x^{-2}} = \lim_{x \to \infty} \left(\dfrac{2x}{x+2}\right) = \lim_{x \to \infty} \dfrac{2}{1} = 2.$$

Hence, $\lim\limits_{x \to \infty} \left(1 + \dfrac{2}{x}\right)^x = e^2$.

- **Indeterminate form** $\infty - \infty$: To evaluate this form, change it into a quotient or product to get a familiar indeterminate form.

Example: Evaluate $\lim\limits_{x \to \left(\frac{\pi}{2}\right)^-} (\tan x - \sec x)$

$$\lim_{x \to \left(\frac{\pi}{2}\right)^-} (\tan x - \sec x) = \lim_{x \to \left(\frac{\pi}{2}\right)^-} \left(\dfrac{\sin x}{\cos x} - \dfrac{1}{\cos x}\right) = \lim_{x \to \left(\frac{\pi}{2}\right)^-} \left(\dfrac{\sin x - 1}{\cos x}\right) \text{ is a } \dfrac{0}{0} \text{ indeterminate}$$

form. $\lim\limits_{x \to \left(\frac{\pi}{2}\right)^-} \left(\dfrac{\sin x - 1}{\cos x}\right) = \lim\limits_{x \to \left(\frac{\pi}{2}\right)^-} \left(\dfrac{\cos x}{-\sin x}\right) = 0$

Review Problems for Section 6.3.3

1. Show that $f(x)=\begin{cases} 3|x| & \text{if } x>0 \\ x^3+3x & \text{if } x\le 0 \end{cases}$ is differentiable at $x=0$. What does this tell us about the continuity of f?

2. Consider $f(x)=\dfrac{1}{x^2}$. $f(1)=f(-1)$ yet there is no value c in $(-1,1)$ where there is a horizontal tangent. Does this contradict Rolle's Theorem? Why?

3. Suzie Swift runs a 100 yard dash in 10 seconds. Assume that the function $s(t)$ that describes her position relative to the starting line is continuous and differentiable. Use the Mean Value Theorem to explain how Suzie must have been running at a speed of 10 yards per second at some point during her run.

4. Give a geometrical interpretation (use words and a drawing) of

    (a) Rolle's Theorem

    (b) the Mean Value Theorem

5. Explain how the following theorem is a consequence of the Mean Value Theorem.
   Theorem: If $f'(x)=0$ for all x in an interval I, then $f(x)=c$, a constant, for all x in I.

6. Use L'Hôpital's Rule to evaluate the following limits:

    (a) $\displaystyle\lim_{x\to 0}\frac{x+\sin x}{x}$

    (b) $\displaystyle\lim_{x\to\infty}\left(\ln x\right)^{\frac{1}{x}}$

    (c) $\displaystyle\lim_{x\to\infty}\left(\sqrt{4x^2+x}-2x\right)$

Detailed Solutions

1. $f(x)=\begin{cases} 3|x| & \text{if } x>0 \\ x^3+3x & \text{if } x\le 0 \end{cases}$. Compute the left and right-hand derivatives:

$$f'_+(0)=\lim_{h\to 0^+}\frac{f(0+h)-f(0)}{h}=\lim_{h\to 0^+}\frac{3|h|-0}{h}=\lim_{h\to 0^+}\frac{3h}{h}=\lim_{h\to 0^+}3=3$$

$$f'_-(0)=\lim_{h\to 0^-}\frac{f(0+h)-f(0)}{h}=\lim_{h\to 0^-}\frac{h^3+3h-0}{h}=\lim_{h\to 0^+}\frac{h(h^2+3)}{h}=\lim_{h\to 0^+}(h^2+3)=3$$

So $f'(0)=3$. Hence, f is continuous at 0 because differentiability implies continuity.

2. This does not contradict Rolle's Theorem because f is not differentiable (nor continuous) at $x=0$.

3. Suzie's position at $t = 0$ is 0 and at $t = 10$ is 100; i.e., $s(0) = 0$, $s(10) = 100$. By the Mean

    Value Theorem, there is at least one c in $(0, 10)$ where $s'(c) = v(c) = \dfrac{s(10) - s(0)}{10 - 0} = \dfrac{100}{10} = 10$. This

    means that at some time c in the run, Suzie's speed was exactly 10 yards/sec.

4. Both of these are given in the section. Practice!

5. If $f'(x) = 0$ for all x in an interval I, then for all $a, b \in I$, f is continuous and differentiable on

    $[a, b]$, so by the Mean Value Theorem, there is a value z in (a, b) such $f'(z) = \dfrac{f(b) - f(a)}{b - a}$. But

    we assume. $f'(z) = 0$. Thus, for all $a, b \in I$, $f(b) - f(a) = 0$. So, f is a constant function on the entire
    interval I.

6. (a) $\lim\limits_{x \to 0} \dfrac{x + \sin x}{x} = \lim\limits_{x \to 0} \dfrac{1 + \cos x}{1} = 2$. (This is an indeterminate form $\dfrac{0}{0}$ problem.)

    (b) Let $y = (\ln x)^{\frac{1}{x}}$ $\ln y = \ln(\ln x)^{\frac{1}{x}} = \dfrac{1}{x}\ln(\ln x)$. Hence, $\lim\limits_{x \to \infty} \ln y = \lim\limits_{x \to \infty} \dfrac{1}{x}\ln(\ln x) = \lim\limits_{x \to \infty} \dfrac{\frac{1}{\ln x} \cdot \frac{1}{x}}{1}$

     $= \lim\limits_{x \to \infty} \dfrac{1}{\ln x} \cdot \dfrac{1}{x} = 0$. So $\lim\limits_{x \to \infty} \ln y = 0$ $\lim\limits_{x \to \infty} (\ln x)^{\frac{1}{x}} = e^0 = 1$. (This is an ∞^0 indeterminate

    form problem.)

    (c) This problem begins as an $\infty - \infty$ indeterminate form and then, by rationalizing the numerator,

    we have an $\dfrac{\infty}{\infty}$ indeterminate form:

$$\lim_{x \to \infty}\left(\sqrt{4x^2 + x} - 2x\right) = \lim_{x \to \infty}\left(\sqrt{4x^2 + x} - 2x\right) \cdot \dfrac{\left(\sqrt{4x^2 + x} + 2x\right)}{\left(\sqrt{4x^2 + x} + 2x\right)} = \lim_{x \to \infty} \dfrac{\left(4x^2 + x\right) - 4x^2}{\sqrt{4x^2 + x} + 2x} = \lim_{x \to \infty} \dfrac{x}{\sqrt{4x^2 + x} + 2x}$$

Now use L'Hôpital's rule for $\dfrac{\infty}{\infty}$:

$$\lim_{x \to \infty}\left(\sqrt{4x^2 + x} - 2x\right) = \lim_{x \to \infty}\dfrac{x}{\sqrt{4x^2 + x} + 2x} = \lim_{x \to \infty}\dfrac{1}{\frac{1}{2}\left(4x^2 + x\right)^{-\frac{1}{2}}(8x + 1) + 2} = \lim_{x \to \infty}\dfrac{1}{\frac{8x + 1}{2\sqrt{4x^2 + x}} + 2}$$

Compute

$$\lim_{x \to \infty}\dfrac{8x + 1}{2\sqrt{4x^2 + x}} = \lim_{x \to \infty}\sqrt{\dfrac{64x^2 + 16x + 1}{16x^2 + 4x}} = \sqrt{\lim_{x \to \infty}\left(\dfrac{64x^2 + 16x + 1}{16x^2 + 4x}\right)} = \sqrt{\lim_{x \to \infty}\left(\dfrac{64x^2}{16x^2}\right)} = \sqrt{\lim_{x \to \infty}(4)} = 2.$$

Therefore, $\lim\limits_{x \to \infty}\left(\sqrt{4x^2 + x} - 2x\right) = \lim\limits_{x \to \infty}\dfrac{1}{\frac{8x + 1}{2\sqrt{4x^2 + x}} + 2} = \dfrac{1}{2 + 2} = \dfrac{1}{4}$.

6.3.4 The California *Mathematics Subject Matter Requirements* stipulate that candidates for any credential program for teaching secondary mathematics must be able to *use the derivative to solve rectilinear motion, related rate, and optimization problems.*

Motion Problems

Rectilinear Motion

Rectilinear motion is motion of an object moving in a straight line. The relationships we can use are:

- $a(t)$ is **acceleration** and is a function of time. Acceleration is the instantaneous rate of change of **velocity**, $v(t)$, which is also a function of time. Hence,

  $\frac{d}{dt}(v(t)) = a(t)$, or the antiderivative of acceleration is velocity.

  Notation: We can use the symbol $\int$ to mean antiderivative, so here we could write $\int a(t)dt = v(t) + c$.

- Velocity is the instantaneous rate of change of **position** (or displacement), $s(t)$, which is a function of time. So,

  $\frac{d}{dt}(s(t)) = v(t)$, so the antiderivative of velocity is position and $\int v(t)dt = s(t) + c$.

  Example: Suppose a particle moves along a straight line with its acceleration given by $a(t) = 12t + 8$, with its initial velocity equal to -3 cm/sec, and its initial displacement equal to 6 cm. Find the position function.

  We are given that $v'(t) = a(t) = 12t + 8$ so that $v(t) = 6t^2 + 8t + A$ by antidifferentiation. We can find $A = -3$, by using $v(0) = -3$. Next we use antidifferentiation to solve $s'(t) = v(t) = 6t^2 + 8t - 3$. We obtain $s(t) = 2t^3 + 4t^2 - 3t + B$. Knowing that $s(0) = 6$, the position function for the particle is $s(t) = 2t^3 + 4t^2 - 3t + 6$.

Related Rates

Related rates problems involve computing the rate of change of a quantity in terms of the rate of change of another quantity that may be more easily measured. For example, a balloon's change in, volume is related to the rate of change in its radius as air is leaked out of the balloon or pumped into it, or a ladder is sliding down a wall and the distance the top of the ladder is above ground is related by the Pythagorean Theorem to the distance the foot of the ladder is from the wall.

Examples:

(a) Air is being pumped into a spherical balloon with the volume increasing at a constant rate of 50 cm³/sec. How fast is the radius of the balloon increasing when the diameter of the balloon is 20 cm?

$V = \frac{4}{3}\pi r^3$, and we are given $\frac{dV}{dt} = 50$. We want to find $\frac{dr}{dt}$ when $d = 20$.

Differentiating with respect to t, $\frac{dV}{dt} = 4\pi r^2 \frac{dr}{dt} \Leftrightarrow 50 = 4\pi (10)^2 \frac{dr}{dt}$, so that $\frac{dr}{dt} = \frac{1}{8\pi} \approx 0.0398$. Thus, the radius of the balloon is increasing at the rate of approximately 0.0398 cm/sec when the diameter is 20 cm.

(b) A cone-shaped filter with radius 4 in. and depth 6 in. contains water that is leaking out of a hole at the bottom at a rate of 1 in.³ per minute. If the filter starts out full, how long does it take to empty? How fast is the radius decreasing when the radius is 2 in.?

For a cone, $V = \frac{1}{3}\pi r^2 h$, and we are given that $\frac{dV}{dt} = -1$. The volume of the filter is

$V = \frac{1}{3}\pi r^2 h = \frac{1}{3}\pi (4)^2 (6) = 32\pi$ in.³. Hence, it will take $32\pi \approx 100.53$ minutes to

empty the tank.

Next using similar triangles (Figure 6.71), $\frac{4}{6} = \frac{r}{h}$.

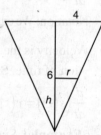

So that $h = 1.5r$. Substituting this in, we get $V = \frac{1}{2}\pi r^3$, so that at $r = 2$,

$\frac{dV}{dt} = \frac{3}{2}\pi r^2 \frac{dr}{dt}$. Thus $-1 = \frac{3}{2}\pi (2)^2 \frac{dr}{dt} \Leftrightarrow \frac{dr}{dt} = -\frac{1}{6\pi} \approx -0.053$.

The radius is decreasing at the rate of about 0.53 in./min when $r = 2$.

Figure 6.71

Optimization Problems

- To find a **global maximum or minimum of a continuous function on a closed and bounded interval [a, b]** where the Extreme Value Theorem guarantees the existence, find all critical points in the interval ($f'(x) = 0$ or does not exist) and compare the values of the function at the critical points and the endpoints.

- To find a **global maximum or minimum of a continuous function on an open interval** (this could be all reals or another infinite interval), find the value of the function at all the critical points and sketch the graph. Consider the limits of the function as x approaches the endpoints of the interval, or $\pm\infty$ if they are involved.

The steps for solving max/min word problems are as follows.

1. Read each problem carefully several times before trying to solve it. Identify what the problem is asking. What are the unknowns?

2. Draw a diagram of the problem to be solved. Pictures can be helpful in organizing and sorting out your thoughts.

3. Define all variables to be used and carefully label your picture or diagram with these variables. This step leads directly or indirectly to the mathematical equations you need to solve the problem.

4. Write down all equations that are related to your problem and/or diagram. Clearly denote the equation you are asked to optimize. Many optimization problems will begin with two equations. One equation is a "constraint" equation and the other is the equation you need to optimize. The "constraint" equation is used to solve for one of the variables. This is then substituted into the equation to be optimized before differentiation occurs. Some problems do not have a constraint equation, and some problems may have two or more constraint equations.

5. Before differentiating, the optimization equation must be a function of only one variable. Differentiate this equation using the rules of differentiation.

6. Verify that your result is a maximum or minimum value. Be sure to consider in what type of interval your variable lies.

Examples:

(a) A farmer has 1000 feet of fencing and wants to fence in a rectangular area using a large barn (length 1000 feet) as one side of the rectangular area (no fencing is needed on that side). What are the dimensions that give the greatest area and what is the maximum area?

Let x be the length of the side of the rectangular area perpendicular to the barn. Then the length of the side across from the barn is $1000 - 2x$ (Figure 6.72).

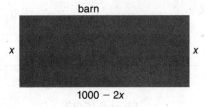

Figure 6.72

The area can be given by $A(x) = x(1000 - 2x) = 1000x - 2x^2$ and $0 \le x \le 500$, even though the values of 0 and 500 give zero area. The Extreme Value Theorem guarantees a maximum area.

$A'(x) = 1000 - 4x$, so there is only one critical value, $x = 250$. $A(250) = 125{,}000$, so this must be the maximum area and it happens when the sides perpendicular to the barn use 250 of fencing with the side parallel to the barn having length 500 feet.

(b) A cylindrical can is needed that will hold 2 liters of liquid. Find the dimensions of the can that will minimize the cost of the metal used to make the can, assuming that the entire surface of the can is made of the same metal.

We want to minimize the surface area of the can, which is $SA = 2\pi r^2 + 2\pi rh$. We know the volume is 2 liters = 2000 cm³, and $V = \pi r^2 h = 2000 \Leftrightarrow h = \dfrac{2000}{\pi r^2}$. We can substitute this into the surface area equation to make it a function of one variable:

$SA = 2\pi r^2 + 2\pi r \left(\dfrac{2000}{\pi r^2}\right) = 2\pi r^2 + \dfrac{4000}{r}$. We know $r > 0$, so we do not have a closed and

bounded interval, and $SA'(r) = 4\pi r - \dfrac{4000}{r^2} = \dfrac{4\pi r^3 - 4000}{r^2}$. Setting the numerator equal to 0

and solving, we get $4\pi r^3 - 4000 = 0 \Leftrightarrow r = \sqrt[3]{\dfrac{1000}{\pi}} = \dfrac{10}{\sqrt[3]{\pi}} \approx 6.828$. A graph of the surface

area function is shown in Figure 6.73. From this, we can see that the function must have a global

minimum at our critical value. $SA\left(\dfrac{10}{\sqrt[3]{\pi}}\right) \approx 878.755$ cm². The dimensions that will minimize the

cost of the metal are: $r \approx 6.828$ cm., $h \approx 16.132$ cm.

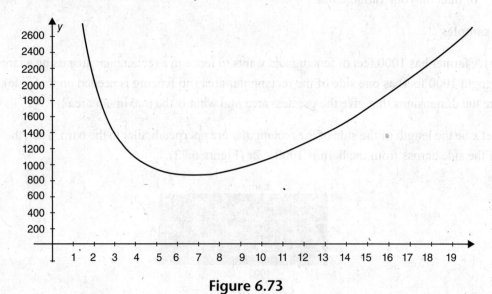

Figure 6.73

Review Problems for Section 6.3.4

1. A particle moves along a straight line and has acceleration given by $a(t) = 6t - 10$. Its initial velocity is 2 cm/sec and its initial displacement is 7 cm. Find the position function.

2. Air is leaking out of a spherical balloon with the radius decreasing at a constant rate of 3 cm/min. How fast is the volume of the balloon decreasing when the diameter of the balloon is 100 cm?

3. A 20 ft ladder is sliding down a vertical wall at a rate of 3 in./sec. How fast is foot of the ladder moving away from the bottom of the wall when the top of the ladder is 8 feet from the top?

4. We want to construct a box whose base length is 4 times the base width. The material used to build the top and bottom cost $5/ft² and the material used to build the sides cost $2/ft². If the box must have a volume of 60 ft³, determine the dimensions that will minimize the cost to build the box.

5. A piece of wire 40 cm long is to be cut into two pieces. One piece is bent into a square and the other into an equilateral triangle. How should the wire be cut so that the total area enclosed is a maximum?

Detailed Solutions

1. $a(t) = 6t - 10 \Rightarrow v(t) = 3t^2 - 10t + A.$ $v(0) = 2$, so $v(t) = 3t^2 - 10t + 2 \Rightarrow$
$\Rightarrow s(t) = t^3 - 5t^2 + 2t + B$ and $s(0) = 7 \Rightarrow s(t) = t^3 - 5t^2 + 2t + 7$ is the position function.

2. We are told $\dfrac{dr}{dt} = -3.$ $V = \dfrac{4}{3}\pi r^3 \Rightarrow \dfrac{dV}{dt} = 4\pi r^2 \dfrac{dr}{dt} = -12\pi r^2.$ What is $\dfrac{dV}{dt}$ when $r = 50$?

$\dfrac{dV}{dt} = -12\pi(50)^2 = -30000\pi \approx -94247.78.$ The volume is decreasing at a rate of approximately 94,247.78 cm³/min when the radius is 50 cm.

3. Let x be the distance the foot of the ladder is from the wall and let y be the distance from the top of the ladder to the ground. The ladder is 20 feet in length (Figure 6.74).

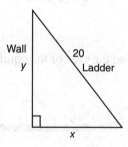

Figure 6.74

By the Pythagorean Theorem $x^2 + y^2 = 400 \Rightarrow 2x\dfrac{dx}{dt} + 2y\dfrac{dy}{dt} = 0$, or $x\dfrac{dx}{dt} + y\dfrac{dy}{dt} = 0.$

$\dfrac{dy}{dt} = -3/12 = -0.25$ ft. If $y = 8$, then $x = \sqrt{20^2 - 8^2} = \sqrt{336} = 4\sqrt{21}$, so

$(4\sqrt{21})\dfrac{dx}{dt} + (8)(-0.25) = 0 \Rightarrow \dfrac{dx}{dt} = \dfrac{1}{2\sqrt{21}} \approx 0.109$ ft/sec. Therefore, the bottom of the ladder is moving away from the wall at a rate of approximately 0.109 feet per second.

4. Let x be the width of the base, then the length of the base is $4x$. The area of two bases $= 2lw = 8x^2$

The volume of the box $V = lwh = 4x^2h = 60 \Rightarrow h = \dfrac{15}{x^2}.$

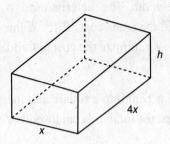

Figure 6.75

The cost function is

$$C(x) = (5)(2lw) + (2)(2lh + 2wh)$$

$$= (5)(8x^2) + (2)\left(\frac{120}{x} + \frac{30}{x}\right) = 40x^2 + \frac{300}{x}$$

$$C'(x) = 80x - \frac{300}{x^2} = \frac{80x^3 - 300}{x^2}$$

$C'(x) = 0$ when $x = \sqrt[3]{\dfrac{30}{8}} \approx 1.544$.

The dimensions that minimize the cost are: base $\dfrac{\sqrt[3]{30}}{2}$ ft by $2\sqrt[3]{30}$ ft and height $2\sqrt[3]{30}$ ft.

5. Let x be the length of the wire that is to be bent into a square and let $40 - x$ be the length of the wire to be bent into an equilateral triangle (Figure 6.76).

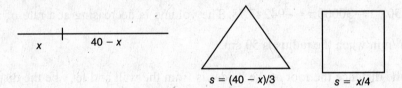

Figure 6.76

The area of the square is $\left(\dfrac{x}{4}\right)^2 = \dfrac{x^2}{16}$ and the area of the equilateral triangle is

$$\frac{\left(\dfrac{40-x}{3}\right)^2 \sqrt{3}}{4} = \frac{\sqrt{3}}{36}(x^2 - 80x + 1600).$$ The total area enclosed is: $A = \dfrac{x^2}{16} + \dfrac{\sqrt{3}}{36}(x^2 - 80x + 1600)$, so

$$A' = \frac{1}{8} \times \frac{\sqrt{3}}{36}(2x - 80) = \left(\frac{1}{8} + \frac{\sqrt{3}}{18}\right) \times -\frac{20\sqrt{3}}{9}.$$ $A' = 0$ when $x = \dfrac{160\sqrt{3}}{9 + 4\sqrt{3}} \approx 17.4$. The wire

should be cut so that approximately 17.4 cm is used for the square and 22.6 cm. is used for the equilateral triangle.

> **6.3.5** The California *Mathematics Subject Matter Requirements* stipulate that candidates for any credential program for teaching secondary mathematics must be able to *use the derivative to analyze functions and planar curves (e.g., maxima, minima, inflection points, concavity).*

Analyzing Functions and Planar Curves

- Let f be a function and let c be in the domain of f. Then if $f'(c) = 0$ or $f(c)$ does not exist, then we call c a **critical value** or **point** of f, and $(c, f(c))$ is also called a **critical point** of f.

- Let c be an interior point of the domain of the function f. Then $f(c)$ is

  (i) **a local maximum value** at $x = c$ if and only if $f(c) \geq f(x)$ for all values of x in some open interval containing c, or

  (ii) **a local minimum value** at $x = c$ if and only if $f(c) \leq f(x)$ for all values of x in some open interval containing c.

- Local extrema are also called **relative extrema**.

- A function f has a **local maximum or minimum at an endpoint** c if the appropriate inequality holds for all x in some half-open interval with c as the included endpoint.

Theorem: If a function f has a local extremum at a number c in an open interval, then either $f'(c) = 0$ or $f'(c)$ does not exist.

Corollary: If $f'(c)$ exists and $f'(c) \neq 0$, then $f(c)$ is *not* a local extremum of the function f.

Theorem (First Derivative Test): Let c be a critical point for f, and suppose f is continuous at c and differentiable on an open interval I containing c, except possibly at c itself.

  (a) If f' changes from positive to negative at c, then $f(c)$ is a local maximum of f.

  (b) If f' changes from negative to positive at c, then $f(c)$ is a local minimum of f.

  (c) If $f'(x) > 0$ or $f'(x) < 0$ for all $x \in I$ except $x = c$, then $f(c)$ is *not* a local extremum of f.

- Recall that if D_f is the domain of the function f, then the maximum and minimum values of f on D_f, if they exist, are called the **global maximum** and **global minimum** of f, respectively.

- A function (or its graph) is called **concave up** (or upward) on an open interval I if f' is an increasing function on I. A function (or its graph) is called **concave down** (or downward) on an open interval I if f' is a decreasing function on I.

- A point $(c, f(c))$ on the graph of f is an **inflection point** if the following two conditions hold:

  (i) f is continuous at c, and

(ii) there is an open interval (a, b) containing c such that the graph is concave upward on (a, c) and concave downward on (c, b) or vice versa.

Theorem The Second Derivative Test: Suppose f'' is continuous near c. Then if

(a) $f'(c) = 0$ and $f''(c) > 0$, then f has a local minimum at c.

(b) $f'(c) = 0$ and $f''(c) < 0$, then f has a local maximum at c.

Examples: Use the derivatives to find all important information about the graph of the function and then sketch a graph of the function.

(a) $f(x) = x^4 - 8x^3$. First note that f is a polynomial of degree 4, so the end behavior of f is like the end behavior of x^4 (ends go up) and also f is continuous everywhere. In addition, $f(x) = x^3(x - 8)$, so f has zeroes when $x = 0$ or 8.

Now, $f'(x) = 4x^3 - 24x^2 = 4x^2(x - 6)$, so the critical values are $x = 0$ and 6. Use the first derivative test; substitute values from each interval into the derivative (Figure 6.77).

Figure 6.77

This tells us that f is increasing on $(6, \infty)$ and decreasing on $(-\infty, 0) \cup (0, 6)$, and so f has a local minimum of $f(6) = -432$.

Next, $f''(x) = 12x^2 - 48x = 12x(x - 4)$, so the critical values are $x = 0$ and 4. Test the sign of the second derivative (Figure 6.78).

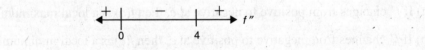

Figure 6.78

This tells us that f is concave up on $(-\infty, 0) \cup (4, \infty)$ and concave down on $(0, 4)$. The graph also has inflection points $(0, 0)$ and $(4, -256)$.

The graph of $f(x) = x^4 - 8x^3$ sketched in Figure 6.79.

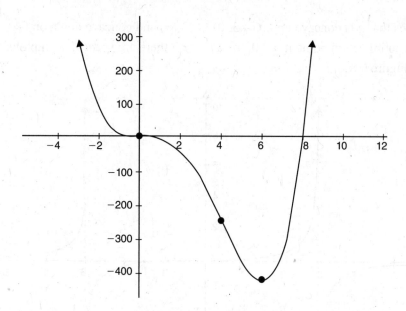

Figure 6.79

(b) $g(x) = \dfrac{x}{x^2 - 9}$. Note that g is a rational function that has a zero at $x = 0$ and vertical asymp-

totes $x = 3$ and $x = -3$.

Then $g'(x) = \dfrac{(x^2 - 9)\cdot 1 - x(2x)}{(x^2 - 9)^2} = \dfrac{-(x^2 + 9)}{(x^2 - 9)^2}$, so that the only important numbers are $x = \pm 3$.

Check the sign of the derivative. Figure 6.80 indicates that g is always decreasing and that there are no local or absolute extrema.

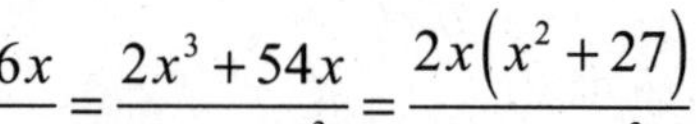

$$\xleftarrow{\quad} \overset{-}{\underset{-3}{|}} \quad \overset{-}{\underset{0}{|}} \quad \overset{-}{\underset{3}{|}} \quad \xrightarrow{\quad} g''$$

Figure 6.80

$$g''(x) = \frac{(x^2 - 9)^2 \cdot (-2x) + (x^2 + 9)2(x^2 - 9)(2x)}{(x^2 - 9)^4} = \frac{(x^2 - 9)\left[(-2x)(x^2 - 9) + 4x(x^2 + 9)\right]}{(x^2 - 9)^4}$$

$$= \frac{-2x^3 + 18x + 4x^3 + 36x}{(x^2 - 9)^3} = \frac{2x^3 + 54x}{(x^2 - 9)^3} = \frac{2x(x^2 + 27)}{(x^2 - 9)^3}$$

So the critical values are $x = 0, \pm 3$. Test the sign of the second derivative (Figure 6.81).

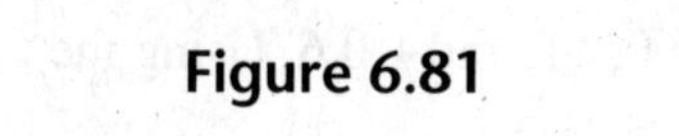

$$\xleftarrow{\quad} \overset{-}{\underset{-3}{|}} \quad \overset{+}{\underset{0}{|}} \quad \overset{-}{\underset{3}{|}} \quad \overset{+}{} \quad \xrightarrow{\quad} g''$$

Figure 6.81

This tells us that g is concave up on $(-3, 0) \cup (3, \infty)$ and concave down on $(-\infty, -3) \cup (0, 3)$; so there is an inflection point at $x = 0$, but at $x = \pm 3$ there are vertical asymptotes. The graph is shown in Figure 6.82.

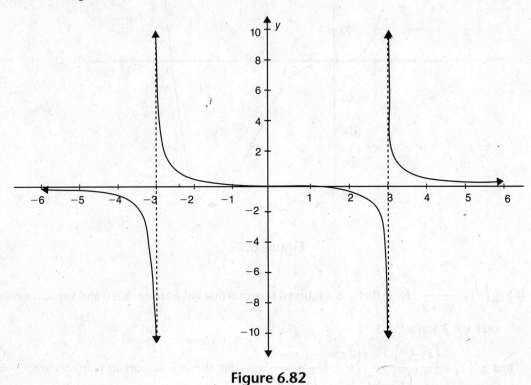

Figure 6.82

Review Problems for Section 6.3.5

Use the first and second derivatives to find all important information about each of these functions and then graph the functions.

1. $f(x) = x^3(x+1)^2$

2. $g(x) = \dfrac{x^2 - 1}{x - 3}$

Detailed Solutions

1. Let $f(x) = x^3(x+1)^2$. This is a polynomial which has zeroes at $x = 0$ and -1.

$$f(x) = x^5 + 2x^4 + x^3 \Rightarrow f'(x) = 5x^4 + 8x^3 + 3x^2 = x^2(5x^2 + 8x + 3) = x^2(5x + 3)(x + 1).$$ So

the zeroes of the derivative are $x = 0$, -1, and -0.6. Using the first derivative test, we look at the

sign of the first derivative (Figure 6.83).

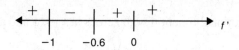

Figure 6.83

This shows us that f is increasing on $(-\infty, -1) \cup (-0.6, 0) \cup (0, \infty)$ and decreasing $(-1, -0.6)$. So f has a local maximum of 0 at $x = -1$ and a local minimum of -0.03456 at $x = -0.6$.

$f'(x) = 5x^4 + 8x^3 + 3x^2 \Rightarrow f''(x) = 20x^3 + 24x^2 + 6x = 2x(10x^2 + 12x + 3)$. Using the quadratic formula on $10x^2 + 12x + 3$ we obtain, $x = \dfrac{-12 \pm \sqrt{144 - 120}}{20} = \dfrac{-12 \pm \sqrt{24}}{20} = \dfrac{-6 \pm \sqrt{6}}{10}$. So the

zeroes of the second derivative are $x = 0$, $\dfrac{-6 + \sqrt{6}}{10} \approx -0.355$, and $\dfrac{-6 - \sqrt{6}}{10} \approx -0.893$. Next, we

test the second derivative's sign (Figure 6.84).

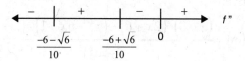

Figure 6.84

From this, we know that f is concave up on $\left(\dfrac{-6 - \sqrt{6}}{10}, \dfrac{-6 + \sqrt{6}}{10} \right) \cup (0, \infty)$ and concave down on $\left(-\infty, \dfrac{-6 - \sqrt{6}}{10} \right) \cup \left(\dfrac{-6 + \sqrt{6}}{10}, 0 \right)$; the graph of f also has inflection points: $(0, 0)$ and approximate inflection points $(-0.355, -0.019)$ and $(-0.893, -0.008)$. The graph is shown in Figure 6.85.

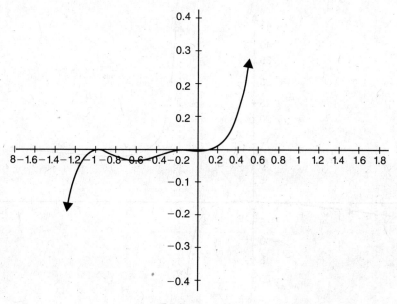

Figure 6.85

2. $g(x) = \dfrac{x^2 - 1}{x - 3}$. This is a rational function with zeroes at $x = \pm 1$ and a vertical asymptote at $x = 3$.

$g(x) = \dfrac{x^2 - 1}{x - 3} \Rightarrow g'(x) = \dfrac{(x-3)(2x) - (x^2 - 1)(1)}{(x-3)^2} = \dfrac{x^2 - 6x + 1}{(x-3)^2}$ does not exist at $x = 3$ and has

zeroes at $x = \dfrac{6 \pm \sqrt{36 - 4}}{2} = 3 \pm 2\sqrt{2}$. Use the first derivative test (Figure 6.86).

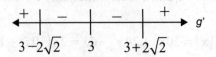

Figure 6.86

From this, we know that g is increasing on $\left(-\infty, 3 - 2\sqrt{2}\right) \cup \left(3 + 2\sqrt{2}, \infty\right)$ and decreasing on $\left(3 - 2\sqrt{2}, 3\right) \cup \left(3, 3 + 2\sqrt{2}\right)$; g has a local maximum of approximately 0.343 at $x = 3 - 2\sqrt{2}$ and a local minimum of approximately 11.657 at $x = 3 + 2\sqrt{2}$.

Next, use the second derivative:

$g'(x) = \dfrac{x^2 - 6x + 1}{(x-3)^2} \Rightarrow g''(x) = \dfrac{(x-3)^2(2x-6) - (x^2 - 6x + 1)2(x-3)}{(x-3)^4} = \dfrac{16}{(x-3)^3}$. This has no

zeroes but does not exist for $x = 3$. Check the second derivative's sign (Figure 6.87).

Figure 6.87

So g is concave down on $(-\infty, 3)$ and up on $(3, \infty)$ with no inflection points. The graph is shown in Figure 6.88.

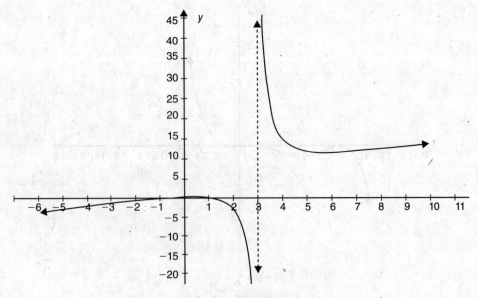

Figure 6.88

First-Order Differential Equations

- A **first-order differential equation** is an equation that involves a first derivative but no higher derivatives.

- A **separable first-order differential equation** is a differentiable equation that can be written in the form $N(y)\dfrac{dy}{dx} = M(x)$. In differential form, this is $N(y)dy = M(x)dx$. This means we can write the equation so that the variables y and x are separated.

  Example: The differential equation $\dfrac{dy}{dx} = \dfrac{x^2}{y^4}$ is separable since we can write it in the form.
  $y^4 dy = x^2 dx$. The differential equation $2xy - 1 + (y^2 + xy + x)\dfrac{dy}{dx} = 0$ is not separable.

- To solve a separable first-order differential equation, write it in differential form and integrate both sides. Then solve for y if possible.

  Example: $\dfrac{dy}{dx} = \dfrac{x^2}{y^4}$ can be written as $y^4 dy = x^2 dx$. To solve:

  $\displaystyle\int y^4\, dy = \int x^2 dx \Rightarrow \dfrac{y^5}{5} = \dfrac{x^3}{3} = C' \Rightarrow y = \sqrt[5]{\dfrac{5}{3}x^2 + C}$. Hence the solution is a family of functions, one for each value of C.

- If an **initial value** is given for a first-order equation, then it should be possible to determine the value of the constant C, and thus there would be a specific solution.

  Example: $\dfrac{dy}{dx} = \dfrac{xy^3}{\sqrt{1+x^2}}, \quad y(0)=2$:

  $\displaystyle\int y^{-3}dy = \int x(1+x^2)^{-\frac{1}{2}} dx \Rightarrow \dfrac{-1}{2}y^{-2} = (1+x^2)^{\frac{1}{2}} + C$. Then, using the initial value, we obtain:

  $(2)^{-2} = (1+(0)^2)^{\frac{1}{2}} + C \Rightarrow C = -\dfrac{9}{8}$.

  The implicit solution $\dfrac{-1}{2}y^{-2} = (1+x^2)^{\frac{1}{2}} - \dfrac{9}{8} \Rightarrow y^2 = \dfrac{4}{9 - 8(1+x^2)^{\frac{1}{2}}}$.

This represents two functions, only one of which satisfies the initial condition:

$$\frac{-1}{2}y^{-2} = \left(1+x^2\right)^{\frac{1}{2}} - \frac{9}{8} \Rightarrow y^2 = \frac{4}{9-8\left(1+x^2\right)^{\frac{1}{2}}} \Rightarrow y = \pm\frac{2}{\sqrt{9-8\left(1+x^2\right)^{\frac{1}{2}}}}, \text{ so we must choose}$$

the explicit function $y = \dfrac{2}{\sqrt{9-8\left(1+x^2\right)^{\frac{1}{2}}}}$ as the solution.

Growth and Decay Problems

Let $y(t)$ represent the number of members of some population at the time t. Then the rate of change of population is $y'(t)$. If it is known that $y'(t)$ is proportional to $y(t)$, $\dfrac{dy}{dt} = ky$, then y can be solved as a separable differentiable equation as follows:

$$\frac{dy}{dt} = ky \Rightarrow \frac{1}{y}dy = kdt \Rightarrow \int\frac{1}{y}dy = \int kdx \Rightarrow \ln|y| = kx+C' \Rightarrow y = e^{kx+C'} = Ce^{kt}$$

We need to be given more information to find C and k.

Examples:

(a) Let $P(t)$ be the population of West Garfield, VT. Assume that the population is changing so that it is proportional to the size of the population. Suppose we know the population of the city was 30,000 in 1990 and it was 50,000 in 2010. Assuming that the population will continue to grow in this manner, find the population of West Garfield in 2016.

So $y = Ce^{kt}$, $y(0) = 30$, $y(20) = 50$; $t = 0$ is 1990, and population is measured in thousands.

$$y(0) = 30 \Rightarrow 30 = Ce^0 \Rightarrow C = 30 \Rightarrow y = 30e^{kt}.$$

$$y(20) = 50 \Rightarrow 50 = 30e^{20k} \Rightarrow \frac{5}{3} = \left(e^k\right)^{20} \Rightarrow \left(\frac{5}{3}\right)^{\frac{1}{20}} = e^k \Rightarrow y = 30\left(\frac{5}{3}\right)^{\frac{t}{20}}.$$

The year 2016 is $t = 26$, $y(26) = 30\left(\frac{5}{3}\right)^{\frac{26}{20}} \approx 58.281$.

So in 2016 there will be approximately 58,281 people in West Garfield, VT.

(b) The half-life of radioactive particle X is 1840 years. Radioactive material is always assumed to decay at a rate proportional to the amount present at any time.

  (i) If a sample of radioactive particle X has a mass of 80 mg now, show how to find a formula for the mass of radioactive particle X that remains after t years using differential equations.

  (ii) Find the mass after 1000 years, correct to the nearest milligram.

  (iii) When will the mass be reduced to 30 mg?

Let $y(t)$ be the amount of radioactive particle X (in mg) at time t (in years), with $t = 0$ representing this year.

(i) $y(0) = 80$ and $y(1840) = 40$.

$$\frac{dy}{dt} = ky \implies \frac{1}{y}dy = kdt \implies \int \frac{1}{y}dy = \int kdx \implies \ln|y| = kx + C' \implies y = e^{kx+C'} = Ce^{kt}$$

Then, $80 = Ce^0 \implies C = 80 \implies y = 80e^{kt}$. Next, use $y(1840) = 40$:

$$40 = 80e^{1840k} \implies \frac{1}{2} = \left(e^k\right)^{1840} \implies y = 80\left(\frac{1}{2}\right)^{\frac{t}{1840}}.$$

(ii) $y(1000) = 80\left(\frac{1}{2}\right)^{\frac{1000}{1840}} \approx 54.8$. So after 1000 years, approximately 55 mg will remain.

(iii) Find t so $30 = 80\left(\frac{1}{2}\right)^{\frac{t}{1840}}$.

$$\frac{3}{8} = \left(\frac{1}{2}\right)^{\frac{t}{1840}} \implies \ln\left(\frac{3}{8}\right) = \frac{t}{1840}\ln\left(\frac{1}{2}\right) \implies t = 1840\frac{\ln\left(\frac{3}{8}\right)}{\ln\left(\frac{1}{2}\right)} \approx 2603.7 \text{ , so it will take about}$$

2603.7 years to reduce the sample to 30 mg.

Review Problems for Section 6.3.6

1. Solve $\frac{dy}{dx} = \frac{y}{x}$, where $y(1) = 4$.

2. A perfectly spherical snowball is melting at a rate proportional to its size. The snowball originally had a diameter of 2 feet but after 10 hours its diameter is 1 foot. Find an equation to represent this situation. How long before the diameter is only 0.4 feet?

3. A population of fish in a lake is growing in proportion to its size at any time t. In 2000, the population was estimated to be 410, and in 2011 it was estimated to be 1205. Write the differential equation for this problem and predict what the fish population will be in 2025.

Detailed Solutions

1. $\frac{dy}{dx} = \frac{y}{x} \implies \frac{1}{y}dy = \frac{1}{x}dx \implies \int \frac{1}{y}dy = \int \frac{1}{x}dx \implies \ln|y| = \ln|x| + C' \implies e^{\ln|y|} = e^{\ln|x|+C'} \implies y = Cx$.

   If $y(1) = 4$, then $C = 4$, so that $y = 4x$ is the solution.

2. Let $V(t)$ be the volume of the snowball at t hours after its diameter was 2 feet. Then the differential equation $\frac{dV}{dt} = kV, V(0) = \frac{4}{3}\pi(1)^3 = \frac{4}{3}\pi, V(10) = \frac{4}{3}\pi\left(\frac{1}{2}\right)^3 = \frac{1}{6}\pi$. To solve this:

$$\frac{dV}{dt} = kV \Rightarrow \int \frac{1}{V}dV = \int k\,dt \Rightarrow \ln|V| = kt + C' \Rightarrow V = Ce^{kt}.$$

$$V(0) = \frac{4}{3}\pi \Rightarrow C = \frac{4}{3}\pi \Rightarrow V = \frac{4}{3}\pi e^{kt}. \text{ Then } V(10) = \frac{1}{6}\pi \Rightarrow \frac{1}{6}\pi = \frac{4}{3}\pi\left(e^k\right)^{10} \Rightarrow e^k = \left(\frac{1}{8}\right)^{\frac{1}{10}}. \text{ Thus,}$$

$$V(t) = \frac{4}{3}\pi\left(\frac{1}{8}\right)^{\frac{t}{10}} \text{ is the solution. If the diameter is 0.4 ft, the radius is 0.2 and the volume is } \frac{4\pi}{375}.$$

Find t when $V = \frac{4\pi}{375}$:

$$\frac{4\pi}{375} = \frac{4}{3}\pi\left(\frac{1}{8}\right)^{\frac{t}{10}} \Rightarrow \frac{1}{125} = \left(\frac{1}{8}\right)^{\frac{t}{10}} \Rightarrow \ln\left(\frac{1}{125}\right) = \frac{t}{10}\ln\left(\frac{1}{8}\right) \Rightarrow t = \frac{10\ln\left(\frac{1}{125}\right)}{\ln\left(\frac{1}{8}\right)} = \frac{10\ln 125}{\ln 8} = \frac{10\ln 5}{\ln 2} \approx 14.65$$

Thus, the diameter will shrink to 0.4 feet after about 14.65 hours.

3. Let $P(t)$ be the fish population at time t years after 2000. Then the differential equation is $\frac{dP}{dt} = kP$. We have $P = Ce^{kt}$, $P(0) = 410$, and $P(11) = 1205$, so $C = 410$, and $P = 410e^{kt}$ and

$$1205 = 410e^{11k} \text{ so } e^k = \left(\frac{241}{82}\right)^{\frac{1}{11}}. \text{ Therefore, } P = 410\left(\frac{241}{82}\right)^{\frac{t}{11}} \text{ is the solution.}$$

$$P(25) = 410\left(\frac{241}{82}\right)^{\frac{25}{11}} \approx 4752. \text{ The fish population should be around 4752 in 2025.}$$

6.4 Integrals and Applications

6.4.1 The California *Mathematics Subject Matter Requirements* stipulate that candidates for any credential program for teaching secondary mathematics must be able to *derive definite integrals of standard algebraic functions using the formal definition of the integral.*

Integrals

Summation Notation

The Greek letter sigma, Σ is used to indicate summation as follows:

$$\sum_{i=1}^{6} i = 1 + 2 + 3 + 4 + 5 + 6$$

The letter i is the **index of summation** and is a dummy variable, meaning that we could change the letter without changing the meaning of the symbols.

Examples:

(a) $\sum_{i=1}^{3} x_i = x_1 + x_2 + x_3$

(b) $\sum_{k=0}^{5} ka^k = 0 + a + 2a^2 + 3a^3 + 4a^4 + 5a^5$

Summation in Relation to Integration

- Some summations needed to calculate definite integrals are the following:

  (a) $1 + 2 + 3 + \cdots + k = \dfrac{k(k+1)}{2}$ for all positive integers k.

  (b) $1^2 + 2^2 + 3^2 + \cdots + n^2 = \dfrac{n(n+1)(2n+1)}{6}$ for all positive integers n.

  (c) $1 + 8 + 27 + \cdots + k^3 = \dfrac{k^2(k+1)^2}{4}$ for all $k = 1, 2, 3, \ldots$.

- A **partition**, P, of a closed interval $[a, b]$ is any decomposition of $[a, b]$ into subintervals of the form

$$[x_0, x_1], \quad [x_1, x_2], \quad [x_2, x_3], \quad \cdots [x_{n-1}, x_n]$$

where $n > 0$ is an integer and the numbers x_i are such that

$$a = x_0 < x_1 < x_2 < \ldots < x_{n-1} < x_n = b$$

The length of the ith subinterval $[x_{i-1}, x_i]$ is $\Delta x_i = x_i - x_{i-1}$.

- Let f be defined on a closed interval $[a, b]$, and let P be the partition of $[a, b]$ in which all the subintervals have the same width, i.e., $\Delta x = \dfrac{b-a}{n}$. For each subinterval choose any value $x_i^* \in [x_{i-1}, x_i]$. Then the **definite integral of f from a to b** is

$$\int_a^b f(x)\,dx = \lim_{n \to \infty} \sum_{i=1}^{n} f(x_i^*)\,\Delta x$$

provided the limit exists. If the limit exists, we say f is **integrable** on $[a, b]$.

- The symbol $\int$ is the **integral sign**; it is like an elongated S (for limit of a sum). The function $f(x)$ is called the **integrand**, a is **the lower limit** of integration, b is the **upper limit** of integration, and dx indicates the **independent variable**.

Theorem: If f is continuous on $[a, b]$ then f is integrable. In fact, if f is continuous except for a finite number of jump discontinuities, then f is integrable.

Theorem: If f is integrable on $[a, b]$, then $\displaystyle\int_a^b f(x)\,dx = \lim_{n\to\infty}\sum_{i=1}^{n} f(x_i)\,\Delta x$, where $\Delta x = \dfrac{b-a}{n}$ and $x_i = a + i\Delta x$ for $i = 1,2,3,\dots n$ (See Figure 6.89).

- The sum $\displaystyle\sum_{i=1}^{n} f(x_i^*)\,\Delta x$ is called a **Riemann sum.**

Note: i here is an index and not the symbol for $\sqrt{-1}$.

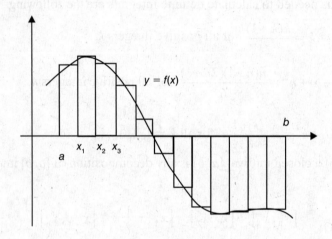

Figure 6.89

Example:

(a) Express $\displaystyle\lim_{n\to\infty}\sum_{i=1}^{n}\left(\frac{3}{\left(x_i^*\right)^2} - 5x_i^* + 2\right)\Delta x$ as a definite integral over $[2, 6]$.

$$\int_2^6 \left(\frac{3}{x^2} - 5x + 2\right)dx$$

(b) Set up the Riemann sum for $f(x) = 2x^2 - x$ on $[0, 4]$ and then evaluate it to give the value of $\displaystyle\int_0^4 (2x^2 - x)\,dx$.

For this problem, $\Delta x = \dfrac{4-0}{n} = \dfrac{4}{n}$, and $x_i = 0 + i\Delta x = \dfrac{4i}{n}$. The Riemann sum is

$$\sum_{i=1}^{n}\left(2x_i^2 - x_i\right)\Delta x = \sum_{i=1}^{n}\left(2\left(i\frac{4}{n}\right)^2 - \left(i\frac{4}{n}\right)\right)\frac{4}{n}$$

$$= \sum_{i=1}^{n}\left(\frac{128}{n^3}i^2 - \frac{16}{n^2}i\right)$$

$$= \frac{128}{n^3}\sum_{i=1}^{n}i^2 - \frac{16}{n^2}\sum_{i=1}^{n}i$$

$$= \frac{128}{n^3}\left(\frac{n(n+1)(2n+1)}{6}\right) - \frac{16}{n^2}\left(\frac{n(n+1)}{2}\right)$$

$$= \frac{128}{3} + \frac{64}{n} + \frac{64}{3n^2} - 8 - \frac{8}{n} = \frac{104}{3} + \frac{56}{n} + \frac{64}{3n^2}$$

So, $\displaystyle\int_0^4 (2x^2 - x)dx = \lim_{n\to\infty}\left(\frac{104}{3} + \frac{56}{n} + \frac{64}{n^2}\right) = \frac{104}{3}.$

(c) Set up the Riemann sum for $f(x) = x^3 + 1$ on $[2, 3]$ and then evaluate it to give the value of $\displaystyle\int_2^3 (x^3 + 1)dx.$

For this problem, $\Delta x = \dfrac{3-2}{n} = \dfrac{1}{n}$ and $x_i = 2 + \dfrac{i}{n}$, so the Riemann sum is

$$\sum_{i=1}^{n}\left(x_i^3 + 1\right)\Delta x = \sum_{i=1}^{n}\left(\left(2 + \frac{i}{n}\right)^3 + 1\right)\frac{1}{n}$$

$$= \sum_{i=1}^{n}\left(\frac{8}{n} + \frac{12}{n^2}i + \frac{6}{n^3}i^2 + \frac{1}{n^4}i^3 + \frac{1}{n}\right)$$

$$= \frac{9}{n}\sum_{i=1}^{n}1 + \frac{12}{n^2}\sum_{i=1}^{n}i + \frac{6}{n^3}\sum_{i=1}^{n}i^2 + \frac{1}{n^4}\sum_{i=1}^{n}i^3$$

$$= \frac{9}{n}(n) + \frac{12}{n^2}\left(\frac{n(n+1)}{2}\right) + \frac{6}{n^3}\left(\frac{n(n+1)(2n+1)}{6}\right) + \frac{1}{n^4}\left(\frac{n(n+1)}{2}\right)^2$$

$$= 9 + 6 + \frac{6}{n} + 2 + \frac{3}{n} + \frac{1}{n^2} + \frac{1}{4} + \frac{1}{2n} + \frac{1}{4n^2}$$

So, $\displaystyle\int_2^3 (x^3 + 1)dx = \lim_{n\to\infty}\left(\frac{69}{4} + \frac{19}{2n} + \frac{5}{n^2}\right) = \frac{69}{4}.$

Review Problems for Section 6.4.1

1. Express $\displaystyle\lim_{n\to\infty}\sum_{i=1}^{n} x_i^* \sin x_i^* \Delta x$ as a definite integral over $[-1, 3]$.

2. Set up the Riemann sum for $f(x) = 4x - 3$ on $[1, 6]$ then evaluate it to give the value of $\displaystyle\int_{1}^{6}(4x-3)\,dx$.

3. Set up the Riemann sum for $f(x) = 2x^3$ on $[0, 3]$ then evaluate it to give the value of $\displaystyle\int_{0}^{3}(2x^3)\,dx$.

Detailed Solutions

1. $\displaystyle\int_{-1}^{3} x\sin x\,dx$.

2. $\Delta x = \dfrac{6-1}{n} = \dfrac{5}{n}$ and $x_i = 1 + \dfrac{5i}{n}$. The Riemann sum is:

$$\sum_{i=1}^{n}(4x_i - 3)\Delta x = \sum_{i=1}^{n}\left(4\left(1+\frac{5i}{n}\right)-3\right)\frac{5}{n}$$

$$= \sum_{i=1}^{n}\left(\frac{5}{n}+\frac{100i}{n^2}\right) = \frac{5}{n}\sum_{i=1}^{n}1 + \frac{100}{n^2}\sum_{i=1}^{n}i$$

$$= \frac{5}{n}(n) + \frac{100}{n^2}\left(\frac{n(n+1)}{2}\right) = 5 + 50 + \frac{50}{n} = 55 + \frac{50}{n}$$

So, $\displaystyle\int_{1}^{6}(4x-3)\,dx = \lim_{n\to\infty}\left(55+\frac{50}{n}\right) = 55$.

3. $\Delta x = \dfrac{3-0}{n} = \dfrac{3}{n}$ and $x_i = \dfrac{3i}{n}$. The Riemann sum is:

$$\sum_{i=1}^{n}(2x_i^3)\Delta x = \sum_{i=1}^{n}2\left(\frac{3i}{n}\right)^3\frac{3}{n}$$

$$= \sum_{i=1}^{n}\frac{162}{n^4}i^3 = \frac{162}{n^4}\sum_{i=1}^{n}i^3$$

$$= \frac{162}{n^4}\left(\frac{n(n+1)}{2}\right)^2 = \frac{81}{2}+\frac{162}{n}+\frac{81}{2n^2}$$

So, $\displaystyle\int_{0}^{3}(2x^3)\,dx = \lim_{n\to\infty}\left(\frac{81}{2}+\frac{162}{n}+\frac{81}{2n^2}\right) = \frac{81}{2}$.

6.4.2 The California *Mathematics Subject Matter Requirements* stipulate that candidates for any credential program for teaching secondary mathematics must be able to *interpret the concept of a definite integral geometrically, numerically, and analytically (e.g., limit of Riemann sums).*

Interpreting Definite Integrals

The Definite Integral as Area

Given a continuous nonnegative function, f, the area of the region, R, bounded above by the graph of $y = f(x)$, below by the x-axis, and on the sides by the vertical lines $x = a$ and $x = b$ is (Figure 6.90):

$$A = \int_a^b f(x)\,dx = \lim_{n \to \infty} \sum_{i=1}^{n} f(x_i)\,\Delta x$$

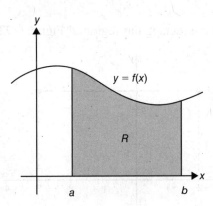

Figure 6.90

But if f takes on both positive and negative values over $[a, b]$ then we can think of both the Riemann sum and the integral as a "signed area." This means the integral over $[a, b]$ counts area above the x-axis as positive and are below the x-axis as negative (Figure 6.91), so

$$A = \int_a^b f(x)\,dx = \lim_{n \to \infty} \sum_{i=1}^{n} f(x_i)\,\Delta x$$

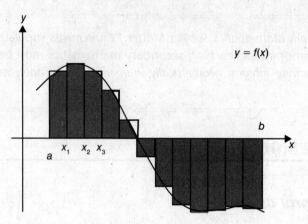

Figure 6.91

Examples: Evaluate each of the following:

(a) $\displaystyle\int_{-2}^{3} 5\,dx$ (b) $\displaystyle\int_{2}^{7}(10-3x)\,dx$ (c) $\displaystyle\int_{-4}^{0}\sqrt{16-x^2}\,dx$

(a) $\displaystyle\int_{-2}^{3} 5\,dx$ is the area in the rectangular region of Figure 6.92, which is $5(5) = 25$.

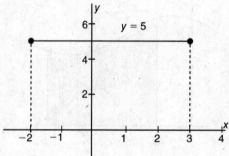

Figure 6.92

(b) Some area is above the x-axis and some is below, so the integral splits the interval up and calculates over each interval separately (Figure 6.93).

$$\int_{2}^{7}(10-3x)\,dx = A_1 - A_2$$

$$= \frac{1}{2}\left(\frac{4}{3}\right)(4) - \frac{1}{2}\left(\frac{11}{3}\right)(11)$$

$$= \frac{-105}{6} = \frac{-35}{2}$$

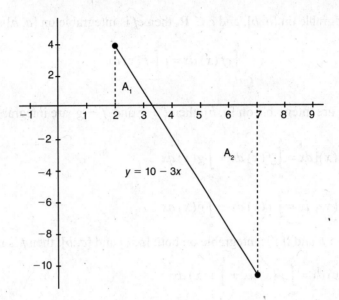

Figure 6.93

(c) $\displaystyle\int_{-4}^{0}\sqrt{16-x^2}\,dx = \frac{1}{4}\pi\left(4\right)^2 = 4\pi$

Figure 6.94 shows the region is a quarter circle with radius of 4.

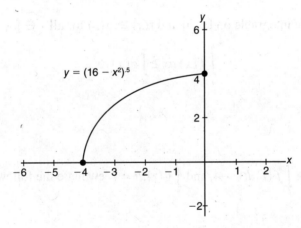

Figure 6.94

Properties of the Definite Integral

Theorem: If $f(a)$ exists, then $\displaystyle\int_{a}^{a} f(x)\,dx = 0$.

Theorem: If $c > d$ then $\displaystyle\int_{c}^{d} f(x)\,dx = -\int_{d}^{c} f(x)\,dx$.

Theorem: If c is a real number, then $\displaystyle\int_{a}^{b} c\,dx = c(b-a)$.

Theorem: If f is integrable on $[a, b]$, and $c \in \mathbf{R}$, then cf is integrable on $[a, b]$ and

$$\int_a^b cf(x)\, dx = c\int_a^b f(x)\, dx.$$

Theorem: If f and g are integrable on $[a, b]$, then $f + g$ and $f - g$ are integrable on $[a, b]$ and

(i) $\int_a^b [f(x) + g(x)]\, dx = \int_a^b f(x)\, dx + \int_a^b g(x)\, dx$

(ii) $\int_a^b [f(x) - g(x)]\, dx = \int_a^b f(x)\, dx - \int_a^b g(x)\, dx$

Theorem: If $a < c < b$ and if f is integrable on both $[a, c]$ and $[c, b]$, then f is integrable on $[a, b]$

and $\int_a^b f(x)\, dx = \int_a^c f(x)\, dx + \int_c^b f(x)\, dx.$

Theorem: If f is integrable on a closed interval and a, b, and c are any three numbers in that interval, then $\int_a^b f(x)\, dx = \int_a^c f(x)\, dx + \int_c^b f(x)\, dx.$

Theorem: If f is integrable on $[a, b]$ and $f(x) \geq 0$ for all $x \in [a, b]$, then $\int_a^b f(x)\, dx \geq 0$.

Corollary: If f and g are integrable on $[a, b]$ and $f(x) \geq g(x)$ for all $x \in [a, b]$, then

$$\int_a^b f(x)\, dx \geq \int_a^b g(x)\, dx.$$

Examples:

(a) Given $\int_0^5 f(t)\, dt = 6$, $\int_2^5 f(t)\, dt = -4$, and $\int_2^0 g(t)\, dt = 7$, evaluate the following:

(i) $\int_0^2 f(t)\, dt$

$$\int_0^2 f(t)\, dt = \int_0^5 f(t)\, dt - \int_2^5 f(t)\, dt = 6 - (-4) = 10$$

(ii) $\int_0^2 f(t) + 3g(t)\, dt$

$$\int_0^2 f(t) + 3g(t)\, dt = \int_0^2 f(t)\, dt + 3\int_0^2 g(t)\, dt = \int_0^2 f(t)\, dt - 3\int_2^0 g(t)\, dt = 10 - 3(7) = -11$$

(b) Consider $\int_{-2}^{2} f(x)\,dx$, where $f(x) = \begin{cases} 2x+4 & \text{when } x < 0 \\ -2x+4 & \text{when } x \geq 0 \end{cases}$ Interpret this integral

(i) geometrically

(ii) numerically

(iii) analytically (as a Riemann sum).

The graph of f is shown in Figure 6.95.

(i) Geometrically, $\int_{-2}^{2} f(x)\,dx$ is the area of $\triangle ABC$.

(ii) Numerically, $\int_{-2}^{2} f(x)\,dx = \dfrac{1}{2}(4)(4) = 8$.

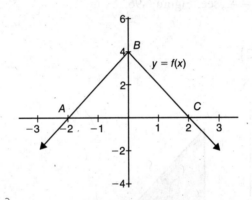

Figure 6.95

(iii) Analytically, $\int_{-2}^{2} f(x)\,dx = 2\int_{0}^{2}(-2x+4)\,dx = \lim_{n \to \infty} 2\sum_{i=1}^{n}\left(-2\left(\dfrac{2}{n}i\right)+4\right)\dfrac{2}{n}$, where the interval being partitioned is $(0, 2)$ and $\Delta x = \dfrac{2}{n}$, $x_i^* = \dfrac{2i}{n}$.

Review Problems for Section 6.4.2

1. Evaluate each of the following as an area (draw the graph!):

(a) $\int_{1}^{4}(6-2x)\,dx$

(b) $\int_{0}^{6} f(t)\,dt$ where $f(t) = \begin{cases} 3 & \text{when } t < 2 \\ -1 & \text{when } t \geq 2 \end{cases}$

2. If $\int_{0}^{3} f(t)\,dt = -2$, $\int_{6}^{3} f(t)\,dt = -5$, $\int_{3}^{0} g(t)\,dt = 3$. Evaluate:

(a) $\displaystyle\int_0^6 f(t)\,dt$

(b) $\displaystyle\int_0^3 2f(t)-g(t)\,dt$

3. Consider $\displaystyle\int_{-2}^2 f(x)\,dx$ where $f(x)=\sqrt{4-x^2}$. Interpret this integral

    (a) geometrically

    (b) numerically

    (c) analytically (as a Riemann sum).

Detailed Solutions

1. (a) $\displaystyle\int_1^4 (6-2x)\,dx = A_1 - A_2$, see. Figure 6.96.

$$= \frac{1}{2}(2)(4) - \frac{1}{2}(1)(2)$$
$$= 4 - 1 = 3$$

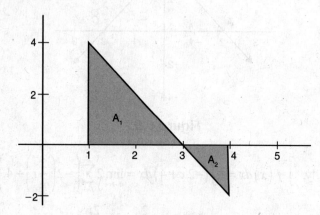

Figure 6.96

(b) $\displaystyle\int_0^6 f(t)\,dt$ where $f(t)=\begin{cases} 3 & \text{when } t < 2 \\ -1 & \text{when } t \geq 2 \end{cases}$

$\displaystyle\int_0^6 f(t)\,dt = A_1 - A_2 = 6 - 4 = 2$ (shown in Figure 6.97).

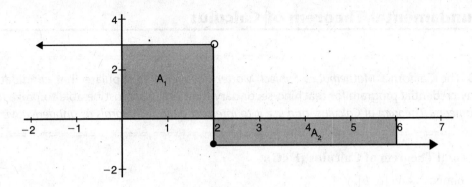

Figure 6.97

2. If $\int_{0}^{3} f(t)\,dt = -2$, $\int_{6}^{3} f(t)\,dt = -5$, $\int_{3}^{0} g(t)\,dt = 3$, Evaluate:

(a) $\int_{0}^{6} f(t)\,dt = \int_{0}^{3} f(t)\,dt + \int_{3}^{6} f(t)\,dt = \int_{0}^{3} f(t)\,dt - \int_{6}^{3} f(t)\,dt = -2 - (-5) = 3$

(b) $\int_{0}^{3} 2f(t) - g(t)\,dt = 2\int_{0}^{3} f(t)\,dt - \int_{0}^{3} g(t)\,dt = 2\int_{0}^{3} f(t)\,dt + \int_{3}^{0} g(t)\,dt = 2(-2) + 3 = -1$

3. $\int_{-2}^{2} \sqrt{4 - x^2}\,dx$

(a) $\int_{-2}^{2} \sqrt{4 - x^2}\,dx$ is the area enclosed in a semicircle of radius 2. (Figure 6.98)

(b) $\int_{-2}^{2} \sqrt{4 - x^2}\,dx = \frac{1}{2}\pi(2)^2 = 2\pi$

(c) $\int_{-2}^{2} \sqrt{4 - x^2}\,dx = 2\int_{0}^{2} \sqrt{4 - x^2}\,dx = 2\lim_{n \to \infty} \sum_{i=1}^{n}\left(\sqrt{4 - \left(\frac{2}{n}i\right)^2}\right)\frac{2}{n}$

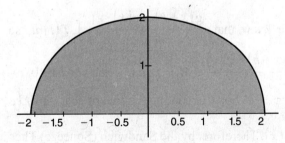

Figure 6.98

The Fundamental Theorem of Calculus

6.4.3 The California *Mathematics Subject Matter Requirements* stipulate that candidates for any credential program for teaching secondary mathematics must be able to *prove the Fundamental Theorem of Calculus, and use it to interpret definite integrals as antiderivatives.*

Fundamental Theorem of Calculus (FTC):

Let f be continuous on $[a, b]$.

I.   If $g(x) = \int_a^x f(t)\,dt$, then $g'(x) = f(x)$.

II. $\int_a^b f(x)\,dx = F(b) - F(a)$, where F is any antiderivative of f over $[a, b]$.

Proof (Part I): Let f be continuous on $[a, b]$.

Assume $g(x) = \int_a^x f(t)\,dt$. Then $g(x+h) - g(x) = \int_a^{x+h} f(t)\,dt - \int_a^x f(t)\,dt$

$$= \int_x^{x+h} f(t)\,dt.$$

So for h not equal to 0, $\dfrac{g(x+h) - g(x)}{h} = \dfrac{1}{h}\int_x^{x+h} f(t)\,dt.$

Now, f is continuous on $[a, b]$, and hence on any subset of it. Assuming that $h > 0$ (the case for $h < 0$ can be proven in the same manner), by the Extreme Value Theorem, f has an absolute minimum, m, and an absolute maximum, M, on $[x, x + h]$; say, $f(c) = m$ and $f(d) = M$, with $c, d \in [x, x + h]$.

Hence, since $m \le f(t) \le M$ for $x \le t \le x + h$, $mh \le \int_x^{x+h} f(t)\,dt \le Mh$. Then $h > 0$, thus

$m \le \dfrac{1}{h}\int_x^{x+h} f(t)\,dt \le M$. We know that $\dfrac{g(x+h) - g(x)}{h} = \dfrac{1}{h}\int_x^{x+h} f(t)\,dt$, so we may substitute this

to obtain $f(c) = m \le \dfrac{g(x+h) - g(x)}{h} \le M = f(d)$. Then as $h \to 0$, $c \to x$, and $d \to x$, since c and d lie between x and $x + h$. So, f is continuous means that $\lim\limits_{h \to 0} f(c) = \lim\limits_{c \to x} f(c) = f(x)$ and

$\lim\limits_{h \to 0} f(d) = \lim\limits_{d \to x} f(d) = f(x)$. Therefore, by the Sandwich (Squeeze) Theorem,

$$g'(x) = \lim_{h \to 0} \frac{g(x+h) - g(x)}{h} = f(x).$$

Q.E.D.

Proof (Part II): Let f be continuous on $[a, b]$ and let F be any antiderivative of f.

Partition $[a, b]$ into n subintervals with endpoints $a = x_0, x_1, x_2,..., x_n = b$ and with length $\Delta x = (b - a)/n$.

Let F be an antiderivative of f. Then:

$$F(b) - F(a) = F(x_n) - F(x_0)$$
$$= F(x_n) - F(x_{n-1}) + F(x_{n-1}) - F(x_{n-2}) + \cdots + F(x_2) - F(x_1) + F(x_1) - F(x_0)$$
$$= \sum_{i=1}^{n} \left[F(x_i) - F(x_{i-1}) \right]$$

Since F is differentiable, it is continuous. The Mean Value Theorem thus is true on each $\left[x_{i-1}, x_i \right]$. Hence, for each i, there is a number $x_i^* \in (x_{i-1}, x_i)$ such that $F(x_i) - F(x_{i-1}) = F'(x_i^*)(x_i - x_{i-1}) = f(x_i^*)\Delta x$. Therefore, $F(b) - F(a) = \sum_{i=1}^{n} \left[F(x_i) - F(x_{i-1}) \right] = \sum_{i=1}^{n} f(x_i^*)\Delta x$. Taking the limit, we have

$$= \lim_{n \to \infty} (F(b) - F(a)) = \lim_{n \to \infty} \sum_{i=1}^{n} f(x_i^*)\Delta x = \int_a^b f(x)\,dx.$$

Q.E.D.

Notation: $F(x)\Big|_a^b = F(b) - F(a)$

Examples:

(a) Find F' for each of the following:

(i) $F(x) = \int_1^x te^t\,dt \implies F'(x) = xe^x$ by a direct application of the FTC, part I.

(ii) $F(x) = \int_0^{x^2} \sin t\,dt \implies F'(x) = \left(\sin(x^2) \right) \cdot \frac{d}{dx}(x^2) = 2x\sin(x^2)$ by the FTC, part I, and the Chain Rule.

(iii) $F(x) = \int_{2x}^{3} 5 + \cos t\,dt = -\int_{3}^{2x} 5 + \cos t\,dt \implies F'(x) = -(5 + \cos x)(2x)' = -2(5 + \cos x)$

(b) Evaluate:

(i) $\int_{-1}^{2} (t - t^2)\,dt$

$$\int_{-1}^{2} (t - t^2)\,dt = \left(\frac{1}{2}t^2 - \frac{1}{3}t^3 \right)\Big|_{-1}^{2} = \left(2 - \frac{8}{3} \right) - \left(\frac{1}{2} + \frac{1}{3} \right) = -\frac{3}{2}$$

(ii) $\int_0^{\frac{\pi}{4}} \left(\sec^2 t\right) dt$

$$\int_0^{\frac{\pi}{4}} \left(\sec^2 t\right) dt = \left(\tan x\right)\Big|_0^{\frac{\pi}{4}} = \tan\frac{\pi}{4} - \tan 0 = 1$$

(iii) $\int_1^0 \left(3^u\right) du$

$$\int_1^0 \left(3^u\right) du = \left(\frac{1}{\ln 3} 3^u\right)\Big|_1^0 = \frac{1}{\ln 3}\left(3^0 - 3^1\right) = \frac{-2}{\ln 3}$$

Review Problems for Section 6.4.3

1. Find F' for each of the following:

   (a) $F(x) = \int_1^x v \ln v \, dv$

   (b) $F(x) = \int_{\sin x}^0 e^\beta \, d\beta$

   (c) $F(x) = \int_2^{3-x} \csc t \, dt$

2. Evaluate:

   (a) $\int_3^e \left(\frac{1}{x} + x^2\right) dx$

   (b) $\int_0^{\frac{\pi}{3}} \left(\cos t + 1\right) dt$

   (c) $\int_1^1 \left(5^t\right) dt$

3. State and prove both parts of the Fundamental Theorem of Calculus.

Detailed Solutions

1. (a) $F(x) = \int_1^x v \ln v \, dv \Rightarrow F'(x) = x \ln x$, using the FTC, part I, directly.

   (b) $F(x) = \int_{\sin x}^0 e^\beta \, d\beta = -\int_0^{\sin x} e^\beta \, d\beta \Rightarrow F'(x) = -e^{\sin x}\left(\sin x\right)' = -e^{\sin x}\cos x$, using the FTC, Part I,

   and the Chain Rule.

   (c) $F(x) = \int_2^{3-x} \csc t \, dt \Rightarrow F'(x) = \csc(3-x)\cdot(3-x)' = -\csc(3-x)$ using the FTC, Part I,

   and the Chain Rule.

2. (a) $\int_{3}^{e}\left(\dfrac{1}{x}+x^{2}\right)dx=\left(\ln|x|+\dfrac{1}{3}x^{3}dx\right)\Big|_{3}^{e}=\left(\ln e+\dfrac{1}{3}e^{3}\right)-\left(\ln 3+9\right)=-8+\dfrac{1}{3}e^{3}-\ln 3.$

    (b) $\int_{0}^{\frac{\pi}{3}}(\cos t+1)dt=(\sin t+t)\Big|_{0}^{\frac{\pi}{3}}=\left(\left(\sin\dfrac{\pi}{3}+\dfrac{\pi}{3}\right)\right)-(\sin 0+0)=\dfrac{\sqrt{3}}{2}+\dfrac{\pi}{3}.$

    (c) $\int_{1}^{1}\left(5^{t}\right)dt=0$ since the interval of integration has 0 width.

3. This is in the section. Practice!

> **6.4.4** The California *Mathematics Subject Matter Requirements* stipulate that candidates for any credential program for teaching secondary mathematics must be able *to apply the concept of integrals to compute the length of curves and the areas and volumes of geometric figures.*

Area

Theorem: If f and g are continuous and $f(x) \geq g(x)$ for all $x \in [a, b]$, then the area A of the region bounded by the graphs of f, g, $x = a$, and $x = b$ is

$$A=\lim_{n\to\infty}\sum_{i=1}^{n}[f(x_{i}^{*})-g(x_{i}^{*})]\,\Delta x=\int_{a}^{b}[f(x)-g(x)]\,dx$$

where $[a, b]$ has been partitioned by $a = x_0, x_1, x_2, \ldots, x_n = b$; $x_{i}^{*} \in \left[x_{i-1}, x_{i}\right]$ for each $i = 1, 2, 3, \ldots,$ n; and $\Delta x_{i} = x_{i} - x_{i-1}$ for all i.

- A region is called an R_{x} **region** if it lies between the graphs of two equations $y = f(x)$ and $y = g(x)$, with f and g being continuous and such that $f(x) \geq g(x)$ for every $x \in [a, b]$. We call the graph of f the **upper boundary** and the graph of g the **lower boundary**.

Finding the Area of an R_{x} Type of Region

1. Sketch the region, labeling the upper boundary $y = f(x)$ and lower boundary $y = g(x)$. Find the least value $x = a$ and the greatest value $x = b$ for points in the region.

2. Sketch a typical vertical rectangle and label its width dx.

3. Express the area of the rectangle as $[f(x) - g(x)]\,dx$.

4. Apply the limit of sums operator $\int_{a}^{b}$ to the expression in step 3 and then evaluate the integral.

- A region is called an R_{y} **region** if it lies between the graphs of two equations $x = f(y)$ and $x = g(y)$, with f and g being continuous and such that $f(y) \geq g(y)$ for every $y \in [c, d]$. We call the graph of f the **right boundary** and the graph of g the **left boundary**.

Examples:

(a) Find the area between the functions $y = x^3$ and $y = 12 - x^2$ over $[0, 4]$.

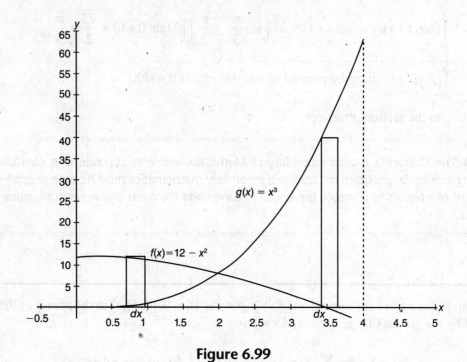

Figure 6.99

This is an R_x region (Figure 6.99) but the upper and lower boundaries switch part way through the interval ($x = 2$). So we will need to use two integrals to find the area.

$$A = \int_0^2 \left[(12 - x^2) - (x^3) \right] dx + \int_2^4 \left[(x^3) - (12 - x^2) \right] dx$$

$$= \left[12x - \frac{1}{3}x^3 - \frac{1}{4}x^4 \right]_0^2 + \left[\frac{1}{4}x^4 - 12x + \frac{1}{3}x^3 \right]_2^4$$

$$= \left(24 - \frac{8}{3} - 4 - 0 \right) + \left(64 - 48 + \frac{64}{3} \right) - \left(4 - 24 + \frac{8}{3} \right)$$

$$= \frac{1076}{3} = 72$$

(b) Find the area enclosed between the curves $x = y^2$ and $x + y = 6$.

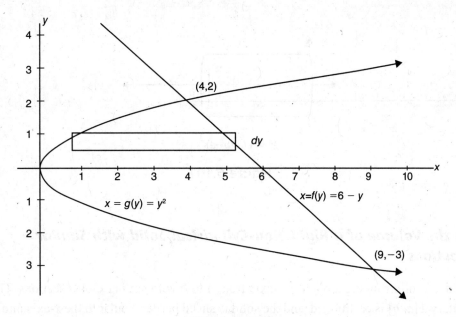

Figure 6.100

This is an R_y region (Figure 6.100).

$$A = \int_{-3}^{2}\left[(6-y)-y^2\right]dy = \left[6y - \frac{1}{2}y^2 - \frac{1}{3}y^3\right]_{-3}^{2} = \left(12 - 2 - \frac{8}{3}\right) - \left(-18 - \frac{9}{2} + 9\right) = 20\frac{5}{6}$$

Volume

Volumes by Cross-Sections

- If a plane intersects a solid, the region common to the plane and the solid is called a **cross-section of the solid**.

- Consider a solid with the following property: For every $x \in [a, b]$, the plane perpendicular to the x-axis at x intersects the solid in a cross-section whose area is $A(x)$, where A is a continuous function of x on $[a, b]$. The solid is called a **right cylinder** if the solid can be generated by translating the cross-section along a line parallel to the x-axis (with the cross-section perpendicular to the line). Note all the cross sections are congruent (Figure 6.101). In this case, the volume of the solid is $A(a) \cdot (b - a)$, where $A(a)$ is the area of the cross-section at $x = a$ (which happens to be the area of every cross-section in this case!)

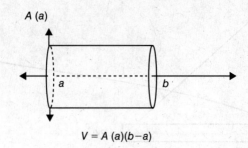

$$V = A(a)(b-a)$$

Figure 6.101

Finding the Volume of a Right Non-Cylindrical Solid with Similar Cross-Sections

Consider a solid running along the x-axis from a to b with similar cross-sections. The idea is that the interval $[a, b]$ is partitioned, and the solid is sliced perpendicular to the x-axis into n pieces, each with volume approximately equal to the area of the cross-section $A(x_i^*)$ times its thickness dx.

Example:

The cross sections in Figure 6.102 are squares. The length of one side of the square is $2y$, so the area of the square is $4y^2$. Assuming the boundary of the circular base has equation $x^2 + y^2 = r^2$, the area of the cross-section is $A(x) = 4(r^2 - x^2)$.

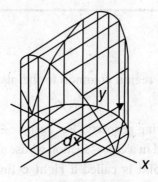

Figure 6.102

Returning to the general problem, after we find $A(x)$ we add up the volumes of the n cross-sections and take the limit. This is an integral

$$V = \lim_{n \to \infty} \sum_{i=1}^{n} A(x_i^*) dx = \int_a^b A(x) dx$$

The steps to finding the volume are as follows:

1. Sketch the solid above and parallel to the x-axis, labeling the x-axis at the right end b and at the left end a.

2. Sketch a typical vertical slice and label its width dx.

3. Express the volume of the slice as $A(x)\,dx$, where $A(x)$ is the area of the cross section.

4. Apply the limit of sums operator to the expression in step 3 and then evaluate the integral (i.e., use the following theorem).

Theorem: Let S be a solid bounded by planes that are perpendicular to the x-axis at a and b. If, for every $x \in [a, b]$, the cross-sectional area of S is given by the function $A(x)$, where A is continuous on $[a, b]$, then the volume of S is:

$$V = \lim_{n \to \infty} \sum_{i=1}^{n} A(x_i)\,dx = \int_a^b A(x)\,dx$$

Example: The base of a solid is the region enclosed by the graph $y = e^{-x}$, the coordinate axes, and the line $x = 3$. If all plane cross sections perpendicular to the x-axis are equilateral triangles, what is the volume of the solid?

The base of the equilateral triangle is shown in Figure 6.103. The base of the equilateral triangle has $y = f(x_i) = e^{-x_i}$.

The equilateral triangles (not shown here) rise out of the xy-plane.

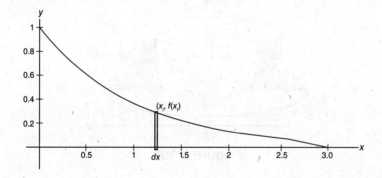

Figure 6.103

The area of an equilateral triangle $\dfrac{s^2\sqrt{3}}{4}$, so $A(x) = \dfrac{\left(e^{-x}\right)^2 \sqrt{3}}{4} = \dfrac{\sqrt{3}e^{-2x}}{4}$, and the volume

is $V = \displaystyle\int_0^3 \dfrac{\sqrt{3}e^{-2x}}{4}\,dx = \left[\dfrac{\sqrt{3}}{-8}e^{-2x}\right]_0^3 = \dfrac{-\sqrt{3}}{8}\left(e^{-6} - 1\right) \approx 0.216$.

Volumes of Solids of Revolution

Type I Problem:

(a) Let f and g be continuous on $[a, b]$ with $f(x) \geq g(x)$ for all $x \in [a, b]$. And let R be the region bounded by the graphs of f and g, and the vertical lines $x = a$ and $x = b$. Find the volume V of the solid of revolution generated by revolving R about the line $y = t$ (Figure 6.104).

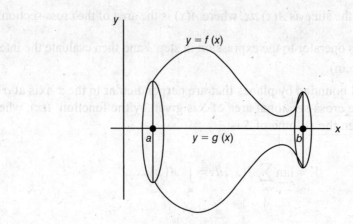

Figure 6.104

Type II Problem:

Let f and g be continuous on $[c, d]$ with $f(y) > g(y)$ for all $y \in [c, d]$. And let R be the region bounded by the graphs of f and g, and the horizontal lines $y = c$ and $y = d$. Find the volume V of the solid of revolution generated by revolving R about the line $x = t$ (Figure 6.105).

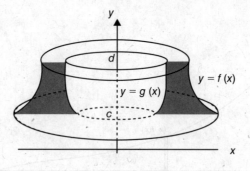

Figure 6.105

• These problems can be solved by using the theorem on volumes of a solid with known cross-section since all the cross- sections in these problems are disks or washers.

To find the volume of a solid of revolution by using disks or washers, follow these steps:

1. Sketch the region P to be revolved and label the boundaries. Sketch a typical vertical rectangle of width dx or a horizontal rectangle of width dy.

2. Sketch the solid generated by P and the disk or washer generated by the rectangle.

3. Express the volume of the disk (πR^2) or washer ($\pi(R^2 - r^2)$) in terms of x or y, depending on whether the thickness is dx or dy.

4. Apply the limit of sums operator to the expression in step 3 and then evaluate the integral.

Example:

(a) The region bounded by the x-axis, the graph of the equation $y = x^2 + 1$, and the lines $x = -1$ and $x = 1$ is revolved about the x-axis. Find the volume of the resulting solid.

Sketch of the region to be revolved.

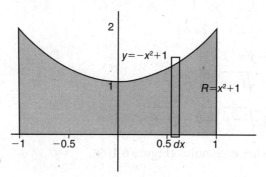

Figure 6.106

Solid resulting from revolution.

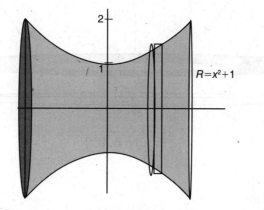

Figure 6.107

$$V = \int_{-1}^{1} \pi\left(x^2 + 1\right)^2 dx$$

$$= \pi\left(\frac{1}{5}x^5 + \frac{2}{3}x^3 + x\right)\Bigg|_{-1}^{1} = 2\pi\left(\frac{1}{5} + \frac{2}{3} + 1\right) = \frac{56}{15}\pi$$

(b) The region in the first quadrant bounded by the graphs of the equations $x^2 = 2x - y$, $x = 1$, and $y = 0$ is revolved about the line $x = 3$. Find the volume of the resulting solid.

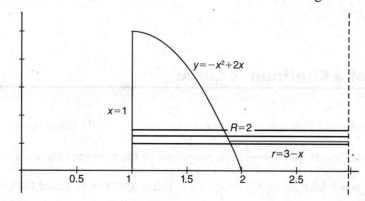

Figure 6.108

Draw Figure 6.108.

$$y = -x^2 + 2x \Leftrightarrow 1 - y = x^2 - 2x + 1$$
$$\Leftrightarrow 1 - y = (x - 1)^2$$
$$\Leftrightarrow 1 + \sqrt{1 - y} = x$$

$$r = 3 - x = 3 - \left(1 + \sqrt{1 - y}\right) = 2 - \sqrt{1 - y}$$

The cross-section is a washer or annulus (Figure 6.109).

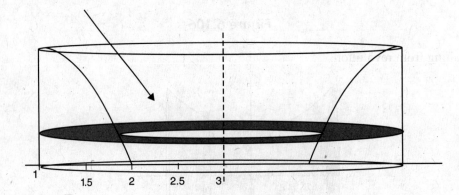

Figure 6.109

$$V = \pi \int_0^1 \left(R^2 - r^2\right) dy$$

$$= \pi \int_0^1 \left[\left(2^2\right) - \left(2 - \sqrt{1 - y}\right)^2\right] dy$$

$$= \pi \int_0^1 \left[y - 1 + 4\sqrt{1 - y}\right] dy$$

$$= \pi \left(\frac{1}{2}y^2 - y - \frac{8}{3}(1 - y)^{\frac{3}{2}}\right)_0^1$$

$$= \pi \left(-\frac{1}{2} - \left(-\frac{8}{3}\right)\right) = \frac{13}{6}\pi$$

Arc Length of a Continuous Curve

Consider a continuous function $y = f(x)$ on an interval $[a, b]$. Partition the interval $[a, b]$ into n subintervals of equal length $\Delta x = \dfrac{b - a}{n}$; the endpoints of the subintervals are $a = x_0$, $x_1 = a + \Delta x$, $x_2 = a + 2\Delta x, ..., x_k = a + k\Delta x, ...,$ so $x_{n-1} = a + (n - 1)\Delta x$, and $x_n = b$. Label the points on the curve (Figure 6.110).

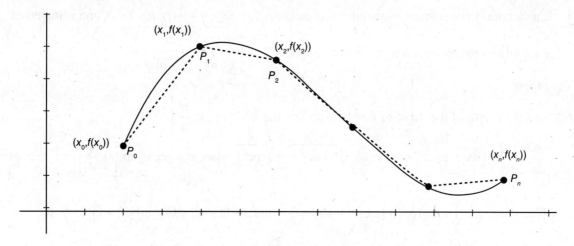

Figure 6.110

The length of the curve is approximated by the sums of the lengths of the line segments joining the consecutive points. Denote the length of the kth segment by $|P_{k-1}P_k|$.

$$|P_{k-1}P_k| = \sqrt{(x_k - x_{k-1})^2 + (f(x_k) - f(x_{k-1}))^2} =$$

$$\sqrt{(\Delta x_k)^2 + (\Delta y_k)^2} = \sqrt{1 + \frac{(\Delta y_k)^2}{(\Delta x_k)^2}}\,\Delta x_k = \sqrt{1 + \frac{(\Delta y_k)^2}{(\Delta x)^2}}\,\Delta x.$$

Since f is differentiable on $[a, b]$, we can apply the Mean Value Theorem. So since f is differentiable in each subinterval of the partition, there exists a value $x_k^* \in \left[x_{k-1}, x_k\right]$ such that

$$f(x_k) - f(x_{k-1}) = f'(x_k^*)(x_k - x_{k-1}) \iff \Delta y_k = f'(x_k^*)\Delta x \iff f'(x_k^*) = \frac{\Delta y_k}{\Delta x}. \text{ Hence, we can}$$

write $|P_{k-1}P_k| = \sqrt{1 + \left(f(x_k^*)\right)^2}\,\Delta x$, and the length of the curve, L, can be approximated by

$$L \approx \sum_{k=1}^{n}\sqrt{1 + \left(f(x_k^*)\right)^2}\,\Delta x.$$

Using the definition of the integral, as we increase the number of subintervals in our partition, the approximation becomes increasingly better, and we have

$$L = \lim_{n \to \infty}\sum_{k=1}^{n}\sqrt{1 + \left(f(x_k^*)\right)^2}\,\Delta x = \int_a^b \sqrt{1 + \left(f'(x)\right)^2}\,dx = \int_a^b \sqrt{1 + \left(\frac{dy}{dx}\right)^2}\,dx$$

Theorem: Let f be a smooth curve on the interval $[a, b]$. Then the length of the

curve is $L = \int_a^b \sqrt{1 + \left(\frac{dy}{dx}\right)^2}\,dx$.

- If a smooth curve has equation $x = g(y)$, $a \le y \le b$, the length is $L = \int_a^b \sqrt{1 + \left(\frac{dx}{dy}\right)^2}\,dy$.

- If a smooth curve is given by parametric equations $x = x(t)$, $y = y(t)$, $a \le t \le b$, and is traversed once as t increases from a to b, then its length is $L = \int_a^b \sqrt{\left(\frac{dx}{dt}\right)^2 + \left(\frac{dy}{dt}\right)^2}\, dt$.

Examples:

(a) Find the length of the curve of $y = \ln(\sec x)$ on the interval $\left[0, \frac{\pi}{4}\right]$.

$\dfrac{dy}{dx} = \dfrac{1}{\sec x}(\sec x \tan x) = \tan x$, so $\sqrt{1 + \tan^2 x} = \sqrt{\sec^2 x} = |\sec x| = \sec x$ on $\left[0, \frac{\pi}{4}\right]$.

Therefore, $L = \int_0^{\frac{\pi}{4}} \sec x\, dx = \ln|\sec x + \tan x|\Big|_0^{\frac{\pi}{4}} = \ln|\sqrt{2} + 1| - \ln|1 + 0| = \ln\left(\sqrt{2} + 1\right)$.

(b) Find the arc length of a curve given parametrically by $x = 2t^2$, $y = 2t^3$ over $[1, 4]$.

$\dfrac{dy}{dt} = 6t^2$ and $\dfrac{dx}{dt} = 4t$, so $\sqrt{\left(\frac{dx}{dt}\right)^2 + \left(\frac{dy}{dt}\right)^2} = \sqrt{(4t)^2 + (6t^2)^2} = \sqrt{16t^2 + 36t^4} = 2t\sqrt{4 + 9t^2}$

Hence, $L = \int_1^4 2t\sqrt{4 + 9t^2}\, dt = \dfrac{1}{9}\int_{13}^{148} \sqrt{u}\, du$ if we set $u = 4 + 9t^2$ so that $du = 18t\,dt$ or this can be

seen as $2t\,dt = \dfrac{1}{9}du$. Note that $u = 13$ when $t = 1$, and $u = 148$ when $t = 4$. Computing, we find

$L = \dfrac{1}{9}\int_{13}^{148} \sqrt{u}\, du = \dfrac{2}{27}u^{\frac{3}{2}}\Big|_{13}^{148} = \dfrac{2}{27}\left(148\sqrt{148} - 13\sqrt{13}\right)$.

■ Review Problems for Section 6.4.4

1. Use the method of volume of a solid of revolution to prove that the volume of a cone is $V = \dfrac{1}{3}\pi r^2 h$.

2. Find the area enclosed between the curves $f(x) = x^2 - 3x + 12$ and $g(x) = -x^2 + x + 18$.

3. The base of a solid is the region bounded by $y = 1 - x^2$ and $y = x^4 - 1$. Cross sections of the solid that are perpendicular to the x-axis are semicircles. Find the volume of the solid.

4. Find the length of the curve $y^2 = (2x - 1)^3$, cut off by the line $x = 4$.

5. Find the arc length of a curve given parametrically by $x = 2\sin t$, $y = 2\cos t$ over $[0, \frac{3}{4}\pi]$.

Detailed Solutions

1. A cone can be generated by revolving a segment of the line $y = \dfrac{r}{h}x$ about the *x*-axis (Figure 6.111 and 6.112).

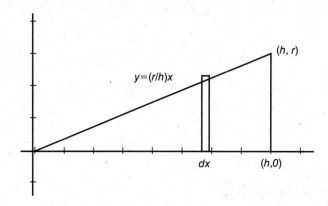

Figure 6.111   **Figure 6.112**

Then using volumes of solids with known cross-sections, the volume of the cone is

$$V = \pi \int_0^h \left(\frac{r}{h}x\right)^2 dx = \pi \frac{r^2}{h^2} \int_0^h x^2 dx = \pi \frac{r^2}{h^2}\left(\frac{1}{3}x^3\right)\Big|_0^h = \pi \frac{r^2}{h^2}\left(\frac{1}{3}h^3\right)\Big| = \frac{1}{3}\pi r^2 h$$

2. Sketch $-x^2 + x + 18 = x^2 - 3x + 12$ to see the desired area (Figure 6.113).

$$2x^2 - 4x - 6 = 0$$
$$2(x-3)(x+1) = 0$$

are the points of intersection.

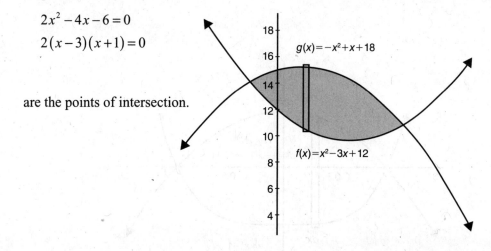

Figure 6.113

$$A = \int_{-1}^{3} \left(-x^2 + x + 18\right) - \left(x^2 - 3x + 12\right) dx$$

$$= \int_{-1}^{3} \left(-2x^2 + 4x + 6\right) dx$$

$$= \left(\frac{-2}{3}x^3 + 2x^2 + 6x\right)\Big|_{-1}^{3}$$

$$= \left(-18 + 18 + 18\right) - \left(\frac{2}{3} + 2 - 6\right)$$

$$= \frac{64}{3}$$

3. Sketch the curves to see the desired volume (Figure 6.114).

$$V = 2\int_{0}^{1} \pi \left(\frac{1}{2}\left(2 - x^2 - x^4\right)\right)^2 dx$$

$$= \frac{\pi}{2} \int_{0}^{1} \left(4 - 4x^2 - 3x^4 + 2x^6 + x^8\right) dx$$

$$= \frac{\pi}{2} \left[4x - \frac{4}{3}x^3 - \frac{3}{5}x^5 + \frac{2}{7}x^7 + \frac{1}{9}x^9\right]_{0}^{1}$$

$$= \frac{\pi}{2} \left[4 - \frac{4}{3} - \frac{3}{5} + \frac{2}{7} + \frac{1}{9}\right]$$

$$\approx 3.87$$

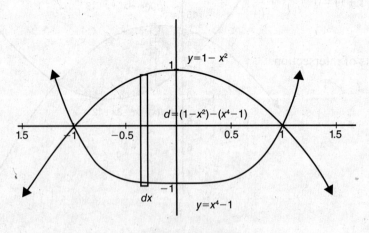

Figure 6.114

4. The curve is symmetric. So we can find the length of the upper portion of the arc and double it.

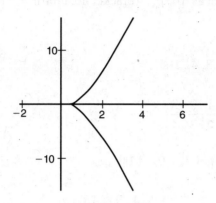

Figure 6.115

$$y = (2x-1)^{\frac{3}{2}} \quad \frac{dy}{dx} = \frac{3}{2}(2x-1)^{\frac{1}{2}}(2) = 3(2x-1)^{\frac{1}{2}},$$

so $\sqrt{1+\left(\dfrac{dy}{dx}\right)^2} = \sqrt{1+9(2x-1)} = \sqrt{18x-8}$.

$$L = 2\int_{\frac{1}{2}}^{4} \sqrt{18x-8}\,dx = \frac{2}{18}(18x-8)^{\frac{3}{2}}\left(\frac{2}{3}\right)\Bigg|_{\frac{1}{2}}^{4} = \frac{2}{27}\left(64^{\frac{3}{2}} - (1)^{\frac{3}{2}}\right) \approx 39.85$$

5. $x = 2\sin t$, $y = 2\cos t$, $\dfrac{dx}{dt} = 2\cos t$, and $\dfrac{dy}{dt} = -2\sin t$. Then $\left(\dfrac{dx}{dt}\right)^2 + \left(\dfrac{dy}{dt}\right)^2 = 4$ and

$$L = \int_{0}^{\frac{3\pi}{4}} \sqrt{4}\,dt = 2t\Big|_{0}^{\frac{3\pi}{4}} = \frac{3}{2}\pi$$

6.5 Sequences and Series

6.5.1 The California *Mathematics Subject Matter Requirements* stipulate that candidates for any credential program for teaching secondary mathematics must be able to *derive and apply the formulas for the sums of finite arithmetic series and finite and infinite geometric series (e.g., express repeating decimals as a rational number).*

Formulas for Sums

A **sequence** is a function, f, whose domain is the set of positive integers, written as

$$f(1), f(2), f(3), f(4), f(5), \cdots, f(n), \cdots$$

or

$$a_1, a_2, a_3, a_4, a_5, \cdots, a_n, \cdots$$

This can also be written as $\{a_n\}_{n=1}^{\infty}$ (bracket notation).

Examples:

(a) $\{n\}_{n=1}^{\infty}$ represents 1, 2, 3, 4,...

(b) $\left\{\dfrac{n}{n+1}\right\}_{n=1}^{\infty}$ represents $\dfrac{1}{2}, \dfrac{2}{3}, \dfrac{3}{4},...$

(c) $\left\{1+(.1)^k\right\}_{k=1}^{\infty}$ represents 1.1, 1.01. 1.001,...

(d) $\left\{(-1)^{n+1}\dfrac{n^2}{3n-1}\right\}_{n=1}^{\infty}$ represents $\dfrac{1}{2}, -\dfrac{4}{5}, \dfrac{9}{8}, -\dfrac{16}{11},...$

Arithmetic Sequence

- An infinite sequence of numbers $\{a_n\}_{n=1}^{\infty}$ is called an **arithmetic sequence** if there exists a number d, such that for every $n \geq 1$, $a_{n+1} = a_n + d$. The number d is called the **common difference**, or just the difference of the arithmetic sequence.

Examples:

(a) $a_1 = 2, d = 3$: 2, 5, 8, 11,...

(b) $a_1 = 7, d = -1$: 7, 6, 5,...

(c) $a_1 = 5, d = 0$: 5, 5, 5,...

Theorem: Let $\{a_n\}_{n=1}^{\infty}$ be an arithmetic sequence. Then:

(a) for all positive integers n, for $a_n = a_1 + (n-1)d$

(b) $S_n = a_1 + a_2 + \cdots + a_n = \dfrac{a_1 + a_n}{2}n$ for all positive integers n.

Proof: Let $\{a_n\}_{n=1}^{\infty}$ be an arithmetic sequence.

(a) Let S be the statement $a_n = a_1 + (n-1)d$, where n is a positive integer and d is the common difference.

Since $a_1 = a_1 + (1-1)d$, S is true for $n = 1$.

Assume S is true for k, where k is any fixed but arbitrary integer greater than or equal to 1. Then $a_k = a_1 + (k-1)d$ and $a_{k+1} = a_k + d = a_1 + (k-1)d + d = a_1 + ((k+1)-1)d$.

Therefore, S is true for $k+1$ whenever it is true for k.

By the Principle of Mathematical Induction, $a_n = a_1 + (n-1)d$ is true for all positive integers n.

(b) Let S be the statement $S_n = a_1 + a_2 + \cdots + a_n = \dfrac{a_1 + a_n}{2} n$, where n is a positive integer.

$S_1 = a_1 = \dfrac{a_1 + a_1}{2}(1)$, so S is true for 1.

Assume S is true for k, where k is any fixed but arbitrary integer greater than or equal to 1.

Then $S_k = a_1 + a_2 + \cdots + a_k = \dfrac{a_1 + a_k}{2} k$ and $S_{k+1} = S_k + a_{k+1} = \dfrac{a_1 + a_k}{2} k + a_{k+1}$. By the defini-

tion of arithmetic sequence, $a_{k+1} = a_k + d$, or $a_k = a_{k+1} - d$. Substituting, we obtain

$$S_{k+1} = \frac{a_1 + (a_{k+1} - d)}{2} k + a_{k+1}$$

$$= \frac{a_1 + (a_{k+1} - d)}{2} k + \frac{2a_{k+1}}{2}$$

$$= \frac{a_1 k + a_{k+1}(k+1) - dk + a_{k+1}}{2}$$

$$= \frac{a_1 k + a_{k+1}(k+1) - dk + (a_1 + kd)}{2}$$

$$= \left(\frac{a_1 + a_{k+1}}{2}\right)(k+1)$$

Therefore, S is true for $k + 1$ whenever it is true for k.

By the Principle of Mathematical Induction, $S_n = a_1 + a_2 + \cdots + a_n = \dfrac{a_1 + a_n}{2} n$ for all $n \geq 1$.

Q.E.D.

Corollary: Let $\{a_n\}_{n=1}^{\infty}$ be an arithmetic sequence. Then:

$$S_n = \frac{2a_1 + (n-1)d}{2} n$$

Examples:

(a) Find the sum of the first 60 terms of the sequence 3, 7, 11, 15,...

$$S_{60} = \frac{2a_1 + (60-1)d}{2}(60) = \frac{2(3) + (59)(4)}{2}(60) = 7260.$$

(b) Find the 40th term of the sequence 4, 7, 10...

$$a_{40} = a_1 + (40-1)(3) = 4 + 39(3) = 121$$

Geometric Sequences

- An infinite sequence of numbers $\{a_n\}_{n=1}^{\infty}$ is called a **geometric sequence** if there exists a number r such that for every $n \geq 1$, $a_{n+1} = a_n r$. The number r is called the **common ratio**, or just the ratio of the geometric sequence.

Examples:

(a) $a_1 = 2, r = 3$: 2, 6, 18, 54,...

(b) $a_1 = 1, r = -2$: 1, -2, 4, -8,...

(c) $a_1 = 5, r$ $\dfrac{1}{4}$: 5, $\dfrac{5}{4}$, $\dfrac{5}{16}$,...

Theorem: Let $\{a_n\}_{n=1}^{\infty}$ be a geometric sequence with common ratio r. Then:

(a) for all positive integers n, $a_n = a_1 r^{(n-1)}$

(b) $S_n = a_1 + a_2 + \cdots + a_n = \dfrac{a_1\left(1 - r^n\right)}{1 - r}$ if $r \neq 1$, for all positive integers n. If $r = 1$, $S_n = na_1$

Proof: Let $\{a_n\}_{n=1}^{\infty}$ be a geometric sequence with common ratio r.

(a) Let S be the statement $a_n = a_1 r^{(n-1)}$, where n is a positive integer and r is the common ratio.

Since $a_1 = a_1 r^{(1-1)}$, S is true for $n = 1$.

Assume S is true for k, where k is any fixed but arbitrary integer greater than or equal to 1. Then $a_k = a_1 r^{(k-1)}$ and $a_{k+1} = a_k r = a_1 r^{(k-1)}\left(r\right) = a_1 r^k$.

Therefore, S is true for $k + 1$ whenever it is true for k.

By the Principle of Mathematical Induction, $a_n = a_1 r^{(n-1)}$ is true for all positive integers n.

(b) Let S be the statement $S_n = a_1 + a_2 + \cdots + a_n = \dfrac{a_1\left(1 - r^n\right)}{1 - r}$ if $r \neq 1$, where n is a positive integer.

$S_1 = \dfrac{a_1\left(1 - r^1\right)}{1 - r} = a_1$, so S is true for 1.

Assume S is true for k, where k is any fixed but arbitrary integer greater than or equal to 1. Then $S_k = a_1 + a_2 + \cdots + a_k = \dfrac{a_1\left(1 - r^k\right)}{1 - r}$ and $S_{k+1} = S_k + a_{k+1}$. Using the definition of geometric sequence, we obtain,

$$S_{k+1} = S_k + a_{k+1}$$

$$= \frac{a_1\left(1-r^k\right)}{1-r} + a_1 r^k$$

$$= \frac{a_1\left(1-r^k\right)}{1-r} + \frac{a_1 r^k\left(1-r\right)}{1-r}$$

$$= \frac{a_1 - a_1 r^k + a_1 r^k - a_1 r^{k+1}}{1-r}$$

$$= \frac{a_1 - a_1 r^{k+1}}{1-r}$$

$$= \frac{a_1\left(1-r^{k+1}\right)}{1-r}$$

Therefore, S is true for $k+1$ whenever it is true for k.

By the Principle of Mathematical Induction, $S_n = a_1 + a_2 + \cdots + a_n = \dfrac{a_1\left(1-r^n\right)}{1-r}$ if $r \neq 1$ for all $n \geq 1$.

If $r = 1$, $S_n = a_1 + a_2 + \cdots + a_n = \displaystyle\sum_{i=1}^{n} a_1 = na_1$.

Q.E.D.

Examples:

(a) Find the 17th term of the sequence $-3, 6, -12, \ldots$

$$a_n = a_1 r^{(n-1)} \Rightarrow a_{17} = a_1 r^{(17-1)} = -3\left(-2\right)^{16} = -196608.$$

(b) Find the sum of the sequence $\dfrac{1}{5}, \dfrac{2}{15}, \dfrac{4}{45}, \ldots, \dfrac{2048}{885735}$.

$a_1 = \dfrac{1}{5}, r = \dfrac{2}{15} \div \dfrac{1}{5} = \dfrac{2}{3}$. So first find the number of terms in this finite sequence:

$$a_n = \frac{2048}{885735} = \left(\frac{1}{5}\right)\left(\frac{2}{3}\right)^{(n-1)} \Rightarrow \frac{2048}{177147} = \left(\frac{2}{3}\right)^{(n-1)} \Rightarrow \left(\frac{2}{3}\right)^{11} = \left(\frac{2}{3}\right)^{(n-1)} \quad \text{so } n = 12.$$

$$S_{12} = \frac{a_1\left(1-r^n\right)}{1-r} = \frac{\left(\frac{1}{5}\right)\left(1-\left(\frac{2}{3}\right)^{12}\right)}{1-\frac{2}{3}} = \frac{\frac{1}{5}\left(\frac{527345}{531441}\right)}{\frac{1}{3}} = \frac{1582035}{2657205} \approx 0.6$$

Theorem: Let $\left\{a_n\right\}_{n=1}^{\infty}$ be a geometric sequence with common ratio $|r| < 1$. Then:

(a) $\displaystyle\lim_{n \to \infty} a_n = 0$, and

(b) $S = \displaystyle\sum_{i=1}^{\infty} a_i = \frac{a_1}{1-r}$

- If the common ratio is such that $|r| \geq 1$, then the series, diverges if $a_1 \neq 0$.

Example: Find the sum of the geometric sequence $\dfrac{-3}{2}, \dfrac{-6}{10}, \dfrac{-12}{50}, \ldots$

$$a_1 = \frac{-3}{2} \text{ and } r = \frac{2}{5}, \text{ so } S = \sum_{i=1}^{\infty} a_i = \frac{a_1}{1-r} = \frac{\dfrac{-3}{2}}{1 - \dfrac{2}{5}} = \frac{-5}{2}.$$

- Repeating decimals may be expressed as an infinite geometric series, and this can be used to write a repeating decimal in the fraction form $\dfrac{p}{q}$.

Example: Write $0.\overline{312}$ in fraction form using series.

$$x = 0.\overline{312} = 0.312 + 0.000312 + 0.000000312 + \cdots$$
$$= 0.312 + 0.312\left(10^{-3}\right) + 0.312\left(10^{-6}\right) + 0.312\left(10^{-9}\right) + \cdots$$
$$= 0.312 + 0.3121\left(10^{-3}\right)^1 + 0.312\left(10^{-3}\right)^2 + 0.312\left(10^{-3}\right)^3 + \cdots$$
$$= \sum_{i=0}^{\infty} (0.312)\left(10^{-3}\right)^i$$

This is an infinite geometric sum with $a_1 = 0.312$ and $r = 10^{-3}$, so $x = \dfrac{a_1}{1-r} = \dfrac{0.312}{1-10^{-3}} = \dfrac{104}{333}$.

Review Problems for Section 6.5.1

1. Find the 15th term of each of the following sequences:

    (a) $7, 2, -3, -8, \ldots$

    (b) $18, -6, 2, \dfrac{-2}{3}, \ldots$

2. Find the sum, if possible, of each of the following:

    (a) $\displaystyle\sum_{i=3}^{14} \frac{2}{3^i}$

    (b) $\displaystyle\sum_{i=0}^{14} (-6 + 2i)$

    (c) $\displaystyle\sum_{i=1}^{\infty} \frac{3}{2^i}$

    (d) $\displaystyle\sum_{i=1}^{\infty} \left(\frac{-3}{2}\right)^i$

3. Write $2.\overline{145}$ in fraction form using geometric series.

Detailed Solutions

1. (a) This is an arithmetic sequence with $a_1 = 7$ and $d = -5$

   $a_{15} = a_1 + (15-1)(d) = 7 + 14(-5) = -63.$

   (b) This is a geometric sequence with $a_1 = 18$ and $r = \dfrac{-1}{3}$

   $a_{15} = a_1 r^{(15-1)} \Rightarrow a_{15} = (18)\left(\dfrac{-1}{3}\right)^{14} = \dfrac{2}{3^{12}} = \dfrac{2}{531441}$

2. $\displaystyle\sum_{i=3}^{14} \dfrac{2}{3^i} = \dfrac{2}{27} + \dfrac{2}{81} + \cdots + \dfrac{2}{3^{14}} = \sum_{i=1}^{12} \dfrac{2}{3^{i+2}}$. This is a geometric finite series (sum of a sequence) with

   12 terms, $a_1 = \dfrac{2}{27}$, and $r = \dfrac{1}{3}$, so

   $S_{12} = \dfrac{a_1(1-r^{12})}{1-r} = \dfrac{\left(\dfrac{2}{27}\right)\left(1-\left(\dfrac{1}{3}\right)^{12}\right)}{1-\dfrac{1}{3}} = \left(\dfrac{1}{9}\right)\left(1-\left(\dfrac{1}{3}\right)^{12}\right) = \dfrac{3^{12}-1}{3^{14}} = \dfrac{531440}{4782969}.$

   (b) $\displaystyle\sum_{i=0}^{14} (-6+2i) = -6 + (-6+2) + (-6+2(2)) + \cdots + (-6+2(14))$ is an arithmetic sequence

   with $a_1 = -6$ and $d = 2$. There are 15 terms, so $S_{15} = \dfrac{2a_1 + (15-1)d}{2}(15) = \dfrac{2(-6)+14(2)}{2}(15) = 120.$

   (c) $\displaystyle\sum_{i=1}^{\infty} \dfrac{3}{2^i} = \dfrac{3}{2} + \dfrac{3}{2^2} + \dfrac{3}{2^3} + \cdots$. This is the sum of an infinite geometric sequence with

   $a_1 = \dfrac{3}{2}$ and $r = \dfrac{1}{2}$, so the geometric series converges (has a finite sum) to $S = \dfrac{a_1}{1-r} = \dfrac{\dfrac{3}{2}}{1-\dfrac{1}{2}} = 3.$

   (d) $\displaystyle\sum_{i=1}^{\infty} \left(\dfrac{-3}{2}\right)^i = \dfrac{-3}{2} + \dfrac{9}{4} - \dfrac{27}{8} + \cdots$. This is a sum of an infinite geometric sequence with

   $|r| = \dfrac{3}{2} > 1$, so this sum does not exist.

3. $x = 2.1\overline{45} = 2.1 + (0.045 + 0.00045 + 0.0000045 + \cdots) = \dfrac{21}{10} + S$ where $S = (0.045 + 0.00045$

   $+\ 0.0000045 + \cdots)$ is a geometric sum with

   $a_1 = 0.045$ and $r = 10^{-2}$.

   So $S = \dfrac{a_1}{1-r} = \dfrac{0.045}{1-10^{-2}} = \dfrac{45}{990}$. Hence, $x = 2.1\overline{45} = \dfrac{21}{10} + \dfrac{45}{990} = \dfrac{2124}{990} = \dfrac{1062}{495}.$

6.5.2 The California *Mathematics Subject Matter Requirements* stipulate that candidates for any credential program for teaching secondary mathematics must be able to *determine convergence of a given sequence or series using standard techniques (e.g., Ratio, Comparison, Integral Tests).*

Convergence

Convergence of Sequence

- A sequence $\{a_n\}_{n=1}^{\infty}$ has the **limit** L, or **converges to** L, denoted by either

  $$\lim_{n \to \infty} a_n = L \text{ or } a_n \to L \text{ as } n \to \infty$$

  if, for all $\varepsilon > 0$, there exists $N > 0$ such that $|a_n - L| < \varepsilon$ whenever $n > N$.

- If such a number L does not exist, then we say the sequence has no limit or **diverges.**

Examples:

(a) $\left\{\dfrac{1}{n}\right\}_{n=1}^{\infty}$. This is $1, \dfrac{1}{2}, \dfrac{1}{3}, \ldots$, which converges to 0.

(b) $\left\{(-1)^n\right\}_{n=1}^{\infty}$. This is $-1, 1, -1, 1, \ldots$, which has no limit because the sequence oscillates between 1 and -1.

(c) Let $a_k = k^2$. Then this sequence is $1, 4, 9, 16, \ldots$, which diverges since the terms increase without bound.

- The notation $\lim_{n \to \infty} a_n = \infty$ means that for all $P > 0$, there exists a number N such that $a_n > P$ for all $n > N$.

  Theorem: Let $\{a_n\}_{n=1}^{\infty}$ be a sequence such that $\lim_{n \to \infty} |a_n| = 0$. Then $\lim_{n \to \infty} a_n = 0$

  Example: Let $a_n = \dfrac{(-1)^n}{n}$. Then the sequence converges to 0 since $|a_n| = \dfrac{1}{n} \to 0$.

- Recall that L'Hôpital's Rule can be used only on continuous functions. Sequences are clearly not continuous, so when studying sequences, we can form a continuous function $f(x)$, where x is real and $f(n) = a_n$, and then use L'Hôpital's Rule.

  Theorem: If f is a continuous function and if $f(n) = a_n$ for all n sufficiently large, then

  (a). if $\lim_{x \to \infty} f(x) = L$, then $\lim_{n \to \infty} a_n = L$.

  (b). if $\lim_{x \to \infty} f(x) = \infty$, then $\lim_{n \to \infty} a_n = \infty$.

Example: Consider $a_n = \dfrac{n}{n+1}$. Let $f(x) = \dfrac{x}{x+1}$. Then f is continuous for all $x > 0$ and it has the

indeterminate form $\dfrac{\infty}{\infty}$ as $x \to \infty$. So we can use L'Hôpital's Rule on f: $\displaystyle\lim_{x\to\infty}\frac{x}{x+1} = \lim_{x\to\infty}\frac{1}{1} = 1$. Thus,

$\displaystyle\lim_{n\to\infty}\frac{n}{n+1} = 1$.

- Many of the theorems we have for limits of functions apply to limits of sequences:

Theorem: If $\displaystyle\lim_{n\to\infty} a_n = A$ and $\displaystyle\lim_{n\to\infty} b_n = B$, then

(a) $\displaystyle\lim_{n\to\infty}(a_n \pm b_n) = A \pm B$

(b) $\displaystyle\lim_{n\to\infty} ka_n = k \cdot A$ for k a real number

(c) $\displaystyle\lim_{n\to\infty}(a_n \cdot b_n) = A \cdot B$

(d) $\displaystyle\lim_{n\to\infty}\frac{a_n}{b_n} = \frac{A}{B}$ if $B \neq 0$ and $b_n \neq 0$, for all n.

Corollary: If $\{a_n\}_{n=1}^{\infty}$ diverges and $c \neq 0$, $\{ca_n\}_{n=1}^{\infty}$ diverges.

Theorem (Squeeze Theorem for Sequences):

If $a_n \leq b_n \leq c_n$ for all $n \geq N$ for some N, and $\displaystyle\lim_{n\to\infty} a_n = L = \lim_{n\to\infty} c_n$, then $\displaystyle\lim_{n\to\infty} b_n = L$.

Example: Consider $\left\{\dfrac{\sin m}{m}\right\}_{m=1}^{\infty}$. Since $-1 \leq \sin m \leq 1$, $-1/m \leq \dfrac{\sin m}{m} \leq 1/m$ and

$\displaystyle\lim_{m\to\infty}\frac{1}{m} = \lim_{m\to\infty}\frac{-1}{m} = 0$, so $\displaystyle\lim_{m\to\infty}\frac{\sin m}{m} = 0$.

- A sequence $\{a_n\}_{n=1}^{\infty}$ is **increasing** if $a_n \leq a_{n+1}$ ($a_1 \leq a_2 \leq a_3 \leq \cdots$) for all n.

- A sequence $\{a_n\}_{n=1}^{\infty}$ is **decreasing** if $a_n \geq a_{n+1}$ ($a_1 \geq a_2 \geq a_3 \geq \cdots$) for all n.

- A sequence is $\{a_n\}_{n=1}^{\infty}$ **monotone** if it is increasing for all n or strictly decreasing for all n.

- To show that $\{a_n\}_{n=1}^{\infty}$ is

  (a) increasing, show
  - (i) $f'(x) > 0$ for all $x \geq 1$, where $f(n) = a_n$.
  - or (ii) $\dfrac{a_{n+1}}{a_n} > 1$ and $a_n > 0$ for all $n = 1, 2, 3, \dots$.
  - or (iii) $a_{n=1} - a_n > 0$ for all $n = 1, 2, 3, \dots$.

  (b) decreasing, show
  - (i) $f'(x) < 0$ for all $x \geq 1$, where $f(n) = a_n$.
  - or (ii) $\dfrac{a_{n+1}}{a_n} < 1$ and $a_n > 0$ for all $n = 1, 2, 3, \dots$.
  - or (iii) $a_{n=1} - a_n < 0$ for all $n = 1, 2, 3, \dots$.

Examples:

(a) $a_n = \dfrac{n}{n+2}$: This sequence is increasing because

$$a_{n+1} - a_n = \frac{n+1}{n+3} - \frac{n}{n+1} = \frac{(n+1)^2 - n(n+3)}{(n+3)(n+1)} = \frac{-n+1}{(n+3)(n+1)} \geq 0 \text{ for all } n.$$

(b) $a_n = e^{-n}$: Set $f(x) = e^{-x}$ then $f'(x) = -e^{-x} < 0$ for all $x \geq 1$, so this sequence is decreasing.

- M is an **upper bound** of a sequence $\{a_n\}_{n=1}^{\infty}$ provided $a_n \leq M$ for all n.

- M is a **lower bound** of a sequence $\{a_n\}_{n=1}^{\infty}$ provided $a_n \geq M$ for all n.

- A sequence is **bounded** provided it has an upper and lower bound.

Examples:

(a) $1, \dfrac{1}{2}, \dfrac{1}{4}, \cdots$ is a bounded sequence since it is bounded above by 1 and below by 0.

(b) $1, 2, 3, \ldots$ is bounded below by 1 but is not bounded above.

Theorem (Bounded Monotone Convergence Theorem (BMCT)):

A bounded monotone sequence converges.

- It is also true that if a sequence is bounded above and increasing, or bounded below and decreasing, the sequence converges.

Example: Prove $a_n = \dfrac{n+1}{5^n}$ converges using the BMCT.

Proof: Let $a_n = \dfrac{n+1}{5^n}$. Then $\dfrac{a_{n+1}}{a_n} = \dfrac{n+2}{5^{n+1}} \div \dfrac{n+1}{5^n} = \dfrac{n+2}{5n+5} < 1$ for all n, so the sequence is monotone.

Also, $0 \leq a_n \leq \dfrac{2}{5}$ for all n, so the sequence is bounded. By the Bounded Monotone Convergence

Theorem, $a_n = \dfrac{n+1}{5^n}$ converges.

Q.E.D.

- Note that the Bounded Monotone Convergence Theorem does not tell us what the sequence converges to, just that it does converge.

Convergence of Series

- A finite series is a sum of a finite sequence: $a_1 + a_2 + a_3 + \ldots + a_N$,

- In terms of sigma notation this is $a_1 + a_2 + a_3 + \ldots + a_N = \displaystyle\sum_{n=1}^{N} a_n$.

- An **infinite series** (or just **series**) is the sum of an infinite sequence: $\sum_{n=1}^{\infty} a_n = a_1 + a_2 + a_3 + \cdots$

- Given an infinite series $\sum_{n=1}^{\infty} a_n = a_1 + a_2 + a_3 + \cdots$, we call the finite sum

  $S_n = \sum_{k=1}^{n} a_k = a_1 + a_2 + a_3 + \cdots + a_n$ the ***n*th partial sum.** These sums themselves
  form a sequence $S_1, S_2, S_3, \ldots$, where $S_1 = a_1$, $S_2 = a_1 + a_2$, $S_3 = a_1 + a_2 + a_3 \ldots$

- An **infinite series converges (diverges)** if and only if its sequence of partial sums converges (diverges).

  Theorem (The *n*th Term Test or the Divergence Test):

  (a) If $\lim_{n \to \infty} a_n \neq 0$, then $\sum_{n=1}^{\infty} a_n$ diverges.

  (b) If $\lim_{n \to \infty} a_n = 0$, further investigation is necessary to determine whether $\sum_{n=1}^{\infty} a_n$ converges or diverges.

  Examples:

  (a) $\sum_{n=1}^{\infty} 1 = 1 + 1 + 1 + \ldots$ diverges since $\lim_{n \to \infty} 1 \neq 0$.

  (b) $\sum_{n=1}^{\infty} \frac{1}{n} = 1 + \frac{1}{2} + \frac{1}{3} + \ldots$ diverges even though $\lim_{n \to \infty} \frac{1}{n} = 0$. This series is called the **harmonic series.**

- The infinite series $\sum_{n=1}^{\infty} a_n$ **converges absolutely** provided $\sum_{n=1}^{\infty} |a_n|$ converges.

- In general, a series that is not absolutely convergent but is convergent may be called **conditionally convergent.**

- Clearly, if a series converges absolutely, we can say the series converges.

  Theorem (The Comparison Test): Let $\sum_{n=1}^{\infty} a_n$ and $\sum_{n=1}^{\infty} b_n$ be series with $0 \leq a_n \leq b_n$ for all n. Then

  (a) if $\sum_{n=1}^{\infty} a_n$ diverges, then so does $\sum_{n=1}^{\infty} b_n$.

  (b) if $\sum_{n=1}^{\infty} b_n$ converges, then so does $\sum_{n=1}^{\infty} a_n$.

Example: $\displaystyle\sum_{n=1}^{\infty}\frac{6^n}{7^n-4^n}=\sum_{n=1}^{\infty}\frac{6^n}{7^n\left(1-\left(\frac{4}{7}\right)^n\right)}\leq\sum_{n=1}^{\infty}\frac{6^n}{7^n\left(1-\left(\frac{4}{7}\right)\right)}=\sum_{n=1}^{\infty}\frac{6^n}{7^n\left(\frac{3}{7}\right)}=\frac{7}{3}\sum_{n=1}^{\infty}\frac{6^n}{7^n}$. This last series is

convergent since it is a geometric series with ratio less than 1. Also, the original series is bounded below by 0. Hence, by the comparison test, $\displaystyle\sum_{n=1}^{\infty}\frac{6^n}{7^n-4^n}$ converges.

Theorem (The Limit Comparison Test): Let $\displaystyle\sum_{n=1}^{\infty}a_n$ and $\displaystyle\sum_{n=1}^{\infty}b_n$ be series such that $b_n>0$ for all n.

$$\text{Let }\rho=\lim_{n\to\infty}\left|\frac{a_n}{b_n}\right|$$

If ρ is finite and non-zero, then the series either both converge (absolutely) or diverge.

Example: $\displaystyle\sum_{n=1}^{\infty}\frac{3n^2-n}{\sqrt[3]{n^8+n^5}}$. To find another sequence to compare this to, consider the terms: $\dfrac{3n^2-n}{\sqrt[3]{n^8+n^5}}$.

The numerator and denominator behave like their dominating terms, so $\dfrac{3n^2-n}{\sqrt[3]{n^8+n^5}}$ can be compared

with $\dfrac{3n^2}{\sqrt[3]{n^8}}=\dfrac{3}{n^{\frac{2}{3}}}$: $\displaystyle\lim_{n\to\infty}\frac{3n^2-n}{\sqrt[3]{n^8+n^5}}\div\frac{3}{n^{\frac{2}{3}}}=\lim_{n\to\infty}\frac{3n^{\frac{8}{3}}-n^{\frac{5}{3}}}{3\sqrt[3]{n^8+n^5}}=\sqrt[3]{\lim_{n\to\infty}\frac{n^8}{n^8+n^5}}-\sqrt[3]{\lim_{n\to\infty}\frac{n^5}{3\left(n^8+n^5\right)}}=1$. Hence by

the Limit Comparison Test, $\displaystyle\sum_{n=1}^{\infty}\frac{3n^2-n}{\sqrt[3]{n^8+n^5}}$ behaves like $\displaystyle\sum_{n=1}^{\infty}\frac{3}{n^{\frac{2}{3}}}$, which is a divergent p-series.

Theorem (The Integral Test): Let $\displaystyle\sum_{n=1}^{\infty}a_n$ be a series such that $a_n\geq0$ for all n, and let $f(x)$ be a continuous decreasing function on $[1,\infty]$ such that $f(n)=a_n$ for all n. Then

(a) if either $\displaystyle\sum_{n=1}^{\infty}a_n$ or $\displaystyle\int_1^{\infty}f(x)dx$ diverges, so does the other;

(b) if either $\displaystyle\sum_{n=1}^{\infty}a_n$ or $\displaystyle\int_1^{\infty}f(x)dx$ converges, so does the other;

(c) if the series converges, then R_n, the "tail" of the series, has the following upper bound:

$$R_n=\sum_{k=n+1}^{\infty}a_k<\int_n^{\infty}f(x)dx$$

- A *p*-series or **hyperharmonic series** is a series of the form

$$\sum_{n=1}^{\infty} \frac{1}{n^p} = 1 + \frac{1}{2^p} + \frac{1}{3^p} + \cdots + \frac{1}{n^p} + \cdots$$

where p is a positive real number.

Theorem: The p-series, $\displaystyle\sum_{n=1}^{\infty} \frac{1}{n^p}$ converges for $p > 1$ and diverges for $p \leq 1$.

Proof: Consider $\displaystyle\int_{1}^{\infty} \frac{1}{x^p}$, where at first $p \neq 1$. This improper integral can be computed as follows:

$$\int_{1}^{\infty} \frac{1}{x^p}dx = \lim_{b\to\infty}\int_{1}^{b}\frac{1}{x^p}dx = \lim_{b\to\infty}\left[\frac{x^{-p+1}}{-p+1}\right]_{1}^{b} = \lim_{b\to\infty}\left[\frac{b^{-p+1}}{-p+1} - \frac{1}{-p+1}\right] = \begin{cases} \dfrac{1}{p-1} & \text{if } p > 1 \\[2mm] \infty & \text{if } p < 1 \end{cases}$$

For $p = 1$, $\displaystyle\int_{1}^{\infty} \frac{1}{x^p}dx = \lim_{b\to\infty}\int_{1}^{b}\frac{1}{x}dx = \lim_{b\to\infty}\Big[\ln x\Big]_{1}^{b} = \lim_{b\to\infty}\Big[\ln b\Big] = \infty.$ (This is the harmonic series.)

Hence, the p-series converges only when $p > 1$.

Q.E.D.

Theorem (The Ratio Test): Let $\displaystyle\sum_{n=1}^{\infty} a_n$ be a series and let $L = \lim_{n\to\infty}\left|\dfrac{a_{n+1}}{a_n}\right|$.

(a) If $L < 1$, then the series is absolutely convergent.

(b) If $L > 1$, then the series is divergent.

(c) If $L = 1$, then this test is inconclusive; apply a different test!

Examples:

(a) Consider $\displaystyle\sum_{n=1}^{\infty} \frac{2^n}{n!}$. Then $\left|\dfrac{a_{n+1}}{a_n}\right| = \left|\dfrac{2^{n+1}}{(n+1)!}\dfrac{n!}{2^n}\right| = \dfrac{2}{n+1} \to 0$ as $n \to \infty$. Hence, by the Ratio

Test, $\displaystyle\sum_{n=1}^{\infty} \frac{2^n}{n!}$ converges absolutely.

(b) Determine whether the series $\displaystyle\sum_{n=1}^{\infty} \frac{(2n)!}{(n!)^2}$ converges or diverges.

$$\left|\frac{(2n+2)!}{((n+1)!)^2}\frac{(n!)^2}{(2n)!}\right| = \frac{(2n+2)(2n+1)}{(n+1)^2} \to 4 \text{ as } n \to \infty; \text{ hence, } \sum_{n=1}^{\infty} \frac{(2n)!}{(n!)^2} \text{ diverges by the Ratio}$$

Test.

Theorem (The Root Test): Let $\displaystyle\sum_{n=1}^{\infty} a_n$ be a series. Let $L = \lim_{n\to\infty}\sqrt[n]{|a_n|}$.

(a) If $L < 1$, then $\sum_{n=1}^{\infty} a_n$ is absolutely convergent.

(b) If $L > 1$, then $\sum_{n=1}^{\infty} a_n$ is divergent.

(c) If $L = 1$, then this test is inconclusive; apply a different test!

Example: Consider the series $\sum_{n=1}^{\infty} \left(\frac{3n-1}{2n+1} \right)^n$. Using the Root Test, we obtain

$$\left(\left| \left(\frac{3n-1}{2n+1} \right)^n \right| \right)^{\frac{1}{n}} = \frac{3n-1}{2n+1} \to \frac{3}{2} \text{ as } n \to \infty \text{, so the series diverges.}$$

Theorem (The Alternating Series Test): Consider the alternating series $\sum_{n=1}^{\infty} (-1)^n a_n$. This series converges provided

1. $\lim_{k \to \infty} a_k = 0$, and

2. $a_1 \geq a_2 \geq a_3 \geq \cdots \geq 0$

Example: Consider the **alternating harmonic series** $\sum_{n=1}^{\infty} \frac{(-1)^n}{n}$. Then $a_k = \frac{1}{k} \to 0$ as $k \to \infty$,

$a_{k+1} < a_k$ all k, so by the Alternating Series Test $\sum_{n=1}^{\infty} \frac{(-1)^n}{n}$ converges.

Review Problems for Section 6.5.2

1.   Determine whether each of the following sequences converges or diverges:

(a) $\left\{ \dfrac{\ln n}{n} \right\}_{n=1}^{\infty}$ (b) $\left\{ \sin \dfrac{n\pi}{2} \right\}_{n=1}^{\infty}$ (c) $a_n = \left(\dfrac{1}{5} \right)^n$, $n = 1, 2, 3,...$ (d) $a_n = -3 + 2n$, $n = 1, 2, 3, ...$

2.   Determine whether each of the following series converges or diverges:

(a) $\sum_{n=2}^{\infty} \dfrac{n}{2n+1}$ (b) $\sum_{k=1}^{\infty} \dfrac{\sin k}{k^3}$ (c) $\sum_{k=1}^{\infty} \dfrac{k!}{k+2}$ (d) $\sum_{n=1}^{\infty} \left(\dfrac{5}{4} \right)^n$ (e) $\sum_{k=1}^{\infty} \dfrac{3}{(k+1)^k}$

3.   If possible, find the sum of the sequence:

(a) $-3, \dfrac{-3}{5}, \dfrac{-3}{25}, ...$

(b) $-10, -4, 2, 8, ..., 128$

Detailed Solutions

1. (a) $\left\{\dfrac{\ln n}{n}\right\}_{n=1}^{\infty}$. Let $f(x) = \dfrac{\ln x}{x}$. We can use L'Hôpital's Rule since $\lim\limits_{x\to\infty}\dfrac{\ln x}{x}$ is an $\dfrac{\infty}{\infty}$ indeter-

minate form. $\lim\limits_{x\to\infty}\dfrac{\ln x}{x} = \lim\limits_{x\to\infty}\dfrac{\frac{1}{x}}{1} = \lim\limits_{x\to\infty}\dfrac{1}{x} = 0$. Thus, $\left\{\dfrac{\ln n}{n}\right\}_{n=1}^{\infty}$ also converges to 0.

(b) $\left\{\sin\dfrac{n\pi}{2}\right\}_{n=1}^{\infty}$. The terms of this sequence are: $1, 0, -1, 0, 1, 0, -1, 0,...$ which has no limit.

(c) $a_n = \left(\dfrac{1}{5}\right)^n$ is a geometric sequence with common ratio 1/5, so it converges to 0.

(d) $a_n = -3 + 2n$ is the arithmetic sequence $-1, 1, 3, 5, ...$, which diverges.

2. (a) $\sum\limits_{n=2}^{\infty}\dfrac{n}{2n+1}$ diverges by the Divergence Test because $\lim\limits_{n\to\infty}a_n = \lim\limits_{n\to\infty}\dfrac{n}{2n+1} = \dfrac{1}{2}$.

(b) $\sum\limits_{k=2}^{\infty}\dfrac{\sin k}{k^3} : \left|\dfrac{\sin k}{k^3}\right| \leq \dfrac{1}{k^3} : \left|\dfrac{\sin k}{k^3}\right| \leq \dfrac{1}{k^3}$, and $\sum\limits_{k=1}^{\infty}\dfrac{1}{k^3}$ is a p-series with $p = 3 > 1$, so it con-

verges. Thus, by the Comparison Test, $\sum\limits_{k=1}^{\infty}\dfrac{\sin k}{k^3}$ converges absolutely.

(c) $\sum\limits_{k=1}^{\infty}\dfrac{k!}{k+2}$. Use the Ratio Test: $\dfrac{(k+1)!}{k+2} \div \dfrac{k!}{k+1} = \dfrac{(k+1)^2}{k+2} \to \infty$. Thus, $\sum\limits_{k=1}^{\infty}\dfrac{k!}{k+2}$ diverges.

(d) $\sum\limits_{n=1}^{\infty}\left(\dfrac{5}{4}\right)^n$ diverges because it is a geometric series with ratio greater than 1.

(e) $\sum\limits_{k=1}^{\infty}\dfrac{3}{(k+1)^k}$. Use the Root Test: $\left(\dfrac{3}{(k+1)^k}\right)^{\frac{1}{k}} = \dfrac{\sqrt[k]{3}}{k+1} \to 0$, and hence $\sum\limits_{k=1}^{\infty}\dfrac{3}{(k+1)^k}$ converges.

3. (a) $-3, \dfrac{-3}{5}, \dfrac{-3}{25}, ...$ is a geometric series with $a_1 = -3$ and $r = 1/5$, so its sum is $S = \dfrac{-3}{1-\frac{1}{5}} = \dfrac{-15}{4}$.

(b) $-10, -4, 2, 8,...$ 128 is a finite arithmetic sequence with $a_1 = -10$ and $d = 6$. To find n:

$a_n = 128 = a_1 + (n-1)d = -10 + (n-1)6 = -16 + 6n \qquad 128 = -16 + 6n \qquad n = 24$.

So the sum is $S_{24} = \left(\dfrac{-10+128}{2}\right)24 = 1416$.

> **6.5.3** The California *Mathematics Subject Matter Requirements* stipulate that candidates for any credential program for teaching secondary mathematics must be able *to calculate Taylor series and Taylor polynomials of basic functions.*

Taylor Series and Taylor Polynomials

Let c be a real number and let f be a function with n continuous derivatives on an open interval I containing c. Then $P_n(x)$ is called the **Taylor polynomial of degree n of f at c**, where

$$P_n(x) = f(c) + f'(c)(x-c) + \frac{f''(c)}{2!}(x-c)^2 + \frac{f'''(c)}{3!}(x-c)^3 + \cdots + \frac{f^{(n)}(c)}{n!}(x-c)^n$$

- Note that $f^{(k)}(c) = P_n^{(k)}(c)$ for all $k = 1, 2, 3, \ldots$

- Also note that $P_1(x) = f(c) + f'(c)(x - c)$ is the equation of the tangent line for f at $x = c$.

- In addition, $P_2(x) = f(c) + f'(c)(x - c) + \frac{f''(c)}{2!}(x-c)^2$ is the parabola that is tangent to f at $x = c$, which "best" fits the graph of f at $x = c$ in the way that the curvature of both graphs are close near $x = c$.

Example: Compute $P_4(x)$ for $f(x) = \ln x$ near $x = 1$.

$$f(x) = \ln x \qquad\qquad f(1) = \ln 1 = 0$$

$$f'(x) = \frac{1}{x} \qquad\qquad f'(1) = \frac{1}{1} = 1$$

$$f''(x) = \frac{-1}{x^2} \qquad\qquad f''(1) = \frac{-1}{1} = -1$$

$$f'''(x) = \frac{2}{x^3} \qquad\qquad f'''(1) = \frac{2}{1} = 2$$

$$f^{(iv)}(x) = \frac{-6}{x^4} \qquad\qquad f^{(iv)}(1) = \frac{-6}{1} = -6$$

So, $P_4(x) = 0 + 1(x-1) - \frac{1}{2}(x-1)^2 + \frac{1}{3}(x-1)^3 - \frac{1}{4}(x-1)^4$. Figure 6.116 shows the graphs of f (solid) and P_4 (dotted). The Taylor polynomial is a reasonable representation of f near $x = 1$.

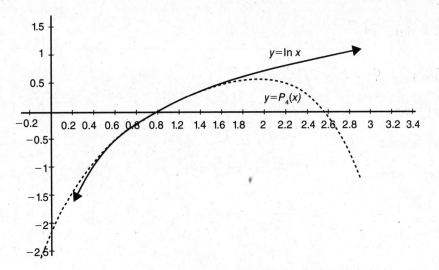

Figure 6.116

Let c be a real number and let f be a function with continuous derivatives of all orders on an open interval I containing c. Then $P(x)$ is called the **Taylor series of f at c**, where

$$P(x) = f(c) + f'(c)(x-c) + \frac{f''(c)}{2!}(x-c)^2 + \frac{f'''(c)}{3!}(x-c)^3 + \cdots + \frac{f^{(n)}(c)}{n!}(x-c)^n + \cdots$$

Examples: Compute the Taylor Series for each of the following:

(a) $f(x) = e^x$, $c = 1$

$f(x) = e^x$

$f^{(n)}(x) = e^x$

$f^{(n)}(1) = e^1 = e$

So, $P(x) = \sum_{n=0}^{\infty} \frac{e}{n!}(x-1)^n$

(b) $f(x) = \sin x$, $c = \dfrac{\pi}{2}$.

$$f(x) = \sin x \qquad\qquad f\left(\dfrac{\pi}{2}\right) = \sin\dfrac{\pi}{2} = 1$$

$$f'(x) = \cos x \qquad\qquad f'\left(\dfrac{\pi}{2}\right) = \cos\dfrac{\pi}{2} = 0$$

$$f''(x) = -\sin x \qquad\qquad f''\left(\dfrac{\pi}{2}\right) = -\sin\dfrac{\pi}{2} = -1$$

$$f'''(x) = -\cos x \qquad\qquad f'''\left(\dfrac{\pi}{2}\right) = -\cos\dfrac{\pi}{2} = 0$$

and then repeats through this pattern.

$$P(x) = 1 + 0\left(x - \dfrac{\pi}{2}\right) - \dfrac{1}{2!}\left(x - \dfrac{\pi}{2}\right)^2 + 0\left(x - \dfrac{\pi}{2}\right)^3 - \cdots$$

$$= \sum_{n=0}^{\infty} \dfrac{(-1)^n}{(2n)!}\left(x - \dfrac{\pi}{2}\right)^{2n}$$

(c) $f(x) = \cos x$, $c = \dfrac{\pi}{4}$.

$$f(x) = \cos x \qquad\qquad f\left(\dfrac{\pi}{4}\right) = \cos\dfrac{\pi}{4} = \dfrac{\sqrt{2}}{2}$$

$$f'(x) = -\sin x \qquad\qquad f'\left(\dfrac{\pi}{4}\right) = -\sin\dfrac{\pi}{4} = -\dfrac{\sqrt{2}}{2}$$

$$f''(x) = -\cos x \qquad\qquad f''\left(\dfrac{\pi}{4}\right) = -\cos\dfrac{\pi}{4} = -\dfrac{\sqrt{2}}{2}$$

$$f'''(x) = \sin x \qquad\qquad f'''\left(\dfrac{\pi}{4}\right) = \sin\dfrac{\pi}{4} = \dfrac{\sqrt{2}}{2}$$

and then repeats through this pattern.

$$P(x) = \dfrac{\sqrt{2}}{2} - \dfrac{\sqrt{2}}{2}\left(x - \dfrac{\pi}{4}\right) - \dfrac{\sqrt{2}}{4}\left(x - \dfrac{\pi}{4}\right)^2 + \dfrac{\sqrt{2}}{12}\left(x - \dfrac{\pi}{4}\right)^3 + \cdots$$

Review Problems for Section 6.5.3

1. Compute the Taylor polynomials for

   (a) $f(x) = 2^x$ at $x = 1$ for $n = 3$.

   (b) $f(x) = \tan x$ at $x = 0$ for $n = 3$.

2. Compute the Taylor series for

   (a) $f(x) = \dfrac{1}{x}$ at $x = 2$

   (b) $f(x) = e^x$ at $x = 0$

   (c) $f(x) = x^5 - 2x^3 + 4x^2$ at $x = -2$

Detailed Solutions

1. (a) $f(x) = 2^x$ $\qquad\qquad f(1) = 2$

   $f'(x) = 2^x \ln 2$ $\qquad\qquad f'(1) = 2\ln 2$

   $f''(1) = 2^x (\ln 2)^2$ $\qquad\quad f''(1) = 2(\ln 2)^2$

   $f'''(1) = 2(\ln 2)^3$ $\qquad\quad\; f'''(1) = 2(\ln 2)^3$

   So, $P_3(x) = 2 + 2\ln 2(x-1) + \dfrac{2(\ln 2)^2}{2!}(x-1)^2 + \dfrac{2(\ln 2)^3}{3!}(x-1)^3$

   $\qquad\quad = 2 + 2\ln 2(x-1) + (\ln 2)^2(x-1)^2 + \dfrac{(\ln 2)^3}{3}(x-1)^3$

   (b) $f(x) = \tan x$

   $f'(x) = \sec^2 x$

   $f''(x) = 2\sec x(\sec x \tan x) = 2\sec^2 x \tan x$

   $f'''(x) = 2\sec^2 x(\sec^2 x) + 2\tan x(\sec x \tan x) = 2\sec x(\sec^3 x + \tan^2 x)$

   $f(0) = \tan 0 = 0$

   $f'(0) = \sec^2 0 = 1$

   $f''(0) = 2\sec^2(0)\tan(0) = 0$

   $f'''(x) = 2\sec(0)(\sec^3(0) + \tan^2(0)) = 2$

   So, $z^4 = \sqrt{2}\left(\cos\left(\dfrac{7\pi}{4}\right) + i\sin\left(\dfrac{7\pi}{4}\right)\right)$

2   (a)

$$f(x) = \frac{1}{x} \qquad\qquad f(2) = \frac{1}{2}$$

$$f'(x) = \frac{-1}{x^2} \qquad\qquad f'(2) = \frac{-1}{4}$$

$$f''(x) = \frac{2}{x^3} \qquad\qquad f''(2) = \frac{2}{8} = \frac{1}{4}$$

$$f'''(x) = \frac{-6}{x^4} \qquad\qquad f'''(2) = \frac{-6}{16} = \frac{-3}{8}$$

$$f^{(n)}(x)\frac{(-1)^n n!}{x^{n+1}} \qquad\qquad f^{(n)}(2) = \frac{(-1)^n n!}{2^{n+1}}$$

So, $P(x) = \sum_{x=0}^{\infty} \frac{\frac{(-1)^n n!}{2^{n+1}}}{n!}(x-2)^n = \sum_{n=0}^{\infty} \frac{(-1)^n}{2^{n+1}}(x-2)^n$

(b) $f(x) = e^x$

$f^{(n)}(x) = e^x$

$f^{(n)}(0) = e^0 = 1$

So, $\beta = \dfrac{7\pi}{16} + \dfrac{\pi}{2}k$

(c)
$$f(x) = x^5 - 2x^3 + 4x^2 \qquad f(-2) = (-2)^5 - 2(-2)^3 + 4(-2)^2 = 0$$
$$f'(x) = 5x^4 - 6x^2 + 8x \qquad f'(-2) = 5(-2)^4 - 6(-2)^2 + 8(-2) = 40$$
$$f''(x) = 20x^3 - 12x + 8 \qquad f''(-2) = 20(-2)^3 - 12(-2) + 8 = -128$$
$$f'''(x) = 60x^2 - 12 \qquad f'''(-2) = 60(-2)^2 - 12 = 228$$
$$f^{(iv)}(x) = 120x \qquad f^{(iv)}(-2) = 120(-2) = -240$$
$$f^{(v)}(x) = 120 \qquad f^{(v)}(-2) = 120$$
$$f^{(vi)}(x) = 0 \qquad f^{(vi)}(-2) = 0$$

So, $P(x) = 40(x + 2) - 64(x + 2)^2 + 38(x + 2)^3 - 10(x + 2)^4 + (x + 2)^5$.

Note that f is a polynomial so that P is a re-factorization of f.

CHAPTER 7

Content Domain 6: History of Mathematics

7.1 Chronological and Topical Developments of Mathematics

This area of the *Mathematics Subject Matter Requirements* states two related objectives that are not easily separated. Hence, we state both here and address them together.

> **7.1.1** The California *Mathematics Subject Matter Requirements* stipulate that candidates for any credential program for teaching secondary mathematics must be able to *demonstrate understanding of the development of mathematics, its cultural connections, and its contributions to society.*

> **7.1.2** The California *Mathematics Subject Matter Requirements* stipulate that candidates for any credential program for teaching secondary mathematics must be able to *demonstrate understanding of the historical development of mathematics, including the contributions of diverse populations as determined by race, ethnicity, culture, geography, and gender.*

One should read many books on the development of mathematics to completely grasp the magnificent achievement that has brought us to where we are now in mathematics. To truly be prepared for the CSET, it is recommended that if the future mathematics teacher has not taken a college-level *History of Mathematics* course he/she should read and work through a textbook on this subject. Some texts that are widely recommended are listed at the end of this chapter. What follows is a summary of the development of mathematics with listed sources that the future teacher may want to read.

435

The Origins of Mathematics

Professor G. Donald Allen of Texas A & M University has a website of lectures on the history of mathematics (*www.math.tamu.edu/*). This section is mainly based on his lecture on the origins of mathematics.

The origins of mathematics are found in the evolution of social systems. Social systems require numbers and calculations, and the ability to compute enables more complex relations and interactions between peoples; this requires a well-organized operational system.

But the origins of mathematics include more than just enumeration, counting, and arithmetic. The concept of *number* was a common link between societies and a basis for communication and trade. However, at the basic level mankind's mathematical needs were counting, calculations, and measurement. For example, herdsmen need to be able to count the herd, inheritance needs to be divided, and building temples requires information about geometric shapes and measurement. So mathematics was born from practical needs and the questions "How many?" and "How much?". This is the *cardinal number* viewpoint of mathematics. The alternative *ordinal* viewpoint is based on the concept of ranking or questions such as "What or who comes first, second, etc.?". This viewpoint also arose from societies' needs.

There are two competing opinions on how counting originated throughout the world; one is that counting developed more or less independently in different societies and cultures, and the other is that counting was invented in one place and then was taught to others as people traveled, such as with the silk trade.

Mathematical artifacts have been discovered from various ancient eras. The oldest mathematical artifact currently known was discovered in Africa near Swaziland. It is a piece of baboon fibula with 29 notches, which indicates tallying, and has been dated to 35,000 BCE. The first known forms of fired clay tokens were used by Neolithic people to record products of farming at sites near present-day Syria and Iran, in 8,000 BCE. Tokens are believed to have been instrumental in separating the ideas of number and written word. In 2002, scientists discovered some paleolithic art in the Blombos cave in the southern tip of South Africa that dates back 70,000 years; these discoveries included two pieces of rock decorated with geometric patterns. Multicolored knotted cords, called quipus, have been found that were used for record-keeping by the Incas of Peru around 1500 CE. Other cultures, such as the Chinese, also used knotted materials for mathematics.

The four places where there is physical evidence of significant mathematical development during early times are China, India, Egypt, and Mesopotamia/Babylonia.

- The earliest mathematical textbook is from China; it was written over a long period of time (circa 1105 BCE–220 CE.) and has the title *Chou Pei Suan Ching* ("The Arithmetical Classic of the Gnomon and the Circular Paths of Heaven"). It is an anonymous collection of more than 240 problems collected by the Duke of Zhou (brother of the King in the Zhou dynasty) and his astrologer Shang Gao. It includes one of the earliest uses of the Pythagorean Theorem but without proof. The Chinese are also credited with the discovery of the magic square puzzles and using mathematics in astronomy.

- The Hindus in India developed mathematics in the areas of number theory, geometry, and astronomy, and their complex computational methods rivaled those of Greece except in geometry. The Hindus first began to use mathematics to serve religion in the study of the stars. The dates of their mathematical accomplishments seem to start around 1000 BCE with some arithmetic operations used in *Narad Vishnu Purana* by Hindu scholar Ved Vyas.

- Evidence of early Egyptian mathematics comes from several famous papyri (the Rhind and Moscow) containing collections of mathematical problems with their solutions. These papyri date from about 1650 BCE, well before the development of Greek philosophy and mathematics. They consist mostly of applied problems written for studies for students, as well as for leaders and builders. Many are logistic problems of the type needed to feed a large army or workforce.

- Babylonian mathematics also was a tool in the service of the state. Babylonian counting was positional and included a numeral zero for place keeping. Both achievements, position and zero, are considered among the greatest inventions of mankind. These allowed the Babylonians to write extremely large numbers with fewer symbols, affording the completion of more difficult computations. There is evidence of interpolation of tables to solve nonlinear equations and an elegant method for computing the square root of two. Most of what we know about Babylonian mathematics has been found on clay tablets that date to before 1600 BCE.

The study of mathematics of these four early civilizations contrasts to that of the Greeks in the classical mathematics period, who were able to develop the model of abstract mathematics by way of geometry, which has continued to be been the model of mathematical achievement until modern times.

The Development of Mathematics

In 2010, Assad Ebrahim, director of engineering at BioSonics Inc., wrote an excellent article titled "The Development of Mathematics." Ebrahim earned his master's degree in applied mathematics at University of Washington in 2001. Since then, he has remained involved in education and has taught workshops and college courses in the Seattle area. Most of what follows in this section is drawn from Ebrahim's article.

Ebrahim believes the development of mathematics can be broken into seven periods:

1. **Proto-Mathematics, circa 30000 BCE to 2000 BCE:** The mathematics of this time was basic and not abstract, and it was more empirical in nature. *Empirical* means learned or presented by experiment and observation. Mathematics was used for practical purposes, such as counting, measuring, shape, and keeping time. As humankind evolved during this period, it had more need to use mathematics in its everyday living—interacting with the environment and pursuing an agricultural lifestyle. Much mathematical evidence is archeological in nature—bone fragments used for counting or time keeping, for instance. Written evidence of mathematics appeared around 3500 BCE. Ebrahim discusses the probable need for humans to use comparison of

numbers of people in tribes or to use timekeeping well before 30,000 BCE. Once humans were capable of speech, there was most likely the usage of mathematics in some form.

2. **Ancient Mathematics, circa 2000 BCE to 800 BCE:** Mathematics is still rather empirical in nature but by around 3500 BCE the Egyptians had developed a number system and the Babylonians, by 300 BCE, had created a pictorial sexagesimal (base 60) number system. Both the Babylonians and Egyptians during this era used mathematics for astronomy, building, surveying, and calculating areas and volumes. The Egyptian pyramids and monuments are evidence of sophisticated calculations and usage of geometry. The astronomical calculations of both cultures were surprisingly precise. Other usages of mathematics during this time include the administration of planning and supplying for large armies, solving quadratic and cubic equations, and other architectural calculations. The Babylonians had introduced place value and a decimal point, but there is no evidence of an axiomatic or formal system for any mathematics. Mathematical proof at the end of this period was informal or demonstrative sometimes with erroneous conclusions.

3. **Classical Mathematics, circa 800 BCE to 1400 CE:** In the earlier part of this time period the Greeks introduced the axiomatic approach, to mathematics bringing a more formal structure to mathematics. This is the time of great advancement in geometry. The Greeks and Romans used this more sophisticated approach in their study of mechanics and astronomy. The realization that rational numbers could not represent the length of the diagonal of a cube with rational side lengths was unsatisfying to the Greeks and led to paradoxes in logical methodology. This in turn, led to accepting mathematics as useful (concrete) but regarding it as something with flaws in the abstract. Euclid's books *The Elements* were written during this time and are still regarded as the great advancement in various mathematical areas including geometry, algebra, and number theory.

In the latter part of this time period, algebra was also sophistically developed in the Arab, Central Asian, and Indian mathematical societies. The algorithmic processes used in modern algebra were developed in these cultures and used in the areas of optics, astronomy, and engineering.

4. **Mercantile Mathematics, circa 1400 CE to 1500 CE:** Computation and calculations, now including negative numbers and symbols, were sophisticatedly developed in the Arab, Central Asian, Indian, and Chinese cultures to be used in various practical areas. These ideas flowed to Italy, also being a mercantile state, and then spread to other parts of Europe. With this resurgence, an interest in solving polynomial equations occurred. The concept of a continuous function was developed during this time by Galileo following his observations and modeling of astronomical situations, and also by Descartes and Fermat in their studies of analytic geometry. Until this period, most functions were discrete or polynomial or rational. The collection of functions under these studies by Galileo, Descartes, Fermat, and others expanded to the trigonometric, logarithmic, and exponential functions. The area of calculus emerged mostly as a geometric area of mathematics with some numerical computation to support ideas concerning the tangent problem (differential calculus) and areas (integral calculus).

5. **Pre-Modern Mathematics, circa 1500 CE to 1700 CE:** The analytic methods of the mercantile era produced progress in the areas of number theory separate from algebra, geometric analysis

without the concept of limits, complex analysis, and probability theory. Mathematicians were still called "geometers" rather than mathematicians.

6. **Modern Mathematics, circa 1700 CE to 1950 CE:** A deep development and synthesis of mathematics occurred in this time period. Euler's ideas at the beginning of this era led the transformation. Mathematicians were now called "mathematicians" rather than "geometers." Many ideas that developed in this period, including the ones below, brought the mathematical world to an incredible understanding and unification of mathematical knowledge.

(a) Galois Theory, which revealed the impossibility of solvability of certain unsolved algebraic problems.

(b) The concept of a limit and the infinite, to be used in calculus as part of the definition of derivatives, integrals, series, sequences, and the completion of our number system with the addition of irrational numbers.

(c) The understanding of a multitude of algebraic structures, including integers, polynomials, number theory, matrices, quaternions, and vectors, and being able to apply algebraic mathematics to geometry and the continuum.

(d) The introduction of non-Euclidean geometries and the resolution of whether Euclid's Fifth Postulate could be proven from the other four postulates of Euclid.

(e) The development of set theory and topology.

(f) The proof of the existence of transcendental numbers and the proof that π and e are transcendental.

(g) The development of real analysis and measure theory.

7. **Post-Modern Mathematics: 1950 CE to present:** In Ebrahim's words: *Post-modern mathematics is thus characterized by the analytic and set theoretic language of mathematical practice and also by the modern algebraic.* Some of what he alludes to is the more standard axiomatic approaches and presentations of mathematics in today's world. This period is also characterized by the increased use of technology to test and model mathematical ideas in mathematics applied to the real world.

Some Famous Problems and Ideas in the History of Mathematics

These problems and ideas are presented here in no special order. Links to websites discussed below can be found at www.rea.com.

1. **The Bridges of Konigsberg:** This problem dates from the mid-1700s. In Konigsberg, Germany, a river ran through the city such that in its center was an island, and after passing the island, the

river broke into two parts. Seven bridges were built so that the people of the city could get from one part to another. A crude map of the center of Konigsberg might be as shown in Figure 7.1:

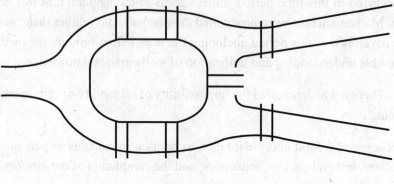

Figure 7.1

The people wondered whether one could walk around the city in a way that would involve crossing each bridge exactly once. Euler's solution can be found at the *mathforum.org/isaac/problems/bridges2.html*. The solution involves ideas from the mathematics area of graph theory.

2. **Squaring the Circle** (Quadrature of the Circle): This problem, first formulated in about 1800 BCE by the Greeks, is to construct a square equal in area to that of a given circle (Figure 7.2). This is one of three big problems of classical geometry; the other two are (i) trisecting an angle and (ii) the duplication of the cube. The construction must be done with only a straightedge and compass.

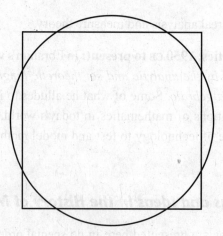

Figure 7.2

To construct such a square, we would need to construct a line segment with length equal to $\sqrt{\pi}r$, where r is the radius of the given circle. In 1882 CE, German mathematician Ferdinand Lindemann proved that π is transcendental; this proved that the construction was impossible with only a straightedge and compass. (see *mathforum.org/isaac/problems/pi3.html*.)

3. **Zeno's Paradoxes.** There are 4 paradoxes presented by the Greek philosopher Zeno of Elea (born circa 490 BCE). These paradoxes stymied mathematicians for centuries, until Cantor's development (in the late nineteenth century) of the theory of infinite sets. Here is one of them:

The Paradox on Motion: A runner wants to run a certain distance—let us say 100 meters—in a finite time. But to reach the 100-meter mark, the runner must first reach the 50-meter mark, and to reach that, the runner must first run 25 meters. But to do that, he/she must first run 12.5 meters. So far there does not seem to be a problem, but this description of the run has the runner travelling an *infinite* number of *finite* distances, which, Zeno would have us conclude, must take an infinite time, so the run is never completed. It follows that no finite distance can ever be traveled, which is to say that all motion is impossible. Understanding that an infinitely long series might equal a limit solves this paradox. An equation that will explain how a convergent series converges to a limit is as follows: "$\frac{1}{2} + \frac{1}{4} + \frac{1}{8} + \frac{1}{16} \cdots = 1$." The end of the race is represented by "1" instead of infinity. To learn more about all of Zeno's paradoxes, go to the website of the *Stanford Encyclopedia of Philosophy, plato.stanford.edu/entries/paradox-zeno/.*

4. **Trisecting an Angle:** The second problem from the ancient Greeks was to be able to divide a given angle into three equal-sized sub-angles (Figure 7.3) using only compass a and straight-edge. In approximately 1836 CE. French mathematician Pierre Wantzel proved that it was impossible to trisect an angle without using other tools; the problem boiled down to being able to construct a segment of length $\sqrt{2}$. (see *mathworld.wolfram.com/AngleTrisection.html.*)

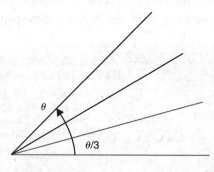

Figure 7.3

5. **The Four-Color Problem:** The four-color Problem originated around 1850 CE when Francis Guthrie, who was trying to color a map of the counties of England, noticed that he needed only four colors. He asked his brother Frederick if he thought it was true that any map can be colored using four colors in such a way that adjacent regions (i.e., those sharing a common boundary segment, not just a point) are given different colors. Such a map of the United States is shown in Figure 7.4 below.) Frederick Guthrie then communicated the conjecture to mathematician Augustus De Morgan. The first printed reference is due to Cayley in 1878. Modern day mathematicians Appel and Haken published their proof that the conjecture is true in 1976. The proof used the area of mathmatics called graph theory.

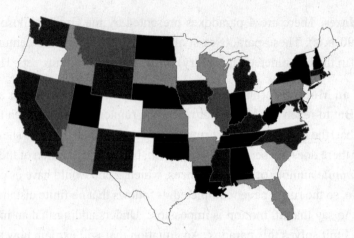

Figure 7.4

6. **The Rhind Papyrus**: The Rhind mathematical papyrus, written about 1650 BCE, was discovered mid-nineteenth century in an archaeological excavation near Thebes and bought by A. Henry Rhind, a Scottish lawyer, who had become interested in Egyptian antiquities when visiting Egypt for health reasons. Other objects and papyri had been discovered in Egypt, but they contained hieroglyphic and hieratic script and non-mathematical writings. The Rhind papyrus has provided the world with a clear view of Egyptian mathematics from ancient times. The first part of the Rhind papyrus consists of reference tables and a collection of 20 arithmetic and 20 algebraic problems ranging from simple fractional expressions to linear equations. The second part of the Rhind papyrus consists of geometry problems. A piece of the papyrus is shown in Figure 7.5.

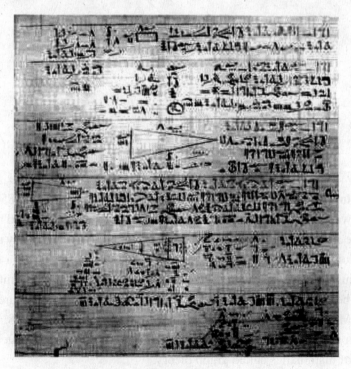

Figure 7.5

7. **The Value of Pi:** Throughout time, different people established what they thought was the value of pi. Around 2000 BCE humans, figured out that the ratio of the circumference of a circle to its diameter was the same no matter the size of the circle. The notation π to represent this number was not used until the 1700s. Figure 7.6 below shows the progress of computing π over time.

The Value of Pi

People/Person	Year	Value of Pi produced
Babylonians	≈ 2000 BCE	$3\frac{1}{8}$
Egyptians	≈ 2000 BCE	$\left(\frac{16}{9}\right)^2 \approx 3.1605$
Chinese	≈ 1200 BCE	3
Old Testament	≈ 550 BCE	3
Archimedes	≈ 300 BCE	proves $3\frac{10}{71} < \pi < 3\frac{1}{7}$
Ptolemy	≈ 200 CE	$\frac{377}{120} = 3.141666...$
Chung Huing	≈ 300 CE	$\sqrt{10} = 3.166...$
Wang Fau	≈ 263 CE	$\frac{157}{50} = 3.14$
Tsu Chung-Chi	≈ 500 CE	proves $3.1415926 < \pi < 3.1415929$
Aryabhatta	≈ 500 CE	3.1416
Brahmagupta	≈ 500 CE	$\sqrt{10}$
Fibonacci	≈ 1220 CE	3.141818
Ludolph van Ceulen	≈ 1596 CE	calculates π correctly to 35 decimal places
Machin	1706 CE	calculates π correctly to 100 places
Lambert	1766 CE	proves π is irrational
Richter	1855 CE	calculates π correctly to 500 places
Lindemann	1882 CE	proves is transcendental
Ferguson	1947 CE	calculates π correctly to 808 places
Pegasus Computer	1957 CE	calculates π correctly to 7840 places
IBM 7090 computer	1961 CE	calculates π correctly to 100,000 places
CDC 6600 computer	1967 CE	calculates π correctly to 500,000 places
multiple scientists	2010 CE	calculates π correctly to more than 5 trillion places

Figure 7.6

8. **Duplicating a Cube:** The third construction problem that the Greeks proposed and struggled with is to find a cube equal in volume to twice a given cube. So, if the edge of the given cube is one unit, the problem is to find a line equal in length to the cube root of two. The cube root of two is an irrational number (approximately 1.2599210498948732...). This problem is equivalent to solving a cubic equation using geometry, and is algebraically similar to trisecting an angle. So since Wantzel showed that $\sqrt{2}$ is not constructible, this problem is also impossible.

9. **The Pythagorean Theorem:** *The square of the length of the hypotenuse of a right triangle is equal to the sum of the squares of the lengths of the legs.*

There are many proofs of this famous theorem and many illustrations to accompany them. One proof using similar triangles is shown in Chapter 4 in section 4.2.2 of this book. There are 35 proofs of the Pythagorean Theorem at the *Cut The Knot* website which has a large collection of interesting mathematics (*www.cut-the-knot.org/pythagoras/index.shtml*). Figures 7.7 and 7.8 are illustrations from different proofs of the Pythagorean Theorem.

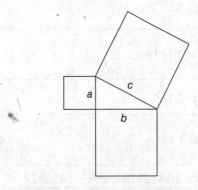

Figure 7.7

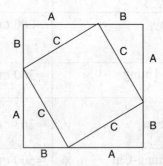

Figure 7.8

10. **There are Infinitely Many Prime Numbers.** This statement was proved by Euclid (circa 300 BCE) as follows: Assume there are only finitely many primes, say $p_1, p_2, p_3, \ldots, p_n$, and let $p = p_1 p_2 p_3 \cdots p_n + 1$. Then every prime number has a remainder of 1 when dividing p. This means that p is prime but this is a contradiction to our assumption. Thus there must be infinitely many prime numbers! A short list of the least primes is shown below. (see *primes.utm.edu/notes/proofs/infinite/euclids.html*.)

2, 3, 5, 7, 11, 13, 17, 19, 23, 29, 31, 37, 41, 43, 47, 53, 59, 61, 67, 71, 73, 79, 83, 89, 97,....

11. **The Number *e* is Transcendental** ($e \approx 2.7182818284590...$): French mathematician Charles Hermite was the first to prove this in 1873. A transcendental number is a real number that is not algebraic, meaning that it is not a root of a non-constant polynomial equation with rational coefficients. There have been various proofs of the transcendentalism of *e* and also that *e* is an irrational number; the proof of the latter statement by French mathematician Jean Baptiste Joseph Fourier (written circa, 1800) is presented on the Math Forum website: *mathforum.org/isaac/*

problems/eproof.html. More on *e* can be found at *www.history.mcs.st-and.ac.uk/HistTopics/e. html*.

12. **Solution of Cubic Equations:** Persian mathematician and philosopher Omar Khayyám of the eleventh and twelfth century is generally credited for establishing solutions of cubic equations using the intersection of a hyperbola with a circle (conic sections). Greek geometer Apollonius of Perga (circa 200 BCE) in the book *Conics* also developed ideas related to the mathematical area of analytic geometry. The work of both men is thought to have led to the work of René Descartes on solving cubic equations approximately 1800 years later.

13. **The Monty Hall Problem:** On the game show *Let's Make a Deal* (1960s–present), the host, Monty Hall, gives contestants the choice of three doors. Behind one door is the grand prize; behind the others—a goat. You want the grand prize, of course, and you pick a door, say door 1. Mr. Hall, who knows what is behind each door, opens another door, say door 2, revealing another goat. Mr. Hall then offers the contestant the opportunity to change the selection to door 3. Should the contestant the stick with the original choice or switch? Does it make any difference? Marilyn vos Savant gives a clear explanation of the probability used to answer these questions at *www.marilynvossavant.com/articles/gameshow.html*.

Figure 7.9

14. **Goldbach's Conjecture:** Christian Goldbach wrote conjecture in a letter to Euler in 1742 as follows: *Every even number greater than 4 can be written as the sum of two odd prime numbers*. Some progress has been made on the proof of this statement by various mathematicians, but it has yet to be proven. Information on Goldbach's Conjecture can be found at *primes.utm.edu/notes/conjectures/*.

15. **The History of Zero:** It is thought that the first use of zero occurred in about 350 BCE by the Babylonians, and sometime after it was also developed by the Indians. It is reported that the concept of zero was brought to Europe by Fibonacci. Zero was first used as a placeholder in the sense of differentiating between numbers such as 23 and 203. The Mayans are thought to have independently discovered and used the concept of zero as a placeholder in their calendar system around the third century CE The Indians were probably the first people to use zero as a number rather than a placeholder in the fifth century CE They spread the use of a number zero to the Chinese and later to the Arabs.

16. **Twin Prime Conjecture:** Twin primes are pairs of prime numbers whose difference is 2; for example, (3, 5), (5, 7), and (11, 13) are three pairs of twin primes. The conjecture is: *There are infinitely many twin primes*. This conjecture dates back at least 150 years, and there is some controversy on who first made the conjecture. This conjecture still has not been proved or disproved. (see *primes.utm.edu/top20/*.)

17. **Fermat's Last Theorem:** Pierre de Fermat was an early seventeenth-century French lawyer and amateur mathematician who made many contributions to mathematics (e.g., number theory, geometry, optics). Around 1637, Fermat was reading the book *Arithmetica* by the Greek mathematician Diophantus, and he wrote in the margin, "I have discovered a truly marvelous proof that it is impossible to separate a cube into two cubes, or a fourth power into two fourth powers, or in general, any power higher than the second into two like powers. This margin is too narrow to contain it."This statement was final proved in 1993 by Princeton University Professor Andrew Wiles.

18. **Euler's Formula in Complex Analysis:** Swiss mathematician Leonard Euler's idea of substituting $i\theta$ into the infinite series representing the exponential function $e^x = \sum_{n=0}^{\infty} \dfrac{x^n}{n!}$, and then collecting the real and imaginary terms to arrive at $e^{i\theta} = \cos\theta + i\sin\theta$ (Figure 7.10) made an important connection between analysis and trigonometry. He included this in his 1748 *Introductio in analysin infinitorum*. (see *en.wikipedia.org/wiki/Euler's_formula*.)

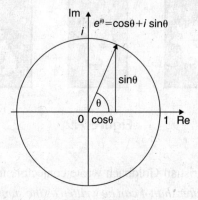

Figure 7.10

19. **Estimating the Circumference of the Earth:** Greek mathematician Eratosthenes, born circa 247 BCE in Cyrene (in current-day Libya), approximated the circumference of Earth. He used the approximate distance between Cyrene and Alexandria, as measured by camel-powered trade caravans, and then he measured the angle of a shadow of a stick in Alexandria on the solstice; this meant the sun was directly overhead in Cyrene at a certain time and there would be no shadow there. The angle of the shadow (7°12'), divided into 360°, and multiplied by the distance between Alexandria and Cyrene, gave Eratosthenes the approximate circumference. In today's measurements, this was 25,000 miles, just 100 miles over the actual circumference at the equator (24,901 miles).

20. **Gödel's Incompleteness Theorem:** Austrian mathematician Kurt Gödel came up with his Incompleteness Theorem in 1931. Gödel's statement is, "Anything you can draw a circle around cannot explain itself without referring to something outside the circle—something you have to assume but cannot prove." For example, we can draw a circle around all of the concepts in a high school geometry book, but they're all built on Euclid's five original postulates, which are assumed to be true. Gödel's Incompleteness Theorem applies to *everything* that is subject to the laws of logic. The theorem implies that if the universe is mathematical and logical, incompleteness also applies to the universe.

21. **Fundamental Theorem of Algebra:** *Every polynomial equation of degree n with complex coefficients has n roots in the complex numbers.* The origin of this theorem is not clear, although various proofs, (both valid and invalid,) of the statement or of a related statement were being generated beginning in the 1500s. German mathematician Johann Carl Friedrich Gauss is credited with the first correct proof of this theorem in 1799 as part of his doctoral dissertation. He also was the first to identify the error in the earlier proofs, which was the assumption of the existence of roots and then deducing properties of them.

22. **First Calculating Machine:** In 1642, Blaise Pascal, the French philosopher, mathematician, and physicist, invented the first mechanical calculating machine. It could add and subtract directly, and multiply and divide by repetition. Pascal developed the machine to aid his father, who was a tax collector. He went through many prototypes before presenting it to the public. These machines are the ancestors of our modern calculators.

23. **The Independence of the Fifth Postulate of Euclid:** During the approximately 20 centuries following Euclid's presentation of his postulates and geometry, a multitude of mathematicians made it their goal to prove that the Fifth Postulate of Euclid was dependent on the first four; (i.e., the Fifth Postulate could be proven from the other four). But in 1868, Italian mathematician Eugenio Beltrami indirectly proved that the Fifth Postulate indeed is independent of the other four in his paper *Essay on an Interpretation of Non-Euclidean Geometry*.

24. **The Fundamental Theorem of Calculus:** Although German mathematician and philosopher Gottfried Leibniz (1646–1716) and English mathematician, physicist, and astronomer Isaac Newton (1642–1727) are considered to be the "inventors of calculus" and it is clear that they intuitively understood the ideas of the Fundamental Theorem of Calculus, French mathematician Augustin Louis Cauchy was the first to write down the rigorous ideas and proofs of calculus. Newton's interpretations of calculus were algebraic and based on physical models of time, motion, and velocity, whereas Leibniz's ideas about integrals, derivatives, and calculus in general were derived from close analogies with finite sums and differences. The modern proof of the Fundamental Theorem of Calculus was written in Cauchy's *Lessons Given at the École Royale Polytechnique on the Infinitesimal Calculus* in 1823, which finally provided the elegant connection between differential and integral calculus.

Mathematicians throughout History

Information about mathematicians of all races, genders, ethnicities, cultures, eras, and countries can be found easily today by searching the internet. A short list of websites can be found at *www.rea.com/studycenter*

As mentioned at the beginning of this chapter, to thoroughly prepare for the CSET, one should either take a *History of Mathematics* course or read and study a good textbook on the subject. Here is a shortlist of good textbooks:

- *History of Mathematics: An Introduction,* 7th edition by David Burton, McGraw-Hill Science, 2010.

- *Journey through Genius: The Great Theorems of Mathematics* by William Dunham, Penguin, 1991.

- *A History of Mathematics* by Victor Katz, HarperCollins, 3rd edition, 2008.

- *Great Moments in Mathematics before 1650 and Great Moments in Mathematics after 1650* by Howard Eves, Mathematical Association of America, 1983.

Review Problems for Section 7.1.1

1. True or False:

   (a) The first mechanical calculating machine was invented in the twentieth century.

   (b) For Euclid, a line was infinite in length.

   (c) The number π is transcendental.

   (d) The Greeks knew how to duplicate the cube using only a compass and straightedge.

   (e) Sir Isaac Newton gave the first formal proof of the Fundamental Theorem of Calculus.

   (f) The four-color problem was solved in the nineteenth century soon after it was discovered.

   (g) Greeks preferred the study of the mathematics area of geometry over algebra because Geometry came from a rigorous (axiomatiic) system, whereas algebra did not.

   (h) Eratosthenes estimated the circumference of Earth using the shadow of a stick.

   (i) Mathematicians were generally called geometers until the modern period.

2. Carefully state and explain the three famous Greek construction problems.

3. Why is Euclid's *Elements* seen as a significant step in the history of mathematics?

4. Who was the first mathematician to use conics to solve cubic equations, leading the way for the later development of analytical geometry?

   (A) Omar Khayyám

   (B) David Hilbert

   (C) René Descartes

(D)   Euclid

5.   Who proved that $\sqrt{2}$ is not constructible, which proves that it is impossible to trisect an angle using only a straightedge and compass?

(A)   Euclid

(B)   Eratosthenes

(C)   David Hilbert

(D)   Pierre Wantzel

6.   Explain Zeno's paradox on motion.

7.   Prove the Pythagorean Theorem in reference to this figure:

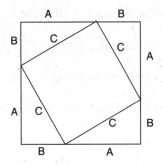

Figure 7.11

8.   Mathematics originally developed as an answer to which of the following?

(A)   Lack of travel

(B)   Societies' needs

(C)   Need for the Pythagorean Theorem

(D)   Logical arguments

9.   Which of the following relates trigonometry to exponentials?

(A)   Goldbach's conjecture

(B)   Spherical geometry

(C)   The Fundamental Theorem of Algebra

(D)   Euler's Formula

10.   Prior to the existence of trigonometric tables, Archimedes found that $\frac{223}{71} < \pi < \frac{22}{7}$ by comparing the perimeters of 96-sided regular polygons inscribed in and circumscribed about a circle of radius 1. Archimedes started with 6-sided polygons and found numerical values of the perimeters of these inscribed and circumscribed hexagons. He then derived a recursive

formula that used the numerical values found to calculate the perimeters of 12-sided polygons. This formula was equivalent to the modern half-angle formulas of trigonometry. The method was then repeated with 24-sided, 48-sided, and 96-sided polygons.

(a) Repeat Archimedes' method using trigonometry to find upper and lower bounds for π determining the perimeters of a hexagon inscribed in and a circumscribed about a circle of radius 1. Express the answer using exact values.

(b) Explain (without actually doing) how the trigonometric half-angle formulas can be used to extend the result to 96-sided inscribed and circumscribed polygons to obtain a more accurate approximation of π.

Detailed Solutions

1. (a) False. Blaise Pascal invented the first mechanical calculating machine in 1642.

   (b) False. For Euclid, a line is what we would call a line segment.

   (c) True. Both e and π are transcendental.

   (d) False. The Greeks proposed the problem but did not know whether it was possible.

   (e) False. Cauchy presented the first formal proof of the Fundamental Theorem of Calculus.

   (f) False. The four-color problem was not proved until the latter part of the twentieth century.

   (g) True. The Greeks originated the axiomatic system.

   (h) True. A shadow of a stick was used in Alexandria.

   (i) True. Mathematicians were not generally referred as "mathematicians" until a few centuries ago.

2. The three famous Greek construction problems are (i) squaring the circle, (ii) trisecting an angle, and (iii) duplicating the cube.

3. Euclid's *The Elements* demonstrated the first systematic treatment of mathematics, which proceeded from clearly stated axioms (postulates and common notions) to theorems (propositions) so that the proofs used only axioms and previously proved results. This ensured that the proofs were not circular and made clear how the theory depended on each particular axiom.

4. A

5. D

6. Zeno's paradox on motion is that it takes an infinite amount of time to travel a finite distance. Thus, motion is not possible.

7. Proof: Given the dissected square in Figure 7.11. The large square, with area $(A + B)^2$, is dissected into four right triangles each, having area $\frac{1}{2}AB$, and a smaller square with area C^2.

Hence, we have: $\left(A + B\right)^2 = 4\left(\frac{1}{2}AB\right) + C^2$. Since $(A + B)^2 = A^2 + 2AB + B^2$, we can substitute

and obtain $A^2 + 2AB + B^2 = 4\left(\frac{1}{2}AB\right) + C^2$. Simplifying, this is equivalent to $A^2 + B^2 = C^2$.

Q.E.D.

8. B

9. D

10. (a) In Figure 7.13, $ABCDEF$ can be partitioned into six equilateral triangles so $m\angle AOB = 60°$, $\theta = 30°$, and $OP = 1$. Using trigonometry, we obtain $\tan(\theta) = AP/PO = AP$, so $AP = \tan 30° = \frac{\sqrt{3}}{3}$. Hence, the circumference of the circumscribed hexagon $ABCDEF$ is $(6)(2)\left(\frac{\sqrt{3'}}{3}\right) = 4\sqrt{3}$.

Therefore, $2\pi < 4\sqrt{3}$.

Now consider the inscribed regular hexagon $PQRSTU$. Its perimeter, $6UP$, is smaller than the circumference of the circle. Using trigonometry, $UP = 2\sin\theta = 2(0.5) = 1$. Hence, the circumference of the inscribed hexagon $PQRSTU$ is 6.

It follows that $6 < 2\pi$.

Therefore, $6 < 2\pi < 4\sqrt{3}$, so that $3 < \pi < 2\sqrt{3}$.

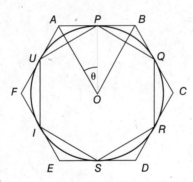

Figure 7.13

(b) If we inscribe and circumscribe a regular dodecagon (12 sides) about a circle of radius 1, we can partition each 12-gon into 12 sub-triangles with central angles half of that of the hexagons in part (a). So instead, calculating the perimeters of the two 12-gons, we obtain:

$12\left(2\sin\left(\dfrac{\theta}{2}\right)\right) < 2\pi < 12\left(2\tan\left(\dfrac{\theta}{2}\right)\right)$, or $12\sin\left(\dfrac{\theta}{2}\right) < \pi < 12\tan\left(\dfrac{\theta}{2}\right)$. So if we then compute the sine and tangent of 15° by using the half angle formulas to obtain a better approximation for π. Then, repeating this for 24-gons, we would have: $24\sin\left(\dfrac{\theta}{4}\right) < \pi < 24\tan\left(\dfrac{\theta}{4}\right)$. We could repeat this for 48-gons and 96-gons, etc., to get better approximations.

CSET: Mathematics

Practice Test 1

This test is also on CD in our special interactive TestWare® for the CSET: Mathematics Test. It is highly recommended that you first take this exam on computer. You will then have the additional study features and benefits of enforced timed conditions and instantaneous, accurate scoring. See page 6 for instructions on how to get the most out of this book and software.

Multiple-Choice Answer Sheet

Use the ovals below and on the next page to indicate your answer choices for the multiple-choice sections of the exam.

Subtest I

1. Ⓐ Ⓑ Ⓒ Ⓓ
2. Ⓐ Ⓑ Ⓒ Ⓓ
3. Ⓐ Ⓑ Ⓒ Ⓓ
4. Ⓐ Ⓑ Ⓒ Ⓓ
5. Ⓐ Ⓑ Ⓒ Ⓓ
6. Ⓐ Ⓑ Ⓒ Ⓓ
7. Ⓐ Ⓑ Ⓒ Ⓓ
8. Ⓐ Ⓑ Ⓒ Ⓓ

9. Ⓐ Ⓑ Ⓒ Ⓓ
10. Ⓐ Ⓑ Ⓒ Ⓓ
11. Ⓐ Ⓑ Ⓒ Ⓓ
12. Ⓐ Ⓑ Ⓒ Ⓓ
13. Ⓐ Ⓑ Ⓒ Ⓓ
14. Ⓐ Ⓑ Ⓒ Ⓓ
15. Ⓐ Ⓑ Ⓒ Ⓓ
16. Ⓐ Ⓑ Ⓒ Ⓓ

17. Ⓐ Ⓑ Ⓒ Ⓓ
18. Ⓐ Ⓑ Ⓒ Ⓓ
19. Ⓐ Ⓑ Ⓒ Ⓓ
20. Ⓐ Ⓑ Ⓒ Ⓓ
21. Ⓐ Ⓑ Ⓒ Ⓓ
22. Ⓐ Ⓑ Ⓒ Ⓓ
23. Ⓐ Ⓑ Ⓒ Ⓓ
24. Ⓐ Ⓑ Ⓒ Ⓓ

25. Ⓐ Ⓑ Ⓒ Ⓓ
26. Ⓐ Ⓑ Ⓒ Ⓓ
27. Ⓐ Ⓑ Ⓒ Ⓓ
28. Ⓐ Ⓑ Ⓒ Ⓓ
29. Ⓐ Ⓑ Ⓒ Ⓓ
30. Ⓐ Ⓑ Ⓒ Ⓓ

Subtest II

1. Ⓐ Ⓑ Ⓒ Ⓓ
2. Ⓐ Ⓑ Ⓒ Ⓓ
3. Ⓐ Ⓑ Ⓒ Ⓓ
4. Ⓐ Ⓑ Ⓒ Ⓓ
5. Ⓐ Ⓑ Ⓒ Ⓓ
6. Ⓐ Ⓑ Ⓒ Ⓓ
7. Ⓐ Ⓑ Ⓒ Ⓓ
8. Ⓐ Ⓑ Ⓒ Ⓓ

9. Ⓐ Ⓑ Ⓒ Ⓓ
10. Ⓐ Ⓑ Ⓒ Ⓓ
11. Ⓐ Ⓑ Ⓒ Ⓓ
12. Ⓐ Ⓑ Ⓒ Ⓓ
13. Ⓐ Ⓑ Ⓒ Ⓓ
14. Ⓐ Ⓑ Ⓒ Ⓓ
15. Ⓐ Ⓑ Ⓒ Ⓓ
16. Ⓐ Ⓑ Ⓒ Ⓓ

17. Ⓐ Ⓑ Ⓒ Ⓓ
18. Ⓐ Ⓑ Ⓒ Ⓓ
19. Ⓐ Ⓑ Ⓒ Ⓓ
20. Ⓐ Ⓑ Ⓒ Ⓓ
21. Ⓐ Ⓑ Ⓒ Ⓓ
22. Ⓐ Ⓑ Ⓒ Ⓓ
23. Ⓐ Ⓑ Ⓒ Ⓓ
24. Ⓐ Ⓑ Ⓒ Ⓓ

25. Ⓐ Ⓑ Ⓒ Ⓓ
26. Ⓐ Ⓑ Ⓒ Ⓓ
27. Ⓐ Ⓑ Ⓒ Ⓓ
28. Ⓐ Ⓑ Ⓒ Ⓓ
29. Ⓐ Ⓑ Ⓒ Ⓓ
30. Ⓐ Ⓑ Ⓒ Ⓓ

(continued on next page)

Multiple-Choice Answer Sheet

Subtest III

1. Ⓐ Ⓑ Ⓒ Ⓓ   9. Ⓐ Ⓑ Ⓒ Ⓓ   17. Ⓐ Ⓑ Ⓒ Ⓓ   25. Ⓐ Ⓑ Ⓒ Ⓓ

2. Ⓐ Ⓑ Ⓒ Ⓓ   10. Ⓐ Ⓑ Ⓒ Ⓓ   18. Ⓐ Ⓑ Ⓒ Ⓓ   26. Ⓐ Ⓑ Ⓒ Ⓓ

3. Ⓐ Ⓑ Ⓒ Ⓓ   11. Ⓐ Ⓑ Ⓒ Ⓓ   19. Ⓐ Ⓑ Ⓒ Ⓓ   27. Ⓐ Ⓑ Ⓒ Ⓓ

4. Ⓐ Ⓑ Ⓒ Ⓓ   12. Ⓐ Ⓑ Ⓒ Ⓓ   20. Ⓐ Ⓑ Ⓒ Ⓓ   28. Ⓐ Ⓑ Ⓒ Ⓓ

5. Ⓐ Ⓑ Ⓒ Ⓓ   13. Ⓐ Ⓑ Ⓒ Ⓓ   21. Ⓐ Ⓑ Ⓒ Ⓓ   29. Ⓐ Ⓑ Ⓒ Ⓓ

6. Ⓐ Ⓑ Ⓒ Ⓓ   14. Ⓐ Ⓑ Ⓒ Ⓓ   22. Ⓐ Ⓑ Ⓒ Ⓓ   30. Ⓐ Ⓑ Ⓒ Ⓓ

7. Ⓐ Ⓑ Ⓒ Ⓓ   15. Ⓐ Ⓑ Ⓒ Ⓓ   23. Ⓐ Ⓑ Ⓒ Ⓓ

8. Ⓐ Ⓑ Ⓒ Ⓓ   16. Ⓐ Ⓑ Ⓒ Ⓓ   24. Ⓐ Ⓑ Ⓒ Ⓓ

Use the space below and on the following page to answer the constructed-response questions.

CSET: Mathematics Practice Test 1, Subtest I

Content Domain I *Algebra & Number Theory*

Directions: This subtest consists of two sections:

(I) thirty multiple-choice questions, and

(II) four constructed-response questions that require written responses.

Note: The use of calculators is NOT allowed for CSET: Mathematics Subtest I.

1. Which of the following is a ring property that $X = I^- \cup \{0\}$, the set of non-positive irrational numbers, with standard addition and multiplication, does not satisfy?

   (A) The Closure Property of Multiplication

   (B) The Associative Property of Multiplication

   (C) The Additive Identity Property

   (D) The Commutative Property of Addition

2. The **center** of a group, G, is the set $Z(G) = \{a \in G | ab = ba$ for all $b \in G\}$. Consider $Z(G)$ when $G = GL_2(R)$, the collection of all invertible 2×2 matrices, with the binary operation of matrix multiplication. Let O_2 be the 2×2 zero matrix, and let I_2 be the 2×2 identity matrix. Which of the following statements confirms that, even though $Z(G)$ is a group under multiplication, $Z(G)$ is not a field with the usual matrix addition and multiplication?

   (A) $I_2 A = A$ for any A in $Z(G)$.

   (B) $\det(I_2) = 1$.

   (C) $I_2 + -I_2 = O_2$.

   (D) AB is in $Z(G)$ for any A and B in $Z(G)$.

3. Which of the following sets is not an ordered field with its standard addition and multiplication?

   (A) The rational numbers

   (B) $\{a + b\sqrt{2} \mid a$ and b are rational numbers$\}$

   (C) The real numbers

   (D) The complex numbers

4. The set $2Z$ of all even integers with standard multiplication is not a group. Name all the group properties to satisfy.

   (A) The Closure Property

   (B) The Inverse Property

   (C) The Identity and Inverse Properties

   (D) The Associative and Identity Properties

5. Which of the steps in the proof shown below illustrates definition of a conjugate?

   Assume that $z = a + bi$ and $w = c + di$ are complex numbers.
   Prove that $\overline{z - w} = \overline{z} - \overline{w}$.

   Proof: Step 1: $\qquad \overline{z - w} = \overline{(a + bi) - (c + di)}$

   Step 2: $\qquad = \overline{(a - c) + (b - d)i}$

   Step 3: $\qquad = (a - c) - (b - d)i$

   Step 4: $\qquad = a - c - bi + di$

   Step 5: $\qquad = (a - bi) - (c - di)$

   Step 6: $\qquad = \overline{a + bi} - \overline{c + di}$

   Step 7: $\qquad = \overline{z} - \overline{w}$

   $\therefore \overline{z - w} = \overline{z} - \overline{w}$ $\qquad$ Q.E.D.

(A) Steps 1 and 7

(B) Steps 2 and 6

(C) Steps 3 and 6

(D) Steps 4 and 7

5. Which of the following graphs represents the solution of the system

$$\begin{cases} x + 2y \leq 8 \\ 3x - y \geq 2 \\ 2x + y < 8 \end{cases}$$

(A)

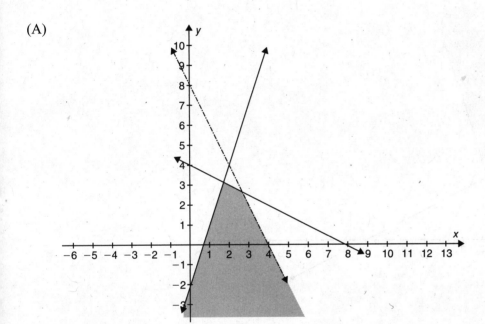

(B)

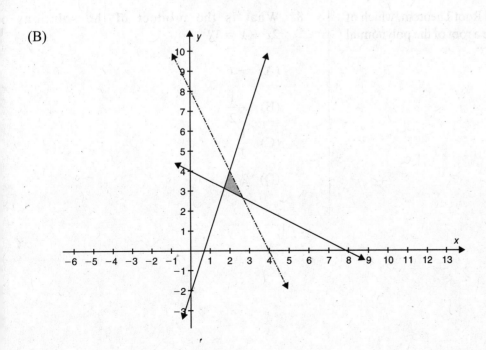

(C)

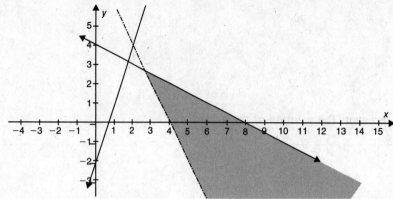

(D)

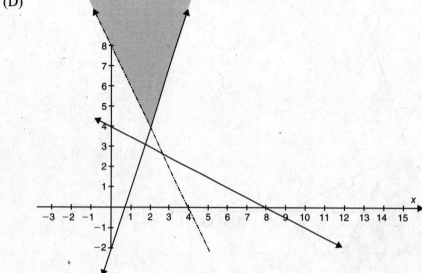

7. According to the Rational Root Theorem, which of the following could not be a root of the polynomial $p(x) = 6x^3 - 5x^2 + x + 3$?

    (A) -2

    (B) $-\dfrac{3}{2}$

    (C) $\dfrac{1}{3}$

    (D) 3

8. What is the product of the solutions of $2x^2 + x = 1$?

    (A) -6

    (B) $-\dfrac{1}{2}$

    (C) $\dfrac{1}{2}$

    (D) 2

9. Find the value of a so that $\dfrac{\left(3x^5 + x^4 - 2x^2 + 1\right)}{x-2}$

   $= q(x) - \dfrac{a}{x-2}$, where q is a polynomial of degree 4.

   (A) -105

   (B) -2

   (C) 2

   (D) 105

10. Which of the following statements is true for the equation $iz^3 + 8 = 0$?

    (A) It has one complex solution, which is not a real number.

    (B) It has two distinct complex solutions, neither of which is a real number.

    (C) It has three distinct complex solutions, with exactly one being a real number.

    (D) It has three distinct complex solutions, with none being a real number.

11. The GHM Co. is planning to build a state-subsidized rehabilitation facility for both homeless and high-income patients. State regulations require that every rehabilitation facility must house a minimum of 840 homeless patients and no more than 1000 high-income patients to qualify for state subsidies. The maximum number the facility can hold is 1500 patients. The board of directors insists that the number of homeless patients must be less than or equal to twice the number of high-income patients. Due to the state subsidy, the rehabilitation facility will make an average profit of $900 per month for every homeless patient it houses, whereas the profit per high-income patient is estimated at $600 per month. What is the maximum profit the GHM Co. can earn each month?

    (A) $1,008,000

    (B) $1,152,000

    (C) $1,200,000

    (D) $1,352,000

12. Which of the following functions does not have an inverse function?

    (A) $f(x) = x^3 + 1$

    (B) $g(x) = \dfrac{2}{x-5}$

    (C) $h(x) = -2x^2 - x + 6$

    (D) $j(x) = 6^x$

13. **Use the graph below to answer the given question.**

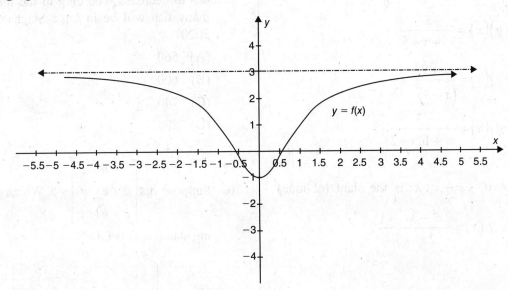

$y = f(x)$

Which of the following statements about the function f must be true?

(A) f is a polynomial.

(B) f is an exponential function.

(C) f is an odd function.

(D) f is an even function.

14. Line m is perpendicular to the line segment with endpoints $A(-3, 5)$ and $B(2, -1)$. If line m passes through the midpoint of $\overline{AB}$, what is the sum of the x-coordinate of m's x-intercept and the y-coordinate of m's y-intercept?

(A) $\dfrac{-29}{60}$

(B) $\dfrac{-13}{12}$

(C) $\dfrac{57}{12}$

(D) $\dfrac{319}{60}$

15. Let $g(x) = \dfrac{3}{x+5}$ and $h(x) = x^2 + x$. What is $(h \circ g)(x)$?

(A) $(h \circ g)(x) = \dfrac{3x^2 + 3x}{x+5}$

(B) $(h \circ g)(x) = \dfrac{3}{x^2 + x + 5}$

(C) $(h \circ g)(x) = \dfrac{3x + 24}{(x+5)^2}$

(D) $(h \circ g)(x) = \dfrac{3}{x^2 + 11x + 25}$

16. What is k if $y = \dfrac{3}{2}x + k$ is the slant (oblique) asymptote $f(x) = \dfrac{3x^4 - 3x^3 + 1}{2x^3 + 5}$?

(A) $-\dfrac{3}{2}$

(B) $-\dfrac{1}{3}$

(C) 0

(D) $\dfrac{1}{2}$

17. Let $f(x) = \log_2 x$ and $g(x) = x^2 - 4$. What is the domain of $\dfrac{f}{g}$?

(A) $(-\infty, -2) \cup (-2, 2) \cup (2, \infty)$

(B) $(0, \infty)$

(C) $(0, 2) \cup (2, \infty)$

(D) $(-\infty, \infty)$

18. Which of the following is a vector that is orthogonal to the plane determined by the triangle with vertices $A(-2, 1, -2)$, $B(-1, -1, 1)$, $C(-1, -2, -1)$?

(A) $\langle -1, 4, 3 \rangle$

(B) $\langle -7, -2, 1 \rangle$

(C) $\langle 3, -2, 1 \rangle$

(D) $\langle 7, 1, -1 \rangle$

19. The fish population in Lake Stagnant is decreasing, and its changes can be modeled by the function $f(t) = P_0 e^{kt}$. The population was first counted in the year 2000 to be 3,500, but in 2010, there were only 1,400 left. If the fish population continues to decrease according to the function f, how many fish will be in Lake Stagnant in the year 2020?

(A) 560

(B) 600

(C) 740

(D) 800

20. Suppose $\det \begin{bmatrix} a & b & c \\ d & e & f \\ g & h & i \end{bmatrix} = 5$. Which of the following statements is false?

(A) $\det \begin{bmatrix} a & b & c \\ d-3a & e-3b & f-3c \\ g & h & i \end{bmatrix} = 5$

(B) $\det \begin{bmatrix} g & h & i \\ a & b & c \\ d & e & f \end{bmatrix} = 5$

(C) $\det \begin{bmatrix} 3a & 3b & 3c \\ 3d & 3e & 3f \\ 3g & 3h & 3i \end{bmatrix} = 15$

(D) $\det \begin{bmatrix} a & b & c \\ d & e & f \\ 2g & 2h & 2i \end{bmatrix} = 10$

21. Let A and B be $n \times n$ matrices. Which of the following does not always equal $(A + B)^2$?

(A) $(B + A)^2$

(B) $A^2 + 2AB + B^2$

(C) $A^2 + AB + BA + B^2$

(D) $(A + B)A + (A + B)B$

22. Which of the following is a true statement?

(A) A linear system can have an infinite number of solutions only if there are more variables than equations.

(B) A linear system with more equations than unknowns cannot have any solutions.

(C) It is possible to have a linear system with exactly three solutions.

(D) Suppose A is an $n \times n$ matrix and $\vec{x}$ is $n \times 1$ such that $A\vec{x} = \vec{0}$ has only the trivial solution, then $A\vec{x} = \vec{b}$ has a solution for every $n \times 1$ vector $\vec{b}$.

23. Let $A = \begin{bmatrix} 2 & -2 \\ -3 & 1 \end{bmatrix}$. If $\det (A - \lambda I) = 0$, where I is the identity matrix, which of the following is a value of λ?

(A) -4

(B) 1

(C) 2

(D) 4

24. Given $q(x) = (x + 4)(x - 1)^2$, find c so that one real zero of $q(x) + c$ is -3.

(A) $c = -16$

(B) $c = -7$

(C) $c = 7$

(D) $c = 16$

25. Which of the following statements is a false statement?

(A) Exponential functions in the form $y = b^x$ are one-to-one functions.

(B) Exponential functions in the form $y = b^x$ are onto functions when considering their codomain to be the set of positive real numbers.

(C) A logarithmic function $y = \log_b x$ is the inverse function of an exponential function $y = b^x$.

(D) Logarithmic functions in the form $y = \log_b x$ are always increasing.

26. Find the greatest common divisor of 252 and 1200.

(A) 4

(B) 12

(C) 16

(D) 24

27. Which of the following statements is true for any a, b, and c nonzero integers?

(A) $\gcd(a, b) \geq \text{lcm}(a, b)$.

(B) If $c|a$ and $c|b$, then $\text{lcm}(a, b) \leq \dfrac{ab}{c}$.

(C) $\gcd(ac, bc) = c \cdot \gcd(a, b)$.

(D) If $a|b$ and $b|c$, then $a|c$.

28. Find the greatest power of 3 that divides 7128.

(A) 3^0

(B) 3^2

(C) 3^4

(D) 3^6

29. In order to identify all the prime divisors of 622, a person needs to check only the primes less than or equal to p, where p equals what prime?

   (A) 17

   (B) 23

   (C) 29

   (D) 31

30. Using the Euclidean Algorithm to determine the gcd(66, 345), a person writes the following first two lines. What is the next line in the algorithm?

   $$345 = 66(5) + 15$$
   $$66 = 15(4) + 6$$

   (A) $15 = 6(2) + 3$

   (B) $15 = 6(3) - 3$

   (C) $15 = 4(3) + 3$

   (D) $15 = 4(4) - 1$

Constructed-Response Problems

31. Use the Principle of Mathematical Induction to prove the following statement.

   $$\sum_{j=1}^{n} \frac{1}{j(j+1)} = \frac{1}{1 \cdot 2} + \frac{1}{2 \cdot 3} + \cdots + \frac{1}{n(n+1)} = \frac{n}{n+1} \text{ for}$$

   all $n = 1, 2, 3, \ldots$

32. Prove that $(Z_6, \oplus, \otimes)$ is a commutative ring with unity but not a field, where $Z_6 = \{0,1,2,3,4,5\}$ and the operations are modular addition and multiplication.

33. Show algebraically that $f(x) = x^3 + 2$ is a one-to-one function; then find its inverse. Then graph both f and its inverse on the same set of axes.

34. Show whether the following set of vectors is linearly independent or dependent: $S = \{\vec{v_1} = \langle 2, 0, -2 \rangle$, $\vec{v_2} = \langle 0, -3, 1 \rangle, \vec{v_3} = \langle 1, 1, -1 \rangle\}$.

Answer Key Subtest I

Question Number	Answer	SMR
1	A	1.1 a
2	C	1.1 a
3	D	1.1 a, c
4	C	1.1 a
5	C	1.1 b
6	A	1.2 a
7	A	1.2 b
8	B	1.2 b, c
9	A	1.2 b
10	D	1.2 b, c
11	C	1.2 a
12	C	1.3 a, b
13	D	1.3 a, b, c
14	A	1.3 a, b
15	C	1.3 a, b
16	A	1.3 b
17	C	1.3 a, c

Question Number	Answer	SMR
18	B	1.4 a
19	A	1.3 c
20	C	1.4 c
21	B	1.4 c
22	D	1.4 c
23	D	1.4 c
24	A	1.2 b
25	D	1.3 a, c
26	B	3.1 a, d
27	D	3.1 a
28	C	3.1 a
29	B	3.1 a
30	A	3.1 c
31	Constructed-Response	3.1 b
32	Constructed-Response	1.1 a
33	Constructed-Response	1.3 a, b
34	Constructed-Response	1.4 c

Practice Test 1: Subtest I Answer Explanations

1. (A)

Since X is a subset of the set of real numbers, the Associative and Commutative Properties hold, so (B) and (D) are satisfied. Also, $0 \in X$, and 0 satisfies the Additive Identity Property, so (C) is satisfied. The product of two negative irrationals is positive and, in addition, may not be an irrational number; therefore, (A) is the correct answer.

2. (C)

Choice (A) is demonstrating that I_2 is the multiplicative identity, and choice (B) indicates that I_2 is invertible since its determinant is non-zero. If A and B are in $Z(G)$ and $C \in G$, then $(AB)C = A(BC)$ by Associativity. Since $B \in Z(G)$, $A(BC) = A(CB)$, and again by Associativity, $A(CB) = (AC)B$. Thus, by the Transitive Property of Equality, $(AB)C = (AC)B$. But $A \in Z(G)$, so $(AC)B = (CA)B$. Associating one last time, we have $(CA)B = C(AB)$, and by transitivity again, we conclude that $(AB)C = C(AB)$; thus, choice (D) is true. Since O_2 is not invertible, $O_2 \notin G$, we see that $Z(G)$ does not have the Closure Property of Addition; hence, (C) confirms that $Z(G)$ with standard matrix addition and multiplication is not a group. The correct answer is (C).

3. (D)

All four sets are fields with their standard addition and multiplication, and the first three sets are ordered fields with the ordering $>$. The complex numbers cannot be ordered by $>$ because we cannot compare the complex number i to 0. If we assume that $i > 0$, then, by the Property of a Total Ordering, which says *if $a > 0$ and $b > 0$, then $ab > 0$*, it must be true that we get $i^2 > 0$. But $i^2 = -1$, so it cannot be non-negative. If i is not greater than 0, then $-i$ would have to be positive. But then again, by the same property, $-i \cdot -i = i^2$ is not negative, which we know is not true. Therefore, the complex numbers cannot be ordered by $>$. The correct answer is (D).

4. (C)

The product of two even integers is an even integer, so $2Z$ has the Closure Property of Multiplication. The identity for $2Z$ would have to be 1, but 1 is not an even integer, so $2Z$ does not have the Multiplicative Identity Property. Since the multiplicative inverse of a non-zero integer is its reciprocal, and the reciprocal of most integers is not an integer, $2Z$ does not satisfy the Inverse Property. Since $2Z$ is a subset of the real numbers, it does satisfy the Associative Property of Multiplication. So the correct answer is (C).

5. (C)

The conjugate property is $\overline{a + bi} = a - bi$ for all a, real numbers, and $i = \sqrt{-1}$. This is illustrated in steps and 6. Steps 1 and 7 are simply the definitions of z and w. Step 2 uses both the Associative and Commutative Properties to gather the real and imaginary terms together. Step 4 is the Distributive Property, and step 5 illustrates both the Distributive and Commutative Properties. The correct answer is (C).

6. (A)

The boundary lines are the same for all four graphs, so just the region needs to be determined. The point $(2, 0)$ satisfies all three inequalities, so $(2, 0)$ is in the solution set. The only shaded region that includes $(2, 0)$ is the graph in (A). The correct answer is (A).

7. (A)

The Rational Root Theorem tells us that the rational roots of a polynomial $p(x) = a_n x^n + a_{n-1}x^{n-1} + \cdots + a_1 x + a_0$ are in the form $\dfrac{r}{q}$, where r is an integer factor of a_0 and q is an integer factor of a_n. Thus, for the polynomial $p(x) = 6x^3 - 5x^2 + x + 3$, $a_0 = 3$ and $a_n = 6$, so $r \in \{\pm 1, \pm 3\}$ and $q \in \{\pm 1, \pm 2, \pm 3, \pm 6\}$. Therefore, $\dfrac{r}{q} \in \left\{ \pm\dfrac{1}{6}, \pm\dfrac{1}{3}, \pm\dfrac{1}{2}, \pm 1, \pm\dfrac{3}{2}, \pm 3 \right\}$

The only choice of answer not in this set is -2, so the correct answer is (A).

8. (B)

$2x^2 + x - 1 = 0 \Leftrightarrow (2x - 1)(x + 1) = 0$. The solutions are $x = \dfrac{1}{2}$ and $x = -1$ so their product is $-\dfrac{1}{2}$. The correct answer is (B).

9. (A)

Use long division: $\left(3x^5 + x^4 - 2x^2 + 1\right)/\left(x - 2\right) = 3x^4 + \left(7x^4 - 2x^2 + 1\right)/\left(x - 2\right)$

$$= 3x^4 + 7x^3 + \left(14x^3 - 2x^2 + 1\right)/\left(x - 2\right)$$

$$= 3x^4 + 7x^3 + 14x^2 + \left(26x^2 + 1\right)/\left(x - 2\right)$$

$$= 3x^4 + 7x^3 + 14x^2 + 26x + \left(52x + 1\right)/\left(x - 2\right)$$

$$= 3x^4 + 7x^3 + 14x^2 + 26x + 52 + \left(105\right)/\left(x - 2\right)$$

$$= 3x^4 + 7x^3 + 14x^2 + 26x - \frac{-105}{x - 2}$$

$$= q(x) - \frac{a}{x - 2}$$

So the correct answer is (A).

10. (D)

$iz^3 + 8 = 0$ is equivalent to $i^3z^3 + i^2 2^3 = 0$, or $i^3 z^3 - 2^3 = 0$. To solve, factor the left side of the equation as the sum of cubes: $(iz - 2)(i^2z^2 + 2iz + 2^2) = 0$, or $(iz - 2)(-z^2 + 2iz + 4) = 0$. Then we have $iz - 2 = 0$ or, after multiplying through by -1, $z^2 - 2iz - 4 = 0$. So $z = \dfrac{2}{i} = -2i$ or $z = \dfrac{2i \pm \sqrt{(-2i)^2 - (-16)}}{2} = i \pm \dfrac{\sqrt{14}}{2}$. The correct answer is (D).

11. (C)

Let x be the number of homeless patients that GHM Co. can house in the rehabilitation facility and let y be the number of high-income patients. With P representing profit, the problem sets up as follows:

Maximize: $P = 900x + 600y$

subject to: $\begin{cases} x \geq 840 \\ y \leq 1000 \\ x + y \leq 1500 \\ x \leq 2y \\ x \geq 0, y \geq 0 \end{cases}$

To solve this linear programming problem, graph the feasible region and then evaluate the objective function (profit) at the corner points.

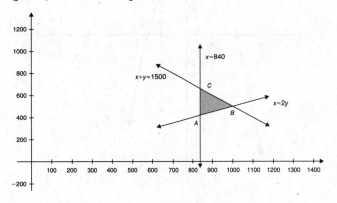

Corner point	Coordinates	$P = 900x + 600y$
A	$(840, 420)$	$P = 756{,}000 + 252{,}000 = 1{,}008{,}000$
B	$(1000, 500)$	$P = 900{,}000 + 300{,}000 = 1{,}200{,}000$
C	$(840, 660)$	$P = 756{,}000 + 396{,}000 = 1{,}152{,}000$

The maximum profit the GHM Co. can make per month is $1,200,000, when they house 1000 homeless and 500 high-income patients. The correct answer is (C).

12. (C)

The graphs of the four functions are shown below. Using the horizontal line test, we can see that all the functions are one-to-one except for h, which is a parabola. Functions that are not one-to-one do not have an inverse function. Therefore, h does not have an inverse function, so the correct answer is (C).

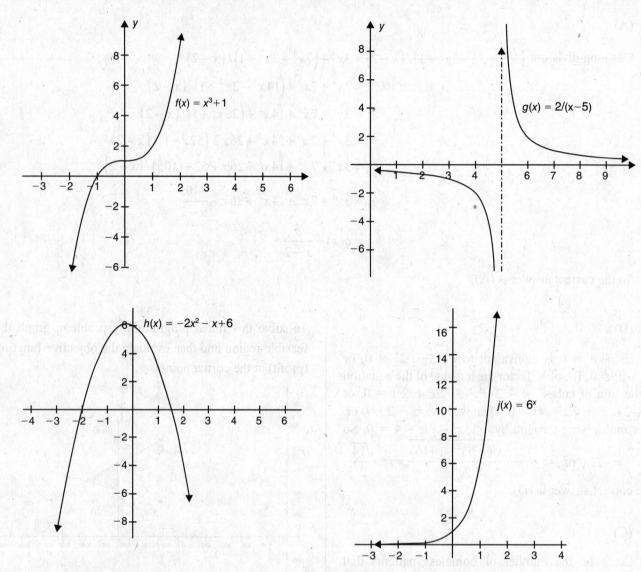

Graphs for problem 12

13. (D)

The graph does not represent a polynomial since polynomials do not have asymptotes, so (A) is not true. The graph does not represent an exponential function (choice B) since b^x either increases without bound as $x \to \infty$ or $x \to -\infty$. Clearly, the graph of f is not symmetric with respect to the origin, so it is not an odd function, so (C) is not true. Since the graph of f is symmetric with respect to the y-axis, f is an even function. The correct answer is (D).

14. (A)

The slope of the line containing points A and B is $\dfrac{5-(-1)}{-3-2} = \dfrac{6}{-5}$. Perpendicular lines have slopes that are negative reciprocals; thus, the slope of line m is $\dfrac{5}{6}$. The midpoint of line segment AB is $\left(\dfrac{-3+2}{2}, \dfrac{5+(-1)}{2}\right) = \left(\dfrac{-1}{2}, 2\right)$.

This point lies on line m; therefore, the equation of line m is $y - 2 = \dfrac{5}{6}\left(x - \left(-\dfrac{1}{2}\right)\right)$, or $y = \dfrac{5}{6}x + \dfrac{29}{12}$. So the x-intercept is $\left(-\dfrac{29}{10}, 0\right)$, and the y-intercept is $\left(0, \dfrac{29}{12}\right)$.

Then $\dfrac{-29}{10} + \dfrac{29}{12} = \dfrac{-174 + 145}{60} = \dfrac{-29}{60}$. The correct answer is (A).

5. (C)

$$(h \circ g)(x) = h\left(\dfrac{3}{x+5}\right) = \left(\dfrac{3}{x+5}\right)^2 + \left(\dfrac{3}{x+5}\right)$$

$\dfrac{9 + 3(x+5)}{(x+5)^2} = \dfrac{3x + 24}{(x+5)^2}$. The correct answer is clearly (C).

6. (A)

$$f(x) = \dfrac{3x^4 - 3x^3 + 1}{2x^3 + 5} = \dfrac{3}{2}x + \dfrac{-3x^3 - \dfrac{15}{2}x + 1}{2x^3 + 5}$$

$$= \dfrac{3}{2}x + \dfrac{-3x^3 - \dfrac{15}{2}x + 1}{2x^3 + 5} = \dfrac{3}{2}x - \dfrac{3}{2} + \dfrac{-\dfrac{15}{2}x + \dfrac{17}{2}}{2x^3 + 5}.$$

So, $k = \dfrac{-3}{2}$, and the correct answer is (A).

17. (C)

The domain of $\dfrac{f}{g}$ is $D_{\frac{f}{g}} = D_f \cap D_g - \left\{x \in D_g \mid g(x) = 0\right\}$. The domains are: $D_f = (0, \infty)$, and $D_g = (-\infty, \infty)$. $\{x \in D_g \mid g(x) = 0\} = \{-2, 2\}$, so $D_{\frac{f}{g}} = (0, 2) \cup (2, \infty)$.

Therefore, the correct answer is (C).

18. (B)

The vector $\vec{v} = \overline{AB} \times \overline{AC}$ is orthogonal to the plane determined by the points $A(-2, 1, -2)$, $B(-1, -1, 1)$, and $C(-1, -2, -1)$. So any vector orthogonal to ABC must be parallel to $\vec{v}$ and so must be a scalar multiple $\vec{v} = <7, 2, -1>$. The correct answer is (B).

19. (A)

The year 2000 is $t = 0$, so $P_0 = 3500$. Also $f(10) = 1400$. Substituting this into the function's equation:

$$1400 = 3500e^{10k} \Rightarrow \dfrac{2}{5} = \left(e^k\right)^{10} \Rightarrow e^k = \left(\dfrac{2}{5}\right)^{\frac{1}{10}};$$

thus, the function can be written in the form

$f(t) = 3500\left(\dfrac{2}{5}\right)^{\frac{t}{10}}$. The year 2020 is represented by

$t = 20$; therefore, $f(20) = 3500\left(\dfrac{2}{5}\right)^2 = 560$. The correct answer is (A).

20. (C)

The elementary row operations affect the determinant of a matrix as follows. If matrix B is matrix A with a row interchanged, then $\det(B) = -\det(A)$. If matrix B is matrix A with a row multiplied by the constant k, then $\det(B) = k \cdot \det(A)$. If matrix B is matrix A with a multiple of one row added to another row, then $\det(B) = \det(A)$. So, given that

$$\det \begin{bmatrix} a & b & c \\ d & e & f \\ g & h & i \end{bmatrix} = 5,$$

$$\det\begin{bmatrix} a & b & c \\ d-3a & e-3b & f-3c \\ g & h & i \end{bmatrix} = 5, \text{ so (A) is ture.}$$

$$\det\begin{bmatrix} g & h & i \\ a & b & c \\ d & e & f \end{bmatrix} = (-1)(-1)5 = 5, \text{ so (B) is true.}$$

$$\det\begin{bmatrix} 3a & 3b & 3c \\ 3d & 3e & 3f \\ 3g & 3h & 3i \end{bmatrix} = 27(5) = 135, \text{ so (C) is false.}$$

$$\det\begin{bmatrix} a & b & c \\ d & e & f \\ 2g & 2h & 2i \end{bmatrix} = (2)5 = 10, \text{ so (D) is true.}$$

So, statement (C) is the correct answer.

21. (B)

Let A and B be $n \times n$ matrices. Then $(B + A)^2 = (A + B)^2$ because of the Commutative Property of Addition of matrices. Then by the Distributive Property for matrices, $(A + B)^2 = (A + B)(A + B) = (A + B)A + (A + B)B$. Using the Distributive Property again, we obtain $(A + B)^2 = (A + B)A + (A + B)B = A^2 + BA + AB + B^2$. However, it is not always true that $AB = BA$, so the expression cannot be reduced to $A^2 + 2AB + B^2$. Therefore, (B) is the correct answer.

22. (D)

Statement (A), *a linear system can have an infinite number of solutions only if there are more variables than equations,* can be seen to be false from the following system: $\begin{cases} 2x - y = 3 \\ -4x + 2y = -6 \end{cases}$. This system has infinitely many solutions since the second equation is the first equation multiplied by -2, yet the number of variables does not exceed the number of equations.

Statement (B), *a linear system with more equations than unknowns cannot have any solutions,* is false, as seen from this example: $\begin{cases} x + y = 1 \\ x - y = 1 \\ 2x + 2y = 2 \end{cases}$. This system has the solution $(1, 0)$.

Statement (C), *it is possible to have a linear system with exactly three solutions,* is false. A system of linear equations has no solutions, exactly one solution, or infinitely many solutions.

Statement (D), *suppose A is an n × n matrix and $\vec{x}$ is n × 1 such that $\vec{x} = B$ has only the trivial solution, then $A\vec{x} = \vec{b}$ has a solution for every n × 1 vector $\vec{b}$,* is true.

The correct answer is (D).

23. (D)

$A = \begin{bmatrix} 2 & -2 \\ -3 & 1 \end{bmatrix}$, so $A - \lambda I = \begin{bmatrix} 2-\lambda & -2 \\ -3 & 1-\lambda \end{bmatrix}$ and

$\det(A - \lambda I) = \lambda^2 - 3\lambda - 4 = (\lambda + 1)(\lambda - 4)$. Therefore,

$\det(A - \lambda I) = 0$ for $\lambda = 4$ or -1. The correct answer is

(D).

24. (A)

$q(-3) + c = (-3 + 4)(-3 - 1)^2 + c = 16 + c = 0$

so c is -16. The correct answer is (A).

25. (D)

Exponential functions are one-to-one and the range is the positive real numbers so (A) and (B) are true. It is true that the inverse of $y = \log_b x$ is $y = b^x$ so (C) is true. Some logarithm functions are decreasing, in particular those with base b where $0 < b < 1$. The correct answer is (D).

26. (B)

Use the Euclidean Algorithm:

$$1200 = 252(4) + 19$$
$$252 = 192(1) + 60$$
$$192 = 60(3) + 12$$
$$60 = 12(5) + 0$$

So the gcd(252, 1200) = 12. The correct answer is (B)

27. (D)

Statement (A) is false; for example, $\gcd(10, 14) = 2$, and $\text{lcm}(10, 14) = 70$, but $2 < 70$. Statement (B) is false; suppose $c = -5$, $a = 5$, and $b = 10$, then $\text{lcm}(a, b) = 10$ but $\dfrac{ab}{c} = -10$, and $10 > -10$. Statement (C) is false; because $\gcd(-8, -12) = 4$, but $-4\gcd(2, 3) = -4$. Statement (D) is true because if $a|b$ and $b|c$, then there exist integers m and n such that $am = b$ and $bn = c$, so $bn = (am)n = a(mn) = c$; since mn is an integer by the Closure Property, $a|b$. The correct answer is (D).

28. (C)

Since $7 + 1 + 2 + 8 = 18$, which is divisible by 9, then 7128 is divisible 3^2. And $7128 = 3^2 \cdot 792$. But $7 + 9 + 2 = 18$, so 792 is also divisible by 9, so $7128 = 3^4 \cdot 88$. But $8 + 8 = 16$ is not divisible by 3, so the greatest power of 3 that divides 7128 is 3^4. Therefore, the correct answer is (C).

29. (B)

To find all primes that divide into 622, we must test all primes p such that $p \leq \sqrt{622} < \sqrt{625} = 25$. The greatest prime less than or equal to 25 is 23; hence, the correct answer is (B).

30. (A)

The correct complete algorithm is

$$
\begin{aligned}
345 &= 66(5) + 15 \\
66 &= 15(4) + 6 \\
15 &= 6(2) + 3 \\
6 &= 3(2) + 0
\end{aligned}
$$

which indicates that $\gcd(345, 66) = 3$. The correct answer is (A).

Constructed-Response Problems

31. Proof: Let $P(k)$ be the statement $\displaystyle\sum_{j=1}^{k} \frac{1}{j(j+1)} = \frac{1}{1 \cdot 2} + \frac{1}{2 \cdot 3} + \cdots + \frac{1}{k(k+1)} = \frac{k}{k+1}$, where k is a natural number.

$P(1)$ is the statement $\dfrac{1}{1(1+1)} = \dfrac{1}{1+1}$ or $\dfrac{1}{2} = \dfrac{1}{2}$, which is true.

Assume that $P(k)$ is true, that is, assume $\dfrac{1}{1 \cdot 2} + \dfrac{1}{2 \cdot 3} + \cdots + \dfrac{1}{k(k+1)} = \dfrac{k}{k+1}$, where k is any fixed but arbitrary integer such that $k \geq 1$.

Note that $P(k + 1)$ is $\dfrac{1}{1 \cdot 2} + \dfrac{1}{2 \cdot 3} + \cdots + \dfrac{1}{k(k+1)} + \dfrac{1}{(k+1)(k+2)} = \dfrac{k+1}{(k+1)+1}$. Then,

$$
\begin{aligned}
\frac{1}{1 \cdot 2} + \frac{1}{2 \cdot 3} + \cdots + \frac{1}{k(k+1)} + \frac{1}{(k+1)(k+2)} &= \frac{k}{k+1} + \frac{1}{(k+1)(k+2)} && \text{by the Induction Hypothesis} \\
&= \frac{k(k+2)+1}{(k+1)(k+2)} && \text{by algebra} \\
&= \frac{(k+1)^2}{(k+1)(k+2)} && \text{by algebra} \\
&= \frac{k+1}{k+2} = \frac{k+1}{(k+1)+1} && \text{by algebra}
\end{aligned}
$$

Hence, for all $k \geq 1$, if $P(k)$ is true, then $P(k + 1)$ is true.

Thus, by the Principle of Mathematical Induction, $P(k)$ is true for all $k = 1, 2,\ldots$

Q.E.D.

32. Proof: Let $X = Z_6$ with modular addition and multiplication.

X is closed under both addition and multiplication by means of the definition of modular arithmetic; i.e., $a \oplus b \mod 6 = r$, where r is the remainder when $a + b$ is divided by 6, and $a \otimes b \mod 6 = r$, where r is the remainder when $a \cdot b$ is divided by 6, so in both cases $0 \leq r < 6$. Since X is a subset of the Reals, the Associative Properties of Addition and Multiplication hold, as well as the Commutative Properties of Addition and Multiplication, and the Distributive Property of Multiplication over Addition (both left and right distributive).

0 and 1 are clearly the additive and multiplicative identities of X.

For addition, each element has an additive inverse $0 \oplus 0 = 0$, $1 \oplus 5 = 0$, $2 \oplus 4 = 0$, $3 \oplus 3 = 0 \mod 6$.

Therefore, $(X, \oplus, \otimes)$ is a commutative ring with unity.

The only property that we have not examined in order for $X - \{0\}$ with modular multiplication to be a field i the inverse property of multiplication. The multiplicativ inverse of 1 is 1, and the multiplicative inverse of 5 is 5 but 2, 3, and 4 do not have multiplicative inverses.

Hence, $(Z_6, \oplus, \otimes)$ is a commutative ring with unit but not a field.

Q.E.D

33. To show that f is one-to-one, assume that $f(p) = f(q)$. This means that $p^3 + 2 = q^3 + 2$. Using the Additio Property of Equality, this equation is equivalent to $p^3 = q^3$. Raising both sides to the 1/3 power results in $p = q$ Therefore, f is one-to-one.

To find the inverse, switch the input and output of the function; i.e., exchange x and y; then solve for y:

$x = y^3 + 2 \Rightarrow x - 2 = y^3 \Rightarrow y = \sqrt[3]{x-2}$, so $f^{-1}(x) = \sqrt[3]{x-2}$. To check, compute the composition:

$f \circ f^{-1}(x) = \left(f^{-1}(x)\right)^3 + 2 = \left(\sqrt[3]{x-2}\right)^3 + 2 = x$ and $f^{-1} \circ f(x) = \sqrt[3]{f(x)-2} = \sqrt[3]{(x^3+2)-2} = \sqrt[3]{x^3} = x$. Thus,

$f^{-1}(x) = \sqrt[3]{x-2}$. The graph is shown below.

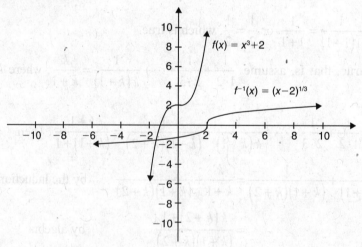

4. Suppose $k_1 \vec{v_1} + k_2 \vec{v_2} + k_3 \vec{v_3} = \vec{0}$. This is equivalent to $\begin{cases} 2k_1 + k_3 = 0 \\ -3k_2 + k_3 = 0 \\ -2k_1 + k_2 - k_3 = 0 \end{cases}$. Using Gauss-Jordan elimination to solve this system, we get

$$\begin{bmatrix} 2 & 0 & 1 & | & 0 \\ 0 & -3 & 1 & | & 0 \\ -2 & 1 & -1 & | & 0 \end{bmatrix} \begin{matrix} R_1 + R_3 \to R_3 \\ \frac{1}{2}R_1 \to R_1 \end{matrix} \begin{bmatrix} 1 & 0 & \frac{1}{2} & | & 0 \\ 0 & -3 & 1 & | & 0 \\ 0 & 1 & 0 & | & 0 \end{bmatrix} \begin{matrix} R_2 \leftrightarrow R_3 \\ 3R_2 + R_3 \to R_3 \end{matrix} \begin{bmatrix} 1 & 0 & \frac{1}{2} & | & 0 \\ 0 & 1 & 0 & | & 0 \\ 0 & 0 & 1 & | & 0 \end{bmatrix} -\frac{1}{2}R_3 + R_1 \to R_1$$

$$\begin{bmatrix} 1 & 0 & 0 & | & 0 \\ 0 & 1 & 0 & | & 0 \\ 0 & 0 & 1 & | & 0 \end{bmatrix}$$

This means that the only solution is the trivial solution $k_1 = k_2 = k_3 = 0$; thus, the set of vectors is linearly independent.

CSET: Mathematics Practice Test 1, Subtest II

Content Domain II *Geometry and Probability & Statistics*

> Directions: This subtest consists of two sections:
>
> (I) thirty multiple-choice questions, and
>
> (II) four constructed-response questions that require written responses.

Note: A calculator will be needed and will be allowed only for CSET: Mathematics Subtest II. You will **required to bring your own graphing calculator. Please check the latest CSET Mathematics Test Guide for a li** **of approved models of graphing calculators.**

1. Which of the following statements is true in elliptic geometry?
   (A) All lines intersect.
   (B) The sum of the angles of any triangle is equal to 180°.
   (C) Through a point outside a given line, exactly one line can be drawn that does not intersect the given line
   (D) Rectangles exist.

Use the incomplete proof below to answer the two questions that follow.

Prove: If two angles are complementary to the same angle, then they are congruent.

Given: $\angle 1$ and $\angle 2$ are complementary angles, and $\angle 2$ and $\angle 3$ are complementary angles.

Prove: $\angle 1 \cong \angle 3$.

Statement	Reason
1. $\angle 1$ and $\angle 2$ are complementary angles. $\angle 2$ and $\angle 3$ are complementary angles.	1. Given
2. $m\angle 1 + m\angle 2 = 90°$ $m\angle 2 + m\angle 3 = 90°$	2. Definition of complementary angles
3.	3.
4. $m\angle 2 = m\angle 2$	4. Reflexive Property of Equality
5. $m\angle 1 = m\angle 3$	5. Addition Property of Equality
6. $\angle 1 \cong \angle 3$	6.

Which of the following is the missing statement and reason for step 3?

(A)

Statement	Reason
3. $m\angle 1 + 2m\angle 2 + m\angle 3 = 180°$	3. Addition Property of Equality

(B)

Statement	Reason
3. $m\angle 2 + m\angle 3 = 90°$	3. Definition of complementary angles

(C)

Statement	Reason
3. $m\angle 1 + m\angle 2 = m\angle 2 + m\angle 3$	3. Addition Property of Equality

(D)

Statement	Reason
3. $m\angle 1 + m\angle 2 = m\angle 2 + m\angle 3$	3. Transitive Property of Equality

Which of the following is the missing reason for step 6?

(A) Definition of complementary angles

(B) Definition of congruent angles

(C) Definition of the measure of an angle

(D) Transitive Property of Equality

Use the given statement to answer the question that follows.

> The sum of the measures of the interior angles of a triangle is 180°.

If the above statement is false, which of the following statements must also be false?

(A) Vertical angles are congruent.

(B) Through a point not on a given line there is exactly one line parallel to the given line.

(C) Equilateral triangles exist.

(D) An acute angle has measure less than 90°.

5. **Use the diagram below to answer the question that follows.**

$\overline{AD} \cong \overline{BC}$, $\overline{BC} \perp \overline{AB}$, and $\overline{AD} \perp \overline{AB}$, what is the reason that $\triangle ABD \cong \triangle BAC$?

(A) SSS

(B) SSA

(C) ASA

(D) SAS

6. **Use the diagram below to answer the question that follows.**

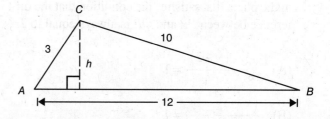

Given that h is the height of the altitude of $\triangle ABC$, which of the following best approximates h?

(A) 1.8

(B) 2.0

(C) 2.2

(D) 2.4

7. **Use the diagram below to answer the question that follows.**

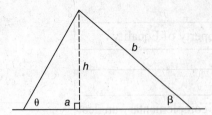

Which of the following statements relating the labeled angles and sides is true?

(A) $\dfrac{a}{b} = \dfrac{\sin \theta}{\tan \beta}$

(B) $\dfrac{a}{b} = \dfrac{\sin \beta}{\tan \theta}$

(C) $\dfrac{a}{b} = \dfrac{\tan \theta}{\sin \beta}$

(D) $\dfrac{a}{b} = \dfrac{\tan \beta}{\sin \theta}$

8. A regular hexagon is inscribed in a circle of diameter 16 cm. What is the area of the hexagon?

(A) 96 square centimeters
(B) $96\sqrt{3}$ square centimeters
(C) 192 square centimeters
(D) $192\sqrt{3}$ square centimeters

9. Let $P(0, 5)$ and $Q(0, -1)$ be fixed points, and let R represent any arbitrary point (x, y) in the Cartesian coordinate system. Find the equation of the locus in the plane that satisfies the condition that the difference between PR and QR is always equal to 2.

(A) $\dfrac{x^2}{8} - \dfrac{(y-2)^2}{1} = 1$

(B) $\dfrac{(x-2)^2}{8} - \dfrac{y^2}{1} = 1$

(C) $\dfrac{y^2}{8} - \dfrac{(x-2)^2}{1} = 1$

(D) $\dfrac{(y-2)^2}{1} - \dfrac{x^2}{8} = 1$

10. Plane M is perpendicular to plane N. Plane N contains line l which is perpendicular to plane M. Line k is parallel to line l. Which of the following statements must be true?

(A) Line k is perpendicular to plane M.
(B) Line k lies in plane M.
(C) Line k intersects plane N.
(D) Line k lies in plane N.

11. A sphere is inscribed in a cube. The surface area of the cube is 240 square inches. What is the surface area of the sphere?

(A) $10\sqrt{10}\pi$ square inches
(B) 32π square inches
(C) 40π square inches
(D) $15\sqrt{10}\pi$ square inches

12. **Use the figure below to answer the question that follows.**

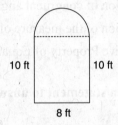

A Norman window, shown in the figure, is a semicircle attached to the top of a rectangle. What is the approximate perimeter of the window?

(A) 36 ft
(B) 41 ft
(C) 48 ft
(D) 53 ft

13. **Use the figure below to answer the question that follows.**

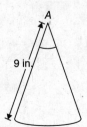

The measure of angle A is 40°. A right circular cone is formed by attaching the sides of the circular sector above. What is the volume of this cone?

(A) 3π cubic inches

(B) $\dfrac{3}{2}\pi$ cubic inches

(C) $\dfrac{4\sqrt{5}}{3}\pi$ cubic inches

(D) $\dfrac{8\sqrt{5}}{3}\pi$ cubic inches

4. Consider the following two statements.

   (I)   A line perpendicular to a given plane is perpendicular to every line in the plane.

   (II) Two distinct lines that are both parallel to the same plane must be parallel to each other.

   Which of the following is correct?

   (A) Only statement I is true.
   (B) Only statement II is true.
   (C) Both statements I and II are true.
   (D) Neither statement I nor II is true.

5. **Use the figure below to answer the question that follows.**

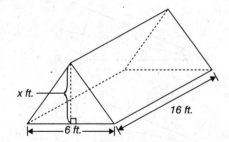

x ft.

16 ft.

6 ft.

The volume of the above prism is 96 cubic feet. What is the best approximation of the surface area of the prism?

(A) 150 square feet
(B) 220 square feet
(C) 270 square feet
(D) 300 square feet

16. Which of the following statements is false?

   (A) In a triangle, an altitude is shorter than either side from the same vertex.

   (B) The centroid of a triangle lies in the interior of the triangle.

   (C) The circumcenter of a triangle may lie in the exterior of the triangle.

   (D) At least one altitude of a triangle lies in the exterior of the triangle.

17. **Use the graphs below to answer the question that follows.**

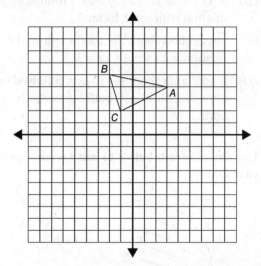

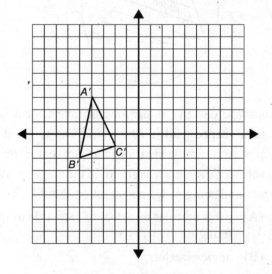

$\triangle ABC$ is the preimage of $\triangle A'B'C'$ under a transformation T. Transformation T is which of the following?

(A) translation

(B) rotation about the origin

(C) reflection about the *y*-axis

(D) reflection about the *x*-axis

18. Consider $T(x,y) = \begin{bmatrix} 3 & 0 \\ 0 & -3 \end{bmatrix}\begin{bmatrix} x \\ y \end{bmatrix}$. This transformation is geometrically:

(A) a reflection about the *x*-axis followed by a translation 3 units both horizontally and vertically.

(B) a reflection about the *y*-axis followed by a dilation with scale factor 3.

(C) a reflection about the *x*-axis followed by a dilation with scale factor 3.

(D) a reflection about the *y*-axis followed by a translation 3 units both horizontally and vertically.

19. **Use the diagram below to answer the question that follows.**

A landscape designer is drawing up plans for a large triangular-shaped garden. She would like to construct a circular path outside the triangular plot that intersects each vertex of the garden as shown in the diagram. What compass and straightedge construction should she use?

(A) perpendicular bisectors of each side of the triangle

(B) angle bisectors

(C) perpendicular lines to each side through the opposite vertex

(D) lines parallel to each side through the opposite vertex

20. **Use the figure below to answer the question that follows.**

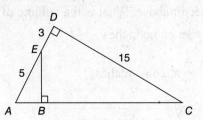

Which of the <u>following</u> is the best approximation of the length *BC* ?

(A) 17.7

(B) 15.8

(C) 14.6

(D) 13. 9

21. Two sides of a triangle have lengths of 6 and 1 inches, respectively. Which of the following could be the length of the third side?

(A) 4 inches

(B) 7 inches

(C) 18 inches

(D) 22 inches

22. Which of the following illustrates the correct construction of an angle bisector?

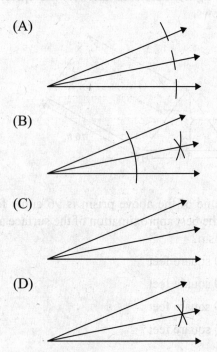

(A)

(B)

(C)

(D)

3. On a quiz with 10 true-false questions, how many different ways can a student answer the questions and earn exactly 60% on the quiz?

(A) 16

(B) 64

(C) 210

(D) 1024

4. Each of the numbers in a normally distributed data set is multiplied by three. How does this transformation affect the mean, median, and shape of the frequency distribution?

(A) The mean and median triple, and the distribution stretches horizontally.

(B) The mean and median triple, and the distribution's shape remains the same.

(C) The mean and median remain the same, and the distribution stretches horizontally.

(D) The mean and median remain the same, and the distribution's shape remains the same.

5. Laptop computers are shipped to the College Bookstore from three factories, A, B and C. It is well known that 22% of factory A's laptop computers are defective, and factories B and C produce 10% and 5% defective laptops, respectively. The manager of the bookstore just received a new shipment of laptops and discovered that 30% are from factory C, 50% are from factory B, and 20% are from factory A. What is the probability that there is at least one defective laptop in this shipment?

(A) 10.9%

(B) 14.2%

(C) 21.8%

(D) 26.6%

6. There are 6 red, 9 blue, and 8 yellow marbles in a box. If we randomly choose four marbles from the box without replacement, what is the probability, to the nearest tenth, that we have chosen exactly two red marbles?

(A) 10.4%

(B) 11.5 %

(C) 16.8%

(D) 23.0%

27. **Use the graph below to answer the question that follows.**

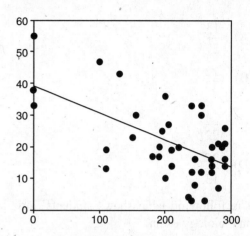

The data and a regression line for an experiment are plotted in the graph. What is the most likely value of the coefficient of correlation for this data and line?

(A) −10

(B) −0.71

(C) 0.9

(D) 40

28. At the Computer Analysis Company, the ages of all new employees hired during the last 10 years are normally distributed. Within this curve, approximately 95% of the ages, centered about the mean, are between 21.6 and 44.4 years. What are the mean age and the standard deviation of the data?

(A) The mean age is 33 and the standard deviation is 5.7.

(B) The mean age is 33 and the standard deviation is 11.4.

(C) The mean age is 31.5 and the standard deviation is 5.7.

(D) The mean age is 31.5 and the standard deviation is 11.4.

29. A student is randomly chosen from a class with 22 history majors, thirteen who are seniors and nine are juniors, and 19 anthropology majors, five of whom are juniors and the rest are seniors. What is the probability that the randomly chosen student is a history major given that the student is a senior?

    (A) $\dfrac{13}{27}$

    (B) $\dfrac{22}{27}$

    (C) $\dfrac{13}{22}$

    (D) $\dfrac{27}{13}$

30. The following table shows students' quiz scores on a biology exam.

Score	10	9	8	7	6	5	4	3	2	1	0
Frequency	3	7	4	2	3	7	8	3	0	2	1

What is the interval of the range of the third quartile of scores?

    (A) 4 – 5
    (B) 4 – 7
    (C) 5 – 8
    (D) 6 – 9

Constructed-Response Problems

31. Use the figure below to answer the question that follows.

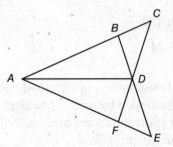

Given: $\angle C \cong \angle E$, $\quad \angle CAD \cong \angle EAD$
Prove: $\overline{BD} \cong \overline{DF}$

32. State the Euclidean Parallel Postulate; then prove that it is equivalent to the following statement:

> *If a line intersects one of two parallel lines, it must also intersect the other.*

33. Find the equation of the curve traced by a point that moves so that the sum of its distances to the points (0, 0) and (8, 0) is 10. Then graph and name the curve.

34. A student wants to test if an octahedral die is fair (unbiased) and rolls the die 160 times with the results shown the table below.

Result of Roll	1	2	3	4	5	6	7	8
Frequency	15	26	31	12	17	27	22	10

(a) State the null hypothesis that the student should use to determine whether these data suggest that the distribution the results shows that the die is fair.

(b) Determine the value of the chi-square (χ^2) test statistic for these sample data, then write the conclusi Determine if, at the 5% significance level, the data suggest that the die is fair.

Here is a chi-square table for the 5% significance level.

Degrees of freedom	1	2	3	4	5	6	7	8
χ^2 values	3.841	5.991	7.815	9.488	11.070	12.592	14.067	15.507

Answer Key Subtest II

Question Number	Answer	SMR	Question Number	Answer	SMR
1	A	2.1 a, b	18	C	2.4 a, b
2	D	2.2 a	19	A	2.2 c, d
3	B	2.2 a	20	C	2.2 b
4	B	2.2 a, b	21	C	2.2 b
5	D	2.2 a	22	B	2.2 d
6	B	2.2 b	23	C	4.1 a, b
7	B	2.2 b	24	A	4.1 b, c, d
8	B	2.2 c	25	A	4.1 a, b, c
9	D	2.2 e	26	D	4.2 d
10	A	2.3 a	27	B	4.2 a, b
11	C	2.3 b	28	A	4.2 a, e
12	B	2.2 c	29	A	4.1e
13	C	2.3 b, 2.2 c	30	C	4.2 b
14	D	2.3 a	31	Constructed-Response	2.2 a
15	B	2.3 b	32	Constructed-Response	2.1 a
16	D	2.2 b	33	Constructed-Response	2.2 e
17	B	2.4 a	34	Constructed-Response	4.2 e

1. (A)

In elliptic geometry, the postulate that replaces the Euclidean Parallel Postulate is: *Through a point outside a given line, no lines can be drawn that do not intersect the given line.* Hence, statement (C) is false. Statements (B) and (D) are equivalent to the Euclidean Parallel Postulate, so they are false. Statement (A) is a consequence of the Elliptic Parallel Postulate and is true; therefore, (A) is the correct answer.

2. (D)

The statement $m\angle 1 + m\angle 2 = m\angle 2 + m\angle 3$ follows from the statements $m\angle 1 + m\angle 2 = 90°$ and $m\angle 2 + m\angle 3 = 90°$ by the Transitive Property of Equality. So the correct answer is (D).

3. (B)

Step 5 to step 6 illustrates the definition of congruent angles: *If the measures of two angles are equal, then the angles are congruent.* The correct answer is (B).

4. (B)

The statements (A), *vertical angles are congruent*, and (C), *equilateral triangles exist* are true in neutral geometry, being two of the 28 propositions in neutral geometry. Statement (D) is a definition that is used in all geometries. Statement (B) is the Euclidean Parallel Postulate, which is equivalent to the given statement. Hence, if the given statement is false, so is the Euclidean Parallel Postulate. So the correct answer is (B).

5. (D)

We separate the triangles to see the congruent parts better. First we are told that

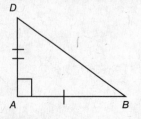
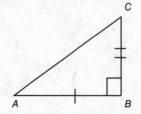

$\overline{AD} \cong \overline{BC}$, $\overline{BC} \perp \overline{AB}$, and $\overline{AD} \perp \overline{AB}$, so $\angle ABC \cong \angle BAD$ because they are both right angles. In addition, $\overline{AB} \cong \overline{AB}$ by the Reflexive Property of Congruence. Thus, $\triangle ABD \cong \triangle BAC$ by SAS. The correct answer is (D).

6. (B)

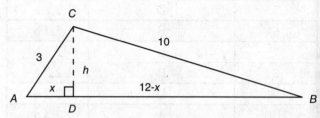

Let the foot of the altitude be point D and let $AD = x$ so that $DB = 12 - x$.

Then, using the Pythagorean Theorem on both right triangles, we obtain: $x^2 + h^2 = 9$ and $h^2 + (12-x)^2 = 100$. Eliminating h^2 by substitution: $(9 - x^2) + (12 - x)^2 = 100$. Solving this equation for x, we have:

$$9 - x^2 + 144 - 24x + x^2 = 100 \qquad 24x = 53 \qquad x = \frac{53}{24}.$$

Then, solving for h in $\triangle ADC$,

$$h = \sqrt{9 - \left(\frac{53}{24}\right)^2} = \sqrt{\frac{5184 - 2809}{576}} = \sqrt{\frac{2375}{576}} = \frac{5\sqrt{95}}{24} \approx 2.0$$

The correct answer is (B).

7. (B)

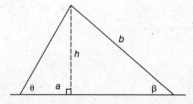

The altitude drawn creates two right triangles. From the right triangle on the left, we see that $\tan(\theta) = \frac{h}{a}$ or $h = a\tan(\theta)$, and from the right triangle on the right, we have $\sin(\beta) = \frac{h}{b}$ or $h = b\sin(\beta)$. Using the ransitive Property of Equality, we obtain $a\tan(\theta) =$

$\sin(\beta)$, or $\dfrac{a}{b} = \dfrac{\sin(\beta)}{\tan(\theta)}$. The correct answer is (B).

(B)

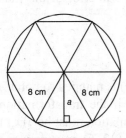

The diameter of the circle is 16, which means that
e can label the hexagon as in the figure above. Each
de of the inscribed hexagon has length 8 cm, so the
erimeter of the hexagon is 48 cm. We need to find a,
e length of the apothem. The triangles formed by the
pothem are 30°-60°-90° triangles, so $a = 4\sqrt{3}$. So the
ea of the hexagon is $A = \frac{1}{2}aP = \dfrac{1}{2}\left(4\sqrt{3}\right)(48) = 96\sqrt{3}$
quare centimeters. The correct answer is (B).

(D)

$PR = \sqrt{(x-0)^2 + (y-5)^2}$ and $QR =$

$\sqrt{(x-0)^2 + (y+1)^2}$, so if we know the difference

etween these lengths is always 2, we have the

ollowing equation:

$\sqrt{x^2 + (y-5)^2} - \sqrt{x^2 + (y+1)^2} = 2$. Isolating the

idicals and squaring both sides of the equation, we

otain:

$\left(\sqrt{x^2 + (y-5)^2}\right)^2 = \left(\sqrt{x^2 + (y+1)^2} + 2\right)^2$

$x^2 + y^2 - 10y + 25 = x^2 + y^2 + 2y + 1 + 4\sqrt{x^2 + (y+1)^2} + 4$

Simplifying and again isolating the radical, then
quaring both sides one more time, we get

$-3y + 5 = \sqrt{x^2 + (y+1)^2} \Rightarrow 9y^2 - 30y + 25 = x^2 + y^2$

$+ 2y + 1$. Then we obtain: $x^2 - 8y^2 + 32y - 24 = 0$

$y^2 - 4y - \dfrac{x^2}{8} = -3 \quad (y-2)^2 - \dfrac{x^2}{8} = -3 + 4 = 1$

which is $\Rightarrow \dfrac{(y-2)^2}{1} - \dfrac{x^2}{8} = 1$. So the correct answer
is (D).

10. **(A)**

Line l is perpendicular to plane M. This implies
that any plane containing line l is perpendicular
to plane M. Lines l and k are parallel and thus are
contained in a plane; call this plane P. So plane P must
be perpendicular to plane M. Let points A and B be the
points of intersection of lines l and k with plane M,
respectively. So $\overleftrightarrow{AB} \perp l$ since l is perpendicular to any
line in plane M that intersects it. This means that line k
is also perpendicular to $\overleftrightarrow{AB}$ since k and l are parallel.
Thus, k must be perpendicular to plane M. The correct
answer is (A).

11. **(C)**

The surface area of a cube is $6s^2$, where s is the length of
each edge. Since the surface area of the cube is 240 square
inches, $s = 2\sqrt{10}$ inches. This means that the diameter
of the inscribed sphere is $2\sqrt{10}$ inches. The surface area
of the sphere is $SA = 4\pi r^2 = 4\pi\left(\sqrt{10}\right)^2 = 40\pi$ square
inches. The correct answer is (C).

12. **(B)**

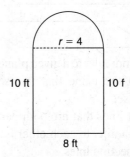

The radius of the semicircle on top of the rectangle
is 4 ft. So the length of the arc of the semicircle is 4π.
Thus, the perimeter of the Norman window is $28 + 4\pi$
≈ 41 ft. The correct answer is (B).

13. (C)

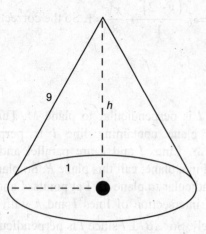

The given sector is $\dfrac{40}{360} = \dfrac{1}{9}$th of a complete circle. The circumference of the complete circle is $C = 18\pi$, and one-ninth of this is 2π. This means that when the cone is formed, the circumference of the base is 2π and its radius is 1. Using the Pythagorean Theorem, we get $h = \sqrt{81-1} = \sqrt{80} = 4\sqrt{5}$. Therefore, the volume of the cone is $V = \dfrac{1}{3}\pi\left(1\right)^2\left(4\sqrt{5}\right) = \dfrac{4\sqrt{5}}{3}\pi$ cubic inches. The correct answer is (C).

14. (D)

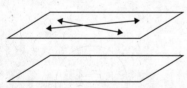

A line perpendicular to a given plane is perpendicular to every line in the plane that intersects the line. So statement I is false.

Two distinct lines that are both parallel to the same plane could be parallel to each other but they could also be skew or intersecting lines.

Both statements are false. The correct answer is (D).

15. (B)

$V = Bh$. We are given $h = 16$ and $B = 1/2x(6) = 3x$. So $V = 96 = 48x$, from which it follows that $x = 2$. The surface area of the prism is $2B$ + area of 3 lateral sides = $2(6) + (16)(6) + 2(16\sqrt{13}) = 108 + 32\sqrt{13} \approx 223$. The correct answer is (B).

16. (D)

The only statement that is false is (D). To se that (D) is false, consider an equilateral triangle; th altitudes coincide with the angle bisectors, which mu all intersect in the interior of the triangle. The corre answer is (D).

17. (B)

Point A (3, 4) is mapped to point A' (−4 , 3). Fro this we see that if the transformation is a translatic then the transformation must be $T(x,y) = (x - 7, y - 1$ But then point B (−2, 5) must map to the point (−9, but instead it maps to (−5, −2). If the transformation a reflection about the y-axis, then point A (3, 4) wou map to (−3, 4) which it doesn't. If the transformation a reflection about the x-axis, then it would map point A (3, −4), which it does not. So by default it is a rotatio But to check this, let us find the angle of rotation. Th transformation for rotation about the origin is $T(x,y)$ ($x\cos\alpha - y\sin\alpha$, $x\sin\alpha + y\cos\alpha$). So for point A, w have $T(3, 4) = (3\cos\alpha - 4\sin\alpha, 3\sin\alpha + 4\cos\alpha)$ (−4, 3). We then set this up as a system of equations ar solve: $\begin{cases} 3\cos\alpha - 4\sin\alpha = -4 \\ 3\sin\alpha + 4\cos\alpha = 3 \end{cases}$. This will give us that α 90°. So the transformation is $T(x,y) = (-y, x)$, which fi with the other two points' transformation. Therefor the correct answer is (B).

18. (C)

$T(x, y) = \begin{bmatrix} 3 & 0 \\ 0 & -3 \end{bmatrix}\begin{bmatrix} x \\ y \end{bmatrix}$ can be viewed as

$T(x, y) = \begin{bmatrix} 3 & 0 \\ 0 & 3 \end{bmatrix}\begin{bmatrix} 1 & 0 \\ 0 & -1 \end{bmatrix}\begin{bmatrix} x \\ y \end{bmatrix}$. The matrix $\begin{bmatrix} 1 & 0 \\ 0 & -1 \end{bmatrix}$

is a reflection about the x-axis. The matrix $\begin{bmatrix} 3 & 0 \\ 0 & 3 \end{bmatrix}$

a dilation by a scale factor of 3. We can check this b looking at a segment with endpoints (1, 2) and (3, 5 These points are sent to (3, −6) and (9, −15). See th figure on the next page. The correct answer is (C).

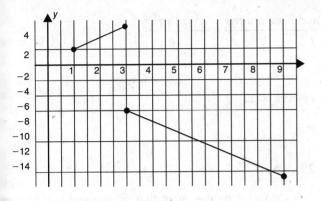

9. (A)

To find the circumcenter of the triangle, construct the perpendicular bisectors of each side. The point of intersection is the center of the circumscribed circle. The correct answer is (A).

0. (C)

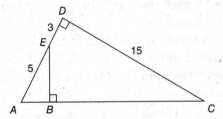

Using the Pythagorean Theorem, $AC = \sqrt{15^2 + 8^2} = \sqrt{289} = 17$. Let $x = BC$. Then using the fact that $\triangle ABE \sim \triangle ADC$, so that the corresponding sides are in proportion, we have $\dfrac{AE}{AC} = \dfrac{AB}{AD}$ or $\dfrac{5}{17} = \dfrac{17-x}{8} \Rightarrow x \approx 14.6$. So, statement (C) is correct.

1. (C)

Let x be the length of the third side. The *Triangle Inequality* tells us that the sum of the lengths of any two sides of a triangle must be greater than the length of the third side. Thus, $x < 6 + 14 = 20$, so x cannot equal 22. Also, $x + 6 > 14$; hence, x cannot be equal to 4 or 8. Thus, x must be equal to 18; (C) is the correct answer.

2. (B)

To construct the angle bisector you must find second point for the ray to pass through. Answers

(A) and (C) have no marks indicating a second point. Answer (D) does have the point but no markings on how the point was found. Answer (B) indicates the correct construction.

23. (C)

To earn 60% on the quiz, a student must answer six correctly and four incorrectly. So the question can be viewed as *how many ways can a student choose 6 questions to answer correctly?* This is a combination of 10 objects taken 6 at a time: $_{10}C_6 = \dfrac{10!}{6!4!} = \dfrac{10 \cdot 9 \cdot 8 \cdot 7}{4 \cdot 3 \cdot 2 \cdot 1} = 210$. The correct answer is (C).

24. (A)

Consider a simple example: Given data 1, 3, 7, 15; the median is 5 and the mean is 6.5. The range of the data is $15 - 1 = 14$. Now multiply each data number by 3: 3, 9, 21, 45. The median is now 15 and the mean is 19.5, so the mean and median have tripled. The range is now $45 - 3 = 42$, so the distribution curve has stretched horizontally. The correct answer is (A).

25. (A)

The complement of the event E: *having at least one defective laptop* is E': *having no defective laptops*. We will compute the probability of E' and then use $P(E) = 1 - P(E')$.

$P(E') = P$(no defective computers have come from factory A) + P(no defective computers have come from factory B) + P(no defective computers have come from factory C) $= P(A) \cdot P(D'|A) + P(B) \cdot P(D'|B) + P(C) \cdot P(D'|C)$, where $P(A)$, $P(B)$, and $P(C)$ is the probability that the computer came from factory A, B, and C, respectively, and $P(D'|A)$, $P(D'|B)$, and $P(D'|C)$ indicate the probability of a computer being not defective, knowing that it came from factory A, B, and C, respectively. Hence, $P(E') = (.2)(.78) + (.5)(.9) + (.3)(.95) = .891$, and $P(E) = 1 - 0.891 = 10.9\%$. The correct answer is (A).

26. (D)

The probability that we choose exactly two red marbles is equal to:

485

the number of ways to choose 4 marbles so that 2 are red and 2 are not red

$$\frac{\text{the number of ways to choose 4 marbles so that 2 are red and 2 are not red}}{\text{the number of ways to choose 4 marbles}} = \frac{_6C_2 \cdot _{17}C_2}{_{23}C_4}$$

$$= \frac{\dfrac{6!}{4!2!} \cdot \dfrac{17!}{15!2!}}{\dfrac{23!}{19!4!}} = \frac{15 \cdot 136}{8855} \approx 0.2303 = 23.03\%. \text{ The correct answer is (D)}.$$

27. (B)

The coefficient of correlation is a number between -1 and 1, inclusive. This eliminates answers (A) and (D). The coefficient of correlation indicates the fit of the regression line to the given data. If the slope of the regression line is negative, so is the coefficient of correlation. Similarly, if the slope of the regression line is positive, so is the coefficient of correlation. The regression line shown in the graph has a negative slope, so the correct answer must be (B).

28. (A)

The mean is the center of the interval [21.6, 44.4], which is $\dfrac{21.6 + 44.4}{2} = 33$. For a normally distributed collection of data, about 95.4% lies within two standard deviations of the mean. This means that $44.4 - 33 = 11.4$ is two standard deviations, so the standard deviation is 5.7. The correct answer is (A).

29. (A)

Let A be the event that the student is a histor major and let B be the event that the student is a senio Then $n(B) = 27$ and $n(A \cap B) = 13$. So the probabilit that the chosen student is a history major given that th student is a senior is $P(A|B) = \dfrac{P(A \cap B)}{P(B)} = \dfrac{n(A \cap B)}{n(B)} = \dfrac{13}{27}$ The correct answer is (A).

30. (C)

There are 40 scores, and $40/4 = 10$; so there ar 10 scores in each quartile. The first quartile (lowes scores) has scores 0, 1, 1, 3, 3, 3, 4, 4, 4, 4. The secon quartile has scores 4, 4, 4, 4, 5, 5, 5, 5, 5, 5. The thir quartile has scores 5, 6, 6, 6, 7, 7, 8, 8, 8, 8. The res of the 10 scores lie in the fourth quartile. The correc answer is (C).

Constructed-Response Problems

31. (B)

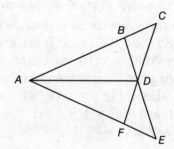

Figure 1

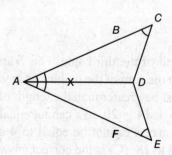

Figure 2

(continued on next page)

Proof:

1.	$\angle C \cong \angle E, \angle CAD \cong \angle EAD$	1.	Given (Figure 1)
2.	$\overline{AD} \cong \overline{AD}$	2.	Reflexive Property of Congruence
3.	$\triangle ADC \cong \triangle ADE$	3.	AAS (Angle-Angle-Side) (Figure 2)
4.	$\angle CAE \cong \angle CAE$	4.	Reflexive Property of Congruence
5.	$\overline{AC} \cong \overline{AE}$	5.	CPCTC (corresponding parts of congruent triangles are congruent)
6.	$\triangle ACF \cong \triangle AEB$	6.	ASA (Angle-Side-Angle) (Figure 3)

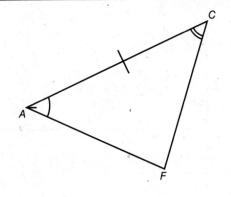 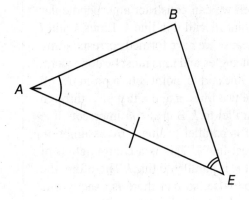

Figure 3

7.	$\overline{BE} \cong \overline{CF}$	7.	CPCTC
8.	$BE = CF$	8.	Definition of congruent segments
9.	$BE = BD + DE, CF = CD + DF$	9.	A whole is equal to the sum of its parts
10.	$BD + DE = CD + DF$	10.	Substitution
11.	$\overline{CD} \cong \overline{DE}$	11.	CPCTC (from step 3)
12.	$CD = DE$	12.	Definition of congruent segments
13.	$BD = DF$	13.	Addition Property of Equality (subtraction)
14.	$\overline{BD} \cong \overline{DF}$	15.	Definition of congruent segments
			Q.E.D.

2. The Euclidean Parallel Postulate states: *Through any point not on a given line there is exactly one line parallel to the given line.*

The given statement is:

> *If a line intersects one of two parallel lines, it must also intersect the other.*

Proof: ($\Rightarrow$) Assume the Euclidean Parallel Postulate holds. Assume lines l and m are parallel and that line t intersects line l; let point A be the point of intersection. Suppose line t does not intersect line m. Then there are two lines through point A parallel to line m, contradicting the Euclidean Parallel Postulate. Thus, line t intersects line m.

($\Leftarrow$) Assume that if a line intersects one of two parallel lines, it intersects the other one. Let l be a line and A a point not on l. First, we know there is at least one line through point A parallel to line l because we can construct a perpendicular to line l through point A; call this line j. Then we can construct a perpendicular to line j through point A; call this line k. Lines k and l must be parallel because we have formed corresponding angles that are right angles and thus must be congruent.

Now, let l be a line and let point A be a point not on l. Suppose there are two lines m and n that pass through point A and are parallel to l. But line m intersects line n, and since line n is parallel to line l, by assumption line m must intersect line l. This is a contradiction of the assumption that m is parallel to line l. Therefore, the assumption must be false, so that there is exactly one line through point A that is parallel to line l.

Q.E.D.

33. Let (x, y) be any point on the curve. Then, since the sum of the distances from this point to the points $(0, 0)$ and $(8, 0)$ is 10, we have the following equation:
$$\sqrt{(x-8)^2+(y-0)^2}+\sqrt{(x-0)^2+(y-0)^2}=10.$$ Isolat-

ing the radicals, one on each side, and squaring, we have $(x-8)^2+y^2=100-20\sqrt{x^2+y^2}+x^2+y^2$. Next, simplify and isolate the radical again. Then
$$4x+9=5\sqrt{x^2+y^2} \qquad 9x^2-72x+25y^2=81.$$

After completing squares, we obtain $\dfrac{(x-4)^2}{25}+\dfrac{y^2}{9}=1$, which is an ellipse with center a (4, 0) and major axis along the x-axis.

Here is the graph:

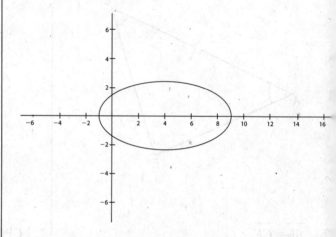

34. (a) The null hypothesis is: *The die is a fair die.*

(b) When using χ^2, the number of degrees of free dom is $8-1=7$, so at the 5% significance level (use the given table), we are looking for a number less than 14.067. We set up the table below assuming a uniform expected distribution.

Result on die	Observed Frequency	Expected Frequency	(Observed − Expected)^2	$\dfrac{(Obs. - Exp.)^2}{Expected}$
1	15	20	25	1.25
2	26	20	36	1.8
3	31	20	121	6.05
4	12	20	64	3.2
5	17	20	9	4.5
6	27	20	49	2.45
7	22	20	4	0.2
8	10	20	100	5.0
				24.45

So $\chi^2 = 24.45$, which exceeds 14.067, so the student can reject the null hypothesis and conclude that the octahedral die is not fair (biased).

CSET Mathematics Practice Test 1, Subtest III

Content Domain III *Calculus & History of Mathematics*

> Directions: This subtest consists of two sections:
>
> (I) thirty multiple-choice questions, and
>
> (II) four constructed-response questions that require written responses.

NOTE: The use of calculators is NOT allowed for CSET: Mathematics Subtest III

1. Find all values of $x \in [0, 2\pi)$ for which the graphs of the functions $f(x) = 2\cos^2 x$ and $g(x) = 1 - \cos x$ intersect.

   (A) $0, \dfrac{\pi}{6}, \pi, \dfrac{11\pi}{6}$

   (B) $\dfrac{\pi}{6}, \dfrac{5\pi}{6}, \pi$

   (C) $0, \dfrac{\pi}{3}, \pi, \dfrac{5\pi}{3}$

   (D) $\dfrac{\pi}{3}, \pi, \dfrac{5\pi}{3}$

2. Which of the following is equivalent to $\dfrac{\sin^2 \beta}{\cos^2 \beta} + \sin^2 \beta \csc^2 \beta$?

   (A) $\sec^2 \beta$

   (B) $\tan^2\beta + \cot^2 \beta$

   (C) $\cot^2 \beta + \cos^2 \beta$

   (D) $\csc^2 \beta$

3. Point P is on the edge of a DVD with a diameter of 12 cm. If $x(t) = 6\cos(400\pi t)$ describes the x-coordinate of the position of point P at time t in minutes, how far does the point P travel in three minutes as the DVD revolves?

   (A) 2400π cm

   (B) 6400π cm

   (C) 7200π cm

   (D) 8600π cm

4. Use the graph below to answer the question that follows.

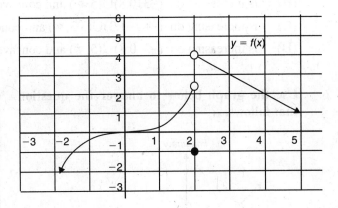

   Which of the following is the reason that f is not continuous at $x = 2$?

   (A) $\lim\limits_{x \to 2} f(x)$ does exist.

   (B) $f(2)$ does not exist.

   (C) $\lim\limits_{x \to 2} f(x) \neq f(2)$.

   (D) $\displaystyle\int_0^4 f(x)\,dx$ does not exist.

5. **Use the graph of f' below to answer the question that follows.**

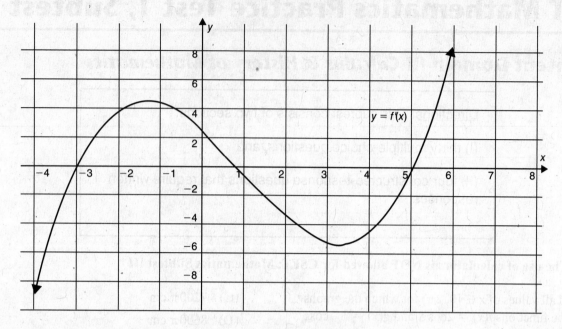

On approximately what intervals is f increasing, and on what intervals is f concave down?

(A) f is increasing on $(-\infty, -1.3)\cup(3.3, \infty)$ and concave down on $(-\infty, 1.5)$.

(B) f is increasing on $(-3, 0.8)\cup(5, \infty)$ and concave down on $(-1.3, 3.3)$.

(C) f is increasing on $(-\infty, -1.3)\cup(3.3, \infty)$ and concave down on $(-1.3, 3.3)$.

(D) f is increasing on $(-3, 0.8)\cup(5, \infty)$ and concave down on $(-\infty, 1.5)$.

6. **Use the graph below to answer the question that follows.**

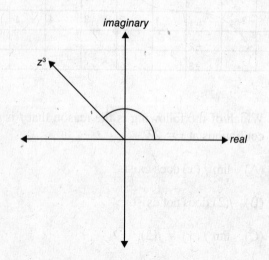

Which of the following complex numbers could be z if the above vector represents z^3, where z^3 is a unit vector?

(A) $\sin(45°) + i\cos(45°)$

(B) $\sin(405°) - i\cos(405°)$

(C) $\cos(45°) + i\sin(45°)$

(D) $-\cos(405°) + i\sin(405°)$

7. Which of the following statements is true?

(A) If a function is continuous at a point, it is differentiable at that point.

(B) If $\lim_{x\to a} f(x) = 0 = \lim_{x\to a} g(x)$, then $\lim_{x\to a} \frac{f(x)}{g(x)}$ does not exist.

(C) If f is continuous on $[2, 6]$ and d lies between the values of $f(a)$ and $f(b)$, then there exists a number $c \in (a, b)$ such that $f(c) = d$.

(D) The derivative of a product of functions is equal to the product of the derivative of the functions.

8. For what value of b will

$$h(x) = \begin{cases} \dfrac{\sin(4x)}{x}, & \text{when } x < 0 \\ x^2 + b - 2, & \text{when } x \geq 0 \end{cases}$$

be continuous at $x = 0$?

(A) 0.25

(B) 2.25

(C) 4

(D) 6

9. A curve in the xy-plane is given by the equation $xy - y^2 = 9x$. At which of the following points is the tangent to the curve vertical?

(A) $(-81, 9)$

(B) $(0, 9)$

(C) $(36, 18)$

(D) $(18, 18)$

10. The population of a certain country has been growing at a rate proportional to its size. If the population in 1990 ($t = 0$ years) was 1 million, and in 2000 it was 4 million, what will the population be in 2025?

(A) 14 million

(B) 28 million

(C) 64 million

(D) 128 million

11. **Use the chart below to answer the question that follows.**

x	$F(x)$	$F'(x)$	$G(x)$	$G'(x)$
1	3	5	2	-1
2	2	9	4	7
3	4	-2	1	8
4	1	6	3	-3

If $H(x) = \dfrac{F(2x) + G\left(\dfrac{x}{2}\right)}{x^2}$, what is the equation of the tangent to the curve $y = H(x)$ at $x = 2$?

(A) $y = \dfrac{17}{8}x - \dfrac{7}{2}$

(B) $y = \dfrac{5}{4}x - \dfrac{7}{2}$

(C) $y = \dfrac{5}{4}x - 5$

(D) $y = \dfrac{17}{8}x - 5$

12. An oil tanker has sprung a leak. The oil is spreading in a circular patch, with 50π m² of oil being added to the patch every minute. How quickly is the circumference of the patch growing when the area of the patch is 8100π m²?

(A) $\dfrac{5}{9}\pi$ meters per minute

(B) $\dfrac{5}{18}\pi$ meters per minute

(C) 10π meters per minute

(D) 90π meters per minute

13. The function $g(x) = \displaystyle\int_1^x \dfrac{t^2 + t - 6}{t^2 - 1}\, dt$ has exactly one critical point in the interval $1.5 \leq x \leq 10.5$. Find this point and classify it as a maximum or a minimum.

(A) The critical point occurs at $x = 2$ and it is a maximum.

(B) The critical point occurs at $x = 2$ and it is a minimum.

(C) The critical point occurs at $x = 3$ and it is a maximum.

(D) The critical point occurs at $x = 3$ and it is a minimum.

14. Let R be the region bounded by the curves $y = \sqrt{\sin x}$, $x = 0$, $x = \pi$, and $y = 0$. What is the volume of the solid created by revolving R about the x-axis?

(A) 1 cubic unit

(B) π cubic units

(C) $\left(1 + \dfrac{\sqrt{2}}{2}\right)$ cubic units

(D) 2π cubic units

15. The acceleration of a particle traveling in one dimension along the x-axis at time t is given by $a(t) = -3t + 4$. At time $t = 2$, the velocity of the particle is 0. If the position of the particle at time $t = 4$ is -10, what is the position of the particle at time $t = 2$?

    (A) -34

    (B) -2

    (C) 0

    (D) 16

16. Find the area under the curve $y = \dfrac{x}{9 + x^2}$ over the interval $[0, 3]$.

    (A) $\ln(2)$

    (B) $\ln(\sqrt{2})$

    (C) $\ln(3)$

    (D) $\ln(\sqrt{3})$

17. **Use the graph shown below and the Fundamental Theorem of Calculus to answer the following question.**

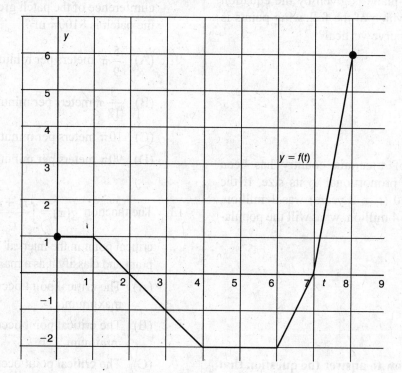

Let $g(x) = \displaystyle\int_0^x f(t)\,dt$. Where in the interval $[0, 8]$ does g have its absolute maximum and minimum values?

(A) Absolute maximum at $x = 8$ and absolute minimum at all points in $[4, 6]$

(B) Absolute maximum at $x = 8$ and absolute minimum at $x = 7$

(C) Absolute maximum at $x = 2$ and absolute minimum at $x = 7$

(D) Absolute maximum at $x = 2$ and absolute minimum at $x = 0$

18. **Use the graph below to answer the question that follows.**

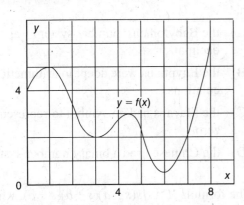

Use the graph of f to estimate a value of c that satisfies the conclusion of the Mean Value Theorem (for derivatives) for the interval $[0, 8]$.

(A) $c = 1$

(B) $c = 2$

(C) $c = 3.2$

(D) $c \doteq 7.3$

19. Use L'Hôpital's Rule to evaluate the limit: $\lim_{x \to 0^+} (\sin x)^x$.

(A) 0

(B) 1

(C) e

(D) The limit does not exist.

20. Find the sum of the series $4 - \dfrac{8}{3} + \dfrac{16}{9} - \dfrac{32}{27} + \dfrac{64}{81} - \cdots$.

(A) 2

(B) $\dfrac{12}{5}$

(C) 4

(D) The series is divergent.

21. For what value(s) of x does $\displaystyle\sum_{k=1}^{\infty} \dfrac{(-1)^k (x+1)^k}{k 2^k}$ converge absolutely?

(A) Only $x = -1$

(B) $x \in (-3, 1]$

(C) $x \in (-\infty, \infty)$

(D) $x \in (-3, 1)$

22. What is the Taylor series for $f(x) = e^{3x}$ at $x = 0$?

(A) $\displaystyle\sum_{n=0}^{\infty} \dfrac{3^n x^n}{n}$

(B) $\displaystyle\sum_{n=0}^{\infty} \dfrac{(n+1)x^n}{n!}$

(C) $\displaystyle\sum_{n=0}^{\infty} \dfrac{3^{n-1} x^n}{n!}$

(D) $\displaystyle\sum_{n=0}^{\infty} \dfrac{3^n x^n}{n!}$

23. Which of the following expressions is equal to $\tan(\arccos(5x))$ for $0 \le x \le \dfrac{1}{5}$?

(A) $\dfrac{\sqrt{1 - 25x^2}}{5x}$

(B) $\dfrac{\sqrt{1 + 25x^2}}{5x}$

(C) $\dfrac{\sqrt{1 + 25x^2}}{x}$

(D) $\sqrt{1 - 25x^2}$

24. Which of the following is the best approximation for the average value of the function $g(x) = xe^{-x}$ over the interval $[0, 2]$?

(A) 0.05

(B) 0.1

(C) 0.2

(D) 0.3

25. Which of the following statements is true?

    (A) The solution of the differential equation
    $\dfrac{dy}{dx} = x^2 y$ is $y = e^{\frac{1}{3}x^3} + C.$

    (B) To obtain the trigonometric iden-
    tity $\cot^2 x + 1 = \csc^2 x$ from the identity
    $\sin^2 x + \cos^2 x = 1$, divide $\sin^2 x + \cos^2 x = 1$ by
    $\cos^2 x.$

    (C) Let f be a function defined on a closed interval
    $[a, b]$ and let v be any real number between
    $f(a)$ and $f(b)$. Then there exists at least one
    number $c \in (a, b)$ such that $f(c) = 0.$

    (D) A polynomial $y = P(x)$ is continuous at every
    real number a because $\lim_{x \to a} P(x) = P(a).$

26. Let $w(t)$ be the number of inches of snow that has
    accumulated on the ground t hours after midnight.
    Which of the following statements is false?

    (A) $w(4) = 3$ means that three inches of snow
    has accumulated by 4 a.m.

    (B) $w^{-1}(1) = 3$ means that at 1 a.m. the snow is
    falling at a rate of 3 inches per hour.

    (C) $w'(4) = 1.2$ means that at 4 a.m. the snow
    is accumulating at a rate of 1.2 inches per
    hour.

    (D) $(w^{-1})'(2.1) = 6$ means that at 6 a.m. the
    snow is accumulating at a rate of 2.1 inches
    per hour.

27. Which of the following statements is true?

    (A) The Pythagorean Theorem was first used by
    Pythagoras.

    (B) Euclid's book *The Elements* studies only
    the mathematical areas of geometry and
    number theory.

    (C) Georg Cantor was one of the first mathema-
    ticians to develop the mathematical area of
    set theory.

    (D) Blaise Pascal was the first mathematician
    to use the famous triangle called *Pascal's
    Triangle* in applying the binomial theorem.

28. The Rhind Papyrus, which dates from around
    1650 BCE, is a document that provides evidence
    that

    (A) the Babylonians' number system was hexa-
    decimal.

    (B) the Egyptians were adept in arithmetic cal-
    culations.

    (C) the Mayans had no symbol to represent
    zero.

    (D) the Chinese used a binary number system.

29. The formula $A = \sqrt{s(s-a)(s-b)(s-c)}$, where a,
    b, and c are the lengths of the sides of a triangle
    and $s = \dfrac{1}{2}(a+b+c)$ is the semiperimeter of the
    triangle, was developed by

    (A) Heron (Hero) of Alexandria

    (B) Leibnitz of Germany

    (C) Hippocrates of Chios

    (D) Panini of Shalatula

30. Which of the following mathematicians is not
    considered to be a pioneer of differential calculus
    as it is known today?

    (A) Albert Einstein

    (B) Blaise Pascal

    (C) Évariste Galois

    (D) Gottfried Leibnitz

Constructed-Response Problems

31. Let $f(x) = x^4 - 4x^3$. Use first and second deriva-
    tives to determine the intervals of increase/de-
    crease and concavity, as well as to find all extrema
    and inflection point. Then sketch the function.

32. Use the formal definition of the derivative to com-
    pute the derivative of $g(x) = \dfrac{1}{x^2}$ at $x = 2$ and then
    write the equation of the tangent line at $x = 2$.

33. Use the definition of the Riemann integral to compute $\int_0^4 (x^2 - 3)\,dx$.

34. Consider this definition from Pythagoras: (x, y, z) forms a **Pythagorean triple** if x, y, and z are positive integers such that $x^2 + y^2 = z^2$. In addition, if a Pythagorean triple is such that x, y, and z have no common factors, then it is called a **primitive** Pythagorean triple.

(a) Suppose n is a positive integer with $z = 2n^2 + 2n + 1$ and $y = 2n + 1$. Prove that there exists some x so that (x, y, z) forms a Pythagorean triple.

(b) Prove that there are infinitely many primitive Pythagorean triples.

(c) Show that if (x, y, z) is a primitive Pythagorean triple, then exactly one of x, y, or z must be an even integer.

Answer Key Subtest III

Question Number	Answers	SMR
1	D	5.1 c
2	A	5.1 c
3	C	5.1 c
4	A	5.2 a
5	B	5.3 b, e
6	C	5.1 e
7	C	5.2 a, c
8	D	5.2 a
9	C	5.3 b, c
10	D	5.3 f
11	A	5.3 b
12	A	5.3 d
13	B	5.4 c, 5.3 e
14	D	5.4 d
15	B	5.3 d
16	B	5.3 b, d
17	C	5.3 e, 5.4 b, c

Question Number	Answers	SMR
18	C	5.3 c
19	B	5.3 c
20	B	5.5 a
21	D	5.5 b
22	D	5.5 c
23	A	5.1 c, d
24	D	5.4 b
25	D	5.1 a, 5.2 b, c
26	B	5.3 b
27	C	6.1 a, b
28	B	6.1 a, b
29	A	6.1 a, b
30	C	6.1 a, b
31	Constructed-Response	5.3 b, e
32	Constructed-Response	5.3 a, b
33	Constructed-Response	5.4 a
34	Constructed-Response	6.1 a, b

Practice Test 1: Subtest III Answer Explanations

1. (D)

$2\cos^2(x) = 1 - \cos(x) \Leftrightarrow 2\cos^2(x) + \cos(x) - 1 = 0$.
Let $u = \cos(x)$ and substitute into the last equation to get $2u^2 + u - 1 = 0$. Factor and solve: $(2u - 1)(u + 1) = 0 \Rightarrow u = \dfrac{1}{2}$ or $u = -1$. Now substitute again: $\cos(x) = \dfrac{1}{2}$ or $\cos(x) = -1$. For $x \in [0, 2\pi)$, the solutions are

$x = \dfrac{\pi}{3}, \dfrac{5\pi}{3}, \pi$. Therefore, (D) is the correct answer.

2. (A)

$\dfrac{\sin^2 \beta}{\cos^2 \beta} + \sin^2\beta \csc^2\beta = \tan^2\beta + 1 = \sec^2\beta$. So the correct answer is (A).

3. (C)

$x(t) = 6 \cos(400\pi t)$. The diameter is 12 cm, so the circumference of the DVD is 12π cm. Since the DVD rotates 2π radians (1 revolution) in $\dfrac{2\pi}{400\pi} = \dfrac{1}{200}$ of a minute, the point P travels 200 revolutions in one minute and 600 in three minutes. The point P therefore travels $12\pi(600) = 7200\pi$ cm in three minutes. The correct answer is (C).

4. (A)

$f(2) = -1$, so the function value exists. The left-hand limit, $\lim\limits_{x \to 2} f(x)$, equals about 2.5, whereas the right-hand limit, $\lim\limits_{x \to 2} f(x)$, equals 4. So the one-sided limits exist, but since they are not equal, the two-sided limit does not exist. The integral does exist. So the correct answer is (A).

5. (B)

The function f is increasing on the intervals where its derivative f' is positive. The given graph is of f', and

according to the graph, $f'(x) > 0$ (graph is above the x-axis) on the intervals $(-3, 0.8) \cup (5, \infty)$. This is where f is increasing. Now f is concave down when $f''(x) < 0$ or when f' is decreasing. According to the graph, f' is decreasing on approximately the interval $(-1.3, 3.3)$. The correct answer is (B).

6. (C)

The polar form of a unit vector in $\mathbf{C}$ is $z = e^{i\theta} = \cos(\theta) + i\sin(\theta)$. Then $z^3 = e^{3i\theta} = \cos(3\theta) + i\sin(3\theta)$. From the unit vector shown in the graph, it appears that its angle is approximately 135° or that $3\theta = 135°$. From this, we see that $\theta = 45°$, so the correct answer is (C).

7. (C)

It is false that continuity at a point implies differentiability at a point, which can be seen from the example $f(x) = |x|$, which is continuous at $x = 0$ but not differentiable at $x = 0$, so statement (A) is false. Statement (B) can be seen to be false: Let $f(x) = x = g(x)$. Then

$$\lim_{x \to 0} f(x) = 0 = \lim_{x \to 0} g(x), \text{ but } \lim_{x \to 0} \frac{f(x)}{g(x)} = \lim_{x \to 0} \frac{x}{x} = \lim_{x \to 0} 1 = 1.$$

To see that statement (D) is false, consider the functions

$$f(x) = x = g(x). \text{ Then } \frac{d}{dx}(f(x)d(x)) = \frac{d}{dx}(x^2) = 2x$$

but $\dfrac{d}{dx}(f(x)) = 1 = \dfrac{d}{dx}(g(x))$ so that the product of the derivatives is equal to 1 rather than $2x$. Statement (C) is the *Intermediate Value Theorem* and is true. The correct answer is (C).

8. (D)

The limit of $h(x)$ must exist at $x = 0$ and must equal $h(0) = b - 2$. The one-sided limits are:

$$\lim_{x \to 0^+} h(x) = \lim_{x \to 0^+}(x^2 + b - 2) = b - 2 \text{ and}$$

$$\lim_{x \to 0} h(x) = \lim_{x \to 0^-}\left(\frac{\sin(4x)}{x}\right) = \lim_{x \to 0^-}\left(\frac{4\sin(4x)}{4x}\right) = 4. \text{ We}$$

need these limits to be equal; so $b - 2 = 4$ or $b = 6$. The correct answer is (D).

9. (C)

We must use implicit differentiation to find $\frac{dy}{dx}$: $x \cdot \frac{dy}{dx} + y - \left(2y\frac{dy}{dx}\right) = 9$. Solving for the derivative, we get: $(x-2y)\cdot\frac{dy}{dx} = 9-y$ $\frac{dy}{dx} = \frac{9-y}{x-2y}$, which represents the slope of the tangent line. The tangent line is vertical when the derivative is infinitely undefined. This occurs when $x - 2y = 0$. The only answer that fits this is (C). You should also use substitution to check that the point (36, 18) satisfies the equation of the given curve: $36(18) - 18^2 = 18^2 = (9(36))$; check! The correct answer is (C).

10. (D)

This is an exponential function since the growth rate is in proportion to its size. The basic equation is $P = P_0 e^{rt}$. Since 1990 is $t = 0$, $P(0) = 1$ (in millions). Hence, the equation becomes $P = e^{rt}$. The year 2000 is $t = 10$, so $4 = e^{10r}$, and $e^r = 4^{\frac{1}{10}} = 2^{\frac{1}{5}}$. Our function is therefore $P = (e^r)^t = 2^{\frac{t}{5}}$. The year 2025 is $t = 35$ so $P(35) = 2^{\frac{35}{5}} = 2^7 = 128$ million people. The correct answer is (D).

11. (A)

$$H(x) = \frac{F(2x) + G\left(\frac{x}{2}\right)}{x^2}, \text{ so, } H'(x) = \frac{x^2\left(2F'(2x) + \frac{1}{2}G'\left(\frac{x}{2}\right)\right) - 2x\left(F(2x) + G\left(\frac{x}{2}\right)\right)}{\left(x^2\right)^2}$$

by the quotient rule. Then the slope of the tangent at $x = 2$ is

$$H'(2) = \frac{2^2\left(2F'(4) + \frac{1}{2}G'(1)\right) - 2(2)(F(4) + G(1))}{(2)^4} = \frac{4\left(2(6) + \frac{1}{2}(-1)\right) - 4(1+2)}{16} = \frac{17}{8}.$$

The point of tangency is $(2, H(2)) = \left(2, \frac{F(4) + G(1)}{2^2}\right) = \left(2, \frac{3}{4}\right)$, so to get the equation of the tangent at $x = 2$, we can use the point-slope formula: $y - \frac{3}{4} = \frac{17}{8}(x-2)$ $y = \frac{17}{8}x - \frac{7}{2}$. The correct answer is (A).

12. (A)

The area and circumference of a circle are related to the radius by the equations $A = \pi r^2$ and $C = 2\pi r$. We are given that $\frac{dA}{dt} = 50\pi$ square meters per minute. We want to know $\frac{dC}{dt}$ when the area is 8100π square meters, or when $r = 90$ meters. We may differentiate the two equations with respect to time to get $\frac{dA}{dt} = 2\pi r\frac{dr}{dt}$ and $\frac{dC}{dt} = 2\pi\frac{dr}{dt}$. We can eliminate the common $\frac{dr}{dt}$ and obtain

$\frac{dC}{dt} = 2\pi\left(\frac{dA}{dt} \cdot \frac{1}{2\pi r}\right) = \frac{1}{r}\frac{dA}{dt}$. So when $r = 90$ meters we have $\frac{dC}{dt} = \frac{1}{90}(50\pi) = \frac{5}{9}\pi$ meters per minute. The correct answer is (A).

13. (B)

Given $g(x) = \int_1^x \frac{t^2 + t - 6}{t^2 - 1}dt$, we can use the Fundamental Theorem of Calculus to differentiate g t

obtain $g'(x) = \dfrac{x^2 + x - 6}{x^2 - 1}$. The critical values of g are where $g'(x) = 0$ or does not exist; this occurs when $x^2 + x - 6 = (x + 3)$
$(x - 2) = 0$ or $x^2 - 1 = (x - 1)(x + 1) = 0$, respectively. These values are -3, 2, 1, and -1, but the only value that
lies in $[1.5, 10.5]$ is $x = 2$. If we evaluate g' for numbers between 1.5 and 2, we see that $g'(x) < 0$, and if we evaluate
g' for numbers between 2 and 2.5, we see that $g'(x) > 0$. This means that g changes from decreasing to increasing at
$x = 2$, so there is a relative minimum at $x = 2$. The correct answer is (B).

14. (D)

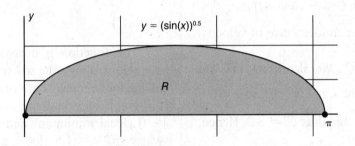

Figure A

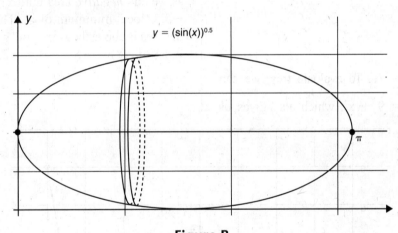

Figure B

R is the region bounded by the curves $f(x) = y = \sqrt{\sin x}$, $x = 0$, $x = \pi$, and $y = 0$; see Figure A. Revolving the
region R about the x-axis gives a solid (Figure B) that can be sliced into disks of width Δx and radius approximately r
$= f(x^*)$ where x^* is a point in the width interval. So the volume of such a disk is $\pi[f(x^*)]^2\Delta x$. Summing up the volumes
of the disks gives $\Sigma \pi[f(x)]^2\Delta x$. If we imagine the number of the slices increasing so that Δx becomes very small, this
makes the problem an integration problem (the method of finding the volume of a solid of revolution by using disks).
The volume is thus

$$V = \int_0^\pi \pi\left[f(x)\right]^2 dx = \pi\int_0^\pi \left[\sqrt{\sin(x)}\right]^2 dx = \pi\int_0^\pi \sin(x)dx = \pi\left[-\cos(\pi) - (-\cos(0))\right] = 2\pi \text{ cubic units. The correct}$$

answer is (D).

15. (B)

The acceleration of a particle traveling in one dimension along the x-axis at time t is given by $a(t) = -3t + 4$. The antiderivative of acceleration is velocity, and in this case we have $v(t) = -\frac{3}{2}t^2 + 4t + C$. We are told that at time $t = 2$ the velocity of the particle is 0, so $0 = -\frac{3}{2}(2)^2 + 4(2) + C$; thus, $C = -2$ and $v(t) = \frac{3}{2}t^2 + 4t - 2$. The position, s, is the antiderivative of velocity, so $s(t) = -\frac{1}{2}t^3 + 2t^2 - 2t + C'$. We also know that the position of the particle at time $t = 4$ is -10, so $-10 = -\frac{1}{2}(4)^3 + 2(4)^2 - 2(4) + C'$, and thus $C' = -2$. Hence, the position function is $s(t) = -\frac{1}{2}t^3 + 2t^2 - 2t - 2$, and $s(2) = -2$. The correct answer is (B).

16. (B)

The area is $\int_0^3 \frac{x}{9+x^2}\,dx$. To evaluate this, we can use the substitution $u = 9 + x^2$, which also gives us

$du = 2x\,dx$, or $x\,dx = \frac{1}{2}du$. In addition, $u = 18$ when $x = 3$ and $u = 9$ when $x = 0$. So, by substitution, we have

$$A = \int_0^3 \frac{x}{9+x^2}\,dx = \frac{1}{2}\int_8^{18} \frac{du}{u} = \frac{1}{2}\ln|u|\Big|_9^{18} = \frac{1}{2}\big((18) - \ln(9)\big)$$

$= \frac{1}{2}\ln\left(\frac{18}{9}\right) = \ln\left(\sqrt{2}\right)$. The correct answer is (B).

17. (C)

The function g measures the signed area (area of regions above the x-axis is positive and the area of regions below the x-axis is negative) between the graph of g and the x-axis from 0 to x. So $g(0) = 0$ (local minimum) and g is growing until $x = 2$ where $g(2) = 1.5$ (local maximum) can be seen as the sum of the areas in the square above the interval $[0,1]$ and the triangle above $[1,2]$. Then g starts to decrease as we add *negative* area until $x = 7$. $g(7) = 1.5 - 7 = -5.5$ (local minimum of g). Then g increases because the area is above the x-axis and g has a local maximum at $x = 8$ of $g(8) = -5.5 + 3 = -2.5$. See the graph below.

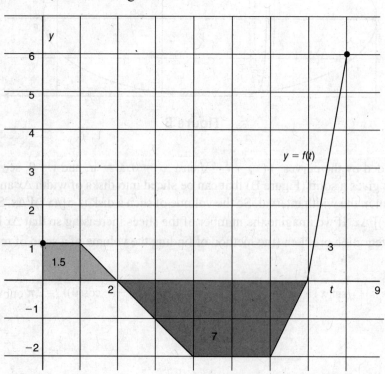

The function g is continuous so the absolute maximum must be at the greatest local maximum which is at $x = 2$, and the absolute minimum must occur at the least of the local minimums which is at $x = 7$. The correct answer is (C).

18. (C)

The Mean Value Theorem says that if f is continuous on $[a, b]$ and differentiable on (a, b), then there exists a $c \in (a, b)$ such that $f'(c) = \dfrac{f(b) - f(a)}{b - a}$. For this problem, $a = 0$, $b = 8$, and $f(8) = 6$, $f(0) = 4$, so $\dfrac{f(b) - f(a)}{b - a} = \dfrac{6 - 4}{8} = \dfrac{1}{4}$; this is the slope of the secant line through the points $(0, 4)$ and $(8, 6)$. We want to find c in $(0, 8)$ such that the tangent line is parallel to the secant line. So where does the tangent line have a slope of ¼? Check the four given numbers for possible answers. At $x = 1$, the slope of the tangent is 0; at $x = 2$, the tangent has a negative slope; at $x = 3.2$, the slope is close to ¼; and at $x = 7.3$, the slope of the tangent is greater than 2 (draw the tangents in and look at them). The correct answer is (C), $c = 3.2$.

19. (B)

Let $y = (\sin x)^x$ so that $\ln(y) = \ln((\sin x)^x) = x \ln(\sin(x)) = \dfrac{\ln(\sin(x))}{\dfrac{1}{x}}$. Taking the limit: $\lim\limits_{x \to 0^+} (\ln(y))$

$= \lim\limits_{x \to 0^+} \left(\dfrac{\ln(\sin(x))}{\dfrac{1}{x}} \right)$. The limit of the right side is

an indeterminate form of the $\dfrac{\infty}{\infty}$ type, so we may use L'Hôpital's Rule and take the derivative of the functions in the numerator and denominator separately to obtain

$\lim\limits_{x \to 0^+} \left(\dfrac{\ln(\sin(x))}{\dfrac{1}{x}} \right) = \lim\limits_{x \to 0^+} \dfrac{\dfrac{1}{\sin(x)} \cdot \cos(x)}{-\dfrac{1}{x^2}} = \lim\limits_{x \to 0^+} (-x^2 \cot(x))$

$= \lim\limits_{x \to 0^+} \dfrac{-x^2}{\tan(x)}$, but this limit is an indeterminate form

of the $\dfrac{0}{0}$ type. So we use L'Hôpital's Rule again:

$\lim\limits_{x \to 0^+} \dfrac{-x^2}{\tan(x)} = \lim\limits_{x \to 0^+} \dfrac{-2x}{\sec^2(x)} = 0$. Hence, $\lim\limits_{x \to 0^+} (\ln(y)) = 0$,

so that taking the exponential of both sides of the equations gives us $e^0 = e^{\lim\limits_{x \to 0^+} (\ln(y))}$ or $1 = \lim\limits_{x \to 0^+} e^{\ln(y)} = \lim\limits_{x \to 0^+} y$, Thus, the correct answer is (B).

20. (B)

The series is a geometric series with initial term $a = 4$, and ratio $r = \dfrac{-2}{3}$. Since $|r| < 1$, the series is convergent and its sum is $\dfrac{a}{1 - r} = \dfrac{4}{1 - \left(\dfrac{-2}{3} \right)} = \dfrac{12}{5}$. So, answer (B) is correct.

21. (D)

Using the ratio test:

$\left| \dfrac{(-1)^{k+1}(x+1)^{k+1}}{(k+1)2^{k+1}} \cdot \dfrac{k \cdot 2^k}{(-1)^k(x+1)^k} \right| = \dfrac{k}{k+1} \cdot \dfrac{1}{2} \cdot |x+1| \xrightarrow{k \to \infty} \dfrac{1}{2}|x+1| \cdot$

So the series is absolutely convergent when

$\dfrac{1}{2}|x+1| < 1$ or $|x+1| < 2$. Thus, the series definitely converges absolutely for $x \in (-3, 1)$. We have to check the endpoints separately:

$x = -3: \sum\limits_{k=1}^{\infty} \dfrac{(-1)^k(-3+1)^k}{k2^k} = \sum\limits_{k=1}^{\infty} \dfrac{(-1)^k(-2)^k}{k2^k} = \sum\limits_{k=1}^{\infty} \dfrac{1}{k},$

which is the harmonic series, and it diverges.

$x = 1: \sum\limits_{k=1}^{\infty} \dfrac{(-1)^k(1+1)^k}{k2^k} = \sum\limits_{k=1}^{\infty} \dfrac{(-1)^k(2)^k}{k2^k} = \sum\limits_{k=1}^{\infty} \dfrac{(-1)^k}{k},$

which is the alternating harmonic series, which converges conditionally but not absolutely.

Therefore, the series converges absolutely only for $x \in (-3, 1)$. The correct answer is (D).

22. (D)

$f(x) = e^{3x} \Rightarrow f'(x) = 3e^{3x}, f''(x) = 9e^{3x}, f'''(x) = 27e^{3x}$, from which we deduce that $f^{(n)}(x) = 3^n e^{3x}$, so that

$f^{(n)}(0) = 3^n$. Thus, the Taylor series for $f(x) = e^{3x}$ at

$x = 0$ is $1 + 3x + \dfrac{9}{2!}x^2 + \cdots + \dfrac{3^n}{n!}x^n + \cdots = \displaystyle\sum_{n=0}^{\infty} \dfrac{3^n x^n}{n!}$.

Answer (D) is correct.

23. (A)

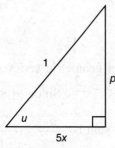

Let $u = \arccos(5x)$, then $\cos u = 5x$, and $0 \le 5x \le 1$. Label a right triangle appropriately (see Figure). Using the Pythagorean Theorem, $p = \sqrt{1 - 25x^2}$

Then $\tan(\arccos(5x)) = \tan(u) = \dfrac{\sqrt{1 - 25x^2}}{5x}$. The correct answer is (A).

24. (D)

The average value of g over $[0, 2]$ is given by $\dfrac{1}{2-0}\displaystyle\int_0^2 xe^{-x}dx$. We can evaluate the integral as an indefinite integral using integration by parts, where $u = x$, $dv = e^{-x}dx$, so that $du = dx$ and $v = -e^{-x}$; thus,

$$\int xe^{-x}dx = -xe^{-x} - \int -e^{-x}dx = -xe^{-x} + (-e^{-x}) + C$$

Then we obtain:

$$\dfrac{1}{2}\int_0^2 xe^{-x}dx = \dfrac{1}{2}\left(-xe^{-x} - e^{-x}\right)\Big|_0^2 = \dfrac{1}{2}(-2e^{-2} - e^{-2} - (0-1))$$

$$= \dfrac{-3}{2}e^{-2} + \dfrac{1}{2} \approx \dfrac{-3}{2(2.7)^2} + 0.5 \approx 0.3.$$ The correct answer is (D).

25. (D)

$$\frac{dy}{dx} = \frac{d}{dx}\left(e^{\frac{1}{3}x^3} + c\right) = x^2 e^{\frac{1}{3}x^3}$$

But $x^2 y = x^2\left(e^{\frac{1}{3}x^3} + c\right) = x^2 e^{\frac{1}{3}x^3} + cx^2$, so (A) is false. If we divide $\sin^2 x + \cos^2 x = 1$ by $\cos^2 x$, we obtain $\tan^2 x + 1 = \sec^2 x$, so (B) is false. Answer option (C) is false: let $f(a) = 1$, $f(b) = 2$ and $f(x) = 1.5$ for all $x \in (a,b)$. Then there is no value $c \in (a,b)$ such that $f(c)=0$. Answer option (D) is true from the definitions of continuity and polynomial.

26. (B)

The statement $w^{-1}(1) = 3$ is equivalent to $w(3) = 1$, which means that at 3 a.m. there is 1 inch of snow accumulation, so this is the incorrect statement. The correct answer is (B).

27. (C)

The true statement is *Georg Cantor was one of the first mathematicians to develop the mathematical area of Set Theory*. The correct answer is (C).

28. (B)

The correct answer is (B), *the Egyptians were adept at arithmetic calculations*.

29. (A)

The formula is well known to be Heron's (Hero's) formula. The correct answer is (A).

30. (C)

Einstein and Leibnitz are considered the main developers of calculus and they both used ideas of Pascals. Galois is an algebraist. The correct answer is (C).

Constructed-Response Problems

31. $f(x) = x^4 - 4x^3$. From this equation, we can see that f is a polynomial and thus does not have any asymptotes. Since $f(x) = x^3(x - 4)$, f has two zeroes, 0 and 4. We also can determine the end behavior of f by comparing it with its dominant term x^4. The graph of $y = x^4$ is such that $\lim_{x \to \infty} x^4 = +\infty(undefined) = \lim_{x \to -\infty} x^4$, so that the ends of the graph point upward; the end behavior of f is the same.

Next, take the first derivative: $f'(x) = 4x^3 - 12x^2 = 4x^2(x - 3)$. The zeroes of the derivative are 0 and 3, and these are the only possible values of x for which local extrema might occur since f' is defined for all real numbers. We test the intervals for the sign of the derivative.

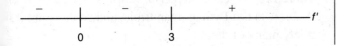

We see from the first derivative test that there is a local minimum when $x = 3$ (the point is $(3, -27)$), whereas there is no extremum at $x = 0$ as there is no change in the sign of the derivative and it is continuous. We also can conclude that f is increasing on $(3, \infty)$ and decreasing on $(-\infty, 0) \cup (0, 3)$.

The second derivative is $f''(x) = 12x^2 - 24x = 12x(x - 2)$. The zeroes of f'' are 0 and 2, and these are the possible values for which there might be inflection points. We test the second derivatve to find when it is positive and negative.

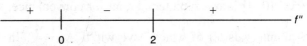

The second derivative test indicates that there are two inflection points, one at 0 and the other at 2. The inflection points are $(0, 0)$ and $(2, -16)$. In addition, we see that f is concave up on $(-\infty, 0) \cup (2, +\infty)$ and concave down on $(0, 2)$.

We use all this information to sketch the graph of f:

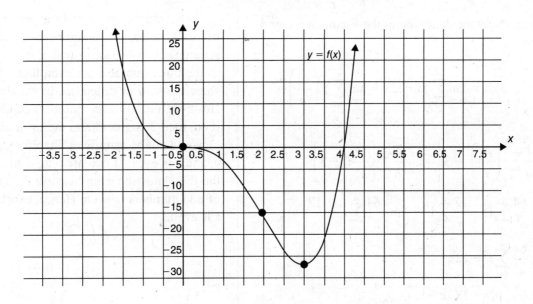

2.

$$g'(2) = \lim_{h \to 0} \frac{g(2+h) - g(2)}{h} = \lim_{h \to 0} \frac{\frac{1}{(2+h)^2} - \frac{1}{4}}{h} = \lim_{h \to 0} \frac{\frac{1}{(2+h)^2} - \frac{1}{4}}{h} \bullet \left(\frac{4(2+h)^2}{4(2+h)^2} \right)$$

$$= \lim_{h \to 0} \frac{4 - (2+h)^2}{4h(2+h)^2} = \lim_{h \to 0} \frac{-h(4+h)}{4h(2+h)^2} = \lim_{h \to 0} = \frac{-(4+h)}{4(2+h)^2} = -\frac{1}{4}$$

So, the slope of the tangent line at $x = 2$ is $\frac{-1}{4}$.

The point of tangency is $(2, g(2)) = (2, \frac{1}{4})$.

Therefore, the equation of the tangent line at $x = 2$ is

$$y - \frac{1}{4} = -\frac{1}{4}(x - 2) \text{ or } y = \frac{-1}{4}x + \frac{3}{4}.$$

33. To compute $\int_0^4 (x^2 - 3)dx$, begin by partitioning the interval $[0, 4]$ into n subinterval, and for convenience, use subintervals all of which have width $\Delta x = \frac{4}{n}$. In each subinterval, choose any point and call it x_i for the ith interval $i = 1, 2, 3, \ldots, n$. Actually, it does not matter which point we choose in each of the n subintervals, since the intervals will be becoming infinitesimal in size once we take the limit; hence, let x_i be the right endpoint of each interval; i.e., $x_i = \frac{4i}{n}$.

Then, using the definition of the Riemann integral, we have:

$$\int_0^4 (x^2 - 3)dx = \lim_{n \to \infty} \sum_{i=1}^n f(x_i)\Delta x = \lim_{n \to \infty} \sum_{i=1}^n f\left(\frac{4i}{n}\right)\frac{4}{n}$$

$$= \lim_{n \to \infty} \frac{4}{n} \sum_{i=1}^n \left[\left(\frac{4i}{n}\right)^2 - 3\right] = \lim_{n \to \infty} \frac{4}{n} \sum_{i=1}^n \left[\frac{16}{n^2}i^2 - 3\right]$$

$$= \lim_{n \to \infty} \left[\frac{64}{n^3} \sum_{i=1}^n i^2 - \frac{12}{n} \sum_{i=1}^n 1\right] = \lim_{n \to \infty} \left[\frac{64}{n^3} \sum_{i=1}^n i^2 - \frac{12}{n}(n)\right]$$

$$= \lim_{n \to \infty} \left[\frac{64}{n^3} \sum_{i=1}^n i^2 - 12\right]$$

$$= \lim_{n \to \infty} \left[\frac{64}{n^3}\left[\frac{n(n+1)(2n+1)}{6}\right] - 12\right]$$

$$= \lim_{n \to \infty} \frac{32}{3}\left[\frac{(n+1)(2n+1)}{n^2}\right] - 12$$

$$= \frac{32}{3} \lim_{n \to \infty} \left(2 + \frac{3}{n} + \frac{1}{n^2}\right) - 12$$

$$= \frac{64}{3} - 12 = \frac{28}{3}$$

34. (a) **Proof:** Let $z = 2n^2 + 2n + 1$ and $y = 2n + 1$. We would like to find x such that $x^2 = z^2 - y^2 = (2n^2 + 2n + 1)^2 - (2n + 1)^2 = (4n^4 + 8n^3 + 8n^2 + 4n + 1) - (4n^2 + 4n + 1) = 4n^4 + 8n^3 + 4n^2 = 4n^2(n^2 + 2n + 1) = 4n^2(n + 1)^2$. Thus, $x = 2n(n + 1)$, so that (x, y, z) is a Pythagorean triple.

Q.E.D

(b) **Proof:** From part (a), we can see that for infinitely many choices of n, $(2n(n + 1), 2n + 1, 2n^2 + 2n + 1)$ is a Pythagorean triple. To see that these are all primitive Pythagorean triples, note that $x = z - 1$, so that x and z have no common factors other than 1 because if j divide x and $z = x + 1$, then j also must divide 1, but that mean $j = 1$. Also, y has no common factor with x or z, because if, say, x and y have a common factor, then z must have that same factor because we know $z^2 = x^2 + y^2$. Therefore, for each integer n, $(2n(n + 1), 2n + 1, 2n^2 + 2n + 1)$ is a Pythagorean triple, and so there are infinitely many of them.

Q.E.D

(c) Assume (x, y, z) is a primitive Pythagorean triple. It is clear that a number is even if and only if its square is even. We know that $z^2 = x^2 + y^2$, so if any two of the three numbers are even then all three are even since the sum or difference of even numbers is even. However, not all three numbers can be even, because if so, then 2 is a common factor of all three and (x, y, z) would not be primitive. Therefore, at most one of x, y, and z is even. If two are odd, then since $z^2 = x^2 + y^2$ the third must be even because the sum or difference of odd numbers is even. Hence, exactly one of x, y, or z is even.

CSET: Mathematics

Practice Test 2

This test is also on CD in our special interactive TestWare® for the CSET: Mathematics Test. It is highly recommended that you first take this exam on computer. You will then have the additional study features and benefits of enforced timed conditions and instantaneous, accurate scoring. See page 6 for instructions on how to get the most out of this book and software.

Multiple-Choice Answer Sheet

Use the ovals below and on the next page to indicate your answer choices for the multiple-choice sections of the exam.

Subtest I

1. Ⓐ Ⓑ Ⓒ Ⓓ
2. Ⓐ Ⓑ Ⓒ Ⓓ
3. Ⓐ Ⓑ Ⓒ Ⓓ
4. Ⓐ Ⓑ Ⓒ Ⓓ
5. Ⓐ Ⓑ Ⓒ Ⓓ
6. Ⓐ Ⓑ Ⓒ Ⓓ
7. Ⓐ Ⓑ Ⓒ Ⓓ
8. Ⓐ Ⓑ Ⓒ Ⓓ

9. Ⓐ Ⓑ Ⓒ Ⓓ
10. Ⓐ Ⓑ Ⓒ Ⓓ
11. Ⓐ Ⓑ Ⓒ Ⓓ
12. Ⓐ Ⓑ Ⓒ Ⓓ
13. Ⓐ Ⓑ Ⓒ Ⓓ
14. Ⓐ Ⓑ Ⓒ Ⓓ
15. Ⓐ Ⓑ Ⓒ Ⓓ
16. Ⓐ Ⓑ Ⓒ Ⓓ

17. Ⓐ Ⓑ Ⓒ Ⓓ
18. Ⓐ Ⓑ Ⓒ Ⓓ
19. Ⓐ Ⓑ Ⓒ Ⓓ
20. Ⓐ Ⓑ Ⓒ Ⓓ
21. Ⓐ Ⓑ Ⓒ Ⓓ
22. Ⓐ Ⓑ Ⓒ Ⓓ
23. Ⓐ Ⓑ Ⓒ Ⓓ
24. Ⓐ Ⓑ Ⓒ Ⓓ

25. Ⓐ Ⓑ Ⓒ Ⓓ
26. Ⓐ Ⓑ Ⓒ Ⓓ
27. Ⓐ Ⓑ Ⓒ Ⓓ
28. Ⓐ Ⓑ Ⓒ Ⓓ
29. Ⓐ Ⓑ Ⓒ Ⓓ
30. Ⓐ Ⓑ Ⓒ Ⓓ

Subtest II

1. Ⓐ Ⓑ Ⓒ Ⓓ
2. Ⓐ Ⓑ Ⓒ Ⓓ
3. Ⓐ Ⓑ Ⓒ Ⓓ
4. Ⓐ Ⓑ Ⓒ Ⓓ
5. Ⓐ Ⓑ Ⓒ Ⓓ
6. Ⓐ Ⓑ Ⓒ Ⓓ
7. Ⓐ Ⓑ Ⓒ Ⓓ
8. Ⓐ Ⓑ Ⓒ Ⓓ

9. Ⓐ Ⓑ Ⓒ Ⓓ
10. Ⓐ Ⓑ Ⓒ Ⓓ
11. Ⓐ Ⓑ Ⓒ Ⓓ
12. Ⓐ Ⓑ Ⓒ Ⓓ
13. Ⓐ Ⓑ Ⓒ Ⓓ
14. Ⓐ Ⓑ Ⓒ Ⓓ
15. Ⓐ Ⓑ Ⓒ Ⓓ
16. Ⓐ Ⓑ Ⓒ Ⓓ

17. Ⓐ Ⓑ Ⓒ Ⓓ
18. Ⓐ Ⓑ Ⓒ Ⓓ
19. Ⓐ Ⓑ Ⓒ Ⓓ
20. Ⓐ Ⓑ Ⓒ Ⓓ
21. Ⓐ Ⓑ Ⓒ Ⓓ
22. Ⓐ Ⓑ Ⓒ Ⓓ
23. Ⓐ Ⓑ Ⓒ Ⓓ
24. Ⓐ Ⓑ Ⓒ Ⓓ

25. Ⓐ Ⓑ Ⓒ Ⓓ
26. Ⓐ Ⓑ Ⓒ Ⓓ
27. Ⓐ Ⓑ Ⓒ Ⓓ
28. Ⓐ Ⓑ Ⓒ Ⓓ
29. Ⓐ Ⓑ Ⓒ Ⓓ
30. Ⓐ Ⓑ Ⓒ Ⓓ

(continued on next page)

Multiple-Choice Answer Sheet

Subtest III

1. Ⓐ Ⓑ Ⓒ Ⓓ
2. Ⓐ Ⓑ Ⓒ Ⓓ
3. Ⓐ Ⓑ Ⓒ Ⓓ
4. Ⓐ Ⓑ Ⓒ Ⓓ
5. Ⓐ Ⓑ Ⓒ Ⓓ
6. Ⓐ Ⓑ Ⓒ Ⓓ
7. Ⓐ Ⓑ Ⓒ Ⓓ
8. Ⓐ Ⓑ Ⓒ Ⓓ

9. Ⓐ Ⓑ Ⓒ Ⓓ
10. Ⓐ Ⓑ Ⓒ Ⓓ
11. Ⓐ Ⓑ Ⓒ Ⓓ
12. Ⓐ Ⓑ Ⓒ Ⓓ
13. Ⓐ Ⓑ Ⓒ Ⓓ
14. Ⓐ Ⓑ Ⓒ Ⓓ
15. Ⓐ Ⓑ Ⓒ Ⓓ
16. Ⓐ Ⓑ Ⓒ Ⓓ

17. Ⓐ Ⓑ Ⓒ Ⓓ
18. Ⓐ Ⓑ Ⓒ Ⓓ
19. Ⓐ Ⓑ Ⓒ Ⓓ
20. Ⓐ Ⓑ Ⓒ Ⓓ
21. Ⓐ Ⓑ Ⓒ Ⓓ
22. Ⓐ Ⓑ Ⓒ Ⓓ
23. Ⓐ Ⓑ Ⓒ Ⓓ
24. Ⓐ Ⓑ Ⓒ Ⓓ

25. Ⓐ Ⓑ Ⓒ Ⓓ
26. Ⓐ Ⓑ Ⓒ Ⓓ
27. Ⓐ Ⓑ Ⓒ Ⓓ
28. Ⓐ Ⓑ Ⓒ Ⓓ
29. Ⓐ Ⓑ Ⓒ Ⓓ
30. Ⓐ Ⓑ Ⓒ Ⓓ

Use the space below and on the following page to answer the constructed-response questions. Additional notes pages can be found after page 558.

CSET: Mathematics Practice Test 2 Subtest I

Content Domain I *Algebra & Number Theory*

Directions: This subtest consists of two sections:

(I) thirty multiple-choice questions, and

(II) four constructed-response questions that require written responses.

Note: The use of calculators is NOT allowed for CSET: Mathematics Subtest I.

1. Which of the following is a group property that $X = \{n \in \mathbf{Z} \mid n \text{ is odd or } n = 0\}$, the set of all odd integers along with 0, with standard multiplication, does not satisfy?

   (A) The Multiplicative Identity Property

   (B) The Associative Property of Multiplication

   (C) The Commutative Property of Multiplication

   (D) The Multiplicative Inverse Property

2. For a real number, a, define the function $f_a : \mathbf{R} \to \mathbf{R}$ by $f_a(x) = x + a$. Also define the set of real-valued functions $F = \{f_a \mid a \text{ is a real number}\}$.
   We define two operations on F as follows:
   (i) addition, $f_a \oplus f_b = f_{a+b}$ and
   (ii) multiplication, $f_a \otimes f_b = f_{ab}$.

   Which of the following statements is true?

   (A) The additive identity element for F is $f(x) = 0$.

   (B) The multiplicative identity element for F is $f(x) = x + 1$.

   (C) The set F with the addition operation is not an abelian group.

   (D) The set F with these two operations is not a field.

3. Which of the following sets is not an ordered fie with its standard addition and multiplication?

   (A) The rational numbers

   (B) $\left\{ bi \mid b \text{ is a rational number and } i = \sqrt{-1} \right\}$

   (C) The real numbers

   (D) $\left\{ a + b\sqrt{5} \mid a \text{ and } b \text{ are rational numbers} \right\}$

4. Which of the following statements is false?

   (A) The union of two subgroups of a group, G could be a subgroup of G.

   (B) The intersection of two subgroups of a group, G, must be a subgroup of G.

   (C) Every group contains at least two subgroups.

   (D) Z_n is not a subgroup of Z.

5. Use the proof below and on the next page to a swer the question that follows.

   Assume that $z = a + bi$ and $w = c + di$ are compl numbers.

Prove that $\overline{z+w} = \overline{z} + \overline{w}$.

Proof:

Step 1: $\overline{z+w} = \overline{(a+bi)+(c+di)}$

Step 2: $= \overline{(a+c)+(b+d)i}$

Step 3: $= (a+c)-(b+d)i$

Step 4: $= a+c-bi-di$

Step 5: $= (a-bi)+(c-di)$

Step 6: $= \overline{a+bi} + \overline{c+di}$

Step 7: $= \overline{z} + \overline{w}$

$\therefore \overline{z-w} = \overline{z} - \overline{w}$

Q.E.D.

Which of the following properties is one justification for Step 4?

(A) Additive Identity Property

(B) Commutative Property of Addition

(C) Definition of an imaginary number

(D) Distributive Property

Use the graph below to answer the question that follows.

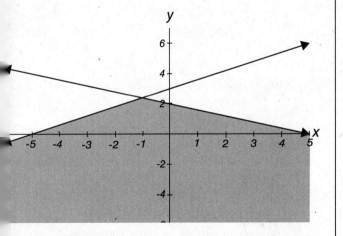

Which of the following systems of inequalities represents the shaded region in the graph?

(A) $\begin{cases} 2x - 5y \le 10 \\ 5y - 3x \le 15 \end{cases}$

(B) $\begin{cases} 2x + 5y \ge 10 \\ 5y + 3x \le 15 \end{cases}$

(C) $\begin{cases} 2x + 5y \le 10 \\ 5y - 3x \le 15 \end{cases}$

(D) $\begin{cases} 2x + 5y \ge 10 \\ 5y - 3x \ge 15 \end{cases}$

7. According to the Rational Root Theorem, which of the following might be a root of the polynomial $p(x) = 4x^3 - 5x^2 + x + 3$?

(A) -4

(B) $-\dfrac{4}{5}$

(C) $\dfrac{1}{3}$

(D) 3

8. What is the sum of the solutions of $x^3 = 8x + 2x^2$?

(A) -2

(B) 0

(C) 2

(D) 7

9. Find a value of a so that $\dfrac{\left(-4x^4 + x^2 + 4\right)}{x-a} = q(x) + \dfrac{1}{x-a}$, where q is a polynomial of degree 3.

(A) 1

(B) $\dfrac{-1}{4}$

(C) 0

(D) 2

10. Which of the following is a polynomial with zeroes $2i$ and $2 + i$, and passing through the point $(1, -10)$?

(A) $P(z) = (3+i)z^2 - (3-11i)z - 10 - 12i$

(B) $P(z) = (3+i)z^2 - (3+11i)z - (10-10i)$

(C) $P(z) = z^3 - (2+3i)z^2 - (2-4i)z - 10$

(D) $P(z) = z^2 - (2+3i)z - 9 + 3i$

11. Courtney is creating a low-fat pie crust recipe for her pie shop. Butter has six grams of saturated fat and one gram of polyunsaturated fat per tablespoon. Vegetable shortening has one gram of saturated fat and four grams of polyunsaturated fat per tablespoon. Courtney does not want the butter and the shortening in the recipe to be more than 30 tablespoons, but the two ingredients will have at least 32 grams of saturated fat and at least 48 grams of polyunsaturated fat. Butter has 100 calories per tablespoon and the shortening has 115 calories per tablespoon. How many tablespoons each of butter and shortening should Courtney use in her pie crust so she can minimize the number of calories in the recipe?

    (A) 30 tablespoons of butter and no shortening

    (B) no butter and 30 tablespoons of shortening

    (C) $3\frac{11}{23}$ tablespoons of butter and $11\frac{3}{23}$ tablespoons of shortening

    (D) $\frac{2}{7}$ tablespoons of butter and $29\frac{5}{7}$ tablespoons of shortening

12. Which of the following is one of the properties that a function f must have in order for its inverse f^{-1} to be a function?

    (A) f has to be a polynomial.

    (B) f has to be onto.

    (C) f has to be symmetric with respect to the y-axis.

    (D) f has to be an odd function.

13. If $a = 3$ and $b = 2 + i$ are two of the zeros of cubic polynomial with real coefficients, with the third root being designated by c, find the product abc.

    (A) -15

    (B) 15

    (C) $-18 - 9i$

    (D) $18 + 9i$

Which of the following lines is perpendicular to line m, which has equation $6x - 4y = 28$, and passes through the y-intercept of m?

(A)

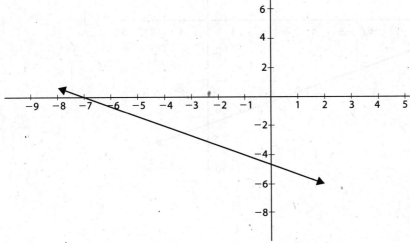

(B)

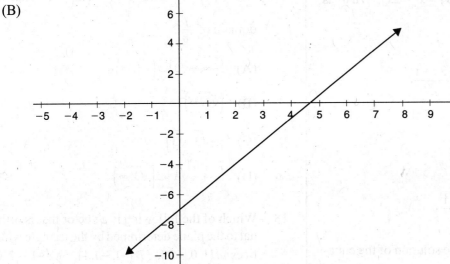

(C)

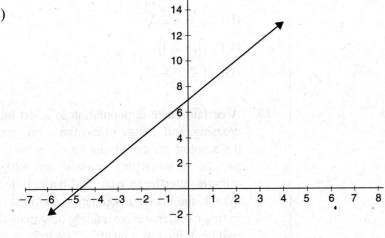

(D)

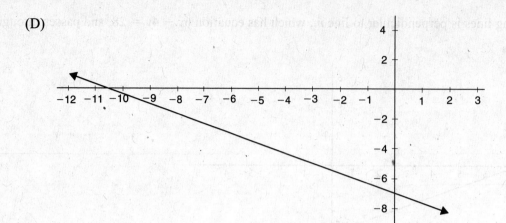

15. Let $g(x) = \dfrac{1}{x} + 1$ and $h(x) = x^3 - 2x$. What is $(g \circ h)(x)$?

(A) $(g \circ h)(x) = \dfrac{-x^3 + x^2 + 3x + 1}{x^3}$

(B) $(g \circ h)(x) = \dfrac{1}{x^3} - \dfrac{2}{x} + 1$

(C) $(g \circ h)(x) = \dfrac{x^3 - 2x + 1}{x^3 - 2x}$

(D) $(g \circ h)(x) = \dfrac{x^4 - 2x^3 + 1}{x + 1}$

16. Which of the following is the solution of the equation $\dfrac{k}{2m+1} = \dfrac{\sqrt{T^2 - h^2}}{T}$ in terms of T?

(A) $T = \dfrac{(2m+1)h}{\pm\sqrt{(2m+1)^2 - k^2}}$

(B) $T = \dfrac{h}{\pm\sqrt{1 - k^2}}$

(C) $T = \dfrac{(2m+1)h}{\pm\sqrt{(2m+1)^2 + k^2}}$

(D) $T = \dfrac{h}{\pm\sqrt{(2m+1)^2 - k^2}}$

17. Let $f(x) = 2^x$ and $g(x) = \sqrt{x^2 - 3}$. What is the domain of $\dfrac{f}{g}$?

(A) $\left(-\infty, -\sqrt{3}\right) \cup \left(\sqrt{3}, \infty\right)$

(B) $\left(\sqrt{3}, \infty\right)$

(C) $\left(-\sqrt{3}, \sqrt{3}\right)$

(D) $\left(-\infty, -\sqrt{3}\right] \cup \left[\sqrt{3}, \infty\right)$

18. Which of the following is a vector that is orthogonal to the plane determined by the triangle with vertices $A(1, 0, -2)$, $B(-1, -1, 1)$, $C(-1, -2, 0)$?

(A) $\langle -8, 2, -9 \rangle$

(B) $\langle -8, -2, 2 \rangle$

(C) $\langle 1, -2, 1 \rangle$

(D) $\langle -2, 1, -1 \rangle$

19. A certain bacteria population in a test tube is increasing, and its rate of change is proportional to the amount present at any time t in minutes. The population when first counted was 400, and 4 minutes later there were 520 bacteria in the test tube. If the bacteria population continues to grow in this manner, approximately how many bacteria will be in the test tube after 2 hours?

(A) 880

(B) 1020

(C) 1560

(D) 4800

0. Suppose $\det \begin{bmatrix} a & b & c \\ d & e & f \\ g & h & i \end{bmatrix} = -6$. Which of the following statements is false?

(A) $\det \begin{bmatrix} a & b & c \\ d+2a & e+2b & f+2c \\ g & h & i \end{bmatrix} = -6$

(B) $\det \begin{bmatrix} g & h & i \\ a & b & c \\ d & e & f \end{bmatrix} = 6$

(C) $\det \begin{bmatrix} 3a & 3b & 3c \\ 3d & 3e & 3f \\ 3g & 3h & 3i \end{bmatrix} = -162$

(D) $\det \begin{bmatrix} a & b & c \\ d & e & f \\ 2g & 2h & 2i \end{bmatrix} = -12$

1. Let a and b be integers. How many different matrices of the form $\begin{bmatrix} 2 & b \\ a & 5 \end{bmatrix}$ are not invertible?

(A) two

(B) four

(C) eight

(D) more than eight

2. Which of the following is a false statement?

(A) It is impossible to have a linear system with exactly two solutions.

(B) Suppose A is an $n \times n$ matrix and $\vec{x}$ is $n \times 1$ such that $A\vec{x} = \vec{0}$ has only the trivial solution, then $A\vec{x} = \vec{b}$ has a solution for

every $n \times 1$ vector $\vec{b}$.

(C) All leading 1's in a matrix in row-echelon form must occur in different columns.

(D) A linear system with more equations than unknowns cannot have infinitely many solutions.

23. Let $A = \begin{bmatrix} 4 & -1 \\ 2 & 1 \end{bmatrix}$. If $\det(A - \lambda I) = 0$ where I is the identity matrix, which of the following is a value of $\lambda + 2$?

(A) -3

(B) 1

(C) 5

(D) 10

24. If $AX = B$ represents a homogeneous linear system of equations in three-dimensional space and $\det(A) = 0$, then the solution set to this system is:

(A) a plane, a line, or empty.

(B) a point or a line.

(C) a plane or a line.

(D) a point, a line, or empty.

25. Which of the following statements is a true statement?

(A) Exponential functions in the form of $y = e^{ax}$ are always decreasing.

(B) A logarithmic function $y = \log_b x$ is the inverse function of an exponential function.

(C) Logarithmic functions in the form $y = \log_b x$ are always increasing.

(D) Exponential functions in the form of $y = e^{ax}$ are onto functions when considering their codomain to be the set of real numbers.

26. Find the greatest common divisor of 660 and 9800.

(A) 10

(B) 20

(C) 60

(D) 300

27. Which of the following statements is true for any $a, b,$ and c nonzero integers?

   (A) If $a, b,$ and c are integers such that $a|b$ and $b|a$, then $a = b$.

   (B) If $a|b$ and $b|c$ then $a|c$.

   (C) $\gcd(ac, bc) = c^2 \cdot \gcd(a, b)$

   (D) If $a|(b + c)$, then $a|b$ and $a|c$.

28. What is the greatest prime divisor of 765?

   (A) 9

   (B) 11

   (C) 17

   (D) 51

29. Let a, b, c be integers such that $0 < a < b < c$. If is divisible by a and also by b, then which of th following is true?

   (A) b is factor of a.

   (B) c is a factor of ab or ab is a factor of c.

   (C) ab is divisible by c.

   (D) c is divisible by ab if $\gcd(a, b) = 1$.

30. Using the Euclidean Algorithm to determine th gcd(115, 396), a person writes the following firs two lines. What is the next line in the algorithm?

$$396 = 115(3) + 51$$
$$115 = 51(2) + 13$$

   (A) $51 = 2(27) - 3$

   (B) $51 = 13(4) - 1$

   (C) $51 = 2(25) + 1$

   (D) $51 = 13(3) + 12$

31. Use the Principle of Mathematical Induction to prove the following statement.

$$\sum_{j=1}^{n} j^2 = 1 + 2^2 + 3^2 + \cdots + n^2 = \frac{n(n+1)(2n+1)}{6} \text{ for all } n = 1, 2, 3, \ldots$$

32. Let $S = \left\{ a + b\sqrt{2} \mid a, b \text{ are rational numbers} \right\}$. Prove that S is a field with the standard addition and multiplication of real numbers.

33. A cubic function of the form $f(x) = x^3 - 4x + a$, where a is a real number, has one zero at $x = 3$.

   (a) Find a.

   (b) Find any other zeroes if they exist.

   (c) Sketch the graph of the function and label any intercepts.

34. Show whether the following set of vectors is linearly independent or dependent:

$$S = \left\{ \vec{v_1} = \langle 1, -1, 2 \rangle, \vec{v_2} = \langle 0, -3, 1 \rangle \vec{v_3} = \langle 1, 1, -1 \rangle \right\}$$

Answer Key Practice Test 2: Subtest I

Question Number	Answer	SMR
1	(D)	1.1 a
2	(B)	1.1 a, b
3	(B)	1.1 b, c
4	(C)	1.1 a, b
5	(D)	1.1 b
6	(C)	1.2 a
7	(D)	1.2 b
8	(C)	1.2 b, c
9	(A)	1.2 b
10	(B)	1.2 c
11	(C)	1.2 a
12	(B)	1.3 a, b
13	(B)	1.2 b, c
14	(D)	1.3 a, b
15	(C)	1.3 a
16	(A)	1.3 b
17	(A)	1.3 a

Question Number	Answer	SMR
18	(D)	1.4 a
19	(A)	1.3 c
20	(B)	1.4 c
21	(C)	1.4 c
22	(D)	1.4 c
23	(C)	1.4 c
24	(C)	1.4 c
25	(B)	1.4 c
26	(B)	3.1 a, d
27	(B)	3.1 a
28	(C)	3.1 a
29	(D)	3.1 a
30	(D)	3.1 c, d
31	Constructed-Response	3.1 b
32	Constructed-Response	1.1 a, b, c
33	Constructed-Response	1.2 b, c, 1.3 b
34	Constructed-Response	1.4 a, b

Practice Test 2: Subtest I Answer Explanations

1. (D)

Since X is a subset of the set of real numbers, the Associative and Commutative Properties hold, so (B) and (C) are satisfied by X (although Commutativity is not a group property!). Also $1 \in X$, and 1 satisfies the Multiplicative Identity Property, so (A) is true. But 5 is an element of X and there is no multiplicative inverse of 5 in X; therefore, (D) is the correct answer.

2. (B)

For $f_a \oplus f_b = f_a, a \in \mathbf{R}$, to be true, since $f_a \oplus f_b = f_{a+b}$, we must have $f_{a+b} = f_a$ or that $b = 0$. But $f_0(x) = x + 0 = x$, so $f(x) = 0$ is not the additive identity; so (A) is false. Choice (B) is true because $f_a \otimes f_1 = f_{a \cdot 1} = f_a$. We see that (C) is false because the set F with addition is an abelian group since it satisfies the Closure, Associativity, Commutativity, Identity, and Inverse Properties for addition due to the fact that the real numbers satisfy these properties under standard addition. Also, $F - \{f_0\}$ with $\otimes$ is also an abelian group since $\mathbf{R} - \{0\}$ with standard multiplication is an abelian group. And the distributive property holds:

$f_a \otimes (f_b \oplus f_c) = f_a \otimes f_{b+c} = f_{a(b+c)} = f_{ab+ac} = f_{ab} \oplus f_{ac}$

$= (f_a \otimes f_b) \oplus (f_a \otimes f_c)$. Hence, F with these two operations is a field, and (D) is false. The correct answer is (B).

3. (B)

All four sets are ordered sets, but only (A), (C), and (D) are fields. Choice (B) is not closed under multiplication since $bi(bi) = -b^2$, which cannot be written as some rational number times i if $b \neq 0$. There are other reasons (including the lack of identities for both addition and multiplication) that the set in (B) is not a field. The correct answer is (B).

4. (C)

Choice (A) is true; for example, let $G = \mathbf{R}$ with standard addition. G is a subgroup of itself, and so is the set of all rational numbers, $\mathbf{Q}$. $G \cup \mathbf{Q} = G$, which is a subgroup of itself. Choice (B) is true because if $(G, \oplus)$ is a group and A and B are subgroups of G, then for

$C = A \cap B$, C is a subgroup if C is closed and has the identity in it. If i is the identity of G, then since A and B are subgroups of G, $i \in A \cap B = C$. Also if $x, y \in C$, then $x, y \in A$ and $x, y \in B$. Since A and B are subgroups, $x \oplus y \in A \cap B = C$. Also, (D) is true because the operations on Z and Z_n are different. Choice (C) is false because the group $\{0\}$ with addition is a group and it has only one subgroup, itself. So the correct answer is (C).

5. (D)

Step 4 is the Distributive Property since it demonstrate the distribution of the -1 to both terms in the second parentheses in step 3. The correct answer is (D).

6. (C)

The given boundary lines are incorrect for (A) and (B) but correct for (C) and (D). The point $(0, 0)$ is in the shaded region, so $(0, 0)$ is in the solution set of the inequalities that represent the shaded region. The system that $(0, 0)$ satisfies is the third one, (C). The correct answer is (C).

7. (D)

The Rational Root Theorem says that the rational roots of a polynomial

$p(x) = a_n x^n + a_{n-1} x^{n-1} + \cdots + a_1 x + a_0$ are in the form $\dfrac{r}{q}$, where r is an integer factor of a_0 and q is an integer factor of a_n. Thus, for the polynomial

$p(x) = 4x^3 - 5x^2 + x + 3$, $a_0 = 3$ and $a_n = 4$, so

$r \in \{\pm 1, \pm 3\}$ and $q \in \{\pm 1, \pm 2, \pm 4\}$. Therefore,

$\dfrac{r}{q} \in \left\{\pm\dfrac{1}{4}, \pm\dfrac{1}{2}, \pm 1, \pm\dfrac{3}{4}, \pm\dfrac{3}{2}, \pm 3\right\}$. The only answer

choice in this set is 3, so the correct answer is (D).

8. (C)

$x^3 = 8x + 2x^2 \Leftrightarrow x^3 - 2x^2 - 8x = 0 \Leftrightarrow x(x-4)(x+2)$
The solutions are $x = 0$, $x = 4$, and $x = -2$, so their sum is 2. The correct answer is (C).

. (A)

$$\left(-4x^4 + x^2 + 4\right)/\left(x-a\right) = -4x^3 + \left(-4ax^3 + x^2 + 4\right)/\left(x-a\right)$$
$$= -4x^3 + -4ax^2 + \left(\left(1 - 4a^2\right)x^2 + 4\right)/\left(x-a\right)$$
$$= -4x^3 + -4ax^2 + \left(1 - 4a^2\right)x + \left(a\left(1 - 4a^2\right)x + 4\right)/\left(x-a\right)$$
$$= 4x^3 + -4ax^2 + \left(1 - 4a^2\right)x + a\left(1 - 4a^2\right) + \left(a^2\left(1 - 4a^2\right) + 4\right)/\left(x-a\right)$$
$$= q(x) + \frac{a^2\left(1 - 4a^2\right) + 4}{x - a}.$$

So we check the answer choices to see if $r(a) = a^2\left(1 - 4a^2\right) + 4 = 1$.

For (A), $r(-1) = (1 - 4) + 4 = 1$, so the correct answer is (A). Answer choices (B), (C), and (D) give

$\left(-\dfrac{1}{4}\right) = \dfrac{1}{16}\left(1 - \dfrac{1}{4}\right) + 4 \neq 1$, $r(0) = 4 \neq 1$, $r(2) = 4(1 - 16) + 4 \neq 1$, respectively.

0. (B)

Since $2i$ and $2 + i$ are zeroes, the polynomial must have $(z - 2i)$ and $(z - 2 - i)$ as factors, so if P is second degree it must have the form $P(z) = a(z - 2i)(z - 2 - i)$. We know $P(1) = -10$, so
$$P(1) = a(1 - 2i)(1 - 2 - i) = a(1 - 2i)(-1 - i) = a(-3 + i)$$
$= -10$ or $a = \dfrac{-10}{-3 + i} = \dfrac{-10}{(-3 + i)}\dfrac{(-3 - i)}{(-3 - i)} = 3 + i$.

The answer must be equivalant:

$P(z) = (3 + i)(z - 2i)(z - 2 - i)$, so

$P(z) = (3 + i)z^2 - (3 + 11i)z - (10 - 10i)$. The correct answer is (B).

11. (C)

Let x be the number of tablespoons of butter to use in the pie crust recipe and let y be the number of tablespoons of vegetable shortening to use in the recipe. With C representing calories, the problem sets up as follows:

Minimize: $C = 100x + 115y$

$$\text{Subject to:} \begin{cases} x + y \leq 30 \\ 6x + y \geq 32 \\ x + 4y \geq 48 \\ x \geq 0, y \geq 0 \end{cases}$$

To solve this linear programming problem, graph the feasible region and then evaluate the objective function (calories) at the corner points. (See the figure on the next page.)

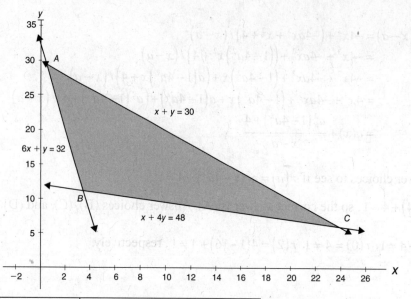

Corner point	Coordinates	$C = 100x + 115y$
A	$\left(\dfrac{2}{7}, 29\dfrac{5}{7}\right)$	$C = \dfrac{200}{7} + \dfrac{23920}{7} = 3445\dfrac{5}{7}$
B	$\left(3\dfrac{11}{23}, 11\dfrac{3}{23}\right)$	$C = \dfrac{800}{23} + \dfrac{29440}{23} = 1314\dfrac{18}{23}$
C	$(24, 6)$	$C = 2400 + 690 = 3090$

The minimum calories the recipe can have from butter and shortening is $1314\dfrac{18}{23}$, when it has $3\dfrac{11}{23}$ tablespoons o

butter and $11\dfrac{3}{23}$ tablespoons of shortening. The correct answer is (C).

12. (B)

A function must be one-to-one and onto in order to have an inverse function. Therefore, the correct answer is (B).

13. (B)

If a cubic polynomial with real coefficients has a zero that is a complex number then the conjugate must also be a zero by the Complex Conjugate Root Theorem. So the product of the roots is $abc = 3(2+i)(2-i) = 15$. The correct answer is (B).

14. (D)

The equation of line m can be rewritten in the form $y = \dfrac{3}{2}x - 7$. Any line perpendicular to line m has slope $\dfrac{-2}{3}$. Answer options (A) and (D) are the only graphs of the four lines that have negative slopes. We want the line that passes though m's y-intercept, which is $(0, -7)$; this is (D). The correct answer is (D).

15. (C)

$$(g \circ h)(x) = g(x^3 - 2x) = \frac{1}{x^3 - 2x} + 1 = \frac{x^3 - 2x + 1}{x^3 - 2x}.$$

The correct answer is clearly (C).

16. (A)

$$\frac{k}{2m+1} = \frac{\sqrt{T^2-h^2}}{T} \Leftrightarrow \frac{k^2}{(2m+1)^2} = \frac{T^2-h^2}{T^2}$$
$$\Leftrightarrow k^2T^2 = (2m+1)^2(T^2-h^2)$$
$$\Leftrightarrow ((2m+1)^2 - k^2)T^2 = h^2(2m+1)^2$$
$$\Leftrightarrow T = \frac{h(2m+1)}{\pm\sqrt{(2m+1)^2 - k^2}}$$

The correct answer is (A).

17. (A)

The domain of $\dfrac{f}{g}$ is

$D_{\frac{f}{g}} = D_f \cap D_g - \{x \in D_g \mid g(x) = 0\}$. The domains are:

$D_f = (-\infty, \infty)$, and $D_g = \left(-\infty, -\sqrt{3}\right] \cup \left[\sqrt{3}, \infty\right)$.

$\{x \in D_g \mid g(x) = 0\} = \{\pm\sqrt{3}\}$, so

$D_{\frac{f}{g}} = \left(-\infty, -\sqrt{3}\right) \cup \left(\sqrt{3}, \infty\right)$. Therefore, the correct

answer is (A).

18. (D)

The vector $\vec{v} = \overrightarrow{AB} \times \overrightarrow{AC}$ is orthogonal to the plane determined by $A(1,0,-2)$, $B(-1,-1,1)$, $C(-1,2,)$. So any vector orthogonal to ΔABC must be parallel to $\vec{v}$ and so must be a scalar multiple of $\vec{v}' = \overrightarrow{AB} \times \overrightarrow{AC}$ $= \langle-2, -1, 3\rangle \times \langle-2, -2, 2\rangle = \langle 4, -2, 2\rangle$. Since $\langle 4, -2, 2\rangle = \langle-2, 1, -1\rangle$, $\langle-2, 1, -1\rangle$ is perpendicular to the place containg triangle ABC, so the correct answer is (D)

19. (A)

When the population was first counted, $t = 0$, and $P_0 = 400$. Then $P(40) = 520$. Substituting this into the function's equation $P = P_0 e^{kt}$, we obtain:

$520 = 400e^{40k} \Rightarrow 1.3 = (e^k)^{40} \Rightarrow e^k = (1.3)^{\frac{1}{40}}$; thus,

the function can be written in the form $P(t) = 400(1.3)^{\frac{t}{40}}$. Two hours later is represented by $t = 120$, therefore,

$P(120) = 400(1.3)^{\frac{120}{40}} = 400(1.3)^3 \approx 878.8 \approx 880$.
The correct answer is (A).

20. (B)

The elementary row operations affect the determinant of a matrix as follows. If matrix B is matrix A with a row interchanged $\det(B) = -\det(A)$. If matrix B is matrix A with a row multiplied by the constant k $\det(B) = k \cdot \det(A)$. If matrix B is matrix A with a multiple of one row added to another row

$\det(B) = \det(A)$. So given $\det \begin{bmatrix} a & b & c \\ d & e & f \\ g & h & i \end{bmatrix} = -6$,

$\det \begin{bmatrix} a & b & c \\ d+2a & e+2b & f+2c \\ g & h & i \end{bmatrix} = -6$,

$\det \begin{bmatrix} g & h & i \\ a & b & c \\ d & e & f \end{bmatrix} = (-1)(-1)(-6) = -6$

$\det \begin{bmatrix} 3a & 3b & 3c \\ 3d & 3e & 3f \\ 3g & 3h & 3i \end{bmatrix} = 3^3(-6) = -162$,

$\det \begin{bmatrix} a & b & c \\ d & e & f \\ 2g & 2h & 2i \end{bmatrix} = 2(-6) = -12$.

So, statement (B) is false.

21. (C)

$\det \begin{bmatrix} 2 & b \\ a & 5 \end{bmatrix} = 10 - ab$. The matrix $\begin{bmatrix} 2 & b \\ a & 5 \end{bmatrix}$ is not invertible if its determinant equals zero, which in this case means $ab = 10$. So, a and b must be integer divisors of 10. Here are the possibilities as pairs (a, b): $(1, 10), (-1, -10), (10, 1), (-10, -1), (2, 5), (-2, -5),$ $(5, 2), (-5, -2)$. Therefore, (C) is the correct answer.

22. (D)

The first statement, *It is impossible to have a linear system with exactly two solutions,* is true since a linear system must have none, one, or infinitely many solutions.

If $A\vec{x} = \vec{0}$ has only the trivial solution, then det(A) is not zero so that $A\vec{x} = \vec{b}$ has exactly one solution for every $n \times 1$ vector $\vec{b}$, so answer (B) is true.

It is also true that *All leading 1's in a matrix in row-echelon form must occur in different columns.*

A linear system with more equations than unknowns cannot have infinitely many solutions is false. Here is an example:

$$\begin{cases} -4x + 2y = -6 \\ 2x - y = 3 \\ -6x + 3y = 9 \end{cases}$$. This system does have infinitely

many solutions since the first equation is the second equation multiplied by -2, and the third equation is two times the first equation added to the second equation, so there are infinitely many solutions of this system. Hence, the correct answer is (D).

23. (C)

$A = \begin{bmatrix} 4 & -1 \\ 2 & 1 \end{bmatrix}$, so $\begin{bmatrix} 4-\lambda & -1 \\ 2 & 1-\lambda \end{bmatrix}$ and

$\det(A - \lambda I) = \lambda^2 - 5\lambda + 6 = (\lambda - 2)(\lambda - 3)$. Therefore, $\det(A - \lambda I) = 0$ for $\lambda = 2$ or 3, and $\lambda + 2 = 4$ or 5. The correct answer is (C).

24. (C)

There are always none, one, or infinitely many solutions for a general linear system of equations. $AX = 0$ is a homogeneous equation that must have at least one solution, so the answer cannot include the empty set, therefore (A) and (D) are incorrect. In three dimensions, linear equations represent planes. The intersection of planes can be a point, line, or plane. But $\det(A) = 0$ means that the intersection is a not unique point, therefore (B) is incorrect. So the interesection must be a line or a plane. The correct answer is (C).

25. (B)

Exponential functions can be either increasing or decreasing. So (A) is false. For example, for $y = b^x$, if $b > 1$ then the graph is increasing, but if $0 < b < 1$ then the graph is decreasing. It is true that the inverse of $y = \log_b x$ is $y = b^x$, and this tells us that some logarithmic functions are increasing while others are decreasing; so (B) is true and (C) is false. (D) is false because the range of a basic exponential function is $(0, \infty)$. The correct answer is (B).

26. (B)

Use the Euclidean Algorithm:

$$9800 = 660(14) + 560$$
$$660 = 560(1) + 100$$
$$560 = 100(5) + 60$$
$$100 = 60(1) + 40$$
$$60 = 40(1) + 20$$
$$40 = 20(2) + 0$$

So the gcd(660, 9800) = 20. The correct answer is (B).

27. (B)

Statement (A) is false; for example, let $a = 3$ and $b = -3$. Statement (C) is false; for examples, if $c = 4$, $a = 5$ and $b = 7$, then, gcd(ac, bc) = 4 and gcd(a, b) = 1. Statement (D) is false; for example, $2|(3 + 5)$ but 2 does not divide 3 or 5. Statement (B) is true because if $a|b$ and $b|c$, then there exists integers m and n such that $am = b$ and $bn = c$, so $bn = (am)n = a(mn) = c$, since mn is an integer by the Closure Property, $a|c$. The correct answer is (B).

28. (C)

$765 = (3)5(51) = 3^2(5)(17)$. The correct answer is (C).

29. (D)

Assume a, b, c be integers such that $0 < a < b < c$ $a|c$ and $b|c$. Statement (A) is false; let $a = 2$, $b = 3$, and $c = 6$, but 3 is not a factor of 2. Statement (B) is false; let $a = 4$, $b = 6$, and $c = 60$, $ab = 24$, which is not a factor of 60 nor divisible by 60. This example also shows that statement (C) is false. Statement (D) is true.

30. (D)

The correct complete algorithm is

$$
\begin{aligned}
396 &= 115(3) + 51 \\
115 &= 51(2) + 13 \\
51 &= 13(3) + 12 \\
13 &= 12(1) + 1 \\
12 &= 1(12) + 0
\end{aligned}
$$

So the third line is $51 = 13(3) + 12$. The correct answer is (D).

Constructed-Response Problems

31.   Proof: Let $P(k)$ be the statement $\displaystyle\sum_{j=1}^{k} j^2 = 1 + 2^2 + 3^2 + \cdots + n^2 = \frac{k(k+1)(2k+1)}{6}$ where k is a natural number.

$P(1)$ is the statement $1^2 = \dfrac{1(1+1)(2+1)}{6}$ or $1 = 1$, which is true.

Assume that $P(k)$ is true, that is, assume $1 + 2^2 + 3^2 + \ldots + k^2 = \dfrac{k(k+1)(2k+1)}{6}$, where k is any fixed but arbitrary integer such that $k \geq 1$.

Note that $P(k+1)$ is $1 + 2^2 + 3^2 + \ldots + k^2 + (k+1)^2 = \dfrac{(k+1)(k+2)(2(k+1)+1)}{6}$.

$$
\begin{aligned}
1 + 2^2 + 3^2 + \ldots + k^2 + (k+1)^2 &= \frac{k(k+1)(2k+1)}{6} + (k+1)^2 && \text{by the induction hypothesis} \\[2mm]
&= \frac{k(k+1)(2k+1) + 6(k+1)^2}{6} && \text{by algebra} \\[2mm]
&= \frac{(k+1)\big(k(2k+1) + 6(k+1)\big)}{6} && \text{by algebra} \\[2mm]
&= \frac{(k+1)(k+2)(2k+3)}{6} && \text{by algebra}
\end{aligned}
$$

Hence, for all $k \geq 1$, if $P(k)$ is true, then $P(k + 1)$ is true.

Thus, by the Principle of Mathematical Induction, $P(k)$ is true for all $k = 1, 2,\ldots$

Q.E.D.

32. Proof: Let $S = \left\{ a + b\sqrt{2} \mid a,b \text{ are rational numbers} \right\}$ with standard addition and multiplication.

S is closed under both addition and multiplication since $(a + b\sqrt{2}) + (c + d\sqrt{2}) = (a + c) + (b + d)\sqrt{2}$ and $(a + b\sqrt{2}) \times (c + d\sqrt{2}) = (ac + 2bd) + (b + d)\sqrt{2}$. And due to the fact that S is a subset of the Reals, the Associative Properties of Addition and Multiplication hold, as well as the Commutative Properties of Addition and Multiplication, and the Distributive Property of Multiplication over Addition (both left and right distributive) is also true.

$0 = 0 + 0\sqrt{2}$ and $1 + 0\sqrt{2}$ are clearly the additive and multiplicative identities of S.

For addition, each element $a + b\sqrt{2}$ has an additive inverse $-a - b\sqrt{2}$.

Therefore, S is a commutative ring with unity.

The only property that we have not examined in order for s to be a field is the inverse property. The multiplicative inverse of the element $a + b\sqrt{2}$ is

$$\frac{1}{a + b\sqrt{2}} = \frac{1}{a + b\sqrt{2}} \frac{a - b\sqrt{2}}{a - b\sqrt{2}} = \frac{a}{a^2 - 2b^2} - \frac{b}{a^2 - 2b^2}\sqrt{2},$$

which is an element of S since $a^2 - 2b^2$ never equals 0, as this would make a a multiple of $\sqrt{2}\, b$.

Hence, S with standard addition and multiplication is a field.

Q.E.D.

33. $f(x) = x^3 - 4x + a$ and $f(3) = 27 - 12 + a = 15 + a$ so $a = -15$. So we have $f(x) = x^3 - 4x - 15$. Using long division or synthetic division to factor f, we obtain $f(x) = (x - 3)(x^2 + 3x + 5)$. To attempt to factor the quadratic, we use the quadratic formula: $x = \dfrac{-3 \pm \sqrt{9 - 20}}{2}$ which shows that the other two roots of f are complex. Since f is a cubic, it can have at most two relative extrema. Here is the graph of f:

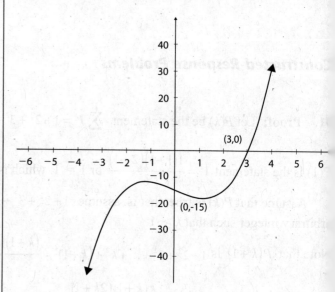

34. Suppose $k_1 \vec{v}_1 + k_2 \vec{v}_2 + k_3 \vec{v}_3 = \vec{0}$. This is equivalent to $\begin{cases} k_1 + k_3 = 0 \\ -k_1 - 3k_2 + k_3 = 0 \\ -2k_1 + k_2 - k_3 = 0 \end{cases}$. Using Gauss-Jordan elimination to sol

this system:

$$\begin{bmatrix} 1 & 0 & 1 & | & 0 \\ -1 & -3 & 1 & | & 0 \\ -2 & 1 & -1 & | & 0 \end{bmatrix} \begin{matrix} R_1 + R_2 \to R_2 \\ 2R_1 + R_3 \to R_3 \end{matrix} \begin{bmatrix} 1 & 0 & 1 & | & 0 \\ 0 & -3 & 2 & | & 0 \\ 0 & 1 & 1 & | & 0 \end{bmatrix} \begin{matrix} R_2 \leftrightarrow R_3 \\ 3R_2 + R_3 \to R_3 \end{matrix} \begin{bmatrix} 1 & 0 & 1 & | & 0 \\ 0 & 1 & 1 & | & 0 \\ 0 & 0 & 5 & | & 0 \end{bmatrix}$$

$$\begin{matrix} \frac{1}{5}R_3 \\ -R_3 + R_1 \to R_1 \\ -R_3 + R_2 \to R_2 \end{matrix} \begin{bmatrix} 1 & 0 & 0 & | & 0 \\ 0 & 1 & 0 & | & 0 \\ 0 & 0 & 1 & | & 0 \end{bmatrix}$$

This means that the only solution is the trivial solution $k_1 = k_2 = k_3 = 0$; thus, the set of vectors is linear independe

CSET: Mathematics Practice Test 2 Subtest II

Content Domain II Geometry and Probability & Statistics

> Directions: This subtest consists of two sections:
>
> (I) thirty multiple-choice questions, and
>
> (II) four constructed-response questions that require written responses.

Note: A calculator will be needed and will be allowed only for CSET: Mathematics Subtest II. You will be required to bring your own graphing calculator. Pleae check the latest CSET: Mathematics Test Guide for a list of the approved models of graphing calculators.

1. Which of the following statements is true in hyperbolic geometry?

   (A) All lines intersect.

   (B) The sum of the angles of any triangle is less than 180°.

   (C) Through a point not on a given line, exactly one line can be drawn that does not intersect the given line.

   (D) Rectangles exist.

2. Which of the following statements is false?

   (A) The Saccheri quadrilateral is a convex quadrilateral with two adjacent angles being right angles.

   (B) The Lambert quadrilateral is a convex quadrilateral with at least three right angles.

   (C) If two lines do not intersect, they are parallel.

   (D) The Pythagorean Theorem is equivalent to Euclid's Fifth Postulate in neutral geometry.

Use the incomplete proof on the next page to answer the two questions that follow.

Prove that if two angles are complementary to the same angle, then they are congruent.

Given: $\angle 1$ and $\angle 2$ are complementary angles and $\angle 2$ and $\angle 3$ are complementary angles.

Prove: $\angle 1 \cong \angle 3$.

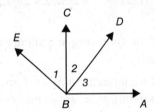

Statement	Reason
1. $\angle 1$ and $\angle 2$ are complementary angles. $\angle 2$ and $\angle 3$ are complementary angles.	1. Given
2. $m\angle 1 + m\angle 2 = 90°$ $m\angle 2 + m\angle 3 = 90°$	2.
3. $m\angle 1 + m\angle 2 = m\angle 2 + m\angle 3$	3. Transitive Property of Equality.
4. $m\angle 2 = m\angle 2$	4. Reflexive Property of Equality.
5.	5. Addition Property of Equality.
6. $\angle 1 \cong \angle 3$	6. Definition of congruent angles.

3. Which of the following is the missing reason for step 2?

   (A) Definition of right angles
   (B) Definition of complementary angles
   (C) Given
   (D) Definition of adjacent angles

4. Which of the following is the missing step 5?

   (A) $m\angle 1 = m\angle 3$
   (B) $m\angle 1 + m\angle 2 = m\angle 2 + m\angle 3$
   (C) $m\angle 1 < m\angle 2 + m\angle 3$
   (D) $m\angle 1 + 2m\angle 2 = 2m\angle 2 + m\angle 3$

5. Which of the following statements is true in neutral geometry?

   (A) Two triangles are similar if and only if corresponding sides are in proportion.
   (B) Through a point not on a given line, there is exactly one line, parallel to the given line.
   (C) Vertical angles are congruent.
   (D) If line $l \perp$ line m and $m \parallel n$ then $l \perp n$.

6. **Use the diagram below to answer the question that follows.**

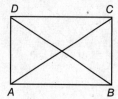

If $\angle ADB \cong \angle ACB$, $\overline{BC} \perp \overline{AB}$, and $\overline{AD} \perp \overline{AB}$, what is the reason that $\triangle ABD \cong \triangle BAC$?

   (A) ASA
   (B) SSA
   (C) SAS
   (D) AAS

7. **Use the diagram below to answer the question that follows.**

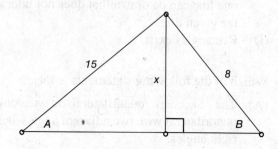

Which of the following is the best approximation of $\cos B$ if $\sin A = 0.4$?

   (A) 0.3
   (B) 0.5
   (C) 0.66
   (D) 0.7

8. A regular hexagon is circumscribed about a circle of diameter 6 cm. What is the area of the hexagon?

   (A) 18 square centimeters
   (B) $18\sqrt{3}$ square centimeters
   (C) 36 square centimeters
   (D) $36\sqrt{3}$ square centimeters

. Let $P(\sqrt{5}, 0)$ and $Q(-\sqrt{5}, 0)$ be fixed points, and let R represent any arbitrary point $(x\ y)$ in the Cartesian coordinate system. Find the equation of the locus in the plane that satisfies the condition that $PR + QR = 6$.

(A) $\dfrac{x^2}{4} + \dfrac{y^2}{9} = 1$

(B) $\dfrac{x^2}{\frac{4}{81}} + \dfrac{y^2}{9} = 1$

(C) $\dfrac{x^2}{9} + \dfrac{y^2}{4} = 1$

(D) $\dfrac{x^2}{\frac{81}{4}} + \dfrac{y^2}{9} = 1$

0. Plane M is parallel to plane N. Line l is perpendicular to plane M. Line k is perpendicular to line l. Which of the following statements must be true?

(A) Line k is perpendicular to plane N.

(B) Line k lies in plane M.

(C) Line k lies in plane N.

(D) Line l intersects plane N.

1. A sphere is inscribed in a right circular cylinder. The surface area of the sphere is 144π square inches. What is the surface area of the cylinder?

(A) 169π square inches

(B) 196π square inches

(C) 216π square inches

(D) 240π square inches

2. **Use the figure below to answer the question that follows.**

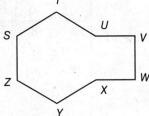

. STUXYZ is a regular hexagon and UVWX is a square with diagonal length of 2 feet. What is the perimeter of polygon STUVWXYZ?

(A) 12 ft

(B) $8\sqrt{2}$ ft

(C) 14

(D) $10\sqrt{2}$

13. **Use the figure below to answer the question that follows.**

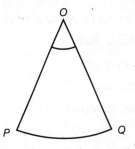

The length of arc PQ is 4π inches, and angle POQ is $60°$. A right circular cone is formed by attaching the sides of the circular sector above. What is the volume of this cone?

(A) 4π cubic inches

(B) $\dfrac{4\sqrt{35}}{3}\pi$ cubic inches

(C) $\dfrac{8\sqrt{35}}{3}\pi$ cubic inches

(D) $\dfrac{64\sqrt{3}}{3}\pi$ cubic inches

14. Consider the following two statements.

(I)	A normal to a given plane is perpendicular to every line in the plane.
(II)	Two skew lines never intersect.

Which of the following is correct?

(A) Only statement I is true.

(B) Only statement II is true.

(C) Both statements I and II are true.

(D) Neither statement I nor II is true.

15. **Use the figure on the below to answer the question that follows.**

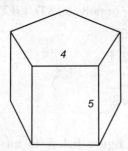

The regular pentagonal prism shown is measured in feet. Which of the following is the best estimate of the volume of the prism?

(A)   100 cubic feet

(B)   138 cubic feet

(C)   200 cubic feet

(D)   276 cubic feet

16. Which of the following statements is false?

(A)   A median bisects a side of the triangle.

(B)   The centroid of a triangle lies in the interior of the triangle.

(C)   The orthocenter of a triangle may lie in the exterior of the triangle.

(D)   An altitude bisects an angle of the triangle.

17. **Use the two graphs to answer the question that follows.**

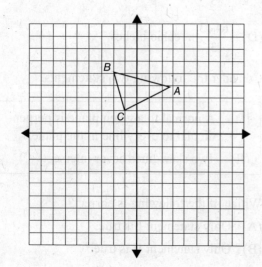

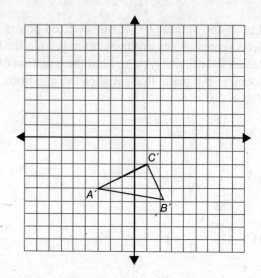

$\triangle ABC$ is the preimage of $\triangle A'B'C'$ under a transformation T. Transformation T is which of the following?

(A)   translation

(B)   rotation about the origin

(C)   reflection about the y-axis

(D)   reflection about the x-axis

18. Which of the following is a transformation that geometrically is a dilation by a scale factor of 4 followed by a rotation 150° counterclockwise?

(A) $T(x, y) = \begin{bmatrix} -2\sqrt{3} & -2 \\ 2 & -2\sqrt{3} \end{bmatrix} \begin{bmatrix} x \\ y \end{bmatrix}$

(B) $T(x, y) = \begin{bmatrix} -2 & -2\sqrt{3} \\ 2\sqrt{3} & 2 \end{bmatrix} \begin{bmatrix} x \\ y \end{bmatrix}$

(C) $T(x, y) = \begin{bmatrix} -2 & -2\sqrt{3} \\ 2\sqrt{3} & -2 \end{bmatrix} \begin{bmatrix} x \\ y \end{bmatrix}$

(D) $T(x, y) = \begin{bmatrix} \dfrac{-\sqrt{3}}{8} & \dfrac{-1}{8} \\ \dfrac{-1}{8} & \dfrac{-\sqrt{3}}{8} \end{bmatrix} \begin{bmatrix} x \\ y \end{bmatrix}$

9. **Use the diagram below to answer the question that follows.**

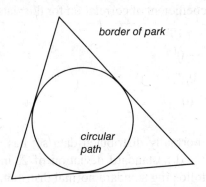

border of park

circular
path

A sports park designer is drawing up plans for a large triangular-shaped park. He would like to construct a circular walking path inside the triangular plot that intersects each side of the park as shown in the figure above. What compass and straightedge construction should he begin with?

(A) perpendicular bisectors of each side of the triangle

(B) angle bisectors

(C) perpendicular lines to each side through the opposite vertex

(D) lines parallel to each side through the opposite vertex

20. **Use the figure below to answer the question that follows.**

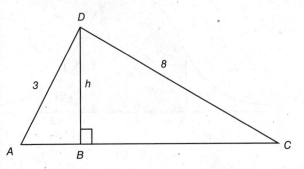

If $AC = 9$, which is the best approximation of h?

(A) 2.65

(B) 2.15

(C) 1.65

(D) 1.40

21. Two sides of a triangle have lengths of 17 and 11 inches. Which of the following could not be the length of the third side?

(A) 8 inches

(B) 10 inches

(C) 25 inches

(D) 29 inches

22. **Use the figure below to answer the question that follows.**

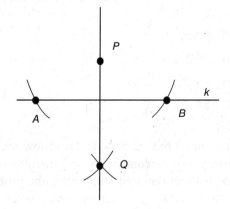

The compass and straightedge construction shown is which of the following?

(A) angle bisection

(B) segment bisection

(C) perpendicular line through a point not on the given line

(D) perpendicular line through a point on the given line

23. For a quiz with 10 multiple-choice questions, each with 4 possible answers, how many different answer keys are possible?

(A) 40

(B) 10,000

(C) 1,048,576

(D) 847,660,528

24. Which of the following is not equivalent to Euclid's Fifth Postulate?

(A) Given an angle, one can construct a congruent angle on a given line segment at a specified point.

(B) The Euclidean Parallel Postulate

(C) The sum of the measures of the interior angles of a triangle is 180°.

(D) If *l* is parallel to lines *m* and *n*, then either *m* is parallel to *n* or *m* = *n*.

25. There are three identical boxes labeled *A, B,* and *C.* Each box has 100 bicycle parts, of which exactly three are defective. If someone randomly chooses one part from each box what is the approximate probability that exactly two of the chosen parts are non-defective?

(A) 8.5%

(B) 16.2%

(C) 28.2%

(D) 84.7%

26. There are 8 red, 12 blue, and 6 yellow marbles in a box. If we randomly choose 3 marbles from the box, without replacement, what is the probability, to the nearest tenth, that we have chosen exactly two red marbles?

(A) 10.8%

(B) 14.3%

(C) 19.4%

(D) 22.9%

27. **Use the graph below to answer the question that follows.**

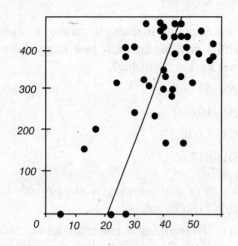

The data and a regression line for an experiment are plotted above. What is the most likely value of the coefficient of correlation for this data and line?

(A) −10

(B) −0.7

(C) 0.7

(D) 10

28. If a normally distributed data set has a mean of 70.0 and a standard deviation of 2, in which of the following standard normal distribution graphs does the shaded area represent the probability that a given member of the set is greater than or equal to 68 and less than or equal to 73?

(A)

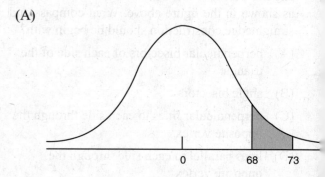

(B)

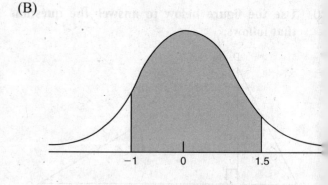

(C)

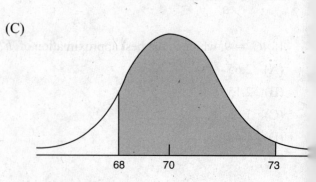

(D)

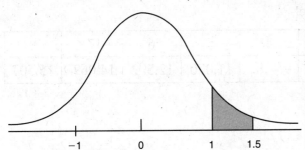

29. A card is randomly chosen from a standard deck of 52 cards. What is the probability that the chosen card is a two or eight, given that the card is not a heart?

(A) $\dfrac{2}{13}$

(B) $\dfrac{3}{26}$

(C) $\dfrac{5}{26}$

(D) $\dfrac{8}{39}$

30. The following table shows the quiz scores for the students on an anthropology exam.

score	10	9	8	7	6	5	4	3	2	1	0
frequency	5	3	7	1	5	8	1	6	0	2	2

What is the interval of the range of the second quartile of scores?

(A) $4 - 6$

(B) $4 - 7$

(C) $5 - 8$

(D) $6 - 9$

31. **Use the figure below to answer the question that follows.**

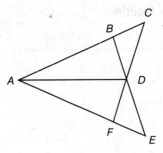

Given: $\angle C \cong \angle E$, $\angle CDA \cong \angle EDA$

Prove: $\overline{AB} \cong \overline{AF}$

32. State the Euclidean Parallel Postulate, then prove that the statement below is true if the Euclidean Parallel Postulate is true:

> *The sum of the measures of the interior angles of a triangle is* $180°$.

33. Given that in $\triangle ABC$ the length of $\overline{BC}$ is 20 cm, the length of $\overline{AB}$ is 9 cm, and $\angle ABC = 21°$, use the Law of Cosines to find the length $\overline{AC}$, and then use the Law of Sines to find $m\angle BAC$.

34. A company wants to test whether a certain drug is effective in curing a disease. Patients in a study were given this drug or a placebo; the results are shown below:

	cured	not cured
drug	31	11
placebo	16	26

(a) State the null hypothesis.

(b) Determine the value of the chi-square (χ^2) test statistic for these sample data, then write the conclusion. Determine if, at the 5% significance level, the data suggest that the drug is not effective.

(continued on next page)

Here is a chi-square table for the 5% significance level.

Degrees of freedom	1	2	3	4	5	6	7	8
χ^2 values	3.841	5.991	7.815	9.488	11.070	12.592	14.067	15.507

Answer Key Subtest II

Question Number	Answer	SMR
1	(B)	2.1 a, b
2	(C)	2.1 a, b
3	(B)	2.2 a
4	(A)	2.2 a
5	(C)	2.1 a, 2.2 a
6	(D)	2.2 a
7	(C)	2.2 b
8	(B)	2.2 c
9	(C)	2.2 e, 2.3 b
10	(D)	2.3 a
11	(C)	2.3 b
12	(B)	2.2 c
13	(C)	2.3 b, 2.2 c
14	(B)	2.3 a
15	(B)	2.3 b, 2.2 c
16	(D)	2.2 b
17	(B)	2.4 a

Question Number	Answer	SMR
18	(A)	2.4 a, b
19	(B)	2.2 b, d
20	(A)	2.2 b
21	(D)	2.2 b
22	(C)	2.2 d
23	(C)	4.1 a, b
24	(A)	2.1 a, b
25	(A)	4.1 a, b, c, d
26	(C)	4.1 a, b, d
27	(C)	4.2 d
28	(B)	4.2 a
29	(A)	4.1e
30	(A)	4.2 b
31	Constructed-Response	2.2 a
32	Constructed-Response	2.1 a
33	Constructed-Response	2.2 b
34	Constructed-Response	4.2 e

Practice Test 2: Subtest II Answer Explanations

1. (B)

In hyperbolic geometry, the postulate that replaces the Euclidean Parallel Postulate is: *Through a point not on a given line, at least two lines can be drawn that do not intersect the given line.* Hence, statements (A) and (C) are false. Statement (D) is equivalent to the Euclidean Parallel Postulate, so it is false in hyperbolic geometry. Statement (B) is a consequence of the Hyperbolic Parallel Postulate and is true; therefore, (B) is the correct answer.

2. (C)

Statements (A) and (B) are definitions of the Saccheri and Lambert quadrilaterals, respectively, and are thus true. (D) is true since, by assuming the rules of neutral geometry, we can show the Pythagorean Theorem is true if and only if Euclid's Fifth Postulate is true. The correct answer is (C) because if two lines do not intersect it could be because they are skew lines.

3. (B)

Step 2 illustrates the definition of complementary angles: *The sum of the measures of two complementary angles is 90°.* The correct answer is (B).

4. (A)

Step 3 is $m\angle 1 + m\angle 2 = m\angle 2 + m\angle 3$ and step 4 is $m\angle 2 = m\angle 2$. The reason for step 5 is the Addition Property so adding the opposite of $m\angle 2$ would give $m\angle 1 = m\angle 3$ as step 6, especially in the light that step 6 is $\angle 1 \cong \angle 3$. So the correct answer is (A).

5. (C)

Vertical angles are congruent because they each are the supplement of the same angle; this is true in neutral geometry. The other three statements need the assumption of Euclid's Fifth Postulate in order to be considered true. The correct answer is (C).

6. (D)

We separate the triangles to see the congruent part better.

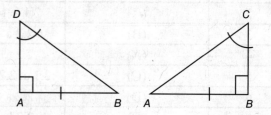

First we are told that $\angle ADB \cong \angle ACB$ and $\overline{AD} \perp \overline{A}$ and $\overline{CB} \perp \overline{AB}$, so that $\angle ABC \cong \angle BAD$ because they ar both right angles. In addition $\overline{AB} \cong \overline{AB}$ by the Reflexiv Property of Congruence. Thus, $\triangle ABD \cong \triangle BAC$ b AAS. The correct answer is (D).

7. (C)

Given that $\sin A = 0.4$, since $\sin A = x/15 = 0.$ then $x = 6$. Label the length of the third side of th triangle on the right as y. Then, using the Pythagorea Theorem, we have: $x^2 + y^2 = 64$ or $36 + y^2 = 64$. Thus $y = 2\sqrt{7}$, so $\cos B = \dfrac{2\sqrt{7}}{8} = \dfrac{\sqrt{7}}{4} \approx 0.66$. So the correc answer is (C).

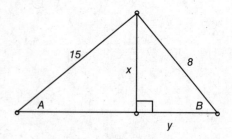

8. (B)

The diameter of the circle is 6 cm, so the radius 3 cm. Triangle BOC is a 30°-60°-90° triangle, so tha $BC = \sqrt{3}$ and the area of $\triangle OCA$ is $3\sqrt{3}$. Therefore, th area of the hexagon is $18\sqrt{3}$ square cm. The correct answer is (B).

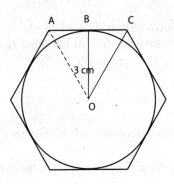

9. (C)

$$PR = \sqrt{\left(x-\sqrt{5}\right)^2+\left(y-0\right)^2} \quad \text{and} \quad QR =$$

$$\sqrt{\left(x+\sqrt{5}\right)^2+\left(y-0\right)^2}, \text{ so if we know the sum of these}$$

lengths is always 6, we have the following equation:

$$\sqrt{\left(x-\sqrt{5}\right)^2+y^2}+\sqrt{\left(x+\sqrt{5}\right)^2+y^2}=6.$$

Isolating the radicals and squaring both sides of the equation, we obtain:

$$\sqrt{\left(x-\sqrt{5}\right)^2+y^2}=6-\sqrt{\left(x+\sqrt{5}\right)^2+y^2} \Rightarrow \left(x-\sqrt{5}\right)^2+y^2$$

$$=36-12\sqrt{\left(x+\sqrt{5}\right)^2+y^2}+\left(x+\sqrt{5}\right)^2+y^2$$

Simplifying and again isolating the radical, we obtain $9+\sqrt{5}x=3\sqrt{\left(x+\sqrt{5}\right)^2+y^2}$ and then we square both sides and simplify:

$$81+18\sqrt{5}x+5x^2=9\left(x^2+2\sqrt{5}x+5+y^2\right) \Rightarrow 4x^2+9y^2=36.$$

Then we obtain: $\dfrac{x^2}{9}+\dfrac{y^2}{4}=1.$ So the correct answer is (C).

10. (D)

Line l is perpendicular to plane M. This implies that any plane parallel to plane M is also perpendicular to line l, thus (D) must be true. Line k is perpendicular to line l means that line k could lie in plane M or N but cannot be perpendicular to either plane. The correct answer is (D).

11. (C)

The surface area of a sphere is $4\pi r^2$ where r is the radius. Since the surface area of the sphere is 144π square inches, $r=6$ inches. This means that the height of the circumscribed cylinder is 12 inches. The surface area of the cylinder is: $SA = 2 \cdot \text{area of the base} + \text{lateral area} = 2\pi r^2 + 2\pi rh = 72\pi + 144\pi = 216\pi$ square inches. The correct answer is (C).

12. (B)

The diagonal of the square is 2 feet, so using the Pythagorean Theorem, the length of the side of the square is $\sqrt{2}$. The length of a side of the regular hexagon is also $\sqrt{2}$. Thus, the perimeter of the figure is $8\sqrt{2}$ feet. The correct answer is (B).

13. (C)

The angle POQ has measure $60 = \dfrac{\pi}{3}$ radians, and arc PQ is 4π inches, so $OP = \dfrac{s}{\angle POQ} = \dfrac{4\pi}{\frac{\pi}{3}} = 12$ in. This means that when the cone is formed, the circumference of the base is 4π, so its radius is 2. Using the Pythagorean theorem, $h = \sqrt{144-4} = \sqrt{140} = 2\sqrt{35}$. Therefore, the volume of the cone is $V = \dfrac{1}{3}\pi\left(2\right)^2\left(2\sqrt{35}\right) = \dfrac{8\sqrt{35}}{3}\pi$ cubic inches. The correct answer is (C).

14. (B)

A line perpendicular to a given plane is perpendicular to every line in the plane that intersects the line but not to the lines in the plane that do not intersect it. So statement I is false. Skew lines are lines that do not intersect and are not coplanar. Thus statement II is true. The correct answer is (B).

15. (B)

$V = Bh$. We are given $h = 5$, and

$B = \dfrac{1}{2}aP = \dfrac{1}{2}a(20) = 10a$ from the pentagon below

$\angle QOP = 36°$, so $\tan(36°) = 2/a$. Using a calculator,

we get $a \approx 2.753$ so that $B \approx 27.53$. Hence, the

volume of the prism is $V \approx (27.53)(5) = 137.65$. The

correct answer is (B).

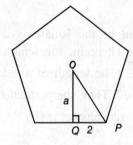

16. (D)

The only statement that is false is (D). An altitude of a triangle is the segment drawn from a vertex to the line containing the opposite side so that it is perpendicular to that line. In general, it does not bisect the angle. The correct answer is (D).

17. (B)

Point $A\,(3, 4)$ is mapped to point $A'\,(-3, -4)$. From this, we see that if the transformation is a translation, then the transformation must $T(x, y) = (x - 6, y - 8)$. Then point $B(-2, 5)$ must map to the point $(-8, -3)$, but instead it maps to $(2, -5)$ so (A) is wrong. If the transformation is a reflection about the y-axis, then point $A\,(3, 4)$ would map to $(-3, 4)$ which it doesn't. If the transformation is a reflection about the x-axis, then it would map point A to $(3, -4)$, which it does not, so (C) and (D) are wrong. So it is a rotation, by default. But to check this, let us find the angle of rotation. The transformation for rotation about the origin is $T(x, y) = (x\cos\alpha - y\sin\alpha,\ x\sin\alpha + y\cos\alpha)$. So for point A, we have

$T(3, 4) = (3\cos\alpha - 4\sin\alpha,\ 3\sin\alpha + 4\cos\alpha) = (-3, -4)$.

We then set this up as a system of equations and solve:

$\begin{cases} 3\cos\alpha - 4\sin\alpha = -3 \\ 3\sin\alpha + 4\cos\alpha = -4 \end{cases}$. This will give us $\alpha = 180°$.

So the transformation is $T(x, y) = (-x, -y)$, which fits with the transformation of the other two points. Therefore, the correct answer is (B).

18. (A)

The matrix that represents dilation by a factor of 4 i

$\begin{bmatrix} 4 & 0 \\ 0 & 4 \end{bmatrix}$. The matrix that represents the transformatio

that rotates a point 150° counterclockwise about th

origin is $\begin{bmatrix} \cos(150°) & -\sin(150°) \\ \sin(150°) & \cos(150°) \end{bmatrix}$. Therefore, the matri

that represents the dilation by a scale factor of 4 followe
by the 150 degree counterclockwise rotation about th

origin is $\begin{bmatrix} \dfrac{-\sqrt{3}}{2} & \dfrac{-1}{2} \\ \dfrac{1}{2} & \dfrac{-\sqrt{3}}{2} \end{bmatrix} \begin{bmatrix} 4 & 0 \\ 0 & 4 \end{bmatrix} = \begin{bmatrix} -2\sqrt{3} & -2 \\ 2 & -2\sqrt{3} \end{bmatrix}$.

The correct answer is (A).

19. (B)

To find the center of the inscribed circle, construc the angle bisectors of the triangle. Only two need to b constructed. In the figure below, $\overrightarrow{AP}$ and $\overrightarrow{CQ}$ are th angle bisectors. The point of their intersection, O, is th center of the inscribed circle. The correct answer is (B To finish the construction, construct a perpendicular fror the point O to one of the sides of the triangle, such as $\overline{OR}$ the perpendicular line through O to $\overline{AC}$. The radius of th circle is segment OR.

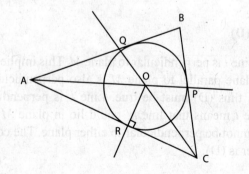

20. (A)

$AC = 9$, so let $AB = x$ and $BC = 9 - x$. Using the Pythagorean Theorem on triangle ABD, $x^2 + h^2 = 9$. Using the Pythagorean Theorem on triangle CBD, $(9-x)^2 + h^2 = 64$. Then, using substitution, we obtain, $(9-x)^2 + (9 - x^2) = 64$, which simplifies to $18x = 26$, so $x \approx 1.4$. Again using substitution, $h^2 \approx 9 - (1.4)^2 = 7.04$ $h \approx 2.65$. So statement (A) is correct.

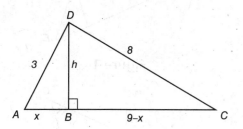

21. (D)

Let x be the length of the third side. The *Triangle inequality* tells us that the sum of the lengths of any two sides of a triangle must be greater than the length of the third side. Thus, $x < 17 + 11 = 28$. So x cannot equal 29. Also $8 + 11 > 17$, $10 + 11 > 17$, and $11 + 17 > 15$. Thus, (D) is the correct answer.

22. (C)

The construction shown is the one of a perpendicular line through a point not on the given line. Answer (C) is correct.

23. (C)

Each question has 4 possible answers and there are 10 questions, so using Fundamental Principle of Counting, there are $4^{10} = 1,048,576$ possible keys. The correct answer is (C).

24. (A)

The only one that does not rely on the existence of parallel lines is *Given an angle, one can construct a congruent angle on a given line segment at a specified point.* The correct answer is (A).

25. (A)

There are three ways of choosing exactly two non-defective out of three bicycle parts; the defective part is in box A, B, or C. The probability that one gets the defective part from A is $(.03)(.97)(.97) = 0.028227$. Then multiply this by 3 since there are three ways to get exactly one defective part to get $0.028227(3) = 0.084681 \approx 8.5\%$. The correct answer is (A).

26. (C)

The probability that we choose exactly 2 red marbles is equal to

$$\frac{\text{the number of ways to choose 3 marbles so that 2 are red and 1 is not red}}{\text{the number of ways to choose 3 marbles}} = \frac{{_8C_2} \cdot {_{18}C_1}}{{_{26}C_3}}$$

$$= \frac{\dfrac{8!}{6!2!} \cdot \dfrac{18!}{17!1!}}{\dfrac{26!}{23!3!}} = \frac{28 \cdot 18}{2600} \approx 0.194 = 19.4\%.$$ The correct answer is (C).

27. (C)

The coefficient of correlation is a number between -1 and 1 inclusive. This eliminates answers (A) and (D). The coefficient of correlation indicates the fit of the regression line to the given data. If the slope of the regression line is negative, so is the coefficient of correlation. Similarly, if the slope of the regression line is positive, so is the coefficient of correlation. The regression line shown in the graph has a positive slope, so the correct answer must be (C).

28. (B)

The mean is standardized so that 70 correlates to a z-score of 0. Then 68 correlates to -1 because 68 is 1 standard deviation below the mean and 73 is 1.5 standard deviations above 70, so it is represented by 1.5. The correct answer is (B).

29. (A)

Let A be the event that the card chosen is a two or an eight, and let B be the event that the card is not a heart. We know there are 3 twos that are not hearts and 3 eights that are not hearts, so $n(A \cap B) = 6$. Also there is a total of 39 cards that are not hearts. So the probability that the chosen card is a two or eight given that the card is not a heart is $P(A|B) = \dfrac{P(A \cap B)}{P(B)} = \dfrac{n(A \cap B)}{n(B)} = \dfrac{6}{39} = \dfrac{2}{13}$.

The correct answer is (A).

30. (A)

There are 40 scores and $40/4 = 10$; so there are 10 scores in each quartile. The first quartile (lowest scores) has scores: 0, 0, 1, 1, 3, 3, 3, 3, 3, 3, 3. The second quartile has scores: 4, 5, 5, 5, 5, 5, 5, 5, 5, 6. The correct answer is (A).

Constructed-Response Problems

31.

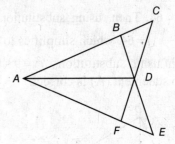

Figure 1

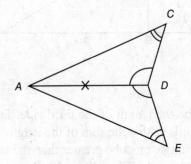

Figure 2

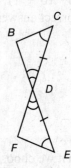

Figure 3

Proof:

1. $\angle C \cong \angle E$, $\angle CDA \cong \angle EDA$	1. Given
2. $\overline{AD} \cong \overline{AD}$	2. Reflexive Property of Congruence
3. $\triangle ADC \cong \triangle ADE$	3. AAS (Angle-Angle-Side) (Figure 2)
4. $\overline{DC} \cong \overline{DE}$, $\overline{AC} \cong \overline{AE}$	4. CPCTC (Corresponding Parts of Congruent Triangles are congruent)
5. $\angle CDB \cong \angle FDE$	5. Vertical angles are congruent
6. $\triangle BCD \cong \triangle FED$	6. ASA (Angle-Side-Angle) (Figure 3)
7. $\overline{BC} \cong \overline{FE}$	7. CPCTC
8. $AC = AE$; $BC = FE$	8. Definition of congruent segments
9. $AC = AB + BC$; $AE = AF + FE$	9. A whole is equal to the sum of its parts.
10. $AB + BC = AF + FE$	10. Substitution
11. $AB = AF$	11. Addition Property of Equality (subtraction)
12. $\overline{AB} \cong \overline{AF}$	12. Definition of congruent segments
	Q.E.D.

2. The Euclidean Parallel Postulate is: *Through any point not on a given line, there is exactly one line parallel to the given line.*

The given statement is: *The sum of the measures of the interior angles of a triangle is 180°.*

Proof: Assume the Euclidean Parallel Postulate is true. Consider $\triangle ABC$ in the figure on the right.

Let line l be the unique line through point B that is parallel to the line through side $\overline{AC}$ as stipulated in the Euclidean Parallel Postulate. Let D be a point on line l on the same side as point C, and let point E be another point on l on the same side as point A.

Then $m\angle EBA + m\angle ABC + m\angle DBC = 180°$. By the converse of Euclid's Proposition 27, the angles $\angle DBC$ and $\angle BCA$ are alternate interior angles, as are the angles $\angle EBA$ and $\angle BCA$, and so $\angle DBA \cong \angle BCA$ and $\angle EBA \cong \angle BCA$ so each pair is congruent.

Thus, by substitution,
$$m\angle BAC + m\angle ABC + m\angle BCA = 180°.$$
Q.E.D.

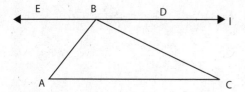

33. Let $a = BC = 20$ cm and $c = AB = 9$ cm. Let b be the length $\overline{AC}$.

Then, using the Law of Cosines, $b^2 = a^2 + c^2 - 2ac\cos B$ computes the following:

$$b^2 = 20^2 + 9^2 - 2(20)(9)\cos(21°) \implies b^2 \approx 400 + 81 - 360(0.9336)$$
$$\implies b^2 \approx 144.90$$
$$\implies b \approx 12.04 \text{ cm}$$

Next, use the Law of Sines to find the measure of $\angle BAC$: $\dfrac{\sin A}{a} = \dfrac{\sin B}{b}$

$$\frac{\sin A}{20} = \frac{\sin(21°)}{12.04} \implies \sin A = 20\frac{\sin(21°)}{12.04} = 0.595$$

$$\implies m\angle A \approx \arcsin(0.595) \approx 36.5°$$

34. (a) The null hypothesis is: *The drug is not effective in curing the disease.*

(b) If the drug is not effective, then one would expect 50% to be cured and 50% not to be cured. But we use the results of the placebo (which is not effective) as the expected value since that is the result with no drug for this disease.

Using χ^2, the number of degrees of freedom is $2 - 1 = 1$, so at the 5% significance level (use the given table) we are looking for a number less than 3.841.

drug	Observed frequency	Expected Frequency	(Observed − Expected)²	$\dfrac{(Obs.-Exp.)^2}{Expected}$
cured	31	16	225	14.06
not cured	11	26	225	8.65
				22.71

So 22.71 exceeds 3.841, so the null hypothesis is rejected and we conclude that the drug is effective.

> Directions: This subtest consists of two sections:
>
> (I) thirty multiple-choice questions, and
>
> (II) four constructed-response questions that require written responses.

Note: The use of calculators is not allowed for CSET: Mathematics Subtest III.

. Find all values of $x \in [0, 2\pi)$ for which the graphs of the functions $f(x) = \sin^2 x$ and $g(x) = -\cos\left(x - \frac{3}{2}\pi\right)$ intersect.

(A) $0, \frac{\pi}{2}, \pi$

(B) $\frac{\pi}{2}, \frac{2\pi}{3}, \pi$

(C) $0, \frac{\pi}{2}, \pi, \frac{3\pi}{2}$

(D) $0, \frac{\pi}{2}, \frac{2\pi}{3}, 2\pi$

Which of the following is equivalent to $\dfrac{\csc^2\beta}{\sec^2\beta} + \tan^2\beta\cot^2\beta$?

(A) $\sec^2\beta$

(B) $\tan^2\beta + \cot^2\beta$

(C) $\cot^2\beta + \cos^2\beta$

(D) $\csc^2\beta$

3. **Use the figure below to answer the question that follows.**

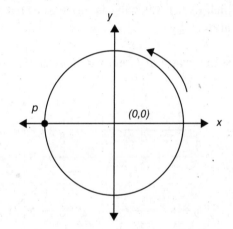

Point P is on a circle that has diameter of 2 feet. If $y(t) = \cos(8\pi t)$ describes the y-coordinate of the position of point P at time t in minutes as the circle rotates counterclockwise, how far does point P travel in five minutes as the circle revolves?

(A) 20π feet

(B) 40π feet

(C) 80π feet

(D) 160π feet

4. Use the graph below to answer the question that follows.

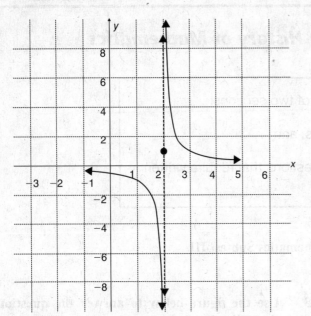

Which of the following is the reason that f is not continuous at $x = 2$?

(A) $\lim\limits_{x \to 2} f(x)$ does not exist.

(B) $f(2)$ does not exist.

(C) $f(2) \neq 0$

(D) f^{-1} does not exist.

5. Which of the following statements is true?

(A) If a function is differentiable at a point, it is continuous at that point.

(B) If $\lim\limits_{x \to a} g(x) = 0$, then $\lim\limits_{x \to a} \dfrac{f(x)}{g(x)}$ does not exist.

(C) If $f(x) > 0$ on the interval (a, b), then f is concave up on (a, b).

(D) The derivative of a product of functions is equal to the product of the derivative of the functions.

6. Use the graph of f below to answer the question that follows.

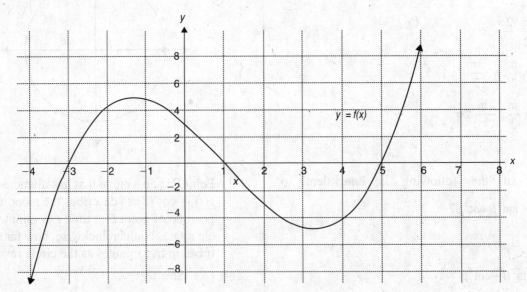

On approximately what intervals is the instantaneous rate of change of f increasing?

(A) $(-\infty, -1.3) \cup (3.3, \infty)$

(B) $(-1.3, 3.3)$

(C) $(1, \infty)$

(D) $(-\infty, 1.5)$

7. Use the figure below to answer the question that follows.

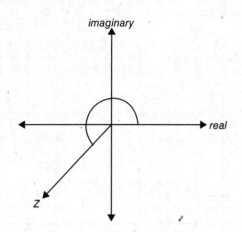

Which of the following complex numbers could be z^3 if the above vector represents z, where z is a unit vector?

(A) $\sin(45°) + i\cos(45°)$

(B) $\sin(405°) - i\cos(405°)$

(C) $\cos(45°) - i\sin(45°)$

(D) $-\cos(405°) + i\sin(405°)$

8. For what value of b will

$$h(x) = \begin{cases} \dfrac{1-\cos(2x)}{x} & \text{when } x < 0 \\ x^2 + b + 3 & \text{when } x \geq 0 \end{cases}$$

be continuous at $x = 0$?

(A) 2

(B) 0

(C) −1

(D) −3

9. A curve in the xy-plane is given by the equation $\ln y - 2x = y^2$. At which of the following points does the tangent to the curve have slope 2?

(A) $(-(0.125 + \ln\sqrt{2}), 0.5)$

(B) $(-0.5, 1)$

(C) $(-0.125 + \ln\sqrt{2}, 0.5)$

(D) $(0.5, -1)$

10. The number of worms in a worm farm has been growing at a rate proportional to its size. If the population of worms at the beginning was 100, and 20 days later it was 300, after how many days will the worm population reach 8100?

(A) 65 days

(B) 80 days

(C) 90 days

(D) 105 days

11. Use the chart below to answer the question that follows.

x	$F(x)$	$F'(x)$	$G(x)$	$G'(x)$
1	3	5	2	−1
2	2	9	4	7
3	4	−2	1	8
4	1	6	3	−3

If $H(x) = \dfrac{x^2 G\left(\dfrac{x}{2}\right)}{F(2x)}$, what is the equation of the tangent to the curve $y = H(x)$ at $x = 2$?

(A) $y = -90x - 188$

(B) $y = -90x + 188$

(C) $y = 8x + 64$

(D) $y = -8x + 64$

12. A water tank has sprung a leak. The water is coming out of the right circular cylinder tank, which has a diameter of 3 feet, at a rate of 1 cubic feet per hour. How quickly is the water level changing while the water is leaking out?

(A) $-\dfrac{4}{3}\pi$ feet per hour

(B) $-\dfrac{4}{9}\pi$ feet per hour

(C) $-\dfrac{4}{3\pi}$ feet per hour

(D) $-\dfrac{4}{9\pi}$ feet per hour

13. The function $f(x) = \int_1^x \dfrac{18 - 5t}{3\sqrt[3]{t-6}}\, dt$ has one inflection point. Find where it occurs.

(A) $x = 6$

(B) $x = 7.2$

(C) $x = 8.4$

(D) $x = 9.6$

14. Let R be the region enclosed by the curves $y = \sqrt{x}$ and $y = x$. What is the volume of the solid created by revolving R about the y-axis?

(A) $\dfrac{2\pi}{15}$ cubic units

(B) $\dfrac{4\pi}{15}$ cubic units

(C) $\sqrt{2}\pi$ cubic units

(D) 2π cubic units

15. The acceleration of a particle traveling in one dimension along the x-axis at time t is given by $a(t) = 5t + 1$. At time $t = 1$ the velocity of the particle is 0. If the position of the particle at time $t = 3$ is 15, what is the position of the particle at time $t = 6$?

(A) -10.5

(B) 84.5

(C) 175.5

(D) 223.5

16. Find the area under the curve $y = \dfrac{x}{\left(1 + x^2\right)^2}$ over the interval $[0, 4]$.

(A) $\dfrac{5}{12}$

(B) $\dfrac{7}{15}$

(C) $\dfrac{8}{17}$

(D) $\dfrac{17}{21}$

17. Use the graph shown below and the Fundamental Theorem of Calculus to answer the following question.

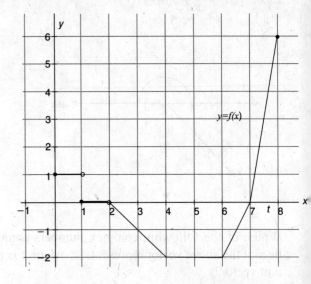

Let $g(x) = \int_0^x \left(1 + f(t)\right) dt$. Where in the interval $[0, 8]$ does g have its absolute maximum and minimum values?

(A) g has its absolute maximum at $x = 8$ and absolute minimum at all points in $[4, 6]$.

(B) g has its absolute maximum at $x = 3$ and absolute minimum at $x = 0$.

(C) g has its absolute maximum at $x = 3$ and absolute minimum at $x = 6.5$.

(D) g has its absolute maximum at $x = 8$ and absolute minimum at $x = 6.5$.

18. Let $f(x) = 3x^2 - 5x + 1$. Find a value of c that satisfies the conclusion of the Mean Value Theorem (for derivatives) for the interval $[-1, 2]$.

(A) $c = -2$

(B) $c = 0.5$

(C) $c = 1$

(D) $c = 2.4$

9. Use L'Hôpital's Rule to evaluate the limit: $\lim\limits_{x\to\infty} x^{\frac{1}{x}}$.

    (A) 1

    (B) e

    (C) 6.

    (D) The limit does not exist.

0. Find the sum of the series:

    $$3 - \frac{9}{4} + \frac{27}{16} - \frac{81}{64} + \frac{243}{256} - \cdots$$

    (A) $\dfrac{12}{7}$

    (B) $\dfrac{18}{7}$

    (C) 3

    (D) The series is divergent

1. For what value(s) of x does $\sum\limits_{k=1}^{\infty} \dfrac{(-1)^k (x-3)^k}{k^k}$ converge absolutely?

    (A) Only $x = 3$

    (B) $x \in (-2, 4]$

    (C) $x \in (-\infty, \infty)$

    (D) $x \in (-2, 4)$

2. What is the Taylor series for $f(x) = \sin(x)$ at $x = \dfrac{\pi}{3}$?

    (A) $\sum\limits_{n=0}^{\infty} \dfrac{\sqrt{3}\left(x - \dfrac{\pi}{3}\right)^n}{n!}$

    (B) $\sum\limits_{n=0}^{\infty} \dfrac{(-1)^n \sqrt{3}\left(x - \dfrac{\pi}{3}\right)^n}{n!}$

    (C) $\sum\limits_{n=0}^{\infty} \dfrac{(-1)^n \left(x - \dfrac{\pi}{3}\right)^{2n}}{2\cdot(2n)!} + \sum\limits_{n=0}^{\infty} \dfrac{(-1)^n \sqrt{3}\left(x - \dfrac{\pi}{3}\right)^{2n+1}}{2\cdot(2n+1)!}$

    (D) $\sum\limits_{n=0}^{\infty} \dfrac{(-1)^n \sqrt{3}\left(x - \dfrac{\pi}{3}\right)^{2n}}{2\cdot(2n)!} + \sum\limits_{n=0}^{\infty} \dfrac{(-1)^n \left(x - \dfrac{\pi}{3}\right)^{2n+1}}{2\cdot(2n+1)!}$

23. Which of the following expressions is equal to $\sin\left(\arctan(3x)\right)$?

    (A) $\dfrac{3x}{\sqrt{1-9x^2}}$

    (B) $\dfrac{3x}{\sqrt{1+9x^2}}$

    (C) $3x$

    (D) $\sqrt{1+9x^2}$

24. Which of the following is the best approximation for the average value of the function $g(x) = x \ln x$ over the interval $[1, e]$?

    (A) 0.78

    (B) 0.95

    (C) 1.22

    (D) 2.08

25. Which of the following statements is false?

    (A) To obtain the trigonometric identity from the identity $\sin^2 x + \cos^2 x = 1$, divide by $\sin^2 x + \cos^2 x = 1$ by $\cos^2 x$.

    (B) Let f be a function defined on a closed interval $[a, b]$ and let v be any real number between $f(a)$ and $f(b)$. Then there exists at least one number $c \in (a, b)$ such that $f(c) = v$.

    (C) A polynomial $y = P(x)$ is continuous at every real number a because $\lim\limits_{x\to a} P(x) = P(a)$.

    (D) The solution of the differential equation $\dfrac{dy}{dx} = xy$ is $y = Ae^{\frac{1}{2}x^2}$.

26. Let $T(t)$ be the temperature in degrees (Fahrenheit) of coffee t minutes after being taken out of a microwave. Which of the following statements is false?

    (A) $T(2) = 100$ means that after 2 minutes, the coffee is 100 degrees F.

    (B) $T^{-1}(90) = 3$ means that after 3 minutes, the temperature of the coffee is 90 degrees F.

(C) $T^1(3) = -6$ means that after 3 minutes, the temperature of the coffee has dropped 6 degrees.

(D) $(T^{-1})(-10) = 1$ means that after 1 minute, the temperature of the coffee is decreasing at a rate of 10 degrees per minute.

27. Which of the following statements is false?

(A) Zeno's paradoxes were written by Zeno of Elea.

(B) Fermat presented the first proof of the theorem named *Fermat's Last Theorem*.

(C) Blaise Pascal invented the first mechanical calculating machine.

(D) Euclid proved there are infinitely many primes.

28. The Rhind Papyrus which dates from around 1650 B.C.E. is a document that provides evidence that

(A) the Chinese number system was hexadecimal.

(B) the Mayans were adept in arithmetic calculations.

(C) the Babylonians had a symbol to represent zero.

(D) the Egyptians studied linear equations.

29. In the nineteenth century, Charles Hermite proved which of the following?

(A) The number e is transcendental.

(B) The number π is irrational.

(C) Duplicating the cube is impossible with only straightedge and ruler.

(D) The twin prime conjecture is true.

30. Which of the following mathematicians is considered to be a pioneer of differential calculus as it is known today?

(A) David Hilbert

(B) Gottfried Leibnitz

(C) Évariste Galois

(D) Pythagoras

Constructed-Response Problems

31. Let $f(x) = \dfrac{4x}{x^2 + 1}$. Use first and second derivative to determine the intervals of increase/decrease and concavity, as well as to find all extrema and inflection points. Then sketch the function.

32. Use the formal definition of the derivative to compute the derivative of $g(x) = \sqrt{3x + 1}$ at $x = 5$ and then write the equation of the tangent line at $x = 5$.

33. **Use the part of the Fundamental Theorem of Calculus stated below to complete the exercise that follows.**

Let f be continuous on a closed interval $[a, b]$ and let x be any point in $[a, b]$. If F is defined by

$F(x) = \int_a^x f(t)\, dt$, then $F'(x) = f(x)$ at each point x in the interval $[a, b]$.

Using the formal definition of the derivative, prove the above theorem.

34. Although Pascal's Triangle is named after a seventeenth-century mathematician, Blaise Pascal, other mathematicians knew about and used the triangle hundreds of years before Pascal's birth (1623). The triangle was discovered independently by both the Persians and the Chinese during the eleventh century. Hundreds of years after it first appeared in Persia and China, the triangle came to be known as Pascal's Triangle after Blaise Pascal's publication of *Traité du triangle arithmétique* in 1654.

(a) Explain how Pascal's Triangle is generated.

(b) Write the Binomial Theorem.

(c) Explain the relationship between Pascal's Triangle and the Binomial Theorem.

Answer Key Subtest III

Question Number	Answer	SMR
1	(A)	5.1 c
2	(D)	5.1 c
3	(B)	5.1 c
4	(A)	5.2 a
5	(A)	5.3 b
6	(C)	5.3 b
7	(C)	5.1 e
8	(D)	5.2 a
9	(A)	5.3 b
10	(B)	5.3 f
11	(B)	5.3 b, c
12	(D)	5.3 d
13	(B)	5.4 c
14	(A)	5.4 d, 5.3 e
15	(C)	5.3 d
16	(B)	5.4 b, d
17	(D)	5.3 e, 5.4 b, c

Question Number	Answer	SMR
18	(B)	5.3 c
19	(A)	5.3 c
20	(A)	5.5 a
21	(C)	5.5 b
22	(D)	5.5 c
23	(B)	5.1 c, d
24	(C)	5.4 b
25	(B)	5.1a, 5.2 b, c
26	(C)	5.3 b
27	(B)	6.1 a, b
28	(D)	6.1 a, b
29	(A)	6.1 a, b
30	(B)	6.1 a, b
31	Constructed-Response	5.3 b, e
32	Constructed-Response	5.3 a, b
33	Constructed-Response	5.3 b, 5.4 c
34	Constructed-Response	6.1 a, b

Practice Test 2: Subtest III Answer and Explanations

1. (A)

$$\sin^2 x = -\cos\left(x - \frac{3}{2}\pi\right) \Leftrightarrow \sin^2 x = -\left(\cos x\cos\left(\frac{3}{2}\pi\right) + \sin x\sin\left(\frac{3}{2}\pi\right)\right)$$
$$\Leftrightarrow \sin^2 x = \sin x$$
$$\Leftrightarrow \sin^2 x - \sin x = 0$$
$$\Leftrightarrow \sin x(\sin x - 1) = 0$$
$$\Leftrightarrow \sin x = 0 \text{ or } \sin x = 1$$
$$\text{Hence, } x = 0, \pi, \text{ or } \frac{\pi}{2}$$

Therefore, (A) is the correct answer.

2. (D)

$$\frac{\csc^2\beta}{\sec^2\beta} + \tan^2\beta\cot^2\beta = \cot^2\beta + 1 = \csc^2\beta. \quad \text{So the}$$
correct answer is (D).

3. (B)

$y(t) = \cos(8\pi t)$. The period of the function is $\frac{2\pi}{8\pi} = \frac{1}{4}$, so the wheel completes 4 revolutions per minute, for a total of 20 revolutions in five minutes. The diameter is 2 feet, so the circumference of the wheel is 2π cm. Thus, the point P travels $2\pi(20) = 40\pi$ feet in five minutes.

The correct answer is (B).

4. (A)

$f(2) = 1$, so the function value exists, hence (B) is not the answer. The left-hand limit, $\lim_{x\to 2^-} f(x)$, decreases without bound while the right-hand limit, $\lim_{x\to 2^+} f(x)$, increases without bound. Then because the one-sided limits do not exist, the two-sided limit does not exist. This is the reason that f is not continuous at $x = 2$ and

(D) is not correct becaue f has an inverse. Answer (C) is not correct because $f(2)$ does not have to equal 0. So the correct answer is (A).

5. (A)

It is true that differentiability at a point implie continuity at a point. So statement (A) is true. Statemen (B) can be seen to be false: Let $f(x) = x = g(x)$. Then

$$\lim_{x\to 0} f(x) = 0 = \lim_{x\to 0} g(x) \text{ but } \lim_{x\to 0}\frac{f(x)}{g(x)} = \lim_{x\to 0}\frac{x}{x} = \lim_{x\to 0} 1 = 1$$

Statement (C) is false; consider $f(x) = -x^2 + 25$ $f(x) > 0$ on $(-5, 5)$, but is concave down on tha interval; the second derivative tells us about concavity Statement (D) is false. Consider the functions $f(x) = x = g(x)$. Then $\frac{d}{dx}(f(x)g(x)) = \frac{d}{dx}(x^2) = 2x$ but $\frac{d}{dx}(f(x)) = 1 = \frac{d}{dx}(g(x))$, so that the product o the derivatives is equal to 1 rather than $2x$. The correc answer is (A).

6. (C)

The instantaneous rate of change of f is th derivative of f. So f' is increasing when its derivative, f'' is positive or when the graph of f is concave up, which i on approximately the interval $(1, \infty)$. The correct answe is (C).

. (C)

The polar form of a unit vector in $\mathbf{C}$ is
$$z = e^{i\theta} = \cos(\theta) + i\sin(\theta). \text{ Then,}$$

$$z^3 = e^{3i\theta} = \cos(3\theta) + i\sin(3\theta).$$

From the unit vector shown in the figure, it appears that its angle is approximately $225°$ so $3\theta = 675°$. Thus, $z^3 = \cos(675°) + i\sin(675°) = \cos(315°) + i\sin(315°)$, or $z^3 = \cos(45°) - i\sin(45°)$. So the correct answer is (C).

. (D)

The limit of h must exist at $x = 0$ and must equal $(0) = b + 3$ in order for h to be continuous at $x = 0$. The one-sided limits are: $\lim\limits_{x\to 0^+} h(x) = \lim\limits_{x\to 0^+}(x^2 + b + 3) = b + 3$

and $\lim\limits_{x\to 0^-} h(x) = \lim\limits_{x\to 0^-}\left(\dfrac{1-\cos(2x)}{x}\right) = \lim\limits_{x\to 0^-}\left(\dfrac{2\sin(2x)}{1}\right)$ by

l'Hôpital's Rule for indeterminate form $\dfrac{0}{0}$, and the last limit equals 0. We need these limits to be equal; hence, $b = -3$. The correct answer is (D).

. (A)

We must use implicit differentiation to find $\dfrac{dy}{dx}$.

$\dfrac{1}{y}\dfrac{dy}{dx} - 2 = 2y\dfrac{dy}{dx}$ solving for the derivative we obtain:

$$\left(\dfrac{1}{y} - 2y\right)\cdot\dfrac{dy}{dx} = 2 \Rightarrow (1 - 2y^2)\dfrac{dy}{dx} = 2y \Rightarrow \dfrac{dy}{dx} = \dfrac{2y}{1 - 2y^2},$$

which represents the slope of the tangent line. The tangent line has slope 2, so

$$\dfrac{2y}{-2y^2} = 2 \Rightarrow 2y = 2 - 4y^2 \Leftrightarrow 4y^2 + 2y - 2 = 0 \Leftrightarrow$$

$y = -1$ or 0.5. But we know that $y > 0$ by the definition of the original function, so $y = 0.5$.

Substitute this into the original equation to find x:

$$\ln(0.5) - 2x = (0.5)^2 \Leftrightarrow x = \dfrac{1}{2}\left(-\dfrac{1}{4} - \ln(2)\right) = -\dfrac{1}{8} - \ln(\sqrt{2}).$$

The correct answer is (A).

10. (B)

This is an exponential function since the growth rate is in proportion to its size. The basic equation is $P = P_0 e^{rt}$. At $t = 0$, $P = 100$. Hence, the equation becomes $P = 100e^{rt}$. Twenty days later, $P = 300$, so

$$300 = 100e^{20r} \text{ and } e^r = 3^{\frac{1}{20}}. \text{ The function is therefore}$$

$P = 100(e^r)^t = 100\left(3^{\frac{1}{20}}\right)^t$. The population will reach

8100 when: $8100 = 100\left(3^{\frac{1}{20}}\right)^t \Rightarrow 81 = 3^{\frac{t}{20}}$, so we need

$\dfrac{t}{20} = 4$, or $t = 80$ days. The correct answer is (B).

11. (B)

$$H(x) = \dfrac{x^2 G\left(\dfrac{x}{2}\right)}{F(2x)}. \text{ So,}$$

$$H'(x) = \dfrac{F(2x)\left[x\,G'\left(\dfrac{x}{2}\right)\dfrac{1}{2} + 2xG\left(\dfrac{x}{2}\right)\right] - x\,G\left(\dfrac{x}{2}\right)(F'(2x)2)}{(F(2x))^2}$$

by the quotient rule. Then the slope of the tangent at $x = 2$

is $H'(2) = \dfrac{F(4)\left[4G'(1)\dfrac{1}{2} + 4G(1)\right] - 4G(1)(F'(4)2)}{(F(4))^2} =$

$$\dfrac{1(2(-1) + 4(2)) - 4(2)(6)(2)}{1^2} = -90.$$

The point of tangency is $(2, H(2)) = \left(2, \dfrac{4G(1)}{1}\right) = (2, 8)$ so to obtain the equation of the tangent at $x = 2$ we can use the point-slope formula:
$y - 8 = -90(x - 2) \Rightarrow y = -90x + 188$

The correct answer is (B).

12. (D)

The volume of the cylindrical can is $V = \pi r^2 h$. We are given that $\dfrac{dV}{dt} = -1$ ft³/hr and $r = 1.5$ ft.

Hence, $V = \dfrac{9}{4}\pi h$. We want to know $\dfrac{dh}{dt}$; so to this

end we differentiate with respect to time: $\dfrac{dV}{dt} = \dfrac{9}{4}\pi\dfrac{dh}{dt}$.

Then substituting, $-1 = \dfrac{9}{4}\pi\dfrac{dh}{dt} \Rightarrow \dfrac{dh}{dt} = -\dfrac{4}{9\pi}$ ft/hr.

The water level is changing at a rate of $-\dfrac{4}{9\pi}$ ft/hr. The

correct answer is (D).

13. (B)

Given $f(x) = \displaystyle\int_1^x \dfrac{18 - 5t}{3\sqrt[3]{t-6}}\, dt$ we can use the

Fundamental Theorem of Calculus to differentiate f to

obtain $f'(x) = \dfrac{18 - 5x}{3\sqrt[3]{x-6}}$. Then

$$f''(x) = \dfrac{3(x-6)^{\frac{1}{3}}(-5) - (18-5x)(x-6)^{-\frac{2}{3}}}{9(x-6)^{\frac{2}{3}}}$$

$$= \dfrac{-15(x-6) - (18-5x)}{9(x-6)^{\frac{4}{3}}}$$

$$= \dfrac{-10x - 72}{9(x-6)^{\frac{4}{3}}}$$

So, f'' changes sign at $x = 7.2$. The correct answer is (B).

14. (A)

Let R be the region bounded by the curves $f(x) =$ $y = \sqrt{x}$ and $g(x) = x$. See Figure A.

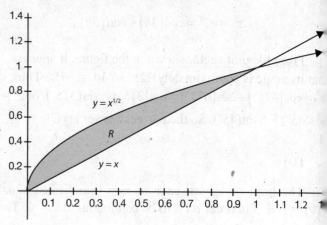

Figure A

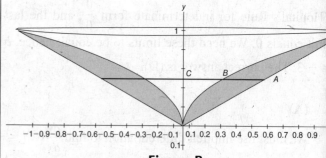

Figure B

Revolving the region R about the y-axis gives a solid B) that can be sliced into washers of width Δy w radius approximately $R = x = y$ (see CA in Figure small radius (the width of the hole) approximately r y^2 (see BA in Figure B). So the volume of such a w $\pi[R^2 - r^2]\Delta y$. Summing up the volumes of the washe us $\sum \pi\left(y^2 - y^4\right)$. If we imagine the number of th increasing so that Δy becomes very small, this ma problem an integration problem (method of finding the of a solid of revolution by using washers (disks with

The volume is $V = \displaystyle\int_0^1 \pi\left(y^2 - y^4\right) dy = \pi\left(\dfrac{1}{3}y^3 - \dfrac{1}{5}y^5\right)$

cubic units. The correct answer is (A).

15. (C)

The acceleration of a particle traveling in one dimension along the x-axis at time t is given by $a(t) = 5t + 1$. The antiderivative of acceleration is velocity, and in this case we have $v(t) = \dfrac{5}{2}t^2 + t + C$. We are told that at time $t = 1$ the velocity of the particle is 0, so $0 = \dfrac{5}{2}(1)^2 + (1) + C$, thus $C = -\dfrac{7}{2}$ and $v(t) = \dfrac{5}{2}t^2 + t - \dfrac{7}{2}$.

The position, s, is the antiderivative of velocity, so that $s(t) = \dfrac{5}{6}t^3 + \dfrac{1}{2}t^2 - \dfrac{7}{2}t + C'$. We also know that the position of the particle at time $t = 3$ is 15, so $\dfrac{5}{6}(3)^3 + \dfrac{1}{2}(3)^2 - \dfrac{7}{2}(3) + C' = 15$, and $C' = -\dfrac{3}{2}$. Hence, the position function is $s(t) = \dfrac{5}{6}t^3 + \dfrac{1}{2}t^2 - \dfrac{7}{2}t - \dfrac{3}{2}$ and $s(6) = 180 + 18 - 21 - 1.5 = 175.5$. The correct answer is (C).

16. (B)

The area is $\displaystyle\int_0^4 \dfrac{x}{\left(1+x^2\right)^2}\,dx$. To evaluate this, we can use the substitution $u = 1 + x^2$, which also gives us $du = 2x\,dx$ or $x\,dx = \dfrac{1}{2}du$. In addition, $u = 1$ when $x = 0$ and $u = 17$ when $x = 4$. So by substitution we have:

$$A = \int_0^4 \dfrac{x}{\left(1+x^2\right)^2}\,dx = \dfrac{1}{2}\int_1^{17}\dfrac{du}{u^2} = -\dfrac{1}{2}u^{-1}\Big|_1^{17} = \dfrac{8}{17}.$$ The correct answer is (B).

17. (D)

The function $g(x) = \displaystyle\int_0^x \left(1 + f(t)\right)dt = x + \int_0^x f(t)\,dt$, where $\displaystyle\int_0^x f(t)\,dt$ measures the signed area (area above the x-axis is positive and area below the x-axis is negative) between the graph of f and the x-axis from 0 to x. Taking the derivative, we obtain $g'(x) = 1 + f(x)$. So $g'(x) = 0$ when $f(x) = -1$, which is when $x = 3$ or 6.5, and $g'(x)$ does not exist at $x = 0, 1, 2, 4, 6, 6.5, 7,$ and 8. Evaluating g at these points gives us: $g(0) = 0$,

$$g(1) = 1 + \int_0^1 f(t)\,dt = 2,\ g(2) = 2 + \int_0^2 f(t)\,dt = 3,$$

$$g(3) = 3 + \int_0^3 f(t)\,dt = 3.5,\ g(4) = 4 + \int_0^4 f(t)\,dt = 3,$$

$$g(6) = 6 + \int_0^6 f(t)\,dt = 1,\ g(6.5) = 6.5 + \int_0^{6.5} f(t)\,dt = 0.75$$

$$g(7) = 7 + \int_0^7 f(t)\,dt = 1,\ g(8) = 8 + \int_0^8 f(t)\,dt = 5.\text{ So}$$

g has an absolute maximum at $x = 8$ and an absolute minimum at $x = 6.5$. The correct answer is (D).

18. (B)

The Mean Value Theorem says that if f is continuous on $[a, b]$ and differentiable on (a, b), then there exists a $c \in (a, b)$ such that $f'(c) = \dfrac{f(b) - f(a)}{b - a}$. For this problem, $a = -1$, $b = 2$, and $f(2) = 3$, $f(-1) = 9$, so $\dfrac{f(b) - f(a)}{b - a} = \dfrac{3 - 9}{3} = -2$; this is the slope of the secant line through the points $(2, 3)$ and $(-1, 9)$. We want to find c in $(-1, 2)$ such that the tangent line is parallel to the secant line. So where does the tangent line have a slope of -2? $f'(x) = 6x - 5$, so we solve $6x - 5 = -2$ to get $c = 0.5$. See the figure on the next page. The correct answer is (B).

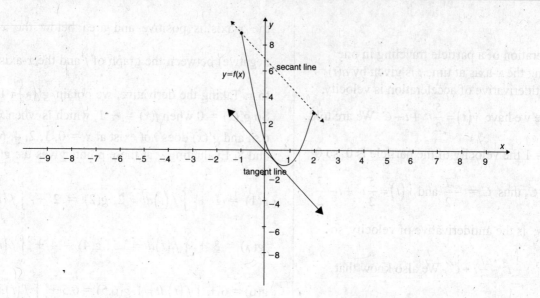

19. (A)

Let $y = x^{\frac{1}{x}}$ so that $\ln(y) = \ln\left(x^{\frac{1}{x}}\right) = \frac{1}{x}\ln x$. Taking the limits: $\lim\limits_{x \to \infty}(\ln(y)) = \lim\limits_{x \to \infty}\left(\dfrac{\ln x}{x}\right)$. The limit of the right side is an indeterminate form of the $\dfrac{\infty}{\infty}$ type, so we may use L'Hôpital's Rule and take the derivative of the functions in the numerator and denominator separately to obtain: $\lim\limits_{x \to \infty}(\ln(y)) = \lim\limits_{x \to \infty}\left(\dfrac{\ln x}{x}\right) = \lim\limits_{x \to \infty}\left(\dfrac{1}{x}\right) = 0$. Hence $\lim\limits_{x \to \infty}(\ln(y)) = 0$, so that taking the exponential of both sides of the equation gives us $e^{0} = e^{\lim\limits_{x \to \infty}(\ln(y))}$ or $1 = \lim\limits_{x \to \infty}e^{\ln(y)} = \lim\limits_{x \to \infty}y$, Thus, the correct answer is (A).

20. (A)

The series is a geometric series with initial term $a = 3$, and ratio $r = \dfrac{-3}{4}$. Since $|r| < 1$, the series is convergent and its sum is $\dfrac{a}{1-r} = \dfrac{3}{1-\left(\frac{-3}{4}\right)} = \dfrac{12}{7}$. So, answer (A) is correct.

21. (C)

Using the Root Test:

$$\left|\dfrac{(-1)^{k}(x-3)^{k}}{k^{k}}\right|^{\frac{1}{k}} = \dfrac{1}{k}\cdot|x-3| \xrightarrow{k \to \infty} 0$$

So the series is absolutely convergent for all real numbers. The correct answer is (C).

22. (D)

$$f(x) = \sin x$$
$$\Rightarrow f'(x) = \cos x,\ f''(x) = -\sin x,\ f'''(x) = -\cos x,\ \text{which}$$
establishes a pattern:

$$f\left(\frac{\pi}{3}\right) = \frac{\sqrt{3}}{2},\, f'\left(\frac{\pi}{3}\right) = \frac{1}{2},\, f''\left(\frac{\pi}{3}\right) = -\frac{\sqrt{3}}{2},\, f'''\left(\frac{\pi}{3}\right) = -\frac{1}{2}$$

Thus, the Taylor series for $f(x) = \sin x$ at $x = \dfrac{\pi}{3}$ is

$$\frac{\sqrt{3}}{2} + \frac{1}{2}\left(x - \frac{\pi}{3}\right) + \frac{-\frac{\sqrt{3}}{2}}{2!}\left(x - \frac{\pi}{3}\right)^{2} + \frac{-\frac{1}{2}}{3!}\left(x - \frac{\pi}{3}\right)^{3} + \cdots$$

$$= \sum_{n=0}^{\infty}\frac{(-1)^{n}\sqrt{3}\left(x - \frac{\pi}{3}\right)^{2n}}{2\cdot(2n)!} + \sum_{n=0}^{\infty}\frac{(-1)^{n}\left(x - \frac{\pi}{3}\right)^{2n+1}}{2\cdot(2n+1)!}.$$

Answer (D) is correct.

3. (B)

Let $u = \arctan(3x)$ then $\tan u = 3x$. Label a right triangle appropriately. (see below). Using the Pythagorean Theorem, $h = \sqrt{1+9x^2}$. Then $\sin\left(\arctan\left(3x\right)\right) = \sin(u) = \dfrac{3x}{\sqrt{1+9x^2}}$.

The correct answer is (B).

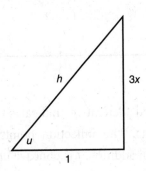

4. (C)

The average value of g over $[1, e]$ is given by $\dfrac{1}{e-1}\displaystyle\int_{1}^{e} x\ln x\, dx$. We can evaluate the integral as an indefinite integral using integration by parts, where $u = \ln x$, $dv = x\,dx$, so that $du = \dfrac{1}{x}$ and $v = \dfrac{x^2}{2}$;

Thus, $\displaystyle\int x\ln x\,dx = \dfrac{x^2}{2}\ln x - \int \dfrac{x}{2}dx = \dfrac{x^2}{2}\ln x - \dfrac{x^2}{4} + C$.

Then we obtain:

$$\dfrac{1}{e-1}\int_{1}^{e} x\ln x\,dx = \dfrac{1}{e-1}\left(\dfrac{e^2}{2}\ln e - \dfrac{e^2}{4} - \left(\dfrac{1}{2}\ln 1 - \dfrac{1}{4}\right)\right)$$

$$= \dfrac{1}{e-1}\left(\dfrac{e^2}{2} - \dfrac{e^2}{4} + \dfrac{1}{4}\right) = \dfrac{1}{e-1}\left(\dfrac{e^2}{4} + \dfrac{1}{4}\right)$$

$$\approx \dfrac{1}{1.7}\left(\dfrac{(2.7)^2}{4} + \dfrac{1}{4}\right) \approx 1.22$$

The correct answer is (C).

25. (B)

Dividing $\sin^2 x + \cos^2 x = 1$ by $\cos^2 x$ results in $\dfrac{\sin^2 x}{\cos^2 x} + \dfrac{\cos^2 x}{\cos^2 x} = \dfrac{1}{\cos^2 x}$, which is equivalent to $\tan^2 x + 1 = \sec^2 x$, so (A) is true. (B) is almost the statement of the *Intermediate Value Theorem*, but the hypothesis condition of f being continuous is missing; the given statement is false, as can be seen from the example $f(x) = \begin{cases} x+1, & x<1 \\ x+2, & x \geq 1 \end{cases}$: On the interval $[0, 3]$, $f(3) = 5$ and $f(0) = 1$, but there is no c in $(0, 3)$ such that $f(c) = 2.5$, so (B) is false. Statement (C) is true by the definition of a polynomial and continuity. Statement (D) can be seen to be true: $y = Ae^{\frac{1}{2}x^2}$, so $\dfrac{dy}{dx} = Ae^{\frac{1}{2}x^2}\left(\dfrac{1}{2}(2x)\right) = Axe^{\frac{1}{2}x^2} = xy$.
The correct answer is (B).

26. (C)

$T'(3) = -6$ that after 3 minutes the temperature is decreasing at a rate of 6 degrees per minute, so this is the incorrect statement. The correct answer is (C).

27. (B)

Fermat wrote his theorem in the margin of a book but did not prove it. The correct answer is (B).

28. (D)

The correct answer is (D), *the Egyptians studied linear equations.*

29. (A)

Hermite proved that e is a transcendental number. The correct answer is (A).

30. (B)

Einstein and Leibnitz are considered the main developers of calculus. The correct answer is (B).

Constructed-Response Problems

31. $f(x) = \dfrac{4x}{x^2 + 1}$.

The domain of f is the set of all real numbers. Also, f has a zero at $x = 0$. Note that this rational function has no vertical asymptotes but does have a horizontal asymptote at $y = 0$ since $\lim\limits_{x \to \pm\infty} f(x) = 0$.

Then, $f'(x) = \dfrac{(x^2 + 1)4 - 4x(2x)}{(x^2 + 1)^2} = \dfrac{4 - 4x^2}{(x^2 + 1)^2} = \dfrac{4(1 - x)(1 + x)}{(x^2 + 1)^2}$

which is defined for all real numbers and has zeroes at $x = 1$ and -1. These are the only possible values of x for which local extrema might occur since f' is defined for all real numbers. We test the intervals for the sign of the derivative.

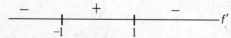

We see from the First Derivative Test that there is a local minimum when $x = 1$ (the point is $(1, 2)$), and a local maximum at $x = -1$ (the point is $(-1, -2)$). We also can conclude that f is decreasing on $(-1, 1)$ and increasing on $(-\infty, -1) \cup (1, +\infty)$.

The second derivative

$$f''(x) = \frac{(x^2 + 1)^2(4(-2x)) - 2(x^2 + 1)(2x)4(1 - x^2)}{(x^2 + 1)^4} =$$

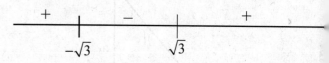

$\dfrac{8x(x - \sqrt{3})(x + \sqrt{3})}{(x^2 + 1)^3}$. The zeroes of f'' are $\pm\sqrt{3}$, and the

are the possible values for which there might be an infle point. We test the second derivatve to find when it is pos and negative.

The second derivative indicates that there are inflection points. The inflection points are $(\sqrt{3}, \sqrt{3}$ $(-\sqrt{3} - \sqrt{3})$. In addition, f is concave up on $(-\infty, -\sqrt{}$ $(\sqrt{3}, +\infty)$ and concave down on $(-\sqrt{3}, \sqrt{3})$.

We use all this information to sketch the graph of g t

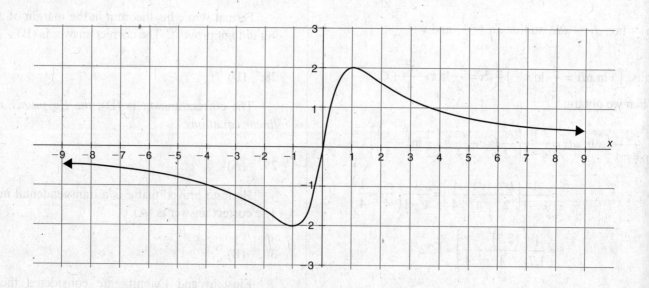

32.

$$g'(5) = \lim_{h \to 0} \frac{g(5+h) - g(5)}{h} = \lim_{h \to 0} \frac{\sqrt{3(5+h)+1} - 4}{h} = \lim_{h \to 0} \frac{\sqrt{3(5+h)+1} - 4}{h} \cdot \left(\frac{\sqrt{3(5+h)+1} + 4}{\sqrt{3(5+h)+1} + 4} \right)$$

$$= \lim_{h \to 0} \frac{3(5+h)+1-16}{h\left(\sqrt{3(5+h)+1}+4\right)} = \lim_{h \to 0} \frac{3h}{h\left(\sqrt{3(5+h)+1}+4\right)} = \lim_{h \to 0} \frac{3}{\left(\sqrt{3(5+h)+1}+4\right)} = \frac{3}{8}$$

So, the slope of the tangent line at $x = 5$ is $\frac{3}{8}$.

The point of tangency is $(5, g(5)) = (5, 4)$. Therefore, the equation of the tangent line at $x = 5$ is $y - 4 = \frac{3}{8}(x-5)$ or $y = \frac{3}{8}x + \frac{17}{8}$.

33. **Proof**: Let f be continuous on $[a, b]$. Assume $g(x) = \int_a^x f(t)dt$. Then

$$g(x+h) - g(x) = \int_a^{x+h} f(t)dt - \int_a^x f(t)dt$$

$$= \int_x^{x+h} f(t)dt.$$

So for h not equal to 0, $\dfrac{g(x+h) - g(x)}{h} = \dfrac{1}{h} \int_x^{x+h} f(t)dt$.

Now, f is continuous on $[a, b]$ and, hence, on any subset of it. Assuming that $h > 0$ (the case for $h < 0$ can be proven in the same manner), by the Extreme Value Theorem, f has an absolute minimum, m, and an absolute maximum, M, on $[x, x + h]$; say $f(c) = m$ and $f(d) = M$ with $c, d \in [x, x + h]$.

Hence, since $m \leq f(t) \leq M$ for $x \leq t \leq x + h$, $mh \leq \int_x^{x+h} f(t)dt \leq Mh$. Then, since $h > 0$,

$$m \leq \frac{1}{h}\int_x^{x+h} f(t)dt \leq M. \text{ We know that } \frac{g(x+h)-g(x)}{h} = \frac{1}{h}\int_x^{x+h} f(t)dt, \text{ so we may substitute this to obtain}$$

$$f(c) = m \leq \frac{g(x+h)-g(x)}{h} \leq M = f(d).$$

Then as $h \to 0$, $c \to x$, and $d \to x$, since c and d lie between x and $x + h$. So, f is continuous means that

$$\lim_{h \to 0} f(c) = \lim_{c \to x} f(c) = f(x) \text{ and } \lim_{h \to 0} f(d) = \lim_{d \to x} f(d) = f(x). \text{ Therefore by the Sandwich or Squeeze Theorem,}$$

$$g'(x) = \lim_{h \to 0} \frac{g(x+h)-g(x)}{h} = f(x)$$

Q.E.D.

34. (a) The first row (call this row 0) of Pascal's Triangle is a single number: 1; the second row (row 1) has two ones. Each following row always begins and ends with a 1 and row n has $n + 1$ numbers. Starting with row 2, the numbers that are not the first or last in the rows are obtained by adding the two numbers in the previous row that are to the left and right of the number; for example to get the second number in row 2 (which has 3 numbers with 1 being first and last), we add $1 + 1 = 2$. To obtain the second number in row 3, we add $1 + 2 = 3$ and for the third number in row 3 we add $2 + 1 = 3$. We show the first six rows of Pascal's triangle here.

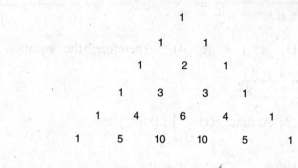

We can also define each entry of Pascal's Triangle by using combinations: For integers n and r, we define

$_nC_r = \begin{pmatrix} n \\ r \end{pmatrix} = \dfrac{n!}{r!(n-r)!}$. Then the entry in the nth row and rth position in that row is $_nC_r$. For example, the 3rd entry

in row 5 (remember: the first row is row 0) we compute as $_5C_3 = \dfrac{5!}{2!\,3!} = 10$

(b) **The Binomial Theorem:** For any natural number n and any real numbers x and y, it is true that

$$(x+y)^n = \sum_{k=0}^{n} \begin{pmatrix} n \\ k \end{pmatrix} x^{n-k} y^k.$$

(c) The relationship between Pascal's Triangle and the Binomial Theorem is that the coefficients of the

expansion of $(x+y)^n$ are the numbers in the nth row of Pascal's Triangle. For example:

$$(x+y)^6 = \sum_{k=0}^{6} \begin{pmatrix} 6 \\ k \end{pmatrix} x^{6-k} y^k$$

$$= \begin{pmatrix} 6 \\ 0 \end{pmatrix} x^{6-0} y^0 + \begin{pmatrix} 6 \\ 1 \end{pmatrix} x^{6-1} y^1 + \begin{pmatrix} 6 \\ 2 \end{pmatrix} x^{6-2} y^2 + \begin{pmatrix} 6 \\ 3 \end{pmatrix} x^{6-3} y^3 + \begin{pmatrix} 6 \\ 4 \end{pmatrix} x^{6-4} y^4 + \begin{pmatrix} 6 \\ 5 \end{pmatrix} x^{6-5} y^5 + \begin{pmatrix} 6 \\ 6 \end{pmatrix} x^{6-6} y^6$$

$$= x^6 + 6x^5 y + 15x^4 y^2 + 20x^3 y^3 + 15x^2 y^4 + 6xy^5 + y^6$$

NOTES

REA's Test Preps

The Best in Test Preparation

- REA "Test Preps" are **far more** comprehensive than any other test preparation series
- Each book contains full-length practice tests based on the most recent exams
- **Every** type of question likely to be given on the exams is included
- Answers are accompanied by **full** and **detailed** explanations

REA publishes hundreds of test prep books. Some of our titles include:

Advanced Placement Exams (APs)
Art History
Biology
Calculus AB & BC
Chemistry
Economics
English Language & Composition
English Literature & Composition
European History
French Language
Government & Politics
Latin Vergil
Physics B & C
Psychology
Spanish Language
Statistics
United States History
World History

College-Level Examination Program (CLEP)
American Government
College Algebra
General Examinations
History of the United States I
History of the United States II
Introduction to Educational Psychology
Human Growth and Development
Introductory Psychology
Introductory Sociology
Principles of Management
Principles of Marketing
Spanish
Western Civilization I
Western Civilization II

SAT Subject Tests
Biology E/M
Chemistry
French
German
Literature
Mathematics Level 1, 2
Physics
Spanish
United States History

Graduate Record Exams (GREs)
Biology
Chemistry
Computer Science
General
Literature in English
Mathematics
Physics
Psychology

ACT - ACT Assessment

ASVAB - Armed Services Vocational Aptitude Battery

CBEST - California Basic Educational Skills Test

CDL - Commercial Driver License Exam

CLAST - College Level Academic Skills Test

COOP, HSPT & TACHS - Catholic High School Admission Tests

FE (EIT) - Fundamentals of Engineering Exams

FTCE - Florida Teacher Certification Examinations

GED

GMAT - Graduate Management Admission Test

LSAT - Law School Admission Test

MAT - Miller Analogies Test

MCAT - Medical College Admission Test

MTEL - Massachusetts Tests for Educator Licensure

NJ HSPA - New Jersey High School Proficiency Assessment

NYSTCE - New York State Teacher Certification Examinations

PRAXIS PLT - Principles of Learning & Teaching Tests

PRAXIS PPST - Pre-Professional Skills Tests

PSAT/NMSQT

SAT

TExES - Texas Examinations of Educator Standards

THEA - Texas Higher Education Assessment

TOEFL - Test of English as a Foreign Language

USMLE Steps 1,2,3 - U.S. Medical Licensing Exams

For information about any of REA's books, visit www.rea.com

Research & Education Association
61 Ethel Road W., Piscataway, NJ 08854
Phone: (732) 819-8880

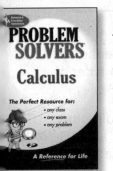

Installing REA's TestWare®

System Requirements

Microsoft Windows XP or later; Internet Explorer 6.0 or higher; 64 MB available RAM.

Installation

1. Insert the CSET: Mathematics TestWare® CD into the CD-ROM drive.

2. If the installation doesn't begin automatically, from the Start Menu choose the RUN command. When the RUN dialog box appears, type d:\setup (where d is the letter of your CD-ROM drive) at the prompt and click OK.

3. The installation process will begin. A dialog box proposing the directory "C:\Program Files\REA\CSET_Math" will appear. If the name and location are suitable, click OK. If you wish to specify a different name or location, type it in and click OK.

4. Start the CSET: Mathematics TestWare® application by double-clicking on the icon.

REA's TestWare® is **EASY** to **LEARN AND USE**. To achieve maximum benefits, we recommend that you take a few minutes to go through the on-screen tutorial on your computer. The "screen buttons" are also explained here to familiarize you with the program.

SSD Accommodations for Students with Disabilities

Many students qualify for extra time to take the CSET: Mathematics exam, and our TestWare® can be adapted to accommodate your time extension. This allows you to practice under the same extended-time accommodations that you will receive on the actual test day.

Technical Support

REA's TestWare® is backed by customer and technical support. For questions about **installation or operation of your software**, contact us at:

> **Research & Education Association**
> **Phone: (732) 819-8880 (9 a.m. to 5 p.m. ET, Monday–Friday)**
> **Fax: (732) 819-8808**
> **Website: *www.rea.com***
> **E-mail: info@rea.com**

NOTE: In order for the TestWare® to function properly, please install and run the application under the same computer administrator-level user account. Installing the TestWare® as one user and running it as another could cause file-access path conflicts.